FINANCIAL MARKETS AND CORPORATE FINANCE

FINANCIAL ECONOMISTS OF THE TWENTIETH CENTURY

This series includes specially invited selections of articles by economists whose work has made an important and distinct contribution to financial economics in the late twentieth century.

Wherever possible, the articles in these volumes have been reproduced as originally published using facsimile reproduction, inclusive of footnotes and pagination to facilitate ease of reference.

Financial Markets and Corporate Finance

Selected Papers of Michael J. Brennan

Michael J. Brennan

Goldyne and Irwin Hearsh Chair in Money and Banking,
The John E. Anderson Graduate School of Management,
University of California, Los Angeles, USA
and Professor of Finance, London Business School, UK

FINANCIAL ECONOMISTS OF THE TWENTIETH CENTURY

Edward Elgar
Cheltenham, UK • Northampton, MA, USA

Published by
Edward Elgar Publishing Limited
Glensanda House
Montpellier Parade
Cheltenham
Glos GL50 1UA
UK

Edward Elgar Publishing, Inc.
136 West Street
Suite 202
Northampton
Massachusetts 01060
USA

A catalogue record for this book
is available from the British Library

Library of Congress Cataloguing in Publication Data

Brennan, Michael J.
    Financial markets and corporate finance : selected papers of
Michael J. Brennan.
(Financial economists of the twentieth century)
Includes bibliographical references.
1. Money market.   2. Corporations—Finance.   I. Title.
II. Series.
HG226.B73   1999
658. 15—dc21   99–11540
                                                                             CIP

ISBN 1 84064 023 5

Printed and bound in Great Britain by Biddles Ltd, Guildford and King's Lynn

Contents

Acknowledgements   vii
Introduction   ix
Complete bibliography: M.J. Brennan   xvii

PART I   CORPORATE FINANCE

 1 'Taxes, Market Valuation and Corporate Financial Policy', *National
    Tax Journal*, **XXIII** (4), December 1970, 417–27   3
 2 'An Approach to the Valuation of Uncertain Income Streams',
    Journal of Finance, **XXVIII** (3), June 1973, 661–74   14
 3 'Corporate Income Taxes, Valuation, and the Problem of Optimal
    Capital Structure', with Eduardo S. Schwartz, *Journal of Business*,
    51 (1), 1978, 103–14   28
 4 'Consistent Regulatory Policy under Uncertainty', with Eduardo S.
    Schwartz, *Bell Journal of Economics*, **13** (2), Autumn 1982, 506–21 40
 5 'Evaluating Natural Resource Investments' with Eduardo S. Schwartz,
    Journal of Business, **58** (2), 1985, 135–57   56
 6 'Efficient Financing under Asymmetric Information', with Alan Kraus,
    Journal of Finance, **XLII** (5), December 1987, 1225–43   79
 7 'Vendor Financing', with Vojislav Maksimovic and Josef Zechner,
    Journal of Finance, **XLIII** (5), December 1988, 1127–41   98
 8 'Latent Assets', *Journal of Finance*, **XLV** (3), July 1990, 709–30 113
 9 'Corporate Finance over the Past 25 Years', *Financial Management*,
    24 (2), Summer 1995, 9–22   135

PART II   OPTION PRICING AND DERIVATIVES MARKETS

10 'The Valuation of American Put Options', with Eduardo S. Schwartz,
    Journal of Finance, **XXXII** (2), May 1977, 449–62   151
11 'Finite Difference Methods and Jump Processes Arising in the Pricing
    of Contingent Claims: A Synthesis' with Eduardo S. Schwartz,
    Journal of Financial and Quantitative Analysis, **XIII** (3),
    September 1978, 461–74   165
12 'A Continuous Time Approach to the Pricing of Bonds', with
    Eduardo S. Schwartz, *Journal of Banking and Finance*, **3**, 1979,
    133–55   178
13 'The Pricing of Contingent Claims in Discrete Time Models',
    Journal of Finance, **XXXIV** (1), March 1979, 53–68   201
14 'Optimal Portfolio Insurance', with R. Solanki, *Journal of Financial
    and Quantitative Analysis*, **XVI** (3), September 1981, 279–300 217

15 'Time-Invariant Portfolio Insurance Strategies', with Eduardo S.
    Schwartz, *Journal of Finance*, **XLIII** (2), June 1988, 283–99   238
16 'Portfolio Insurance and Financial Market Equilibrium', with
    Eduardo S. Schwartz, *Journal of Business*, **62** (4), 1989, 455–72   255
17 'Information, Trade, and Derivative Securities', with H. Henry Cao,
    Review of Financial Studies, **9** (1), Spring 1996, 163–208   273
18 'Stripping the S&P 500 Index', *Financial Analysts Journal*,
    January/February 1998, 12–22   319

PART III   INFORMATION AND PRICE FORMATION IN FINANCIAL
           MARKETS

19 'International Portfolio Investment Flows', with H. Henry Cao,
    Journal of Finance, **LII** (5), December 1997, 1851–80   333
20 'Stock Prices and the Supply of Information', with Patricia J. Hughes,
    Journal of Finance, **XLVI** (5), December 1991, 1665–91   363
21 'Investment Analysis and the Adjustment of Stock Prices to Common
    Information', with Narasimhan Jegadeesh and Bhaskaran
    Swaminathan, *Review of Financial Studies*, **6** (4), Winter 1993,
    799–824   390
22 'Investment Analysis and Price Formation in Securities Markets',
    with Avanidhar Subrahmanyam, *Journal of Financial Economics*,
    38, 1995, 361–81   416
23 'Alternative Factor Specifications, Security Characteristics, and the
    Cross-Section of Expected Stock Returns', with Tarun Chordia and
    Avanidhar Subrahmanyam, *Journal of Financial Economics*,
    49, 1998, 345–73   437

Name index   467

Acknowledgements

The author and publishers wish to thank the following who have kindly given permission for the use of copyright material.

American Finance Association for the following articles from *Journal of Finance*: 'An Approach to the Valuation of Uncertain Income Streams', **XXVIII** (3), June 1973, 661–74; 'Efficient Financing under Asymmetric Information', with Alan Kraus, **XLII** (5), December 1987, 1225–43; 'Vendor Financing', with Vojislav Maksimovic and Josef Zechner, **XLIII** (5), December 1988, 1127–41; 'Latent Assets', **XLV** (3), July 1990, 709–30; 'The Valuation of American Put Options', with Eduardo S. Schwartz, **XXXII** (2), May 1977, 449–62; 'The Pricing of Contingent Claims in Discrete Time Models', **XXXIV** (1), March 1979, 53–68; 'Time-Invariant Portfolio Insurance Strategies', with Eduardo S. Schwartz, **XLIII** (2), June 1988, 283–99; 'International Portfolio Investment Flows' with H. Henry Cao, **LII** (5), December 1997, 1851–80; 'Stock Prices and the Supply of Information', with Patricia J. Hughes, **XLVI** (5), December 1991, 1665–91.

Association for Investment Management and Research for article: 'Stripping the S&P 500 Index', *Financial Analysts Journal*, January/February 1998, 12–22.

Elsevier Science for articles: 'A Continuous Time Approach to the Pricing of Bonds', with Eduardo S. Schwartz, *Journal of Banking and Finance*, **3**, 1979, 133–55; 'Investment Analysis and Price Formation in Securities Markets', with Avanidhar Subrahmanyam, *Journal of Financial Economics*, **38**, 1995, 361–81; 'Alternative Factor Specifications, Security Characteristics, and the Cross-Section of Expected Stock Returns', with Tarun Chordia and Avanidhar Subrahmanyam, *Journal of Financial Economics*, **49**, 1998, 345–73.

Financial Management Association International for article: 'Corporate Finance over the Past 25 Years', *Financial Management*, **24** (2), Summer 1995, 9–22.

Journal of Financial and Quantitative Analysis for articles: 'Finite Difference Methods and Jump Processes Arising in the Pricing of Contingent Claims: A Synthesis' with Eduardo S. Schwartz, **XIII** (3), September 1978, 461–74; 'Optimal Portfolio Insurance' with R. Solanki, **XVI** (3), September 1981, 279–300.

National Tax Association for article: 'Taxes, Market Valuation and Corporate Financial Policy', *National Tax Journal*, **XXIII** (4), December 1970, 417–27.

Oxford University Press for articles: 'Information, Trade, and Derivative Securities', with H. Henry Cao, *Review of Financial Studies*, **9** (1), Spring 1996, 163–208;

'Investment Analysis and the Adjustment of Stock Prices to Common Information' with Narasimhan Jegadeesh and Bhaskaran Swaminathan, *Review of Financial Studies*, **6** (4), Winter 1993, 799–824.

RAND Journal of Economics for article: 'Consistent Regulatory Policy under Uncertainty', with Eduardo S. Schwartz, *Bell Journal of Economics*, **13** (2), Autumn 1982, 506–21.

University of Chicago Press for the following articles from *Journal of Business*; 'Corporate Income Taxes, Valuation, and the Problem of Optimal Capital Structure', with Eduardo S. Schwartz, **51** (1), 1978, 103–14; 'Evaluating Natural Resource Investments', with Eduardo S. Schwartz, **58** (2), 1985, 135–57; 'Portfolio Insurance and Financial Market Equilibrium', with Eduardo S. Schwartz, **62** (4), 1989, 455–72.

Introduction

My education in economics began at Oxford University in 1961 where I studied Philosophy, Politics and Economics. I was not so much drawn towards economics by enthusiasm, as deterred from the pursuit of philosophy by the rigours of mathematical logic. On graduating, I was able to continue my studies in economics on a fellowship at Nuffield College. Completing the graduate B.Phil degree in one year, and by then somewhat dillusioned about the practical relevance of economics as I had learned it, I was invited by Professor Bela Gold of the University of Pittsburgh to pursue an MBA degree at that university. Pitt was then offering a one year MBA that was taught in large part by Carnegie Tech Ph.D. students; it was therefore at the forefront of the new movement in graduate education in business that had been stimulated by the recent Ford and Carnegie Foundation reports on business education. Pitt proved a good choice for me, providing an excellent grounding in accounting, statistics, and computer programming, as well as such esoterica as linear and dynamic programming – all within the space of one year.

This year at Pitt restored the faith that I had lost at Oxford in the relevance of economic analysis for practical men, and I applied to MIT for a Ph.D., and was accepted in 1967. Unfortunately my father died after only one month, and I returned to England for the balance of the academic year, only to re-enroll, newly married, in September 1968. My initial plan was to study marketing but I was persuaded by Professor Dan Holland to switch to finance. At that time, the field of finance was sparse, being divided between, on the one hand, the newly developed mathematical programming techniques and, on the other, the neoclassical economics models of Modigliani and Miller. Sprouting between these was the newly emergent theory of asset pricing which, at least in Bill Sharpe's case, owed as much to mathematical programming as it did to economics. Working as a research assistant, I was surprised to find Myron Scholes and Franco Modigliani actually attempting to test the Capital Asset Pricing Model (CAPM) on data from the newly constructed Center for Research into Security Prices (CRSP) tapes. I was surprised, because it had never occurred to me that one could substitute for the moments of subjective probability distributions that enter the theory, the sample moments estimated from historical data. Although routine today and grounded in the theory of rational expectations, at that time the idea that one could replace the subjective expectations of the theory by outcomes seemed bold to say the least. But when the time came for me to do my own work, I not only turned to working on the CAPM, modestly extending it to allow for tax rates that differ across investors (see Chapter 1), but actually tried to estimate the average tax rate using the same techniques. However, I had little faith in the empirical estimates and left it to others[1] to tease the truth from the data. One lesson that this experience taught me was the important role of the investigator's prior beliefs – coming from England where tax rates had been punitive, I was convinced that the tax authorities were serious so that there must be a tax effect in returns. Black and Scholes, reflecting the more tolerant tax environment of the US, thought that taxes could be avoided, reducing the effective tax rate to zero – thus they reported that 'it is not possible to demonstrate that the returns on high yield securities are different from the returns on low yield securities either before taxes or after taxes'. I was fortunate to have both Franco and Myron on my dissertation committee. Graduating with a student visa meant that I would have to leave the US within two years. Receiving an attractive offer from the University of British Columbia (UBC) and finding the environment there ideal for my growing family, we moved there in 1970.

UBC proved to be a supportive setting for me, and in the next two years I published two papers clearing up confusions in the corporate finance literature (Brennan, 1971b, 1973a)[2], but my major effort was in trying to extend the CAPM so that it could be used to value cash flows more than one period in the future. This culminated in Chapter 2 which owed much to what I had learned from Bob Merton about continuous time processes. The idea that asset prices should satisfy a partial differential equation had been anticipated in an unpublished paper by Jack Treynor. It was to be further developed by Bhattacharya (1978), Constantinides (1978) and Cox, Ingersoll and Ross (1985), though there has unfortunately been relatively little recent work on developing this framework for valuing risky cash flows. During this time I was also working on extending the CAPM to allow for differential borrowing and lending rates (Brennan 1971a) and transaction costs (Brennan 1975). Rolf Banz told me that the latter paper inspired his empirical work which was to uncover the 'small firm effect', probably the first of an increasing collection of empirical anomalies that were to plague the asset pricing paradigm as soon as Michael Jensen (1978) declared that: 'there is no other proposition in economics that has more solid empirical evidence supporting it than the Efficient Market Hypothesis.'

While UBC was a comfortable environment, it was not especially challenging until Alan Kraus arrived in the mid-1970s. A scholar of exceptional depth and ability, he encouraged me to read carefully for the first time the more technical papers that I had previously regarded as falling outside the applied field of finance. The result was a series of joint papers, including (1976) and (1978), in which we attempted to exposit the peculiar features of the HARA (Hyperbolic abolute risk aversion) class of utility functions that made them so useful. We showed that portfolio separation, the aggregation property, and the property that the Bellman function retains the HARA characteristic could all be traced back to the homotheticity of the indifference curves in state contingent claim space for this class of utility functions.

I had left MIT in 1970 with an early draft of the Black–Scholes manuscript in my satchel but, while I taught this to several generations of MBA students, I was not able to see how to apply the principles more generally until I met Eduardo Schwartz. A Chilean mining engineer, he had come to Canada to escape the political disruptions in his native country. Phelim Boyle, a former actuary from the UK, explained to us the problems that UK insurance companies had experienced during the market drop in 1974 because they had sold guarantees on the value of equity portfolios. We recognized that what was involved was a put option but one that did not fit the standard Black–Scholes assumptions. However, Eduardo knew that such partial differential equations could be solved numerically and the result was Brennan and Schwartz (1976, 1979a) in which we showed how to price such contracts and to hedge them, well before the technique of dynamic asset allocation or portfolio insurance became notorious.

Armed with numerical skills, we discovered that the solution to a whole range of problems was now within our reach. We valued American put options using over the counter price data from Myron Scholes (see Chapter 10), and found that before the Black–Scholes era there were very big differences between the Black–Scholes prices and the market prices. Contemporaneously with Oldrich Vasicek we began to apply the same principles to interest rate contingent claims (Brennan and Schwartz 1977a); our inspiration was the humble savings bond which gave the investor the right to redeem early and at that time played a major role in Canadian government finance. We valued puttable bonds as well as callable bonds and, turning to corporate finance, showed how to value callable convertible bonds (1977c, 1980b), and for the first time were able to model in a dynamic context the twin pillars of capital structure theory, tax deductibility of interest and bankruptcy costs which we captured by a loss of the debt tax shield (Chapter 3)[3]. In Chapter 11 we explored the relation between the standard finite difference approximation procedures we were using to solve the Black–Scholes equation and the approximation of the underlying diffusion process by a jump process, demonstrating that the finite difference procedure is equivalent to a certain numerical integration. I was intrigued by the finding of Rubinstein (1976) that the Black–Scholes model could be obtained in a discrete time setting without the usual arbitrage arguments if one was willing to assume a representative investor with power utility. Further explorations along these lines led to Chapter 13 in which I showed that Rubinstein's results were in a sense necessary as well as sufficient and that they could be extended to the normal-exponential case, a result Henry Cao and I were to find useful in Chapter 17.[4]

In 1977 I was eligible for my first sabbatical leave. Casting about for a reason to spend it in England, I decided to study savings bonds in different countries. As part of this project, Eduardo and I developed a model for valuing the put feature on Canada Savings Bonds, and predicting redemptions. We realized that it was not possible to do serious empirical work on interest-dependent claims with the single factor model of the yield curve that we had already developed, since it was obvious to us that the curve twisted as well as shifted vertically. We therefore developed a two factor model in which the second factor was the yield on a consol bond which we called the long rate. In our empirical work we took care to estimate the parameters of the joint process for the two interest rates taking account of the discreteness of the sample data – we later found that for short sampling intervals this was an unnecessary refinement. Although much effort has been devoted to improving estimation techniques for diffusion processes, recent investigations have confirmed the robustness of discrete time approximations.[5] In addition to a monograph published by the New York Institute of Finance, our work on interest-dependent claims was published in Brennan and Schwartz (1980a, 1982c,d, 1983, 1985d) as well as Chapter 12, and led to several Wall Street opportunities for us as trading in interest derivatives began to develop in the early 1980s.

In the early 1980s Eduardo and I began to apply our knowledge of derivatives pricing and stochastic optimal control theory to valuation problems in corporate finance. Stimulated by consulting assignments on utility regulation, we developed the concept of a consistent regulatory policy in Chapter 4. We had been struck by the conceptual inconsistency of most rates of return regulation in which risk and required rates of return were estimated as though these were exogenous data. We showed that these variables depended on the *future* policy of the regulator, which implies that regulatory policy cannot be determined myopically from rate hearing to rate hearing, but must be set as an internally consistent *policy* in which the investor is fairly compensated today for the risks that the regulatory policy will impose tomorrow. We applied variants of the same corporate valuation model to show the dynamic effects on corporate investment policy of regulation (1982a), and the agency problem is induced by corporate debt (1984). Perhaps our most influential papers in this series were Chapter 5 and Brennan and Schwartz (1985c) in which we showed how option pricing methods could be applied to real investment projects where, as in most cases, there is scope for managerial discretion about future output rates and so on; in one sense we were doing no more than integrate the decision tree analysis that had figured in standard texts for 20 years with modern valuation techniques.

In the early 1980s my interests broadened from a concern solely with valuing securities and real assets to a concern with why particular securities existed and had particular characteristics. In Chapter 14 Solanki and I asked what type of insurance contract on his portfolio return a rational investor would demand if the contract were priced by Black–Scholes principles. This paper was of interest, not only because it was one of the first to introduce the concept of portfolio insurance[6] but because it showed for the first time how a dynamic portfolio problem could be reduced to a static problem in a complete market – this idea was to be pursued more rigorously in a series of papers by Cox and Huang (1989) and others. In Brennan and Schwartz (1982b), Schwartz and I proposed an informal theory of convertible bond issuance in which we argued that convertibles could mediate differences of opinion between investors and firms about the underlying risk of the firm. In Chapter 6 Alan Kraus and I developed the idea more formally by showing that the terms of a convertible bond issue could be designed to signal the risk characteristics of the firm to investors, the possibility of capital structure being used as a signal having been proposed earlier by Ross (1977).[7]

In Chapter 15 Schwartz and I defined and explored the class of portfolio insurance strategies that were 'time-invariant' in the sense that the fraction of wealth allocated to risky securities is time-independent. In Chapter 16, chastened by the blame that portfolio insurance strategies had attracted in the 1987 Stock Market Crash, we investigated the effect of portfolio insurance strategies on stock market volatility – we concluded that the effect was likely to be modest so long as the portfolio insurance was fully anticipated by market participants.[8] Our attention was next attracted by the increasingly popular strategy of arbitraging away discrepancies in the pricing of stock index futures – this strategy is limited by the transaction costs that must be incurred and made more attractive by the possibility that a mispricing in one direction may evolve into mispricing in the other direction before cash and futures coincide at maturity – the interplay of these factors creates a nice problem that we analysed in Brennan and Schwartz (1988b, 1990).

Following the pioneering work of Modigliani and Miller, the financial policies of corporations for a long time defied satisfactory explanation. In the late 1980s I worked on two issues of financial policy: trade credit and stock splits. In Chapter 7 Maksimovic, Zechner and I offered a theory of why corporations often act as financial intermediaries by providing credit to their customers: an offer of financing by the vendor may allow him to price discriminate between different classes of customer.[9] Grinblatt *et al.* (1984) had shown that stock splits were accompanied by abnormal stock returns despite the fact that a split is apparently without economic significance. Copeland and I (1988b) developed a signalling theory of stock splits which relied on the fact that lower priced stocks had higher brokerage trading costs – we showed that it was possible to construct a signalling equilibrium in which firms with good private information could signal their quality by splitting, essentially because, given their good prospects the expected transaction costs associated with a lower share price would be lower for them than for lower quality firms; the model explained around 28 per cent of the split announcement returns. I returned to this theme with Hughes (see Chapter 20) In that paper we argued that the higher brokerage commissions associated with low priced stocks provided an additional incentive to sell side analysts to produce information about these stocks. A stock split therefore allows management to attract the attention of analysts: firms with good private information will have an incentive to split. We found evidence that the number of analysts following a stock increased after a split.

Chordia and I (1993) pursued the brokerage commission–information link further by exploring the optimality of selling information by charging a brokerage commission on trades – we showed that, depending on the quality of the information and the heterogeneity of the information purchasers a brokerage commission might offer significant advantages over either a fixed fee as charged by a newsletter or a proportional asset management fee as charged by mutual funds. At the empirical level, Copeland and I (1988a) had found that the apparent rise in stock betas following stock splits was due to a more timely adjustment in stock prices which made stock and market returns more contemporaneous. In Chapter 21 Jegadeesh, Swaminathan and I showed that the lagged price adjustment of small firms that had been uncovered by Lo and MacKinlay (1988) was in fact attributable to differences in the number of analysts following the firms rather than to firm size *per se*.[10] Subrahmanyam and I in Chapter 22 identified another role for investment analysis – we showed that an increase in the number of analysts following a firm tended to increase the liquidity of a firm's shares as measured by the Kyle (1985) lambda; this is inconsistent with the notion that increased competition between information producers will reduce the information asymmetry problem which causes illiquidity. The final link between investment analysis and a firm's cost of capital was established in Brennan and Subrahmanyam (1996), where we showed that the risk-adjusted expected return on equities depended on the (il)liquidity of the firm's shares as measured by the Kyle lambda. Brennan and Subrahmanyam (1998) provided the empirical support for the Kyle model by showing that investor order placing strategies are consistent with the assumptions of the Kyle model.

In Chapter 22 Subrahmanyam and I had been able to use only a short sample to explore the relation between returns and illiquidity because transaction by transaction data were required to estimate the Kyle lambda. We therefore decided that since trading volume was the major determinant of liquidity, we would look for a relation between risk-adjusted returns and several other firm characteristics including trading volume. With Chordia as a co-author in Chapter 23 we developed a novel statistical approach in which we used the risk-adjusted returns on individual securities instead of returns on portfolios as the dependent variables in our regressions. Among other things, we found that the firm size effect was completely subsumed by a trading volume effect which is consistent with required returns being influenced by liquidity considerations.

Returning to the corporate finance theme, Anjan Thakor and I (1990) argued that dividend payments might be preferred to share repurchases under certain circumstances because the *pro rata* nature of dividends protects uninformed investors from the possible wealth redistribution effects associated with repurchases. In Chapter 8 I returned to a puzzle which had intrigued me since my work on natural resource investments, namely why firms dig up gold from the ground when the world stocks of gold are so large that the value of an additional unit of stocks as measured by the convenience yield is effectively zero. Why not defer the extraction to a later date when the present value of the extraction costs will be lower? I provided an explanation rooted in information asymmetry: the only way to demonstrate the value of a deposit to outsiders is to extract it. I demonstrated that the higher quality deposits would be exploited first, and drew implications for the management of other 'latent' corporate assets. I also demonstrated that security analysis and valuation may have an element of the 'conventional' about them – there is little benefit to discovering important information about the value of firm assets unless it will be recognized by other analysts and be reflected in the share price soon.[10] Most recently, Julian Franks and I (1997) added one more brick to the edifice explaining initial public offerings (IPO) underpricing by showing that firms that were more underpriced tend to have a more diffuse ownership structure – we also found that the costs of underpricing are not on the whole borne by boards of directors who tend not to be sellers at the IPO. Chapter 9 reflects my views of 25 years of progress and development in the field of corporate finance.

A major new research theme I developed in the 1990s with Henry Cao is the analysis of multi-period markets with asymmetric information. In Chapter 17 we analysed a dynamic noisy rational expectations economy, demonstrating among other things that less well informed investors would prefer securities whose pay-offs are convex functions of the pay-off on an underlying asset (while better informed investors would prefer concave functions); such convex pay-off functions are reminiscent of portfolio insurance pay-offs and, in the absence of the requisite securities, we showed how investors would attempt to synthesize their own pay-offs by dynamic replication. In Chapter 19 we applied these ideas to international portfolio flows: if foreigners are less well informed about domestic capital markets we should expect them to behave as trend-followers, buying on market rises and selling on declines; this seems to capture a signficant aspect of international portfolio flows.

Concerned like others with the giddy heights to which equity markets have risen in the 1990s, I conceived of a new security in Chapter 18 which I believe would serve to focus investor attention on the cash flow streams that are the ultimate source of value for securities, as well as providing improved risk sharing opportunities for investors. In other work, Schwartz and I, along with Lagnado (1997), have been exploring the implications of the predictability of asset returns for dynamic portfolio strategies. We find that for utility functions which are different from the log, the optimal dynamic portfolio strategy differs significantly from the optimal one period strategy which is the basis for most applied 'tactical asset allocation' models. A weakness of our approach is that it assumes that the parameters of the system generating expected returns are known rather than estimated. Therefore in Brennan (1998b) I turned my attention to the problem of learning about the parameter values, and showed that the fact that the parameters are only estimated can have a dramatic effect on the optimal strategy of an investor who has a long horizon. As yet this work is at a rudimentary stage. However, in unpublished work, Yihong Xia and I have shown that, in an equilibrium setting, learning about the aggregate dividend process can account for the variability of stock prices relative to dividends that some authors have regarded as *prima facie* evidence of investor irrationality.

Looking back on almost 30 years of work, I am struck by how much our field has advanced over this period. In many respects of course the field is still in its infancy, and there are many things that we still only see 'as through a glass, darkly'. For this reason financial economics exerts a continuing fascination for me, and attracts a stream of bright young people into the field. No less than 17 of the 23 papers in this collection are co-authored and, of these, 14 are co-authored with my former doctoral students. I am grateful to have had the opportunity to work with such exciting colleagues, and particularly with Eduardo Schwartz, my first and most frequent co-author. These papers are as much theirs as mine.

Notes
1. Black and Scholes (1974), Litzenberger and Ramaswamy (1979), Miller and Scholes (1978).
2. References for all of Brennan's publications are in the Bibliography.
3. This led to subsequent work by Zechner *et al.* (1989), and more recently Leland (1994).
4. The result was extended by Heston (1993), and used by Amin and Ng (1993) among others.
5. See Stanton (1997).
6. The other was Leland (1980).
7. More recent papers which have rationalized the role of convertibles includes Harris and Raviv (1985) and Stein (1992).
8. This theme has been pursued more recently by Basak (1995) and Grossman and Zhou (1996) among others.
9. Petersen and Rajan (1997) find evidence that is consistent with the price discrimination hypothesis.
10. This is consistent with the theoretical analysis of Holden and Subrahmanyam (1992).
11. This phenomenon has been analysed further by Froot *et al.* (1992), and Hirshleifer *et al.* (1994).

References
Amin, K. and V.K. Ng (1993), 'Option valuation with stochastic volatility', *Journal of Finance*, **XLVIII**, 881–910.
Basak, S. (1995), 'A general equilibrium model of portfolio insurance', *Review of Financial Studies*, **8**, 1059–90.
Bhattacharya, S. (1978), 'Project valuation with mean reverting cash flows', *Journal of Finance*, **XXXIII**, 1317–31.
Black, F. and M.S. Scholes (1974), 'The effects of dividend yield and dividend policy on common stock prices and returns', *Journal of Financial Economics*, **1**, 1–22.
Constantinides, G.M. (1978), 'Market risk adjustment in project valuation', *Journal of Finance*, **XXXIII**, 606–16.
Cox, J.C. and Chi-fu Huang (1989), 'Optimal consumption and portfolio policies when asset prices

follow a diffusion process', *Journal of Economic Theory*, **49**, 33-83.

Cox, J.C., J.E. Ingersoll and S.A. Ross (1985), 'A theory of the term structure of interest rates', *Econometrica*, **53**, 385-408.

Froot, K.A., D.S. Scharfstein and J. Stein (1992), 'Herd on the street: Informational efficiencies in a market with short-term speculation', *Journal of Finance*, **XLVII**, 1461-84.

Grinblatt, M., R. Masulis and S. Titman (1984), 'The valuation/effects of stock splits and stock dividends', *Journal of Financial Economics*, **13**, 461-90.

Grossman, S.J. and Z. Zhou (1996), 'Equilibrium analysis of portfolio insurance', *Journal of Finance*, **LI**, 1379-404.

Harris, M. and A. Raviv (1985), 'A sequential signalling model of convertible debt call policy', *Journal of Finance*, **XLI**, 1263-81.

Heston, S. (1993), 'Invisible parameters in option prices', *Journal of Finance*, **XLVIII**, 933-47.

Hirshleifer, D., A. Subrahmanyam and S. Titman (1994), 'Security analysis and trading patterns when some investors receive information before others', *Journal of Finance*, **XLIX**, 1665-98.

Holden, C. and A. Subrahmanyam (1992), 'Long-lived private information and imperfect competition', *Journal of Finance*, **XLVII**, 247-70.

Jensen, M.C. (1978), 'Some anomalous evidence regarding market efficiency', *Journal of Financial Economics*, **6**, 5-101.

Kyle, A.S. (1985), 'Continuous Auctions and Insider Trading', *Econometrica*, **53**, 1315-35.

Leland, H.E. (1980), 'Who should buy portfolio insurance?', *Journal of Finance*, **XXXV**, 581-94.

Leland, H.E. (1994), 'Corporate debt value, debt covenants, and optimal capital structure', *Journal of Finance*, **XLIX**, 1213-52.

Litzenberger, R.H. and K. Ramaswamy (1979), 'The effect of personal taxes and dividends on capital asset prices: Theory and empirical evidence', *Journal of Financial Economics*, **7**, 163-96.

Lo, A. and C. MacKinlay (1988), 'Stock prices do not follow random walks: evidence from a simple specification test', *Review of Financial Studies*, **1**, 175-206.

Miller, M.H. and M.S. Scholes (1978), 'Dividends and taxes', *Journal of Financial Economics*, **6**, 333-64.

Petersen, M.A. and R.G. Rajan (1997), 'Trade credit: Theories and evidence', *Review of Financial Studies*, **10**, 661-92.

Ross, S.A. (1977), 'The determination of financial structure: The incentive-signalling aproach', *Bell Journal of Economics and Management Science*, **8**, 23-40.

Rubinstein, M. (1976), 'The valuation of uncertain income streams and the pricing of options', *Bell Journal of Economics and Management Service*, **7**, 407-25.

Stanton, R. (1997), 'A nonparametric model of term structure dynamics and the market price of interest rate risk', *Journal of Finance*, **LII**, 1973-2002.

Stein, J.C. (1992), 'Convertible Bonds as Backdoor Equity Financing', *Journal of Financial Economics*, **32**, 3-21.

Zechner, J., E.O. Fischer and R. Heinkel (1989), 'Dynamic capital structure choice: Theory and tests', *Journal of Finance*, **XLIV**, 19-40.

Complete bibliography: M.J. Brennan

Brennan, M.J. (1970), 'Taxes, market valuation and corporate financial policy', *National Tax Journal*, **XXIII** (4), December, 417–27.

Brennan, M.J. (1971a), 'Capital market equilibrium with divergent borrowing and lending rates', *Journal of Financial and Quantitative Analysis*, **VI** (5), December, 1197–206.

Brennan, M.J. (1971b), 'A note on dividend irrelevance and the Gordon valuation model', *Journal of Finance*, **XXVI** (5), December, 1115–21.

Brennan, M.J. (1973a), 'A new look at the weighted average cost of capital', *Journal of Business Finance*, **5** (1), 24–30.

Brennan, M.J. (1973b), 'An approach to the valuation of uncertain income streams', *Journal of Finance*, **XXVIII** (3), July, 661–73.

Brennan, M.J. (1975), 'The optimal number of securities in a risky asset portfolio when there are fixed costs of transacting: Theory and some empirical results', *Journal of Financial and Quantitative Analysis*, **X** (4), September, 483–96.

Brennan, M.J. and A. Kraus (1976), 'The geometry of separation and myopia', *Journal of Financial and Quantitative Analysis*, **XI** (2), June, 171–93.

Brennan, M.J. and E.S. Schwartz (1976), 'The pricing of equity-linked life insurance policies with an asset value guarantee', Journal of Financial Economics, 3, 195–213.

Brennan, M.J. and E.S. Schwartz (1977a), 'Savings bonds, retractable bonds and callable bonds', *Journal of Financial Economics*, **5**, 67–8.

Brennan, M.J. and E.S. Schwartz (1977b), 'The valuation of American put options', *Journal of Finance*, **XXXII** (2), May, 449–62.

Brennan, M.J. and E.S. Schwartz (1977c), 'Convertible bonds: Valuation and optimal strategies for call and conversion', *Journal of Finance*, **XXXII** (5), December, 1699–715.

Brennan, M.J. and A. Kraus (1978), 'Necessary conditions for aggregation in securities markets', *Journal of Financial and Quantitative Analysis*, **XIII** (3), September, 407–18.

Brennan, M.J. and E.S. Schwartz (1978a), 'Corporate income taxes, valuation and the problem of optimal capital structure', *Journal of Business*, **51** (1), January, 103–14.

Brennan, M.J. and E.S. Schwartz (1978b), 'Finite difference methods and jump processes arising in the pricing of contingent claims: A synthesis', *Journal of Financial and Quantitative Analysis*, **XIII** (3), September, 461–74.

Brennan, M.J. (1979), 'The pricing of contingent claims in discrete time models', *Journal of Finance*, **XXXIV** (1), March, 53–68.

Brennan, M.J. and E.S. Schwartz (1979a), 'Alternative investment strategies for the issuers of equity-linked life insurance policies with an asset value guarantee', *Journal of Business*, **52** (1), January, 63–93.

Brennan, M.J. and E.S. Schwartz (1979b), 'A continuous time approach to the pricing of bonds', *Journal of Banking and Finance*, **3** (2), July, 133–55; reprinted in Lane Hughston (ed.) (1996), *Vasicek and Beyond*, London: Risk Publications.

Brennan, M.J. and E.S. Schwartz (1980a), 'Conditional predictions of bond prices and returns', *Journal of Finance*, **XXXV** (2), May, 405–17.

Brennan, M.J. and E.S. Schwartz (1980b), 'Analyzing convertible securities', *Journal of Financial and Qualitative Analysis*, **XV** (4), November, 907–29.

Brennan, M.J. and R. Solanki (1981), 'Optimal portfolio insurance', *Journal of Financial and Quantitative Analysis*, **XVI** (3), September, 279–300.

Brennan, M.J. and E.S. Schwartz (1982a), 'Regulation and corporate investment policy', *Journal of Finance*, **37** (2), May, 289–300.

Brennan, M.J. and E.S. Schwartz (1982b), 'The case for convertibles', *Chase Financial Quarterly*, **1** (3), Spring, 27–46.

Brennan, M.J. and E.S. Schwartz (1982c), 'Bond pricing and market efficiency', *Financial Analysts Journal*, **38** (5), September/October, 49–56.

Brennan, M.J. and E.S. Schwartz (1982d), 'An equilibrium model of bond pricing and a test of market efficiency', *Journal of Financial and Quantitative Analysis*, **XVII** (3), September, 301–29.

Brennan, M.J. and E.S. Schwartz (1982e), 'Consistent regulatory policy under uncertainty', *Bell Journal of Economics*, **13** (2). Autumn, 506–21.

Brennan, M.J. and E.S. Schwartz (1983), 'Alternative methods for valuing debt options', *Finance*, **4** (2), October, 119–37.

Brennan, M.J. and E.S. Schwartz (1984), 'Optimal financial policy and firm valuation', *Journal of Finance*, **XXXIX** (3), July, 593–607.

Brennan, M.J. and E.S. Schwartz (1985a), 'A note on the geometric mean index', *Journal of Financial and Quantitative Analysis*, **XX** (1), March, 119–22.

Brennan, M.J. and E.S. Schwartz (1985b), 'Evaluating natural resource investments', *Journal of Business*, **58** (2), April, 135–57.

Brennan, M.J. and E.S. Schwartz (1985c), 'A new approach to evaluating natural resource investments', *Midland Corporate Finance Journal*, **3** (1), Spring, 37–47.

Brennan, M.J. and E.S. Schwartz (1985d), 'Determinants of GNMA mortgage prices', *Journal of the American Real Estate and Urban Economics Association*, **13** (3), Fall, 209–28.

Brennan, M.J. (1986), 'A theory of price limits in futures markets', *Journal of Financial Economics*, **16** (2), June, 213–34.

Brennan, M.J. and A. Kraus (1987), 'Efficient financing under asymmetric information', *Journal of Finance*, **XLII** (5), December, 1225–44.

Brennan, M.J. and T.E. Copeland (1988a), 'Beta changes around stock splits: A note', *Journal of Finance*, **XLIII** (4), September, 1009–14.

Brennan, M.J. and T.E. Copeland (1988b), 'Stock splits, stock prices and transaction costs', *Journal of Financial Economics*, **22**, 83–102.

Brennan, M.J., V. Maksimovic and J. Zechner (1988), 'Vendor financing', *Journal of Finance*, **XLIII** (5), December, 1127–41.

Brennan, M.J. and E.S. Schwartz (1988a), 'Time-invariant portfolio insurance strategies', *Journal of Finance*, **XLIII** (2), June, 283–300.

Brennan, M.J. and E.S. Schwartz (1988b), 'Optimal arbitrage strategies under basis variability', *Journal of Banking and Finance*, **5**, 167–80.

Brennan, M.J. and E.S. Schwartz (1989), 'Portfolio insurance and financial market equilibrium', *Journal of Business*, **62**, 455–72.

Brennan, M.J. and B. Solnik (1989), 'International risk sharing and capital mobility', *Journal of International Money and Finance*, **8**, 359–73.

Brennan, M.J. and E.S. Schwartz (1990), 'Arbitrage in stock index futures', *Journal of Business*, **63**, S7–S53.

Brennan, M.J. (1990), 'Latent assets', *Journal of Finance*, **XLV**, 709–30.

Brennan, M.J. and A.V. Thakor (1990), 'Shareholder preferences and dividend policy', *Journal of Finance*, **XLV**, 993–1018.

Brennan, M.J. (1991), 'A perspective on accounting and stock prices', *Accounting Review*, **66**, 67–79; reprinted in *Journal of Applied Corporate Finance*, 1995, **8**.

Brennan, M.J. and Hughes, P.J. (1991), 'Stock prices and the supply of information', *Journal of Finance*, **XLVI** (5), 1665–91.

Brennan, M.J. (1993), 'Aspects of insurance intermediation and finance', *Geneva Papers on Risk and Insurance Theory*, **18** (1), 7–30.

Brennan, M.J. and T. Chordia (1993), 'Brokerage commission schedules', *Journal of Finance*, **XLVIII**, 1379–402.

Brennan, M.J., J. DeTemple and A. Kalay (1993), 'Une nouvelle optique d'evaluation de la dette contractuelle', *Fineco*, **2**, 183–204.

Brennan, M.J., N. Jegadeesh and B. Swaminathan (1993), 'Investment analysis and the adjustment of stock prices to common information', *Review of Financial Studies*, **6**, 799–824.

Brennan, M.J. (1994), 'Incentives, rationality and society', *Journal of Applied Corporate Finance*, **7**, 31–9.

Brennan, M.J. (1995a), 'The individual investor', *Journal of Financial Research*, **18**, 59–74.

Brennan, M.J. (1995b), 'Corporate finance over the past 25 years', *Financial Management*, **24** (2), Summer, 9–22.

Brennan, M.J. and A. Subrahmanyam (1995), 'Investment analysis and price formation in securities markets', *Journal of Financial Economics*, **38** (3), July, 361–81.

Brennan, M.J. (1996), 'Executive compensation in the UK', *Journal of Applied Corporate Finance*, **9**, 88–93.

Brennan, M.J. and H.H. Cao (1996), 'Information, trade and derivative securities', *Review of Financial Studies*, **9** (1), 163–208.

Brennan, M.J. and A. Subrahmanyam (1996), 'Market microstructure and asset pricing: On the compensation for market illiquidity in stock returns', *Journal of Financial Economics*, **41**, 441–64.

Brennan, M.J. (1997), 'The term structure of discount rates', *Financial Management*, **26**, 9–24.

Brennan, M.J. and H.H. Cao (1997) 'International portfolio investment flows', *Journal of Finance*, **LII** (5), 1851–80.

Brennan, M.J. and Julian Franks (1997), 'Underpricing, ownership and control in initial public offerings of equity securities in the UK', *Journal of Financial Economics*, 45, 391–410.

Brennan, M.J., E.S. Schwartz and R. Lagnado (1997), 'Strategic asset allocation', *Journal of Economic Dynamics and Control*, **21**, 1377–403.

Brennan, M.J. (1998a), 'Stripping the S&P 500', *Financial Analysts Journal*, January/February, 12–22.

Brennan, M.J. (1998b), 'The role of learning in dynamic portfolio decisions', *European Finance Review*.

Brennan, M.J., T. Chordia and A. Subrahmanyam (1998), 'Alternative factor specifications, security characteristics, and the cross-section of expected security returns, *Journal of Financial Economics*, **49**, 345–73.

Brennan, M.J. and A. Subrahmanyam (1998), 'The determinants of average trade size', *Journal of Business*.

PART I

CORPORATE FINANCE

[1]

TAXES, MARKET VALUATION AND CORPORATE FINANCIAL POLICY

M. J. BRENNAN*

IN A well-known series of papers Franco Modigliani and Merton Miller[1] have outlined a general framework for the analysis of the effects of capital structure and dividend policies on the valuation of the corporation under uncertainty. What disagreement remains about their conclusions stems mainly from different beliefs about the effects of various market imperfections on their analysis.[2] Modigliani and Miller themselves have dealt comprehensively with one such imperfection, namely the tax system as it affects corporations directly.[3] However, while they have directed attention to the effects of the tax system as it relates to the taxation of corporate income, their papers are characterized by an almost total neglect of the complementary aspect of the system, which is the taxation of individuals. It is the purpose of this paper to extend their analysis to incorporate the effects of those features of the personal tax structure which are relevant for the valuation of the corporation.

Two features of the personal tax structure stand out in importance for the theory of valuation. First is the provision of the existing tax code which permits individuals as well as corporations to deduct interest payments from the computation of their taxable income. Second is the asymmetric tax treatment of income received in the form of dividends and of capital gains. The difficulty of introducing these institutional imperfections into the analysis arises from the progressive nature of the personal tax structure, which causes the relevant marginal tax rates to vary between investors in different income classes.

An important step towards recognizing the effects of the personal tax structure on corporate financial policy was made in a 1967 article in this journal by Farrar and Selwyn.[4] However, their analysis is limited by its concentration on the net income received by an investor with given tax rates from a share in a corporation, as that corporation pursues alternative financial policies. Their use of this net income concept as a criterion of optimality suffers by its implicit neglect of the market exchange opportunities open to an investor who does not find a particular set of financial policies congenial. To take into account these market exchange opportunities requires the development of a market valuation principle, so that the impact of alternative financial policies on the value of the corporation may be calculated: the Farrar-Selwyn paper lacks such a valuation principle.

The outline of this paper is as follows: in Section I the Farrar-Selwyn analysis and its results are considered in more detail. In Section II a market equilibrium condition is developed which takes account of the diversity of investor marginal tax rates. From this equilibrium condition a market valuation equation is developed in Section III. This is then used to discuss the effects of alternative dividend policies on the valuation of the corporation. In Section IV the effects of alternative capital structures are discussed within the framework of the same

*University of British Columbia. This paper represents a substantial part of a thesis completed at M.I.T. in June 1970. The author is grateful to the Sloan School for financial support and to his thesis committee, especially Franco Modigliani, for his help and encouragement. Daniel Rie and a referee have also made helpful comments. The author is responsible for remaining errors. An abbreviated version of this paper was presented at the Second World Econometric Congress in Cambridge, September 1970.

[1][4, 5, 6, 7]

[2]Major attention has been focused on the effects of bankruptcy costs by P. A. Tinsley [12]. There remains also some dispute about the effects of dividend policy under uncertainty.

[3][7].

[4][1].

valuation model. In Section V attention is directed to the interactions of capital structure and dividend policies when the firm is subject to a share re-purchase constraint.

Throughout the paper we abstract from the postponability feature of the capital gains tax, and assume that taxes on capital gains as on dividends must be paid each period.

I

We summarize here the most general part of the Farrar-Selwyn analysis of corporate financial policy, in which they take into account the full array of personal and corporate tax rates.[5] They consider three different sets of corporate and personal financial strategies, but we shall restrict our attention to the first two, since the third concentrates on the postponability feature of the capital gains tax which we are neglecting. The strategies we shall consider are:

(i) Corporate earnings are paid out entirely as dividends and are taxed as personal income.

(ii) Corporate earnings are translated into capital gains with all gains being realized immediately by investors and taxed at capital gains rates.[6]

Farrar and Selwyn consider a single investor with given marginal tax rates, owning a share in a corporation and having a desired total (corporate and personal) debt per share. Within this framework they evaluate alternative corporate financial policies in terms of the after-tax income received by the investor.

For this purpose define:[7]

$\widetilde{Y}$—the net income stream (including

[5]The three other cases considered by Farrar and Selwyn may be obtained from this one by setting one or more of the tax rates equal to zero.

[6]As Myers [9] has pointed out, Farrar and Selwyn make an error in their computation of the capital gains tax liability. However, their error corresponds to our assumption that capital gains are taxed when earned rather than when realized.

[7]Those symbols covered with a tilde denote random variables.

capital gains) available to an investor from holding one share of stock after all interest and taxes, personal and corporate, have been paid.

$\widetilde{X}$—the operating income per share of the company before interest and tax payments.

r —the market rate of interest faced by personal and corporate borrowers and lenders alike.

D_c—the amount of corporate debt outstanding per share of common stock.

D_p—the amount of personal debt outstanding per share of common stock.

T_c, T_p, T_g—the marginal corporate, personal income, and capital gains tax rates.

Strategy 1: Earnings Paid as Dividends and Taxed as Income.

When all the earnings of the corporation are paid out as dividends and are taxed as the personal income of the investor, his net income per share is given by:

$$\widetilde{Y}=[(\widetilde{X}-rD_c)(1-T_c)-rD_p](1-T_p)$$

(1.1)

Then the after-tax costs to the investor of personal and corporate debt are found by differentiating (1.1) partially with respect to D_p and D_c.

$$\frac{\partial \widetilde{Y}}{\partial D_p} = -r(1-T_p)$$

(1.2)

$$\frac{\partial \widetilde{Y}}{\partial D_c} = -r(1-T_p)(1-T_c)$$

It follows from (1.2) that an investor's net income per share is reduced less by additional corporate debt than it is by additional personal debt; this is on account of the additional tax shield for corporate interest payments offered by the corporate income tax. In this sense corporate debt is 'cheaper' than personal debt for all investors, whatever their marginal tax rates.

Strategy 2: Earnings Transformed into Capital Gains and Taxed Immediately.

In this case the net income available to the investor may be written:

$$\widetilde{Y} = (\widetilde{X} - rD_c)(1 - T_c)(1 - T_g)$$
$$- rD_P(1 - T_P)$$

(1.3)

The costs of personal and corporate debt are again found by partial differentiation with respect to D_p and D_c.

$$\frac{\partial \widetilde{Y}}{\partial D_p} = -r(1 - T_p)$$

(1.4)

$$\frac{\partial \widetilde{Y}}{\partial D_c} = -r(1 - T_c)(1 - T_g)$$

Now corporate debt is 'cheaper' for an investor only if:

$$(1 - T_c)(1 - T_g) < (1 - T_p)$$

or

$$T_p < T_c + T_g + T_c T_g$$

(1.5)

(1.5) indicates that the relative effects of corporate and personal debt on the net income per share received by the investor will depend upon his marginal tax rates T_p and T_g: in general, low tax bracket investors will find the impact of corporate debt on their net income relatively more favourable than will high tax bracket investors.

Thus if the criterion of maximizing the net income per share received by investors is accepted, the following conclusions may be drawn. First, as Farrar and Selwyn also show, and as is readily apparent, it will always be optimal for a corporation to use any residual earnings for share re-purchase rather than for dividend payment, so long as the investor's marginal tax rate on dividends exceeds his marginal tax rate on capital gains. Secondly, corporate debt will be advantageous for all investors in dividend-paying corporations, although the value of corporate debt to different investors will depend directly upon their marginal tax rates T_p. Finally, for a non-dividend paying corporation, different financial policies may be optimal for different investor groups, according to their marginal tax rates: for example, high marginal tax rate investors for whom $T_p > T_c + T_g + T_c T_g$ would appear to prefer

the corporation to pursue a zero debt strategy[8] to maximize the amount of debt the investors may issue on their personal account, consistent with their desired total debt per share. Low marginal tax rate investors on the other hand would appear to prefer the corporation to pursue a maximum debt strategy: if such a strategy results in excessive debt per share from the investor's point of view it can always be partially undone by personal lending.

This possibility of a conflict of aims between different investor groups within the same corporation raises serious problems, both for the financial theorist in search of clear decision rules for corporate financial policy, and for the financial manager who must somehow reconcile these divergent interests. Farrar and Selwyn suggest tentatively that investors within a single corporation may be relatively homogeneous with respect to marginal tax rates, if different tax clienteles of investors find different characteristics of operating income streams $\widetilde{X}$ attractive; but they conclude that "a certain amount of creative artistry will continue to be needed in the design of optimal financial policies."[9]

Fortunately we need only accept the Farrar-Selwyn conclusion if we accept their criterion of optimality, namely the maximization of the after-tax income flow to the investor. As we have previously suggested, such a criterion is open to objection. Its validity relies on the implicit assumption that the investor is locked into his existing shareholding, and hence is interested only in the net income per share which will accrue to him from that shareholding. A more reasonable assumption is that the investor's opportunity set includes not only the possibility of borrowing and lending but also of trading securities in the capital market. If, following the usual assumptions of a perfect market for securities,[10] this oppor-

[8]Or even a negative debt strategy! i.e. they would prefer the corporation to become a net lender.

[9][1, p. 454].

[10]The assumptions required are that all market participants are price-takers and that transactions costs may be neglected. Note that "transac-

tunity set can be regarded as independent of the decisions of a single firm, then it follows that the welfare of all investors in the firm is maximized by the maximization of the market value of the firm. Thus once the investor's market exchange opportunities are recognized the potential conflict of aims suggested by Farrar and Selwyn is shown to be nugatory.

A related criticism of the Farrar-Selwyn approach is that it is essentially comparative static, and takes no account of any possible dynamic impact of the issuance of corporate debt on the net income of the investor $\widetilde{Y}$, in the period in which the debt is issued. There will be such a dynamic impact to the extent that the value of the corporation is changed by the issuance of debt.

Hence the fundamental limitation of the Farrar-Selwyn approach stems from its lack of a market valuation principle; this prevents it from taking into account the market exchange opportunities open to the investor, or dealing with the dynamic effects of debt issue. The basis for such a market valuation principle will be developed in the following section.

II

In this section we develop the basic condition for capital market equilibrium under uncertainty when investors have different marginal tax rates. The basic framework of analysis is the Capital Asset Pricing Model of Lintner,[11] Sharpe[12] and Mossin,[13] generalized to incorporate the effects of the taxes investors must pay on their income from dividends and capital gains.

Following the usual assumptions of this model, we take the market for securities to consist of m risk-averse investors who are concerned with selecting portfolios to hold over the same single-period horizon. We assume that the utility functions U_i $(i=1,$

tions costs" in this context includes any unpaid capital gains tax liability: we have assumed capital gains taxes are payable when the gains are made.

[11] [3]

[12] [11]

[13] [8]

$\ldots, m)$ of the investors may be defined on the mean V_i, and variance S^2_i, of the *after-tax* returns on the portfolios, so that

$$U_i = U_i(V_i, S^2_i)$$

$$\text{where} \quad U'_i = \frac{\partial U_i}{\partial V_i} > 0 \qquad \left. \begin{array}{c} \\ \\ \end{array} \right\} \ i = 1, \ldots, m$$

$$U''_i = \frac{\partial U_i}{\partial S^2_i} < 0 \qquad (2.1)$$

The investors trade in $(n+1)$ securities; security 0 is assumed to have an initial unit price of unity, and a known terminal unit price q, and the whole of the return from this security is assumed to be subject to tax as ordinary income. The remaining n securities have initial unit prices p_j $(j=1, \ldots, n)$ and uncertain terminal unit prices $\widetilde{\pi}_j$; in addition, each unit of security j $(j=1, \ldots, n)$ pays a terminal dividend d_j which is known at the beginning of the period. Thus the return on each risky security has two components, a known dividend and an uncertain terminal price. It is assumed that all investors agree in their assessments of the mean values of terminal price $\widetilde{\pi}_j$ $(j=1, \ldots, n)$, and of the covariances between the terminal prices of the securities s_{jk} $(j=1, \ldots, n; k=1, \ldots, n)$. Each investor i $(i=1, \ldots, m)$ comes to the market with an initial endowment of x^0_{ji} units of security j $(j=0, 1, \ldots, n)$, and by trading with other investors achieves an equilibrium asset position x_{ji} $(j=0, 1, \ldots, n)$. We are concerned with the conditions for all the investors to be in personal portfolio equilibrium and for the security markets to clear. Finally, we assume for simplicity that each investor has marginal tax rates on dividend and capital gains income t_{di} and t_{gi} which are constant and independent of his portfolio choice.

Individual Portfolio Equilibrium

The expected after-tax return on investor i's portfolio is given by:

$$V_i = \sum_{j=1}^{n} [\overline{\pi}_j \cdot (\overline{\pi}_j - p_j) t_{gi} + d_j (1 - t_{di})] x_{ji}$$
$$+ [q \cdot (q - 1) t_{di}] x_{oi} \qquad (2.2)$$

and the variance of the after-tax return is:

$$S^2_i = \sum_{j=1}^{n} \sum_{k=1}^{n} s_{jk} x_{ji} x_{ki} (1 - t_{gi})^2$$

(2.3)

Thus the investor may be represented as maximizing a utility function

$$U_i = U_i(V_i, S^2_i)$$ (2.4)

subject to his budget constraint

$$\sum_{j=1}^{n} p_j(x_{ji} - x^o_{ji}) + (x_{oi} - x^o_{oi}) = 0$$ (2.5)

where V_i and S^2_i are given by (2.2) and (2.3).

The first-order conditions for the constrained maximum are found by setting up the Lagrangean expression

$$L = U_i(V_i, S^2_i) - \lambda [\sum_{j=1}^{n} p_j(x_{ji} - x^o_{ji}) + (x_{oi} - x^o_{oi})]$$ (2.6)

and setting equal to zero its partial derivatives with respect to $x_{ji} (j=0, 1, \ldots, n)$ and λ.

$$\frac{\partial L}{\partial x_{ji}} = U'_i \frac{\partial V_i}{\partial x_{ji}} + U''_i \frac{\partial S^2_i}{\partial x_{ji}} - \lambda p_j = 0$$

$$j = 0, 1, \ldots, n$$ (2.7)

$$\frac{\partial L}{\partial \lambda} = \sum_{j=1}^{n} p_j(x_{ji} - x^o_{ji}) + (x_{oi} - x^o_{oi}) = 0$$

(2.8)

But from (2.2) we see that:

$$\frac{\partial V_i}{\partial x_{oi}} = q - (q - 1)t_{di}$$ (2.9)

$$\frac{\partial V_i}{\partial x_{ji}} = \bar{\pi}_j - (\bar{\pi}_j - p_j)t_{gi} + d_j(1 - t_{di})$$

(2.10)

$$j = 1, \ldots, n$$

and from (2.3)

$$\frac{\partial S^2_i}{\partial x_{oi}} = 0$$ (2.11)

$$\frac{\partial S^2_i}{\partial x_{ji}} = 2 \sum_{k=1}^{n} s_{jk} x_{ji} x_{ki} (1 - t_{gi})^2$$

(2.12)

$$j = 1, \ldots, n$$

Substituting for these expressions in (2.7) we obtain as conditions for the constrained maximum, in addition to the budget equation (2.8):

$$\frac{\partial L}{\partial x_{oi}} - U'_i[q - (q - 1)t_{di}] - \lambda = 0$$ (2.13)

$$\frac{\partial L}{\partial x_{ji}} = U'_i[\bar{\pi}_j - (\bar{\pi}_j - p_j)t_{gi} + d_j(1 - t_{di})]$$

$$+ U''_i[2 \sum_{k=1}^{n} s_{jk}(1 - t_{gi})^2 x_{ki}]$$

$$- \lambda p_j = 0$$ (2.14)

$$j = 1, \ldots, n$$

Eliminating λ between (2.13) and (2.14) and re-arranging, we obtain:

$$\sum_{k=1}^{n} s_{jk} x_{ki} = \frac{w_i}{(1-t_{gi})^2} [\bar{\pi}_j(1 - t_{gi}) + p_j t_{gi}$$

$$+ d_j(1 - t_{di}) - p_j(q - (q - 1)t_{di})]$$

(2.15)

$$j = 1, \ldots, n$$

Where $w_i = - \frac{1}{2} \frac{U'_i}{U''_i}$, is proportional to

the investor's marginal rate of substitution between expected return and variance.

Assuming that the second order conditions for the constrained maximum are satisfied, equations (2.15) give the equilibrium relationship between the per unit covariance of return on security j $(j=1, \ldots, n)$ and the after-tax risk premium expected per unit of security j. The n equations (2.15) in conjunction with the budget equation (2.8) suffice to determine uniquely the investor's equilibrium holding of each of the $(n+1)$ securities. It may be observed that since w_i enters only as a scaling constant in (2.15), the investor's relative holdings of the n risky securities are independent of the exact shape of his utility function, but not of his marginal tax rates t_{di} and t_{gi}.

Market Equilibrium

Equilibrium in the securities market requires first that each individual investor be in portfolio equilibrium, so that (2.8) and (2.15) must hold for all investors ($i = 1$, ..., m); and secondly that the market for all securities clears so that:

$$\sum_{i=1}^{m} x_{ji} = \sum_{i=1}^{m} x^{o}_{ji} = x^{o}_{j}$$

$$j=0, 1, \ldots, n$$

(2.16)

where x^{o}_{j} is the outstanding supply of security j.[14]

Then summing (2.15) over all investors ($i = 1, \ldots, m$) we obtain

$$h \sum_{k=1}^{n} s_{jk} x^{o}_{k} = [\overline{\pi}_j + d_j - qp_j]$$

$$- T_g[\overline{\pi}_j - p_j] \quad j=1, \ldots, n$$

$$- T_d[d_j - p_j(q-1)] \quad (2.17)$$

where

$$h = \left[\sum_{i=1}^{m} \frac{w_i}{(1-t_{gi})^2} \right]^{-1}$$

$$T_g = \left[\sum_{i=1}^{m} \frac{w_i t_{gi}}{(1-t_{gi})^2} \right] \left[\sum_{i=1}^{m} \frac{w_i}{(1-t_{gi})^2} \right]^{-1}$$

$$T_d = \left[\sum_{i=1}^{m} \frac{w_i t_{di}}{(1-t_{gi})^2} \right] \left[\sum_{i=1}^{m} \frac{w_i}{(1-t_{gi})^2} \right]^{-1}$$

Note that T_d and T_g are weighted averages of investors' marginal tax rates on dividends and capital gains, where the weights depend upon investors' marginal rates of substitution between expected return and variance of return.

Define the following new variables:

$r = q - 1$ the riskless rate of interest

$\delta_j = \dfrac{d_j}{p_j}$ the prospective dividend yield on security j ($j=1, \ldots, n$)

[14]As usual in a general equilibrium system one of these equations is redundant since it can be obtained from the other equations and the summation of investors' budget equations.

$$\widetilde{R}_j = \frac{\widetilde{\pi}_j + d_j - p_j}{p_j}$$ the rate of return on security j ($j=1, \ldots, n$)

Note that

$$\sum_{k=1}^{n} \frac{s_{jk}}{p_j} x^{o}_{k} = M \sum_{k=1}^{n} Q_k \text{COV}(\widetilde{R}_j \widetilde{R}_k)$$

where M is the total market value of all securities and Q_k ($k=1, \ldots, n$) is the share of security k in that total market value.[15]

Then dividing (2.17) by p_j, transposing terms and making the above substitutions yields:

$$\overline{R}_j - r = hM \sum_{k=1}^{n} Q_k \text{COV}(\widetilde{R}_j \widetilde{R}_k)$$

$$+ T_d(\delta_j - r) + T_g(\overline{R}_j - r)$$

$$j=1, \ldots, n$$

(2.18)

or $$\overline{R}_j - r = HM \sum_{k=1}^{n} Q_k \text{COV}(\widetilde{R}_j \widetilde{R}_k)$$

$$+ T(\delta_j - r)$$

$$j=1, \ldots, n$$

(2.19)

where $H = h/(1 - T_g)$[16]

$T = (T_d - T_g)/(1 - T_g)$[17]

Finally (2.19) may be simplified by noting

that $\sum_{k=1}^{n} Q_k M \widetilde{R}_k = \widetilde{R}_m$ where $\widetilde{R}_m$ is the rate

[15]This is because

$$\sum_{k=1}^{n} \frac{s_{jk}}{p_j} x^{o}_k = \sum_{k=1}^{n} \frac{\text{COV}(\widetilde{\pi}_j \widetilde{\pi}_k)}{p_j p_k} p_k x^{o}_k$$

$$= \sum_{k=1}^{n} M Q_k \text{COV}(\widetilde{R}_j \widetilde{R}_k)$$

[16]The value of H may be found by multiplying equation (2.19) by $p_j x^{o}_j$ and summing over j ($j=1, \ldots, n$). This yields

$$H = \overline{R}_m - r - T(\delta_m - r)$$

where $\overline{R}_m$ and δ_m are the expected return and dividend yield on a value-weighted market portfolio.

[17]If $t_{di} \geq t_{gi} \geq 0$ for all investors, then $0 \leq T \leq 1$.

of return on the whole market portfolio, so that

$$M \sum_{k=1}^{n} Q_k \, COV(\widetilde{R}_j \, \widetilde{R}_k) = COV(\widetilde{R}_j \, \widetilde{R}_m) \tag{2.20}$$

and (2.19) becomes:

$$\overline{R_j} - r = H \, COV(\widetilde{R}_j \, \widetilde{R}_m) + T(\delta_j - r) \tag{2.21}$$

$$j = 1, \ldots, n$$

Equation (2.21) then expresses the basic principle of market valuation under uncertainty when different investors have different marginal tax rates. It asserts that the expected or required risk premium on security j ($j = 1, \ldots, n$), $(\overline{R_j} - r)$, is a function of that security's risk characteristics $COV(\widetilde{R}_j \widetilde{R}_m)$, and of its expected dividend yield δ_j. The intuitive interpretation of this result is that for a given level of risk, investors require a higher total return on a security the higher is its prospective dividend yield, because of the higher rate of tax levied on dividends than on capital gains.

III

In the previous section we have derived a market equilibrium condition relating the required rate of return on a security to its risk characteristics and its expected dividend yield. For the discussion of dividend and capital structure policies it is helpful to transform this equation into a relationship between the value of a firm, the characteristics of its operating income stream, and its financial policies. For this purpose we restrict our attention to the convenient no-growth case and assume that the future may be regarded as a series of identical periods in each of which the market equilibrium condition (2.21) is expected to hold.

Each period the corporation[18] has an uncertain operating income stream $\widetilde{X}$, and the joint probability distribution of $\widetilde{X}$ and the returns on all other assets in the economy is

[18]In this and the following section we drop the firm subscript since we are always referring to the same firm.

assumed to be stable through time; corporate tax at the rate τ is levied on this income stream each period. The corporation is assumed to pay a constant dividend, D, each period, and to repurchase or issue stock at the end of each period so that its market value at the beginning of the following period is a constant, V. If we assume also that investors' risk preferences and tax rates remain constant through time, then all periods are identical and the expected future earnings of the corporation will be capitalized at a constant rate we shall denote by ρ. We have excluded the possibility of a change in the value of the firm due to a recapitalization of future earnings prospects; therefore, the uncertain end-of-period value of the firm, $\widetilde{V}_t$, after dividends have been paid but before any shares have been issued or repurchased, will be equal to the beginning-of-period value of the firm, V, plus the net operating income stream, $\widetilde{X}(1 - \tau)$, less the amount of dividends paid, D.

i.e. $\widetilde{V}_t = V + \widetilde{X}(1 - \tau) - D \tag{3.1}$

It follows then that if $\widetilde{R}$ is the rate of return on the corporation's securities

$$1 + \widetilde{R} = (\widetilde{V}_t + D)/V \tag{3.2}$$

and $COV(\widetilde{R}, \widetilde{R}_m) - COV[(V + \widetilde{X}(1 - \tau))$

$$/V, \widetilde{R}_m] = COV[\widetilde{X}(1 - \tau)/V, \widetilde{R}_m] \tag{3.3}$$

Hence, the value of the corporation, V, may be written as the capitalized value of the expected earnings after tax

$$V = \frac{\overline{X}(1 - \tau)}{\rho} \tag{3.4}$$

where the capitalization rate ρ is given by the market equilibrium condition (2.21)

$$\rho = r + H \, COV(\widetilde{R}, \widetilde{R}_m) + T[\frac{D}{V} - r]$$

$$= r + H \, COV[\widetilde{X}(1 - \tau)/V, \widetilde{R}_m] +$$

$$T[\frac{D}{V} - r], \tag{3.5}$$

for $\frac{D}{V}$ will be the prospective dividend yield

on the corporation's securities. Then substituting for ρ in (3.4) and rearranging, we obtain:

$$V = \frac{\overline{X}(1-\tau) - H \, COV[\widetilde{X}(1-\tau), \widetilde{R}_m] - TD}{r(1-T)}$$

(3.6)

(3.6) is a general valuation equation for the corporation, expressing its value as function of the net operating income stream, $\widetilde{X}(1-\tau)$, and the amount of dividends paid each period, D.

To calculate the effect of alternative dividend policies on the value of the corporation it is only necessary to differentiate (3.6) partially with respect to D.

$$\frac{\partial V}{\partial D} = \frac{-T}{r(1-T)}$$

(3.7)

(3.7) shows that if the criterion of market value maximization is accepted and if $T > 0$, it is non-optimal for all investors in a corporation for the corporation to pay dividends: share re-purchase is a preferred alternative for all investors, whatever their marginal tax rates. Since we observe that most corporations do in fact pay regular dividends, such behavior must be rationalized by the assumption that such corporations are behaving under an actual or perceived constraint on systematic share re-purchase as an alternative to dividend payment. In our discussion of capital structure policy we shall assume that the corporation is subject to such a constraint.

IV

Suppose that a corporation has an amount of bonds B outstanding at an interest cost r. Then the market value of the corporation's equity E, is given by:

$$E = V - B$$

(4.1)

But E may also be regarded as the expected net earnings of equity holders $(\widetilde{X} - rB) (1-\tau)$, capitalized at a rate ρ_E appropriate to the risk and composition of the equity income stream.

$$E = \frac{(\overline{X} - rB)(1-\tau)}{\rho_E}$$

(4.2)

An argument analogous to that used in the previous section to derive ρ, shows that ρ_E is given by:

$$\rho_E = r + H \, COV[\widetilde{X}(1-\tau)/E, \widetilde{R}_m]$$

$$+ T[\frac{D}{E} - r]$$

(4.3)

Substituting for ρ_E in (4.2) and rearranging yields:

$$E = \frac{(\overline{X} - rB)(1-\tau) - H \, COV[\widetilde{X}(1-\tau), \widetilde{R}_m] - TD}{r(1-T)}$$

(4.4)

The constraint on systematic share re-purchase may be written:

$$D + (1-\tau) \, rB \geq \overline{X}(1-\tau)$$

(4.5)

(4.5) requires that the amount paid out in dividends and net interest payments be at least as great as the mean net income stream.

Note that since

$$V = B + E$$

$$\frac{dV}{dB} = 1 + \frac{dE}{dB}$$

(4.6)

We shall consider the effects of alternative debt levels on the value of the corporation under two assumptions:

(i) Constraint on share re-purchase not binding so that

$$D + (1-\tau) \, rB > \overline{X}(1-\tau)$$

Then from (4.4)

$$\frac{dE}{dB} = -\frac{(1-\tau)}{(1-T)}$$

(4.7)

and

$$\frac{dV}{dB} = \frac{\tau - T}{1 - T} \text{ from } (4.6)$$

(4.8)

(4.8) shows that a high leverage strategy will maximize the value of the corporation, and hence will be advantageous for all investors so long as the corporate tax rate

τ exceeds the market's "effective tax rate" T. However, the relative advantage of corporate debt is reduced by the existence of investor taxes $(T>0)$.

(ii) Constraint on share re-purchase binding so that

$$D+(1-\tau)\ rB=\overline{X}(1-\tau)$$

Note that this constraint now implies that

$$\frac{dD}{dB}=-(1-\tau)r \qquad (4.9)$$

so that the issuance of debt reduces the amount of dividends that must be paid by the net interest cost of the debt.

Then taking into account this relationship,

$$\frac{dV}{dB}=\frac{\partial V}{\partial B}+\frac{\partial V}{\partial D}\cdot\frac{dD}{dB} \qquad (4.10)$$

$$=-\frac{\tau-T}{1-T}+\frac{T(1-\tau)}{(1-T)}$$

$$\frac{dV}{dB}=\tau \qquad (4.11)$$

But this is precisely the result obtained by Modigliani and Miller neglecting investor taxes:[19] that is, if an amount of bonds B is issued, the value of the corporation is increased by τB. We conclude then that if the corporation is subject to a binding constraint on share re-purchase, the original Modigliani-Miller cost-of-capital propositions are unaffected by the existence of investor taxes.

However, the whole of the above argument has been conducted on the assumption that there is no relationship between the amount of debt issued in a period and the amount of dividends that must be paid in that period. In fact, if there is a constraint on share repurchase which precludes use of the proceeds of a bond issue to repurchase shares and if the share repurchase constraint is binding, there will be a necessary connection between the amount of debt issued in a period and the amount of dividends paid in that period. Since this consequent change in dividends paid

will affect valuation, a full analysis of the effects of debt issuance must take this effect into account. To this problem we turn in the next section.

V

We now consider the effect on the current value of the corporation V, of an expected issue of debt $\triangle$B, at the end of the first period, assuming that the corporation pays a constant dividend and issues no further debt in subsequent periods. We assume also that the corporation is subject to a binding constraint on share re-purchase.

Denote by $\widetilde{V}'_t$ the value of the corporation at the end of one period after the debt has been issued and dividends have been paid. Then the argument of the previous section implies that with a binding constraint on share re-purchase

$$\frac{d\widetilde{V}'_t}{d\triangle B}=\tau \qquad (5.1)$$

and hence

$$\frac{d\overline{V}'_t}{d\triangle B}=\tau \qquad (5.2)$$

so that the end-of-period expected value of the corporation is increased by τ times the amount of debt issued.

The total return to investors from owning the corporation over this period is

$$\frac{\widetilde{V}'_t+\widetilde{X}_1(1-\tau)-V}{V} \qquad (5.3)$$

where $\widetilde{X}_1(1-\tau)$ is the realized net operating income of the corporation during the period. Market equilibrium requires that the expected value of (5.3) be equal to:

$$r(1-T)+H\ COV[(\widetilde{V}'_t+\widetilde{X}_1(1-\tau))/V,\widetilde{R}_m]$$
$$-T\frac{D_1}{V} \qquad (5.4)$$

where D_1 is the amount of dividends paid in the first period.

Then equating these two expressions and solving for V, we obtain:

$$V = \frac{\overline{V}'_t + \overline{X}_1(1-\tau)}{1+r(1-T)}$$

$$\text{(5.5)}$$

$$\frac{-H\,COV[\widetilde{V}'_t + \widetilde{X}_1(1-\tau, \widetilde{R}_m] - TD_1}{1+r(1-T)}$$

The constraint on share re-purchase for the first period may be written:

$$D_1 + (1-\tau)\,rB \geqq \overline{X}_1(1-\tau) + \triangle B \quad \text{(5.6)}$$

Note that (5.6) explicitly excludes use of the proceeds of the bond issue for share repurchase.

$$\text{Now} \quad \frac{dV}{d\triangle B} = \frac{\partial V}{\partial \triangle B} + \frac{\partial V}{\partial D_1} \cdot \frac{dD_1}{d\triangle B}$$

$$\text{(5.7)}$$

(5.7) shows that the total impact of the expected debt issue on the value of the corporation has two components: the direct impact, $\frac{\partial V}{\partial \triangle B}$, and an indirect impact, $\frac{\partial V}{\partial D_1} \cdot \frac{\partial D_1}{\partial \triangle B}$, due to the consequent change in first period dividends. If the repurchase constraint (5.6) is binding, $\frac{\partial D_1}{\partial \triangle B} = 1$, so that:

$$\frac{dV}{d\triangle B} = \frac{\tau - T}{1+r(1-T)} \quad \text{(5.8)}$$

Thus when the repurchase constraint is binding, (5.8) shows that corporate debt issuance will be advantageous so long as the corporate tax rate τ exceeds T. However, it is clear that when a binding repurchase constraint requires the proceeds of a bond issue to be paid out in dividends, the prima facie advantage of adding debt to the capital structure may be substantially reduced. The reason for this is that, while the value of the corporation will tend to be raised by the expected corporate tax savings due to the bond issue, it will tend to be reduced by the higher personal taxes which investors must pay on the increased first period dividend entailed by the bond issue.

VI

In this paper we have discussed the impact of the personal tax structure on optimal corporate financial policy. In Section 1, we argued that the Farrar-Selwyn analysis was misleading on account of its neglect of the market trading opportunities open to investors. It was argued that once these were acknowledged, the welfare of all investors in the corporation would be maximized by the maximization of the market value of the firm. This was therefore accepted as the appropriate criterion of financial policy. Section III was concerned with the effect of dividend policy on the value of the corporation within the framework of the market equilibrium condition developed in Section II. It was shown that so long as the market's "effective tax rate" T, exceeds zero, the payment of dividends will be detrimental to the interests of all investors. A constraint on systematic share repurchase was then invoked to explain the observed behavior of corporations.

Section IV analyzed the effect of alternative capital structure policies on the value of the corporation allowing for this repurchase constraint. It was shown that if the constraint is binding the effects of alternative capital structures are the same as found by Modigliani and Miller neglecting investor taxes. However, if the constraint is not binding then the advantages of a high debt capital structure are reduced by the existence of investor taxes.

Finally, Section V extended the analysis of the previous section to the case in which a binding share repurchase constraint precludes use of the proceeds of a bond issue to repurchase outstanding shares. It was shown that in this case the advantages of issuing corporate debt may be substantially reduced by the consequent need to pay out the proceeds in dividends.

The author hopes to present in a later paper the results of some attempts to derive empirical estimates of the market's "effective tax rate" T. If T is approximately zero, then the Modigliani-Miller propositions concerning capital structure and dividend policies remain substantially unaltered by the existence of investor taxes. But if T is non-zero, then their results must be altered along the lines suggested in this paper.

REFERENCES

1. Farrar, Donald E. and Lee L. Selwyn, "Taxes, Corporate Financial Policies and Returns to Investors", *National Tax Journal*, Vol. 20, No. 4 (December 1967), pp. 444-454.

2. Gordon, Myron J., "The Savings Investment and Valuation of a Corporation", *Review of Economics and Statistics*, Vol. 45, No. 1, (February 1962), pp. 37-51.

3. Lintner, John, "The Valuation of Risk Assets and the Selection of Risky Investments in Stock Portfolios and Capital Budgets", *Review of Economics and Statistics*, Vol. 47, No. 1 (February 1965), pp. 13-37.

4. Miller, Merton H. and Franco Modigliani, "Dividend Policy, Growth and the Valuation of Shares", *Journal of Business*, Vol. 34, No. 4 (October 1961), pp. 411-433.

5. Modigliani, Franco and Merton H. Miller, "The Cost of Capital, Corporation Finance, and the Theory of Investment", *American Economic Review*, Vol. 48, No. 3, (June 1958), pp. 261-297.

6. ————, "The Cost of Capital, Corporation Finance, and the Theory of Investment: Reply", *American Economic Review*, Vol. 49, No. 4, (September 1959), pp. 655-669.

7. ————, "Corporate Income Taxes and the Cost of Capital: A Correction", *American Economic Review*, Vol. 53, No. 3, (June 1963), pp. 433-443.

8. Mossin, Jan. "Equilibrium in a Capital Asset Market", *Econometrica*, Vol. 34, No. 4 (October 1966), pp. 768-783.

9. Myers, S. C., "Taxes, Corporate Financial Policy and the Return to Investors: Comment", *National Tax Journal*, Vol. 20, No. 4 (December 1967), pp. 455-462.

10. Robichek, Alexander A. and Stewart C. Myers, *Optimal Financing Decisions*, Englewood Cliffs, Prentice-Hall, 1965.

11. Sharpe, W. F., "Capital Asset Prices: A Theory of Market Equilibrium Under Conditions of Risk", *Journal of Finance*, Vol. 19, No. 3 (September, 1964), pp. 425-442.

12. Tinsley, P.A., "Capital Structure, Precautionary Balances, and Valuation of the Firm: The Problem of Financial Risk", *Journal of Financial and Quantitative Analysis*, Vol. 5, No. 1 (March 1970), pp. 33-62.

[2]

Reprinted from THE JOURNAL OF FINANCE, Vol. XXVIII, No. 3, June, 1973

AN APPROACH TO THE VALUATION OF
UNCERTAIN INCOME STREAMS

M. J. BRENNAN*

I. INTRODUCTION

IN THE LAST DECADE substantial advances have been made in the theory of the valuation of assets under uncertainty, such work being based mainly on what has come to be known as the Capital Asset Pricing Model,[1] which itself grew out of the static theory of portfolio selection originally due to Markowitz [1959].

More recently the theory of portfolio selection has been extended under certain assumptions to the problem of an individual planning his investment and consumption under uncertainty over a multi-period horizon.[2] As yet, however, the theory of the market valuation of individual assets has not paralleled this development, and remains almost entirely within a one-period context. Exceptions of this generalization are the work of Black and Scholes [1971] on warrant valuation, and an unpublished paper by Black [1969], recently brought to the author's attention, which, drawing on some earlier work by Treynor, anticipates in a more general context part of the theoretical development presented here. Other efforts to apply modern capital market theory to multi-period asset valuation and investment decisions include the work of Tuttle and Litzenberger [1968] and that of Stapleton [1971], both of which differ in significant respects from the approach adopted here.

The Tuttle and Litzenberger paper, which derives appropriate criteria for optimal corporate investment decisions, takes as given the effects on a firm's market risk[3] of adopting a particular investment project. The paper therefore leaves open the questions both of the determinants of this risk effect, and of the way in which the risk of projects is to be assessed. The model presented here is more complete, in that investment decision criteria are developed assuming only that the decision-maker has information on the conditional distributions of the project's cash flows.

Stapleton, on the other hand, while purporting to develop a theory of stock valuation using a multi-period portfolio model,[4] actually employs a single-period certainty-equivalent approach in which it is assumed that the joint probability distribution of all the future dividend payments on a share can be reduced to a probability distribution on the present values at the end of one

---

* Assistant Professor of Finance, University of British Columbia. The author is grateful for helpful discussion with Fischer Black and Irwin Tepper, as well as for the suggestions of a referee.

1. See Jensen [1971].
2. See Merton [1969], Samuelson [1969], and others.
3. By 'market risk' is meant the risk characteristics of a firm's securities as perceived by investors.
4. Stapleton [1971], pp. 95-96.

period of all the possible future dividend streams. The probability distribution of these deferred present values is then valued using the single-period Capital Asset Pricing Model. This procedure would be legitimate only if, at the end of one period, the investor were to know with certainty the precise pattern of dividend payments over the remainder of the horizon; this of course is highly unrealistic and ignores the fact that information about future dividends becomes available only gradually through time.

As a result of its predominantly one-period framework, the relevance of the theory of valuation under uncertainty is severely restricted, for most assets provide risky income streams over an indefinite future life, and unless these income streams can be valued in a market equilibrium context, there can exist no theory of the valuation of the assets which provide them. The most obvious consequence of this lack of available theory lies in the unsatisfactory state of normative models of the corporate investment decision under uncertainty; such models, when they incorporate the maximization of the current value of the firm as an appropriate objective of policy, either rely on a risk-adjusted discount rate to value the uncertain future income stream of the investment, or make use of certainty-equivalents to adjust the expected cash flows, before discounting them at the risk-free rate of interest.[5] Lacking in both approaches is any theory for the determination of the appropriate discount rate or certainty-equivalent adjustment.

A further consequence of the single-period nature of available valuation models is the lack of any rigorous theory of the determinants of the market risk of firms;[6] this has impeded the integration of corporate finance with modern capital market theory except within the confines of a limited single-period model.[7]

This paper has as its major aim, the development of a theory of the valuation of uncertain future cash flows and hence of the valuation of the assets which provide them. The basic framework is a model of multi-period capital market equilibrium developed from an optimizing model of the individual's lifetime portfolio selection problem due to Merton [1969], to which the reader is referred. To this model of capital market equilibrium is introduced an extremely simple expectations generating mechanism which, it is hoped, will serve to capture the basic dynamic nature of information arrival. It is then shown that the behavior of the value of a cash flow claim must follow a simple differential equation: this differential equation approach to valuation was inspired by the article of Black and Scholes on warrant valuation, referred to above. Solution of this differential equation yields the present value of a claim to a risky future cash flow. By aggregating the market values of claims to risky cash flows in different periods, the net present values of risky income streams and therefore of the assets which provide them may be computed, permitting a relatively straightforward approach to the problem of the corporate investment decision under uncertainty.

5. For an excellent discussion of these two approaches see Robichek and Myers [1965].

6. Some progress towards developing such a theory has been made by Pettit and Westerfield [1971], drawing on some unpublished work by Daniel Rie.

7. See for example Mossin [1969].

In Section II the conditions for equilibrium in a multi-period capital market are derived. Section III introduces the expectations generating mechanism and gives the present value of a risky cash flow claim. Some implications of the model are discussed in Section IV.

II.   Multi-Period Capital Market Equilibrium

We shall consider first the conditions for the instantaneous portfolio equilibrium of an individual investor planning his consumption and investment under uncertainty: aggregation of the resulting individual asset demands will then yield a condition for instantaneous capital market equilibrium.

Individual Equilibrium

Assume that the investor is concerned with maximizing the expected utility of both consumption over a known lifespan and terminal wealth; that he has no labour income, and that he is free to adjust his investment portfolio instantaneously without incurring transactions costs. The investor may place his wealth in two types of asset: first, a riskless asset whose yield at each future instant in time is a known constant, r; second, in risky assets whose yields are uncertain but are assumed to be serially independent.

The investor may then be represented at time t as maximizing expected utility, given by:

$$E\left[\int_t^H e^{-\rho s}\, U(C_s)\, ds + B(W_H)\right]$$

constrained by his initial wealth $W(t)$, and investment opportunities. $U(C_s)$ is his utility function, defined on his instantaneous rate of consumption, C_s; ϱ is his rate of time preference; H is his date of death; and $B[W_H]$ is the utility to be gained from dying with net worth W_H. The investor is assumed to exhibit risk aversion so that U and B are strictly concave. The decision variables in this planning problem are C_s, the instantaneous rate of consumption, and $w_j(s)$, the proportion of instantaneous wealth, W_s, that the investor places in each of the risky assets ($j = 1..n$) at each instant of time, s.

Define the investor's optimal value function (i.e., the maximum expected value of discounted utility at time t), $\phi[W_t, t]$ as:

$$\phi[W_t, t] \equiv \mathop{Max}\limits_{C_s,\, w_j(s)}\ E\left[\int_t^H e^{-\rho s}\, U(C_s)\, ds + B(W_H)\right] \tag{1}$$

Note that the optimal value function, which may also be referred to as the investor's derived utility function, depends only on current wealth and time, because of the posited serial independence of asset yields.

Then it may be shown that, providing the risky asset yields possess 'compact' probability distributions,[8] the optimal instantaneous consumption and investment decisions are found by maximizing G

w.r.t. $w_j(t)$ and C_t, where

---

8. Merton [1969] obtains this result when asset yields are generated by a Wiener Brownian motion process. The extension to the more general case of compact probability distributions follows from Samuelson [1970].

$$G \equiv e^{-\rho t}\, U(C_t) + \frac{\partial \phi}{\partial W_t}$$

$$\left\{ W_t \left[\sum_{j=1}^{n} w_j(t)\,(\alpha_{jt} - r) + r \right] - C_t \right\} + \frac{1}{2}\,\frac{\partial^2 \phi}{\partial W2}\, W_t^2 \sum_{j=1}^{n} \sum_{k=1}^{n} w_j(t)\, w_k(t)\, \sigma_{jkt}$$

(2)

and

α_{jt} — the expected instantaneous rate of return on asset j (j $= 1..n$)

σ_{jkt} — the instantaneous rate of covariance between the yields on assets j and k.

r — the risk free rate of interest.

Differentiating w.r.t. $w_j(t)$ and C_t, we obtain the following first order conditions for the maximum of G:[9]

$$\frac{\partial G}{\partial C_t} = e^{-\rho t}\, U' - \frac{\partial \phi}{\partial W} = 0$$

(3)

$$\frac{\partial G}{\partial w_j(t)} = \frac{\partial \phi}{\partial W_t}\, W_t(\alpha_{jt} - r) + \frac{\partial^2 \phi}{\partial W_t^2}\, W_t^2 \sum_{k=1}^{n} w_k(t)\, \sigma_{jkt} = 0.$$

(4)

Then the vector of the ith investor's equilibrium *dollar holdings* of the n risky assets, $Z^i(t)$, is given by

$$Z^i(t) = a_t^i\, \Omega_t^{-1}\, (\alpha_t - rj)$$

(5)

where

$$a_t^i = - \left(\frac{\partial \phi}{\partial W_t} \Big/ \frac{\partial^2 \phi}{\partial W_t^2} \right)$$

—a measure of the investor's absolute risk aversion.

Ω_t—the instantaneous variance-covariance matrix of risk asset yields.

α_t—the vector of expected instantaneous risk asset yields.

j—an n-dimensional vector of units.

The superscript i has been added to a_t^i and $Z^i_{(t)}$ to show that these symbols refer to the ith investor (i $= 1 .. n$).

Market Equilibrium

To obtain the conditions for instantaneous capital market equilibrium we set the vector of aggregate dollar amounts demanded of each risky asset equal to the vector of aggregate dollar supplies, S_t, assuming that all investors agree on the joint probability distribution of asset yields,

$$\text{i.e.,} \quad \sum_{i=1}^{m} Z_{(t)}^i = \left(\sum_{i=1}^{m} a_t^i \right) \Omega_t^{-1}(\alpha_t - j) = S_t.$$

(6)

9. See Merton [1969]. Satisfaction of the second-order conditions is guaranteed by the concavity of U and B.

Re-arranging equation (6) we obtain:

$$\alpha_t - rj = \left(\sum_{i=1}^{m} a_t^i \right)^{-1} \Omega_t S_t \tag{7}$$

which may be interpreted as an equation for the vector of expected asset yields α_t conditional on the vector of asset supplies, S_t. Equation (7) states that, in equilibrium, the excess of the expected instantaneous yield of each risky asset over the risk-free rate of interest is proportional to its weighted average instantaneous rate of covariance with the yields on all the risky assets. It is the continuous time analogue of the single period Capital Asset Pricing Model.

This market equilibrium condition may be readily, if somewhat tediously, transformed in the familiar way[10] to yield

$$\alpha_{jt} - r = \beta_{jt} \, (\mu_t - r) \qquad (j = 1..n) \tag{8}$$

where β_{jt} is the instantaneous slope of the regression of the yield on asset j $(j = 1..n)$ against the yield on the market portfolio of all risky assets, and μ_t is the instantaneous expected yield on this same market portfolio.

It will be recalled that when the conditions for the instantaneous portfolio equilibrium of the individual investor were being derived, it was assumed that individual asset yields were serially independent. Conditions for such independence and for the expected yield on the market portfolio to be a constant are discussed in an Appendix. Assuming that such conditions are satisfied, the market equilibrium condition may be written

$$\alpha_{jt} - r = \beta_{jt} \, (\mu - r). \tag{8'}$$

It is this relationship we shall use in the following section.

III.   THE VALUATION OF RISKY CASH FLOW CLAIMS

At every instant in time, t, investors are assumed to trade in claims to uncertain future cash flows which will be realized at instants in time T, where $T > t$. Initially we assume that the total quantity of such claims is given; later we shall allow an individual firm to create additional claims to finance investment projects, but maintain the assumption that the total quantity of such issues is arbitrarily small so that the market equilibrium conditions are not affected. A particular cash flow will be denoted generically by $\tilde{C}_{jT}$, and the problem to be considered is the determination of the value at time t of a claim to such a cash flow, which value we shall denote generically by $V_t(\tilde{C}_{jT})$. First it is necessary to describe the process by which expectations about future cash flows are generated.

The Expectations Generating Mechanism

Investors are assumed to form their expectations about future cash flows conditional on an index of expectations for the economy as a whole,

$$\text{i.e., } E_t[\tilde{C}_{jT} \mid \tilde{I}_t] = {}_t a_{jT} + b_{jT} \tilde{I}_t \tag{9}$$

where $\tilde{I}_t$ is the current value of the expectations index; $b_{jT} \tilde{I}_t$ is the index-

10. See Fama [1968].

dependent component of the jth cash flow expected at time T; and $_ta_{jT}$ is the index-independent component, as assessed at time t.

It is apparent that changes in the expected value of a particular cash flow can come from two sources: changes in the overall index, $\tilde{I}_t$, and changes in $_ta_{jT}$. We make the diagonal assumption about the expectations generating mechanism, that all the covariance between expectations about different cash flows is due to changes in the index, $\tilde{I}_t$; in other words, changes in $_ta_{jT}$ are independent across securities. We further assume that claims to index-dependent components and index-independent components of claims to future cash flows may be traded separately.[11]

It is a property of rational expectations that such expectations should follow a martingale sequence, since by definition rational expectations can change only on receipt of new (i.e. unexpected) information.

Hence

$$E_t[\tilde{I}_{t+h}] = \tilde{I}_t$$

$$E_t[_{t+h}a_{jT}] = {}_ta_{jT}$$

$$h > 0.$$

We assume that the variance rate on the expectations index is $I_t^2\sigma^2$, and that all random variables possess compact probability distributions.

At any instant in time, the market value of all claims to future cash flows will consist of two components: the market value of claims to all index-independent cash flows and the market value of all index-dependent cash flows. Given the existence of a large number of such claims the market value of the former will be a function of time only, since by construction it is independent of the other state variable, $\tilde{I}_t$. Investment in the portfolio of all index-independent claims will therefore be essentially riskless, and we may, without loss of generality, define the net value of all index-independent claims to be part of the net supply of riskless securities so that the true risky asset portfolio consists only of claims to index-dependent cash flows.

We denote the current value of this risky asset portfolio by $\tilde{M}_t$, and assume that it has a constant cash flow yield or dividend yield, δ, and a constant expected rate of price appreciation γ.

Since $E_t[\tilde{I}_{t+h}] = \tilde{I}_t$, this implies

$$\tilde{M}_t = K_0 e^{\gamma t}\tilde{I}_t \qquad (10)$$

where K_0 is an arbitrary scaling constant, assuring that the rate of return on the risky asset portfolio has a constant variance, σ^2. The reasonableness of these assumptions about the risky market portfolio will be examined in more detail below.

A Differential Equation for the Value of a Claim

The value of a cash flow claim at any instant in time depends upon:

(i) the current instant of time t

---

11. This assumption guarantees satisfaction of condition (ii) for the serial independence of asset yields. See Appendix.

(ii) the current value of the market index, $\widetilde{I}_t$

(iii) the current assessment of the index-independent component of the cash flow expectation, $_t a_{jT}$.

Since there is a one-to-one relationship between the current value of the expectations index and the current value of the risky market portfolio, M_t, given by (10), we may write

$$V_t(\widetilde{C}_{jT}) = y(\widetilde{M}_t, t, {_t}a_{jT}) \tag{11}$$

where $y_1 = \dfrac{\partial y}{\partial \widetilde{M}_t}$; $y_2 = \dfrac{\partial y}{\partial t}$; $y_3 = \dfrac{\partial y}{\partial {_t}a_{jT}}$.

Then, invoking the market equilibrium condition (8′) for the expected return on a security, we see that over any short period of time h, the expected return from holding a cash flow claim must be given by

$$\frac{1}{y} E[\Delta y] = r.h. + \frac{M y_1}{y} \sigma^2(\gamma + \delta - r)h \tag{12}$$

for $\dfrac{M y_1}{y} \sigma^2$ is the instantaneous rate of covariance between the yield on the claim and the yield on the risky market portfolio.

Now $\Delta y = y[M + \Delta M, t + h, {_{t+h}}a_{jT}] - y[M, t, {_t}a_{jT}]$

$$= y_1 \Delta M + y_2 h + y_3 \Delta a + \frac{1}{2} y_{11}(\Delta M)^2 + \frac{1}{2} y_{22} h^2$$

$$+ \frac{1}{2} y_{33}(\Delta a)^2 + \frac{1}{2} y_{12} \Delta M.h + \frac{1}{2} y_{21} \Delta M.h$$

$$+ \frac{1}{2} y_{13}(\Delta M.)(\Delta a) + \frac{1}{2} y_{31}(\Delta M)(\Delta a)$$

$$+ \frac{1}{2} y_{23}(\Delta a)h + \frac{1}{2} y_{32}(\Delta a).h$$

where terms of higher order than the second in h have been dropped, and $\Delta a = {_{t+h}}a_{jT} - {_t}a_{jT}$.

Then, taking the expectation and dropping terms in h^2,

$$E[\Delta y] = y_1 M\gamma h + y_2 h + \frac{1}{2} y_{11} M^2 \sigma^2 h + \frac{1}{2} y_{33} \xi^2 h \tag{13}$$

where $\xi^2 h = E[\Delta a]^2$.

Substitute for $E[\Delta y]$ in (12), divide by h, and let $h \to 0$.

$$M y_1 \gamma + y_2 + \frac{1}{2} y_{11} M^2 \sigma^2 + \frac{1}{2} y_{33} \xi^2 - yr - M y_1(\gamma + \delta - r) = 0$$

or

$$y_2 + \frac{1}{2} y_{11} M^2 \sigma^2 + \frac{1}{2} y_{33} \xi^2 - yr + y_1 M(r - \delta) = 0. \tag{14}$$

(14) is then a differential equation governing the behavior of the value of a claim to a risky cash flow. The equation is formally almost identical to that employed by Black and Scholes [1971] for valuing warrants.

The boundary condition for the differential equation is in terms of the expectations index, $\tilde{I}_T$,

$$\text{i.e., } V_T(\tilde{C}_{jT}) = y(M_T, T, {}_Ta_{jT}) = {}_Ta_{jT} + b_{jT}\tilde{I}_T. \tag{15}$$

For this reason we write the solution to the differential equation in terms of I_t, as

$$V_t(\tilde{C}_{jT}) = {}_ta_{jT}e^{-r(T-t)} + b_{jT}\tilde{I}_te^{-(\gamma+\delta)(T-t)}. \tag{16}$$

It is apparent from inspection that this equation satisfies the boundary condition (15).

Writing this solution in terms of $\tilde{M}_t$

$$V_t(C_{jT}) - {}_ta_{jT}e^{-r(T-t)} + \frac{b_{jT}}{K_0} M_t e^{\delta t - (\gamma+\delta)T} \tag{17}$$

it is readily verified that this expression also satisfies the differential equation (14) for

$$y_1 = \frac{b_{jT}}{K_0} e^{\delta t - (\gamma+\delta)T}$$

$$y_{11} = 0$$

$$y_{33} = 0$$

$$y_2 = \delta \frac{b_{jT}}{K_0} \tilde{M}_t e^{\delta t - (\gamma+\delta)T} + r\, {}_ta_{jT}e^{-r(T-t)}.$$

Characteristics of the Risky Market Portfolio and the Structure of Security Returns

Having derived an expression for the value of an individual cash flow claim we are now in position to examine the implications of our earlier assumptions that the value of the risky market portfolio has a constant expected rate of appreciation γ, and a constant dividend yield δ. For this to hold, it is sufficient that $b_T = \sum_j b_{jT}$, be given by:

$$b_T = b_0 e^{\gamma T} \tag{18}$$

$$\text{for then } K_t = \int_{T>t} b_T e^{-(\gamma+\delta)(T-t)}\, dT$$

$$= \int_{T>t} b_0 e^{(\gamma+\delta)t - \delta T}\, dT$$

$$= \frac{b_0}{\delta} e^{\gamma t} \tag{19}$$

and K_t grows at the constant rate γ, so that the risky market portfolio also has a constant rate of expected appreciation, γ. Moreover, the dividend yield is given by

$$\frac{b_t I_t}{K_t I_t} = \frac{b_0 e^{\gamma t}}{b_0 e^{\gamma t}} . \delta = \delta \tag{20}$$

and is a constant, independent of time and the current level of the expectations index.

Thus the nature of investors' wealth in this simple capital market is as follows: the supply of securities representing claims to future cash flows is given. One component of net wealth consists of claims to riskless future cash flows, while the other consists of claims to index-dependent cash flows. Investors always expect the sum of these index-dependent cash flows to grow at the same rate γ. However the actual growth rate is stochastic.

In spite of the extremely simplistic nature of this model, it does have one feature which is consistent with the observed nature of security returns. Specifically, it implies that security returns will be generated by a diagonal model, which several authors have found to represent adequately the actual security return generating process.[12] The diagonal return generating process in this model stems of course from the assumption that changes in expected cash flows are linked only through the single common index of expectations, I_t.

IV. SOME IMPLICATIONS OF THE CASH FLOW VALUATION EQUATION

Investment Criteria

Under the usual assumptions of a perfectly competitive securities market the individual firm is able to take market prices as given in making its investment decisions. Hence, although the valuation equation (16) was derived on the assumption of fixed security supplies, it may be used to value marginal increases in the supply of securities (cash flow claims) of an individual firm such as accompany on investment decision.

Re-writing the valuation equation (16) as

$$V_t(\widetilde{C}_{jT}) = {}_t a_{jT} e^{-r(T-t)} + b_{jT} \widetilde{I}_t e^{-\mu(T-t)} \tag{16'}$$

where $\mu = \gamma + \delta$ permits a fairly straightforward approach to the corporate investment decision under uncertainty. The information requirements include the index-independent and index-dependent components of all the cash flows associated with the project, viz. ${}_t a_{jT}$ and b_{jT} for all $T > t$, where the subscript j refers to the jth project. Given these, and knowledge of the expected return on the market portfolio, μ, the decision-maker may compute the net present value of the project by applying the valuation equation (16') to each individual cash flow. Given the assumption of perfect security markets, the resulting net present value represents the effect on stockholder wealth of adopting the project, and hence provides a simple criterion for project acceptance.

The similarity of this result to that obtained by Mossin [1969] in a single-period framework may be noted. In particular, although both models are

---

12. See King [1966] and Blume [1970]. However, for evidence of departures from the diagonal model see Black, Jensen and Scholes [1970], and Brennan [1971].

founded upon the portfolio equilibrium of the individual investor, they do not require the firm itself to adopt a portfolio selection approach to project selection as has been suggested by several writers;[13] in other words projects are risk-independent.[14] Furthermore, the net present value of a particular project is a given number in this model, and not a random variable the properties of whose distribution must be examined before the decision on project acceptance can be made. Despite the simplifying assumptions made in this model it seems probable that these conclusions hold more generally.

This model also throws further light on the certainty-equivalent and cost-of-capital approaches to the investment decision. The certainty-equivalent of a particular cash flow, C_{jT}, is now an objective, market-determined phenomenon, and not derived from a manager's utility function. It is defined by

$$CE_t(\widetilde{C}_{jT}) = V_t(\widetilde{C}_{jT})e^{r(T-t)}$$

where $CE_t(\widetilde{C}_{jT})$ denotes the certainty-equivalent at time t.

Substituing for $V_t(\widetilde{C}_{jT})$ from (16′) and recalling the expression for the expected value of the cash flow (9), the relationship between the expected value and the certainty-equivalent of a cash-flow is:

$$CE_t(\widetilde{C}_{jT}) = E_t(\widetilde{C}_{jT}) - b_{jT}\widetilde{I}_t e^{-(\mu-r)(T-t)}. \qquad (21)$$

Thus the risk premium $(E_t(\widetilde{C}_{jT}) - CE(\widetilde{C}_{jT}))$ is a simple exponential function of the time to realization of the cash flow.

While there always exists a number, the 'cost of capital' which, if used to discount the expected cash flows from an investment project, will yield the net present value, it should be clear from (16′) that this number is an extremely complex function of $_ta_{jT}$ and b_{jT} (T=t . . .); the very difficulty of computing the cost of capital even for a single project should give pause to those who would apply a single cost of capital standard for all of a company's investments.[15] However, it is outside the scope of this paper to consider the nature of the biases likely to result from such a procedure.

Finally, because of its explicit consideration of risk in a multi-period context, the model should permit examination of such questions as the conditions under which it is optimal to substitute fixed for variable costs, e.g., by accepting a new labour contract, or by installing automated machinery with high fixed and low variable costs.

Security Risk Measures

It is well-known that the relevant measure of the risk of a security in the framework of capital market equilibrium is the covariance between the rate of return on the security and the rate of return on the market portfolio, or more

13. For example Van Horne [1969], Cohen and Elton [1967].

14. The term is Myers' [1968].

15. This procedure is usually justified on the assumption that the new investment has risk characteristics similar to those of the firm's existing assets. Since new investments will generally have income streams stretching further ahead than the income stream of the existing assets of the firm, it is unlikely that the same cost of capital will be appropriate for both existing assets and new investment.

simply its beta coefficient, β_{jt}. For an individual cash flow claim the beta coefficient is given by:

$$\beta_{jt} = \frac{M}{V}\frac{dV}{dM} \tag{22}$$

$$= \frac{b_{jT}\tilde{I}_t e^{-\mu(T-t)}}{{}_t a_{jT}e^{-r(T-t)} + b_{jT}I_t e^{-\mu(T-t)}} \tag{23}$$

from equations (16) and (17).

Assuming that $b_{jT} > 0$

$$\beta_{jT} \; \genfrac{}{}{0pt}{}{>}{<} \Bigg\} \; 1 \qquad as \qquad {}_t a_{jT} \; \genfrac{}{}{0pt}{}{<}{>} \Bigg\} \; 0.$$

Moreover if ${}_t a_{jT} > 0$ so that $\beta_{jT} < 1$, then with unchanged expectations, β_{jT} will increase as the cash flow realization date approaches; on the other hand, if ${}_t a_{jT} < 0$, β_{jT} will decline towards unity from above as the realization date approaches.

The beta coefficient for a firm is of course simply the market value weighted average of the betas of all the firm's expected cash flows. It is difficult to derive a simple expression for this save under highly restrictive assumptions. However, if both components of a firm's expected cash flows grow at a constant rate g, (where $g < r$), so that

$$_t a_{fT} = a_f e^{gT}$$

$$b_{fT} = b_f e^{gT}$$

where the subscript f refers to the firm, then the value of the firm at time t, V_{ft}, is given by

$$\tilde{V}_{ft} = e^{gT} \int_{T>t} [a_f e^{(g-r)(T-t)} + b_f I_t e^{(g-\mu)(T-t)}]\, dT = \left[\frac{a_f}{r-g} + \frac{b_f\tilde{I}_t}{\mu-g}\right] e^{gt}. \tag{24}$$

The firm's beta coefficient, β_{ft}, is given by

$$\tilde{\beta}_{ft} = \frac{1}{\tilde{V}_{ft}} \int_{T>t} \frac{b_{fT}\tilde{I}_t e^{-\mu(T-t)}}{{}_t a_{fT}e^{-r(T-t)} + b_{fT}I_t e^{-\mu(T-t)}} ({}_t a_{fT}e^{-r(T-t)} + b_{fT}\tilde{I}_t e^{-\mu(T-t)})\, dT$$

$$= \frac{(r-g)\, b_f\tilde{I}_t}{a_f(\mu-g) + (r-g)b_f\tilde{I}^t}. \tag{25}$$

Note that equation (25) implies that the beta coefficient of the firm is non-stationary but depends upon the level of the expectations index, $\tilde{I}_t$.[16] Moreover the beta coefficient of the firm is clearly shown to depend upon the conditional distributions of the firm's underlying cash flows.

16. For the suggestion that empirical beta coefficients are non-stationary, see Fisher [1971].

The Journal of Finance

V. Conclusion

In this paper we have developed, under highly simplified assumptions about the process by which investors' expectations are generated, a model for the valuation of risky future cash flows and income streams. Despite the simplicity of the expectations mechanism, the model has two features which accord well with the observed nature of security returns: it implies that they will be generated by a diagonal model and that the beta coefficients will be non-stationary. Nevertheless, a more sophisticated model of expectations is obviously desirable, and further empirical research is required on the process by which investors form expectations.

However, within the limited scope of this paper, we have been able to show the crucial role of dynamic expectations formation in determining the risk of cash flows, and to demonstrate the possibility of incorporating the investment decision under uncertainty into the mainstream of finance, by employing the same net present value tools employed elsewhere.

APPENDIX

Inspection of (7) shows that expected risky asset yields at time t are dependent on the vector of dollar values of all risky assets outstanding in the market at time t. The instantaneous market values of these risky assets will depend upon the capital gains and hence the yields realized on these assets in previous instants, thus introducing a dependence between realized asset yields in one instant and expected asset yields in the following instant. This dependence will be compounded by any possible effects on the term $\left(\sum_{i=1}^{m} a_i^t \right)^{-1}$ of unanticipated capital gains and losses in the previous instant.[17] Therefore it is necessary to examine in more detail the conditions under which this serial dependence will be absent, for only under such conditions will the model of capital market equilibrium developed above be internally consistent.

The market equilibrium relationship (7) may be written

$$\alpha - rj = M \left(\sum_{i=1}^{m} \phi^i W^i \right)^{-1} \Omega w \tag{26}$$

where

M—the value of the market portfolio of all risky assets
w—an n-dimensional vector giving the proportion of M accounted for by each risky asset
$\phi^i = a^i/W^i$—the relative risk aversion of the derived utility function of investor $i(i=1-m)$
W^i—the wealth of investor i.

The time-subscripts have been removed from the variables to avoid unnecessary complexity. The sufficient conditions for the serial independence of asset yields are then:

(i) $\lambda = M \left(\sum_{i=1}^{m} \phi^i W^i \right)^{-1}$ is constant, and

(ii) the vector w is known.

17. It will be recalled that this term reflects the risk aversion of investors which may well be different at different wealth levels.

(iii) If ϕ^i and W^i are uncorrelated we may write $\lambda = \dfrac{M}{WR}$, where $R = \dfrac{1}{m} \displaystyle\sum_{i=1}^{m} \phi^i$, and

$W = \displaystyle\sum_{i=1}^{m} W^i$. But $W = M + B$, where B is the net value of riskless assets held in investor portfolios, so that $\lambda = \dfrac{M}{(M + B)R}$.

Therefore, sufficient conditions for λ to be independent of realized yields on investment portfolios are that:

a) the derived utility functions of all investors exhibit constant relative risk aversion, and ϕ^i is uncorrelated with W^i.

b) B is small relative to M.

ii) w will be known if the market value of each risky asset bears a known relationship to the value of the market portfolio of all risky assets. It is a property of the cash flow claims considered in this paper that they either have values bearing a known relationship to that of the risky market portfolio or have returns uncorrelated with the returns on the market portfolio, which therefore have constant expected values equal to the risk-free rate of interest.

While the above assumptions are somewhat restrictive, they have some empirical support in that extensive tests indicate that equity security returns tend to be distributed independently through time.[18]

Finally, premultiplying equation (26) by w' it is readily seen that the market portfolio will have a constant expected rate of return, $= w'\alpha$, so long as the variance rate $w'\Omega w$ is constant.

REFERENCES

1. Fischer Black. "Corporate Investment Decisions", Associates in Finance, Financial Note No. 2B, May 1969.
2. Fischer Black, Michael C. Jensen and Myron S. Scholes. "The Capital Asset Pricing Model: Some Empirical Tests", University of Rochester Systems Analysis Program Working Paper No. 57030, November, 1970.
3. Fischer Black and Myron S. Scholes. "Capital Market Equilibrium and the Pricing of Corporate Liabilities", Associates in Finance, Financial Note No. 16C, January 1971.
4. Marshall Blume. "Portfolio Theory: A Step Towards its Practical Application", *Journal of Business*, Vol. 43, (April 1970), pp. 152-174.
5. Michael J. Brennan. "Capital Asset Pricing and the Structure of Security Returns", paper presented at the Wells Fargo Symposium on Modern Capital Theory, San Francisco, 1971.
6. Kalman J. Cohen and Edwin J. Elton. "Inter-Temporal Portfolio Analysis Based Upon Simulation of Joint Returns", *Management Science*, Vol. 14 (September 1967), pp. 5-18.
7. Paul Cootner (ed). *The Random Character of Stock Market Prices*, M.I.T. Press, Cambridge, 1964.
8. Eugene, F. Fama. "Risk, Return and Equilibrium: Some Clarifying Comments", *Journal of Finance*, Vol. 23, (March 1968), pp. 29-40.
9. Lawrence Fisher. "On the Estimation of Systematic Risk", paper presented at the Wells Fargo Symposium on Modern Capital Theory, San Francisco, 1971.
10. Michael C. Jensen. "The Foundations and Current State of Capital Market Theory", forthcoming in *Studies in the Theory of Capital Markets*, M.C. Jensen (ed.), Praeger Publishers, 1971.
11. Benjamin, F. King. "Market and Industry Factors in Stock Price Behavior", *Journal of Business*, Vol. 39, (January 1966), pp. 139-189.
12. Harry Markowitz. *Portfolio Selection*, John Wiley & Sons, New York, 1959.
13. Robert C. Merton. "Lifetime Portfolio Selection Under Uncertainty: The Continuous Time Case", *Review of Economics and Statistics*, Vol. 51, (August 1969), pp. 247-257.
14. Jan Mossin. "Security Pricing and Investment Criteria in Competitive Markets", *American Economic Review*, Vol. 59, (December 1969) pp. 749-756.
15. Stewart Myers Co. "Procedures for Capital Budgetary Under Uncertainty", *Industrial Management Review*, Vol. 9 (Spring, 1968), pp. 1-15.

18. See, for example, the papers contained in Cootner [1964].

16. R. Richardson Pettit and Randolph Westerfield. "A Model of Market Risk", paper presented at the annual meetings of the Western Finance Association, Vancouver, 1971.
17. Alexander A. Robichek and Stewart C. Myers. *Optimal Financing Decisions,* Prentice-Hall, Englewood Cliffs, 1965.
18. Paul A. Samuelson. "Lifetime Portfolio Selection by Dynamic Stochastic Programming", *Review of Economics and Statistics,* Vol. 51, (August 1969), pp. 239-246.
19. Paul A. Samuelson. "The Fundamental Approximation Theorem of Portfolio Analysis in Terms of Means, Variances and Higher Moments", *Review of Economic Studies,* Vol. 37, (October 1970), pp. 538-542.
20. Richard C. Stapleton. "Portfolio Analysis, Stock Valuation and Capital Budgeting Rules for Risky Projects", *Journal of Finance,* Vol. 26 (March 1971), pp. 95-118.
21. Donald L. Tuttle and Robert H. Litzenberger. "Leverage, Diversification and Capital Market Effects on a Risk Adjusted Capital Budgeting Framework", *Journal of Finance,* Vol. 23, (June 1968), pp. 427-444.
22. James C. Van Horne. "Capital Budgeting Decisions Involving Combinations of Risky Investments", *Management Science,* Vol. 13 (October 1966), pp. 84-92.

[3]

M. J. Brennan and E. S. Schwartz*

University of British Columbia

Corporate Income Taxes, Valuation, and the Problem of Optimal Capital Structure

I

Most aspects of the theory of capital structure and valuation in perfect capital markets with no corporate income tax have by now been investigated.[1] Somewhat less attention, however, has been directed to the effects of the corporate income tax on the relationship between capital structure and valuation,[2] although it is the corporate income tax which lends most of the interest to the optimal capital structure problem and although the conclusions reached by Modigliani and Miller (1963) were much more tentative when corporate income taxes were introduced.

Analysis of the effects of the corporate income tax is of interest not only because corporate income taxes do in fact exist but because the analysis appears to lead to the conclusion that an optimal capital structure will consist almost entirely of debt. This conclusion leads to inconsistency between the premise that managements act so as to maximize the wealth of stockholders and the empirical observation that most firms eschew highly levered capital structures. Modigliani and Miller themselves attribute this discrepancy be-

This paper is concerned mainly with the effects of corporate income taxes on the relationship between capital structure and valuation. If the interest tax savings cease once a firm has gone bankrupt, it is apparent that the issue of additional debt will have two effects on the value of the firm: on one hand, it will increase the tax savings to be enjoyed so long as the firm survives; on the other hand, it will reduce the probability of the firm's survival for any given period. Depending on which of these conflicting influences prevails, the value of the firm may increase or decrease as additional debt is issued. The option pricing framework is used to relate the value of a levered firm to the value of an unlevered firm, the amount of debt, and the time to maturity of the debt.

* The authors are grateful to Robert Hamada for helpful comments.

1. Durand (1952), Modigliani and Miller (1958), Solomon (1963), Stiglitz (1969, 1972), Smith (1972), and Milne (1975).

2. See, however, Hamada (1969), Kraus and Litzenberger (1973), and Rubinstein (1973).

(*Journal of Business*, 1978, vol. 51, no. 1)
© 1978 by The University of Chicago
0021-9398/78/5101-0003$01.09

tween the predictions of their model and the observed reality to the effects of the personal income tax, which may make retained earnings a cheaper source of finance than debt, and to "the need for preserving flexibility," which is "not fully comprehended within the framework of static equilibrium models, either our own or those of the traditional variety" (1963, p. 443). Subsequent writers have attempted to explain the low levels of leverage observed by resort to "bankruptcy costs" (Robichek and Myers 1965; Kraus and Litzenberger 1973), though the nature and empirical significance of these costs has received scant attention (however, see Baxter 1967; Warner 1975), suggesting that they may perhaps be no more than a convenient hypothesis to reconcile the theory with the data. Finally, observed capital structures may be explained by the hypothesis that managements are more interested in their own job security and other agency costs, and hence in the avoidance of bankruptcy, than they are in the maximization of the wealth of stockholders (Donaldson 1963; Jensen and Meckling 1976).

This paper is concerned mainly with relaxing the assumption that the tax savings due to debt issuance constitute a "sure stream." Modigliani and Miller themselves acknowledge that "some uncertainty attaches even to the tax savings, though, of course, it is of a different kind and order from that attaching to the stream generated by the assets" (1963, n. 5). They attribute this uncertainty to two causes: first, the possibility of future changes in the tax rate and, second, the possibility that at some future date the firm may have no taxable income against which the interest payments on the debt may be offset.

In this paper we consider the latter possibility, noting in particular that once a firm has gone bankrupt the interest tax savings will cease. Once this possibility is acknowledged, it is apparent that the issue of additional debt will have two effects on the value of the firm: on one hand, it will increase the tax savings to be enjoyed so long as the firm survives; on the other hand, it will reduce the probability of the firm's survival for any given period. Depending on which of these conflicting influences prevails, the value of the firm may increase or decrease as additional debt be issued. It seems reasonable to suppose a priori that, as additional debt is issued from a small base, the survival probabilities of the firm will not be substantially affected, so that the former influence will outweigh the latter and the value of the firm will increase, but that at high initial levels of debt further increments of debt may so affect the survival probabilities that the value of the firm will actually decrease. If such is the case, then an optimal capital structure may exist even without the existence of bankruptcy costs.

The analysis of this paper rests on the Modigliani-Miller (1958) risk-class assumption and compares the value of the levered firm with an otherwise-identical unlevered firm. By assuming that the levered and unlevered firms are identical in all respects save their capital structures, we are neglecting the possibility that the managers of the levered firms will be induced to alter their investment decisions by the structure of the firm's liabilities. This may occur first because managers are concerned to avoid bankruptcy and its attendant costs and second because in making investment decisions they take account of redistribution effects between bondholders and stockholders.[3] Following Modigliani and Miller, we take as given the existence of an unlevered firm and do not enquire why such a firm should exist if there is any advantage to the issue of debt. The value of the levered firm is assumed to be a function of the value of the unlevered firm, the amount of debt outstanding, and the time to maturity of the debt. This specification, together with the assumption that the value of the unlevered firm follows a Gauss-Wiener process, enables us to derive a differential equation relating the values of the unlevered firm and the levered firm. This differential equation is identical with that derived by Black and Scholes (1973) and Merton (1973) for the option-pricing problem. Specification of appropriate boundary conditions then permits a solution of the differential equation, yielding the value of the unlevered firm in terms of the value of the levered firm, the par value of the outstanding debt (and the interest rate on the debt), and the maturity of the debt. Since the methodology employed is sufficiently flexible to allow for bankruptcy costs also, without significant additional complications, and since many authors have regarded these as important, they are included in the model formulation and in one of the numerical examples which follow.

II

It is assumed that the market value of a levered firm, V, may be written solely as a function of the value of an otherwise identical unlevered firm, U, which belongs to the same risk class and has the same earnings and investment policy; the face value of the debt outstanding, B, and the coupon rate on the debt, i; and time, t, which enters the valuation expression because the debt is assumed to have a finite maturity, T. Thus the value of the levered firm may be written as

$$V \equiv V(U,B,i,t). \tag{1}$$

Simple equilibrium considerations dictate that the ratio V/U must be a function solely of the leverage ratio[4] B/U, i, and t, so that (1) may be written as

$$V = UV(1,B/U,i,t). \tag{2}$$

3. Note that the firm-value-maximizing investment policies will be dependent on capital structure to the extent that bankruptcy costs are significant. For a detailed discussion of the distinction between firm-value-maximizing investment decisions and equity-value-maximizing decisions, see Galai and Masulis (1976).

4. This follows from the basic homogeneity property that two levered firms with the same leverage ratio have twice the value of one.

Equation (2) will prove useful when we wish to examine the relationship between V and the leverage ratio for a given value of U. We shall actually solve (1) for different values of U and a fixed value of B. Equation (2) then permits us to derive from that solution V in terms of B for a given value of U.

Since we shall be considering the relationship between V and U for fixed values of B and i, it will be convenient to write (1) as

$$V \equiv V(U,t). \tag{3}$$

In between dividend payments which are assumed to occur at discrete intervals, the value of the unlevered firm is assumed to follow the Gauss-Wiener process[5]

$$\frac{dU}{U} = \mu\, dt + \sigma\, dz, \tag{4}$$

where dz is a Gauss-Wiener process and $E[dz] = 0$, $E(dz)^2 = dt$.

Then, assuming that trading takes place continuously, it can be shown that arbitrage considerations imply that the value of the levered firm between dividend dates must follow the differential equation

$$\tfrac{1}{2}\sigma^2 U^2 V_{uu} + rUV_u + V_t - Vr = 0, \tag{5}$$

where r is the known, constant, risk-free rate of interest and subscripts denote partial derivatives. Equation (5) is derived by forming a zero net investment portfolio consisting of investments in the levered firm, the unlevered firm, and the risk-free asset such that the return on this portfolio must be nonstochastic; its return must therefore be zero.

We consider next the boundary conditions which must be satisfied by the differential equation.

First, at the maturity of the debt, T, we have

$$\begin{aligned} V(U,T) &= U \text{ for } U \geqslant B, \\ &= U\text{-}C(U), \text{ for } U < B, \end{aligned} \tag{6}$$

where $C(U)$ is the bankruptcy costs that will be incurred if a firm whose unlevered value is U files for bankruptcy. To consider first the case in which $U \geqslant B$ so that bankruptcy at maturity is avoided, the value of the levered firm is equal to the value of the unlevered firm. This is because we are considering the effect on firm value of a single issue of debt, so that when that debt matures, if bankruptcy is avoided, levered and unlevered firms are in all respects identical and must therefore command the same market value. No loss of generality is involved in this assumption, since the date at which the levered firm reverts to being an

---

5. This stochastic process has been frequently employed in models of this kind (Black and Scholes 1973; Merton 1973); it implies that the value of U at any future instant follows the lognormal distribution.

unlevered firm may be made as distant as desired.[6] If $U < B$, the levered firm must file for bankruptcy, in which case costs $C(U)$ are incurred which serve to reduce the value of the levered firm below that of the corresponding unlevered firm.

Since the assets of the levered and unlevered firms are at all times identical, we assume that they both pay identical constant dividends,[7] D. Then at a dividend date the following boundary condition holds:

$$V(U,t^-) = V(U-D,t^+) + D, \tag{7}$$

where t^- and t^+ denote the instants before and after the dividend, respectively. Equation (7) expresses the cum-dividend value of the levered firm as the sum of its ex-dividend value and the value of the dividend paid. Note that the dividend payment causes the value of the unlevered firm to fall by the amount D.

The dividend may be made a function of the firm's economic fortunes by making it a function of U and t. Moreover, a negative value of D may be introduced to represent the issue of additional stock. In the interests of simplicity, we assign a fixed value to D.

In addition to paying dividends, the levered firm must also make periodic coupon payments, iB. Each coupon payment will reduce the value of the firm's assets by $iB(1-\tau)$ after giving effect to the concomitant tax savings, where τ is the corporate tax rate. Since the assets of the levered firm are by assumption identical with those of the unlevered firm which makes no such coupon payments, it is necessary to assume that the assets of the levered firm are restored by the issue of stock in the amount $iB(1-\tau)$. Then at a coupon payment date, t,

$$\begin{aligned} V(U,t^-) &= V(U,t^+) + iB - (1-\tau)iB, \\ &= V(U,t^+) + \tau iB. \end{aligned} \tag{8}$$

Equation (8) is derived by expressing the precoupon value of the levered firm as the sum of its postcoupon value and the coupon received, less the value of the stock sold to make the coupon payment $(1-\tau)iB$.

To simplify subsequent numerical examples, it is assumed that dividend and coupon payments are made on the same day, so that, if (7) and (8) are combined, the joint effects of coupon and dividend payments are represented by the boundary condition

$$V(U,t^-) = V(U-D,t^+) + D + \tau iB. \tag{9}$$

The remaining boundary condition relates to the conditions under which the firm becomes bankrupt and the value of the firm when it becomes bankrupt. The value of a bankrupt levered firm is equal to the

---

6. This point will be illustrated later in conjunction with figs. 5 and 6.

7. We could have assumed equivalently that the levered firm retired a corresponding amount of debt and equity as long as the ratio B/U was maintained.

value of an identical unlevered firm less the costs of bankruptcy, since the assets of the levered firm, to be taken over by the creditors, are by definition identical with those of the unlevered firm before allowance is made for the costs of bankruptcy.

It is assumed that the firm will become bankrupt if, on a coupon date, the value of its assets (i.e., the corresponding value of an unlevered firm) is less than some critical value. The lowest conceivable critical value is $(1-\tau)iB$, the net interest obligation; a more reasonable one, and the one adopted here, is the par value of the outstanding bonds, B, so that the firm is assumed to become bankrupt when its value falls to the par value of its outstanding bonds.

Then, if we combine this condition with (9), the value of the firm on a coupon/dividend date is given by

$$V(U,t^-) = V(U-D,t^+) + D + \tau iB \text{ for } U \geq B,$$
$$= U-C(U) \qquad\qquad \text{for } U < B. \tag{10}$$

In summary, the value of the levered firm is given by the solution to the differential equation (5), subject to the boundary conditions (6) and (10). One further boundary condition is required for the solution algorithm: This is

$$\lim_{U \to \infty} V_u = 1. \tag{11}$$

Equation (11) follows from the consideration that, as the value of a levered firm becomes indefinitely large for a given level of debt commitments, the probability of default becomes arbitrarily small, so that the tax savings become essentially riskless, and the formula analysis of Modigliani and Miller (1963) applies, which implies (11).

Although there exists no closed-form solution to the differential equation subject to the foregoing boundary conditions, a solution may be readily obtained by the use of numerical methods (Brennan and Schwartz 1977). The following section presents the results of such numerical analysis.

III

The data for the basic example, given in table 1, relate to a 25-year bond issue by a firm which pays no dividends and would issue no stock if it were not debt financed.[8] The differential equation was solved for a given level of B ($200), yielding V as a function of U. Equation (2) was then used to derive the ratio V/U as a function of the ratio B/U, and in figure 1 V/U is plotted as a function of the leverage ratio B/V. As is evident from this figure the conjecture is borne out that the possibility

---

8. To avoid confounding the effect of investment policy and financing policy, it will be recalled that we assumed that the levered firm issues sufficient stock to offset its net interest payment; see eq. (8).

TABLE 1   **Parameters for Basic Example**

Debt maturity (T)	25 years
Debt par value (B)	$200
Debt coupon rate (i)	.07/year
Risk-free interest rate (r)	.06/year
Corporate tax rate (τ)	.50
Unlevered-firm variance rate (σ^2)	.05/year
Aggregate annual dividend (D)	$0
Bankruptcy cost (as fraction of firm value at bankruptcy) (BC)	.00

of a bankruptcy, with the resulting uncertainty of tax savings, is sufficient to lead to an optimal capital structure even in the absence of bankruptcy costs. For the given parameters, the optimal leverage ratio, B/V, is 54%, and at the optimum the value of the levered firm exceeds that of the unlevered firm by 23%—the maximum leverage premium.[9]

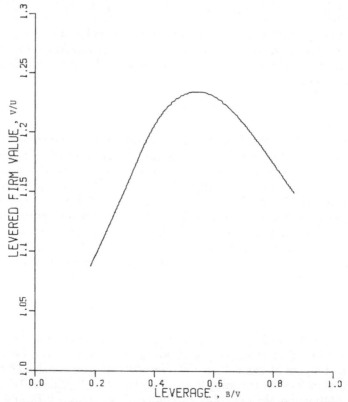

FIG. 1.—Firm value as a function of leverage: basic example

9. Care should be taken in interpreting this leverage ratio, which is the ratio of the book value of a 7% bond to the market value of the firm. It is likely that this ratio understates the true market-value leverage ratio for low values of the ratio and overstates it for high values of the ratio, since the relationship between the bond's market and book values will depend on the risk of the bond and hence on the leverage ratio.

Figure 2 illustrates the effect of business risk on the value of the levered firm and the optimal leverage ratio. Different levels of business risk are represented by different variance rates for the unlevered firm. As would be expected, the more risky the firm (the higher the variance rate), the less the advantage of debt and the lower the optimal leverage ratio, because of the higher probability of bankruptcy for a given leverage ratio. Thus for a variance rate of 0.02 the optimal leverage ratio is 60% and the maximum leverage premium is 30%, while for a variance rate of 0.08 these figures drop to 51% and 22%, respectively.

In figure 3 the relationship between value and leverage is shown for different payout policies. This figure should not be construed as indicating that dividend policy matters in the Modigliani-Miller sense (Miller and Modigliani 1961), for in this model dividends are not offset by stock issues while investment remains constant: rather, the different dividends represent different investment policies, so that a bigger dividend corresponds to a reduction in the exogenously determined asset growth rate. Not surprisingly, the reduced asset growth rate, like

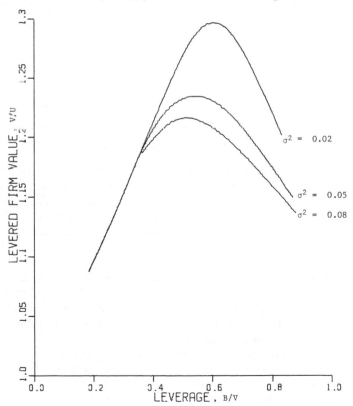

FIG. 2.—Business risk, firm value, and leverage

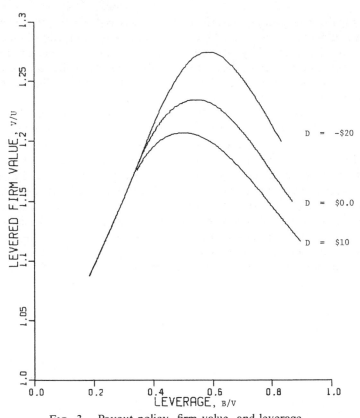

Fɪɢ. 3.—Payout policy, firm value, and leverage

increased business risk, raises the probability of bankruptcy for a given leverage ratio, so that the greater the dividend, the less the advantage of debt and the lower the optimal leverage ratio. The negative dividend of $20 represents an annual stock issue of $20 (10% of the par value of the debt); this exogenous infusion of funds enhances the security of the debt and reduces the probability of bankruptcy. For $D = -\$20$ the optimal leverage ratio is 59% and the maximum leverage premium is 27%, while for $D = \$10$ the corresponding figures are 50% and 21%. Clearly an important determinant of the value of a levered firm and of its optimal capital structure is its investment policy (stock issues less dividends): the lower this net investment, the lower the value of the firm and the optimal leverage ratio.

   In figure 4, the influence of proportional bankruptcy costs is de-picted; the differential bankruptcy costs are assumed to be pro-portional to the value of the unlevered firm at the time of bankruptcy. The additional influence of bankruptcy costs over and above the tax effect is perhaps surprisingly small at the optimum. Even with a

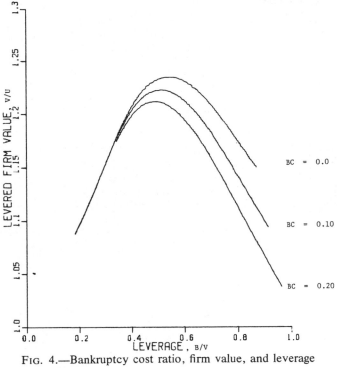

FIG. 4.—Bankruptcy cost ratio, firm value, and leverage

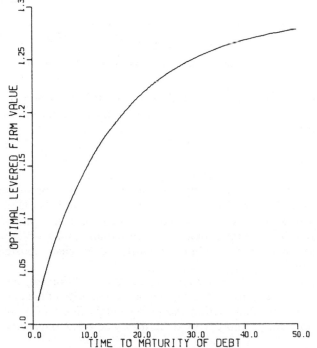

FIG. 5.—Optimal levered-firm value and time to maturity of debt

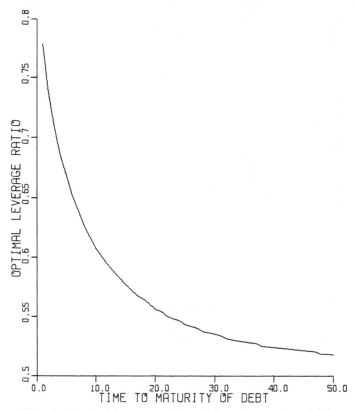

FIG. 6.—Optimal leverage ratio and time to maturity of debt

differential bankruptcy cost ratio (*BC*) of 20%, the optimal leverage
ratio only falls from 54% to 49%, while the maximum leverage premium
falls from 23% to 21%.

Finally, figures 5 and 6 show the effect of the maturity of the debt on
the optimal value of the levered firm and the optimal leverage ratio,
respectively, for the basic example. As the maturity of the debt increases, the corresponding maximum leverage premium tends
asymptotically to 28% and the optimal leverage ratio to 52%. We see
that, by making the date at which the levered firm reverts to being an
unlevered firm distant enough, we can obtain results which approximate the permanent (infinite maturity) debt case considered by
Modigliani and Miller.

Note that, due to the terminal boundary condition (6), the optimal
leverage ratio and firm value depend on the maturity of the debt. This is
because we are considering the incremental effects of a single debt
issue. In reality, short-term debt may be rolled over, and, in the

absence of transactions costs, it will be optimal to issue and redeem debt continuously, for in this way bankruptcy may be avoided while the tax savings are still enjoyed.

References

Baxter, N. D. 1967. Leverage, risk of ruin, and the cost of capital. *Journal of Finance* 22 (September): 395–404.

Black, F., and Scholes, M. 1973. The pricing of options and corporate liabilities. *Journal of Political Economy* 81 (May–June): 637–59.

Brennan, M. J., and Schwartz, E. S. 1977. Convertible bonds: valuation and optimal strategies for call and conversion. *Journal of Finance* (December).

Donaldson, G. 1963. Financial goals: management vs. stockholders. *Harvard Business Review* 41 (May–June): 116–29.

Durand, D. 1952. Cost of debt and equity funds for business: trends and problems of measurement. Conference on Research in Business Finance. New York: National Bureau of Economic Research.

Galai, D., and Masulis, R. W. 1976. The option pricing model and the risk factor of stock. *Journal of Financial Economics* 3 (January): 53–82.

Hamada, R. S. 1969. Portfolio analysis, market equilibrium, and corporation finance. *Journal of Finance* 24 (March): 13–31.

Jensen, M. C., and Meckling, W. H. 1976. Theory of the firm: managerial behavior, agency costs and ownership structure. *Journal of Financial Economics* 3 (October): 305–60.

Kraus, A., and Litzenberger, R. H. 1973. A state-preference model of optimal financial leverage. *Journal of Finance* 28 (September): 911–22.

Merton, R. C. 1973. Theory of rational option pricing. *Bell Journal of Economics and Management Science* 4 (Spring): 141–83.

Miller, M. H., and Modigliani, F. 1961. Dividend policy, growth, and the valuation of shares. *Journal of Business* 34 (October): 411–33.

Milne, F. 1975. Choice over asset economics: default risk and corporate leverage. *Journal of Financial Economics* 2 (June): 165–85.

Modigliani, F., and Miller, M. H. 1958. The cost of capital, corporation finance and the theory of investment. *American Economic Review* 48 (June): 261–97.

Modigliani, F., and Miller, M. H. 1963. Taxes and the cost of capital: a correction. *American Economic Review* 53 (June): 433–43.

Robichek, A. A., and Myers, S. C. 1965. *Optimal Financing Decisions.* Englewood Cliffs, N.J.: Prentice-Hall.

Rubinstein, M. E. 1973. A mean-variance synthesis of corporate financial theory. *Journal of Finance* 28 (March): 167–82.

Smith, V. 1972. Default risk, scale, and the homemade leverage theorem. *American Economic Review* 62 (March): 66–76.

Solomon, E. 1963. Leverage and the cost of capital. *Journal of Finance* 18 (May): 273–79.

Stiglitz, J. 1969. A reexamination of the Modigliani-Miller theorem. *American Economic Review* 59 (December): 784–93.

Stiglitz, J. 1972. Some aspects of the pure theory of corporate finance: bankruptcies and take-overs. *Bell Journal of Economics and Management Science* 3 (Autumn): 458–82.

Warner, J. B. 1975. Bankruptcy and optimal capital structure: issues and evidence. Unpublished manuscript.

[4]

Consistent regulatory policy under uncertainty

Michael J. Brennan*

and

Eduardo S. Schwartz**

This article is concerned with the effects of regulation on the risk and value of the regulated firm in a dynamic context. Current regulatory practice is shown to be logically deficient, since it ignores the effect of regulatory policy on the cost of capital and therefore on the appropriate allowed rate of return. A notion of consistency in regulatory policy is developed, and it is shown how consistent regulatory policies may be implemented once the valuation problem is solved.

1. Introduction

■   The problems of equity and of efficiency in resource allocation that arise from the existence of natural monopolies may be dealt with either by socialization or by regulation: the latter approach is especially common in the United States, while the former is favored in most other jurisdictions. In this article we analyze the dynamic effects of regulation on firm risk and value and show how a consistent regulatory policy may be determined. The valuation model is simple and, in the interest of analytic tractability, abstracts from many features of the regulatory environment. Nevertheless, the general approach lends itself to further elaboration and realism, so that the article represents a first step in the theory of the valuation of the regulated firm. No such theory currently exists and yet, as will become apparent below, such a theory is a prerequisite for the determination of a consistent regulatory policy.

A major task of the regulator is to set the prices at which the output of the regulated firm must be sold. His decisions affect the costs borne and the quantity purchased by consumers on the one hand and the returns received by investors on the other. These decisions must, therefore, be tempered by considerations of equity. At the same time, regulatory decisions, by influencing incentives, also affect the behavior of the regulated firm with attendant implications for economic efficiency; it is these efficiency aspects of regulation which have in the main attracted the attention of economists.

Thus there exists an extensive literature concerned with the effects of regulation on firm behavior: most of this literature assumes certainty and a static setting in which only a single regulatory decision is made.[1] Das (1980), Perrakis (1976), and Peles and Stein (1976) have extended this type of analysis to uncertainty, relying on Leland's (1972) model of the expected utility-maximizing firm. This model, however, is unsatisfactory as

---

* University of British Columbia.

** University of British Columbia.

Previous versions of this article have been presented at seminars at Northwestern, Ohio State, Wisconsin, Yale, New York University, and the London Business School. The comments and suggestions of seminar participants are gratefully acknowledged. We wish to thank especially Fischer Black and the Editorial Board for helpful comments. We retain responsibility for the final contents of the article.

[1] The seminal article here is by Averch and Johnson (1962). Many of the subsequent articles are surveyed in Baumol and Klevorick (1970) and Stein and Borts (1972).

a basis for a theory of the regulated firm, since it ignores the role of the capital market in allocating risk and in providing investment alternatives which affect the incentives of the owners. These capital market alternatives are taken into account by Myers (1973) in his analysis of a value-maximizing regulated firm in a state preference framework. More recently, Marshall *et al.* (1981) have studied the input choices of a regulated value-maximizing firm in the context of the capital asset pricing model. Like us, they treat the risk of the firm as endogenous and affected by the regulatory decision; unlike us, they retain the static framework of the other articles.

Klevorick (1973) has analyzed the dynamic effects of regulation on firm behavior. In his model, regulatory decisions are made at stochastic intervals with the regulator setting output prices according to some known rule. The firm rationally anticipates future regulatory decisions and determines its behavior to maximize the discounted expected value of future cash flows. In keeping with most of the preceding literature on regulation and firm behavior, Klevorick pays no attention to risk, and the discount rate in the firm's objective function is taken as exogenous.[2]

In this article we are concerned, like Klevorick, with the dynamic aspects of regulation. But, while he is concerned with firm behavior and ignores issues of valuation, we are concerned with valuation and therefore suppress the issue of the influence of regulatory policy on firm behavior until Section 6, where we discuss it briefly. The dynamic aspects of regulation arise in our model, as in that of Klevorick, because regulation is an ongoing process in which new regulatory decisions are made as conditions change. In Klevorick's model, rational anticipations of these decisions by the management of the firm affect firm behavior; in our model, rational anticipations of these decisions by investors affect firm risk and value.[3] Consider, for example, the range of possible regulatory responses to the accidental destruction of a plant owned by a regulated firm. At one extreme, the regulatory authority may fail to respond at all, leaving the shareholders of the firm to bear the entire loss; at the other extreme, the plant may be left in the rate base and output prices adjusted so that the regulated firm continues to earn its allowed rate of return on the original investment in the now useless plant. In the latter case, the whole of the loss would be borne by consumers.

This ability of the regulator to allocate stochastic future costs and benefits between consumer and investor means that the investment risk of the regulated firm is endogenous, being a function not only of technological and market uncertainties but also of regulatory policy. It follows that insofar as current regulatory procedures take the investment risk of the regulated firm as exogenous and attempt to determine an allowed rate of return appropriate to this risk, they are conceptually deficient. As Robichek (1978) has remarked, "[F]or a regulated company, the business (and hence, investment) risk depends on the regulatory decision. To require that the rates be set after giving due consideration to 'risk' is circular when such 'risk' is determined to a large extent by the rate-making process." What is required instead is a regulatory procedure or policy that is consistent in the sense that it yields an allowed rate of return which is appropriate for the risk of the firm under that policy.[4] A wide range of regulatory policies are consistent in this sense: they involve different allocations of risk between consumers and investors and, consequently, different allowed rates of return are appropriate for each. The choice between alternative regulatory policies may be made on grounds of efficiency. We shall, however, ignore efficiency considerations by taking the productive decisions of the regulated firm as exogenous.

---

[2] In a more recent article, Bawa and Sibley (1980) also analyze the dynamic behavior of the regulated firm. In their model, as in the one presented here, the probability that a hearing will be held is endogenous; however, as in Klevorick, the discount rate in the firm's objective function is exogenous.

[3] Sometimes the decisions will follow explicit rules, such as automatic fuel adjustment clauses; more frequently the decision rules are implicit.

[4] We defer until the following section a consideration of what constitutes an appropriate rate of return.

Given these productive decisions, the regulatory authority is able to affect the returns to investors in the firm by changing output prices.

In Section 2, we discuss the nature of the regulatory criterion and its implicit justification which, we argue, is inadequate once attention is given to the effects of uncertainty: we therefore offer an alternative definition of a consistent regulatory policy. Section 3 develops the valuation framework, which is specialized in Section 4 to apply to regulated firms under alternative regulatory policies. In Section 5 we present a numerical example. Finally, Section 6 considers the implications of the model for current procedures used to determine the allowed rate of return, and for the investment incentive implications of regulatory lag.

2. The regulatory criterion and consistent regulatory policy

■   A principal task of the regulatory authority in setting output prices for the regulated firm is to determine the appropriate rate of profit for the shareholders. In this, its objective is to combine equity between investors and consumers with appropriate incentives for the management of the firm. The legal criteria for an appropriate rate of profit are enshrined in the *Bluefield* and the *Hope* decisions of the United States Supreme Court,[5] which define what have become generally known as the "comparable earnings standard" and the "capital attraction standard." Some authorities have maintained that the comparable earnings standard requires that the accounting rate of return of the regulated firm correspond to that for unregulated firms of similar risk, and that this principle also satisfies the capital attraction standard.[6] The modern consensus, however, appears to be that both standards require that the allowed rate of return earned by shareholders on the rate base should be equal to the firm's cost of capital, which is defined as the rate of return an investor could expect to earn on investment in other firms of equivalent risk. Thus, the distinction between the modern consensus and the earlier view is that the former takes as its standard a market determined prospective rate of return, whereas the latter relies on retrospective accounting returns on similar risk firms. The implicit justification of the principle that the allowed rate of return be set equal to the cost of capital appears to be the belief that this will cause the market value of the firm to be equal to the value of the rate base on which the return is allowed. Indeed, this result can be rigorously derived within the quasi-uncertainty valuation model of Miller and Modigliani (1961) in which stochastic cash flows are replaced by their expected values and the effects of uncertainty are assumed to be captured in the discount rate.[7]

But this approach to regulation is, in fact, fundamentally deficient because it neglects entirely the role of future regulatory decisions. This deficiency is not apparent in the Miller and Modigliani quasi-uncertainty valuation model because in this model regulation is a one-shot affair, and it is implicitly assumed that the realized return on the rate base is equal to the allowed return. Nor is the deficiency any more apparent in the models of Myers (1973) and Leland (1974), which do explicitly account for uncertainty in a capital markets context but consider only a single period. In both models a role for regulatory response to future uncertainties is effectively precluded—in the one because there is no uncertainty; in the other because there is no future.

Since regulation is a continuing process, the regulatory policy that is anticipated by investors affects the risk and the value of the regulated firm.[8] For this reason, the principle

---

[5] *Bluefield Water Works and Investment Co.* v. *Public Service Commission of the State of West Virginia* (262 U.S. 679, 1923) and *Federal Power Commission* v. *Hope Natural Gas Company* (320 U.S. 591, 1944).

[6] See Myers (1972) for relevant citations and for a forceful critique of this "traditional" position.

[7] Davis and Sparrow (1972) argued that all extant models for the valuation of regulated firms rested on the same set of assumptions. This state of affairs appears to be unchanged.

[8] Empirical evidence of this is provided by Clarke's (1980) study of the introduction of fuel adjustment clauses.

that the allowed rate of return be set equal to the cost of capital is logically incomplete, since the cost of capital is a function of the risk of the firm which, in turn, depends *inter alia* upon the anticipated regulatory policy. That policy includes both the timing of regulatory decisions and the rule for setting the allowed rate of return when those decisions are made. To escape fatal circularity this principle must be replaced by one that takes account of the endogeneity of the risk of the firm. We define a *consistent regulatory policy* as a procedure for determining the holding of a rate hearing and setting the allowed rate of return at the hearing such that, when properly anticipated by investors, the procedure causes the market value of the regulated firm to be equal to the value of the rate base at the time the hearing is held.

Implementation of a consistent regulatory policy presupposes that the regulatory authority is able to assess the effect of alternative regulatory policies on the value of the firm. As we have already noted, however, there exists no model for the valuation of regulated firms which takes account of regulatory policy. In the following section, we present a simplified model that captures the essence of valuation under regulation. A more general model is developed in the Appendix.

3. The valuation framework

■ In the interest of simplicity, we restrict our attention to a regulated firm which is financed entirely by equity funds. Then, under the assumptions described below, the value of the firm may be written as a function of the current rate base, B, and the instantaneous rate of return currently earned on the rate base, x: $F(x, B)$. The rate of return on the rate base is defined as the ratio of the instantaneous earnings rate to the rate base. The instantaneous earnings rate, xB, is locally riskless in the sense that it follows a continuous sample path between regulatory hearings. In nontechnical terms, this means that changes in the earnings rate from week to week are small.

As a result of the business risk to which the firm is exposed, the rate of return x evolves stochastically over time. In a complete model, the resulting stochastic process for the rate of return would be derived from fundamental assumptions about demand and cost conditions. But to derive the rate of return from optimizing behavior in the face of stochastic production and demand functions and stochastic input prices would require the introduction of additional state variables and would substantially increase the complexity of the analysis without contributing further insights. It is therefore assumed, for the sake of tractability, that the rate of return on the rate base follows an exogenously determined stochastic process of the general type

$$dx = \mu(x)dt + \sigma(x)dz_x . \tag{1}$$

Here $\mu(x)$ represents the expected rate of change in x and t is calendar time; dz_x is a standard Gauss-Wiener process with mean zero and variance dt. Thus, the business risk of the firm is represented by the variance of the change in x, $\sigma^2(x)$.

The rate of increase in the rate base is equal to the difference between the instantaneous earnings rate, xB, and the aggregate dividend payout rate net of stock issues.[9] This net payout rate, $\delta(\cdot)$, is assumed to be expressible as

$$\delta(x, B) = p(x)B. \tag{2}$$

Then the instantaneous change in the rate base is given by

$$dB = (x - p(x))Bdt. \tag{3}$$

---

[9] Note that the particular accounting conventions used to determine earnings are irrelevant so long as the same definition is used for x and B and the definition is consistent with the assumed stochastic processes.

In this model, regulatory policy is defined in terms of the rule for holding a regulatory hearing and the rule for determining the outcome of the hearing. It is assumed that the rule for determining a hearing takes the form of a function $\pi(x)$, which is the probability per unit time that a hearing will be held. The motivation for this specification is that a high rate of return will lead to pressure from consumers for a regulatory hearing to reduce the output price of the regulated firm; conversely, should the rate of return fall too low, the firm will press for a hearing to raise output prices.[10]

The outcome of the regulatory hearing is an allowed rate of return $x^*(x)$, which may depend upon the currently earned rate of return, x. The regulator is assumed to be able to adjust output prices instantaneously so that the earned rate of return adjusts immediately to the new allowed rate of return and, starting from this new base, continues to follow the exogenously determined stochastic process (1). We are implicitly assuming that demand for the output of the regulated firm is sufficiently inelastic that there always exists an output price which will yield the allowed rate of return.[11] Furthermore, it should be recognized that, in general, the output price will have implications for the risk of the earnings: in taking the stochastic process (1) as exogenous, we are treating these effects as being of second-order importance.

With the foregoing assumptions, the market value of the regulated firm can be written as $F(x, B)$ and, using equation (A7) in the Appendix, satisfies the partial differential equation:

$$\tfrac{1}{2}\sigma^2(x)F_{xx} + \mu(x)F_x + (x - p(x))BF_B + p(x)B$$
$$+ \pi(x)[F(x^*(x), B) - F(x, B)] = rF + \lambda\sigma(x)F_x . \quad (4)$$

The left-hand side of equation (4) represents the expected return on the firm: the first three terms give the expected change in the value of the firm owing to changes in the state variables x and B, assuming no regulatory hearing takes place. The fourth term, $p(x)B$, is the net dividend received by the owners of the firm, and the last term is the capital gain expected to result from a regulatory hearing. The right-hand side of the equation is the return required on the firm's securities in equilibrium. Here r is the riskless interest rate, which is taken as constant.[12] The second term is a capital asset pricing model type risk premium: $\lambda\sigma(x)$ is the instantaneous covariance between changes in x and the rate of return on aggregate wealth; and an increase in λ represents an increase in the systematic risk of the firm.

The market value of the firm is homogeneous of degree one in the value of the rate base, so that making the substitution $y(x) \equiv F(x, B)/B$, we obtain the following ordinary differential equation for y, the normalized firm value:

$$\tfrac{1}{2}\sigma^2(x)y_{xx} + y_x(\mu(x) - \lambda\sigma(x)) + (x - r - p(x))y + p(x) + \pi(x)[y(x^*(x)) - y(x)] = 0. \quad (5)$$

In this equation the influence of regulatory policy on valuation is captured in the last term, which depends both on the rule for holding hearings, $\pi(x)$, and on the rule for setting the allowed rate of return, $x^*(x)$. It may be noted that if $\partial x^*/\partial x = 0$ and

---

[10] In a study of regulated electric utilities in Florida, Roberts *et al.* (1978) found that the probability that the regulatory authority would require a decrease in rates was an increasing function of the amount by which the earned rate of return exceeded the previously allowed rate of return. The earned rate of return appeared to have no effect on the probability that the company would seek higher rates, perhaps because company requests were based on prospective rather than current rates of return.

[11] This assumption could be relaxed at the expense of introducing additional variables affecting the value of the firm.

[12] The model can be expanded to incorporate a stochastic interest rate. In general, the resulting partial differential equation will not have a closed-form solution. A restrictive example with a stochastic interest rate for which there exists an analytic solution was included in an earlier draft of this article and is available from the authors. The qualitative results are similar to those of the model presented in this article.

$\partial \pi / \partial x = 0$, then as $\pi \to \infty$, $y(x) \to y(x^*)$. This represents a policy of continuous regulation under which the firm always earns the allowed rate of return; consumers bear all of the risk and investors bear none. This is a polar case, the other being that in which $\pi = 0$ and there is no future regulation. To analyze this and intermediate cases, it will be necessary to specify our model further.

4. An explicit model

■   We assume the following:

Assumption 1. The rate of return on the rate base follows an arithmetic Brownian motion, which permits the possibility that, in the absence of regulatory action, the regulated firm may incur losses:

$$dx = \mu dt + \sigma dz. \tag{6}$$

Assumption 2. The output capacity of the firm is proportional to the rate base, B.

Assumption 3. The firm is required by the regulator to maintain capacity equal to potential demand which is growing at the exogenously determined rate g.

Assumptions 2 and 3 imply that the rate base must also grow at the rate g. Equation (3) then defines the dividend payout policy $p(x) = x - g$.
With these substitutions, the differential equation for y is

$$\tfrac{1}{2}\sigma^2 y_{xx} + (\mu - \lambda\sigma)y_x - (r - g)y + (x - g) + \pi(x)[y(x^*(x)) - y(x)] = 0. \tag{7}$$

We shall use equation (7) to discuss the effects of alternative regulatory policies on the value and risk of the equity.

□   **The unregulated case.** The case $\pi(x) \equiv 0$ is of interest not only because it is polar to the case of continuous regulation, but also because it is consistent with current approaches to regulatory issues, which neglect the possibility of future regulatory action. When $\pi(x) = 0$, the complete solution to equation (7) is

$$y(x) = C_1 e^{\gamma_1 x} + C_2 e^{\gamma_2 x} + \frac{x - g}{r - g} + \frac{\mu - \lambda\sigma}{(r - g)^2}, \tag{8}$$

where

$$\gamma_1 = a_1 + a_2,$$

$$\gamma_2 = a_1 - a_2,$$

$$a_1 = -(\mu - \lambda\sigma)/\sigma^2,$$

$$a_2 = [(\mu - \lambda\sigma)^2 + 2\sigma^2(r - g)]^{1/2}/\sigma^2,$$

and C_1 and C_2 are constants to be determined by the boundary conditions.
We restrict our attention to the case $r > g$:[13] then $C_1 = 0$ if $y(x)/x$ is to remain finite as $x \to \infty$. The constant C_2 is determined by the value of x for which the value of the equity is zero: denote this value by $\hat{x}$. There are in principle two ways in which $\hat{x}$ may be determined. First, if the firm has bonds outstanding, the provisions of the bond indenture may allow bondholders to foreclose when the rate of return drops to a critical level,[14] $\hat{x}$. Even in the absence of debt, shareholders may find it to their advantage to declare bankruptcy voluntarily, since continuing to operate the firm requires them to put

---

[13] If $r < g$, the present value of future investments in the rate base is infinite.
[14] When the rate of return drops to this level, the interest coverage ratio will have fallen below a critical level as well.

up the funds to finance the exogenously determined expansion of the rate base; for $x < g$ this will involve a negative cash flow. We shall assume that $\hat{x}$ is chosen by the shareholders to maximize $y(x)$ or, equivalently, to maximize $C_2(\hat{x})$, where $C_2(\hat{x})$ is given by the condition that $y(\hat{x}) = 0$:

$$C_2(\hat{x}) = -e^{-\gamma_2 \hat{x}} \left[\frac{\hat{x} - g}{r - g} + \frac{\mu - \lambda\sigma}{(r - g)^2} \right]. \tag{9}$$

Carrying out the maximization of (9) yields

$$\hat{x} = \gamma_2^{-1} + g - \frac{\mu - \lambda\sigma}{r - g}. \tag{10}$$

Then the ratio of the market value of the firm to the rate base is given by expression (8), where $C_1 = 0$ and C_2 is defined by equations (9) and (10).

It is of interest to note that for large x

$$y(x) \rightarrow \frac{x - g}{r - g} + \frac{\mu - \lambda\sigma}{(r - g)^2}. \tag{11}$$

Recalling that $x - g = p$, the instantaneous dividend rate per unit of the rate base, it is seen that the first term of (11) corresponds to the familiar Gordon (1962) growth model when the riskless interest rate is used for discounting; the second term adjusts both for the trend in the rate of return and for risk. The risk adjustment is independent of x for large x because of our assumption that the variance of the stochastic process (6) is independent of x. For small x, the risk adjustment enters the valuation expression (8) in a nonlinear fashion, reflecting its influence on the bankruptcy condition.

We shall contrast this no regulation case with two classes of regulatory policy. In the first class, there is a constant probability rate for the holding of a hearing as in Klevorick's (1973) model of the regulated firm. Under the second class of policy, hearings are held only when the rate of return reaches predetermined upper and lower bounds. Joskow (1974) argues that regulatory reviews are initiated mainly by firms whose profits have dropped below an acceptable level. On the other hand, Roberts et al. (1978) found that the probability of a hearing increased as the rate of return became high. Hendricks (1975) and Burness et al. (1980) have also constructed models of the regulated firm in which regulatory policy is represented by predetermined bounds on profits. These two classes of regulatory policy were chosen with an eye to tractability and are not intended to be representative of the policies followed by regulatory hearings; nor are they exhaustive of the policies that could be considered within this framework. They are intended, however, to be illustrative of the hitherto largely neglected effects of the possibility of future regulation on the value of the equity of regulated firms and therefore on the choice of regulatory policy.

☐ **Stochastic regulatory hearings.** With a constant probability rate for regulatory hearings, the normalized firm value satisfies equation (5) with $\pi(x) \equiv \pi$. We shall assume that the allowed rate $x^*(x)$ is also independent of x. Two cases will be considered: when x^* is arbitrary and when x^* is chosen so that $y(x^*) = 1$. The latter policy is what we have referred to as a consistent regulatory policy.

Under the consistent regulatory policy, equation (7) becomes

$$\tfrac{1}{2}\sigma^2 y_{xx} + (\mu - \lambda\sigma)y_x - (r - g^*)y + (x - g^*) = 0, \tag{12}$$

where $g^* = g - \pi$. Except for the replacement of g by g^*, this equation is identical to that obtained in the unregulated case, the complete solution of which is given in (8). Therefore, the solution in this special case of stochastic regulation and a consistent regulatory policy is obtained from the unregulated case by reducing the exogenously specified growth rate, g, by the probability rate, π. The value of x^* which yields a consistent regulatory policy is obtained by solving the equation $y(x^*) = 1$, where $y(x^*)$ is the valuation function yielded by a particular value of π.

For arbitrary values of the allowed rate, x^*, the solution to equation (7) is more complex. The complete solution to the equation is

$$y(x) = C_1 e^{\gamma_1 x} + C_2 e^{\gamma_2 x} + \frac{x - g + \pi y(x^*)}{r - g + \pi} + \frac{\mu - \lambda\sigma}{(r - g + \pi)^2}. \tag{13}$$

The argument used in the unregulated case implies that $C_1 = 0$. Then, setting $x = x^*$ in equation (13), we may solve for $y(x^*)$. Substituting the resulting expression for $y(x^*)$ into (13) yields

$$y(x) = C_2(\hat{x})\left[e^{\gamma_2 x} + \left(\frac{x - g}{r - g + \pi}\right)e^{\gamma_2 x^*}\right] + \left(\frac{x - g}{r - g + \pi}\right) + \frac{\pi(x^* - g) + \mu - \lambda\sigma}{(r - g)(r - g + \pi)}. \tag{14}$$

In equation (14) we have explicitly shown the dependence of C_2 on $\hat{x}$, which is defined by $y(\hat{x}) = 0$. Setting $x = \hat{x}$ yields the following expression for $C_2(\hat{x})$:

$$C_2(\hat{x}) = -\left[e^{\gamma_2 \hat{x}} + \frac{\pi}{r - g}e^{\gamma_2 x^*}\right]^{-1}\left[\left(\frac{\hat{x} - g}{r - g + \pi}\right) + k(x^*)\right], \tag{15}$$

where $k(x^*) = (\pi(x^* - g) + \mu - \lambda\sigma)/(r - g)(r - g + \pi)$.

Then, assuming again that $\hat{x}$ is chosen by the shareholders to maximize y (and therefore C_2), $\hat{x}$ is given by the solution to the nonlinear equation:

$$\gamma_2 e^{\gamma_2 \hat{x}}\left[\left(\frac{\hat{x} - g}{r - g + \pi}\right) + k(x^*)\right] - \frac{e^{\gamma_2 \hat{x}} + \pi(r - g)^{-1}e^{\gamma_2 x^*}}{r - g + \pi} = 0. \tag{16}$$

Thus, for arbitrary allowed rates under stochastic regulation, the normalized equity value, $y(x)$, is given by equations (14), (15), and (16).

□ **Deterministic regulatory hearings.** Under the particular deterministic policy which we consider, regulatory hearings are held only when the current rate of return reaches predetermined upper and lower bounds, x_u and x_l, respectively. This is represented by setting $\pi(x) = 0$ for $x \neq x_u, x_l$ in equation (7) and $\pi(x_u) = \pi(x_l) = \infty$. Then the normalized firm value satisfies the differential equation,

$$\tfrac{1}{2}\sigma^2 y_{xx} + (\mu - \lambda\sigma)y_x - (r - g)y + (x - g) = 0, \tag{17}$$

subject to the boundary conditions

$$y(x_u) = y(x^*(x_u))$$

$$y(x_l) = y(x^*(x_l)). \tag{18}$$

The complete solution to this equation is given by (8), where the constants C_1 and C_2 are determined by the boundary conditions (18).

If the regulatory policy is consistent so that $y(x^*(x_u)) = y(x^*(x_l)) = 1$, it may be verified that the constant terms are

$$C_1 = \frac{b_u b_{2l} - b_l b_{2u}}{b_{1u}b_{2l} - b_{1l}b_{2u}}$$

$$C_2 = \frac{b_l b_{1u} - b_u b_{1l}}{b_{1u}b_{2l} - b_{1l}b_{2u}}, \tag{19}$$

where $b_{1i} = e^{\gamma_1 x_i}$, $b_{2i} = e^{\gamma_2 x_i}$ and $b_i = 1 - (x_i - g)/(r - g) + (\mu - \lambda\sigma)/(r - g)^2$ for $i = u, l$. Similar expressions may be derived for the general case in which

$$x^*(x_u) = x_u - \epsilon_u, \quad x^*(x_l) = x_l + \epsilon_l.$$

TABLE 1   Firm Parameter Values

$\sigma = 0.005$	$r = 0.08$
$\mu = 0.0$	$g = 0.06$
	$\lambda = .14$

5. A numerical example

◾ To illustrate the possible effects of alternative regulatory policies, valuation functions, $y(x)$, were computed for the parameter values given in Table 1, assuming no regulation, stochastic regulatory hearings, and deterministic regulatory hearings. In the examples with regulation, the regulatory policies are assumed to be consistent, so that $y(x^*) = 1$, where x^* is the allowed rate of return.

Table 2 presents some summary statistics for three deterministic and three stochastic policies as well as for the no-regulation case ($\pi = 0$). The allowed rate of return x^* appropriate under the different regulatory policies varies widely as one would expect, and it is noteworthy that the appropriate allowed rate of return may even be less than the riskless interest rate as shown by policy (vii).

The second line of Table 2 indicates the value of $y_x(x^*)$, a scalar measure of the absolute risk borne by shareholders of the firm when the return on the rate base is equal to the allowed rate of return. It is greatest in the unregulated case and decreases monotonically in the stochastic policy case as the probability rate of a hearing rises: in the limit the shareholders bear no risk, since all risk is borne by consumers. The beta coefficient, $\beta(x^*)$, shown on the third line of the table is simply a scalar multiple of $y_x(x^*)$.[15] The last three lines of the table illustrate the dramatically different firm values that may result from the same rate of return on the rate base under different regulatory policies.

Figure 1, which shows the valuation schedules obtained under three different regulatory policies, serves to emphasize the importance of regulatory policy for valuation. In the unregulated case, the schedule resembles that between the value of a call option and the value of the underlying stock.[16] As the probability rate of a hearing increases from zero, the valuation schedule rotates clockwise: the reason for this is that if x is high, there is a probability that it will be subject to a discrete downward adjustment, and conversely

TABLE 2   Alternative Regulatory Policies

	No Regulation	Stochastic Policies			Deterministic Policies		
	(i)	(ii)	(iii)	(iv)	(v)	(vi)	(vii)
		$\pi = 0.1$	0.5	10.0	$x_u = 0.12$	0.18	0.18
					$x_l = 0.01$	0.03	0.06
x^*	.099	.086	.081	.080	.106	.092	.073
$y_x(x^*)$	33.1	8.3	1.9	.1	14.2	25.4	6.2
$\beta(x^*)$	.57	.15	.03	.00[a]	.25	.44	.12
$y(.06)$	.08	.78	.96	1.00	.10	.53	1.00
$y(.08)$	.46	.95	1.00	1.00	.44	.75	1.06
$y(.10)$	1.05	1.12	1.04	1.00	.89	1.23	1.44

[a] Subject to rounding error.

---

[15] $\beta(x^*) = y^{-1}y_x(x^*)\lambda\sigma/\sigma_w^2$. The variance of aggregate wealth σ_w^2 is set equal to .2.

[16] Black and Scholes (1973) were the first to point out that the equity in a firm could be regarded as a call option to purchase the firm from the bondholders.

FIGURE 1

NORMALIZED FIRM VALUE FOR DIFFERENT REGULATORY POLICIES

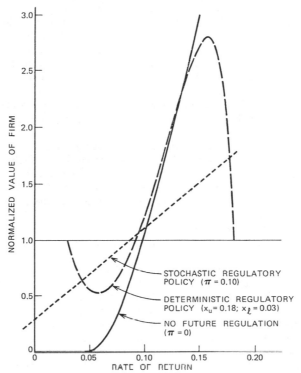

if x is low. These discrete adjustments, which occur when a rate hearing is held, cause capital gains or losses for investors as the normalized equity value reverts to unity. If, as is more realistic, the probability rate of a hearing were an increasing function of the absolute deviation of x from x^*, the valuation schedule would be more S-shaped. An extreme example of this is provided by the deterministic regulatory policy: under this policy the equity value actually decreases as the rate of return approaches the upper control limit, x_u, since as soon as the rate of return reaches x_u, it will be reduced to x^*. A similar phenomenon is apparent in the vicinity of x_l.

6. Implications of the model

◼ **Setting the allowed rate.** As described in Section 2, the modern consensus approach to regulation implies that the allowed rate of return should be set equal to the cost of capital, and in practice much attention is given at regulatory hearings to determination of the appropriate cost of capital.

Current methods of assessing the cost of capital may be classified according to whether they follow an individual firm approach or a risk class approach. The former method involves forecasting the long-run rate of return that an investor might reasonably expect to earn by purchasing shares in the firm at their current price. Unfortunately, this rate of return will depend upon future regulatory policy and in particular upon the allowed rate of return set as a result of the hearing; but it is the appropriate allowed rate which is at issue. Thus, this individual firm approach is beset by a fatal circularity.

Two variants of the risk class approach may be distinguished. According to the first, the regulated firm's cost of capital is assumed to be equal to that of unregulated firms with similar earnings risk. A reasonable interpretation of the earnings risk approach is that the allowed rate of return should be set at the level which would cause an unregulated firm with similar earnings characteristics to sell at book value.[17] This, however, neglects the fact that the risk of the regulated firm depends not only on the stochastic characteristics of the earnings stream but also on regulatory policy. To illustrate, it may be seen from Table 2 that a return on book value of 10% would cause the market value of an unregulated firm to approximate book value. The same rate of return earned on the rate base of a regulated firm with identical earnings risk[18] may cause the market value to range from 89% to 144% of the value of the rate base, depending on which regulatory policy is followed.

The second variant of the risk class approach assumes that the capital asset pricing model holds and that therefore risk can be measured appropriately by the beta coefficient. Although this is consistent with our valuation model which rests upon an intertemporal version of the capital asset pricing model, the beta coefficient, which is equal to $y^{-1}y_x\lambda\sigma/\sigma_w^2$, is stochastic and depends upon x. Therefore, there can be no assurance, and indeed it would be only by coincidence, that the beta coefficient estimated from the nonstationary time series of equity returns would yield a cost of equity capital close to the appropriate allowed rate of return under the consistent regulatory policy.[19]

☐   **Investment incentives.** To this point we have neglected the effects of regulatory policy on the incentives of the regulated firm. To illustrate the effects of regulation on investment incentives in the context of this article suppose that, in the absence of regulation, the rate of return on the rate base would follow the same stochastic process as under regulation. Then the effect of regulation on investment incentives may be measured by the difference in the present value of the same investment project to a regulated and an unregulated firm. The investment project is assumed to generate an instantaneous earnings rate ρI, where ρ follows the same stochastic process as, and is perfectly correlated with, x_0, the rate of return on the preexisting rate base, B, and I is the amount invested in the new project. Then the effect of the new investment on the rate of return is given by

$$x(I) = \frac{x_0 B + \rho I}{B + I}. \tag{20}$$

Recalling the expression for the value of the equity of a regulated firm, $F(x, B)$, the gross present value to the stockholders of a marginal dollar invested is given by

$$\frac{dF}{dI} = F_x \frac{dx}{dI} + y(x), \tag{21}$$

where we have used the assumption that the whole investment is added to the rate base so that $dB/dI = 1$. Then, differentiating equation (20) with respect to I, setting $I = 0$, and substituting the result in (21), we obtain the following expression for the gross present value of a marginal investment:

$$\left.\frac{dF}{dI}\right|_{I=0} = y(x) + y_x(x)(\rho - x). \tag{22}$$

---

[17] This assumes that the book value of the unregulated firm is determined in the same way as the rate base of the regulated firm.

[18] That is, the regulated firm's earnings risk was identical to that of the unregulated firm *before* regulation was imposed on the former.

[19] See Breen and Lerner (1972) and Myers (1972) for a discussion of the problems of using beta in regulatory hearings.

FIGURE 2

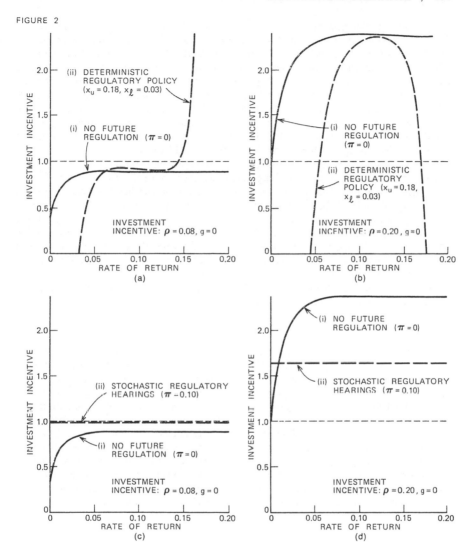

Under the standard assumption of stock price maximization, a project will be undertaken only if this expression, which we refer to as the "investment incentive," exceeds unity.

In Figure 2a, the value of the investment incentive is plotted as a function of x for a marginal investment with $\rho = .08$ for regulatory policy (i), no future regulation, and for policy (vi), a deterministic regulatory policy. The parameter values for these cases are given in Tables 1 and 2, except that g has been set equal to zero. Inspection of the figure reveals that this project would never be accepted by the unregulated firm, but that it becomes highly desirable to the regulated firm as the rate of return approaches x_u, 18%. The explanation of this phenomenon is simple: adoption of the project reduces the currently earned rate of return and thereby postpones the day on which a regulatory hearing takes place, thus prolonging the period for which high returns may be earned. This makes the project desirable despite its low value *per se*. On the other hand, as x approaches x_l, 3%, the project becomes highly undesirable to the regulated firm by postponing a hearing which would raise the overall rate of return. This latter effect is also visible in Figure 2b which depicts the investment incentive for a highly profitable project under the same conditions. However, this profitable project is undesirable to the regulated firm as the rate of return approaches x_u because of its effect in hastening a regulatory hearing. The effects of regulation are proportional to the vertical distance between the schedules in these figures, and it is apparent that under this type of regulatory policy, extreme incentives for the regulated firm may be induced because of the effect of a marginal investment project on the probability that a regulatory hearing will be held.

In Figures 2c and 2d the investment incentives arising from the same projects are illustrated for policy (ii), stochastic regulatory hearings with $\pi = .10$, as well as for the unregulated case. Under these policies adoption of the project has no influence on the probability of regulatory hearings, and the extreme impact of the deterministic regulatory policies is eliminated. Realistic regulatory policies would seem likely to lie between the extremes of our stochastic and deterministic policies, with the probability of a hearing being positively related to the absolute deviation of x from the current allowed rate of return. It seems that even under such policies, regulatory lag will tend to have a substantial effect on investment incentives. Of course, without knowing whether the investment incentives for the unregulated firm are Pareto optimal, it is not possible to make any statements about welfare gains and losses.

7. Conclusion

■   In this article we have analyzed the problem of determining a consistent regulatory policy in a dynamic setting. Contemporary approaches to regulation, which set the allowed rate of return equal to the cost of capital, were shown to be deficient insofar as they take the cost of capital as exogenous, when it is in fact a product of the regulatory policy chosen. To devise a consistent regulatory policy, it is necessary to have a valuation model that explicitly incorporates the effects of regulatory policy. Such a valuation model was constructed, and it was shown how the appropriate allowed rate of return and the risk borne by investors varied as the regulatory policy was changed. Finally, current practices for estimating the appropriate allowed rate of return were analyzed, and a simple analysis was made of the effect of regulatory lag on investment incentives. The models developed in this article are highly simplified, and much work remains to be done in developing more realistic yet tractable models for valuing regulated firms and analyzing the effects of alternative regulatory policies.

Appendix

The general valuation model

■   The valuation model employed in Section 3 is a special case of a general model of the valuation of financial claims. Necessary conditions for equilibrium in the capital market yield a partial differential equation which must be satisfied by the pricing function of any financial claim.

Thus, consider an economy in which:

(1) All investors have time-additive von Neumann-Morgenstern utility functions of the logarithmic form defined over the rate of consumption of a single consumption good.
(2) There are no taxes or transactions costs, trading takes place continuously, and the capital market is always in equilibrium.
(3) The state of the economy is completely described by aggregate wealth, W, and an s-dimensional vector of state variables, X, whose behavior is governed by a system of

stochastic differential equations:

$$dX_j = \mu_j(X, t)dt + \eta_j(X, t)dz_j + (X_j^* - X_j)dq_j, \qquad j = 1, \ldots, s, \tag{A1}$$

where t denotes calendar time and dz_j is a standard Gauss-Wiener process. $q_j(t)$ is an independent Poisson process with intensity $\pi_j(X, t)$, and $(X_j^* - X_j)$ is the change in the state variable if the Poisson event occurs.[20] Jumps in the state variables are assumed to be uncorrelated with the return on aggregate wealth.

Merton (1973) has shown, in a related context, that under such assumptions the equilibrium expected rates of return on individual assets will satisfy the specialized version of the intertemporal capital asset pricing model:[21]

$$\alpha_i - r = \sigma_{iw}, \tag{A2}$$

where α_i is the expected instantaneous rate of return on asset i, σ_{iw} is the covariance of the rate of return on asset i with the rate of return on aggregate wealth, and r is the instantaneously riskless interest rate.

Cox, Ingersoll, and Ross (1978) have shown that if investors possess rational expectations, so that the price functions they use to make their optimal decisions are the equilibrium price functions that continuously clear the market, then the equilibrium condition (A2) implies a fundamental partial differential equation which must be satisfied by the value of all financial assets.

Thus, define $F_i \equiv F_i(W, X, t)$ as the market value of asset i; then the instantaneous change in the value of the asset is given by:[22]

$$dF = [\sum_{j=1}^{s} F_{x_j}\mu_j + F_w(W\alpha_w - C) + F_t + \tfrac{1}{2}\sum_{j=1}^{s}\sum_{k=1}^{s} F_{x_jx_k}\rho_{jk}\eta_j\eta_k$$

$$+ \tfrac{1}{2}\sum_{j=1}^{s} F_{x_jw}\rho_{jw}\eta_j\sigma_w W + \tfrac{1}{2}F_{ww}\sigma_w^2 W^2]dt + \sum_{j=1}^{s} F_{x_j}\eta_j dz_j$$

$$+ F_w\sigma_w W dz_w + \sum_{j=1}^{s} [F(W, X + \Delta X_j, t) - F(W, X, t)]dq_j, \tag{A3}$$

where α_w is the instantaneous expected rate of return on aggregate wealth, C is the rate of aggregate consumption, ρ_{jk} and ρ_{jw} are the instantaneous correlations between the rates of return on asset j and on asset k, and on asset j and on aggregate wealth, respectively. The symbol ΔX_j denotes an s-dimensional vector all of whose elements are equal to zero except element j, which is equal to $(X_j^* - X_j)$.

The expected instantaneous rate of return on asset i, α_i, is the sum of the payout rate on the asset, $\delta_i(W, X, t)$, and the expected price change, divided by the current value of the asset:

$$\alpha_i = F^{-1}[\cdot] + F^{-1}\delta + F^{-1}\sum_{j=1}^{s} [F(W, X + \Delta X_j, t) - F(W, X, t)]\pi_j(X, t), \tag{A4}$$

where $[\cdot]$ is the coefficient of dt in equation (A3).

Since jumps in the state variables are uncorrelated with the return on aggregate wealth, the instantaneous covariance between the return on asset i and the return on

---

[20] For a detailed discussion of such mixed processes, see Merton (1976).

[21] The specialization arises from the assumption of logarithmic utility, which permits us to omit the additional terms relating to stochastic shifts in the investment opportunity set that would otherwise appear in equation (A2).

[22] See Merton (1976) for the necessary extension of Ito's lemma. The subscript i is omitted for the sake of clarity, and the partial derivatives of F are denoted by the appropriate subscripts.

aggregate wealth is

$$\sigma_{iw} = F^{-1}[\sum_{j=1}^{s} F_{x_j}\eta_j\rho_{jw}\sigma_w + F_w\sigma_w^2 W^2].$$ (A5)

Finally, multiplying the equilibrium condition (A2) by the fraction of aggregate wealth accounted for by asset i, and summing over i, we obtain

$$\alpha_w - r = \sigma_w^2.$$ (A6)

Then, substituting for α_i and σ_{iw} in the equilibrium condition (A2) and using (A6), we obtain the basic partial differential equation which is satisfied by the values of all assets:

$$\sum_{j=1}^{s} F_{x_j}(\mu_j - \eta_j\rho_{jw}\sigma_w) + F_w(rW - C) + F_t + \frac{1}{2}\sum_{j=1}^{s}\sum_{k=1}^{s} F_{x_jx_k}\rho_{jk}\eta_j\eta_k + \sum_{j=1}^{s} F_{x_jw}\rho_{jw}\eta_j\sigma_w W$$

$$+ \frac{1}{2}F_{ww}\sigma_w^2 W^2 - rF + \delta + \sum_{j=1}^{s} [F(W, X + \Delta X_j, t) - F(W, X, t)]\pi_j = 0.$$ (A7)

This equation, which is the basis of our valuation model for the regulated firm, corresponds to equation (25) of Cox, Ingersoll, and Ross (1978) under the assumption of logarithmic utility when there are state variables with discontinuous sample paths. When the appropriate boundary conditions are appended, this equation suffices to determine the value of any security.

References

AVERCH, H. AND JOHNSON, L.L. "Behavior of the Firm under Regulatory Constraint." *American Economic Review*, Vol. 52, No. 5 (December 1962), pp. 1062–1069.

BAUMOL, W.J. AND KLEVORICK, A.K. "Input Choices and Rate of Return Regulation: An Overview of the Discussion." *Bell Journal of Economics and Management Science*, Vol. 1, No. 2 (Autumn 1970), pp. 162–190.

BAWA, V.S. AND SIBLEY, D.S. "Dynamic Behavior of a Firm Subject to Stochastic Regulatory Review." *International Economic Review*, Vol. 21, No. 3 (October 1980), pp. 627–642.

BLACK, F. AND SCHOLES, M. "The Pricing of Options and Corporate Liabilities." *Journal of Political Economy*, Vol. 81, No. 3 (May–June 1973), pp. 637–654.

BREEN, W.J. AND LERNER, E.M. "On the Use of β in Regulatory Proceedings." *Bell Journal of Economics and Management Science*, Vol. 3, No. 2 (Autumn 1972), pp. 612–621.

BURNESS, H., MONTGOMERY, D., AND QUIRK, J. "Capital Contracting and the Regulated Firm." *American Economic Review*, Vol. 70, No. 3 (June 1980), pp. 342–354.

CLARKE, R.G. "The Effect of Fuel Adjustment Clauses on the Systematic Risk and Market Values of Electric Utilities." *Journal of Finance*, Vol. 35, No. 2 (May 1980), pp. 347–358.

COX, J.C., INGERSOLL, J.E., AND ROSS, S.A. "A Theory of the Term Structure of Interest Rates." Stanford University Research Paper No. 468, August 1978.

DAS, S.P. "On the Effect of Rate of Return Regulation under Uncertainty." *American Economic Review*, Vol. 70, No. 3 (June 1980), pp. 456–460.

DAVIS, B.E. AND SPARROW, F.T. "Valuation Models in Regulation." *Bell Journal of Economics and Management Science*, Vol. 3, No. 2 (Autumn 1972), pp. 544–567.

GORDON, M.J. *The Investment, Financing and Valuation of the Corporation.* Homewood, Ill.: Richard D. Irwin, Inc., 1962.

HENDRICKS, W. "The Effect of Regulation on Collective Bargaining in Electric Utilities." *Bell Journal of Economics*, Vol. 6, No. 2 (Autumn 1975), pp. 451–465.

JOSKOW, P. "Inflation and Environmental Concern: Structural Change in the Process of Public Utility Regulation." *Journal of Law and Economics*, Vol. 17 (October 1974), pp. 291–327.

KLEVORICK, A.K. "The Behavior of a Firm Subject to Stochastic Regulatory Review." *Bell Journal of Economics and Management Science*, Vol. 4, No. 1 (Spring 1973), pp. 57–88.

LELAND, H.E. "Theory of the Firm Facing Uncertain Demand." *American Economic Review*, Vol. 62, No. 3 (June 1972), pp. 278–291.

———. "Regulation of Natural Monopolies and the Fair Rate of Return." *Bell Journal of Economics and Management Science*, Vol. 5, No. 1 (Spring 1974), pp. 3–15.

MARSHALL, W.J., YAWITZ, J.B., AND GREENBERG, E. "Optimal Regulation under Uncertainty." *Journal of Finance*, Vol. 36, No. 4 (September 1981), pp. 909–922.

MERTON, R. "An Intertemporal Capital Asset Pricing Model." *Econometrica*, Vol. 41, No. 4 (September 1973), pp. 867–888.

———. "Option Pricing When Underlying Stock Returns Are Discontinuous." *Journal of Financial Economics*, Vol. 3, Nos. 1–2 (January/March 1976), pp. 125–144.

MILLER, M.H. AND MODIGLIANI, F. "Dividend Policy, Growth, and the Valuation of Shares." *Journal of Business*, Vol. 34, No. 4 (October 1961), pp. 411–433.

MYERS, S.C. "The Application of Finance Theory to Public Utility Rate Cases." *Bell Journal of Economics and Management Science*, Vol. 3, No. 1 (Spring 1972a), pp. 58–97.

———. "On the Use of β in Regulatory Proceedings: A Comment." *Bell Journal of Economics and Management Science*, Vol. 3, No. 2 (Autumn 1972b), pp. 622–627.

———. "A Simple Model of Firm Behavior under Regulation and Uncertainty." *Bell Journal of Economics and Management Science*, Vol. 4, No. 1 (Spring 1973), pp. 57–88.

PELES, Y.C. AND STEIN, J.L. "The Effect of Rate of Return Regulation Is Highly Sensitive to the Nature of Uncertainty." *American Economic Review*, Vol. 66, No. 3 (June 1976), pp. 278–289.

PERRAKIS, S. "On the Regulated Price-Setting Monopoly Firm with a Random Demand Curve." *American Economic Review*, Vol. 66, No. 3 (June 1976), pp. 410–416.

ROBERTS, R.B., MADDALA, G.S., AND ENHOLM, G. "Determinants of the Requested Rate of Return and the Rate of Return Granted in a Formal Regulatory Process." *Bell Journal of Economics*, Vol. 9, No. 2 (Autumn 1978), pp. 611–621.

ROBICHEK, A.A. "Regulation and Modern Finance Theory." *Journal of Finance*, Vol. 33, No. 3 (June 1978), pp. 693–705.

STEIN, J.L. AND BORTS, G.H. "Behavior of the Firm under Regulatory Constraint." *American Economic Review*, Vol. 62, No. 5 (December 1972), pp. 964–970.

[5]

Michael J. Brennan
Eduardo S. Schwartz
University of British Columbia

Evaluating Natural Resource Investments*

Notwithstanding impressive advances in the theory of finance over the past 2 decades, practical procedures for capital budgeting have evolved only slowly. The standard technique, which has remained unchanged in essentials since it was originally proposed (see Dean 1951; Bierman and Smidt 1960), derives from a simple adaptation of the Fisher (1907) model of valuation under certainty: under this technique, expected cash flows from an investment project are discounted at a rate deemed appropriate to their risk, and the resulting present value is compared with the cost of the project. This standard textbook technique reflects modern theoretical developments only insofar as estimates of the discount rate may be obtained from crude application of single period asset pricing theory (but see Brennan 1973; Bogue and Roll 1974; Turnbull 1977; Constantinides 1978).

The inadequacy of this approach to capital budgeting is widely acknowledged, although not widely discussed. Its obvious deficiency is its

The evaluation of mining and other natural resource projects is made particularly difficult by the high degree of uncertainty attaching to output prices. It is shown that the techniques of continuous time arbitrage and stochastic control theory may be used not only to value such projects but also to determine the optimal policies for developing, managing, and abandoning them. The approach may be adapted to a wide variety of contexts outside the natural resource sector where uncertainty about future project revenues is a paramount concern.

* Research support from the Corporate Finance Division of the Department of Finance, Ottawa, is gratefully acknowledged. We especially thank the referee whose insightful comments have enabled us to eliminate several errors and to improve the presentation. We also thank Robert Pyndyck, Rene Stulz, Suresh Sundaresan, Merton Miller, and participants at seminars in London, Stockholm, Stanford, and Los Angeles.

(*Journal of Business*, 1985, vol. 58, no. 2)

total neglect of the stochastic nature of output prices and of possible managerial responses to price variations. While price uncertainty is unimportant in applications for which the relevant prices are reasonably predictable, it is of paramount importance in many natural resource industries, where price swings of 25%–40% per year are not uncommon.[1] Under such conditions the practice of replacing distributions of future prices by their expected values is likely to cause errors in the calculation both of expected cash flows and of appropriate discount rates and thereby to lead to suboptimal investment decisions.

The model for the evaluation of investment projects presented in this paper treats output prices as stochastic. While this makes it particularly suitable for analyzing natural resource investment projects, where uncertain prices are a particular concern, the model may be applied in other contexts also. The model also takes explicit account of managerial control over the output rate, which is assumed to be variable in response to the output price; moreover, the possibility that a project may be closed down or even abandoned if output prices fall far enough is also considered. Variation in risk and the discount rate due both to depletion of the resource and to stochastic variation in the output price are explicitly taken into account in deriving the equilibrium condition underlying the valuation model.

Two essentially distinct approaches may be taken to the general problem of valuing the uncertain cash flow stream generated by an investment project. First, the market equilibrium approach requires both complete specification of the stochastic properties of the cash flow stream and an underlying model of capital equilibrium whose parameters are known.[2] A general limitation of this approach is that it is difficult to devise adequately powerful tests of the model of market equilibrium and to obtain refined estimates of the model parameters. In the present instance, the market equilibrium approach is further hampered by the difficulty of determining the stochastic properties of the cash flow stream that depend on the stochastic process of the output price: as we have already remarked, it is often very difficult to estimate the expected rate of change in commodity prices. Therefore in this paper we resort to a second approach, which yields the value of one security relative to the value of a portfolio of other traded securities.

Our approach is to find a self-financing portfolio whose cash flows replicate those which are to be valued.[3] The present value of the cash

1. Bodie and Rosansky (1980) report that the standard deviation of annual changes in futures prices over the period 1950–76 was 25.6% for silver, 47.2% for copper, and 25.2% for platinum.

2. See, e.g., the framework developed by Cox, Ingersoll, and Ross (1978); this was used by Brennan and Schwartz (1982a, 1982b) to analyze the valuation of regulated public utilities.

3. A self-financing portfolio has the property that its value at any time is exactly equal to the value of the investment and cash flow distributions required at that time. See

flow stream is then equal to the current value of this replicating portfolio. When a replicating self-financing portfolio can be constructed, our approach offers several advantages over the market equilibrium approach; not only does it obviate the need for a discount rate derived from an inadequately supported model of market equilibrium but, most important in the current context, it eliminates the need for estimates of the expected rate of change of the underlying cash flow and therefore of the output price.

Construction of the requisite replicating self-financing portfolio rests on the assumption that the convenience yield on the output commodity can be written as a function of the output price alone and that the interest rate is nonstochastic. These assumptions suffice to yield a deterministic relation between the spot and futures price of the commodity, and the cash flows from the project can then be replicated by a self-financing portfolio of riskless bills and futures contracts.

Specific limitations of the valuation model include the assumptions that the resource to be exploited is homogeneous and of a known amount, that costs are known, and that interest rates are nonstochastic. Any one of these assumptions may be relaxed at the expense of adding one further dimension to the state space on which the model is defined: as a practical matter it would be difficult to obtain tractable results if more than one of these assumptions were relaxed at a time. While the model as presented here presupposes the existence of a futures market in the output commodity, it would be straightforward to derive an analogous model in a general equilibrium context similar to that employed by Brennan and Schwartz (1982a, 1982b).

To allow for dependence of the output rate on the stochastic output price the capital budgeting decision is modeled as a problem of stochastic optimal control. Stochastic optimal control theory has been applied to the investment decision in a general context by Constantinides (1978), and in the specific context of a regulated public utility by Brennan and Schwartz (1982a, 1982b). Dothan and Williams (1980) have also analyzed the capital-budgeting decision within a similar framework. Pindyck (1980), like us, applies stochastic optimal control to the problem of the optimal exploitation of an exhaustible resource under uncertainty. In some respects Pindyck's analysis is more general than ours: in particular, he allows the level of reserves of the resource to vary stochastically and to be influenced by exploration activities. On the other hand, by confining his attention to risk-neutral firms he neglects the issues of risk and valuation that are the focus of the capital-budgeting decision and of this paper. Other writers who have recognized the importance of the option whether or not to exploit a natural

---

Harrison and Kreps (1979). The notion of a replicating self-financing portfolio is closely related to the option-pricing models of Black and Scholes (1973) and Merton (1973).

resource, which is inherent in the ownership of the resource, include Tourinho (1979); Brock, Rothschild, and Stiglitz (1982); and Paddock, Siegel, and Smith (1982). These writers have not however analyzed the present value of the decision to exploit a given resource or the optimal operating policy for a given facility, as we do, and Brock et al. do not exploit the arbitrage implications of a replicating self-financing portfolio.

Miller and Upton (1985) develop and test empirically a model for the valuation of natural resources based on the Hotelling model. Although it is close in spirit to our model, in that the spot price of the commodity is a sufficient statistic for the value of the mine, unlike ours their model assumes no upper limit on the output rate and ignores the possibility of closing and reopening the mine in response to current market conditions. As they point out this may be a good approximation when output prices exceed extraction costs by a wide margin, just as the value of a stock option approaches its intrinsic value when it is deep in the money.

The general type of model presented here lends itself to use in a number of related contexts—most obviously, to corporations considering when, whether, and how, to develop a given resource; to financial analysts concerned with the valuation of such corporations; and to policymakers concerned with the social costs of layoffs in cyclical industries and with policies to avert them. The model is well suited to analysis of the effects of alternative taxation, royalty, and subsidy policies on investment, employment, and unemployment in the natural resource sector.

Section I develops a general model for valuing the cash flows from a natural resource investment. A specialized version of the general model is presented in Section II. Under the assumption of an inexhaustible resource the model allows for only a single feasible operating rate when the project is operating but includes the possibility of costs of closing and reopening the project. Section III discusses a numerical example based on the general model. Section IV considers the problem, previously raised by Tourinho (1979), of the optimal timing of natural resource investments. Section V discusses briefly the application of the model to the analysis of fixed price long term purchase contracts for natural resources.

I. The General Valuation Model

The first step in analyzing an investment project is to determine the present value of the future cash flows it will generate and to compare this present value with the required investment. If the present value exceeds the investment a further decision is whether to proceed with the project immediately or to wait. We shall postpone consideration of this second, dynamic aspect of the capital-budgeting decision until Section III and in this and the following section will restrict our attention to the problem of determining the present value of the cash flows from a project. In this section we develop a general model, a specialization of which is considered in Section II.

To focus discussion we will suppose that the project under consideration is a mine that will produce a single homogeneous commodity, whose spot price, S, is determined competitively and is assumed to follow the exogenously given continuous stochastic process

$$\frac{dS}{S} = \mu \, dt + \sigma \, dz, \tag{1}$$

where dz is the increment to a standard Gauss-Wiener process; σ, the instantaneous standard deviation of the spot price, is assumed to be known; and μ, the local trend in the price, may be stochastic.

As a preliminary to developing the valuation model it will prove useful to consider the relation between spot and futures prices and the convenience yield on the commodity. The convenience yield is the flow of services that accrues to an owner of the physical commodity but not to the owner of a contract for future delivery of the commodity (see Kaldor 1939; Working 1948; Brennan 1958; Telser 1958). Most obviously, the owner of the physical commodity is able to choose where it will be stored and when to liquidate the inventory. Recognizing the time lost and the costs incurred in transporting a commodity from one location to another, the convenience yield may be thought of as the value of being able to profit from temporary local shortages of the commodity through ownership of the physical commodity. The profit may arise either from local price variations or from the ability to maintain a production process as a result of ownership of an inventory of raw material.[4]

The convenience yield will depend on the identity of the individual holding the inventory and in equilibrium inventories will be held by individuals for whom the marginal convenience yield net of any physical storage costs is highest. We assume that a positive amount of the commodity is always held in inventory, and note that competition among potential storers will ensure that the net convenience yield of the marginal unit of inventory will be the same across all individuals who hold positive inventories. This marginal (net) convenience yield can be expected to be inversely proportional to the amount of the commodity held in inventory. Moreover, when stocks of the physical commodity are high, not only will the marginal convenience yield tend to be low, but so also will be the spot price S, and conversely when

4. Cootner (1967, p. 65) defines the convenience yield of inventory as "the present value of an increased income stream expected as a result of conveniently large inventories." This contrasts with our definition of the convenience yield as a flow.

stocks of the physical commodity are low. We make the simplifying assumption that the marginal net convenience yield of the commodity can be written as a function of the current spot price and time, $C(S, t)$. Detailed modeling of the behavior of the convenience yield is beyond the scope of this paper, and in the interest of tractability we shall sometimes assume simply that the convenience yield is proportional to the current spot price.

Our assumption that the convenience yield is a function only of the current spot price, together with the further assumption which we maintain throughout the paper, that the interest rate is a constant, ρ, suffices to yield a determinate relation between the spot and futures prices of the commodity. Thus let $F(S, \tau)$ represent the futures price at time t for delivery of one unit of the commodity at time T where $\tau = T - t$. The instantaneous change in the futures prices is given from Ito's lemma by

$$dF = (-F_\tau + \tfrac{1}{2}F_{SS}\, \sigma^2 S^2)\, dt + F_S\, dS. \qquad (2)$$

Then consider the instantaneous rate of return earned by an individual who purchases one unit of the commodity and goes short $(F_S)^{-1}$ futures contracts. Since entering the futures contract involves no receipt or outlay of funds, his instantaneous return per dollar of investment including the marginal net convenience yield, using (2), is

$$\frac{dS}{S} + \frac{C(S)dt}{S} - (SF_S)^{-1}dF$$

$$= (SF_S)^{-1}[F_S C(S) - \tfrac{1}{2}F_{SS}\, \sigma^2 S^2 + F_\tau]\, dt. \qquad (3)$$

Since this return to nonstochastic and since $C(S)$ is defined as the (net) convenience yield of the marginal unit of inventory, it follows that the return must be equal to the riskless return $\rho\, dt$. Setting the right hand side of (3) equal to $\rho\, dt$, we obtain the partial differential equation

$$\tfrac{1}{2}F_{SS}\, \sigma^2 S^2 + F_S(\rho S - C) - F_\tau = 0. \qquad (4)$$

Thus the futures price is given by the solution to (4) subject to the boundary condition

$$F(S, 0) = S. \qquad (5)$$

This establishes that the futures price is a function of the current spot price and the time to maturity. Moreover, the parameters of the convenience yield function may be estimated directly from the relation between spot and futures prices. If the convenience yield is proportional to the spot price,

$$C(S, t) = cS, \qquad (6)$$

then following Ross (1978) the futures price is given by

$$F(S, \tau) = Se^{(\rho - c)\tau}, \tag{7}$$

independent of the stochastic process of the spot price. For more general specifications of the convenience yield it is necessary to solve (4) and (5) directly.

Finally, using (4) in expression (2), the instantaneous change in the futures price may be expressed in terms of the convenience yield and the instantaneous change in the spot price as

$$dF = F_S[S(\mu - \rho) + C]dt + F_S S\sigma \, dz. \tag{8}$$

We are now in a position to derive the partial differential equation that must be satisfied by the value of the mine and to characterize the optimal output policy of the mine.

The output rate of the mine, q, is assumed to be costlessly variable between the upper and lower bounds $\bar{q}$ and $\underline{q}$.[5] The output rate can be reduced below $\underline{q}$ only by closing the mine, and it is costly both to close the mine and to open it again. For this reason the value of the mine will depend on whether it is currently open or closed. The value of the mine will also depend on the current commodity price, S; the physical inventory in the mine, Q; calendar time, t; and the mine operating policy, ϕ. We write the value of the mine as

$$H \equiv H(S, Q, t; j, \quad \phi). \tag{9}$$

The indicator variable j takes the value one if the mine is open and zero if it is closed. The operating policy is described by the function determining the output rate when the mine is open $q(S, Q, t)$, and three critical commodity output prices: $S_1(Q, t)$ is the output price at which the mine is closed down or abandoned if it was previously open; $S_2(Q, t)$ is the price at which the mine is opened up if it was previously closed; $S_0(Q, t)$ is the price at which the mine is abandoned if it is already closed. The distinction between closure and abandonment is that a closed mine incurs fixed maintenance costs but may be opened up again. An abandoned mine incurs no costs but is assumed to be permanently abandoned. It is assumed that abandonment involves no costs.

Applying Ito's lemma to (9), the instantaneous change in the value of the mine is given by

$$dH = H_S \, dS + H_Q \, dQ + H_t \, dt + \tfrac{1}{2} H_{SS}(dS)^2, \tag{10}$$

5. These bounds may depend on the amount of inventory remaining in the mine and time.

where the instantaneous change in the mine inventory is determined by the output rate

$$dQ = -q \, dt. \tag{11}$$

The after-tax cash flow, or continuous dividend rate, from the mine is

$$q(S - A) - M(1 - j) - \lambda_j H - T, \tag{12}$$

where

$A(q, Q, t)$ is the average cash cost rate of producing at the rate q at time t when the mine inventory is Q;

$M(t)$ is the after-tax fixed-cost rate of maintaining the mine at time t when it is closed;

$\lambda_j (j = 0, 1)$ is proportional rate of tax on the value of the mine when it is closed and open; and

$T(q,Q,S,t)$ is the total income tax and royalties levied on the mine when it is operating. While alternative forms are possible we shall assume that the tax function is

$$T(q, Q, S,t) = t_1 q S + \max\{t_2 q[S(1 - t_1) - A],0\}, \tag{13}$$

where

t_1 is the royalty rate and t_2 is the income tax rate.[6]

The parameters λ_0 and λ_1 are interpreted most simply as property tax rates. However an alternative interpretation may be apposite in some contexts: they may represent the intensities of Poisson processes governing the event of uncompensated expropriation of the owners of the mine. Then the expected loss rate from expropriation is $\lambda_j H$ and expression (12) represents the cash flow net of the expected cost of expropriation. Under this interpretation the arbitrage strategy outlined below is not entirely risk free; however, we shall assume that there is no risk premium associated with the possibility of expropriation.

To derive the differential equation governing the value of the mine under the output policy ϕ consider the return to a portfolio consisting of a long position in the mine and a short position in (H_S/F_S) futures contracts. The return on the mine is given by (10)–(12) and the change in the futures price is given by (8). Combining these and using (1), the return on this portfolio is

$$\tfrac{1}{2} \sigma^2 S^2 H_{SS} - q H_Q + H_t + q(S - A)$$
$$- M(1 - j) - T - \lambda_j H + (\rho S - C) H_s. \tag{14}$$

6. For simplicity we have ignored depreciation tax allowances.

Ignoring the possibility of expropriation, this return is nonstochastic, and to avoid riskless arbitrage opportunities it must be equal to the riskless return on the value of the investment. Setting expression (14) equal to the riskless return ρH, the value of the mine must satisfy the partial differential equation

$$\tfrac{1}{2}\,\sigma^2 S^2\, H_{SS} + (\rho S - C)H_S - qH_Q + H_t + q(S - A) - M(1 - j) - T$$
$$- (\rho + \lambda_j)\, H - 0 \tag{15}$$
$$(j = 0, 1).$$

The mine value satisfies (15) for any operating policy $\phi \equiv \{\, q, S_0, S_1, S_2 \}$. Under the value maximizing operating policy $\phi^* = \{q^*, S_0^*, S_1^*, S_2^*\}$, the values of the mine when open, $V(S, Q, t)$, and when closed, $W(S, Q, t)$ are given by

$$V(S, Q, t) \equiv \max_{\phi}\, H(S, Q, t;\ 1, \phi) \tag{16}$$

$$W(S, Q, t) \equiv \max_{\phi}\, H(S, Q, t;\ 0, \phi). \tag{17}$$

The value-maximizing output and the value of the mine under the value-maximizing policy satisfy the two equations

$$\max_{q \in (q,\bar{q})}\, [\tfrac{1}{2}\,\sigma^2 S^2 V_{SS} + (\rho S - C)V_S - qV_Q$$
$$+ V_t + q(S - A) - T - (\rho + \lambda_1)V] = 0, \tag{18}$$

$$\tfrac{1}{2}\,\sigma^2 S^2 W_{SS} + (\rho S - C)\, W_S + W_t - M - (\rho + \lambda_0)W = 0 \tag{19}$$

(see Merton 1971, theorem 1; Fleming and Rishel 1975, chap. 6; Cox, Ingersoll, and Ross 1978, lemma 1).

Since the policies regarding opening, closing, and abandoning the mine are known to investors, we have

$$W(S_0^*, Q, t) = 0 \tag{20}$$

$$V(S_1^*, Q, t) = \max[W(S_1^*, Q, t) - K_1(Q, t), 0] \tag{21}$$

$$W(S_2^*, Q, t) = V(S_2^*, Q, t) - K_2(Q, t) \tag{22}$$

where $K_1(\cdot)$ and $K_2(\cdot)$ are the cost of closing and opening the mine respectively. Assuming that the value of an exhausted mine is zero we also have the boundary condition

$$W(S, 0, t) = V(S, 0, t) = 0. \tag{23}$$

Finally, since S_0^*, S_1^*, S_2^* are chosen to maximize the value of the mine it follows from the Merton-Samuelson high-contact condition (Samuelson 1965; Merton 1973) that

$$W_S(S_0^*, Q, t) = 0; \tag{24}$$

$$V_S(S_1^*, Q, t) = \begin{cases} W_S(S_1^*, Q, t) & \text{if } W(S_1^*, Q, t) - K_1(Q, t) \geq 0, \\ 0 & \text{if } W(S_1^*, Q, t) - K_1(Q, t) < 0; \end{cases} \quad (25)$$

$$W_S(S_2^*, Q, t) = V_S(S_2^*, Q, t). \quad (26)$$

The value of the mine depends on calendar time only because the costs A, M, K_1, and K_2 and the convenience yield C depend on time. If there is a constant rate of inflation π in all of these and if $C(S, t)$ may be written as κS, then equations (18)–(26) may be simplified as follows: Define the deflated variables

$$a(q, Q) = A(q, Q, t) e^{-\pi t},$$

$$f = M(t) e^{-\pi t},$$

$$k_1(Q) = K_1(Q, t) e^{-\pi t}, k_2(Q) = K_2(Q, t) e^{-\pi t},$$

$$s = S e^{-\pi t},$$

$$v(s, Q) = V(S, Q, t) e^{-\pi t},$$

$$w(s, Q) = W(S, Q, t) e^{-\pi t}.$$

Then it may be verified that the deflated value of the mine satisfies

$$\max_{q \in (\underline{q}, \bar{q})} [\tfrac{1}{2} \sigma^2 s^2 v_{ss} + (r - \kappa) s v_s - q v_Q$$
$$+ q(s - a) - \tau - (r + \lambda_1) v] = 0, \quad (27)$$

$$\tfrac{1}{2} \sigma^2 s^2 w_{ss} + (r - \kappa) s w_s - f - (r + \lambda_0) w = 0, \quad (28)$$

where $r = \rho - \pi$ is the real interest rate,

$$\tau = t_1 q s + \max \{t_2 q[s(1 - t_1) - a], 0\}; \quad (29)$$

$$w(s_0^*, Q) = 0; \quad (30)$$

$$v(s_1^*, Q) = \max[w(s_1^*, Q) - k_1(Q), 0]; \quad (31)$$

$$w(s_2^*, Q) = v(s_2^*, Q) - k_2(Q); \quad (32)$$

$$w(s, 0) = v(s, 0) = 0; \quad (33)$$

$$w_s(s_0^*, Q) = 0; \quad (34)$$

$$v_s(s_1^*, Q) = \begin{cases} w_s(s_1^*, Q) & \text{if } w(s_1^*, Q, t) - k_1(Q, t) \geq 0, \\ 0 & \text{if } w(s_1^*, Q, t) - k_1(Q, t) < 0; \end{cases} \quad (35)$$

$$w_s(s_2^*, Q) = v_s(s_2^*, Q). \quad (36)$$

Equations (27)–(36) constitute the general model for the value of a mine. They suffice to determine not only the (deflated) value of the mine when open and closed, but also the optimal policies for opening, closing, and abandoning the mine and for setting the output rates. In general there exists no analytic solution to the valuation model, though it is straightforward to solve it numerically. In the next section we present a simplified version of the model.

II.   The Infinite Resource Case

To obtain a model that is analytically tractable we assume that the physical inventory of the commodity in the mine, Q, is infinite. This infinite resource assumption enables us to replace the partial differential equations (27) and (28) for the value of the mine with ordinary differential equations, since the mine inventory, Q, is no longer a relevant state variable. To facilitate the analysis further we assume that the tax system allows for full loss offset so that (29) becomes

$$\tau(q, s) = t_1 qs + t_2 q[s(1 - t_1) - a]. \tag{29'}$$

Finally, we assume that the mine has only two possible operating rates, q^* when it is open, and zero when it is closed; furthermore, because it is costly to open or close the mine, costs must be incurred in moving from one output rate to the other.[7]

Under the foregoing assumptions the (deflated) value of the mine when it is open and operating at the rate q^* satisfies the ordinary differential equation

$$\tfrac{1}{2} \sigma^2 s^2 v_{ss} + (r - \kappa)sv_s + ms - n - (r + \lambda)v = 0, \tag{37}$$

where $m = q^*(1 - t_1)(1 - t_2)$, and $n = q^*a(1 - t_2)$.

If we assume that f, the periodic maintenance cost for a closed mine, is equal to zero, then the value of the mine when closed satisfies the corresponding differential equation

$$\tfrac{1}{2} \sigma^2 s^2 w_{ss} + (r - \kappa)sw_s - (r + \lambda)w = 0. \tag{38}$$

The boundary conditions are obtained by ignoring Q in (31), (32), (35), and (36) and by setting $w(0) = 0$.[8]

The complete solutions to equations (37) and (38) are

$$w(s) = \beta_1 s^{\gamma_1} + \beta_2 s^{\gamma_2}, \tag{39}$$

$$v(s) = \beta_3 s^{\gamma_1} + \beta_4 s^{\gamma_2} + \frac{ms}{\lambda + \kappa} - \frac{n}{r + \lambda}, \tag{40}$$

7. The App. develops the model under the neoclassical assumption of a continuously variable output rate with convex costs.

8. In the absence of maintenance costs it is never optimal to abandon a closed mine so long as there is a possibility that it will be optimal to reopen it. Hence $w(0) = 0$ and $w(s) > 0$ for $s > 0$.

where the β's are constants to be determined by the boundary conditions and

$$\gamma_1 = \alpha_1 + \alpha_2, \quad \gamma_2 = \alpha_1 - \alpha_2,$$

$$\alpha_1 = \tfrac{1}{2} - \frac{r - \kappa}{\sigma^2}, \quad \alpha_2 = \left[\alpha_1^2 + \frac{2(r + \lambda)}{\sigma^2}\right]^{\tfrac{1}{2}}.$$

If we assume that $(r + \lambda) > 0$,[9] then $\beta_2 = 0$ since γ_2 is negative and $w(s)$ must remain finite as s approaches zero. Similarly, since $\gamma_1 > 1$, $\beta_3 = 0$ if we impose the requirement that v/s remain finite as $s \to \infty$. Thus the value of the mine when closed is given by $w(s) = \beta_1 s^{\gamma_1}$, and the value when open is

$$v(s) = \beta_4 s^{\gamma_2} + \frac{ms}{\lambda + \kappa} - \frac{n}{r + \lambda}. \tag{41}$$

If the possibility of closing the mine when output prices are low is ignored, the value of the mine is given by the last two terms in (41); thus the first term represents the value of the closure option.

The remaining constants β_1 and β_4, as well as the optimal policy for closing and opening the mine represented by the output prices s_1^* and s_2^*, are determined by conditions (31), (32), (35), and (36), which imply that

$$\beta_1 = \frac{d\, s_2^*(\gamma_2 - 1) + b\gamma_2}{(\gamma_2 - \gamma_1)\, s_2^{*\gamma_1}}, \quad \beta_4 = \frac{d\, s_2^*(\gamma_1 - 1) + b\gamma_1}{(\gamma_2 - \gamma_1)\, s_1^{*\gamma_2}},$$

$$s_2^* = \gamma_2(e - bx^{\gamma_1})/(x^{\gamma_1} - x)\, d\,(\gamma_2 - 1),$$

$$\frac{s_1^*}{s_2^*} = x,$$

where $e = k_1 - n/(r + \lambda)$, $b = -k_2 - n/(r + \lambda)$, $d = m/(\lambda + \kappa)$, and x, the ratio of the commodity prices at which the mine is closed and opened, is the solution to the nonlinear equation

$$\frac{(x^{\gamma_2} - x)(\gamma_1 - 1)}{\gamma_1(e - bx^{\gamma_2})} = \frac{(x^{\gamma_1} - x)(\gamma_2 - 1)}{\gamma_2(e - bx^{\gamma_1})}. \tag{42}$$

The solution is illustrated in figure 1. In this figure the dotted line represents the present value of the cash flows from the mine assuming that it can never be shut down; this is obtained by setting $\beta_4 = 0$ in equation (42). Since $\gamma_2 < 0$, the value of the closure option diminishes and approaches zero for high output prices. For very low output prices the mine is worth more when it is closed than when it is open and making losses because of the cost of closure. However, for higher output prices the mine is worth more when open, and at the commodity

9. This is necessary for the present value of the future costs to be finite.

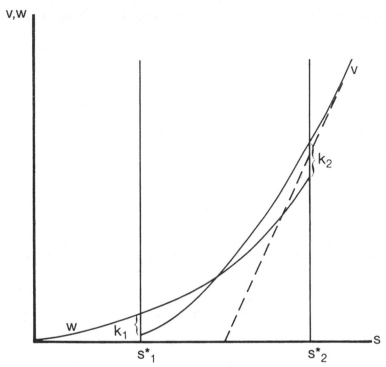

Fig. 1.—Mine value when open (v) and closed (w) as a function of the commodity price (s); k_1: cost of closing mine; k_2: cost of opening mine.

price s_2^* it is worth just enough more to warrant the outlay k_2 to open it. It is clear from the figure and can be demonstrated analytically that as the costs of opening and closing the mine approach zero, s_1^* and s_2^* approach the same value and the mine value schedule becomes a single curve. On the other hand, as the cost of mine closure becomes very large the closure option becomes worthless, and in the limit the value schedule for the open mine approaches the dotted line. Changes in the cost of mine closure, brought about for example by government regulation, will alter the optimal policy for closing the mine, s^*: however, they will also affect the original decision to invest in the mine by changing the present value of the future cash flows. Such effects, or those induced by changes in the tax regime, are readily analyzed in the context of this simplified model or the general model of the previous section.

III.   An Example

To illustrate the nature of our solution we consider a mine example based on the stylized facts for copper. In this example there is a finite

TABLE 1   Data for a Hypothetical Copper Mine

Mine:
  Output rate (q^*): 10 million pounds/year
  Inventory (Q): 150 million pounds
  Initial average cost of production $a(q^*, Q)$: $0.50/pound
  Initial cost of opening and closing (k_1, k_2): $200,000
  Initial maintenance costs (f): $500,000/year
  Cost inflation rate (π): 8%/year
Copper:
  Convenience yield (κ): 1%/year
  Price variance (σ^2): 8%/year
Taxes:
  Real estate (λ_1, λ_2): 2%/year
  Income (t_2): 50%
  Royalty (t_1): 0%
  Interest rate (ρ): 10%/year

mine inventory so that the stochastic optimal control problem represented by equations (27)–(36) must be solved numerically. To simplify matters somewhat we assume that there is a single feasible operating rate when the mine is open. The mine may be closed down or opened at a cost of $200,000 in current prices; it may also be abandoned. Other data required for this example are contained in table 1.[10]

Given an inventory equal to 15 years production, we find that the cost of production is 50 cents per pound, but it is not optimal to incur the cost of opening the mine until the price of copper rises to 76 cents. On the other hand, if the mine is already open and operating, it is not optimal to close it down until the copper price drops to 44 cents. Finally, the mine should be abandoned if the price drops below 20 cents. Obviously these critical prices depend on the assumed costs of opening, closing, and maintaining the mine: they also depend upon the remaining inventory in the mine. The greater the inventory in the mine the greater is the incentive to extract the copper immediately, since the opportunity cost of immediate extraction falls as the expected life of the mine increases. Thus the greater the inventory the lower is the price at which the mine is opened and closed and, since the mine value is a nondecreasing function of the inventory, the lower the price at which it is abandoned.

Table 2 summarizes the results when the mine has a 15-year inventory. Columns 1 and 3 give the present values of the future cash flows from the mine, assuming that it is open and closed, respectively, for different copper prices. These are the relevant values for the investment decision. Column 4 gives the value of the mine assuming that it

10. The variance rate and convenience yield used in table 1 compare with a variance rate for COMEX monthly settlement prices for copper of 7.8% per year for 1971–82 and an average convenience yield of 0.7% per year computed from annual data on the May contract for the same period, using eq. (7).

TABLE 2   Value of Copper Mine for Different Copper Prices

Copper Price ($/pound) (1)	Mine Value ($ million)		Value of Fixed-Output-Rate Mine ($ million) (4)	Value of Closure Option ($ million) (5)	Risk (6)	Value of Mine under Certainty, $\sigma^2 = 0$ ($ million) (7)
	Open (2)	Closed (3)				
.30	(1.25)*	1.45	.38	1.07		0
.40	(4.15)*	4.35	3.12	1.23		0
.50	7.95	8.11	7.22	.89	.75	1.85†
.60	12.52	12.49	12.01	.51	.66	7.84†
.70	17.56	17.38	17.19	.37	.59	13.87†
.80	22.88	(22.68)†	22.61	.27	.54	19.91†
.90	28.38	(28.18)†	28.18	.20	.50	25.94†
1.00	34.01	(33.81)†	33.85	.16	.47	31.98†

 * Optimal to close mine
 † Optimal to open mine

cannot be closed down but must be operated at the rate of 10 million pounds per year until the inventory is exhausted in 15 years. The difference between column 4 and the greater of the values shown in columns 2 and 3 represents the value of the option to close down or abandon the mine if the price of copper falls far enough. The value of this closure option is shown in column 5: it amounts to 12% of the value of the fixed-output-rate mine when the copper price is equal to the variable cost of 50 cents per pound; of course this would represent a much higher proportion of the *net* present value of an investment in the mine.

Column 6 of the table reports the instantaneous risk of the mine at different copper prices. This is the instantaneous standard deviation of the mine value, defined as $(v_s/v)\sigma s$ when the mine is open and $(w_s/w)\sigma s$ when the mine is closed. As we would expect, the risk of the mine decreases as the copper price and hence the operating margin increases. Since the copper price is stochastic, so also is the risk of the mine and the instantaneous rate of return required by investors, pointing to the dangers of assuming a single discount rate in a present value analysis.

Ownership of a mine that is not currently operating involves three distinct types of decision possibilities or options: first, the decision to begin operations; second, the decision to close the mine when it is currently operating (and possibly to reopen it later), which we have referred to as the closure option; and third, the decision to abandon the mine early, before the inventory is exhausted.

The decision to begin operations depends in our model on the current spot price of the commodity and the mine inventory. When there is no uncertainty, so that the time path of the commodity price is deterministic, the optimal decision rule for beginning operations can be expressed in calendar time (and the mine inventory). This certainty

case, which has been analyzed extensively under the rubric of the
"timing option" (see, e.g., Solow 1974), corresponds to column 7, of
table 2: this gives the value of the closed mine under the assumption of
certainty, which may be contrasted with the uncertainty case of column 3. For our parameter values it is never optimal under certainty to
close or abandon the mine, once it is open, before the inventory is
exhausted,[11] so that the closure and early abandonment options are
worthless. When the commodity price is in the neighborhood of the
production costs the elimination of uncertainty reduces the value of the
mine dramatically. Of course this depends on the particular values of
the convenience yield and other parameters.

IV. The Investment Decision

Thus far, only the valuation of the cash flows from an investment
project has been considered. The investment decision itself requires
that a comparison be made between the present value of the project
cash flows and the initial investment needed for the project. Continuing
with the example of a mine, $V(S, Q^*, t)$ represents the (nominal) value
at time t of a completed operating mine with inventory Q^* when the
current output price is S; $V(\cdot)$ is equal to the present value of the cash
flows that will be realized from the mine under the optimal operating
policy. Similarly, let $I(S, Q^*, t)$ represent the investment required to
construct an operating mine with inventory Q^* on a particular property: the amount of this initial investment may obviously depend on
calendar time and upon the size of the mine as represented by Q^*, and
S is included as an argument for the sake of generality. Then, assuming
that construction lags can be neglected, the net present value (NPV) at
time t of constructing the mine immediately is given by

$$\text{NPV}(S, Q^*, t) = V(S, Q^*, t) - I(S, Q^*, t). \tag{43}$$

However, once the possibility of postponing an investment decision
is recognized, it is clear that it is not in general optimal to proceed with
construction simply because the net present value of construction is
positive: there is a "timing option" and it may pay to wait in the
expectation that the net present value of construction will increase.
This dynamic aspect of the investment decision is closely related to the
problem of determining the optimal strategy for exercising an option on
a share of common stock: the right to make the investment decision
and to appropriate the resulting net present value is the ownership right
in the undeveloped mine property, and the value of this ownership
right corresponds to the value of the stock option.

Define $X(S, Q^*, t)$ as the value of the ownership right to an unde-

---

11. Because the commodity price is increasing faster than the production costs.

veloped mine with inventory Q^* at time t when the current output price is S. The stochastic process for $X(\cdot)$ is obtained from Ito's lemma, using the assumption about the stochastic process for S embodied in expression (1). Then the arbitrage argument used to derive the differential equation (15) for the value of a completed mine may be repeated to show that $X(\cdot)$ must satisfy the partial differential equation

$$\tfrac{1}{2}\,\sigma^2 S^2 X_{ss} + (\rho S - C)X_s + X_t - (\rho + \lambda)X = 0, \qquad (44)$$

where, as before, λ represents either the rate of tax on the value of the property or the intensity of a Poisson process governing the event of expropriation.[12]

Since the origin is an absorbing state for the commodity price, S, we have the boundary condition

$$X(0, Q^*, t) = 0, \qquad (45)$$

and if the ownership rights are in the form of a lease which expires at time T, then

$$X(S, Q^*, T) = 0. \qquad (46)$$

Assuming that the size of the mine inventory, Q^*, is predetermined by technical and geological factors, the optimal strategy for investment can be characterized in terms of a time dependent schedule of output prices $S^I(t)$ such that

$$X(S^I, Q^*, t) = V(S^I, Q^*, t) - I(S^I, Q^*, t), \qquad (47)$$

$$X_S(S^I, Q^*, t) = V_S(S^I, Q^*, t) - I_S(S^I, Q^*, t). \qquad (48)$$

Equation (47) states simply that the value of the property is equal to the net present value of the investment at the time it is made. Equation (48) is the Merton-Samuelson high-contact or envelope condition for a maximizing choice of S^I.

If the amount of the accessible inventory in the mine, Q^*, depends on the amount of the initial investment instead of being determined exogenously, then we have the additional value-maximizing condition to determine the size of the initial mine inventory, Q^*:

$$V_Q(S^I, Q^*, t) = I_Q(S^I, Q^*, t). \qquad (49)$$

Thus the optimal investment strategy is obtained by solving the partial differential equation (44) for the value of the ownership right, subject to boundary conditions (45)–(49). The optimal time to invest is determined by the series of critical output prices $S^I(t)$ described by (47) and (48); the optimal amount to invest is determined by the first order condition (49). Note that the boundary conditions for this problem

---

12. An alternative assumption is that all costs inflate at the common rate π; this would convert (44) into an *ordinary* differential eq. for the deflated mine value $x = Xe^{-\pi t}$.

involve $V(S, Q, t)$, the present value of the cash flows from a completed mine. Thus solving the cash flow valuation problem is a prerequisite for the investment decision analysis described in this section.

V.   Long-Term Supply Contracts

It is not uncommon for the outputs of natural resource investments to be sold under long-term contracts that fix the price of the commodity but leave the purchase rate at least partially to the discretion of the purchaser. Where they exist, such contracts must be taken into account in valuing ongoing projects. Therefore in this section we show briefly how these contracts may be valued and the equilibrium contract price determined.

Let $Y(S, t; p, T)$ denote the value at time t of a particular contract to purchase the commodity up to time T at the contract price p, when the current spot price of the commodity is S. The contract is assumed to permit the purchaser to vary the price rate, q, between the lower and upper bounds $\underline{q}$ and $\bar{q}$. Since the commodity is by assumption available for purchase at the prevailing spot price S, ownership of the contract yields an instantaneous benefit or cash flow $q(S - p)$.

Using Ito's lemma and the stochastic process for S, the instantaneous change in the value of the contract is given by

$$dY = (\tfrac{1}{2} \sigma^2 S^2 \, Y_{ss} + Y_t)dt + Y_s \, dS. \tag{50}$$

Then an arbitrage argument analogous to that presented in Section I implies that the value of the contract must satisfy the partial differential equation:

$$\max_{q \in (\underline{q}, \bar{q})} [\tfrac{1}{2} \sigma^2 S^2 \, Y_{ss} + (\rho S - C)Y_s + Y_t + q(S - p) - \rho Y] = 0. \tag{51}$$

The value of the contract at maturity, $t = T$, is equal to zero, so that

$$Y(S, T; p, T) = 0. \tag{52}$$

In addition, the origin is an absorbing state for the spot price S. This implies that if $S = 0$, the holder of the contract must incur certain losses at the rate $\underline{q}p$ up to the maturity of the contract, so that

$$Y(0, t; p, T) = \frac{-p\underline{q}}{\rho} [1 - e^{-\rho(T-t)}]. \tag{53}$$

Finally, for sufficiently high values of S, the value of the right to vary the purchase rate approaches zero and the value of the contract approaches that of a series of forward contracts to purchase at the rate $\bar{q}$

at the fixed price p. Noting that forward and futures prices are equivalent when the interest rate is nonstochastic (see Cox et al. 1981; Jarrow and Oldfield 1981; Richard and Sundaresan 1981), this implies that

$$\lim_{s \to \infty} \frac{\partial Y(S, t; \ p, T)}{\partial S} = \frac{\partial}{\partial S} \int_0^{T-t} \bar{q} \, F(S, \tau) \, d\tau, \qquad (54)$$

where $F(S, \tau)$ is the futures price for delivery in τ periods as defined previously.

The equilibrium contract price (or price schedule) is that which makes the value of the contract at inception equal to zero, given the prevailing spot price, S, and maturity, T. Writing the equilibrium contract price as $p^*(S, T)$, we have

$$Y[S, 0; p^*(S, T), T] = 0 \qquad (55)$$

In general there does not exist a closed-form solution for $Y(\cdot)$ or $p^*(\cdot)$. However, if the convenience yield can be written as $C(s) = \kappa S$, then closed-form solutions may be obtained in two special cases.

First, if the purchaser has no discretion over the purchase rate, so that $\bar{q} = q = q^*$, then the contract is equivalent to a series of forward contracts with value given by[13]

$$Y(S, t; \ p, T) = q^* \left\{ \frac{S}{\kappa} [1 - e^{-\kappa(T-t)}] - \frac{p}{\rho} [1 - e^{-\rho(T-t)}] \right\}. \qquad (56)$$

This implies that the equilibrium contract price is

$$p^*(S, T) = \frac{\rho S}{\kappa} \left(\frac{1 - e^{-\kappa T}}{1 - e^{-\rho T}} \right). \qquad (57)$$

Second, if the contract has an infinite maturity, the value of the contract is equal to the sum of the values of two assets we have already valued: a perpetual contract to purchase the commodity at the fixed rate q and a mine with infinite inventory, an average cost of production p, feasible production rates $\bar{q} - q$, and with no taxes, maintenance costs, or costs of opening and closing. The former may be valued using equation (56) and the latter is a special case of Section II.[14] It can then be shown that

$$Y(S, t; \ p, \infty) = \begin{cases} \beta_1 \, S^{\gamma_1} + q \left(\dfrac{S}{\kappa} - \dfrac{p}{\rho} \right), & S < p \\[2ex] \beta_4 \, S^{\gamma_2} = \bar{q} \left(\dfrac{S}{\kappa} - \dfrac{p}{\rho} \right), & S \geq p, \end{cases} \qquad (58)$$

13. We thank the referee for this point.
14. As the referee remarks, this contract is equivalent to a perpetuity of European options on the commodity.

where

$$\beta_1 = \frac{1}{2\alpha_2\kappa} \left[1 - \gamma_2 \left(\frac{\rho - \kappa}{\rho} \right) \right] q^d p^{1-\gamma_1},$$

$$\beta_4 = \frac{1}{2\alpha_2\kappa} \left[1 - \frac{\gamma_1}{\rho} (\rho - \kappa) \right] q^d p^{1-\gamma_2},$$

$$q^d = \bar{q} - \underline{q},$$

and γ_1, γ_2, and α_2 are as defined following equation (40). The equilibrium price $p^*(S, \tau)$ is found from the nonlinear equation obtained by setting either of the expressions (58) equal to zero.

VI. Conclusion

We have shown in the paper how assets whose cash flows depend on highly variable output prices may be valued and how the optimal policies for managing them may be determined by exploiting the properties of replicating self-financing portfolios. The explicit analysis rests on the assumption that such portfolios may be formed by trading in futures contracts in the output commodity, but the general approach can also be developed in a general equilibrium context if the relevant futures markets do not exist.

In addition to providing a rich set of empirical predictions for empirical research, this framework should be useful for the analysis of capital-budgeting decisions in a wide variety of situations in which the distribution of future cash flows is not given exogenously but must be determined by future management decisions.

Appendix

In contrast to the assumption of Section II that there are only two feasible output rates, zero and q^*, and that it is costly to shift from one to the other, we assume in this case that the output rate is continuously and costlessly variable between zero and $\bar{q}$; in keeping with this assumption, costs of opening and closing the mine are neglected and this renders the distinction between an open and a closed mine otiose.

We assume that no costs are incurred if the output rate is zero and that for positive output rates the total cost per unit time of the output rate q is $c(q) = q \cdot a(q) = a_0 + a_1q + a_2q^2$, where $a_1, a_2 > 0$; this represents a (linearly) increasing marginal cost schedule.

Using these assumptions in equation (27), the optimal output policy and the value of the mine satisfy

$$\tfrac{1}{2} \sigma^2 s^2 v_{ss} + (r - \kappa)vs + (1 - t_2) \max_{q \in (0,\bar{q})} [(1 - t_1)qs$$

$$- a_0 - a_1q - a_2q^2, 0] - (r + \lambda)v = 0. \tag{A1}$$

Carrying out the maximization we find that the optimal output policy is

$$q^*(s) = \begin{cases} \bar{q} & s > \bar{s} \\ \dfrac{(1 - t_1) s - a_1}{2a_2} & \bar{s} > s > s^* \\ 0 & s \leq s^*, \end{cases}$$

where $s^* = (a_1 + 2\sqrt{a_0 a_2})/(1 - t_1)$ and $\bar{s} = (a_1 + 2a_2\bar{q})/(1 - t_1)$. Thus the optimal output policy maximizes the instantaneous profit rate; since the profit rate is zero when the output rate is zero, the output rate is positive whenever the net-of-royalty output price exceeds the minimum average cost of production.

The after-tax cash flow from the mine under the optimal output policy, $p(s)$, is given by

$$p(s) = \begin{cases} (1 - t_2)[(1 - t_1)\bar{q}s - a_0 - a_1\bar{q} - a_2\bar{q}^2] & s > \bar{s}, \\ (1 - t_2)\dfrac{(1 - t_1)(s - a_1)^2}{4a_2 - a_0} & \bar{s} > s > s^*, \\ 0 & s \leq s^*. \end{cases}$$

When $p(s)$ is substituted for the maximand in equation (A1), the complete solutions for the three regions are

$$v(s) = \beta_1 s^{\gamma_1} + \beta_2 s^{\gamma_2} \qquad\qquad s \leq s^*, \qquad (A2)$$

$$v(s) = \beta_3 s^{\gamma_1} + \beta_4 s^{\gamma_2} + \delta(s) \qquad\qquad \bar{s} > s > s^*, \qquad (A3)$$

$$v(s) = \beta_5 s^{\gamma_1} + \beta_6 s^{\gamma_2} + \dfrac{ms}{\lambda + \kappa} - \dfrac{n}{r + \lambda} \qquad s > \bar{s}. \qquad (A4)$$

where

$$\delta(s) = \frac{(1 - t_2)}{r + \lambda}\left[\frac{a_1^2}{4a_2} - a_0\right] - \left[\frac{a_1(1 - t_1)(1 - t_2)}{2a_2(\lambda + c)}\right]s,$$

$$\qquad + \left[\frac{(1 - t_1)^2 (1 - t_2)}{4a_2(\lambda + 2c - \sigma^2 - r)}\right]s^2,$$

$$m = \bar{q}(1 - t_1)(1 - t_2),$$

$$n = (1 - t_2)(a_0 + a_1\bar{q} + a_2\bar{q}^2).$$

Variables γ_1 and γ_2 are as defined following equation (40), and the coefficients β_i ($i = 1, \ldots, 6$) are constants determined as follows. As in the case of Section II the requirements that v and v/s remain finite for very small and very large s, respectively, imply that $\beta_2 = \beta_5 = 0$. The remaining four constants are obtained by solving the four linear equations yielded by imposing the condition that the valuation schedule $v(s)$ be continuous and have a finite second derivative at s^* and $\bar{s}$:

$$\beta_1 s^{*\gamma_1} = \beta_3 s^{*\gamma_1} + \beta_4 s^{*\gamma_2} + \delta(s^*), \qquad (A5)$$

$$\gamma_1\beta_1 s^{*\gamma_1 - 1} = \gamma_1\beta_3 s^{*\gamma_1 - 1} + \gamma_2\beta_4 s^{*\gamma_2 - 1} + \delta'(s^*), \qquad (A6)$$

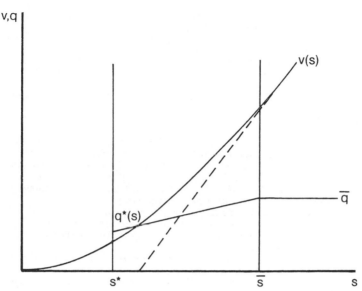

Fig. 2.—Case ii: Mine value (v) and optimal output as a function of the output price (s).

$$\beta_3\bar{s}^{\gamma_1} + \beta_4\bar{s}^{\gamma_2} + \delta(\bar{s}) = \beta_6\bar{s}^{\gamma_2} + \frac{m\bar{s}}{\lambda + \kappa} - \frac{n}{r + \lambda}, \tag{A7}$$

$$\gamma_1\beta_3\bar{s}^{\gamma_1-1} + \gamma_2\beta_4\bar{s}^{\gamma_2-1} + \delta'(\bar{s}) = \gamma_2\beta_6\bar{s}^{\gamma_2-1} + \frac{m}{\lambda + \kappa}. \tag{A8}$$

Thus the value of the mine is given by the solution to equations (A2)–(A8) with $\beta_2 = \beta_5 = 0$. Since the equation system (A5)–(A8) is linear it is a straightforward if tedious task to obtain an explicit valuation expression which may be used for comparative statics. The valuation schedule and the optimal output policy are illustrated in figure 2. In this figure the dotted line corresponds to the value of the mine if it is required to operate perpetually at its maximum rate $\bar{q}$: thus the difference between the $v(s)$ schedule and this line represents the value of the option to vary the output rate in response to changing output prices.

References

Bierman, H., and Smidt, S. 1960. *The Capital Budgeting Decision*. New York: Macmillan.

Black, F., and Scholes, M. 1973. The pricing of options and corporate liabilities. *Journal of Political Economy* 81 (May–June): 637–54.

Bodie, Z., and Rosansky, V. I. 1980. Risk and return in commodity futures. *Financial Analysts Journal* 36 (May–June): 27–40.

Bogue M. C., and Roll, R. 1974. Capital budgeting of risky projects with imperfect markets for physical capital. *Journal of Finance* 29 (May): 601–13.

Brennan, M. J. 1958. The supply of storage. *American Economic Review* 48 (March): 50–72.

Brennan, M. J. 1973. An approach to the valuation of uncertain income streams. *Journal of Finance* 28 (July): 661–73.

Brennan, M. J., and Schwartz, E. S. 1982a. Consistent regulatory policy under uncertainty. *Bell Journal of Economics* 13 (Autumn): 506–21.

Brennan, M. J., and Schwartz, E. S. 1982b. Regulation and corporate investment policy. *Journal of Finance* 37 (May): 289–300.

Brock, W. A.; Rothschild, M.; and Stiglitz, J. E. 1982. Stochastic capital theory. Financial Research Center Memorandum no. 40. Princeton, N.J.: Princeton University, April.

Constantinides, G. M. 1978. Market risk adjustment in project valuation. *Journal of Finance* 33 (May): 603–16.

Cootner, P. 1967. Speculation and hedging. *Food Research Institute Studies* 7 (Suppl.): 65–106.

Cox, J. C.; Ingersoll, J. E.; and Ross, S. A. 1978. A theory of the term structure of interest rates. Research Paper no. 468. Stanford, Calif.: Stanford University.

Cox, J. C.; Ingersoll, J. E.; and Ross, S. A. 1981. The relation between forward prices and futures prices. *Journal of Financial Economics* 9 (December): 321–46.

Dean, Joel 1951. *Capital Budgeting; Top Management Policy on Plant Equipment and Product Development.* New York: Columbia University.

Dothan, U., and Williams, J. 1980. Term-risk structures and the valuation of projects. *Journal of Financial and Quantitative Analysis* 15 (November): 875–906.

Fama, E. F. 1977. Risk-adjusted discount rates and capital budgeting under uncertainty. *Journal of Financial Economics* 5 (August): 3–24.

Fisher, Irving. 1907. *The Rate of Interest: Its Nature, Determination and Relation to Economic Phenomena.* New York: Macmillan.

Fleming, W. H., and Rishel, R. W. 1975. *Deterministic and Stochastic Optimal Control.* New York: Springer-Verlag.

Harrison, J. M., and Kreps, D. M. 1979. Martingales and arbitrage in multiperiod securities markets. *Journal of Economic Theory* 20:381–408.

Jarrow, R. A., and Oldfield, G. S. 1981. Forward contracts and futures contracts. *Journal of Financial Economics* 9 (December): 373–82.

Kaldor, N. 1939. Speculation and economic stability. *Review of Economic Studies* 7:1–27.

Merton, R. C. 1971. Optimum consumption and portfolio rules in a continuous time model. *Journal of Economic Theory* 3 (December): 373–413.

Merton, R. 1973. The theory of rational option pricing. *Bell Journal of Economic and Management Science* 4 (Spring): 141–83.

Miller, M. H., and Upton, C. W. 1985. A test of the Hotelling valuation principle. *Journal of Political Economy* 93 (February): in press.

Myers, S. C., and Turnbull, S. M. 1977. Capital budgeting and the capital asset pricing model: Good news and bad news. *Journal of Finance* 32 (May): 321–32.

Paddock, J. L.; Siegel, D. R.; and Smith, J. L. 1982. Option valuation of claims on physical assets: The case of off-shore petroleum leases. Unpublished manuscript. Evanston, Ill.: Northwestern University.

Pindyck, R. S. 1980. Uncertainty and exhaustible resource markets. *Journal of Political Economy* 88 (December): 1203–25.

Richard, S. F., and Sundaresan, M. 1981. A continuous time equilibrium model of forward prices and futures prices in a multigood economy. *Journal of Financial Economics* 9 (December): 347–72.

Ross, S. A. 1978. A simple approach to the valuation of risky streams. *Journal of Business* 51 (July): 453–75.

Samuelson, P. A. 1965. Rational theory of warrant pricing. *Industrial Management Review* 6 (Spring): 3–31.

Solow, R. M. 1974. The economics of resources or the resources of economics. *American Economic Review* 64 (May): 1–14.

Telser, L. G. 1958. Futures trading and the storage of cotton and wheat. In A. E. Peck, ed., *Selected Writings on Future Markets.* Chicago, 1977.

Tourinho, O. A. F. 1979. The option value of reserves of natural resources. Unpublished manuscript. Berkeley: University of California.

Working, H. 1948. The theory of price of storage. *Journal of Farm Economics* 30:1–28. Reprinted in *Selected Writings of Holbrook Working.* Chicago: Chicago Board of Trade, 1977.

6

THE JOURNAL OF FINANCE • VOL. XLII, NO. 5 • DECEMBER 1987

Efficient Financing under Asymmetric Information

MICHAEL BRENNAN and ALAN KRAUS*

ABSTRACT

This paper characterizes the conditions under which the adverse-selection problem, which may prevent a firm from issuing securities to finance an otherwise profitable investment, may be costlessly overcome by an appropriate choice of financing strategy. The conditions are specialized when the information asymmetry may be characterized by either a first-degree-stochastic-dominance or a mean-preserving-spread ordering across possible distributions of firm earnings. Possible financing strategies that resolve the information asymmetry are discussed, and the results are related to recent empirical findings concerning security issues.

IT HAS BEEN DEMONSTRATED by Myers and Majluf [17] that, to the extent that firms are unable to communicate their future prospects credibly to investors, the resulting adverse-selection problem may cause significant social welfare losses by inducing firms to forego investment opportunities that would otherwise be profitable. In this paper, we explore the possibility that, despite the information asymmetry, the investment opportunities may yet be efficiently financed by an appropriate choice of financing instruments that reveals the private information of corporate insiders to investors. In doing so, we are able to explain some of the complexities of corporate financings and to offer at least a partial interpretation for so far anomalous findings concerning the effects of corporate financings on security prices.

It is natural to consider the firm's choice of financing as a communication device since these choices are easily verifiable and, to the extent that the conditions of the Modigliani-Miller propositions are satisfied, they are costless. Therefore, if the adverse-selection problems due to information asymmetry in capital markets can be overcome by financial policy, it will be efficient to do so, and other more costly forms of communication will be eschewed.

Of course, we are not the first to see the communication possibilities of financial policy. Stiglitz [19] remarked that "changes in financial policy may be an important signal for the real prospects of the firm", and there is now extensive literature exploring the signalling aspects of financial policy. The models in most of the earlier papers rely either on an ad hoc managerial-compensation function

* UCLA and the University of British Columbia, respectively. An earlier version of this paper appeared as "Notes on Costless Financial Signalling" in *Risk and Capital*, edited by G. Bamberg and K. Spreman, Springer-Verlag, Berlin, 1984. Previous versions of the paper have been presented at the Western Finance Association Meetings (1982) and seminars at Yale University (1981) and Columbia University (1982). The authors thank J. Williams and the referee for suggestions that have improved the clarity and focus of the paper.

or on exogenously specified costs in order to achieve a signalling equilibrium. This paper, in contrast, considers only *costless* signalling possibilities so that, to the extent that the choice of cost functions is arbitrary, our analysis is more robust. This paper also differs from the foregoing in providing a general characterization of the conditions under which a fully revealing equilibrium can be obtained; these conditions involve joint restrictions on the nature of the information asymmetry and the set of financing strategies open to the firm. Since the equilibria we explore are efficient or costless and since any deviation of investment policy from the full-information optimum implies deadweight costs, we take the firm's investment policy as given and restrict the range of possible signals to the pure financing decisions of the firm.

The model we present is most closely related to that of Heinkel [11], in which the firm's choice of debt ratio serves as a costless signal of firm value since the distribution of firm earnings is characterized by a single unknown parameter. However, a significant distinction between Heinkel's analysis and our own is that, while he takes the security types as given and demonstrates the existence of a fully revealing equilibrium for a particular type of information asymmetry, we derive the properties the securities must have in order to be informative for general types of information asymmetry. In more recent work, Constantinides and Grundy [4] develop a financial signalling model in which the amount of investment by the firm and the stock-repurchase decision of inside equityholders act as signals about a single unknown parameter of the distribution of earnings.

There have also been extensive empirical investigations of the effects of announcements of corporate financings on security prices.[1] The first general finding is that financing announcements are associated with security price declines. This is usually interpreted as being consistent with a model such as that of Miller and Rock [16], in which the net payouts of the firm are related to cash flow realizations, which in turn are correlated with future cash flows. However, the Miller-Rock model would also predict a negative association between the size of the issue and the security price response; while such a relation has been detected for equity issues, there appears to be no such relation for debt issues.[2] The second general finding is that the more junior and equity-like the security issued, the more negative is the price response. This has been interpreted as being consistent with the spirit of the Myers-Majluf [17] model, in which insiders with privileged information about firm value tend to sell equity securities when they are overvalued. Such an interpretation may be premature, however, for, not only does the Myers-Majluf model not explicitly incorporate any securities except equity and riskless debt, but in addition there are several empirical findings that are difficult to reconcile with it. First, there appears to be no clear relation between bond rating and price response.[3] Second, low-rated convertibles are associated with a significantly *smaller* negative price response than are more

---

[1] For an excellent survey, see Smith [18], which is part of a symposium in the *Journal of Financial Economics*.

[2] Asquith and Mullins [2] and Masulis and Korwar [14] report finding an association for equity issues. Mikkelson and Partch [15] and Eckbo [7] could find no such association for debt issues.

[3] Mikkelson and Parch [15] and Eckbo [7] report a weak negative association.

highly rated convertibles.[4] Third, firms that issue sufficient equity to retire debt as well as finance their capital expenditures experience significantly *smaller* negative price reactions than do firms with equity issues that are used only for capital expenditures.[5] The examples we present below are consistent with any price response to convertible issues and offer an explanation for the simultaneous issue of equity and retirement of debt that is consistent with a smaller negative price reaction for these issues than for simple equity financings.

The remainder of the paper is organized as follows. In Section I, we develop a general characterization of a costless signalling equilibrium and give necessary and sufficient conditions for the existence of such an equilibrium. Section II analyzes the case in which the family of possible distributions of firm earnings is ordered by first-degree stochastic dominance and presents an example in which an equilibrium financing strategy consists of an equity issue combined with a debt retirement. Section III is concerned with the case in which the family of possible distributions is ordered by mean-preserving spread and shows that the convertible bond provides a possible resolution of the information asymmetry. Section IV offers some observations of the possibility of costless signalling of multiple attributes. Section V concludes.

I. Characterization and Existence of a Signalling Equilibrium

We consider initially a general situation in which a firm has private information about its "type", which refers to the joint probability distribution of earnings on its existing assets and on a new investment project. The new project is assumed to be indivisible and to require finance by the sale of securities to uninformed investors. Throughout the analysis, we make the following two assumptions:

(A1) The firm chooses its financing instruments so as to maximize the difference between the price it receives for the package of securities it sells, and the true, full-information, value of the securities, subject to the constraint that it raises K, the amount required for the investment, which is common knowledge.

(A2) Securities are traded in competitive markets, and investors possess rational expectations.

While (A2) is standard, (A1) merits some discussion. Combined with the assumption that original claimants are protected by appropriate me-first clauses, (A1) is tantamount to the assumption that the firm is maximizing the true, full-information, value of the securities held by its original shareholders. It can be shown that this criterion of true or intrinsic value maximization will be unanimously supported by the original shareholders, assuming competition in the capital markets and no redistributions to senior security holders, if the shareholders do not indulge in side bets about the characteristics of firms (either because the market is not rich enough to permit such side bets or because investors share common prior beliefs about firm characteristics so that they do

---

[4] See Mikkelson and Parch [15], Table 7.
[5] See Masulis and Korwar [14], Table 6.

not wish to make such bets).[6] (A1) implicitly ignores any agency problems and corresponds to the classical assumption that the board of directors, in selecting a financing strategy, identifies with the interests of all existing shareholders. This is consistent with the managerial objective implicit in Heinkel [11] but contrasts with that of Constantinides and Grundy [4], who assume that financing strategies are chosen to benefit a group of insider shareholders.

In what follows, we shall distinguish between a "security" and a "financing". Securities are the basic claims traded in capital markets: bonds, stocks, warrants, etc. A financing, on the other hand, refers to the complete set of financial decisions announced by a firm at a point in time; thus, a financing will typically include the issue of more than one type of security—for example, bonds and warrants—and may include retirements or repurchases of existing securities. The aggregate net claim issued in a financing is the difference between the payoffs due to security holders (excluding current shareholders) before and after the financing is announced. For example, if a firm announces a financing consisting of a stock issue and a debt retirement, the aggregate net claim consists of the future dividends on the stock and the immediate payment required to retire the debt, less the future payments that would have been due on the debt if it were not retired.

We then define a *value-revealing* costless signalling equilibrium as a choice of financing by each firm and an assignment of a market price to each traded security that is consistent with assumptions (A1) and (A2), such that the aggregate net claim issued under every financing is priced at its true, full-information, value. With these preliminaries, a value-revealing equilibrium can be characterized by the following theorem.

THEOREM 1 (Property of a Value-Revealing Equilibrium): *A value-revealing costless signalling equilibrium requires that the net claim issued under each financing be priced on the supposition that it was made by that firm (type) with characteristics that would cause the net claim to have the lowest true, full-information, value, and that supposition is correct.*

Proof: Define

z: a vector of parameters describing the aggregate net claim issued under a financing.

Z: the set of feasible financings; Z is common knowledge.

$V(z, t)$: the market value of the aggregate net claim issued under financing, $z \in Z$, when the financing is made by a firm of type t and t is common knowledge. Thus, $V(z, t)$ is the true, full-information, value of financing z when made by firm t.

T: the set of possible firm types, which is common knowledge.

$P(z)$: the funds subscribed by investors under financing z when investors are unable to observe the characteristics of the issuing firm but have rational expectations about them.

[6] Compare Feltham and Christianson [8].

$z^*(t)$: the financing chosen by firm t from the set $Z = \{z \mid z \in Z$ and $P(z) = K\}$, where K is the amount required for the investment.

$\tau(z) \equiv \{t \mid z^*(t) = z\}$: the set of firms that choose financing z.

We shall show that, if $\tau(z)$ is not empty (i.e., some firm chooses financing z), then

$$P(z) = \min_{\{t \in T\}} V(z, t). \tag{1}$$

Assumption (A1) implies that $z^*(t)$ satisfies

$$P(z^*(t)) - V(z^*(t), t) \geq P(z) - V(z, t), \quad \forall z \in \bar{Z}. \tag{2}$$

For every z for which $\tau(z)$ is not empty, a value-revealing equilibrium requires that $V(z, t)$ be constant over all $t \in \tau(z)$. Then, assumption (A2) implies that the market price of the financing be equal to its true, full-information value:

$$P(z) = V(z, t), \quad \text{where } t \in \tau(z). \tag{3}$$

Now suppose that (1) did not hold for some $\hat{z} \in \bar{Z}$ for which $\tau(\hat{z})$ were not empty. This would imply the existence of some set of firm characteristics, t_0, such that

$$V(\hat{z}, t_0) < P(\hat{z}) = K. \tag{4}$$

Then, (2) and (4) imply that

$$P(z^*(t_0)) - V(z^*(t_0), t_0) \geq P(\hat{z}) - V(\hat{z}, t_0) > 0, \tag{5}$$

and this contradicts (3). Therefore, (1) must hold for $z \in Z$. Q.E.D.

If $\tau(z)$ is a singleton for all z, then any particular financing is chosen in equilibrium by only one firm type. In this case, it will be possible for investors to infer the type of any firm from the financing it chooses, and such an equilibrium may be described as *fully revealing*.

Theorem 1 establishes that value-revealing equilibria are characterized by a "lemons property"; each financing strategy is chosen by the worst possible type of firm for that financing strategy (from the investor's viewpoint), and investors anticipate this in pricing the aggregate net claim issued under the financing. If investors did not always expect the worst, there would be scope for cheating or misrepresentation by firms. Figure 1 illustrates a fully revealing equilibrium. By hypothesis, firm 1 selects the financing, $z^*(1)$, with a value that in equilibrium satisfies $V(z^*(1), 1) = P(z^*(1)) = K$. The lemons property states that there can exist no other firm t such that $V(z^*(1), t) < P(z^*(1))$. This is contradicted by the hypothetical $V(z, 2)$ schedule in the figure. However, recalling that, by assumption, firm 2 will select the financing that maximizes $P(z) - V(z, 2)$, it is apparent that, if $V(z, 2)$ is as drawn, firm 2 will not select financing $z^*(2)$ or any other financing that is properly priced. Hence, $V(z, 2)$ cannot lie below $V(z, 1)$ at $z = z^*(1)$ if there is to be a fully revealing equilibrium.

While Theorem 1 provides a general characterization of a value-revealing equilibrium, if one exists, we require a more specific framework within which to

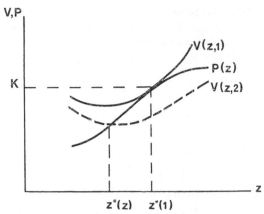

Figure 1. A Costless Signalling Equilibrium

analyze the question of existence itself.[7] Therefore, we consider a two-date world in which the firm arrives at time 0 with a predetermined capital structure and with private information about the time-1 returns on its existing assets and on a new investment opportunity. K, the amount required for this opportunity, is common knowledge.

If the firm decides to undertake the investment, it must raise K by a financing. Let x represent the time-1 return on the total assets (including the new project) of the firm, the probability distribution of which is private information, and let $y(x; z)$ represent the present value of the aggregate net claim issued in the financing as a function of the realized return x. Recall that z is a vector of parameters describing the financing—the terms and numbers of the constituent bonds, stocks, warrants, etc. We assume that, at the time of the financing, the firm is able to precommit to the investment.

The capital market is assumed to be complete, and the true, full-information, value of any claim is given by the expected value of its payoff.[8] Thus, the true value of the (aggregate net claim issued under) financing z when made by a firm of type t can be written as

$$V(z, t) = \int y(x; z) f(x; t) \, dx, \tag{6}$$

where $f(x; t)$ is the density function for the returns on a firm of type t. As we shall see, the possibility of a signalling equilibrium depends on the properties of the class of possible probability density functions governing the returns on the firm's assets. In order to describe the class of densities that do admit signalling equilibria, the following definitions will be useful.

---

[7] As the maximum net present value of new investment projects approaches zero, the only possible signalling equilibrium in which financings are carried out is a value-revealing equilibrium.

[8] This involves no loss of generality since, by an appropriate choice of numeraire, the value of any claim in a market that does not permit arbitrage can be expressed as the expected value of its payoff under an appropriately defined density function. Compare Harrison and Kreps [10].

Definition: Financing z is a *worst-case financing* for a firm of type $\hat{t}$ if $\hat{t} =$ argmin$_{\{t \in T\}} V(z, t)$. Thus, the payoff $y(x; z)$ of the aggregate net claim under a worst-case financing satisfies

$$\min_{\{t \in T\}} \int y(x; z) f(x; t) \, dx = \int y(x; z) f(x; \hat{t}) \, dx. \tag{7}$$

Definition: A family of probability density functions $\{f(\cdot; t)\}$ and a set, Z, of feasible financings are *K-compatible* if, for each $\hat{t}$, there exists a worst-case financing $z^*(\hat{t})$ such that $z^* \in Z$ and

$$\int y(x; z^*(\hat{t})) f(x; \hat{t}) \, dx = K. \tag{8}$$

If, in addition, the minimum in (7) is unique, then $\{f(\cdot, t)\}$ and z are *strongly K-compatible*.

Clearly, a worst-case financing is one for which the firm can be assured that the market price will not be below the true, full-information, value of the financing. The following lemma, the proof of which is immediate, states that compatible financings and probability densities ensure the existence of worst-case financings that raise the necessary investment amount.

LEMMA: *If a family of probability densities and a set of feasible financings are K-compatible, then, for each $\hat{t}$, there exists a worst-case financing $z^*(\hat{t})$ with a true, full-information, value of K.*

The link between worst-case financings and a revealing equilibrium is intuitively clear. If firms believe that investors will price financings at their worst-case values, then the best that a firm can achieve in seeking to maximize the difference between the price of its financing and the true, full-information, value of the financing is achieved by making a worst-case financing. This achieves a difference of zero, but any other choice of financing would produce a negative difference. Thus, if firms believe that investors will price financings at their worst-case values, firms will indeed be induced to make worst-case financings, confirming investors' beliefs. Furthermore, Theorem 1 shows that no other revealing equilibrium is possible. We formalize this intuition in the following:

THEOREM 2 (Existence of a Value-Revealing Equilibrium): *A necessary and sufficient condition for the existence of a value-revealing (fully revealing) equilibrium is that the family of possible risk-adjusted density functions of firm returns and the set of feasible financings be (strongly) K-compatible.*

Proof: We shall prove the theorem for the general case; extension to the fully revealing case is immediate.

Necessity: Combining equation (1) of Theorem 1 with the valuation function (6), a necessary condition for a value-revealing equilibrium is that, for each $\hat{t}$, there exist $z^*(\hat{t}) \in Z$ such that

$$P(z^*(\hat{t})) = \min_{\{t \in T\}} V(z^*(\hat{t}), t) = \min_{\{t \in T\}} \int y(x; z^*(\hat{t})) f(x, t) \, dx = K, \tag{9}$$

where $y(x; z)$ is the net payoff function for financing z. If $f(\cdot, t)$ and Z are not K-compatible, no solution can exist in (9) so that the property of a value-revealing equilibrium cannot be satisfied.

Sufficiency: If the family of possible distributions and the set of feasible financings are K-compatible, the lemma implies that there exists for each firm $\hat{t}$ a worst-case financing $z^*(\hat{t}) \in Z$ such that

$$\min_{\{t \in T\}} \int y(x; z^*(\hat{t})) f(x; t) \, dx$$

$$= \int y(x; z^*(\hat{t})) f(x; \hat{t}) \, dx \equiv V(z^*(\hat{t}), \hat{t}) = K. \qquad (10)$$

Suppose now that investors price all financings according to the "lemons principle", expressed in (1). Then $P(z^*(\hat{t})) = K$, so that financing $z^*(t)$ raises the required amount. Moreover, since, from (10), $V(z^*(\hat{t}), t) \geq K$ for all t, assumption (A1) implies that no firm t for which $V(z^*(\hat{t}), t) \neq K$ will have an incentive to choose financing $z^*(\hat{t})$. Therefore, investor inferences about the value of the financing, as reflected in (1), are correct, and all financings are properly priced.   Q.E.D.

Since, in a revealing equilibrium, the worst-case financing $z^*(\hat{t})$ is chosen by firm $\hat{t}$ and by no other firm that would cause its true value to be different, the financing is a signal of the characteristics of the firm. The existence of a revealing equilibrium then turns on the existence of a worst-case financing for each firm type, and that depends on the set of allowable financings, Z, and the set of possible firm types, T.

A significant implication of Theorems 1 and 2 is that, if the family of probability densities of firm returns and the set of feasible financings are K-compatible, then the investment inefficiency described by Myers and Majluf [17] may be eliminated. Myers and Majluf show that a firm that is restricted to financing through equity may fail to undertake a positive NPV investment project or may undertake a negative NPV project. If the density function of firm returns and the set of financing strategies are K-compatible, then we have shown that the firm can make a worst-case financing that raises K and is properly priced. Therefore, if the investment has a positive NPV, it will be undertaken. Similarly, a negative NPV investment will not be undertaken.

This demonstrates the fundamental importance of assumptions about the feasible set of financing strategies. In the following sections, we shall consider the type of securities that may be required to achieve a value-revealing equilibrium for particular assumptions about the firm's private information.

II. First-Degree Stochastic-Dominance Orderings

In this section, we specialize our general result in order to characterize the aggregate net payoff functions that are required for a value-revealing equilibrium under a first-degree stochastic-dominance ordering and show that these payoff functions may correspond to a financing consisting of an equity issue combined with a debt retirement.[9]

THEOREM 3: *If the firm's type, t, orders the family of possible probability density functions of the firm's total returns $\{f(\cdot, t)\}$ by first-degree stochastic dominance, then a value-revealing equilibrium requires that the first derivative of the net payoff function chosen by firm t in the interior of $\{T\}$ change sign over the allowed range of x.*

Proof: If $y(x; z)$ were monotone in x, (7) implies that $V(z, t)$ would be monotone in t, and no minimum would exist in (1) for interior values of t.   Q.E.D.

If the first-degree stochastic dominance takes the form of a shift in the mean of the distribution holding the other central moments constant, then the net payoff function of the chosen financing must exhibit a minimum in order that a value-revealing equilibrium exist; a V-shaped payoff function is the simplest example. The intuition underlying this theorem is straightforward; if the possible probability densities differed, say, only in their means, the value of the financing would be least if it were made by the firm with the lowest mean. It was shown in Theorem 1 that, in a revealing equilibrium, investors (correctly) infer the issuer type as that which minimizes the value of the financing. Therefore, such a monotone payoff function would be inconsistent with a revealing equilibrium if it were the result of a financing by any firm except that with the lowest possible mean.

Whether there will exist a revealing equilibrium in which financings are properly priced will depend on both the family of possible probability densities of firm earnings and the set of feasible financing strategies; the latter may depend on the pre-existing capital structure of the firm. Some cases in which revealing equilibria can be constructed involve the following kinds of worst-case financing: a debt repurchase and the issue of equity and possibly warrants, the granting of a guarantee to the debt of a subsidiary combined with an equity issue by the subsidiary, and the retirement of one convertible bond or preferred and its replacement by another.

Figure 2 illustrates how a V-shaped net payoff function results from a debt repurchase combined with an equity issue. In this figure, *ABCD* is the payoff function to bondholders from the debt repurchase, and *OFG* is the payoff function to purchasers of the new stock issue. The two functions are added vertically to yield a V-shaped aggregate net payoff function *ABHI*. In this figure, *OE* is the original par value of debt outstanding, and the par amount *FE* was repurchased for a consideration *OA*,[10] which corresponds to a discount of *CE*. The schedule *ABCD* reflects the sure payment of *OA* that bondholders receive as a result of the repurchase; this gives them an incremental gain for low levels of earnings realizations.[11] On the other hand, for high levels of earnings realizations, they

---

[9] This type of financing is quite common. Masulis and Korwar [14] report that the proceeds of 179 out of the 372 equity issues they examined were used for both capital expenditures and debt retirement.

[10] By setting the interest rate equal to zero, we have been able to ignore issues of timing; *OA* is, in fact, the repurchase price compounded for one period.

[11] Note that, as a result of the repurchase, bondholders receive *OA* even if the subsequently realized earnings turn out to be zero.

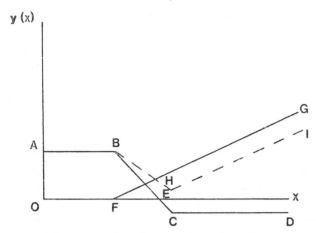

Figure 2. Payoff function for stock issue and debt repurchase. *ABHI*, aggregate net payoff; *ABCD*, net payoff to bondholders; *OFG*, net payoff to new stockholders; *OE*, par value of original debt; *FE*, par value of repurchased debt; *OA*, repurchase price of debt.

suffer an incremental loss corresponding to the discount, *CE*, at which the debt was repurchased. The payoff to the new stockholders, *OFG*, reflects the fact that they receive a constant fraction of earnings in excess of *OF*, the par value of debt outstanding after the repurchase.

We illustrate the possibilities for value-revealing equilibria under first-degree stochastic-dominance orderings by two examples. In the first example, there are only two possible firm types; in the second example, there is a continuum of types. In both examples, the firm has debt outstanding at time 0 and the amount of debt repurchased in the financing is a bullish signal of firm type. The reason for this is that debt retirements increase the firm's payouts to bondholders for low levels of earnings realizations by making the payout independent of the subsequent earnings realization; investors correctly infer from this that low levels of earnings are less probable. For example, a firm with debt that is, in fact, riskless can costlessly retire it at par. Since this would be costly for a firm with debt that is risky, the retirement is bullish information.

Example 1: The data for this example are given in Table I. At time 0, the firm has an opportunity to invest 10. The distribution of returns on the investment depends on the current state of the world; this state, denoted A or B, is private information to the firm. Under either state, the earnings of the firm at time 1 follow a symmetric two-point distribution; the distribution in state A dominates the distribution in state B. Since valuation is by expected value, the investment opportunity has a full information net present value of $150 - 120 - 10 = 20$ in state A, and of $137.5 - 120 - 10 = 7.5$ in state B. Part 3 of the table gives the full-information values of the firm's debt and equity when the investment policy and state are known but before the financing is completed.

Consider now the following (fully) revealing equilibrium. If state A prevails, the firm undertakes the following worst-case financing: it retires the debt at its

Efficient Financing 1235

Table 1

A Revealing Equilibrium for Two Possible States

1. Distribution of Earnings at Time 1

	Probability $= \frac{1}{2}$	Probability $= \frac{1}{2}$	Expected Value
With No Investment	100	140	120
With Investment of 10:			
In State A	100	200	150
In State B	80	195	137.5

2. Initial Capital Structure

100 face value of debt maturing at time 1; 40 shares of equity.

3. Full-Information Security Values at Time 0

	Debt	Equity	Total
With No Investment	100	20	120
With Investment of 10:			
In State A	100	40	140
In State B	90	37.5	127.5

4. Worst-Case Financings

In State A: Retire debt at 100
           Issue 110 shares at 1.00 per share
In State B: Issue 10.67 shares at 0.937 per share

full-information value of 100 and raises 110 to pay for this and the 10 of new investment by the sale of 110 new shares at the full-information value of 1.00 per share; the true, full-information, value of the original equity is then 40. If state B prevails, the firm raises the 10 of new investment by the sale of 10.67 new shares at their full-information value of 0.937 per share; the true, full-information, value of the original equity is then $(40/50.67) \times 47.5 = 37.5$. This equilibrium is possible only if there is no incentive for the firm to misrepresent the state that prevails at time 0 by adopting the financing we have proposed for the other state. If the true state is A, the firm has no incentive to adopt the simple equity financing since $(40/50.67) \times 50 = 39.47 < 40$. If the true state is B and the firm adopts the financing we have proposed for state A, the original shareholders will own 40/150 of the equity, which will be worth $(40/150) \times 137.5 = 36.67$. Since this is less than the 37.5 they obtain with the simple equity financing, there is no incentive for misrepresentation and the equilibrium is fully revealing.

This example, in which the firm repurchases debt when the better state prevails, is consistent with the finding of Masulis and Korwar that firms that use part of their equity issues to finance debt repurchases have higher abnormal returns than do firms that use the whole of the equity issue for capital expenditure.[12]

---

[12] −2.52 percent versus −3.75 percent for industrial firms. See Masulis and Korwar [14], Table 6. This difference is statistically significant on the usual criteria.

Example 2: For this example, we assume that the probability density of firm returns at time 1, $f(x; t)$, is given by

$$f(x; t) = \begin{cases} \pi, & x = X, \\ (1 - \pi)/d, & t \le x \le t + d \le X, \\ 0 & \text{otherwise,} \end{cases} \quad (11)$$

so that t, which is private information, orders the distributions by first-order stochastic dominance. The distribution may be thought of as resulting from a situation in which, if the firm experiences no adversity, the return is X, but there is a probability $(1 - \pi)$ that adversity will be experienced, and conditional on this, the returns are distributed uniformly on the interval $[t, t + d]$. The firm is assumed to have an outstanding bond issue with face value B_0 that matures at time 1. Financings, which take place at time 0, are restricted to equity issues combined with partial debt retirements, so that each possible financing may be described by a pair $z = (\alpha, B_1)$, where α is the fraction of the equity owned by the new shareholders and B_1 is the par value of the debt outstanding after the financing is completed.

Let $V(\alpha, B_1; t)$ denote the true, full-information, value of the financing. It is shown in the Appendix that, for $t \le B_1$,

$$V(\alpha, B_1; t) = \alpha\pi(X - B_1)$$
$$+ (1 - \pi) [\alpha(t + d - B_1)^2 + (B_0 - B_1) (B_0 + B_1 - 2t)]/2d$$
$$- B_0 + B_1, \quad (12)$$

and, for $t \ge B_1$,

$$V(\alpha, B_1; t) = \alpha\pi(X - B_1) + (1 - \pi)\alpha(t + d/2 - B_1)$$
$$- B_0 + B_1 + (1 - \pi)(B_0 - t)^2/2d. \quad (12')$$

For a revealing equilibrium, a firm of type t^i must find a worst-case financing (α^i, B^i) such that

$$V(\alpha^i, B_1^i; t^i) = K \quad (13)$$

and

$$t^i = \underset{\{t \in T\}}{\operatorname{argmin}} \, V(\alpha^i, B_1^i; t). \quad (14)$$

In order to find the worst-case financing for a given firm, equations (13) and (14) are solved for (α, B_1) under an assumption about the relative values of t and B_1 that dictates the use of (12) or (12$'$). If the resulting value of B_1 violates the initial assumption, the alternative assumption is made; if the new value of B_1 violates this assuption, then no worst-case financing exists.[13]

---

[13] It is quite possible that only a subset of firms will be able to find worst-case financings; the remaining firms will be valued at one of two values of t according to whether the intrinsic values of their financings are increasing or decreasing in t. These two values of t will depend upon investors' prior distributions over possible values of t. Investigation of such semipooling equilibria is beyond the scope of this paper.

Instead of solving directly for the worst-case financing for each value of t and K, we shall consider the inferences about t that investors will draw from a given financing (α, B_1).

We know from Theorem 1 that $\hat{t}(\alpha, B_1)$ in a value-revealing equilibrium is the type that minimizes the true, full-information, value $V(\alpha; B_1; t)$. Thus, setting the derivatives of (12) and (12') with respect to t equal to zero[14] and solving for $\hat{t}$, we have

$$\hat{t} = (B_0 - B_1)/\alpha + B_1 - d, \qquad \text{for } \alpha > (B_o - B_1)/d,$$

$$\hat{t} = B_0 - \alpha d, \qquad \text{for } \alpha \le (B_o - B_1)/d. \qquad (15)$$

Equation (15) implies

$$\partial \hat{t}/\partial \alpha < 0, \qquad (16)$$

$$\frac{\partial \hat{t}}{\partial B_1} \begin{array}{l} \le 0 \quad \text{for } \alpha > (B_o - B_1)/d, \\ = 0 \quad \text{for } \alpha \le (B_o - B_1)/d. \end{array} \qquad (17)$$

Equation (16) is consistent with empirical finding by Masulis and Korwar of a negative association between announcement returns and the proportional size of common stock offerings. As we have already mentioned, condition (17) is consistent with the finding, also by Masulis and Korwar, of a significantly smaller announcement-related price drop for firms that use part of their equity issues to retire debt than for those that make a simple equity issue; moreover, the signal of firm value, $\hat{t}$, is nondecreasing in the amount of debt retired for a given initial debt level.

It might appear that our results are inconsistent with the empirical findings of Masulis [13] that, for pure exchange offers, announcement returns are negatively associated with the amount of debt retired. However, it should be clear that our theory relates only to firms that wish to make a financing to raise capital. In a revealing equilibrium, there is nothing to be gained by a pure exchange offer since the true, full-information, values of the securities issued and retired must be identical. Thus, a theory of exchange offers must rely on considerations not encompassed by our model.

Table II shows, for a specific example, the value of t signalled and the amount of capital raised by different financings. Note that the marginal signalling effect of debt repurchases becomes zero once a threshold is reached and that, despite the negative signal associated with an increase in α, the amount of capital raised is increasing in α.

III. Mean-Preserving-Spread Orderings

In this section, we consider the possibility that the information asymmetry concerns the "riskiness" of the distribution of returns. While the riskiness of firm returns is not relevant for valuation of the firm itself, given our assumption

---

[14] It may be verified that the second-order conditions for a minimum in (12) and (12') are satisfied.

Table 2

Firm Type and Capital Raised under Alternative Financings in a
Revealing Equilibrium[a]

B_1	$\alpha = 0.1$	0.2	0.3	0.4	0.5	0.6
975	925, 34	800, 88	758,140	734,192	725,243	717,295
950	970, 12*	900, 72	817,128	775,182	750,235	733,289
925	970, −11*	940, 52*	875,113	813,171	775,227	750,282
900	970, −33*	940, 32*	910, 96*	850,158	800,217	767,274
850	970, −78*	940, 8*	910, 61*	880,128*	850,194	800,258
800	970,−123*	940,−48*	910, 26*	880, 98*	850,169*	820,238*
750	970,−168*	940,−88*	910, −9*	880, 68*	850,144*	820,218*

[a] Each cell contains $(t, V(\alpha, B_1; t))$. Initial data: $X = 2000$, $\pi = 0.5$, $d = 300$, $B_0 = 1000$.
* The remaining debt outstanding is riskless $(t > B_1)$.

that financial assets are valued at the expected value of their payoffs, it is relevant for separate valuation of the constituent securities of the firm's capital structure. Therefore, if a firm has pre-existing debt in its capital structure, resolution of the information asymmetry about the riskiness of its returns is necessary for the proper pricing of new security issues.

THEOREM 4: *If the firm's type, t, orders the family of possible probability density functions of the firm's total returns* $\{f(\cdot, t)\}$ *by mean-preserving spread, then a value-revealing equilibrium requires that the net payoff function chosen by firm t in the interior of* $\{T\}$ *be neither convex nor concave.*

Proof: If $y(x; z)$ were convex or concave, $V(z, t)$ would be monotone in t and no minimum would exist in (1) for interior values of t.[15]   Q.E.D.

The intuition underlying this theorem is analogous to that of Theorem 3. If the payoff function were, say, convex and the probability distributions differed only in, say, the variance, the financing would have least value if made by the lowest variance firm. In a revealing equilibrium, investors will always expect this to be the firm that made the financing; therefore, it cannot be made by any other firm if the equilibrium is indeed to be revealing.

Examples of financings that may lead to a revealing equilibrium for a mean-preserving spread ordering include issues of convertible bonds, junior bonds, or packages of bonds and warrants. We shall illustrate the possibility of achieving a revealing equilibrium when firm returns are ordered by mean-preserving spread by means of an example in which the firm issues a subordinated convertible bond. Such securities are commonly issued, yet there is no widely accepted explanation for their use.[16]

Example 3: For this example, we assume that the probability density of firm returns at time 1 is uniform on the interval $(m - t, m + t)$. At time 0, when a

[15] Note that, if the private information related to a second-degree stochastic-dominance ordering were only upward-sloping concave or downward-sloping convex, payoff functions could be excluded from a revealing equilibrium a priori.

[16] Green [9] argues that convertibles may reduce agency costs.

Efficient Financing 1239

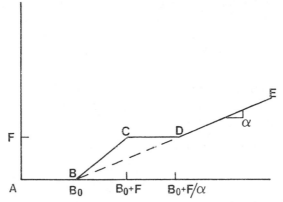

Figure 3. Payoff function for a subordinated convertible bond. B_0, face value senior debt; F, face value of convertible bond; α, conversion ratio.

financing must be made, m is common knowledge, but t, which orders the distributions by mean-preserving spread, is private information to the firm. The firm is assumed to have an outstanding bond issue with face value B_0 that matures at time 1. Financings are restricted to subordinated convertible bonds so that each possible financing may be described by a pair $z \equiv (\alpha, F)$, where F is the face value of the covertible and α is the fraction of the firm's equity into which it is convertible. The payoff function for the convertible is marked $ABCDE$ in Figure 3.

Inspection of Figure 3 reveals that a necessary condition for the true, full-information, value of the convertible to achieve a minimum for an interior value of t is that there be a positive probability that the subordinated convertible bond will be converted at time 1:

$$t \geq B_0 - m + F/\alpha. \tag{18}$$

We assume that it is common knowledge that the outstanding bond is not riskless: $t \geq m - B_0$. Then the full-information value of the convertible, $V(\alpha, F; t)$ is given by

$$V(\alpha, F; t) = \{F^2(1 - \alpha)/\alpha + \alpha(m + t - B_0)^2\}/4t. \tag{19}$$

A revealing equilibrium requires that

$$\min_{\{t \in T\}} V(\alpha, F; t) = K, \tag{20}$$

where K is the amount of capital to be raised. Using (19), the first-order condition from (20)[17] implies that, under the worst-case financing for a firm of type t, the bond is convertible into a fraction $\alpha(t)$ of the equity where

$$\alpha(t) = 2K/(m + t - B_0). \tag{21}$$

Thus, a revealing equilibrium is possible only if the set, T, of possible firm types is such that $t > 2K + m - B_0$ for $t \in T$.

---

[17] It may be verified that the second-order conditions for a minimum are satisfied.

Solving (19) and (20) for $F(t)$, the face value of the bond under the worst-case financing is given by

$$F(t) = \sqrt{\frac{\alpha}{1 - \alpha} [4Kt - \alpha(m + t - B_0)^2]}, \tag{22}$$

it being understood that the terms of the financing satisfy condition (18).

To find $\hat{t}(\alpha, F)$, the firm type that investors infer from the financing (α, F), we eliminate K between (21) and (22) to obtain

$$\hat{t}(\alpha, T) = \sqrt{(m - B_0)^2 + F^2(1 - \alpha)/\alpha^2}. \tag{23}$$

This implies for $\alpha < 1$ that

$$\partial\hat{t}/\partial\alpha < 0, \quad \partial\hat{t}/\partial F > 0. \tag{24}$$

Since the payoff on equity is a convex function of the firm return, this model predicts that the announcement-period stock returns will be negatively associated with the conversion ratio, α, and positively associated with the convertible-debt par value, F. While there is as yet no formal test of this prediction, it is interesting to note that Dann and Mikkelson [6] report a positive association between the increase in the book debt ratio and the stock announcement-period returns for convertible debt issues.[18]

IV. Multiparameter Private Information and the Prospects for Financial Efficiency

We have seen that, when the information asymmetry can be described in terms of a single parameter, it may nevertheless be possible for each firm type to make a worst-case financing so that new financings are properly priced and Pareto efficiency is achieved. When the information asymmetry concerns more than one parameter of the probability distribution of future earnings, the principles remain the same; full Pareto efficiency and correct pricing will follow if a worst-case financing can be constructed for each firm type.

However, when private information is characterized by several parameters, the aggregate net payoff function of a worst-case financing satisfying (9) becomes considerably more complex. For example, if the earnings of the firm follow a uniform distribution, both parameters of which are private information, then it can be shown that the aggregate net payoff function of the worst-case financing must have a section with a shape similar to that of a capital W. Such a payoff function could result, for example, from a financing in which one convertible bond was replaced by another and simultaneously one warrant issue was replaced by another.

Although such financings are possible, they do not seem to correspond with what we observe in practice. There are several alternative conclusions that could

---

[18] The twenty issues with the largest increase in the debt ratio were associated with announcement-period stock returns of -1.82 percent. The corresponding figure for the twenty issues with the lowest increase was -2.85 percent. See Dann and Mikkelson [6], Table 10.

be drawn from this. First, it is possible that multiparameter private information of the type we describe is rare. Second, it may be that we must broaden our definition of financings if the full range of signalling possibilities is to be understood. For example, firms enter into long-term contracts with customers and suppliers, and these contracts often contain complex provisions for setting prices and quantities that, taken in conjunction with the contracts agreed to with capital suppliers, may serve to reveal the private information.[19] Such long-term supply contracts often play an integral role in the financing of natural-resource projects.

A third possibility is that our assumed objective function of maximizing the true, full-information, value of the outstanding shares is not the appropriate one. An obvious alternative assumption that is commonly employed is that the managers of the firm act to maximize their own pecuniary and nonpecuniary rewards. Vermaelen [20] uses this assumption as the basis for a signalling model of the stock-repurchase decision. The analytical advantage of this assumption is that contracts for management remuneration are often highly complex and therefore possess the richness necessary to reveal multiparameter private information. However, in view of the disparate interests of different members of management and the board of directors, it is by no means clear that corporate financings can be better understood in terms of some composite management utility function than in terms of the more traditional objective of share-price maximization, and, for this reason, we have chosen to explore the implications of the classical assumption of value maximization.

V. Conclusion

In this paper, we have characterized the conditions under which the adverse-selection problem that may prevent a firm from issuing securities to finance an otherwise profitable investment may be costlessly overcome by an appropriate choice of financing strategy. The conditions require a certain compatibility between the nature of the information asymmetry and the set of financing strategies available to the firm, which may depend upon its pre-existing capital structure. What is required is that the economic value of the net claim issued by the firm take on its lowest possible value when issued by that firm; the firm has to be the worst possible issuer of that claim from the viewpoint of the investor. This requirement imposes conditions on the function relating the payoff on the net claim to the future earnings of the firm; for example, if the information asymmetry is about the mean of the earnings distribution, the payoff function must be V-shaped.

The conditions on the net payoff function required for a revealing equilibrium are not, in general, sufficient to yield a unique financing strategy; on the other hand, depending on the nature of the information asymmetry and the firm's prior capital structure, there may exist no strategy that satisfies the conditions. As examples of financings that resolve particular types of information asymmetry,

---

[19] However, unless the provisions of contacts with customers and suppliers are public information, investors will not be able to infer the firm's private information.

we considered equity issues combined with debt retirements, as well as junior convertible bond issues. For these financings, our theory provides a consistent rationale for the stock price reactions that have been found to be associated with their announcement.

Appendix

We assume that $t \leq B_0 \leq t + d$. The full-information discount from face value of the original debt is $(1 - \pi)(B_0 - t)^2/2d$. After the debt repurchase, the full-information value of the remaining debt is $B_1 - (1 - \pi)(B_1 - t)^2/2d$ if $t < B_1$ and B_1 otherwise. If $t < B_1$, the full-information value of the equity issue is $\alpha\pi(X - B_1) + (1 - \pi)\alpha[t + d - B_1]^2/2d$. The value of the debt repurchase is the difference between the discounted value of the original debt and the full-information value of the debt remaining after the repurchase. Combining these expressions for the equity issue and the debt repurchase yields (12). If $t \geq B_1$, the full-information value of the equity issue is $\alpha\pi(X - B_1) + (1 - \pi)\alpha[t + d/2 - B_1]$. Combining this with the full-information value of the debt repurchase yields (12').

REFERENCES

1. G. Akerlof. "The Market for Lemons: Qualitative Uncertainty and the Market Mechanism." *Quarterly Journal of Economics* 84 (August 1970), 488–500.
2. P. Asquith and D. W. Mullins. "Equity Issues and Offering Dilution." *Journal of Financial Economics* 15 (January/February 1986), 61–89.
3. F. Black and M. Scholes. "The Pricing of Options and Corporate Liabilities." *Journal of Political Economy* 81 (May/June 1973), 637–54.
4. G. Constantinides and B. Grundy. "Optimal Investment with Stock Repurchase and Financings as Signals." Mimeo, 1986.
5. J. Cox and S. Ross. "The Valuation of Options for Alternative Stochastic Processes." *Journal of Financial Economics* 3 (January/March 1976), 145–66.
6. L. Y. Dann and W. H. Mikkelson. "Convertible Debt Issuance, Capital Structure Change and Financing Related Information: Some New Evidence." *Journal of Financial Economics* 13 (June 1984), 157–86.
7. B. E. Eckbo. "Valuation Effects of Corporate Debt Offerings." *Journal of Financial Economics* 15 (January/February 1986), 119–52.
8. G. A. Feltham and P. Christianson. "The Value of Firm Specific Information in Efficient Capital Markts." Mimeo, 1986.
9. R. Green. "Investment Incentives, Debt, and Warrants." *Journal of Financial Economics* 13 (March 1984), 115–36.
10. J. Harrison and D. Kreps. "Martingales and Arbitrage in Multiperiod Securities Markets." *Journal of Economic Theory* 20 (June 1979), 381–408.
11. R. Heinkel. "A Theory of Capital Structure Relevance under Imperfect Information." *Journal of Finance* 37 (December 1982) 1141–50.
12. J. Ingersoll. "A Contingent-Claims Valuation of Convertible Securities." *Journal of Financial Economics* 4 (May 1977), 289–321.
13. R. W. Masulis. "The Impact of Capital Structure Change on Firm Value: Some Estimates." *Journal of Finance* 38 (March 1983), 107–26.
14. —— and A. N. Korwar. "Seasoned Equity Offerings: An Empirical Investigation." *Journal of Financial Economics* 15 (January/February 1986), 91–118.
15. W. H. Mikkelson and M. M. Partch. "Valuation Effects of Security Offerings and the Issuance Process." *Journal of Financial Economics* 15 (January/February 1986), 31–60.

16. M. Miller and K. Rock. "Dividend Policy under Asymmetric Information." *Journal of Finance* 40 (September 1985), 1031–51.

17. S. C. Myers and N. Majluf. "Corporate Financing and Investment Decisions When Firms Have Information That Investors Do Not Have." *Journal of Financial Economics* 13 (June 1984), 187–221.

18. C. W. Smith. "Investment Banking and the Capital Acquisition Process." *Journal of Financial Economics* 15 (January/February 1986), 3–30.

19. J. Stiglitz. "On the Irrelevance of Corporate Financial Policy." *American Economic Review* 63 (June 1981), 851–66.

20. T. Vermaelen. "Common Stock Repurchases and Market Signalling: An Empirical Study." *Journal of Financial Economics* 9 (June 1981), 139–83.

7

THE JOURNAL OF FINANCE • VOL. XLIII, NO. 5 • DECEMBER 1988

Vendor Financing

MICHAEL J. BRENNAN, VOJISLAV MAKSIMOVIC, and JOSEF ZECHNER*

ABSTRACT

This paper shows that, even in the presence of a perfectly competitive banking industry, it is optimal for firms with market power to engage in vendor financing if credit customers have lower reservation prices than cash customers or if adverse selection makes it infeasible to write credit contracts that separate customers according to their credit risk. We analyze how the advantage of vendor financing depends on the relative size of the cash and credit markets, the heterogeneity of credit customers, and the number of firms in the industry.

IN ADDITION TO THE pure financial intermediation that is provided by banks and other specialized financial institutions, intermediary services are also provided by sellers of goods, such as firms in the automobile industry, that borrow in order to provide long-term credit to the purchasers of their products. We refer to this form of financial intermediation, performed by goods sellers, as vendor financing. While there is now an extensive literature concerned with the role of pure financial intermediaries,[1] the conjunction of financial intermediation with the sale of goods remains largely unexplored. In this paper, we provide a theory of vendor financing that is quite distinct from recent theories of pure financial intermediation and that explains both why firms offer vendor financing and why the financing may be below market rates.

Classical models of financial and product markets without transactions costs or informational asymmetries leave no room for financial intermediation, so that it is necessary to relax one or more of the classical assumptions in order to provide a role for financial intermediaries. Thus, Townsend [12, 13] develops a model in which transactions costs in financial markets provide a reason for the development of intermediaries. More recent models, such as those of Diamond [2] and Ramakrishnan and Thakor [10], which follow from the early work of Leland and Pyle [8], emphasize the information-gathering role of financial intermediaries and show that the cost of delegating the information gathering is reduced by the diversification possible in the intermediary. In Boyd and Prescott [1], the emphasis is also on transaction gathering although the "financial intermediary coalitions" are more closely related to cooperatives than to traditional forms of financial intermediation; they are formed to overcome problems of

* Brennan is from Graduate School of Management, University of California, Los Angeles. Maksimovic and Zechner are from Faculty of Commerce and Business Administration, University of British Columbia. We would like to thank James Brander, Rob Heinkel, Gordon Sick, Joseph Williams, an anonymous referee, and the participants of the UBC Finance Workshop for their comments. We are responsible for all remaining errors.

[1] Diamond [3] provides a useful survey.

adverse selection in an environment in which information about investment projects is a public good that may be acquired at private expense. In a somewhat different vein, Diamond and Dybvig [4] construct a model of the banking firm in which the primary focus is on the bank as a provider of liquidity services.

In contrast to the foregoing, the model of vendor financing that we present here relies primarily on lack of competition in the product market, which, possibly in conjunction with adverse-selection problems, makes price discrimination potentially profitable. Vendor financing makes it possible to price discriminate between cash and credit customers, and this will be advantageous whenever the elasticity of demand of cash customers exceeds that of credit customers or whenever cash customers' reservation prices are systematically higher than those of credit customers. In Section I, we present a simple model in which a monopolist selling to cash and credit customers finds it profitable to price discriminate in favor of credit customers by setting credit terms that are attractive to them but not to the cash customers. In this model, the incentive to price discriminate is created by exogenous differences in the reservation prices of cash and credit customers. In Section II, we show that, even when there is no systematic difference between the reservation prices of cash and credit customers, adverse selection in the credit market is sufficient to provide the incentive for price discrimination and hence for vendor financing. Section III relaxes the assumption of a monopolistic goods market. We show that vendor financing may also arise in an oligopolistic setting and demonstrate its role as a strategic instrument. In Section IV, we contrast our theory with earlier explanations of trade credit and argue that our theory is in broad agreement with the available empirical evidence.

I. Homogeneous Credit Customers

Consider a company that manufactures tractors for sale to farmers. The tractors that are produced at a constant marginal cost, v, may be purchased by the farmers either for cash or on credit. Credit is offered by a competitive banking system, and we shall contrast the system in which banks are the only source of credit with that in which credit is also offered by the company itself or, equivalently, by a captive finance subsidiary. We assume that there are two classes of farmers, rich and poor, and that class membership is public information. Rich farmers have sufficient cash to purchase a tractor outright if they wish; alternatively, they may purchase on credit. However, we assume that, in contrast with the poor farmers, the rich farmers have sufficient other assets that there is a zero probability that they will default on a credit contract. Poor farmers, on the other hand, have no immediate cash,[2] and, therefore, if they are to purchase the tractor, they must use credit that is provided either by the banking system or by the vendor. Moreover, the only collateral that poor farmers can pledge for their loans is the return on the tractor itself. Both types of farmers have a demand for only a single tractor.

---

[2] This assumption is made for simplicity; all that is important is that the poor farmers have to finance at least a part of the purchase.

Each tractor lasts for one period and yields a return of $R_i + h$ or $R_i - h$ with equal probability for $i = \{r, p\}$, where r and p refer to the rich and poor farmers, respectively. Both rich and poor farmers are risk neutral, and there is no discounting, so that the reservation price for rich farmers is R_r and for poor farmers is R_p. The tractors are less productive in the hands of the poor farmers, so that $R_r > R_p$. The variable cost, v, is assumed to be less than R_p. There are N_r rich farmers and N_p poor farmers.

The competitive banking system faces a perfectly elastic supply of funds at an exogenously determined interest rate, which we take as zero. Then, since class membership is public information, competition will force the banks to charge a zero interest rate on their loans to the rich farmers who never default. Let $r(C)$ denote the interest rate charged by the banks to poor farmers when the manufacturer charges a cash price C for each tractor and there is no vendor financing.

The banks must break even on their loans, so that the rate they must charge to the poor farmers is given by

$$r(C) = \begin{cases} 0 & \text{if } C \le R_p - h, \\ 1 - (R_p - h)/C & \text{if } R_p > C > R_p - h, \end{cases} \tag{1}$$

since, in the bad state, the bank will collect only the return from the tractor if $C > R_p - h$.

A necessary condition for the poor farmers to purchase a tractor is that there must be a positive expected net return for them after loan repayments; therefore, $r(C)$ must satisfy

$$C(1 + r) \le R_p + h. \tag{2}$$

Substituting for $r(C)$ from equation (1), a necessary and sufficient condition for the poor farmers to purchase is that $C \le R_p$. Similarly, rich farmers will purchase if and only if $C \le R_r$.

Consider the profit opportunities of a tractor manufacturer who does no financing but relies on the banking sector to provide credit to the poor farmers. If the manufacturer sets $C = R_p$, he or she will sell to both classes of farmers, whereas, if the manufacturer sets $C = R_r$, he or she will sell only to the rich farmers. Assume that the relative number of members of the two classes and their reservation prices are such that it is optimal to sell to both rich and poor farmers. Then the tractor manufacturer's profit, $\pi(C)$, is given by

$$\pi(C) = (N_p + N_r)(R_p - v). \tag{3}$$

Now suppose that the manufacturer offers vendor financing and competes with the banks by offering credit at the rate r^*. His or her profit now depends on both the price of the tractor and the interest rate offered. Assuming that it is optimal to sell to both classes of farmers, the manufacturer's expected profit is $\pi(C, r^*)$ $= N_r(C - v) + (N_p/2)(C(1 + r^*) + R_p - h - 2v).$[3] The tractor manufacturer's

---

[3] The manufacturer will find it optimal to sell to both the rich and the poor farmers if $R_r \le$ $R_p + h + \dfrac{N_p}{N_r}(R_p - v).$

optimization problem can be written as

$$\max_{C, r^*} \pi(C, r^*),\tag{4}$$

subject to

$$C(1 + r^*) \le R_p + h,\tag{5}$$

$$C \le R_r,\tag{6}$$

and

$$r^* \ge 0.\tag{7}$$

Condition (5) guarantees that the poor farmers will purchase, and (6) is the corresponding condition for rich farmers. Condition (7) ensures that the manufacturer does not charge an interest rate below the risk-free rate of return, which is assumed to be zero. If the manufacturer did charge a negative interest rate, rich farmers would also seek vendor financing, so that a negative interest rate is equivalent to a reduction in the cash price, C.[4] There are two cases to consider according to whether the non-negative interest rate restriction is binding:

Case A: $R_r \le R_p + h$. Nonbinding interest rate constraint.

It may be verified that the optimal strategy is to set $C = R_r$ and to charge the highest interest rate consistent with condition (5): $r^*(R_r) = (R_p + h)/R_r - 1$. Then the manufacturers' total expected profit $\pi(R_r, r^*)$ is given by

$$\pi(R_r, r^*) = N_r[R_r - v] + N_p[R_p - v].\tag{8}$$

It is evident in this case that the manufacturer is able to extract all of the farmers' surplus. Note that, although the manufacturer is charging a positive contractual interest rate, his or her expected rate of return on the vendor financing is $R_p/R_r - 1 < 0$; therefore, there is no incentive for the banks to compete for this business since the manufacturer is offering subsidized financing as a way of discriminating in favor of the poor farmers. On the other hand, the positive contractual interest rate is sufficient to deter the rich farmers from applying for credit from the manufacturer.

Case B: $R_r > R_p + h$. Binding interest rate constraint.

In this case, it is not possible to simultaneously sell to the rich farmers at their reservation price and sell to the poor farmers without charging the latter a negative interest rate, which, we here argued, is tantamount to a reduction in the cash price. The optimal price and interest rate are given by $C = R_p + h$, $r^* = 0$. Under this policy, the firm extracts all of the surplus from the poor farmers, and its profit is given by

$$\pi(R_p + h, 0) = N_r[R_p + h - v] + N_p[R_p - v].\tag{9}$$

---

[4] Note that a negative interest rate will benefit rich farmers more than poor ones, as long as there is any probability that the latter will default.

Again, the banks have no incentive to compete with the manufacturer in offering credit to the poor farmers since the expected rate of return on vendor financing is $R_p/(R_p + h) - 1 < 0$.

Contrast the manufacturer's profit with vendor financing, as given by expressions (8) and (9), with his or her profit without vendor financing, which is given by expression (3). Whether or not the non-negativity constraint on the contractual interest rate is binding, manufacturer's profit with vendor financing strictly dominates the profit without vendor financing, so that in this context there is a role for vendor financing.

It has been suggested to us that the price discrimination accomplished by vendor financing might also be achieved by subsidizing bank loans to customers. In fact, this is being done by some manufacturers.[5] This is equivalent to vendor financing if the manufacturer can restrict the subsidy to loans made to poor farmers. However, this might well be difficult to enforce, for, to the extent that rich farmers have ongoing customer relationships with their banks, there will be scope for the banks to claim the subsidy on loans to rich farmers, also charging them the same rates as the poor farmers, but then rebating the interest charge and a portion of the subsidy through other transactions.

The model in this section has relied on exogenously specified differences in the reservation prices of rich and poor farmers to demonstrate a potential role for vendor financing. In the following section, we shall demonstrate that vendor financing may be optimal, even if rich and poor farmers are identical, if there is a problem of adverse selection in the credit market.

II. Heterogeneous Credit Customers

Assume now that $R_p = R_r = R$, so that the return on the tractor is $R + h$ or $R - h$, with equal probability. However, in contrast to the case considered in the previous section, we now assume that the risk parameter, h, varies across farmers and, for both classes of farmers, is uniformly distributed on the interval $(\underline{h}, \overline{h})$. The risk parameter, h, is known by the farmer but cannot be observed by the lender.

A rich farmer will purchase a tractor as long as the cash price, C, is less than R, and a poor farmer with risk parameter h_i will purchase on credit as long as $C(1 + r) \leq R + h_i$. Let h^* denote the lowest level of risk of a poor farmer who purchases on credit. Then

$$h^* = C(1 + r) - R. \tag{10}$$

Note that credit sales are made to the high-risk farmers and that the average risk of credit customers increases with both the cash price and the loan rate. To analyze the manufacturer's optimization problem in the absence of vendor financing, consider first the loan rate $r(C)$, which will be set by the competitive banking system when the cash price is C. Assuming that $C(1 + r) > R - h_i$, the profit on a loan to farmer i is $\{R - h_i + C(1 + r)\}/2 - C$.

---

[5] See *Business Week*, August 26, 1986, p. 77.

Then, since only farmers with $h > h^*$ take loans, the expected profit on a bank loan is

$$\{R - (h^* + \bar{h})/2 + C(1 + r)\}/2 - C.$$

Setting this expression equal to zero and substituting for h^* from equation (10), the competitive-loan rate is given by

$$r(C) = 3 + (\bar{h} - 3R)/C. \tag{11}$$

Substituting for the loan rate from equation (11) in equation (10), the lowest risk level of a poor farmer who purchases is $h^* = \bar{h} - 4(R - C)$; then the number of tractors sold to poor farmers, q_p, is given by

$$q_p(C) = 4(R - C)N_p/d, \tag{12}$$

where $d = \bar{h} - \underline{h}$. Thus, in the absence of vendor financing, the problem of the tractor manufacturer may be written as

$$\max_{C} \pi(C) = (N_r + q_p(C))(C - v), \tag{13}$$

subject to

$$C \le R. \tag{14}$$

Differentiating (13) with respect to C and using equations (12) and (14), the expression for C^*, the optimal price, depends on whether $z + v$ is greater or less than R, where $z = N_r d/4N_p$.

Case A: $z + v < R$. Tractors bought by rich and poor farmers.

In this case, the optimal cash price charged is $C^* = (z + v + R)/2$, and the profit realized by the manufacturer is

$$\pi(C^*) = \left[\frac{N_r}{2} + \frac{N_p}{d}(R - v - z)\right][R - v + z]. \tag{15}$$

It is apparent from the form of the objective function (13) that, since $C^* < R$, sales are made to both rich and poor farmers.[6]

Case B: $z + v > R$. Tractors bought by rich farmers only.

In this case, the optimal price is $C^* = R$, and

$$\pi(C^*) = N_r(R - v). \tag{15a}$$

No sales are made to the poor farmers, for, when the cash price is R, there is no loan rate at which the banks can break even on their sales to credit customers. Thus, the credit market collapses due to the adverse-selection problem.

Consider now the role of vendor financing. The problem of the manufacturer who offers vendor financing is most easily analyzed by reference to equation (13). Thus, let C_1 denote the price charged to the cash customers, and let C_2 denote

---

[6] It can be verified that, if $z + v < R$, all poor farmers who purchase tractors also default in the bad state.

the internal transfer price at which tractors are sold to a captive finance subsidiary that just breaks even on its loans. The situation is then precisely as described above except that the manufacturer is able to charge a lower price to the poor farmers by setting the internal transfer price below the cash market price, so that the manufacturer's profit becomes[7]

$$\pi(C_1, C_2) = N_r(C_1 - v) + q_p(C_2 - v).$$

The maximization can now be written as

$$\max_{C_1, C_2} \pi(C_1, C_2) \tag{13a}$$

subject to

$$C_1 \le R, \tag{14a}$$

$$4C_2 + \bar{h} - 3R \ge C_1, \tag{16}$$

and

$$C_2 \le C_1. \tag{17}$$

Constraint (16) serves to ensure that the quoted credit price $C_2(1 + r)$ is not less than the cash price, for this would cause the rich farmers also to buy on credit;[8] constraint (17) ensures that the effective credit price is no greater than the cash price, so that there is no incentive for the banks to offer better credit terms than the captive finance company. The optimal prices to charge in the two markets are then $C_1^* = R$ and $C_2^* = (R + v)/2$.

These prices satisfy constraints (14a) and (17); constraint (16) also will be satisfied provided that $R < v + \bar{h}/2$, and, to avoid unnecessary complexity, we assume that this condition is met. Then the expected profit of the manufacturer with vendor financing is

$$\pi(C_1, C_2) = N_r(r - v) + N_p(R - v)^2/d. \tag{15b}$$

Comparing expression (15b) with the corresponding expressions for the profit in the absence of vendor financing, (15) and (15a), we see that the profit gained from vendor financing, g, is

$$g = \begin{cases} N_p(R - v)^2/d & \text{if } z + v \ge R, \\ N_r^2 d/16N_p & \text{otherwise.} \end{cases} \tag{18}$$

If $z + v \ge R$, vendor financing opens the market to poor farmers who had previously not been able to buy tractors; in the other case, it makes it possible for the manufacturer to extract all the rents from the rich farmers while still selling to poor farmers.

---

[7] It is assumed that manufacturers can legally set internal transfer prices below the cash market price. Alternatively, the manufacturer can set transfer prices equal to the market price and make losses on their financing operations.

[8] This constraint is obtained by substituting for $r(C)$ from equation (11) in the condition $C_2(1 + r) > C_1$.

Inspection of equation (15b) reveals that the gain from forming a captive is always positive, and the following comparative-static results can be verified for $z + v \geq R$:

$$(\partial g/\partial v) < 0;$$

$$(\partial g/\partial N_r) > 0;$$

$$(\partial g/\partial N_p) > 0;$$

$$(\partial g/\partial h) < 0.$$

Higher variable costs decrease the optimal quantity of tractors sold to the poor farmers and, therefore, if there is no vendor financing, increase the resulting equilibrium price. This reduces the advantage from price discrimination. Similarly, as the number of farmers in either the cash market or the credit market increases, it becomes more profitable to service the credit market by providing the vendor financing. Finally, as h increases, i.e., as the adverse-selection problem becomes more severe, it becomes less profitable to sell to credit customers with or without vendor financing, and the absolute advantage from vendor financing declines.

III. Vendor Financing and Market Structure

In the previous section, it was shown that the existence of adverse selection in the credit market makes it advantageous for a monopolist to offer vendor financing, even though customers in the cash and credit markets are identical except for their credit risk. In this section, we relax the assumption of monopoly and evaluate the gains from vendor financing in an industry in which rival firms compete for market share. We demonstrate how vendor financing can affect the ability of the firms to exploit product-market opportunities in an oligopolistic setting by increasing their market power. Counterintuitively, in some cases all the firms can extract greater rents if only some of them offer vendor financing. The characteristics of farmers are as described in the previous section. Thus, there is adverse selection in the credit market.

We restrict our attention to a duopoly and compare the profits with and without vendor financing.[9] Each firm is assumed to set its production to maximize profits, given the production level of its rival, so that, in equilibrium, each firm's choice of production level is the best response to its rival's choice of production level.[10] We begin with the case in which sales to the poor farmers are financed by competitive banks. As before, banks realize revenue either from the repayment of loans or, in the case of bankruptcy, from the return of the tractor. Since the banks' expected profits are zero, their expected revenue curve is also the demand curve of poor farmers. Equation (12) corresponds to the following inverse demand curve for poor farmers:

$$C = R - q_p d/4N_p. \tag{19}$$

[9] In the Appendix, we also analyze the case of an oligopoly with n firms.
[10] Market equilibrium in oligopolies is discussed in Friedman [5].

The total demand for tractors is obtained by aggregating the demand curves of rich and poor farmers. Let q be the total quantity of tractors sold. The aggregated inverse demand curve for both rich and poor farmers is then

$$C = \begin{cases} R & \text{if } q < N_r, \\ R - (q - N_r)d/4N_p & \text{otherwise.} \end{cases} \quad (20)$$

We assume that it is optimal for the duopolists to sell to at least some poor farmers, so that $q > N_r$. This will be the case if

$$N_r < 2(R - v)N_p/d. \quad (21)$$

Then the optimal production level of firm i, q^{i*}, is given by

$$q^{i*} = \arg \max_{q^i} \{q^i(a - v - b(q^i + q^{j*}))\}, \quad i \neq j,$$

where $a = R + N_r d/4N_p$, $b = d/4N_p$, and q^{j*} is the equilibrium output of the rival firm. In equilibrium, each firm produces $q^* = (a - v)/3b$. The corresponding equilibrium price is given by $C = (a + 2v)/3$, and profit of each firm is

$$\pi = (a - v)^2/9b. \quad (22)$$

We shall now compare the profits in this base case with profits attainable when one or both firms offer vendor financing. We assume that firms have already made their decisions on whether to engage in vendor financing in the current period, and we determine their equilibrium outputs and profits.[11]

Case A: One firm offers vendor financing.

Consider the case in which one firm, firm f, offers vendor financing and its rival, firm c, bills only for cash. Firm f can, by varying the credit terms, decide whether to sell the marginal unit of output to a rich or to a poor farmer. Firm c can only choose its total output. We first show that vendor financing can only be advantageous to firm f if, in equilibrium, banks find it unprofitable to extend credit to poor farmers.

Let the number of tractors sold by firm f to rich and poor farmers be q_r^f and q_p^f, respectively, and the total number sold by firm c be q^c. The number of tractors financed by banks and bought by poor farmers is $q^b = q_r^f + q^c + N_r$. The expected profits of the two firms are

$$\pi^f = q_r^f[C - v] + q_p^f[R - d[q_p^f + q^b]/4N_p - v] \quad (23a)$$

and

$$\pi^c = q^c[C - v]. \quad (23b)$$

---

[11] Engaging in vendor financing usually involves the setting up of financial captives and changes in marketing strategy. The decision on whether to engage in vendor financing is thus costly to reverse in the short run. The analysis can be formalized if we view duopolists as playing a two-stage game. The equilibria discussed in Section III can be interpreted as subgame perfect Nash equilibria of that game. See Kreps and Scheinkman [7] for such an analysis in another context.

If the banks offer credit, competition ensures that the average revenue realized on a loan equals the cash price of a tractor, so that, using equation (20),

$$C = R - d[q_p^f + q_r^f + q^c - N_r]/4N_p. \tag{24}$$

Then, substituting for c from (24) in (23a) and (23b), we obtain

$$\pi^f = q^f[R + N_r d/4N_p - d[q^f + q^c]/4N_p - v] \tag{25a}$$

and

$$\pi^c = q^c[R + N_r d/4N_p - d[q^f + q^c]/4N_p - v], \tag{25b}$$

where $q^f \equiv q_p^f + q_r^f$ is the total sales by firm c.

Since the two expressions are identical, firm f does not derive any benefit from vendor financing. The reason for this is that prices in the cash and credit markets are linked by the banks' zero-profit condition (24), so that the expected revenue from sale to a rich or a poor farmer is equalized, and there is no possibility of segmenting the markets.

This does not rule out the existence of other equilibria in which firm f sells to the poor farmers on credit but the banks do not offer loans. For this to be possible, firm f must leave firm c a sufficiently large share of the sales to rich farmers so that it is optimal for the latter to produce for that market only and not to lower the cash price enough for it to be feasible for the banks to finance sales to poor farmers. Under these conditions, firm f is able to act as a monopolist in the poor-farmer market. This is optimal for the industry taken as a whole since the reduction of competition in the poor-farmer market will increase the economic rents that may be earned there. To investigate this possibility, we derive the minimum market share of the rich-farmer market that will induce firm c to forego sales to poor farmers by maintaining the cash price above the banks' break-even level. Firm c can choose between a high-price, low-output policy in which the banks do not offer credit to poor farmers and a low-price, high-output policy in which (24) is satisfied and the banks finance purchases by poor farmers.

If the banks do not finance purchases by poor farmers, firm c's output will be purchased only by rich farmers and its profit will be

$$\pi^c = (N_r - q_r^f)(R - v). \tag{26a}$$

Alternatively, firm c can decide to produce enough to drive down the price to a level at which banks will find it profitable to finance purchases by poor farmers. If it does so, it will take firm f's output of $(q_p^f + q_r^f)$ as given and will produce the quantity that is its best response to that output, or $(a - v - b(q_p^f + q_r^f))/2b$. Firm c's profit from producing optimally when the price is sufficiently low for the banks to break even on their loans is

$$\pi^c = (a - v - b(q_p^f + q_r^f))^2/4b. \tag{26b}$$

Hence, firm c confines itself to the low-output policy that leaves the credit market to firm f if

$$(N_r - q_r^f)(R - v) > (a - v - b(q_p^f + q_r^f))^2/4b. \tag{27}$$

Substituting the monopoly output in the credit market for q_p^f, inequality (27) can be solved for q_r^f (and therefore for $q^c = N_r - q_r^f$):

$$q^c \geq 4N_p(R - v)/d(\tfrac{3}{2} - \sqrt{2}). \tag{28}$$

If condition (28) is satisfied, firm c has no incentive to follow the high-output policy. It produces q^c tractors and sells to rich farmers at the price R. Firm f sells $N_r - q_r^c$ tractors for cash to rich farmers and the monopoly quantity, $(R - v)/2b$, on credit, to poor farmers. The expected revenue per tractor sold to a poor farmer is $(R + v)/2$. The joint profits of the two firms are given by

$$\pi^c + \pi^f = N_r(R - v) + N_p \frac{(R - v)^2}{d}. \tag{29}$$

The total industry gain from offering vendor financing is the difference between the profit given by equation (29) and twice the profit of a duopolist given by equation (22):

$$g = \frac{7}{9} N_r(R - v) + \frac{N_p}{9d}(R - v)^2 - \frac{dN_r^2}{36N_p}. \tag{30}$$

For the relevant range of N_r, defined by inequality (21), g is positive. Comparing expression (30) with expression (18), it can be verified that the total gain from vendor financing is greater in the duopolistic market than in the monopolistic market in Section II. The comparative-static results derived from equation (18) also hold for equation (30).

Case B: Both firms offer vendor financing.

In this case, both firms will find it optimal to treat the rich and poor farmers as distinct markets and to set production levels for each market separately. In the symmetric Nash equilibrium, each firm will produce $N_r/2$ units for sale to rich farmers and $(\bar{R} - v)4N_p/3d$ for the poor farmers. The equilibrium cash price, C_1, is equal to R, and the expected revenue from a sale to a poor farmer is $(R + 2v)/3$.[12] Since v is less than R, the "effective" price charged to poor farmers is again less than the cash price, C_1. Each firm's expected profit will be

$$\pi = [N_r(R - v)/2] + [(R + v)^2 N_p 4/9d]. \tag{31}$$

By comparing expression (31) with the corresponding expression for profit when neither firm uses vendor financing, equation (22), we see that the gain to each firm due to vendor financing is given by

$$g = 5N_r(R - v)/18 - dN_r^2/18N_p. \tag{32}$$

Comparison of equations (18) and (32) shows that, over the relevant range of N_r, defined by inequality (21), the advantage of vendor financing to each firm is smaller for a duopolist than for a monopolist. In contrast, the *total* advantage, if both firms engage in vendor financing, is greater in a duopoly than in a monopoly.

---

[12] This result can be verified by inserting the total number of tractors sold to poor farmers, $4N_p(R - v)/3d$, into equation (19).

Doubling the profit given in equation (31) and comparing with equation (29) shows that the joint profits of the two firms are greater if only one of them offers vendor financing. The reason for this is that the full advantage of vendor financing is realized when one of the firms is able to act as a monopolist in the credit market and maximize the economic rent that is extracted from poor farmers. In this case, vendor financing allows price discrimination and eliminates competition in the credit market. This will be feasible—as can be seen from condition (28)—if the credit market is not too large and if there is sufficient heterogeneity across farmers. As the credit market grows relative to the cash market, or if there is less heterogeneity across farmers, condition (28) will not hold for any $q_r^c < N_r$. Then only the equilibrium in which both firms offer vendor financing is sustainable.

The foregoing analysis generalizes readily to industries with more than two firms. As in the duopoly, economic rents are increased if only some of the firms service the credit market by supplying vendor financing and all the remaining firms sell to rich farmers only. In the Appendix, we derive a lower bound for the proportion of firms engaging in vendor financing that is necessary to make price discrimination feasible.

IV. Conclusion

The models we have presented in this paper suggest that vendor financing may be optimal for a firm when demand is less elastic in the credit market than in the cash market because of adverse selection and when the reservation prices of credit customers are systematically lower than those of cash customers. We have also shown that, in oligopolistic markets, vendor financing can be used to reduce competition since some firms can concentrate on the credit market while other firms maintain a larger market share in the cash market.

In all cases in which vendor financing is advantageous, the firms offering vendor financing offer subsidized loans. This seems to accord well with casual empiricism concerning the experience of captive finance companies in the automobile industry, which have offered subsidized credit when they have been allowed to do so without restrictions. In 1941, Ford and Chrysler both signed consent decrees according to which they agreed to allow outside lenders such as banks to participate in their subsidized interest rate programs; GM, which had fought similar charges brought against it, finally signed a consent decree in 1952. These consent decrees expired in 1982; since then, the auto companies have renewed their subsidized financing programs and have captured a much larger share of the new-car financing market, to the consternation of the banks.[13]

In our model, it is not optimal for the manufacturer to offer credit at a rate below the riskless interest rate, for then all purchasers would select credit financing, reducing the ability of the manufacturer to price discriminate. While

---

[13] A vice-president of a major bank was reported as saying: "We simply can't compete with those subsidized interest rates. Our costs of funds are higher than the rates that the captive finance companies were offering." *ABA Banking Journal*, Vol. 77, No. 12, December 1985.

this appears to be contradicted by the offers of credit by the auto companies at well below comparable market rates for riskless investments, these offers are accompanied by cash discounts that effectively raise the interest rate above the quoted rate. The substantial increase in market share gained by the auto finance captives suggests, however, that there remains a net subsidy in their credit terms.[14]

An alternative theory of vendor financing to the one we have proposed here rests on the notion that tax savings are possible through vendor financing, on account of the IRS treatment of installment sales, under which a vendor reports taxable income in proportion to the payments received. It is certainly the case that installment sales give rise to tax deferrals; however, they also give rise to a deferral of cash income. If the cost basis of the sale is zero and the present value of the sales price is maintained despite the installment terms, then the present value of the taxes payable will be the same whether or not the sale is made on an installment basis and there will be no tax advantage to vendor financing. On the other hand, if the cost of goods sold is positive, the installment method will delay recognition of the cost, giving rise to a tax *disadvantage* of installment financing. For this reason, we do not believe that tax considerations provide an adequate rationale for vendor financing; nor, of course, are they capable of explaining the subsidized vendor financing we observe.

Our theory also casts some light on the puzzling empirical evidence concerning security price reactions to the establishment of captive finance companies. Both Kim, McConnell, and Greenwood (KMG) [6] and Malitz [9] report stockholder gains of the order of seventeen to eighteen percent at the time of the establishment of a captive. KMG interpret this finding in terms of a bondholder expropriation hypothesis, according to which the captive allows the firm to expand its debt financing against a given level of receivables. They do find evidence of negative bondholder returns at the time a captive is established. However, this is not confirmed by Malitz [9], who uses a more carefully selected control sample of bonds (except in one case where the firm was already in financial distress); nor is the magnitude of the bond price reaction found by KMG commensurate with that required to explain the stockholder gains.

An alternative hypothesis suggested by our theory is that captives are established as a prelude to an extensive program of vendor financing[15] and that the stock price reaction is a reaction to the improved profitability this will make possible. More subtly, since vendor financing is profitable only for firms that have some kind of market power in the cash market, establishment of a captive, insofar as it is costly, may serve as a signal of this market power.

---

[14] According to the President of the Consumer Bankers' Association, "A significant shift of auto loan business from traditional lending organizations to finance companies, including those owned by the 'Big Three' auto makers, makes it essential that consumer banks, savings and loans and credit unions be allowed access to the loan subsidies paid by GM, Ford and Chrysler" (press release September 15, 1986).

[15] Malitz [9] provides evidence that firms that establish captives subsequently increase their receivables. Roberts and Viscione [11] discuss how establishment of a captive will facilitate the provision of intermediation services by a manufacturer.

Appendix

Define

n = total number of firms,
m = number of firms engaging in vendor financing, and
$\hat{q}(m)$ = the quantity of tractors sold to rich farmers by a firm without vendor
     financing.

To induce a firm not engaging in vendor financing to stay out of the credit market, it is necessary that

$$\hat{q}(m)(R - v) > (a - v - b(N_r - \hat{q}(m) = q_p^m))^2/4b, \qquad (A1)$$

where q_p^m is the total number of tractors sold to poor farmers by firms offering vendor financing. Inequality (A1) states that the profit to the firm from selling $\hat{q}$ to rich farmers exceeds the profit from producing optimally for both markets, foregoing the advantage from price discrimination. Inequality (A1) holds if[16]

$$\hat{q}(m) \geq (R - v)/b \left[\frac{2m + 1}{m + 1} - \sqrt{\frac{m}{m + 1}} \right]. \qquad (A2)$$

The upper bound on the number of such firms, $n - \bar{m}$, is given by

$$(n - \bar{m}) = N_r/\hat{q}_{\min}(\bar{m}), \qquad (A3)$$

where $\hat{q}_{\min}(m)$ is determined by (A2) holding as an equality.

Similarly, the maximum ratio of firms not offering vendor financing, M, is

$$M = \frac{N_r}{\hat{q}_{\min}(\bar{m})}. \qquad (A4)$$

To analyze the relationship between industry concentration and M, we take the partial derivative of M with respect to n:

$$\frac{\partial M}{\partial n} = \frac{N_r \left[\hat{q}_{\min}(\bar{m}) - \dfrac{\partial \hat{q}_{\min}(\bar{m})}{\partial n} n \right]}{\hat{q}_{\min}^2(\bar{m})}. \qquad (A5)$$

To determine the sign of $\delta M/\delta n$, note that we can write

$$\frac{\partial \hat{q}_{\min}(\bar{m})}{\partial n} = \frac{\partial \hat{q}_{\min}(m)}{\partial \bar{m}} \times \frac{\partial \bar{m}}{\partial n}.$$

From (A2), it follows that $\dfrac{\partial \hat{q}_{\min}(\bar{m})}{\partial \bar{m}} < 0$. Totally differentiating equation (A2), we obtain $\dfrac{\partial \bar{m}}{\partial n} > 0$ and, hence, $\partial \hat{q}_{\min}(\bar{m}) < 0$. Thus, expression (A5) is positive. The minimum fraction of firms offering vendor financing that allows the industry to derive economic rents is higher in more concentrated industries.

---

[16] Equation (A1) can be derived by substituting the oligopoly output for q_p^m, i.e., $q_p^m = \dfrac{(R - v)m}{(m + 1)b}$.

REFERENCES

1. J. II. Boyd and E. C. Prescott. "Financial Intermediary Coalitions." *Journal of Economic Theory* 38 (April 1986), 211–33.
2. D. W. Diamond. "Financial Intermediation and Delegated Monitoring." *Review of Economic Studies* 51 (July 1984), 392–414.
3. ———. "Asset Services and Financial Intermediation." CRSP Working Paper No. 182, 1986.
4. ——— and P. H. Dybvig. "Bank Runs, Deposit Insurance, and Liquidity." *Journal of Political Economy* (June 1983), 401–19.
5. J. W. Friedman. *Game Theory with Applications to Economics.* New York: Oxford University Press, 1986.
6. E. H. Kim, J. J. McConnell, and P. R. Greenwood. "Capital Structure Rearrangement and Me First Rules in an Efficient Capital Market." *Journal of Finance* 32 (June 1977), 789–810.
7. D. M. Kreps and J. A. Scheinkman. "Quality Precommitment and Bertrand Competition Yield Cournot Outcomes." *Bell Journal of Economics* 14 (Autumn 1983), 326–37.
8. H. E. Leland and D. H. Pyle. "Informational Asymmetries, Financial Structure, and Financial Intermediation." *Journal of Finance* 32 (May 1977), 372–87.
9. I. B. Malitz. "Claim Dilution: A Real Phenomenon." University of Illinois at Chicago working paper, May 1986.
10. T. S. Ramakrishnan and A. V. Thakor. "Information Reliability and a Theory of Financial Intermediation." *Review of Economic Studies* 51 (July 1984), 415–32.
11. G. S. Roberts and J. A. Viscione. "Captive Finance Subsidiaries and the M-Form Hypotheses." *Bell Journal of Economics* (Spring 1981), 285–95.
12. R. M. Townsend. "Optimal Contracts and Competitive Markets with Costly State Verification." *Journal of Economic Theory* 21 (October 1979), 265–93.
13. ———. "Theories of Intermediation Structures." *Rochester Conference Series on Public Policy* 18 (1983), 221–72.

[8]

THE JOURNAL OF FINANCE • VOL. XLV, NO. 3 • JULY 1990

Latent Assets

MICHAEL J. BRENNAN*

IT IS NOW A commonplace that corporate insiders possess an informational advantage over investors at large. On the one hand, the imperfect observability of the actions of corporate managements and of corporate investment opportunities has given rise to a now extensive literature on the problems of agency and adverse selection that arise in the corporate context. On the other, since Ross (1972) there has been considerable interest in the possibility of signaling resolutions to the problems arising from the superior information of management about corporate prospects. Nevertheless, it seems that signaling can provide only a partial resolution of the information asymmetry, and in this paper I want to consider some implications of the fact that it is costly for investors at large to determine the value of the assets held by the corporation. At the risk of oversimplification I shall distinguish between those assets whose values are known and agreed on by investors and reflected in share prices and those assets whose values are not reflected in share prices; the latter I shall refer to as latent assets. Investor rationality requires that the expected value of latent assets for any given firm be equal to zero, so that latent assets may be negative as well as positive.

Systematic evidence that share prices do not always fully reflect the value of assets held for corporations is hard to come by, not least because of the tenuous relation between our valuation models for most assets and observable variables. Nevertheless, there is considerable anecdotal and indirect evidence to this effect. For example, the substantial bid premia that are observed in the current wave of takeovers constitute prima facie evidence of the existence of latent assets, even though the premia themselves may be made possible by tax and operating efficiencies and wealth redistributions rather than the exploration of undervaluation. Thus a bid premium of 30% of the pre-bid market price can be consistent with the market knowing that the value of the assets in their alternative use is 30% higher than in their current use, only if the market assigns a zero probability to the emergence of the bid—that seems unreasonable. If the market assigns only a 20% probability to the bid, then a 30% bid premium implies that the assets are worth 49% more in the alternative than in the current use—but then a 20% probability seems implausibly low, and a 50% probability implies an 86% differential.[1] If investors can be so ignorant of the value of assets in alternative

* Anderson Graduate School of Management, UCLA. I thank Phelim Boyle, Craig Holden, Tim Opler, Richard Roll, Mark Rubinstein, and particularly Julian Franks and Alan Kraus for helpful comments on an earlier draft. The usual disclaimer applies.

[1] Let A denote the value of assets in current use and V their value to a bidder. If M is the current market value of the firm then $M = pV + (1 - p)A$, where p is the probability of a succesful bid. The example in the text assumes $V = 1.3M$.

uses it is reasonable to assume that they have less than perfect information about their values in current use. Further evidence to this effect lies in stock price reactions to many corporate announcements.

I shall consider the implications of latent assets from two perspectives. First I shall take an extreme case in which investors are unable to observe the value of the firm's assets at any cost, and consider some implications of this for corporate policy. In doing so I shall offer an explanation for a problem that has puzzled me for some time—namely the fact that gold mines are widely exploited despite the fact that standard present value analyses generally imply that it is optimal to defer exploitation indefinitely. Generalizing from the example of the gold mine, I shall argue that the latency of asset values induces firms to convert them into cash when they are positive, even when it is costly to do so—and conversely, to postpone realization when they are negative, even when that is costly. Among other things, our results point to the dangers of making inferences from stock price reactions to the announcement of corporate decisions, without giving due attention to the objective of the management.

Secondly, I shall consider the other extreme case in which corporate policies are fixed, but investors are able to acquire information about the value of latent assets at a cost. The main point I shall stress here is the interdependence of individual information acquisition decisions. In a market populated by small investors, the advantage to any individual of acquiring information about the latent assets of a firm may be very small if those assets have a low current yield and no other investor acquires the same information. On the other hand, if many other investors acquire the same information the share price will adjust to reflect it, rewarding those who acquired the information first. Thus, while too much information acquisition activity will compete away the rewards to acquiring information as in the classical efficient market, too little information acquisition activity also may make it not worthwhile for any individual to undertake it. What is true about information acquisition is also true about modes of analysis. If the market follows a demonstrably inappropriate procedure in valuing a particular asset, the rewards to having the correct procedure may yet be small, unless others can be persuaded of the superiority of your approach, and this may be difficult since, by definition, it does not correspond to market prices as well as the conventional procedure. Pity the man who alone knows how to value gold mines, for his reward shall be slight. Thus, I argue, market prices may reflect a large element of convention without there existing a strong tendency for this to be corrected. Of course there are some corrective forces. First among these is the activity of corporations themselves which have so far held fixed. To the extent that assets remain latent or under-valued by the market, there will be an incentive for managements to convert them to cash or run the risk of being acquired by someone else who will convert them. Thus the market for corporate control exerts a corrective force and even tends to increase the incentives for private information acquisition by hastening the day when the rewards of such activity will be enjoyed. Secondly, there are obviously benefits to our atomistic investors of coordinating their information gathering activities to ensure that when latent assets are discovered there is sufficient investment activity that the asset values come to be reflected in market prices. Strict coordination of investment, as in the mutual fund form, will not do the trick, for then the group claiming the information has an obvious incentive to misrepresent, since it will also have taken a position in the securities. However, a "disinterested" third party which is paid only for information acquisition, and gains a reputation for accuracy, may be able to provide the degree of coordination across investors necessary for its information to be quickly and profitably reflected in security prices. Brokerage house analysts provide a possible example.

I. The Gold Mine

My thinking about latent assets was stimulated by a puzzle that arose some years ago in developing with Eduardo Schwartz a model for valuing mineral resources.[2] A distinguishing feature of these assets is the highly unpredictable nature of the price of the extracted resource which, we argued, makes application of traditional valuation techniques extremely difficult. At the same time, this unpredictability provides the impetus for the development of futures markets, and these in turn provide information that can be used to infer the risk adjusted expected price change of the extracted mineral. Although we have used this model quite successfully, it had one embarrassing feature when applied to gold—it was very difficult to find parameter values that would make it optimal to extract the gold at all.

The reason for this apparent perversity is not hard to find. Stocks of gold in the world far exceed commercial inventory needs, and the bulk of the gold is held by individuals and central banks for investment purposes. This means that gold is an asset like a share of common stock, except that it does not pay a dividend.[3] Therefore, the present value of an ounce of gold deliverable at any time in the future is equal to the current spot price. However, it takes resources to extract the gold from the mine; and, assuming that the cost of extraction is rising at a rate less than the rate of interest, it will always pay to defer extraction. So our advice to owners of gold mines was always the same: "Wait!"[4] This makes perfectly good sense when it is just as good to own shares in a gold mine as it is to own the bullion directly.

Nevertheless, we observe that in practice most firms do extract the gold. In an opportunistic compromise between the descriptive and the prescriptive we added a knob to our model that could make this the optimal policy: we allowed for the possibility that the mine could be expropriated without compensation.[5] This

---

[2] See Brennan and Schwartz (1985).

[3] Nor does it cost much to store. In what follows we shall neglect storage costs. Other commodities that are held for commercial purposes are said to yield "convenience services" which correspond to the dividend on a share of common stock. See Brennan (1958).

[4] Keynes (1936) also though it was a (social) mistake to extract the gold: "··· the form of digging holes in the ground known as gold mining, which not only adds nothing whatever to the real wealth of the world, but involves the disutility of labour ···"

When I offered this same advice to a friend who was promoting a gold mine he thought it so laughable that he used to repeat it as evidence of the folly into which one could be led by excessive ratiocination.

[5] Our position was similar to that of Coleridge who one remarked to his dinner partner, "Madam, I accept your conclusion, but you must allow me to provide the logic for it."

means that the mine itself is no longer such a good store of value as the bullion itself. There are other considerations that may also serve to induce immediate extraction; for example, a government which is anxious to get its hands on the tax and royalty revenues from the mine may award a lease which will lapse if the mine is not developed. Rather than pursue these possibilities I shall focus on the asymmetry of the information between corporate insiders and investors about the value of the resource.

Asymmetry of information about the true value of a firm's assets seems particularly likely when those assets consist of a mineral resource, for not only is it difficult to communicate the raw information on which the valuation of the deposit depends and difficult to interpret those data, but there is also always the possibility that the information communicated is incomplete[6]: the market for unused gold mines suffers from much the same problems as the market for used cars. The information asymmetry will include such matters as amounts and grades of ore, costs of extraction and so on. In order to capture the information asymmetry in a simple fashion, we shall assume that it is common knowledge that the mine contains a unit of gold and that the gold can be extracted instantaneously, but that the cost of extraction is known only to management. We shall assume that the management of the mine is precluded from any signaling activities that would reveal its private information; in the appendix we consider a scenario in which the management can reveal its private information by precommitting to an output policy.[7]

Let g denote the current price of a unit of gold, which is also the value of a unit deliverable for sure at any time in the future, and let $M(s)$ denote the market value of the firm at time s. We assume that the future price path of the gold is known with certainty and that management maximizes a weighted average of present values of future stock prices:

$$\max \alpha \int_0^\infty e^{-(\alpha+r)s} M(s) \; ds, \tag{1}$$

where r is the interest rate and α is a parameter.

Let τ denote the date on which the gold is extracted from the mine. Since this cannot be signaled in advance, all firms with unexploited mines will be valued identically. Without loss of generality, we may write the value of such a firm as

$$M(s) = ge^{rs} - Q(s), \qquad s < \tau, \tag{2}$$

where $Q(s)$ is the present value at time s of the expected future costs of extraction

---

[6] See discussion by Grossman and Hart (1980). When one gold mining company was bid for, a commentator remarked: "It (Newmont Gold Mining Company) may also be a company of sizeable *hidden* value." *Los Angeles Times*, September 20, 1989 (emphasis added).

[7] Gold loans whose repayments are in bullion or bullion equivalent are a recent innovation which may function as precommitment devices. Such loans typically carry interest rates of 1.5–3% and are used to finance mine development. Note that while these loans provide a price hedge for the producer, this cannot be their sole purpose for such hedges are available more cheaply in the futures market. Since lenders send in their own analysts to evaluate a mine before making a loan, the size and yield on the loan also serve as signals of the quality of the mine. For a formal model of third party information production see Thakor (1982).

and ge^{rs} is the price of gold at time s, since under certainty the price will appreciate at the riskless rate. Note that since no firm will extract the gold if the cost of extraction exceeds the current gold price, it must be the case that $M(s) \geq 0$, or

$$Q(s) \leq ge^{rs}. \tag{3}$$

Extraction costs grow continuously over time at the known rate m. For ease of reference we shall refer to the extraction costs measured at time 0 as the real cost of extraction and denote it by C. Consider then a firm that extracts the gold at time τ. Its value at that time, $M^*(\tau)$, is equal to the difference between the value of the gold and the, now known, cost of extraction:

$$M^*(\tau) = ge^{r\tau} - Ce^{m\tau}. \tag{4}$$

Finally, for $s > \tau$, the true value of the firm is known so that

$$M(s) = M^*(\tau)e^{r(s-\tau)}. \tag{5}$$

Substituting for $M(s)$ and $M^*(s)$ from equations (2), (4) and (5) in (1), the objective function of the firm may be written as

$$\max_{\tau} V = g - \alpha \int_0^{\tau} Q(s)e^{-(\alpha+r)s}\, ds - Ce^{-(\alpha+r-m)\tau}. \tag{6}$$

The first and second order conditions for a maximum in (6) are

$$V' = -\alpha Q(\tau)e^{-(\alpha+r)\tau} + (\alpha + r - m)Ce^{-(\alpha+r-m)\tau} = 0, \tag{7}$$

$$V'' = [\alpha(\alpha + r)Q - \alpha Q' - (\alpha + r - m)^2 Ce^{m\tau}]e^{-(\alpha+r)\tau} < 0. \tag{8}$$

Solving the first order condition (7) for $C(t)$, the real cost of a mine for which it is optimal to produce at time t:

$$C(t) = \left(\frac{\alpha}{\alpha + r - m}\right)Q(t)e^{-mt}. \tag{9}$$

So

$$Q(0) = \left(\frac{\alpha + r - m}{\alpha}\right)C(0),$$

where $C(0)$ is the cost of the producing mine at time 0.

Then, substituting from (9) in (8), the second order condition may be written as

$$Q'/Q > m. \tag{10}$$

Under risk neutrality, equilibrium in the capital market requires that the expected rate of increase in the value of unexploited mines be equal to the risk-free interest rate. This expected rate of increase has two components—the rate of increase in the value of mines which remain unexploited, M', and the instantaneous capital gain or loss on a mine when it is brought into production, $(M^* - M)$, times the proportional rate at which new mines are brought into production. This rate is equal to the product of the hazard rate of the cost distribution function,[8] $h(C)$, and the time derivative of the real cost of the currently producing mine, $C'(t)$. Thus the condition for equilibrium in the capital market may be written as

$$(M^* - M)hC' + M' = Mr. \tag{11}$$

In order to complete the characterization of the equilibrium, it is necessary to specify the probability distribution function for the costs. For analytical convenience we take this as

$$F(C) = 1 - a/C^k, \qquad a > 0, \quad C > a^{1/k}. \tag{12}$$

This implies the hazard rate function $h(C) = k/C$. Then, computing M' from equation (2), and substituting for h and for M and M^* from (2) and (4) in (11) and using (9), we obtain

$$\eta(C'/C)Q - Q' + rQ = 0, \tag{13}$$

where $\eta \equiv k(r - m)/(\alpha + r - m) > 0$. But from (9) $C'/C = Q'/Q - m$, so that (13) may be written as

$$Q'/Q = (r - m\eta)/(1 - \eta) \equiv \gamma. \tag{14}$$

It may be verified that $\gamma > m$ as required by the second order condition (10) if $r > m$.[9]

The solution to equation (14) may be written as[10]

$$Q(t) = Q(0)e^{\gamma t}, \tag{15}$$

where $Q(0)$ is the present value at time 0 of the expected future costs of extraction, given that the cost of the mine which is producing at time t satisfies condition (18). Define $f(C) \equiv akC^{-(1+k)}$, the density function of extraction costs. Then $Q(0)$ may be written as

$$Q(0) = \int_0^\infty C(t)e^{(m-r)t} f[C(t)] \, dt. \tag{16}$$

Then, substituting for $f(\ )$ and for $C(t)$ from (9), and using (15) it is seen that

$$Q(0)^{1+k} = \left(\frac{\alpha}{\alpha + r - m}\right)^{-k} ak \int_0^\infty \exp\{\{m - r + k(m - \gamma)\}t\} \, dt, \tag{17}$$

or

$$Q(0) = \left[\left(\frac{\alpha}{\alpha + r - m}\right)^{-k} \frac{ak}{[k(\gamma - m) + r - m]}\right]^{1/(1+k)}. \tag{18}$$

---

[8] The fraction of mines producing in the interval $(t, t + dt)$ is $\{F[C(t + dt)] - F[C(t)]\}\{1 - F[C(t)]\}^{-1}$, where F is the distribution function of real costs. Taking limits, this may be written as $h[C(t)]C'(t)dt$, where $h(C) \equiv F'(C)/(1 - F(C))$ is the hazard rate and primes denote derivatives.

[9] Note that this is just the condition required for it to be costly to advance production.

[10] In the interest of tractability we are assuming that all mines are expected to produce eventually. Alternatively, $Q(0)$ could be determined by the assumption that all mines, if they are to produce, must do so by some final date T^*.

The cost of the mine which produces at time t in equilibrium is given by equation (9) where $Q(t)$ is defined by equations (15) and (18).

All mines with real costs less than $C(0)$ produce immediately at time 0. The remaining mines defer production until their cost satisfies condition (9). Thus in equilibrium the current cost of the currently producing mine rises at the rate γ. Each mine finds it worthwhile to postpone production until the cost of further postponement due to continuing as a member of the remaining pool of high cost mines exceeds the cost of advancing production. Since, under symmetric information, it would be optimal to postpone production indefinitely, the timing of production can be regarded as a costly "signal" of firm type. Then the model is one of dynamic costly signaling in which firms reveal their types sequentially. However, to treat the act of production as a costly signal is to strain usage, and the equilibrium is perhaps better described as one of sequential type revelation. In any case, we note that in this model the announcement of production is greeted with an immediate increase in the stock price, as the cost of production of the currently producing firm is a fraction $\mu \equiv \alpha/(\alpha + r - m) < 1$ of the present value of the costs of the average firm which is yet to produce.

Our results thus far rely on the somewhat ad hoc specification of the firm's objective function (1). It is instructive to consider how our results change if the firms pursue a more classical policy of (market) value maximization. Under a policy of value maximization, a mine with real cost C will produce if and only if its cost of extraction does not exceed $Q(s)$:

$$Ce^{ms} \leq Q(s). \tag{19}$$

To avoid technical difficulties, it is convenient to assume that each firm follows a policy of *virtual* continuous value maximization, so that a firm with initial cost $C(t)$ produces at time t where

$$C(t) = \mu Q(t)e^{-mt} \tag{20}$$

and $\mu < 1$. This policy approaches continuous value maximization as $\mu \to 1$.

Suppose that the probability distribution of mine costs is given as before by expression (12). Then, noting the similarity between expressions (9) and (20) which determine the optimal production policies under the two policies, it is apparent that the equilibrium under value maximization is identical to that derived above when $\alpha/(\alpha + r - m) = \mu$. In particular, the optimal production policy is given by (20), where

$$Q(0) = \mu^{-k}\left[\frac{ak}{k(\gamma - m) + (r - m)}\right]^{1/(1+k)}, \tag{21}$$

$$Q(t) = Q(0)e^{\gamma t}, \tag{22}$$

and $\gamma = (r - m\eta)/(1 - \eta)$, where $\eta = k(1 - \mu)$. Thus as $\mu \to 1$, $\gamma \to r$, and the current cost of the currently producing mine grows at a rate approaching the riskless interest rate. Moreover, since $C(t)e^{mt} \to Q(t)$ as $\mu \to 1$, as the policy

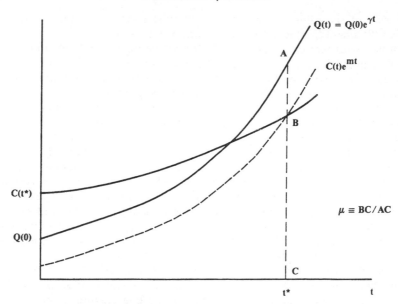

Figure 1. Equilibrium extraction policy for alternative objective functions. A mine with real cost $C(t^*)$ produces at t^*, where its cost of extraction is a fraction μ of the present value of the average costs of extraction of remaining undeveloped mines, $Q(t^*)$. Under objective function (1), $\mu \equiv \alpha/(\alpha + r - m)$; under value maximization, $\mu \to 1$.

approaches that of pure value maximization, the capital gain on the announcement of production approaches zero.[11]

Figure 1 illustrates the nature of the equilibrium under the alternative objective functions. The ratio of the distances $AB:AC$ is equal to $\mu \equiv \alpha/(\alpha + r - m)$. This represents the ratio of the average cost imputed by the market to unexploited mines to the cost of the currently producing mine.

The mines in our model are atomistic, each producing unit output. Real mines correspond to collections of these mines. The model thus predicts that within a given mine the low cost ore will tend to be exploited first, which corresponds with the conventional view, though for different reasons.

II. Generalization from the Gold Mine Example

We have shown that, even under a policy of value maximization the classical NPV rule need not emerge as the criterion of (private) investment optimality under conditions of information asymmetry. Once again we see how critical is the assumption of symmetric information for the simple decision rules yielded by the classical theory of corporate finance; unfortunately, the decision rules which emerge from informational considerations seem much harder to imple-

---

[11] Note that market value maximization in this case is not equivalent to full information value maximization because of the effect of the (non)-production decision on investor perceptions. For a similar point in a different context see Rotemberg and Scharfstein (1989).

ment,[12] and while our result has been derived under the assumption that the firm has no means of signaling its quality, it seems likely that a similar result will emerge so long as there is any residual uncertainty about the quality of the mine.

Our analysis yields in principle a test of whether or not firms follow a policy of value maximization. A non-zero price reaction to the announcement that a mine is to be put into production is inconsistent with value maximization, and if the alternative is the objective function (1) which is a generalization of the type usually found in signaling models,[13] then the price reaction may be used to estimate the discount factor, α.[14]

Although we have considered a gold mine for reasons of analytical tractability,[15] similar results follow in more complex settings, and the gold mine example is intended as a parable of a more general phenomenon of latent, or only partially observed, asset values. As we saw, the effect of latency was to induce managers to realize the asset value early by converting it into cash whose value is universally observable. Other authors have suggested the possibility of a similar outcome,[16] and the financial press contains frequent references to hidden or latent assets.[17]

McConnell and Muscarella (1985) report that stock prices react positively to the announcement of investment projects; this is consistent with the view that the value of the investment opportunities is known only imperfectly to the market. Our theory then suggests that if management places any weight on the current stock price in their objective function, then these opportunities will be exploited too early relative to the usual NPV criterion.

Similarly, Klein (1986) reports that announcements of asset sales are accompanied by positive stock price rections.[18] Again, if the current stock price is an element of the managerial objective function, it follows that asset sales are at least partially motivated by the desire to signal value, and that they will be made even when the sale price does not reflect the full value of the asset. In the model of the previous section, the lower is the discount factor α the more weight is placed on the current stock price and the earlier are the mines exploited. It follows that an exogenous shock that decreases α, such as a sudden threat of takeover, can be expected to trigger increased asset disposals that are costly to

[12] See Heinkel (1978), Miller and Rock (1985), and Constantinides and Grundy (1989) have also presented models in which informational considerations affect investment policy. Dividend policy, capital structure decisions, and optimal call strategies inter alia are all affected by similar considerations.

[13] See Miller and Rock, op. cit, and Harris and Raviv (1985) for example. For a criticism of these objective functions see Dybvig and Zender (1987).

[14] Farrow (1985) provides evidence that actual resource extraction policies are inconsistent with value maximization.

[15] This allowed us to ignore the effect of timing on the present value of the revenues.

[16] Stein (1988) has developed a model somewhat similar to ours, in which for certain parameter values, managers may advance the exploitation of a resource in order to forestall a takeover. Narayanan (1985) presents a model in which the manager chooses projects with short payback periods in order to signal his own ability.

[17] The *Wall Street Journal* (January 20, 1989) in an article on "Hidden Assets" in Japan reported that many U.S. companies were sitting on "potential gold mines," that some companies were moving to "reap value" from these assets, while some bankers wonder if "companies are moving too hastily to reap one time gains."

[18] Interestingly, the positive reaction is only for announcements in which the sale price is specified.

the firm. The takeover threat forces the incumbent management to prove the value of its assets, and the only way in which this can be accomplished is by sale.

It has been suggested that real estate holdings which have relatively low yields may be difficult for the market to reflect accurately in share prices.[19] Consider for example an industrial company that owns its own head office building, or a chain of supermarkets that owns its stores. Ownership will contribute to earnings only by the amount of the rent savings, and it may be difficult for investors to distinguish that part of earnings which is implicitly rental income and should be capitalized at a low rate from that which arises from industrial or grocery product sales and should be capitalized at a higher rate.[20] We might therefore expect those companies whose stock prices do not fully reflect the value of their real estate holdings to sell them and lease them back, even if it is costly to do so.[21] And we might expect a positive stock price reaction to the announcement of such transactions even though the transaction has a negative net present value for, as we argued above, the stock price will depend on whether the firm is continuously maximizing its stock price.

As a final example of a class of assets which may be hard for the market to value, consider the net pension assets of a company which depend on the value of the pension rights held by employees. Prior to the tax imposed by the Miscellaneous Revenue Act of 1988, terminations of defined benefit plans were not infrequent; Alderson and Chen (1986) find a positive stock price response to the announcement of plan termination; this is consistent with the values of pension assets being only partially known to the market and the management maximizing an objective function similar to expression (1). On the other hand, Vanderhei (1987) finds a positive stock price response for only part of his sample, and Bruner, Harrington, and Marshall (1987) find no abnormal returns. While the lack of a stock price response may be interpreted in terms of market efficiency and certain theories of pension property rights, it should be noted that it is consistent also with the hypothesis that investors do not possess detailed knowledge of individual plans, but that firm managements follow policies of market value maximization. This points to the care that must be taken in interpreting event studies when the event in question is a corporate action.[22]

Our analysis of the extraction policy of the gold mine has rested on the assumption that it was not possible for the firm to communicate information about its costs to investors. This is not an unreasonable assumption so long as the investors are small. However, it is not plausible for large investors who might buy up the whole mine. How is our analysis changed by the existence of large investors who can assess mine costs? If the large investors are individuals, then they do not have an incentive to buy up high cost mines that are just about to

---

[19] Hite et al. (1987) report that firm liquidations are frequently associated with management complaints of "undervaluation of natural resources and real estate holdings, assets that had appreciated in relation to their historical cost carrying value" (p. 233).

[20] We shall argue below that, depending on the convention, it may not be worthwhile for the individual investor to make such calculations.

[21] "Investors can profit from real estate · · · provided a company exploits the value of its holdings. It can do this by swelling, leveraging, or upgrading properties · · · ." Heard on the street. *Wall Street Journal*, January 29, 1989.

[22] A similar point is made by Acharya (1988) and by Eckbo, Maksimovic, and Williams (1989).

produce and to hold them out of production, thereby reducing the present value of the extraction costs. More generally, it seems that large investors or corporate insiders may have an advantage in operating latent assets, since such investors need not concern themselves with market values.[23] Note that this does not apply to large *corporate* investors who must themselves be concerned about market values unless they in turn are owned by large individual investors. Thus a firm will be worth more if it is controlled by a large investor who is concerned with intrinsic value as well as market value.[24] And second, a firm will be worth more if it is owned by the managers rather than publicly held, since it will then be free to pursue the goal of intrinsic value maximization. This accords well with the popular view that firms go private in order to free themselves from the pressures for short term performance that a stock market quotation engenders. Of course in practice there are riskbearing costs associated with management ownership and dominant shareholdings; therefore, these are not necessarily optimal ownership arrangements.

III. Equilibrium Information Collection in a Market of Small Investors

Let us turn now from the problem of a firm which owns latent assets to the incentives for individual investors to collect information about firm asset values when it is costly to do so. The main point I shall make in this section is that for long-lived assets the incentive for an individual investor to collect information may depend heavily upon whether other investors are collecting information and that, as a result, there may exist more than one equilibrium, in only one of which investors collect information; in the other equilibrium the assets remain latent.

Assume without loss of generality that each of N individual investors can collect information about the latent asset value of any one of M firms at a cost c, but that this information cannot be communicated credibly to other investors. Consider then an overlapping generations economy in which each generation lives for three, not necessarily equally spaced periods, and a new generation is born every second period at t, $t + 2$, $t + 4$, etc.[25] In the first period of life (period t) generation i ($i = t/2 + 1$) uses its labor income to purchase shares from the previous generation, which in turn uses the proceeds for consumption. Labor

---

[23] Of course, they must be concerned with market values when they come to sell, but there is a presumption that market value maximization will not be a continual concern to them as it is to the management of a firm owned by small investors. It is possible that a managerial policy of acquiring latent assets, rather than simply agency costs, accounts in part for the association between undistributed cash flow and premiums in going private transactions observed by Lehn and Poulson (1989).

[24] This complements the theory of Shleifer and Vishny (1986) which also predicts that firms will be worth more when there is a large shareholder.

[25] The intent of this assumption is to represent the short decision horizon of most investors. The effect of this is to make non-income yielding assets whose value cannot be realized by sale or borrowing and which cannot appear on a balance sheet for, say, 10 years essentially valueless. Even institutional investors with long apparent horizons may have short effective horizons because of agency problems which induce frequent monitoring of the investment manager's performance.

DeLong, Shleifer, Summers, and Waldmann (1989) also employ an overlapping generations assumption to develop a model in which market values depart from fundamentals. However, in their model the departure is caused by the existence of noise traders. Common, and essential to both models, is the market incompleteness captured by the overlapping generations assumption.

Table I
Overlapping Generations Model with Information Production

	Generation i			Generation $(i+1)$
Time	t	$t+1$	$t+2$	$t+3$
Firm Assets	$a_{i-1} + l_{i-1}$ $+l_i$	$a_i + l_i$	$a_i + l_i$ $+l_{i+1}$	$a_{i+1} + l_{i+1}$
Generation i	Receives labor income. Purchases shares from generation $(i-1)$. Purchases information about l_i.	Receives information about l_i purchased at t. Trades.	Sells shares to $(i+1)$. Consumes. Dies.	
Share Price: Reflects l_i?	No	Not at open. At close if $j > m$ investors purchased information.	If reflected at $(t+1)$ or publicly revealed (probability:μ).	Yes
Share Price: At open[a] At close:		$a_i - D(1+r)^2$		$a_{i+1} - D(1+r)^2$
if l_i reflected		$a_i + l_i - D$	$a_i + (l_i - D)(1+r)$	
if l_i not reflected		$a_i - D$	$a_i - D(1+r)$	

[a] If different from closing price.

income in the first period of life may also be used to purchase information about the latent asset values of individual firms: this information becomes available at random times during trade in the second period. In the second period $(t+1)$ individuals suffer random wealth shocks that induce them to trade; at this time individuals who purchased information in the first period may use it to trade as it becomes available. Individuals are assumed to be risk neutral, but to be restricted in the amounts they can purchase or sell short. The key assumption we shall make is that the market price of a firm does not reflect the private information of investors in the second period, until there is some minimum number of investors informed about the firm. In the third period $(t+2)$ the current generation sells its shares to the new generation of individuals, consumes, and dies.

The information structure of the model is illustrated in Table I. In the first period of life of generation i, time t, a fraction f of firms are endowed with latent assets, $l_i/(1+r)$, where $l_i = \pm\Pi$ with equal probability, and r is the riskless interest rate; latent assets yield no current return but appreciate in value at the riskless interest rate. At the beginning of $(t+1)$, before trade occurs, the value of latent assets held by the firm in *generation* $i-1$ is revealed if it is not already known to its investors. Hence the public assets of the firm (in the second period of life of generation i) at time $t+1$, a_i[26] are equal to the sum of the public and latent assets from the previous generation: $a_i = a_{i-1} + l_{i-1}$. Public assets yield a

[26] All asset values are expressed on a per share basis.

certain return each period equal to the interest rate. Information about l_i becomes available at random times during trading at period $t + 1$ to all investors who paid the information acquisition cost c at time t.

For simplicity we shall assume that share prices react in a discontinuous fashion to the purchases and sales of informed investors. In particular, we assume that each informed investor is able to buy/sell a maximum of one share, and that the share price does not reflect the private information until m shares have been purchased/sold by the informed, at which point the price changes to reflect the private information[27] which is thereby revealed.

If the latent asset value l_i is not reflected in the share price as a result of trading at time $t + 1$, there is an (exogenous) probability, μ, that the value will be revealed prior to the opening of trading at $t + 2$; failing this, the latent asset value will certainly be revealed prior to the opening of trading at $t + 2$ (period 2 of generation $i + 1$). The important feature of the model for our purposes is that information about latent asset values may not be reflected in asset values until the next generation.

Note that uninformed investors lose on average by trading with the informed in period 2, because informed investors are more likely to be sellers of shares with latent liabilities (<0), and purchasers of shares with latent assets. Let the expected loss per share for the uninformed from trading with the informed in the second period of life be d, and denote by D the value of the perpetuity of these expected losses, $D \equiv d/R$ where $R \equiv [(1 + r)^2 - 1]$. Then it may be verified that the following is an equilibrium: The share price at the open of trade at $t + 1$ is given by $a_i - D(1 + r)^2$. The price at the close of trade at $t + 2$, if the latent asset value has not been revealed by trade, is $a_i - D$. If the latent asset value has been revealed, the price is $a_i + l_i - D$. Similarly, the price at $t + 2$ is $a_i - D(1 + r)$ if the latent asset value has not been revealed, and $a_i + l_i(1 + r) - D(1 + r)$ if it has. Finally, the price at the open of trade at $t + 3$ of the following generation is $a_{i+1} - D(1 + r)^2$.

An informed investor who is able to transact at the opening price at $t + 1$ will realize an immediate expected profit of $f\Pi$ if l_i is revealed in the course of trading. Given our assumption about price adjustment, if j, the number of investors who acquire information about a frim, exceeds m, the first m of them will realize an expected profit of $f\Pi$ when the price adjusts after the transaction of investor m, while the remaining $(j - m)$ will realize no profit since they will not be able to transact at the full information price. Therefore, if there are $j \geq m$ informed investors, the expected profit per investor from price adjustment in period 2 is $f\Pi(m/j)$. If $j < m$, there will be no price adjustment in period 2; however, informed investors may yet profit from asset value revelation in period $t + 2$. The present value of the expected profit (as of period 2) is $\mu f\Pi$ where μ is the previously defined exogenous probability of value revelation in period $t + 2$.

Define η_{jt} as the probability that exactly j investors in generation t become informed about a particular firm. Then V, the Period 2 present value of the expected reward to becoming informed about a particular firm, given that a

---

[27] The model can be thought of as a simplification of that of Diamond and Verrecchia (1987), which has the same implications for information collection in our intertemporal setting.

fraction f of firms have latent assets, may be written as

$$V = f \Pi [\sum_{j \geq m} \eta_{jt} (m/j) + \mu \sum_{j < m} \eta_{jt}]. \tag{23}$$

The first term in the parentheses corresponds to the event that at least m investors are informed about the firm, so that its value is revealed in the course of trading at $(t + 1)$; the second term corresponds to the possibility of a public announcement of the latent asset value at $(t + 2)$. We consider a stationary environment in which M, the number of firms, and N, the number of individuals who decide to become informed, are time invariant. It is assumed that each individual acquires information about no more than one firm and that firm is chosen at random. Then the probability that a given firm is chosen by a particular investor is M^{-1}, and the distribution of the number of investors who become informed about any firm is binomial, where N is the number of trials, and M^{-1} is the probability of success on a given trial.

Under these assumptions V is a function of N, the number of investors who decide to become informed, and may be written as

$$V(N) = f \Pi [\sum_{j=m}^{N} b_j (M/j) + \mu \sum_{j=1}^{m-1} b_j], \tag{24}$$

where $\eta_{jt} = b(N, j, M^{-1}) \equiv b_j$, the binomal probability of j successes in N trials.

Equilibrium in the market for information requires that all those who acquire information earn an expected return that compensates them for the cost of acquiring information, and that there be no incentive for further information acquisition: the equilibrium number of investors who acquire information, N^e, must satisfy

$$V(N^e) \geq \hat{c} \equiv c(1 + r), \qquad V(N^e + 1) < \hat{c}. \tag{25}$$

At low levels of N, and for small μ, $V(N)$ is increasing, because an increase in the number of informed investors increases the probability that the price will reflect that latent asset value. However, for larger N the probability of immediate price adjustment is already high, and further increases in N tend simply to increase the number of informed individuals over whom the reward of the price adjustment must be spread.

Figure 2 illustrates the two possible types of equilibria in the market for information. The $V(N)$ schedule is drawn for $\mu = 0$ and for $\mu > \hat{c}/f\pi$.[28] When $\mu = 0$, $V(N) = 0$ for $N < m$, because there is no possibility of price adjustment in the current generation; $V(N)$ increases at first for $N > m$ as the probability of price adjustment increases, but eventually turns down as the increase in the number of individuals among whom the fruits of price adjustment must be shared outweighs the increased probability of adjustment. $V(N)$ is a strictly increasing function of μ as shown, and for sufficiently large μ will be a monotone negative function of N.

It is helpful to distinguish two types of market according to the probability of exogenous information revelation. If $\mu > \hat{c}/f\Pi$, there is only one equilibrium in

[28] It is also possible that the $V(N)$ schedule is everywhere below $\hat{c}$. In that case it is never worth collecting information.

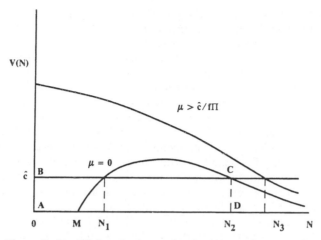

Figure 2. Equilibrium in the market for information acquisition.

the market for information at $N = N_3$. We might describe the security market in such an information gathering equilibrium as stochastically efficient since the probability that the period $(t + 1)$ closing price reflects the value of the firm's latent assets is $B(N_3, m; M^{-1})$ where $B(\ )$ is the probability of m or more successes in N trials. Note that as the cost of information acquisition approaches zero, $N_1 \rightarrow \infty$ and the probability that security prices fully reflect asset values approaches unity.

Consider the situation on the other hand when μ, the probability of exogenous information revelation, is low: $\mu < \hat{c}/f \Pi$. Now there exist two equilibria. $N = 0$ is an "informationless" equilibrium. In this equilibrium it is not worthwhile for anyone to gather information because no one else is gathering information and there is no way to profit from price adjustment. There is also an information gathering equilibrium at $N = N_2$; note that $N = N_1$ is not an equilibrium since at that point there is an incentive for additional investors to become informed.

The first lesson of this simple model is that there may be externalities to the collection of information in securities markets. For example, if oil company shares do not reflect the option value of reserves that can only be developed profitably at a higher oil price, there may be no incentive for individual analysts to estimate the value of these reserves and share prices may continue to ignore them. Nor will this problem be rectified by a single large investor (not included in our model) buying up the whole company unless this investor has an investment horizon which stretches over into the next generation.

While in this model we have made a simple distinction between assets whose values are publicly known and assets which are latent or observable only at a cost, it should be clear that almost all assets possess aspects of latency, and that the uncertainty surrounding corporate asset values can be progressively reduced as the cost incurred in investigation is increased. Our analysis suggests that it may not be worthwhile for an individual to invest heavily in information acquisition unless a sufficient number of other investors are also doing so.

Second, since there is more than one possible equilibrium, the particular equilibrium that prevails may be a matter of convention or of historical accident. For example, it has often been noted that the discounts from net asset value of closed end investment companies show considerable intertemporal variation. However, as Thompson (1978) has shown, the rewards from buying "underpriced" funds are quite modest, because prices do not adjust rapidly[29]—because not many investors attempt to arbitrage these securities. If, on the other hand, there were a well-agreed-on-formula for the appropriate discount based on expense ratios, investment performance, etc., then it is at least possible that there would exist an equilibrium in which it was worthwhile for investors to estimate the appropriate discount and adjustments to this would be rapid. The now abandoned proposal for Unbundled Securities Units may represent a case in which the bad equilibrium prevailed. Reputedly this innovation failed because of concern that the market for USUs would be insufficiently liquid, causing them to trade at a discount to the underlying securities. There is another equilibrium in which the USUs are regarded as perfect substitutes for the underlying security, thereby gain liquidity, and are priced as perfect substitutes.[30]

Third, note that in an information gathering equilibrium the number of individuals who collect information at time t is an increasing function of μ, the probability of exogenous information revelation at $t + 2$. The reason for this of course is that the greater the value of μ, the higher the probability that the asset will trade at its full information value during the life of the current generation, so that purchasers will realize the true full information value rather than handing the asset on to the following generation at a price which does not reflect this information. In a more general model, the higher the income stream and the longer the individual investor horizon, the higher is the proportion of the return realized by the investor that depends on fundamentals and the lower the proportion that depends on the terminal price; consequently, the greater is the incentive to collect information. Thus we should expect the prices of high payout assets to reflect the underlying asset values more precisely than those of low payout assets, ceteris paribus.

Consider next the determinants of D, the expected discount from asset value at which shares trade at the end of period $(t + 1)$. First, note that in an informationless equilibrium the discount will be zero, for then uninformed investors would experience no adverse selection in their period $(t + 2)$ trading. In the information gathering equilibrium informed investors exactly recoup their information costs by trading with the uninformed. Hence d, the expected trading losses of the uninformed per period per share, are equal to $(N_e/M)\hat{c}$ where N_e is the equilibrium number of informed investors. Hence the discount from asset value, D, is given by

$$D = \frac{N^e \hat{c}}{MR},$$ (26)

where $R \equiv (1 + r)^2 - 1$, is the two period interest rate.[31]

---

[29] A similar point has been made by Summers (1986).

[30] Cornell and Shapiro (1989) present an interesting example of the failure of arbitrage in the U.S. Treasury bond market.

[31] See also Heinkel and Kraus (1987) for a model of differential returns to insiders and outsiders.

Equation (26) implies that the discount from asset value is proportional to the area of the rectangle $ABCD$ in Figure 2. Since, from equation (24), the expected reward to information collection, V, is increasing in both $f\Pi$ and μ, it follows from inspection of Figure 2 that in an information gathering equilibrium D, the expected discount from asset value, is an increasing function of

    (i) the uncertainty about latent asset value, as measured by $f\Pi$, since the greater is this uncertainty, the greater is the adverse selection problem faced by the uninformed. It follows that value maximizing firms have an incentive to reveal their values as accurately as possible.[32]

    (ii) μ, the probability that the value of the latent assets will be revealed in period $t + 2$. Not surprisingly, information that is not likely to be revealed does not pose a threat to the uninformed.

It seems likely that information acquisition costs, c, would be higher for multidivisional conglomerate firms which are spread across unrelated industries. Although the effect of c on the discount is ambiguous, it is at least possible in this model that the diversified conglomerate pays a valuation penalty on account of the difficulty of evaluating its assets.

IV. Conventional Valuation

In the model of Section IV, share values may fail to reflect intrinsic values for two distinct reasons. First, the shares may be valued in an informationless equilibrium in which there is no incentive for individuals to collect information because an insufficient number of other individuals are collecting information. Second, in an informed equilibrium, the cost of information collection must be extracted from the uninformed: responding to their resulting losses from adverse selection, the uninformed will be willing to pay less than the expected value of the assets for the shares they purchase. There is also a third way in which prices may fail to reflect fundamental values, for the particular informed equilibrium that prevails may also be a matter of convention—the market may systematically employ the "wrong" model to value a particular class of securities, and yet there may be no natural forces tending to return the market to the "right" model.

To see this, assume now that the value of the latent asset, l is normally distributed with mean zero and variance, σ_1^2, and suppose that there exists a noisy signal of l:

$$s = l + \epsilon, \tag{27}$$

where $\epsilon = N(0,\ \sigma_\epsilon^2)$. s may be thought of as the valuation implied by an inappropriate model. Assume that the cost of observing l or the noisy signal is c, the same for both.

Then from equation (24) and the properties of the normal distribution it follows that $V^l(N)$, the expected reward of observing l when N investors observe l is

$$V^l(N) = f\sigma_1 \sqrt{\frac{2}{\pi}} \{\Sigma_{j=m}^{N} b_j(m/j) + \mu \Sigma_{j=1}^{m-1} b_j\}. \tag{24'}$$

[32] Cf. Diamond (1985) and Ross (1989).

Consider next $V^s(N)$, the expected return from observing the noisy signal s when N investors also observe the same signal. If m investors acquire information about the same firm, the time period $(t + 1)$ price adjustment will be equal to $\hat{l} = E[l \mid s]$, then the expected additional price change at time $(t + 2)$, conditional on information revelation and the signal will be zero. If no information is revealed in the course of trading at $(t + 1)$, the expected profit conditional on information revelation at $(t + 2)$ for an investor who received the signal s is $\mid E[l \mid s] \mid = \mid \hat{l} \mid$. Thus $V^s(N)$ is given by

$$V^s(N) = f\sigma_1 \sqrt{\frac{2k}{\pi}} \{\textstyle\sum_{j=m}^{N} b_j (m/j) + \mu \sum_{j=1}^{m-1} b_j\}, \tag{28}$$

where $E[|\hat{l}|] = \sigma_1 \sqrt{\dfrac{2k}{\pi}}$ and $k = \sigma_1^2/(\sigma_1^2 + \sigma_\epsilon^2)$. Comparing $(24')$ and (28), it is seen that for all N $V^l(N) > V^s(N)$, so that given the number of investors who collect information, they would, not surprisingly, be better off collecting information about l rather than about s, the noisy signal of l. Despite this, we shall see that if N investors are collecting information about s, it may not pay any of them to switch to collection of information about l.

An individual who knows l will make an expected profit of $\mid E[\hat{l} \mid l] \mid$ in Period 2 if m or more investors collect information about s,[33] and, if the information is revealed at $(t + 2)$, will make a further profit whose expected value is $\mid E[l - \hat{l} \mid l] \mid$. If the price does not adjust at $(t + 1)$, then his or her profit at $(t + 2)$, conditional on information revelation, is $\mid l \mid$. Thus $\phi(N)$, the expected reward to collecting information about l when N investors collect information about s is given by

$$\phi(N) = f\{\textstyle\sum_{j=m}^{N} b_j [(m/j)E[\mid E[\hat{l} \mid l]\mid] + \mu E[\mid E[l - \hat{l} \mid l]\mid]]$$
$$+ \mu \textstyle\sum_{j=1}^{m-1} b_j E[\mid l \mid]\}, \tag{29}$$

where b_j is the binomial probability that j investors collect information about s.

Using the properties of the normal distribution, this may be written as

$$\phi(N) = f\sigma_1 \sqrt{\frac{2}{\pi}}\{\textstyle\sum_{j=m}^{N} b_j [km/j + \mu(1 - k)] + \mu \sum_{j=1}^{m-1} b_j\}. \tag{30}$$

Thus, the incentive for an individual to collect information about s, or to use the "wrong" model, rather than collect information about l is proportional to

$$\textstyle\sum_{j=m}^{N} b_j [(m/j)(\sqrt{k} - k) - \mu(1 - k)] - \mu \sum_{j=1}^{m} b_j (1 - \sqrt{k}), \tag{31}$$

and this expression may clearly be positive for small μ—it is more likely to be positive the less noisy the signal (the larger is k).

The incentive to deviate from the equilibrium convention of collecting information on the noisy signal or imperfect model, s, is increasing in μ because the

---

[33] We are assuming that our deviant individual has no effect on price setting.

higher is μ the greater is the probability that the payoff received by the current generation will depend upon the underlying fundamentals rather than the noise signal s. Similarly, the more noisy is the signal, the greater is the incentive to deviate by collecting information on the underlying asset value, because the more noisy is the signal the greater is the reward from knowing the underlying asset value if it is revealed at $t + 2$; offsetting this is the consideration that the noisier is the signal, the less useful is knowledge of the underlying asset value for predicting the change in price during trading at $t + 1$; nevertheless, it can be shown that the former effect outweighs the latter.

Thus, we have shown that it may be advantageous for an investor to stick with the conventional valuation model even though that model is incorrect in the sense that there may be another model which predicts the asset payoffs better. The reason for this paradox of course is that the investor has only limited interest in the ultimate asset payoffs—he is also interested in the resale value of the asset, and that may depend on the conventional valuation model. Note that this result does not depend on the cost of information since we have assumed that the cost of both signals is the same.[34]

It is an interesting empirical issue whether asset market values are ever based on inferior valuation models. This will not be easy to determine, because for few assets is there a close relation between theoretical values and observable variables. Nevertheless, Modigliani and Cohn (1979) have suggested that the whole market was undervalued at times of high inflation because of mistaken conventions in treating real and nominal interest rates, and this hypothesis may be tested. As another example, consider gold again. Casual empiricism suggests that gold mines are valued by traditional discounting of expected net cash flows, although it is well known that the present value of an ounce of gold deliverable in the future is exactly equal to the current spot price. The question then is whether the difference between the value of gold computed at the current spot price and the value obtained by discounting projected sales revenues adds explanatory power to a regression in which the market value is the dependent variable and conventional brokerage house valuations are the independent variable.

V. Summary and Conclusion

We have considered the implications of costly information acquisition by investors from two perspectives. First, we have shown, using the parable of the gold mine, that if market prices do not reflect asset values and the managerial objective function places any weight on the current market price, then there will be an incentive to realize asset values early. We also showed that the market price reaction to the announcement of an asset realization will depend on the precise managerial objective function, and that in particular there will be no price reaction if the manager continuously maximizes the current stock price. If the cost of following such a policy is high, there will be a substantial advantage to

---

[34] The result is similar to sunspot theories of asset market equilibrium.

being owned by a single large investor or by management, since this will shift concern from the market price.

Second, we showed that in a market of small investors the rewards of information collection will depend in a non-monotonic fashion on the number of investors who collect information, since this will affect not only the frequency with which mispriced assets can be discovered, but also the speed at which the pricing discrepancies are eliminated and their discoverers rewarded. Thus it is possible to have equilibria in which assets remain latent despite relatively small information acquisition costs. Such situations create incentives for both managers and large investors who can gain control to convert assets to cash to demonstrate values. The externalities to the collection of information suggest that there may be advantages for small investors in delegating their information acquisition to a single entity; not only does this allow a sharing of costs, but also, by coordinating the investment decisions of the investors, ensures that the information acquired will be rapidly reflected in market prices to their mutual advantage.[35] It is possible that brokerage house analysts play such a role.

Appendix: An Equilibrium with Precommitment

Assume that the manager of the mine can precommit to an extraction policy and that the cost of extraction is not publicly observable. Then, if the interest rate is r, the real cost of extraction is C, and the rate of growth in the nominal cost of extraction is $m < r$, the intrinsic value of time 0 of a mine which is committed to producing at time τ is $g - Ce^{(m-r)\tau}$. Let $V(\tau)$ denote the market value at time 0 of a mine which precommits to producing at time τ, and assume that the manager of the mine maximizes a weighted average of the current market value of the mine and its intrinsic value:[36]

$$\max_{\tau} \alpha V(\tau) + (1 - \alpha)[g - (e^{(m-r)\tau}]. \tag{A1}$$

The first and second order conditions for a maximum in this problem are

$$\alpha V' - (1 - \alpha)(m - r)Ce^{(m-r)\tau} = 0, \tag{A2}$$

$$\alpha V'' - (1 - \alpha(m - r)^2)Ce^{(m-r)\tau} < 0. \tag{A3}$$

Rational expectations require that the market value be equal to the intrinsic value:

$$V(\tau) = g - C(\tau)e^{(m-r)\tau}, \tag{A4}$$

where $C(\tau)$ is the real (time 0) cost of a mine that precommits to produce at time τ in equilibrium. Differentiating expression (A4) with respect to τ,

$$V' = -[C'(\tau) + (m - r)C(\tau)]e^{(m-r)\tau}. \tag{A5}$$

---

[35] Of course, to keep individual investors in the coalition, it will be necessary to randomize the order in which they receive the information. This differs from the randomization of messages by a monopoly information supplier in Admati and Pfleiderer (1986).

[36] This type of objective function which is virtually canonical in models of this kind contrasts with the market value maximization role considered in the body of the paper.

Substitution for V' from (A5) in condition (A2) yields, after some simplification:

$$\alpha C' = (r - m)C. \tag{A6}$$

Solving (A6) and imposing the condition that the lowest cost mine produces immediately, yields the equilibrium time to produce schedule:

$$\tau(c) = \left(\frac{\alpha}{r - m}\right)\ln(C/\underline{C}), \tag{A7}$$

where $\underline{C} \leq g$ is the real extraction cost of the lowest cost mine.

The equilibrium valuation schedule is obtained by solving (A7) for $C(\tau)$ and substituting in (A4):

$$V(\tau) = g - \underline{C} \exp\{(r - m)(1 - \alpha)\tau/\alpha\}. \tag{A8}$$

It can be shown that this schedule satisfies the second order condition (A3), and that (A8) is the unique valuation schedule to satisfy the Cho-Kreps (1987) Intuitive Criterion. Finally, we can calculate the market value assigned to a mine with initial cost C by subsituting for $\tau(C)$ from (A7) in (A8) to obtain

$$V(C) = g - \underline{C}^{\alpha}C^{1-\alpha}. \tag{A9}$$

As with the model without precommitment presented in the text, the information asymmetry induces early extraction, and it is the mines with the lowest cost that produce first. Thus the equilibrium in qualitatively similar to that of Section II.

REFERENCES

Acharya, S., 1988, A generalized econometric model and tests of a signalling hypothesis, *Journal of Finance* 43, 413–430.

Alderson, M., and K. C. Chen, 1986, Excess asset reversions and shareholder wealth, *Journal of Finance* 41, 225–241.

Brennan, M. J., 1958, The supply of storage, *American Economic Review* 48, 50–72.

—— and E. S. Schwartz, 1985, Evaluating natural resource investments, *Journal of Business* 58, 135–158.

Bruner, R. F., D. R. Harrington and S. B. Marshall, 1987, A test of ownership of excess pension assets, Unpublished manuscript, Darden School.

Butz, D. A., 1989, A theory of bust-up takeovers and takeover defenses, Unpublished manuscript, UCLA.

Cho, I. K. and D. M. Kreps, 1987, Signalling games and stable equilibria, *Quarterly Journal of Economics* 101, 179–221.

Constantinides, G. M. and B. D. Grundy, 1989, Optimal investment with stock repurchase and financing as signals, *Review of Financial Studies* Forthcoming.

Cornell, B. and A. C. Shapiro, 1989, The mispricing of U.S. Treasury bonds: A case study, *Review of Financial Studies* Forthcoming.

DeLong, J. B., A. Shleifer, L. H. Summers, and R. J. Waldmann, 1989, The size and incidence of the losses from noise trading, *Journal of Finance* 44, 681–698.

Diamond, D. W., 1985, Optimal release of information by firms, *Journal of Finance* 40, 1071–1094.

—— and R. E. Verrecchia, 1987, Constraints on short-selling and asset price adjustment to private information, *Journal of Financial Economics* 18, 277–312.

Dybvig, P. H. and J. F. Zender, 1987, Capital structure and dividend irrelevance, Unpublished manuscript.

Eckbo, B. E., V. Maksimovic, and J. Williams, 1990, Cross-sectional models in event studies: Econometric issues with an application to horizontal mergers, *Review of Financial Studies* Forthcoming.

Farrow, S., 1985, Testing the efficiency of extraction from a stock resource, *Journal of Political Economy* 93, 452–487.

Grossman, S. J. and O. D. Hart, 1980, Disclosure law and takeover bids, *Journal of Finance* 35, 323–334.

Harris, M. and A. Raviv, 1985, A sequential signalling model of convertible debt call policy, *Journal of Finance* 40, 1263–1281.

────── and A. Raviv, 1988, Corporate control contests and capital structure, *Journal of Financial Economics* 20, 55–86.

Heinkel, R., 1978, Dividend policy as a signal of firm value, in: *Essays on Financial Markets with Imperfect Information*. Ph.D. dissertation, Berkeley.

────── and A. Kraus, 1987, The effect of insider trading on average rates of return, *Canadian Journal of Economics* 20, 588–611.

Hite, G., J. E. Owens, and R. C. Rogers, 1987, The market for interfirm asset sales, *Journal of Financial Economics* 18, 229–252.

Jensen, M. C., 1986, Agency costs of free cash flow, corporate finance and takeovers, *American Economic Review* 76, 323–329.

Keynes, J. M., 1936, *The General Theory of Employment, Interest, and Money* (MacMillan, London).

Klein, A., 1986, The timing and substance of divestiture announcements: Individual, simultaneous, and cumulative effects, *Journal of Finance* 41, 685–695.

Lehn, K. and A. Poulsen, 1989, Free cash flow and stockholder gains in going private transactions, *Journal of Finance* 44, 771–787.

McConnell, J. J. and C. J. Muscarella, 1985, Corporate capital expenditure decisions and the market value of the firm, *Journal of Financial Economics* 14, 399–422.

Miller, M. H. and K. Rock, 1985, Dividend policy under asymmetric information, *Journal of Finance* 40, 1031–1051.

Modigliani, F. and R. A. Cohn, 1979, Inflation and the stock market, *Financial Analysts Journal* 35, 24–44.

Morck, R., A. Shleifer, and R. Vishny, 1988, Management ownership and market valuation: An empirical analysis, *Journal of Financial Economics* 20, 293–316.

Narayanan, M. P., 1985, Observability and the payback criterion, *Journal of Business* 58, 309–323.

Ross, S. A., 1972, The determination of financial structure: The incentive-signalling approach, *The Bell Journal of Economics* 8, 23–40.

──────, 1989, Information and volatility: The no-arbitrage martingale approach to timing and resolution irrelevancy, *Journal of Finance* 44, 1–17.

Rotemberg, J. J. and D. S. Scharfstein, 1989, Shareholder value maximization and product market competition, *Review of Financial Studies* Forthcoming.

Scholes, M. S., G. P. Wilson, and M. A. Wolfson, 1989, Tax planning, regulatory capital planning, and financial reporting strategy for commercial banks, G.S.B., Stanford.

Shleifer, A. and R. W. Vishny, 1986, Large shareholders and corporate control, *Journal of Political Economy* 94, 461–488.

Stein, J., 1988, Takeover threats and managerial myopia, *Journal of Political Economy* 96, 61–80.

Stulz, R., 1988, Managerial control of voting rights: Financing policies and the market for corporate control, *Journal of Financial Economics* 20, 25–54.

Summers, L., 1986, Does the stock market rationally reflect fundamental values?, *Journal of Finance* 41, 591–600.

Thakor, A. V., 1982, An exploration of competitive signalling equilibria with third party information, *Journal of Finance* 37, 717–739.

Thompson, R., 1978, The information content of discounts and premiums on closed end fund shares, *Journal of Financial Economics* 6, 151–186.

Vanderhei, J., 1987, The effect of voluntary termination of overfunded pension plans on shareholder wealth, *Journal of Risk and Insurance* 131–156.

[9]

Corporate Finance Over the Past 25 Years

Michael J. Brennan

Michael J. Brennan is Irwin and Goldyne Hearsh Professor of Banking and Finance, University of California, Los Angeles, CA and Professor of Finance, London Business School.

This paper traces developments in the theory of corporate finance over the past 25 years. These include a shift from consideration of how the value of a *given* cash flow stream is affected by its division among different classes of security holders to a consideration of how the structure of claims affects the cash flow stream itself. A major reason for this shift of emphasis is the attention now paid to the role of individually motivated agents in the corporation. Other important developments include recognition of information asymmetries, the role of private benefits of control, and the application of the option pricing paradigm to the evaluation of real investments.

In fearless youth we tempt the heights of Arts;
While from the bounded level of our mind
Short views we take, nor see the lengths behind,
But, more advanced, behold with strange surprise
New distant scenes of endless science rise!

Alexander Pope

■ It is natural for any generation to think of itself as the culmination of the past—the tip of the arrow of progress. It is less easy for it to see itself as the stepping stone of future generations—to recognize that its perspectives and modes of analysis are likely to appear as limited to them as do the efforts of the past appear to contemporaries. It is therefore instructive to review the history of a science, to see what was unconsciously overlooked, and to recognize the limitations of past perspectives, not to provide a source of self-congratulation to our more enlightened age but rather to provide a sense of humility about our own vision.

I thank the Editors for useful suggestions and editorial comments, and I thank the following individuals who have commented on previous drafts: David Hirshleifer, Ivo Welch, Stewart Myers, and Fred Weston. I retain responsibility for the views expressed.

Editors' Note: Michael J. Brennan is a long-time member of FMA, and currently serves as an Associate Editor of *Financial Management*. He graciously agreed to write this review article for the journal to commemorate the Association's twenty-fifth anniversary. Professor Brennan started in the profession after graduating from MIT 25 years ago, as it happens, in the same year FMA was founded. Since then, he has given tremendously to the profession. In addition to his many significant contributions to the finance literature, he has served in numerous capacities, including as the Editor of the *Journal of Finance* (1980-1983), the founding Executive Editor of the *Review of Financial Studies* (1987-1990), and President of the American Finance Association (1989).

For just as earlier ages may appear to us as blinkered and obtuse, so are we likely to appear to future generations, and by recognizing this fact, we may possibly become more sensitive to the limitations of our contemporary paradigm. Twenty-five years after the founding of *Financial Management*, it is an appropriate moment to stop and take stock of what we have accomplished during this quarter century.

From one perspective, the development of corporate finance since 1970 can be thought of in terms of a shift from exploring the valuation implications of alternative ways of allocating *given* cash flow streams to exploring the implications for the cash flow stream itself of the allocation mechanism used to distribute it: in other words, in terms of the relaxation of the major *ceteris paribus* assumptions underlying the MM propositions concerning dividend and, particularly, capital structure policy. Whereas MM had taken the firm's net operating income as given and had asked what effect its allocation among different claim holders would have on the total value of the income stream, the new theorists were increasingly concerned with the effect of the structure of claims on the incentives of the individuals whose decisions would determine the income stream. Increased recognition of the importance of the structure of claims to the firm's cash flows has led to a renewed attention to the roles of different types of security issue; under the MM paradigm, these were for the most part a "mere detail" and therefore not amenable to serious analysis. At the same time, recognition that contracts are necessarily incomplete and fail to constrain future decisions completely has led to analysis

Financial Management, Vol. 24, No. 2, Summer 1995, pages 9-22.

10   **FINANCIAL MANAGEMENT / SUMMER 1995**

of the allocation of control or decision rights across claimholders. On the asset side of the balance sheet, there has been a corresponding shift in focus, from asking what investment decision rule investors would unanimously support to asking what rules decision makers are likely to follow, given their incentives. Finally, whereas the old approach was essentially comparative static in nature, comparing corporations with different financial structures, the modern theory has a much more dynamic flavor to it, with analysis focused on particular events or transactions in the life of the corporation, such as initial public offerings, subsequent financings of debt and equity, repurchases of securities and exchange offers, takeover, and bankruptcy.

From a second perspective, the fundamental change has been the recognition of the decisive role of individually motivated agents, both those within the corporation and those with whom the corporation must deal. The corporation of financial theory in the early 1970s ignored individual agents within the corporation either by assuming that they acted as well-trained robots (as in the investment decision)[1] or by paralyzing them with the *ceteris paribus* assumptions that underlie the classical capital structure propositions. Similarly, it rendered the individuals with whom the corporation must deal—investors, bankers, underwriters, bidders, customers, employees, and others—essentially uninteresting, by treating them as price takers who suffered from no informational disadvantage and had no relevant aims beyond expanding their budget sets. In economic analysis, agents are described by their tastes and their opportunities, and the new theories that have been developed have relied on a more careful (or perhaps more imaginative!) description of both tastes and opportunities. Important features of the opportunity set that have been newly recognized include the informational endowments of agents, their discretionary powers, and the nature of the implicit and explicit contracts that link their actions to their rewards. Newly recognized aspects of tastes include perquisite consumption, control benefits and other non-pecuniary benefits, reputation, and effort aversion. These new concepts have provided richer explanations for newly recognized phenomena.

From a third perspective, the shift can be seen in large part as one of technique. The new technology of games under incomplete information has replaced the price-taking assumption throughout much of the corporate finance literature, and traditional discounted cash flow approaches to valuation have begun to give way to techniques derived from those used to price stock options.

From a fourth perspective, the shift can be seen as a move from analyzing the implications of existing institutional arrangements, to that of justifying such arrangements as optimal responses to particular problems, then to considering alternative institutions. In parallel to this, efforts have shifted from the development of normative rules for corporate decision makers to the development of normative propositions about such institutional arrangements as insider trading rules, disclosure, the payment of greenmail, and the erection of other takeover defenses.

The reader should be aware that a survey of this nature is likely to suffer from the ex-post selection bias that plagues many empirical studies: it will concentrate on what turned out to be successful and of enduring interest. The historian of science is likely to be as interested in those avenues of endeavor that were subsequently abandoned or became moribund. It is therefore worth recalling that in 1970 the term "financial economics" was not yet in common usage, and the battle between finance as a subfield of management science and as a subfield of economics was not yet over. Major research topics at that time included the use of linear programming to design capital budgets, models of cash management based on inventory theory, models for accounts receivable management based on credit scoring, and Markov Chain models of credit losses. All of these topics have since been abandoned by most scholars in finance and now find only occasional mention in the standard textbooks. Other topics such as leasing, bond refunding, and the estimation of discount rates for capital budgeting,[2] once the focus of considerable research effort, have fallen out of fashion, either because the problems are deemed to have been "solved" or to be intractable so that further progress seems impossible or because the research paradigms that are of most interest today have little or nothing to say about them.

I start this brief survey by sketching the state of corporate financial theory 25 years ago and then describing how the prevailing paradigm broke down under the weight of new developments. In the balance of the paper, I identify some new key concepts and theoretical drivers that have fundamentally changed our way of looking at the world of corporate finance. My focus is on the changing conceptual framework within which problems in corporate finance are analyzed, and I make no attempt to provide an exhaustive survey of the various topics, such as mergers and acquisitions, initial public offerings, etc., that now fall within the purview of the subject, since that would be a considerably more ambitious undertaking. Nor do I give more than passing attention to the now voluminous empirical literature.

---

[1] However, the potential for conflict between managers and stockholders had been recognized by Donaldson (1963), although formal models were lacking.

[2] See for example (1972), Bower (1973), and Van Horne (1980).

I. The State of Financial Theory 25 Years Ago

In 1970, the corpus of corporate financial theory was, on the one hand, the Fisherian separation of consumption and investment decisions that gave rise to the unanimous support among stockholders for value-maximizing decisions, at least in a world of complete capital markets, and on the other hand, the Modigliani-Miller irrelevance propositions and their tax-adjusted counterparts. The pure theory of corporate investment was supplemented for practical purposes by the recently developed Capital Asset Pricing Model, which offered new insights into the determinants of investors' required rates of return, and although management science techniques, such as Monte Carlo analysis and decision trees, were advocated as practical decision tools, little effort was made to integrate these into the corpus of financial theory. Thus, it remained unclear, for example, either what discount rates were to be employed in computing the present values generated by the simulations or how the distribution of present values yielded by the simulations was to be interpreted. However, it was becoming widely recognized that corporate valuations of investment projects could not be divorced from investor valuations of securities. The state of the art in valuing corporate securities was a poorly integrated combination of discounted cash flow analysis, as represented for example by the dividend discount model, which is essentially multi-period, and the capital asset pricing model, which at that time was strictly a single-period model. At this juncture, the abstract simplicity of the Arrow-Debreu model yielded few insights for corporate finance beyond the principle of value additivity that was used to refute the conventional wisdom that conglomerate mergers added value by providing corporate diversification.

The spare elegance of the neo-classical world of the hard core theory of MM, Fisher Separation, and the Arrow-Debreu model was a reaction to the detailed institutional fussiness of the previous era of financial research, represented by Dewing (1920) and other institutionalists—it was in itself a "back to basics" movement, an attempt to focus on essentials while relegating institutional details to footnotes. Of course, the distinction between essentials and details reflects a particular point of view, and the MM decision to focus on the valuation of a given cash flow stream rather than on the effects of the financing method on the cash flow stream was decisive; while the irrelevance propositions of MM were not without their critics, it is notable to the modern eye that none of these critics focused on the critical *ceteris paribus*

assumption about the income stream to be allocated. The reason was of course that this assumption was not recognized as significant—"we are talking here about financing and 'by definition' this has nothing to do with investment or the size of the revenue stream." It is interesting to speculate what comparable oversimplifications future generations will discern in our current modes of analysis and points of view.

On the empirical front, major efforts were devoted to confirming or refuting the MM capital structure and dividend propositions, using the kind of cross-sectional regressions that have recently become popular once more in the form of Tobin's q regressions, the earlier econometric criticisms of this approach having evidently been forgotten.[3] Probably the most significant paper in empirical corporate finance, "The Adjustment of Stock Prices to New Information," by Fama, Fisher, Jensen, and Roll, was published in 1969. This was to be the precursor of an avalanche of "event studies." While many of these are of modest individual value, they have collectively created a whole new body of empirical knowledge, which has at once stimulated theoretical development and disciplined that development by subjecting it to empirical tests.

II. The Breakdown of the Neoclassical Paradigm

The first signs of breakdown in the neoclassical paradigm resulted from confusion as to how the CAPM should be used to determine appropriate value-maximizing investment criteria. This debate about the appropriate definition of price-taking behavior concerned the conditions under which investors in the corporation would be unanimous on the choice of investment policy. It was eventually settled that such unanimity (in support of value maximization) would be achieved if a project's cash flows were spanned by existing securities in the capital market.[4]

It was similar considerations of market spanning and completeness that underlay the first attacks on the MM capital structure propositions,[5] and it was not until 1978 that this issue seems finally to have been laid to rest by Fama (1978), whose "equal access" assumption implies that risk-sharing opportunities are unaffected by corporate capital structure decisions.

However, the implications of market incompleteness for both investment and financing policy have remained largely

---

[3]See Friend and Puckett (1964) and Keenan (1970).

[4]See Jensen and Long (1972) and the Symposium in the *Bell Journal of Economics and Management Science* (Spring 1974).

[5]Stiglitz (1969 and 1974).

unpursued, perhaps because of the lack of tractable results.[6] Thus, it was primarily the papers of Jensen and Meckling (1976), Leland and Pyle (1977), Myers (1977), and Ross (1977) that led to the abandonment of the neo-classical paradigm. Both Fama and Miller (1972) and Stiglitz (1972) had recognized that, when debt is risky, maximizing shareholder wealth may not imply the same decisions as maximizing firm value. Although Stiglitz argued that firms were in fact more likely to maximize shareholder wealth, as late as 1978 Fama was invoking the Coase theorem to argue that if the firm did not maximize total firm value there would be incentives for others to buy up the firm's bonds and equity and follow the value maximizing policy.[7] Neither of these authors pursued the implications of the distinction between firm value and equity value maximization, and as a result, it was left to Jensen and Meckling (1976) and Myers (1977) to provide the first serious arguments that capital structure was more than simply a way of allocating an existing income stream and that it could affect the nature of the income to be distributed. This struck a decisive blow at the fundamental *ceteris paribus* assumption of the MM paradigm. Jensen and Meckling, Leland and Pyle, and Ross were epochal in introducing into financial economics an owner-manager decision maker within the corporation.

The advance of the new paradigms of capital structure was to be further hastened by the growing realization that the old story of taxes and bankruptcy costs was inadequate to explain industry capital structures. The empirical evidence of Warner (1977) on the modest size of the direct costs of bankruptcy was to lead Miller (1977) to label the theory "horse and rabbit stew." Interestingly, Miller, having shown that there might be no tax effects associated with capital structure, went on to suggest that practical concern over capital structure might represent no more than an evolutionarily neutral heuristic!

While the direction of advance has a certain inevitability about it when seen in retrospect, the direction was by no means so obvious to contemporaries. For example, in 1972, Stiglitz published a paper, modestly entitled "Some Aspects

of the Pure Theory of Corporate Finance," in which he developed a theory of capital structure that was based on the assumptions that investors have heterogeneous beliefs about firm payoffs and are prohibited from short selling. In this setting, a value-maximizing debt ratio emerges as the result of a divergence in the estimation of the chances of bankruptcy between the lender and the borrower. Despite the existence of significant costs of short sales for many market participants, this line of inquiry was not pursued further for another 20 years.[8]

III. Adverse Selection, Signaling, and Screening in Financial Markets

Although Miller and Modigliani (1961) had recognized that managerial actions could convey information to less well-informed outsiders, the first formal models of this phenomenon were developed by Leland and Pyle (LP) and by Ross in 1977, applying and extending the work of Rothschild and Stiglitz (1976) and Spence (1973). LP were perhaps the first to address a particular event or transaction in corporate history,[9] while Ross was the first to draw attention to the importance of the managerial compensation function, although this was taken as exogenous in his model.

Asquith and Mullins (1983), using the now common event study methodology, found that share prices tended to fall on the announcement of a common stock issue. This raised the fundamental question of why managers should take actions that impoverished the shareholders. Myers and Majluf (1984) presented an elegant explanation in terms of adverse selection. In their model, unlike those of LP and Ross, privately informed managers were assumed to act in the interest of (old) shareholders.[10]

The underpricing of initial public offerings was recognized as early as 1973 by Logue, but it was not until 1986 that a plausible account of this phenomenon was offered by Rock in terms of the adverse selection problem faced by uninformed investors. This explanation finds empirical support in Koh and Walter (1989), and more recent

---

[6]For recent attention to this theme, see Allen and Gale (1994). DeTemple and Jorion(1990), Jarrow and O'Hara (1989), and Vijh (1994) offer empirical evidence that capital structure changes that affect the span of the market may have significant valuation consequences; of course, the span of the market may be changed not only by the corporation but also by financial intermediaries and the opening of new markets. Boot and Thakor (1993), DeMarzo and Duffie (1993), and Ross (1989) have drawn attention to the possibility that the mix of securities sold by the firm may affect the costs of marketing the securities and investor incentives to collect information about their payoffs, which in turn may affect the price the firm is able to realize for its securities.

[7]This of course is to ignore the free-rider problem stressed by Grossman and Hart (1980).

[8]See Allen and Gale (1994) and the references therein for recent attention to models in which a short sales constraint is important.

[9]While the theory of games under incomplete information has undoubtedly played a major role in the development of new theories of corporate transactions, it is worth noting that considerable progress was made by LP, Myers and Majluf (1984), and others prior to the formal application of this theory in finance.

[10]A not quite resolved difficulty in the Myers-Majluf model concerns the use of rights issues. However, the still not well-understood demise of the rights issue in the U.S. suggests that they were right in concluding that it does not resolve the issue they address.

attempts to explain underpricing as a signal of quality have met with less empirical success.[11] The Rock model would seem particularly applicable to the institutional arrangements in Britain and those Commonwealth countries that have adopted the British system of a formal public offering and less applicable in the book-building environment of the U.S. than the model of Spatt and Srivastava (1991), which emphasizes the incentives for potential investors to reveal their valuations truthfully, or the model of Welch (1992), which analyzes the consequences of approaching potential purchasers of an issue *seriatim*. Both types of models assume strategic behavior on the part of either underwriters or investors, and the differing models point to the importance of attention to details concerning institutional mechanism.[12] The recently noted apparent long-run overpricing of both seasoned issues and initial public offerings poses a continuing challenge to theorists.

Given that issuers of new securities face an adverse selection problem, it was natural to consider how firms could signal their types by the choice of securities or other means. Masulis (1980) had provided evidence that pure capital structure changes brought about by exchange offers caused stock price changes,[13] Brennan and Kraus (1987), Constantinides and Grundy (1989), and Heinkel (1982), all developed signaling models in which a firm could reveal its type by its choice of financing package.

The empirically documented information content of dividend announcements also provided a natural target for the construction of signaling rationales. Bhattacharya (1979) and John and Williams (1985) developed models that relied on the taxability of dividends, while the Miller and Rock (1985) model rested on a link between dividends and investment to provide the required signaling costs. All these models assume implicitly that the informed insider places positive weight on both the current and future stock prices.

Other contexts in which signaling models have been developed are the choice of debt maturity structure when the firm has private information about its future credit rating (Flannery, 1986) and tender offers when the bidding firm has private information about synergy gains (Hirshleifer and Titman, 1990). Brennan (1990) and Stein (1988) have also shown that signaling considerations may influence not only

financial decisions but also real investment decisions, if the manager is concerned about the current level of the stock price.

The accounts provided by these signaling models have an inherent plausibility, yet they often lack the bite of a Popperian conjecture since they generally fail to yield empirical predictions beyond the ones for which they were custom tailored: Williamson labels this style of theorizing "naive functionalism."[14] In particular, while the models show that particular instruments can be used as signals, they generally fail to show why one instrument should be chosen over another.[15] Moreover, the choice of objective function for the informed insider in signaling models has remained a matter of *ad hoc* convenience, and sometimes controversy. Thus, Dybvig and Zender (1991) have objected to "suboptimal contracts imposed by fiat" and propose a simple profit-sharing contract that leads to efficient investment decisions and removes the managerial concern with the current stock price that provides the motivation for many signaling models. However, Persons (1994) shows that the Dybvig-Zender contract is not time consistent in the sense that there will be incentives for shareholders and managers to renegotiate the contract in certain states. As yet there has been no positive analysis of the bargaining, and essentially political process, by which executive compensation contracts are determined, although there is now a growing literature on optimal compensation contracts for managers under moral hazard:[16] in most of the literature, the manager is assumed to receive no more than his reservation wage.

IV. Moral Hazard and Agency in the Theory of the Corporation

The implications of the separation of ownership and control of the modern corporation first noted by Berle and Means (1932) had been further developed by Marris (1964) and Penrose (1959), among others, but it was Jensen and Meckling (1976) (JM) who were the first to emphasize the role of financial contracts in creating and controlling agency problems. Agency problems arise because of the impossibility of contracting perfectly on the actions of an

[11]See Michaely and Shaw (1994).

[12]Benveniste and Wilhelm (1990) and Chowdhry and Sherman (1994) explicitly analyze the implications of different institutional arrangements for IPO pricing.

[13]The Masulis paper is particularly interesting from an historical viewpoint in that it appeared just as the old tax/bankruptcy theories were giving way to the new information-based theories. Masulis is aware of the signaling models but explicitly claims that "the signaling hypothesis will not be tested."

[14]"Naive functionalism supplies *ex post* rationalizations for outcomes in which some intent is purportedly served. That is an easy exercise, but it is irrefutable and undisciplined" (Williamson, 1994).

[15]Ambarish, John, and Williams (1987) do address this issue by analyzing the combination of signals that will yield a separating equilibrium at minimum cost. While almost all signaling models assume that there is only a single parameter of the return distribution to be signaled, Hughes (1986) develops a model in which both the mean and variance of the return distribution are revealed by the insider's choice of action.

[16]See below.

agent whose actions influence both his own welfare and that of others. JM drew attention to the implications of managerial discretion for the welfare of shareholders and explained how agency costs could be minimized by more fully aligning the interests of shareholders and managers. They also drew attention to the agency problem that exists between shareholders, assuming that they have decision rights, and other claimholders, particularly bondholders. These considerations led to an informal theory of capital structure based on the minimization of the sum of these agency costs. In advancing this theory, JM introduced to the finance literature a rich vocabulary of terms, such as costly contracting, perquisites, bonding, and monitoring, that have inspired subsequent investigators.

JM drew further attention to the incentive of shareholders to choose risky projects that would expropriate wealth from creditors and pointed out that convertible securities might mitigate these risk-shifting incentives.[17] This seems to have been the first time in the modern era that an explicit rationale was offered for the existence of these hybrid securities. Myers (1977) extended the JM analysis of the conflict of interest between bondholders and stockholders by showing that it could lead to the failure of the corporation to undertake valuable investment projects. While the nature of managerial perquisite consumption in JM was left somewhat vague, Jensen (1986) claimed to identify a Penrose-Marris concern with growth as a besetting managerial vice that could be constrained by limiting the access of the manager to free cash flow through the issuance of bonds; these securities would represent a pre-commitment to pay out the cash rather than to waste it on unprofitable projects. This represented a turning on its head of one of the major arguments for the conglomerate form that had been popular in the 1960s—the ability of a well-informed management of a conglomerate to allocate capital more efficiently than the capital market could. Hart and Moore (1990) and Stulz (1990) combined these Jensen and Myers arguments into a theory of optimal debt ratio that traded off the costs of good projects foregone against the cost of poor projects undertaken.

Under the standard assumptions, managerial behavior will be influenced by the choice of compensation function as well as by the threat of replacement. Optimal managerial compensation functions that take account of managerial moral hazard have been extensively analyzed.[18] One puzzle that has attracted attention is the heavy dependence of executive compensation on accounting earnings rather

than stock prices, since it is the stock price that investors are assumed to want to maximize. Paul (1992) shows that stock-based compensation can lead to substantial inefficiency because making compensation depend on the stock price constrains the manner in which information about individual project payoffs enters the compensation function. Perhaps a more general limitation of the moral-hazard-based theories of executive compensation is an overly stylized representation of the moral hazard problem itself as one simply of effort aversion: While this may be a major problem in share-cropping on which much of this literature is based, it may well be that shareholders are more concerned with counteracting managerial risk aversion, discouraging the pursuit of grandiose managerial visions at their expense, or ensuring that managers distribute the rents earned by the firm to shareholders rather than to employees or other groups.[19] As yet, little attention has been directed to the effect of managerial compensation on the ability of the manager to successfully lead a team of employees,[20] or to bargain with other stakeholders in the corporation.[21] Hirshleifer and Thakor (1992) and Narayanan (1985) analyze the effects of managerial career considerations on compensation schemes and managerial behavior.

V. Corporate Control, Monitoring, and Financial Intermediation

A new concept or motive for behavior introduced in the corporate finance literature is the non-pecuniary benefit allegedly received by those in control of the corporation. This non-pecuniary benefit has implications for the voting structure of the corporation and has been used to justify the assignment of votes to equity on a one-share-one-vote basis by Grossman and Hart (1988) and Harris and Raviv (1989).

More significantly, the non-pecuniary benefits obtained by the manager of an operating corporation may make him

---

[17]Chiesa (1992) and Green (1984) develop further the effects of convertibles and warrants on risk-shifting incentives.

[18]For early examples in the finance literature, see Diamond and Verrecchia (1982) and Ramakrishnan and Thakor (1984).

[19]Dofusco, Johnson, and Zorn (1990) report that the introduction of executive stock option plans is accompanied by an increase in the stock price but a decrease in the price of the firm's outstanding debt. This is consistent with the hypothesis that stock option plans induce managers to take on more risk than they otherwise would.

[20]It is possible that employee morale may be adversely affected by what is perceived as excessive managerial compensation. While this has received attention in the popular press and Kahneman, Knetsch, and Thaler (1986) present evidence that considerations of equity may affect economic behavior, models that incorporate such considerations have yet to appear in mainstream corporate finance. Baker, Jensen, and Murphy (1988) note that observed compensation schemes are not easily explained by traditional economic theory.

[21]The shape of the managerial compensation function may affect a management's willingness to withstand a strike that will reduce the current year's profits but increase profitability in subsequent years.

reluctant to liquidate the corporation even when it is socially optimal to do so. The infeasibility of writing contracts that will compel the manager to liquidate at the optimal time has led to the development of a line of theory in which the role of capital structure is to ensure socially optimal liquidation. The earliest paper to be concerned with socially optimal liquidation was Titman (1984) although, unlike subsequent writers, his analysis omitted any reference to the non-pecuniary benefits of control. More recent work by Aghion and Bolton (1992) has focused on the role of securities in re-allocating control between different contracting parties in a world of incomplete contracts.

The non-pecuniary benefits of control and the consequent tendency of managers to continue projects when it would be socially efficient to liquidate them have provided the basis also of theories of debt maturity (Diamond, 1993) and the role of financial intermediaries as monitors (Rajan, 1992).[22]

Shleifer and Vishny (1986) focus on the role of large shareholders as monitors who can facilitate the replacement of management by takeover, while Admati, Pfleiderer, and Zechner (1994) stress the free-rider problem in stockholder monitoring and the costs that this implies for large shareholders. A complete theory of the structure of shareholdings is yet to emerge, although Demsetz and Lehn (1985) represents a promising beginning. Maug (1994) and Warther (1994) analyze the role of the board of directors as monitors.

VI. Reputation

The idea that a firm or manager might care about their reputation for quality, skill, or some other attribute, is a new one in corporate finance. Gibbons and Murphy (1992), Hirshleifer and Thakor (1992), and Narayanan (1985) show how concern with personal reputation may be a consideration in managerial decision making. Diamond (1989) shows how a firm's reputation may affect its access to debt markets and demonstrates how this can influence the investment projects it chooses. Boot, Greenbaum, and Thakor (1993) argue that limitations in contracting technology may mean that it is efficient to have some contractual provisions that are legally unenforceable[23] and to rely on reputational considerations for enforcement in most but not all states of the world. They cite as an example the behavior of mutual fund management companies in making voluntary contributions to restore

losses on money market funds. Maksimovic and Titman (1991) analyze the interaction between a firm's reputation for product quality and its financial structure. The lack of a legal requirement for a firm to pay preferred dividends, and the *prima facie* interest of common shareholders to suspend them, appears to be a puzzle that may be explicable in terms of reputational considerations. However, a difficulty with the reputational concept as applied to firms is that it is unclear precisely where the reputation resides if a firm is no more than a "nexus of contracts;" what is it about firms that makes some "good types," and can this not be changed by a new management?

VII. Pre-Commitment and Bonding with Financial Contracts

While outstanding debt can create adverse incentives for investment, which can only be mitigated by the design of appropriate bond indentures (Smith and Warner, 1979), several authors have argued that the risk-increasing incentives of debt can be put to creative use by pre-committing the firm to a particular output policy that will give it a competitive advantage in the product market.[24] Empirical evidence of such effects appears to be lacking,[25] however, and the analysis of Scharfstein and Bolton (1990) suggests rather the reverse. Jensen (1986) claims that an important role of debt is to precommit the firm to pay out its free cash flow rather than wasting it on unprofitable investments, and it is argued that the high leverage employed in many takeovers represents a commitment to dispose of assets. On the other side of the coin, a distinction that is sometimes made between bank debt and publicly held debt is that the former can be renegotiated while the latter is very hard to renegotiate. As Bergman and Callen (1991) show, a firm may sometimes wish to precommit not to renegotiate its debt by issuing public debt.

VIII. Bankruptcy

No subject of study better exemplifies the developments that have taken place in the field of corporate finance than that of bankruptcy. Twenty-five years ago bankruptcy was a neglected topic in the theory of corporate finance, being taken as virtually synonymous with liquidation, its unverified costs used to provide a counterbalance to tax savings in the analysis of capital structure, the absolute priority rule being implicitly assumed to hold, and the details

---

[22]Diamond (1984) had originally proposed that financial intermediaries provided efficiency gains in monitoring, but in his model monitoring was limited to ensuring truthful reporting of project outcomes.

[23]Cornell and Shapiro (1987) had earlier drawn attention to the role of implicit contracts between the corporation and its stakeholders and the incentives of the corporation to honor these contracts.

[24]See Brander and Lewis (1986) and Maksimovic (1988).

[25]For evidence that increases in leverage "soften" product market competition, see Chevalier (1995).

of the legal code neglected. All this has changed. The absolute priority rule was found to be more commonly observed in the breach than the observance by Franks and Torous (1989), and, once studied by Warner (1977) and later by Wruck (1990), the direct costs of bankruptcy appeared too meager to carry out their assigned task in the theory of capital structure. Haugen and Senbet (1978) had argued that capital structure theories that relied on bankruptcy costs implicitly neglected the possibility of informal reorganizations and workouts. Modern analyses pay careful attention to the distinction between reorganization, liquidation, and bankruptcy, and indeed a major focus of concern has become the conditions under which the current bankruptcy code will lead to efficient liquidation.[26] At the same time, reflecting the trend in all aspects of corporate finance, attention is paid to problems raised by asymmetric information about the value of the firm's assets, strategic behavior,[27] free-rider problems, and to how they can be ameliorated by the bankruptcy code, and more generally, the incentives of the various parties to a bankruptcy or reorganization. Noteworthy also is the close attention paid to the details of the bankruptcy code. Going beyond positive analyses of the current code, some authors have even proposed modifications which, they argue, will lead to an increase in efficiency.[28]

IX. Taxes, Valuation, and Capital Allocation Decisions

The implications of corporate and personal taxation for capital structure and dividend policy were a major focus of research 25 years ago. Attention was first directed to the appropriate personal tax rate for analyzing the benefits of corporate debt and the costs of corporate dividends in the Brennan (1970) incomplete markets model of personal taxation.[29] Miller (1977) transformed the debate on capital structure by introducing personal taxes and allowing for adjustments in the supply of debt in a complete markets model; his perfectly elastic supply was modified by the DeAngelo-Masulis (1980) analysis, which took account of the limited nature of corporate tax deductions. Relatively little progress has been made in testing the new tax-based

theories because of the growing recognition of the non-tax effects of debt.[30] However, Green (1993), Skelton (1983), and Trezinka (1982) provided evidence that the spread between yields on Treasury bonds and non-taxable municipal bonds corresponded to the corporate tax rate as predicted by the Miller model.

A central concern of neoclassical finance is the valuation of real assets since this is required to implement the NPV criterion. At first, the CAPM seemed to offer a practical procedure for calculating discount rates.[31] However, the CAPM was a single-period model and early efforts to derive workable multi-period versions proved nugatory.[32] Moreover, disenchantment with the results of empirical tests of the CAPM, combined with the effect of the Roll (1977) critique, has meant that, whereas once instructors were able to present the material on capital budgeting with the greatest confidence while feeling comparatively diffident about the usefulness of the irrelevance propositions that constituted our knowledge of financial policy, today's instructor is likely to feel that he has more to say about financial policy than about capital budgeting;[33] and while the Arbitrage Pricing Theory represents an elegant and more general alternative to the CAPM, its lack of a generally accepted canonical set of factors has so far impeded its widespread adoption.

Bhattacharya (1978), Brennan (1973), and Constantinides (1978) all developed partial differential equation models for asset prices based on Merton's (1973) continuous time intertemporal capital asset pricing model, and this approach reached its final form in the elegant general equilibrium model of Cox, Ingersoll, and Ross (1985); however, while this model has proven a useful workhorse for the valuation of fixed income securities that have known payoffs, it has not been applied directly to the valuation of real assets, perhaps because of the practical difficulty of identifying a system of Markov state variables that are sufficient to determine asset payoffs.

However, improved understanding of the economics of valuation is beginning to lead to the application of the

---

[26]See Gertner and Scharfstein (1991).

[27]An early application of game theoretic considerations in bankruptcy analysis was Bulow and Shoven (1978).

[28]See, for example, Aghion, Hart, and Moore (1992) and Bebchuk (1992).

[29]Miller and Scholes (1978) argued that the payment of taxes on dividend income was essentially voluntary under the U.S. tax code, and Litzenberger and Ramaswamy (1982) and Miller and Scholes (1982) engaged in an inconclusive empirical debate about the size of the representative individual's marginal tax rate on dividend income.

[30]Recognition of the non-tax-related effects of capital both made it harder to devise tests of the pure tax theories (See fn. 12) and made them seem less interesting. As Kuhn (1962, p. 37) notes, "one of the things a scientific community acquires with a paradigm is a criterion for choosing problems that...can be assumed to have solutions.... Other problems, including many that had previously been regarded as standard, are rejected...sometimes as just too problematic to be worth the time."

[31]See Weston (1973).

[32]See Bogue and Roll (1974) and Myers and Turnbull (1977).

[33]A further difficulty in applying simple asset pricing models to the determination of discount rates is the growing evidence of time-varying discount rates. In particular, the finding that the expected return on stocks is inversely related to the level of short-term interest rates casts doubt on the usefulness of techniques that assume that the market risk premium is an intertemporal constant.

martingale pricing principle[34] to the pricing of real assets. Pioneers in this effort include Black (1988) and Sick (1986). As a special case of martingale pricing, more rapid progress on a narrower front has been made by carrying over directly the principles of the Black-Scholes option pricing model to the pricing of real assets.[35] The trick here was to find a traded security whose return was perfectly correlated with that of the underlying cash flow claim: For example, Brennan and Schwartz (1985) valued a mine using futures contracts as the traded security. The option pricing paradigm was also useful in making possible the assimilation of the two old management science techniques of decision trees and Monte Carlo simulation into the mainstream of financial theory. Boyle (1977) had shown how Monte Carlo simulation could be combined with the martingale pricing principle to value financial options—clearly the same principles applied to the pricing of claims to cash flows from real assets.[36] This solved in principle the problems of what discount rate to use in Monte Carlo analyses and how to evaluate the resulting distribution of discounted present values.[37] The growing literature on "real options" has shown how the problem of what discount rate to apply in using decision trees could be solved in principle; it has also brought renewed attention to the relatively neglected topic of the timing of investment outlays[38] and the strategic aspects of investment decisions.[39]

The neoclassical treatment of the capital budgeting problem as essentially one of valuation neglects the incentives of decision makers. Recent work stresses the incentives of privately informed managers and the organizational responses to these incentives. Thus, Antle and Eppen (1985) and Harris and Raviv (1995) assume that managers derive utility from the capital resources under their control, while in Holmstrom and Ricart i Costa (1986) the convexity of the optimal managerial reward function induces excessive risk-taking. The managerial agency problem in these cases is mitigated by capital rationing imposed by the headquarters.

Thus, the focus on capital rationing has come full circle. Twenty-five years ago, attention was directed to devising

optimal procedures for capital budgeting in the presence of capital rationing; these approaches fell out of favor both because the information required to implement them was unlikely to be available in practice and because the evidence of Scholes (1968) on the elasticity of the demand for stock was taken to imply that capital rationing was unlikely to be important in practice. However, the debt overhang problem of Myers (1977) and the adverse selection costs of issuing equity described by Myers-Majluf (1984) make constraints on *external* capital more plausible, while the rationalization of limited capital budgets as optimal responses to agency problems makes constraints on internal capital allocations more plausible. This cycle is illustrative of the more general trend in corporate finance, the shift away from attempts to *prescribe* normative rules for decision makers that would assist them to take decisions that are optimal from the point of view of shareholders and towards attempts to *describe* more realistically the way that decisions are actually made.

The option pricing model of Black and Scholes has permitted a more sophisticated analysis of the valuation of other corporate securities than had hitherto been possible,[40] though surprisingly little attention has been paid to the call feature on corporate bonds, which had been a topic of major interest in the 1960s. Even more surprisingly, empirical work on the application of these models has been very slow in forthcoming.

X. Unfinished Business

While impressive progress has been made in enriching the corporate finance paradigm, it would certainly be a mistake to think that the work is near to complete. Undoubtedly, new problems, techniques, and avenues of investigation that are as yet hidden to us will appear. One of the more obvious areas that calls for further analysis is the transactions of corporations in efficient capital markets, where they can be expected to possess no informational advantages. The primary examples are the management of corporate pension funds and the explosive growth of corporate hedging in derivatives markets. Black (1980) and Tepper (1981) have offered tax-based theories that predict that pension funds will be entirely invested in debt investments, while Sharpe (1976) has argued that the existence of the PBGC put provides an offsetting incentive to invest in risky assets: Neither of these theories seems entirely satisfactory. It is interesting to note that the model of Tepper (1974) for optimal pension funding and the more recent model of Froot, Scharfstein, and Stein

---

[34]See Harrison and Kreps (1979).

[35]Myers (1977) appears to have been the first to treat investment opportunities as options, but his focus was not on valuation but on the incentives to exercise these options.

[36]Though where the underlying asset is not a traded claim, application of the martingale pricing principle may be difficult in practice.

[37]That is, only the mean of the distribution is relevant.

[38]See Ingersoll and Ross (1992).

[39]See Kester (1984). Dixit and Pindyck (1994) present a detailed survey of models in which the analogy between real investment opportunities and options on common stocks is exploited.

---

[40]See Leland (1994) and Merton (1974) for analyses of risky debt and Ingersoll (1977) for an analysis of convertible securities.

(1993) for optimal corporate hedging policy both rely on an exogenously specified rising marginal cost of funds to the corporation to yield an optimal policy; in the latter paper, this is justified by a potential Myers-Majluf-type underinvestment problem. DeMarzo and Duffie (1991) argue that investor ignorance of firm risk exposures is sufficient to justify firm hedging, but unfortunately their theory is not rich enough to specify the optimal risk exposures.[41] In an unpublished paper, the same authors develop a model that relies on managerial career considerations and the ability of the accounting system to reveal or conceal the hedging transactions: As the recent catastrophes in municipal investments and corporate derivatives transactions suggest, there is room for additional work on the agency and incentive aspects of corporate policies in these markets.

A second area in which research effort lags practical developments is the proliferation of corporate security types, such as LYONS, PERCS, and ELKS. While general accounts of securities innovation have been offered, there appears as yet to be no systematic study of the nature of the benefits offered by these and other tailored securities. Related to this is the role of marketing in the sale of securities

and the implications for corporate policy of the growing institutionalization of equity markets, which reduces the cost of transacting for the individual investor at the expense of introducing an additional layer of agency problems.[42] The importance of marketing considerations will be enhanced if the preliminary evidence of Bagwell (1992) and Loderer, Cooney, and Van Drunen (1991), that the supply of funds to the corporation is not as elastic as once believed, is borne out.[43]

The growth of firms whose major asset consists of human rather than physical capital, prominent examples being in computer software and film production, poses a new challenge to theorists and empiricists alike, for the paradigm example underlying most of our theoretical models is the manufacturing firm, which dominated the growth of the economy around mid-century. The new knowledge-based firms have quite different characteristics, since their major assets are autonomous agents rather than inert machines.

Finally, relatively little progress has been made in understanding the international dimension of corporate finance. The continuing trend towards the globalization of business activities suggests that transnational considerations will become more important in the future. ∎

References

Admati, A., P. Pfleiderer, and J. Zechner, 1994, "Shareholder Activism, Risk Sharing and Financial Market Equilibrium," *Journal of Political Economy* (December), 1097-1130.

Aghion, P. and P. Bolton, 1992, "An Incomplete Contracts Approach to Financial Contracting," *Review of Economic Studies* (July), 473-494.

Aghion, P., O.D. Hart, and J. Moore, 1992, "The Economics of Bankruptcy Reform," *Journal of Law, Economics and Organizations* (October), 523-546.

Allen, F. and D. Gale, 1994, *Financial Innovation and Risk Sharing,* Cambridge, MA, MIT Press.

Ambarish, R.K., K. John, and J. Williams, 1987, "Efficient Signalling with Dividends and Investments," *Journal of Finance* (June), 321-344.

Antle, R. and G.D. Eppen, 1985, "Capital Rationing and Organizational Slack in Capital Budgeting," *Management Science* (February), 163-174.

Asquith, P. and D. Mullins, 1983, "Equity Issues and Stock Price Dilution," Harvard Business School unpublished manuscript.

Bagwell, L.S., 1992, "Dutch Auction Repurchases: An Analysis of Shareholder Heterogeneity," *Journal of Finance* (March), 71-106.

Baker, G.P., M.C. Jensen, and K.J. Murphy, 1988, "Compensation and Incentives: Practice vs. Theory," *Journal of Finance* (July), 593-616.

Bebchuk, L.A., 1992, "A New Approach to Corporate Reorganizations," *Harvard Law Review* (February), 775-804.

Benveniste, L.M. and W.J. Wilhelm, 1990, "A Comparative Analysis of IPO Proceeds under Alternative Regulatory Environments," *Journal of Financial Economics* (November/December),173-208.

Bergman, Y.Z. and J.L. Callen, 1991, "Opportunistic Underinvestment in Debt Renegotiation and Capital Structure," *Journal of Financial Economics* (March), 137-172.

Berle, A.A. and G.C. Means, 1932, *The Modern Corporation and Private Property,* New York, NY, Macmillan.

Bhattacharya, S., 1978, "Project Valuation with Mean-Reverting Cash Flow Streams," *Journal of Finance* (December), 1317-1331.

Bhattacharya, S., 1979, "Imperfect Information, Dividend Policy and the 'Bird in the Hand' Fallacy," *Bell Journal of Economics* (Spring), 259-270.

---

[41]All that is required for optimality is that the firm maintain exposures that are known to investors.

[42]See Admati et al. (1994). Some of these issues are discussed in Brennan (1995).

[43]The limited diversification model of Merton (1987) implies that the demand for a firm's stock will be less than perfectly elastic and will depend on marketing efforts.

Bierman, H., 1972, "The Bond Refunding Decision," *Financial Management* (Summer), 27-29.

Black, F., 1988, "A Simple Discounting Rule," *Financial Management* (Summer), 7-11.

Black, F., 1980, "The Tax Consequences of Long-Run Pension Policy," *Financial Analysts Journal* (July-August), 21-29.

Bogue, M.C. and R. Roll, 1974, "Capital Budgeting of Risky Projects with 'Imperfect' Markets for Physical Capital," *Journal of Finance* (May), 601-613.

Boot, A.W.A., S.I. Greenbaum, and A.V. Thakor, 1993, "Reputation and Discretion in Financial Contracting," *American Economic Review* (December), 1165-1183.

Boot, A.W.A. and A.V. Thakor, 1993, "Security Design," *Journal of Finance* (September), 1349-1378.

Bower, R.S., 1973, "Issues in Lease Financing," *Financial Management* (Winter), 25-34.

Boyle, P.P., 1977, "Options: A Monte Carlo Approach," *Journal of Financial Economics* (May), 323-338.

Brander, J.A. and T.R. Lewis, 1986, "Oligopoly and Financial Structure," *American Economic Review* (December), 956-971.

Brennan, M.J., 1970, "Taxes, Market Valuation, and Corporate Finance Policy" *National Tax Journal* (December), 417-427.

Brennan, M.J., 1973, "An Approach to the Valuation of Uncertain Income Streams," *Journal of Finance* (June), 661-673.

Brennan, M.J., 1990, "Latent Assets," *Journal of Finance* (July), 709-730.

Brennan, M.J., 1995, "The Individual Investor," *Journal of Financial Research* (Spring), 59-74.

Brennan, M.J. and A. Kraus, 1987, "Efficient Financing under Asymmetric Information," *Journal of Finance* (December), 1224-1244.

Brennan, M.J. and E.S. Schwartz, 1985, "Evaluating Natural Resource Investments," *Journal of Business* (April), 135-157.

Bulow, J.I. and J.B. Shoven, 1978, "The Bankruptcy Decision," *Bell Journal of Economics* (Autumn), 437-456.

Chevalier, J.A., 1995, "Capital Structure and Product-Market Competition: Empirical Evidence from the Supermarket Industry," *American Economic Review* (June), 415-435.

Chiesa, G., 1992, "Debt and Warrants: Agency Problems and Mechanism Design," *Journal of Financial Intermediation* (September), 237-254.

Chowdhry, B. and A. Sherman, 1994, "International Differences in Oversubscription and Underpricing of IPO's," UCLA Working Paper #12-94.

Constantinides, G.M., 1978, "Market Risk Adjustment in Project Valuation," *Journal of Finance* (May), 603-616.

Constantinides, G.M. and B.D. Grundy, 1989, "Optimal Investment with Stock Repurchase and Financing as Signals," *Review of Financial Studies* (Vol. 2, No. 4), 445-466.

Cornell, B. and A.C. Shapiro, 1987, "Corporate Stakeholders and Corporate Finance," *Financial Management* (Spring), 5-14.

Cox, J.C., J.E. Ingersoll, and S.A. Ross, 1985, "An Intertemporal General Equilibrium Model of Asset Prices," *Econometrica* (March), 363-384.

DeAngelo, H. and R.W. Masulis, 1980, "Optimal Capital Structure under Corporate and Personal Taxation," *Journal of Financial Economics* (March) 3-29.

DeMarzo, P.M. and D. Duffie, 1991, "Corporate Financial Hedging with Proprietary Information," *Journal of Economic Theory* (April) 261-286.

DeMarzo, P.M. and D. Duffie, 1993, "A Liquidity Based Model of Asset-Backed Security Design," Northwestern University unpublished manuscript.

Demsetz, H. and K. Lehn, 1985, "The Structure of Corporate Ownership: Causes and Consequences," *Journal of Political Economy* (December), 1155-1177.

Detemple, J. and P. Jorion, 1990, "Option Listing and Stock Returns: An Empirical Analysis," *Journal of Banking and Finance* (October),781-801.

Dewing, A.S., 1920, *The Financial Policy of Corporations*, New York, NY, The Ronald Press.

Diamond, D., 1984, "Financial Intermediation and Delegated Monitoring," *Review of Economic Studies* (July), 393-414.

Diamond, D., 1989, "Reputation Acquisition in Debt Markets," *Journal of Political Economy* (August), 828-862.

Diamond, D., 1993, "Seniority and Maturity of Debt Contracts," *Journal of Financial Economics* (June), 341-368.

Diamond, D.W. and R. Verrecchia, 1982, "Optimal Managerial Contracts and Equilibrium Security Prices," *Journal of Finance* (May), 275-288.

Dixit, A.K. and R.S. Pindyck, 1994, *Investment Under Uncertainty*, Princeton, NJ, Princeton University Press.

Dofusco, R.A., R.R. Johnson, and T.S. Zorn, 1990, "The Effect of Executive Stock Option Plans on Stockholders and Bondholders," *Journal of Finance* (June), 617-628.

Donaldson, G., 1963, "Financial Goals: Managers versus Stockholders," *Harvard Business Review* (May-June), 116-129.

Dybvig, P.H. and J.F. Zender, 1991, "Capital Structure and Dividend Irrelevance with Asymmetric Information," *Review of Financial Studies* (Vol. 4, No. 1), 201-220.

Fama, E.F., 1978, "The Effects of a Firm's Investment and Financing Decisions on the Welfare of Its Security Holders," *American Economic Review* (June), 272-284.

Fama, E.F. and M.H. Miller, 1972, *The Theory of Finance*, New York, NY, Holt, Rinehart and Winston.

Fama, E.F., L. Fisher, M.C. Jensen, and R. Roll, 1969, "The Adjustment of Stock Prices to New Information," *International Economic Review* (February), 1-21.

Flannery, M.J., 1986, "Asymmetric Information and Risky Debt Maturity Choice," *Journal of Finance* (March), 19-38.

Franks, J.R. and W.N. Torous, 1989, "An Empirical Investigation of U.S. Firms in Reorganization," *Journal of Finance* (July), 747-770.

Friend, I., and M. Puckett, 1964, "Dividends and Stock Prices," *American Economic Review* (September), 656-682.

Froot, K.A., D.S. Scharfstein, and J.C. Stein, 1993, "Risk Management: Coordinating Corporate Investment and Financing Policies," *Journal of Finance* (December), 1629-1658.

Gertner, R. and D. Scharfstein, 1991, "A Theory of Workouts and the Effects of Reorganization Law," *Journal of Finance* (September), 1189-1222.

Gibbons, R. and K.J. Murphy, 1992, "Optimal Incentive Contracts in the Presence of Career Concerns: Theory and Evidence," *Journal of Political Economy* (June), 468-505.

Green, R.C., 1984, "Investment Incentives, Debt, and Warrants," *Journal of Financial Economics* (March), 115-136.

Green, R.C., 1993, "A Simple Model of the Taxable and Tax-Exempt Yield Curves," *Review of Financial Studies* (Vol. 6, No. 2), 233-264.

Grossman, S.J. and O.D. Hart, 1980, "Takeover Bids, the Free-Rider Problem, and the Theory of the Corporation," *Bell Journal of Economics* (Spring), 42-64.

Grossman, S.J. and O.D. Hart, 1988, "One Share-One Vote and the Market for Corporate Control," *Journal of Financial Economics* (January/March), 175-202.

Harris, M. and A. Raviv, 1989, "The Design of Securities," *Journal of Financial Economics* (October), 255-287.

Harris, M. and A. Raviv, 1995, "The Capital Budgeting Process, Incentives and Information," unpublished manuscript.

Harrison, J.M. and D.M. Kreps, 1979, "Martingales and Arbitrage in Multiperiod Securities Markets," *Journal of Economic Theory* (June), 381-408.

Hart, O.D. and J. Moore, 1990, "A Theory of Corporate Financial Structure Based on the Seniority of Claims," MIT Working Paper 560.

Haugen, R.A. and L.W. Senbet, 1978, "The Insignificance of Bankruptcy Costs to the Theory of Optimal Capital Structure," *Journal of Finance* (May), 383-394.

Heinkel, R., 1982, "A Theory of Capital Structure Relevance under Imperfect Information," *Journal of Finance* (December), 1141-1150.

Hirshleifer, D. and A.V. Thakor, 1992, "Managerial Conservatism, Project Choice, and Debt," *Review of Financial Studies* (Vol. 5, No. 3), 437-470.

Hirshleifer, D. and S. Titman, 1990, "Share Tendering Strategies and the Success of Hostile Takeover Bids," *Journal of Political Economy* (April), 295-324.

Holmstrom, B. and J. Ricart i Costa, 1986, "Managerial Incentives and Capital Management," *Quarterly Journal of Economics* (November), 835-860.

Hughes, P.J., 1986, "Signalling by Direct Disclosure Under Asymmetric Information," *Journal of Accounting and Economics* (June), 119-142.

Ingersoll, J.E., Jr., 1977, "A Contingent-Claim Valuation of Convertible Securities," *Journal of Financial Economics* (May), 289-321.

Ingersoll, J.E., Jr. and S.A. Ross, 1992, "Waiting to Invest: Investment and Uncertainty," *Journal of Business* (January), 1-29.

Jarrow, R.A. and M. O'Hara, 1989, "Primes and Scores: An Essay on Market Imperfections," *Journal of Finance* (December), 1263-1288.

Jensen, M.C., 1986, "Agency Costs of Free Cash Flow, Corporate Finance, and Takeovers," *American Economic Review* (May), 323-329.

Jensen, M.C. and J.B. Long, Jr., 1972, "Corporate Investment Under Uncertainty and Pareto Optimality in the Capital Markets," *Bell Journal of Economics and Management Science* (Spring), 151-174.

Jensen, M.C. and W.H. Meckling, 1976, "Theory of the Firm: Managerial Behavior, Agency Costs and Ownership Structure," *Journal of Financial Economics* (October), 305-360.

John, K. and J. Williams, 1985, "Dividends, Dilution, and Taxes: A Signalling Equilibrium," *Journal of Finance* (September), 1053-1070.

Kahneman, D., J.L. Knetsch, and R. Thaler, 1986, "Fairness as a Constraint on Profit Seeking: Entitlements in the Market," *American Economic Review* (September), 728-741.

Keenan, M., 1970, "Models of Equity Valuation: The Great SERM Bubble," *Journal of Finance* (May), 243-273.

Kester, W.C., 1984, "Today's Options for Tomorrow's Growth," *Harvard Business Review* (March/April), 153-160.

Koh, F. and T. Walter, 1989, "A Direct Test of Rock's Model of the Pricing of Unseasoned Issues," *Journal of Financial Economics* (August), 251-272.

Kuhn, T.S., 1962, *The Structure of Scientific Revolutions*, Chicago, IL, University of Chicago Press.

Leland, H.E., 1994, "Corporate Debt Value, Bond Covenants, and Optimal Capital Structure," *Journal of Finance* (September), 1213-1252.

Leland, H.E. and D.H. Pyle, 1977, "Informational Asymmetries, Financial Structure, and Financial Intermediation," *Journal of Finance* (May), 371-387.

Litzenberger, R.H. and K. Ramaswamy, 1982, "The Effects of Dividends on Common Stock Prices: Tax Effects or Information Effects," *Journal of Finance* (May), 429-443.

Loderer, C., J.W. Cooney, and L.D. Van Drunen, 1991, "The Price Elasticity of Demand for Common Stock," *Journal of Finance* (June), 621-651.

Logue, D., 1973, "On the Pricing of Unseasoned Equity Issues: 1965-1969," *Journal of Financial and Quantitative Analysis* (January), 91-103.

Maksimovic, V., 1988, "Capital Structure in Repeated Oligopolies," *Rand Journal of Economics* (Autumn), 389-407.

Maksimovic, V. and S. Titman, 1991, "Financial Policy and Reputation for Product Quality," *Review of Financial Studies* (Vol. 4, No. 1), 175-200.

Marris, R., 1964, *The Economic Theory of Managerial Capitalism*, London, Free Press.

Masulis, R., 1980, "The Effects of Capital Structure Change on Security Prices: A Study of Exchange Offers," *Journal of Financial Economics* (June), 139-178.

Maug, E., 1994, "Boards of Directors and Capital Structure: Alternative Forms of Corporate Restructuring," London Business School Working Paper 184.

Merton, R.C., 1973, "An Intertemporal Capital Asset Pricing Model," *Econometrica* (September), 867-887.

Merton, R.C., 1974, "On the Pricing of Corporate Debt: The Risk Structure of Interest Rates," *Journal of Finance* (May), 449-470.

Merton, R.C., 1987, "A Simple Model of Capital Market Equilibrium with Incomplete Information," *Journal of Finance* (July), 483-510.

Michaely, R. and W.H. Shaw, 1994, "The Pricing of Initial Public Offerings: Tests of Adverse-Selection and Signaling Theories," *Review of Financial Studies* (Summer), 279-320.

Miller, M.H., 1977, "Debt and Taxes," *Journal of Finance* (May), 261-275.

Miller, M.H. and F. Modigliani, 1961, "Dividend Policy, Growth, and the Valuation of Shares," *Journal of Business* (October), 411-433.

Miller, M.H. and K. Rock, 1985, "Dividend Policy under Asymmetric Information," *Journal of Finance* (September), 1031-1051.

Miller, M.H. and M.S. Scholes, 1978, "Dividends and Taxes," *Journal of Financial Economics* (December), 333-364.

Miller, M.H. and M.S. Scholes, 1982, "Dividends and Taxes: Some Empirical Evidence," *Journal of Political Economy* (December), 1118-1141.

Myers, S.C., 1977, "Determinants of Corporate Borrowing," *Journal of Financial Economics* (November), 147-175.

Myers, S.C. and N.S. Majluf, 1984, "Corporate Financing and Investment Decisions When Firms Have Information That Investors Do Not Have," *Journal of Financial Economics* (June), 187-221.

Myers, S.C. and S.M. Turnbull, 1977, "Capital Budgeting and the Capital Asset Pricing Model: Good News and Bad News," *Journal of Finance* (May), 321-333.

Narayanan, M.P., 1985, "Managerial Incentives for Short-Term Results," *Journal of Finance* (December), 1469-1484.

Paul, J., 1992, "On the Efficiency of Stock-Based Compensation," *Review of Financial Studies* (Vol. 5, No. 3), 471-502.

Penrose, E.T, 1959, *The Theory of the Growth of the Firm*, Blackwell, Oxford.

Persons, J.C., 1994, "Renegotiation and the Impossibility of Optimal Investment," *Review of Financial Studies* (Summer), 419-449.

Rajan, R.G., 1992, "Insiders and Outsiders: The Choice between Informed and Arm's-Length Debt," *Journal of Finance* (September), 1367-1400.

Ramakrishnan, R.T.S. and A.V. Thakor, 1984, "The Valuation of Assets under Moral Hazard," *Journal of Finance* (March), 229-238.

Rock, K., 1986, "Why New Issues are Underpriced," *Journal of Financial Economics*, (January/February), 187-212.

Roll, R., 1977, "A Critique of the Asset Pricing Theory's Tests; Part I: on Past and Potential Testability of the Theory," *Journal of Financial Economics* (March), 129-176.

Ross, S.A., 1977, "The Determination of Financial Structure: The Incentive Signalling Approach," *Bell Journal of Economics* (Spring), 23-40.

Ross, S.A., 1989, "Institutional Markets, Financial Marketing, and Financial Innovation," *Journal of Finance* (July), 541-556.

Rothschild, M. and J.E. Stiglitz, 1976, "Equilibrium in Competitive Insurance Markets: An Essay on the Economics of Imperfect Information," *Quarterly Journal of Economics* (November), 629-649.

Scharfstein, D.S. and P. Bolton, 1990, "A Theory of Predation Based on Agency Problems in Financial Contracting," *American Economic Review* (March), 93-106.

Scholes, M.S., 1968, "The Market for Securities: Substitution versus Price Pressure and the Effects of Information on Share Prices," *Journal of Business* (April), 179-211.

Sharpe, W.F., 1976, "Corporate Pension Funding Policy," *Journal of Financial Economics* (June), 183-193.

Shleifer, A. and R.W. Vishny, 1986, "Large Shareholders and Corporate Control," *Journal of Political Economy* (June) 461-488.

Sick, G.A., 1986, "A Certainty-Equivalent Approach to Capital Budgeting" *Financial Management* (Winter), 23-32.

Skelton, J.L., 1983, "Banks, Firms, and the Relative Pricing of Tax-Exempt and Taxable Bonds," *Journal of Financial Economics* (November), 343-356.

Smith, C.W., Jr. and J.B. Warner, 1979, "On Financial Contracting: An Analysis of Bond Covenants," *Journal of Financial Economics* (June), 117-161.

Spatt, C. and S. Srivastava, 1991, "Preplay Communication, Participation Restrictions and Efficiency in Initial Public Offerings," *Review of Financial Studies* (Vol. 4, No. 4), 709-726.

Spence, M., 1973, "Job Market Signalling," *Quarterly Journal of Economics* (August), 355-379.

Stein, J., 1988, "Takeover Threats and Managerial Myopia," *Journal of Political Economy* (February), 61-80.

Stiglitz, J.E., 1969, "A Re-examination of the Modigliani-Miller Theorem," *American Economic Review* (December), 784-793.

Stiglitz, J.E., 1972, "Some Aspects of the Pure Theory of Corporate Finance: Bankruptcies and Take-overs," *Bell Journal of Economics and Management Science* (Autumn), 458-482.

Stiglitz, J.E. 1974, "On the Irrelevance of Corporate Financial Policy," *American Economic Review* (December), 851-866.

Stulz, R.M., 1990, "Managerial Discretion and Optimal Financing Policies," *Journal of Financial Economics* (July), 3-27.

Tepper, I., 1974," Optimal Financial Strategies for Trusteed Pension Plans," *Journal of Financial and Quantitative Analysis* (June), 357-376.

Tepper, I., 1981, "Taxation and Corporate Pension Policy," *Journal of Finance* (March), 1-13.

Titman, S., 1984, "The Effect of Capital Structure on a Firm's Liquidation Decision," *Journal of Financial Economics* (March), 137-151.

Trezinka, C., 1982, "The Pricing of Tax-Exempt Bonds and the Miller Hypothesis," *Journal of Finance* (September), 907-923.

Van Horne, J.C., 1980, "An Application of the CAPM to Divisional Required Returns," *Financial Management* (Spring), 14-19.

Vijh, A.M., 1994, "The Spinoff and Merger Ex-Date Effects," *Journal of Finance* (June), 581-609.

Warner, J.B., 1977, "Bankruptcy Costs: Some Evidence," *Journal of Finance* (May), 337-347.

Warther, V., 1994, "Board Effectiveness and Board Dissent: A Model of the Board's Relationship to Management and Shareholders," University of Southern California unpublished manuscript.

Wruck, K.H., 1990," Financial Distress, Reorganization and Organizational Efficiency," *Journal of Financial Economics* (October), 419-444.

Welch, I., 1992, "Sequential Sales, Learning, and Cascades," *Journal of Finance* (June), 695-732.

Weston, J.F., 1973, "Investment Decisions Using the Capital Asset Pricing Model," *Financial Management* (Spring), 25-33.

Williamson, O.E., 1994, "Visible and Invisible Governance," *American Economic Review* (May), 323-326.

PART II

OPTION PRICING AND DERIVATIVES MARKETS

[10]

Reprinted from
THE JOURNAL OF FINANCE · VOL. XXXII, NO. 2 · MAY 1977

SESSION TOPIC: OPTIONS

SESSION CHAIRPERSON: ROBERT C. MERTON*

THE VALUATION OF AMERICAN PUT OPTIONS

MICHAEL J. BRENNAN AND EDUARDO S. SCHWARTZ**

I

WHILE THE PROBLEM OF PRICING European put options on non-dividend paying stocks was solved under certain conditions by Black-Scholes [2] in their seminal article on option pricing, no closed form solution exists for the valuation of American put options which permit exercise prior to maturity, except for the case of a perpetual put option on a non-dividend paying stock: this was treated by Merton [6]. In this paper we present an algorithm for the put pricing problem when the put has a finite life and may or may not be protected against dividend payments on the underlying stock. The algorithm is then used to evaluate the pricing of put contracts traded in the New York dealer market. Black and Scholes [1] have previously examined the pricing of calls in this market, while Gould and Galai [3] have documented violations of put call parity. A recent paper by Parkinson [7] applies numerical integration to the pricing of puts.

II

Define:

S—the market price of one share of stock on which the put is written
E_t—the exercise price of the put at time t.
$P(S, t)$—the value at time t of a put to sell one share of stock at the exercise price E_τ, $(\tau = t, \ldots, T)$ until expiration, T.
r—the continuously compounded risk free rate of interest.
D_t—the amount of the discrete dividend payment on the underlying stock at time t.

In between dates of dividend payments the stock price is assumed to follow the stochastic process

$$\frac{dS}{S} = \mu \, dt + \sigma \, dz \tag{1}$$

where dz is a Gauss-Wiener process. Then, as shown by Black-Scholes [2] and Merton [6], arbitrage considerations dictate that the value of the put must obey the partial differential equation

$$\tfrac{1}{2}\sigma^2 S^2 P_{SS} + rSP_S - rP + P_t = 0 \tag{2}$$

* Massachusetts Institute of Technology.

** The University of British Columbia. M. J. Brennan is grateful for financial support from the Leslie Wong Research Fellowship.

151

where the subscripts denote partial differentiation.

In addition, $P(S,t)$ must satisfy certain further conditions:

$$P(S,T) = \max[E_T - S, 0] \tag{3}$$

The value of the put at expiration is equal to the greater of its exercise value and zero.

$$P(S,t) \geqslant \max[E_t - S, 0] \tag{4}$$

The possibility of early exercise prevents the value of an American put falling below the exercise value.

$$P(S,t) \leqslant E_t \tag{5}$$

(5) holds if the exercise price is a non-decreasing function of time to maturity. Then the maximum value the put can attain is the current exercise price, if the stock price falls to zero. Simple considerations of stochastic dominance indicate that the value of the put can never exceed this maximum value.

$$P(S,t) \geqslant 0 \tag{6}$$

Since the put contract is an option its value can never fall below zero, as shown by (4).

Further, like a warrant, the value of a put is a convex function of the stock price. Writing the put value explicitly as a function of the stock price and the exercise price, the put price must satisfy.

$$\lambda P(S_1, E) + (1-\lambda)P(S_2, E) \geqslant P(\lambda S_1 + (1-\lambda)S_2, E), \qquad 0 \leqslant \lambda \leqslant 1 \tag{7}$$

To see this, let $S_1 = h_1 E, S_2 = h_2 E$. Then we wish to establish that

$$\lambda P(h_1 E, E) + (1-\lambda)P(h_2 E, E) \geqslant P(\lambda h_1 E + (1-\lambda)h_2 E, E) \tag{8}$$

Assuming that the option price is homogeneous of degree one in the stock price and the exercise price (Cf. Merton [6, p. 146]), then (8) is equivalent to

$$\lambda h_1 P(E, E/h_1) + (1-\lambda)h_2 P(E, E/h_2) \geqslant (\lambda h_1 + (1-\lambda)h_2)P(E, E/(\lambda h_1 + (1-\lambda)h_2)) \tag{9}$$

Then consider forming a portfolio consisting of λh_1 puts with an exercise price of E/h_1, and $(1-\lambda)h_2$ puts with an exercise price of E/h_2. The value of this portfolio when the stock price is equal to E is given by the left hand side of (9). Correspondingly, the right hand side of (9) is the value of a portfolio of $(\lambda h_1 + (1-\lambda)h_2)$ puts with an exercise price of $E/(\lambda h_1 + (1-\lambda)h_2)$, when the stock price is E. Then, following Smith [8] it is readily shown that the returns on the first portfolio exhibit first degree stochastic dominance over the returns on the second portfolio. Hence the value of the first portfolio must exceed that of the second which implies (9) and (7).

The convexity of the put price together with the upper and lower bounds on the value of the put given by (4) and (5) imply:

$$\lim_{S \to \infty} P_S(S,t) = 0 \tag{10}$$

Since the put is a convex function of the stock price, it may be shown that the equilibrium put price is an increasing function of the riskiness of the stock. The proof of this proposition is not offered here since it parallels Merton's [6] proof that the value of a warrant is an increasing function of the riskiness of the stock.

Figure 1 illustrates the boundary conditions which must be satisfied by the put price prior to maturity and shows the relationship between the put price and the stock price for two stocks with different variance rates. S_c is the critical stock price, to be discussed below.

Finally, the possibility of discrete dividends on the underlying stock and of changes in the exercise price introduce a further boundary condition. Thus, suppose that at time t there is change in the exercise price, and a discrete dividend D_t is paid. Let t^- denote the instant before the dividend/exercise price change, and t^+ the instant after. Then the put value must satisfy

$$P(S,t^-) = \max[E_{t^-} - S, P(S - D_t, t^+)] \tag{11}$$

where $P(S,t^+)$ is the put value when the exercise price changes to E_{t^+}. Equation (11) reflects the fact that the put value before the dividend/exercise price change is equal to the greater of its immediate exercise value ($E_{t^-} - S$) and the value after the dividend/exercise price change, $P(S - D_t, t^+)$. If a dividend is paid with no offsetting change in the exercise price,[1] then it will never pay the put holder to exercise immediately before the dividend for then

$$P(S - D_t, t^+) \geq E - (S - D_t) > E - S$$

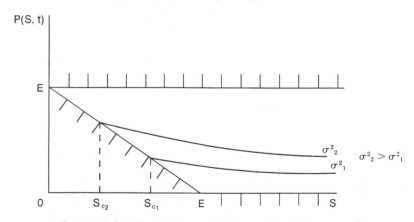

FIGURE 1.   Relationship Between Put Price and Stock Price

1. Cf. Merton [6] for a discussion of the exercise price adjustment which will leave the put-holder indifferent to the amount of the dividend.

and the ex-dividend value of the put exceeds its pre-dividend exercise value.

The problem of valuing the put is then that of solving the differential equation (2) subject to the boundary conditions (3), (4), (5), (6), (10) and (11). A numerical procedure is employed to obtain an approximate solution to the equation. First re-write (2) using the variable τ, time to maturity, instead of t, calendar time

$$\tfrac{1}{2}\sigma^2 S^2 P_{SS} + rSP_S - rP - P_\tau = 0 \qquad (2')$$

Then approximating the partial derivatives in $(2')$ by finite differences, $(2')$ may be written as[2]

$$a_i P_{i-1,j} + b_i P_{i,j} + c_i P_{i+1,j} = P_{i,j-1}; \qquad i = 1,\ldots,(n-1), \quad j = 1,\ldots,m \qquad (12)$$

where

$$a_i = \tfrac{1}{2} r \, ki - \tfrac{1}{2}\sigma^2 ki^2$$

$$b_i = 1 + rk + \sigma^2 ki^2$$

$$c_i = -\tfrac{1}{2} r \, ki - \tfrac{1}{2}\sigma^2 ki^2$$

$$P(S,\tau) = P(S_i,\tau_j) = P(ih,jk) = P_{i,j}$$

h and k are the discrete increments in the stock price and time to maturity respectively. m and n are the number of discrete increments in the time to maturity and stock price respectively; the former corresponds to the time to expiration of the put, while the latter is chosen so that the boundary condition (10) is well approximated at the highest stock price value considered.

The boundary condition (10) which holds for all values of j is approximated by

$$P_{n-1,j} - P_{n,j} = 0 \qquad (j = 1,\ldots,m) \qquad (13)$$

(12) and (13) constitute a set of n linear equations in the $(n+1)$ unknowns $P_{i,j}$ $(i = 0,1,\ldots,n)$ and with the addition of one further equation enable us to solve for $P_{i,j}$ in terms of $P_{i,j-1}$. Since $P_{i,0}$ is given by the condition governing the value of the put at expiration (3), the whole set of $P_{i,j}$ may be solved for by repeated solution of the set of equations.

Note that the solutions to the differential equation must satisfy the boundary condition (4) which may be written as

$$P_{i,j} \geqslant E_j - ih \qquad (i = 0,1,\ldots,n) \qquad (14)$$

where E_j is the exercise price ruling at time increment j $(\tau = jk)$; the differential equation holds only for those values of $P_{i,j}$ for which (14) holds as a strict inequality. The maximum stock price for which (14) holds as an equality, the "critical stock price" is the price at which the put should rationally be exercised. The problem then is to determine the value of i, i_c, corresponding to the critical stock price $S_c (i_c h = S_c)$. The system of equations (12–13) then holds for values of $i \geqslant i_c$.

First, note that by successive subtraction of each equation of (12–13) from a

2. See McCracken and Dorn [5] for further discussion.

suitable multiple of its predecessor (i.e. subtract the last equation from a multiple of equation n; subtract the transformed n^{th} equation from equation $(n-1)$ etc.), the system (12–13) may be transformed into:

$$e_i P_{i-1,j} + f_i P_{i,j} = g_i \qquad (i=1,\ldots,n) \qquad (15)$$

where e_i, f_i, g_i are coefficients of the transformed system.

Let $P_{0,j} = E_j$ from (4) and (5), and use the first equation of (15) to solve for $P_{1,j}$. If $P_{1,j} < E_j - h$, let $P_{1,j} = E_j - h$ and solve for $P_{2,j}$; if $P_{1,j} \geq E_j - h$ solve the remaining equations for $P_{i,j}$ $(i=2,\ldots,n)$. Continue in this manner until a complete set of $P_{i,j}$ are obtained which satisfy the differential equation and the boundary condition. The maximum value of i for which $P_{i,j} = E_j - ih$ is the critical value of i, i_c and the critical stock price is $S_c = i_c h$.

Finally, on the date of a dividend, D, or change in conversion terms, condition (11) is written

$$P_{i,j^-} = P_{i-D/h,j^+}, \qquad \text{for} \quad P_{i-D/h,j^+} > E_{j^-} - ih$$

$$= E_{j^-} - ih, \qquad \text{for} \quad P_{i-D/h,j^+} < E_{j^-} - ih \qquad (16)$$

In the application of the model to empirical data on 6 month puts the time increment k was set equal to one day, and the stock price increment, k, was set equal to 1% of the striking price. As a crude test of the accuracy of the above procedure several puts were valued assuming a zero rate of interest, and the result compared to the corresponding Black-Scholes solution.[3] The numerical method was accurate to within about 0.1%, at option prices corresponding to the exercise price.

III

The model was used to evaluate 55 put options traded in the New York dealer market between May 1966 and May 1969.[4] These were all the put contracts for which a call contract of the same maturity was traded on the same day, and for which the rates of return on the underlying security were available on the Wells Fargo Daily Return file. The risk free rate of interest for each contract was constructed by taking the price of the Treasury Bill maturing closest to the expiration date of the option and computing the continuously compounded rate of return per trading day. A synthetic stock price series was constructed by taking the closing stock price on the day the option was written, and treating the return relatives on the Wells Fargo file as price relatives to generate a stock price series throughout the life of the contract. This procedure is equivalent to assuming that no dividends were paid and is appropriate if the options are perfectly protected against dividends by adjustment of the strike price. In fact, as Merton [6] has pointed out, the actual adjustment of the strike price is not quite the correct one.

---

3. If the interest rate is non-positive the value of a European put always exceeds its exercise value prior to maturity, so that it is equivalent to that of an American put. To see this note that the put-call parity theorem holds for European options [2], so that $p = c - S + Ee^{-rt} > E - S$ if $r \leq 0$ where p and c are the values of a European put and call.

4. The authors are most grateful to Myron Scholes for making this data available to them.

1. Model and Market Put Prices

The only parameter of the valuation model which is not directly observable is the variance rate on the stock. While this may be estimated from historical data, such estimates are necessarily subject to error. Therefore in this paper we restricted our sample to put contracts for which an equivalent call contract was written on the same day. The put pricing model employed here is based on exactly the same set of assumptions as the Black-Scholes option pricing model which may be used to price call contracts. Therefore, if these assumptions correctly describe the option pricing process, the put and the call should be priced on the basis of the same variance estimate.[5] Therefore for each put contract we used the associated call contract to estimate the implied variance rate, which is defined as that variance rate for which the Black-Scholes valuation of the call is equal to the market price.[6] We also obtained an historical variance estimate using the prior 250 trading day returns and an estimated variance rate over the life of each contract (the "actual variance rate").

Then, for each of the 55 put options an estimate of the equilibrium price at the time of issue was computed using the numerical method described earlier and the three different estimates of the variance. Additionally, the options were valued as if they were European options by using the Black-Scholes [2] model for pricing European put options. Table 1 contains the frequency distributions of the ratios of the model prices to the market prices at time of issue, where the model price is derived using both the numerical solution technique (NS) and the Black-Scholes model (BS) for all three variance estimates.

TABLE 1

FREQUENCY DISTRIBUTION OF MODEL TO MARKET PUT PRICE RATIOS

Ratio of Model Price to Market Price	Historical Variance		Implied Variance		Actual Variance	
	BS 1	NS 2	BS 3	NS 4	BS 5	NS 6
> 1.80	10.91	12.73	7.27	10.91	7.27	7.27
> 1.70	5.45	5.45	5.45	1.82	0.0	0.0
> 1.60	3.64	3.64	9.09	10.91	3.64	5.45
> 1.50	3.64	3.64	9.09	7.27	7.27	9.09
> 1.40	7.27	5.45	1.82	3.64	9.09	7.27
> 1.30	7.27	12.73	27.27	30.91	5.45	5.45
> 1.20	14.55	12.73	18.18	21.82	10.91	16.36
> 1.10	7.27	9.09	18.18	9.09	23.64	21.82
> 1.00	9.09	9.09	0.0	0.0	12.73	9.09
> 0.90	18.18	12.73	1.82	1.82	10.91	12.73
> 0.80	7.27	7.27	0.0	0.0	3.64	1.82
< 0.80	5.45	5.45	1.82	1.82	5.45	3.64
Std. Err.	0.44	0.46	0.47	0.50	0.41	0.43
Mean ratio	1.257	1.287	1.390	1.420	1.249	1.278
t-statistic	4.33	4.63	6.16	6.23	4.51	4.80

5. Even if the Black-Scholes model is incorrect, both options will appear to be priced on the basis of the same variance if the options are European and the put-call parity theorem holds.

6. Latane and Rendleman [4] also derived implied variances from the Black-Scholes model.

Using the implied variance rate, the numerical solution model value exceeds the market price by 42% on average, and the t-statistic for the null hypothesis that the mean model to market put price ratio is unity is 6.23; the model put value is less than the actual market value in less than 4% of the cases. Based on this evidence it is easy to reject the hypothesis that puts and calls are priced consistently and in accordance with this model, and our results confirm the findings of Gould and Galai [3] of frequent violations of put-call parity.[7] The puts appear to be significantly underpriced relative to the calls.

Even when the historical or actual variance estimate is used in the numerical solution, the model prices the puts significantly higher than the market price, the mean excess of the model price over the market price being 28.7% and 27.8% respectively. The t-ratios for the null hypothesis that the mean ratio is unity are 4.63 and 4.80, and the model overprices 75% and 82% of the contracts depending on whether the historical or actual variance rate is used.

Much the same distribution of price ratios is obtained when the Black-Scholes model for European options is used to price the contracts. Indeed the magnitude of the discrepancies between the Black-Scholes (European) option values and the numerical solution (American) option values is surprisingly small as shown in Table 2. As is to be expected, the European option value is always less than the corresponding American option value, but the small differences in the computed values suggest that the right to early exercise contained in the American option is not of great economic value, so that the Black-Scholes model may reasonably be used to value 6-month dividend protected American puts. The discrepancies will of course be greater for unprotected puts, for puts of longer maturity or when the stock is selling for below the striking price.

The model prices were further compared with the market prices by cross-section regression of the market price of the put on the model prices, both prices being

---

7. To see the relationship between these results and those of Gould and Galai consider the second column of their Table 5 (p. 118) which gives values of ϵ, the violation of put-call parity, defined by:

$$\epsilon = \frac{C-P}{V} - \frac{i}{(1+i)}$$

Taking as the model price, the put-call parity price, $\hat{P}$, defined by

$$\frac{C-\hat{P}}{V} - \frac{i}{(1+i)} = 0$$

and combining these two expressions, the ratio of model price to market price is

$$\frac{\hat{P}}{P} = \epsilon \frac{V}{P} + 1$$

Using the average ϵ from Table 5 (.0349) and the average P/V (.085) we obtain

$$\frac{\hat{P}}{P} = 1.41$$

Now the model price derived from put call parity should be identical to that derived using BS model with the implied variance. Hence the mean ratio of model to market price for BS (implied variance) should be about 1.41. In fact from our Table 1 the mean ratio is 1.39. The differences may be accounted for by sample correlation between ϵ and V/P and by the fact that our sample contains 6 more observations than Gould and Galai.

TABLE 2

DISTRIBUTION OF DIFFERENCES (D) BETWEEN EUROPEAN (E) AND AMERICAN (A) PUT VALUES
(HISTORICAL VARIANCE ESTIMATE)
$$D \equiv (E-A)/A$$

$D > -.01$	$D > -.02$ $D < -.01$	$D > -.03$ $D < -.02$	$D > -.04$ $D < -.03$	$D < -.04$
0	17	27	5	6
Mean Difference	$-.025$			

TABLE 3

REGRESSION OF NORMALIZED MARKET PRICE,
P/S, ON NORMALIZED MODEL PRICE USING
HISTORICAL VARIANCE $NS(H)$, IMPLIED VARIANCE
$NS(I)$, AND ACTUAL VARIANCE $NS(A)$

$P/S = \underset{(6.80)}{.059} + \underset{(3.15)}{.245} NS(H)/S \qquad R^2 = .16$

$P/S = \underset{(3.56)}{.031} + \underset{(6.35)}{.454} NS(I)/S \qquad R^2 = .43$

$P/S = \underset{(5.85)}{.050} + \underset{(4.30)}{.331} NS(A)/S \qquad R^2 = .26$

11 groups on $NS(I)/S$

$P/S = \underset{(2.51)}{.039} + \underset{(3.02)}{.431} NS(H)/S \qquad R^2 = .50$

11 groups on $NS(H)/S$

$P/S = \underset{(3.78)}{.036} + \underset{(5.16)}{.411} NS(I)/S \qquad R^2 = .78$

11 groups on $NS(H)/S$

$P/S = \underset{(6.60)}{.043} + \underset{(6.43)}{.390} NS(A)/S \qquad R^2 = .82$

t-ratios in parenthesis.

measured as a fraction of the striking price. The results are given in Table 3. While these regressions should be evaluated with care, since we have no assurance that the relationship is linear or that the errors are normally distributed, it is clear that the slope coefficient is far from its theoretical value of unity. One reason for this is that the independent variable, the numerical solution value, impounds errors in the variance estimate. To mitigate this problem, the observations were grouped on an instrumental variable, the numerical solution based on one of the other variance estimates: even with the grouping procedure the slope coefficient is still less than 0.5. We have argued that both puts and calls should be priced on the basis of the same variance, so that the problem of errors-in-variables bias does not arise with the implied variance, and indeed we find that the slope coefficient does not improve with grouping when the implied variance is used to derive the model value. These results indicate that not only are market put prices in general lower than the model prices but that, accepting the model prices as equilibrium prices, put prices on high variance stocks (those with a high ratio of put price to striking price) are systematically underpriced relative to put prices on low variance stocks. This latter result is in accord with the Black-Scholes [1] finding that call prices on high variance stocks are underpriced relative to those on low variance stocks. However, while Black-Scholes found some slight evidence that call contracts in general tended to be overpriced, our evidence thus far is that puts tend to be underpriced, at least relative to model prices. However the real test of the model is its ability, not to predict market prices, but to yield prices which are equilibrium in the sense that they yield no arbitrage profits: such tests are discussed below. First however we discuss the optimal exercise strategy.

2.   The Exercise Strategy

An integral part of the numerical algorithm for valuing American put options is the determination of the optimal exercise strategy to be followed. This is described by a time series of critical stock prices, such that the put is exercised optimally as soon as the stock price drops below the critical stock price. Figure 2 shows the time series of critical stock prices expressed as a fraction of the striking price for a 131 day put on Atlas Chemical Industries, using the three different variance estimates. Since the equilibrium put price is an increasing function of the variance rate, the critical stock price is a decreasing function of the variance rate as shown in Figure 1; consequently, the historical variance rate, which is the lowest of the three variance estimates for this company, yields the uniformly highest critical stock price series. The general pattern of critical stock prices indicates that the optimal strategy is to pursue an aggressive policy at first by requiring a high exercise value (low stock price) before exercising, but that as time runs out on the contract to reduce rapidly the minimum required exercise value so that immediately before expiration it becomes optimal to exercise so long as the exercise value is positive.

Table 4 shows the distributions of exercise dates relative to maturity for the sample of 55 put options. The first column shows the timing of exercise by the actual purchasers of the options as recorded in the option dealer's diary. Only 15 of the 55 contracts were actually exercised and of these, 14 were exercised at maturity. We then calculated when the options would have been exercised had the optimal policy been followed, by comparing the time series of critical stock prices with the time series of actual stock prices adjusted for dividends, and assuming that the option was exercised the first time the stock price fell below the critical stock price. The second and third columns of Table 4 show the distribution of optimal exercise times assuming that the optimal exercise policy is determined using the historical and implied variance estimates respectively. Under either estimate of the optimal policy 20 contracts would have been exercised, of which only seven would have been exercised at maturity. It is of interest to note that the optimal policy using the historical variance resulted in a higher exercise value than was actually achieved by the purchasers of the puts for 16 contracts, while the reverse was true for only 3 contracts; when the optimal policy was derived from the implied variance, the corresponding figures were 13 contracts and 3 contracts.

As a further measure of the departure of the actual exercise strategies followed from the optimal strategies of the model, we calculated for each contract a "maximum return differential." The return differential for a contract on a particular day is defined as the difference between the return the option purchaser would have earned if the contract were exercised at the prevailing stock price and the return the purchaser would have earned if the contract were exercised at the critical

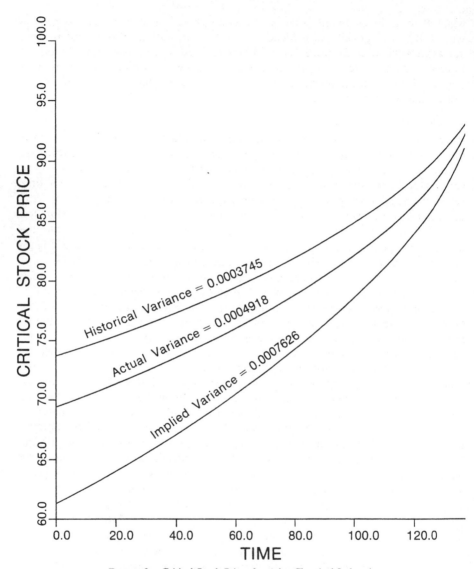

FIGURE 2.   Critical Stock Prices for Atlas Chemical Industries

The Valuation of American Put Options 459

TABLE 4

DISTRIBUTION OF EXERCISE DATES RELATIVE TO MATURITY

	Actual Policy	Policy Historical Variance	Optimal Implied Variance
At expiration	14	7	7
1–5 days before expiration		0	2
6–10 days before expiration	1	1	2
11–20 days before expiration		6	2
21–40 days before expiration		3	5
>40 days before expiration		3	2
Number of contracts exercised	15	20	20

stock price for that day. For example, if the put were originally sold for $5, the striking price were $50, the critical stock price were $40 and the stock price were only $35, the return if the put were exercised at the prevailing stock price would be $(50-35)/5 = 300\%$, and the return if the put were exercised at the critical stock price would be $(50-40)/5 = 200\%$, so that the return differential would be 100%. The maximum return differential is the maximum of these daily return differentials over the time the contract was unexercised. The maximum return differential will be zero if the contract is exercised optimally, and positive if it is exercised too late. The magnitude of the positive differential is an indication of the holder's reluctance to exercise relative to the optimal policy. The distribution of the maximum return differentials for the 55 contracts is shown in Table 5 where the optimal policy is derived using both the historical variance estimate and the implied variance.

TABLE 5

DISTRIBUTION OF "MAXIMUM RETURN DIFFERENTIAL"

	Historical Variance	Implied Variance
No discrepancy	39	39
<10%	1	3
11–30%	1	1
31–50%	5	3
51–100%	3	4
101–150%	4	3
>150%	2	2

The evidence from the distributions of both the exercise dates and the maximum return differentials indicates that the option purchasers were markedly reluctant to exercise their options prior to maturity even though the model indicated that it was optimal to do so. This may be attributable, first, to the failure of the model to value the puts correctly: this seems unlikely since, as we have seen, the model values the puts more highly than does the market and would therefore tend to set the critical stock price too high, delaying exercise. Secondly, it may be attributable to gamblers' greed which causes put purchasers to hold out against exercise in the hope of higher profits in the future. However, a more probable explanation is the tax system with its preferential treatment for long term capital gains.

3.   *The Model Prices as Equilibrium Prices*

We have found that the model tends to systematically over-value the put contracts relative to the observed market prices. The question then arises as to whether the model prices are equilibrium prices in the sense that they yield no arbitrage profits, for if they are, then the market prices are not equilibrium and present the opportunity for arbitrage profits, at least in a world without transaction costs. To determine whether or not the model prices are equilibrium prices we employ a test procedure based on that used by Black and Scholes [1]. That is, we simulated a strategy of purchasing all the put contracts at the model prices and selling short each day $P_S(S,t)$ shares of the underlying stock to obtain a hedged position. Values of $P_S(S,t)$ were obtained from the matrix of $P(S,\tau)$ values generated by the valuation model. Excess dollar returns were computed daily for each contract from the date it was written to the date it was exercised according to the optimal exercise policy, in a manner similar to that described by Black-Scholes. The excess dollar returns were aggregated each day over all contracts outstanding that day to yield a series of portfolio returns for 710 trading days from June 10, 1966 to April 16, 1969.[8] To avoid giving excessive weight to contracts on high priced stocks we assumed that instead of purchasing one put contract for 100 shares, we purchased a put contract with a striking price of $1,000; so if the striking price was $50 we assumed that we bought 1/5 of a contract ($5,000/$1,000).

In addition to computing the total dollar returns per day from this strategy we computed the dollar returns per day per contract by dividing the total dollar returns for each day by the number of unexercised contracts outstanding that day. The total dollar returns per day and the dollar returns per day per contract were then regressed on the rate of return on the market portfolio to allow for systematic risk in the returns due to imperfect hedging. The systematic risk estimates were all insignificantly different from zero and in Table 6 we report only the constant terms from these regressions as estimates of the excess returns. To overcome the problem of heteroscedasticity caused by the different numbers of contracts outstanding on each day, we also employed a weighted regression procedure, which weighted the total dollar returns by $\sqrt{1/N_t}$ and the dollar returns per contract by $\sqrt{N_t}$, where N_t was the number of contracts outstanding on day t. The weighted regression results are reported in the lower half of Table 6.

From the weighted regression results we see that the excess total dollar return per day using the implied variance was − $0.59 while the excess dollar return per contract was − $0.086 per day. The associated t-statistics indicate that these are both significantly different from zero and that therefore the model values obtained using the implied variance are in excess of the equilibrium values. Assuming that the average contract was outstanding for about 125 days the daily loss per contract

---

8. The sample period was actually two days shorter when the implied variance was used, since the optimal strategy derived using the implied variance caused the final put contract to be exercised two days earlier.

The Valuation of American Put Options   461

TABLE 6

EXCESS RETURNS FROM PURCHASING CONTRACTS AT MODEL PRICES AND FOLLOWING OPTIMAL EXERCISE STRATEGY

| | Total Dollar Returns per day | | | | | | Dollar Returns per day per contract | | | | | |
| | Implied Variance | | | Historical Variance | | | Implied Variance | | | Historical Variance | | |
	α	$t-\alpha$	ρ	α	$t-\alpha$	ρ	α	$t-\alpha$	ρ	α	$t-\alpha$	ρ
Unweighted				$x10^{-1}$			$x10^{-1}$			$x10^{-2}$		
Total Period	−1.02	−4.76	.11	− .37	− .17	.11	− .53	−2.05	.15	.68	.27	.12
First Half	0.04	0.25	.17	.97	.64	.08	.82	1.89	.14	6.90	1.67	.12
Second Half	−2.08	−5.31	.07	−1.73	− .42	.11	−1.88	−7.10	.09	− 5.57	−1.99	.11
First Quarter	.66	2.96	.10	4.40	2.22	.06	2.45	3.03	.09	16.64	2.17	.10
Second Quarter	− .58	−2.76	.16	−2.33	−1.01	.08	− .79	−2.81	.18	− 2.68	− .89	.16
Third Quarter	−2.30	−4.61	−.02	−2.30	− .44	−.02	−1.30	−4.98	−.00	− 1.64	− .58	−.01
Fourth Quarter	−1.88	−3.11	.12	−1.44	− .23	.20	−2.48	−5.40	.11	− 9.61	−1.98	.15
Weighted												
Total Period	− .59	−5.18	.12	− .10	− .09	.11	− .86	−2.27	.16	− .12	− .03	.12
First Half	.18	1.67	.17	1.78	1.75	.08	.42	.74	.14	4.19	.78	.12
Second Half	−1.75	−9.01	.07	−2.93	−1.45	.11	−1.66	−3.37	.10	− 2.84	− .55	.11
First Quarter	.63	3.69	.10	4.19	2.76	.06	2.40	2.36	.09	15.97	1.69	.10
Second Quarter	− .56	−4.40	.16	−2.07	−1.50	.08	− .78	−1.74	.18	− 2.93	− .60	.16
Third Quarter	−2.30	−9.66	−.02	−2.64	−1.04	−.02	−1.28	−2.35	−.00	− 1.42	− .24	−.01
Fourth Quarter	−1.46	−4.77	.12	−3.31	−1.05	.20	−2.23	−2.72	.11	− 5.20	− .60	.15

ρ—Serial Correlation of Residuals.

per day corresponds to a total loss per contract of $10.57. This measure of the extent to which the implied variance model overprices the contract may be compared with a mean model price of $118.77 which is therefore about 9% above the equilibrium price.

However, when we simulate a policy of buying at the model prices derived from the historical variance and hedging on the same basis, the excess total dollar returns and dollar returns per contract rise to − $0.01 and − $0.0012 per day respectively, and the associated *t*-values become very small, so that we cannot reject the null hypothesis that the model values are equilibrium values. Note that the excess dollar returns per contract per day are equivalent to only about − $0.15 over a 125 day life contract; this may be compared with an average model put premium of $106.68 on a contract with a striking price of $1,000. For individual subperiods the magnitude of the absolute excess dollar returns per contract per day are somewhat larger, but in no case are they statistically significant. The largest excess dollar return per contract per day is $0.016 which is equivalent to $2.00 over the life of the average contract. Hence the average model price obtained using the historical variance estimate appears to be very close to the equilibrium price.

Since the market prices tend to be below the model prices we may infer that the market prices are below the equilibrium prices, and therefore give rise to profit opportunities. To evaluate these profit opportunities further, we calculated the incremental profit to be derived by purchasing the puts at the market prices rather than at the model prices derived from the historical variance estimate. This was done by converting the dollar profits (losses) for all the contracts due to the difference between market and model prices into an equivalent daily annuity over the whole sample period. The incremental daily profit was $1.68 per day or $0.19 per day per contract.[9] These incremental profits are respectively 170 and 160 times the average daily losses on the hedge portfolio constructed using the model prices. Combining the annuitized profits from purchasing at market rather than model prices with the daily returns on the hedge portfolio, the resulting returns yield t-ratios of 14.5 on a total dollar basis and 4.6 on a dollar per day per contract basis.

While further tests could be employed to evaluate the ability of the model to discriminate between under-priced and over-priced contracts, the above results leave little doubt that this sample of put contracts was on average under-priced and offered the opportunity for profit by following the naive strategy of purchasing all the put contracts. However, as Black and Scholes [1] have pointed out the very high level of transactions costs in this market would almost certainly render it impossible to profit by this evidence of market inefficiency.

REFERENCES

1. F. Black and M. Scholes. "The Valuation of Option Contracts and a Test of Market Efficiency," *Journal of Finance* 27, 1972, 399–417.
2. ———— and ————. "The Pricing of Options and Corporate Liabilities," *Journal of Political Economy* 81, 1973, 637–659.
3. J. P. Gould and D. Galai. "Transactions Costs and the Relationship Between Put and Call Prices," *Journal of Financial Economics* 1, 1974, 105–129.
4. H. A. Latane and R. J. Rendleman. "Standard Deviations of Stock Price Ratios Implied in Option Prices," unpublished draft, 1975.
5. D. D. McCracken and W. S. Dorn. *Numerical Methods and Fortran Programming*, John Wiley and Sons, Inc., 1964.
6. R. C. Merton. "The Theory of Rational Option Pricing," *Bell Journal of Economics and Management Science* 4, 1973, 141–193.
7. M. Parkinson. "Option Pricing: The American Put," forthcoming in *The Journal of Business*.
8. C. W. Smith Jr. "Option Pricing: A Review," *Journal of Financial Economics* 3, 1976, 3–51.

9. $0.19 per day per contract is equivalent to $23.80 over the whole life of an average contract, compared with an average market price per contract of $84.97.

[11]

JOURNAL OF FINANCIAL AND QUANTITATIVE ANALYSIS
September 1978

FINITE DIFFERENCE METHODS AND JUMP PROCESSES ARISING

IN THE PRICING OF CONTINGENT CLAIMS: A SYNTHESIS

Michael J. Brennan and Eduardo S. Schwartz*

Since the seminal article by Black and Scholes on the pricing of corporate liabilities, the importance in finance of contingent claims has become widely recognized. The key to the valuation of such claims has been found to lie in the solution to certain partial differential equations. The best known of these was derived by Black and Scholes, in their original article, from the assumption that the value of the asset underlying the contingent claim follows a geometric Brownian motion.

Depending on the nature of the boundary conditions which must be satisfied by the value of the contingent claim, the Black-Scholes partial differential equation and its extensions may or may not have an analytic solution. Analytic solutions have been derived under certain conditions for the values of a call option (Black and Scholes [1], Merton [11]),of a risky corporate discount bond (Merton [12]), of European put options (Black and Scholes [1], Merton [11]), of the capital shares of dual funds (Ingersoll [8]), and of convertible bonds (Ingersoll [9]). In many realistic situations, however, analytic solutions do not exist, and the analyst must resort to other methods. These include the finite difference approximation to the differential equation employed extensively by Brennan and Schwartz [3, 4, 5], numerical integration used by Parkinson [13], and Monte Carlo methods advocated by Boyle [2].

Complementing the above work, Cox and Ross [6, 7] have analyzed the pricing of contingent claims when the value of the underlying asset follows a jump process rather than a diffusion process, and have shown that in the limit the jump process approaches a pure diffusion process. The major purpose of this paper is to demonstrate that approximation of the Black-Scholes partial differential equation by use of the finite difference method is equivalent to approximating the diffusion process by a jump process and that therefore the finite difference approximation is a type of numerical integration. In particular, we establish

**Both, University of British Columbia. The authors gratefully acknowledge
financial support from The S. S. Huebner Foundation, The Wharton School, University of Pennsylvania. They also thank Phelim Boyle for helpful comments.*

that the simpler explicit finite difference approximation is equivalent to approximating the diffusion process by one of the jump processes described by Cox and Ross, while the implicit finite difference approximation amounts to approximating the diffusion process by a more general type of jump process. As a preliminary to this, we show that certain simplifications of the numerical procedure are made possible by taking a log transform of the Black-Scholes equation. In the subsequent sections we discuss the explicit and implicit finite difference approximations, respectively.

I.   The Log Transform of the Black-Scholes Equation

The basic Black-Scholes equation is

(1) $$\tfrac{1}{2}\sigma^2 S^2\, H_{SS} + rS\, H_S + H_t - rH = 0$$

where S is the value of the underlying asset, t is time, H(S,t) is the value of the contingent claim, r is the riskless rate of interest, σ^2 is the instantaneous variance rate of the return on the underlying asset, and subscripts denote partial differentiation.

To obtain the log transform of (1) we define

(2) $y \quad\equiv\, \ln S$

(3) $W(y,t) \equiv H(S,t)$

so that

(4) $H_S \quad= W_y\, e^{-y}$

(5) $H_{SS} \quad= (W_{yy} - W_y)\, e^{-2y}$

(6) $H_t \quad= W_t.$

Then, making the appropriate substitutions in (1), we obtain the transformed equation:

(7) $$\tfrac{1}{2}\sigma^2\, W_{yy} + (r - \tfrac{1}{2}\sigma^2)W_y + W_t - rW = 0.$$

Notice that (7) unlike (1) is a partial differential equation with constant coefficients. This simplifies the numerical analysis, and, as we shall

see below, makes it possible to employ an explicit finite difference approximation to (7), whereas the explicit finite difference approximation to (1) is
in general unstable.

II.   The Explicit Finite Difference Approximation

To obtain a finite difference approximation to (7), we replace the partial
derivatives by finite differences, and to this end define

$$W(y,t) = W(ih, jk) = W_{i,j}$$

where h and k are the discrete increments in the value of the underlying asset
and the time dimension, respectively. For the explicit approximation, the
partial derivatives are approximated by

$$W_y = (W_{i+1,j+1} - W_{i-1,j+1})/2h$$

$$W_{yy} = (W_{i+1,j+1} - 2W_{i,j+1} + W_{i-1,j+1})/h^2$$

$$W_t = (W_{i,j+1} - W_{i,j})/k$$

so that the corresponding difference equation is

$$(8) \quad W_{i,j}(1+rk) = aW_{i-1,j+1} + b\,W_{i,j+1} + c\,W_{i+1,j+1} \qquad \begin{matrix} i = 1, \ldots, (n-1) \\ j = 1, \ldots, m \end{matrix}$$

where

$$a = [\tfrac{1}{2}(\sigma/h)^2 - \tfrac{1}{2}(r - \tfrac{1}{2}\sigma^2)/h]k,$$

$$b = [1 - (\sigma/h)^2 k], \text{ and}$$

$$c = [\tfrac{1}{2}\sigma/h)^2 + \tfrac{1}{2}(r - 1/2\sigma^2)/h]k .$$

For any given value of j, (8) allows us to solve for $W_{i,j}$ (i = 1, ..., n-1)
in terms of $W_{i,j+1}$. The extreme values of $W_{i,j}$, $W_{o,j}$, and $W_{n,j}$, must be given
by the boundary conditions to the problem.[1] Then, given the values of $W_{i,j}$
corresponding to the maturity of the contingent claim, we may solve (8)

---

[1] Note that we are implicitly assuming that the lower boundary condition
is of the form $W(0,t) = Z_t$. More generally the boundary condtion may be $W(i_jh,t)$
$= Z_t$; this will simply change the range of i in (8) without changing anything
essential.

recursively for all values of $W_{i,j}$.

Notice that the coefficients of (8) are independent of i and that $a + b + c = 1$. For the stability of the explicit solution, it is necessary that the coefficients of (8) be nonnegative (McCracken and Dorn [10]). While appropriate choice of h and k may guarantee this for (8), the corresponding coefficients of the explicit approximation to (1) depend on i, and will be negative for sufficiently large values of i, so that this explicit finite difference approximation may not be applied to the untransformed equation (1).

For the nonnegativity condition to be satisfied, it is necessary that h and k be chosen so that

$$h \leq \sigma^2 / |(r - \tfrac{1}{2}\sigma^2)|$$

(9)   and

$$k \leq \sigma^2 / (r - \tfrac{1}{2}\sigma^2)^2 .$$

If the conditions (9) are satisfied, the coefficients of the RHS of (8) may be interpreted as probabilities since they are nonnegative. Writing p^- for a, p for b and p^+ for c, (8) becomes

(10) $$W_{i,j} = \frac{1}{(1+rk)} \; p^- \, W_{i-1,j+1} + p \, W_{i,j+1} + p^+ \, W_{i+1,j+1}$$

Thus the value of the contingent claim at time instant j may be regarded as given by its expected value at (j+1) discounted at the riskless rate, r. The expected value of the claim at the next instant is obtained by assuming that y, the logarithm of the stock price follows the jump process

(11)
$$dy = \begin{cases} p^+ & h \\ p & 0 \\ p^- & -h \end{cases}$$

which is formally identical to a jump process discussed by Cox and Ross [6, equation (8)], where $\mu = 0$. The local mean and variance of (11) are

(12) $$E[dy] = h[p^+ - p^-]$$

$$= (r - \tfrac{1}{2}\sigma^2)k .$$

(13) $$V[dy] = h^2[p^+ + p^-] - (E[dy])^2$$

$$= \sigma^2 k - (r - \tfrac{1}{2}\sigma^2)^2 k^2 .$$

Thus the diffusion limit of (11) is

$$(14) \qquad dy = (r - 1/2\sigma^2)\,dt + \sigma\,dz$$

where dz is a Gauss-Wiener process with $E[dz] = 0$, $E[dz^2] = dt$; this implies that the diffusion limit of dS is

$$(15) \qquad \frac{dS}{S} = r\,dt + \sigma\,dz.$$

Now as Cox and Ross [6] have pointed out, if a riskless arbitrage portfolio can be established between the contingent claim and the underlying asset, the resulting valuation equation is preference free. Therefore we may value the contingent claim under any convenient assumption about preferences, in particular under the assumption of risk neutrality, which implies that the diffusion process for the underlying asset is (15) and that the value of the contingent claim is obtained by discounting its expected future value at the riskless rate of interest as is done in (10).

We have established therefore that the explicit finite difference approximation to the Black-Scholes differential equation is equivalent to making the permissible assumption of risk-neutrality and approximating the diffusion process (15) by the jump process (11). Notice however that the variance of the approximating jump process given by (13) is a downward biased estimate of the variance of the approximated diffusion process (14). The bias is equal to the square of the expected jump, $(r - \frac{1}{2}\sigma^2)k$. Using the stability condition (9), the upper bound on this bias is σ^4.

The recursive valuation equation (10) may be regarded as a type of numerical integration where the probabilities are taken, not from the normal density function, but from a jump process, (11), approximating the Gauss-Wiener process (14). This approach is almost identical to the numerical integration procedure employed by Parkinson [13], who also approximated the normal distribution by a related but different three-point distribution.

III. The Implicit Finite Difference Approximation

The implicit finite difference approximation to (7) is obtained by approximating the partial derivatives by the finite differences

$$(16) \qquad W_{yy} = (W_{i+1,j} - 2W_{i,j} + W_{i-1,j})/h^2$$

$$(17) \qquad W_y = (W_{i+1,j} - W_{i-1,j})/2h$$

(18)
$$W_t = (W_{i,j+1} - W_{i,j})/k$$

so that the differential equation is written in finite difference form as:

(19) $a\,W_{i-1,j} + b\,W_{i,j} + c\,W_{i+1,j} = (1-rk)W_{i,j+1}$ $i = 1, \ldots n$
                                                                        $j = 1, \ldots m$

where

(20)
$$a = [-\frac{1}{2}(\sigma/h)^2 + \frac{1}{2}(r - \frac{1}{2}\sigma^2)/h]k$$

(21)
$$b = 1 + (\sigma/h)^2 k$$

(22)
$$c = [-\frac{1}{2}(\sigma/h)^2 - \frac{1}{2}(r - \frac{1}{2}\sigma^2)/h]k$$

For any value of j, (19) constitutes a system of n equations in the (n+2) unknowns $W_{i,j}(i = 0,1, \ldots, n+1)$. To complete the system, it is necessary to introduce two boundary conditions. Assume that these are given by knowing $W_{0,j}$ and $W_{n+1,j}$:

(23)
$$W_{0,j} = \alpha_j$$

(24)
$$W_{n+1,j} = \beta_j$$

Then we may eliminate $W_{0,j}$ and $W_{n+1,j}$ from the first and last equations of (19) to obtain:

$b\,W_{1,j} + c\,W_{2,j}$ $= (1-rk)W_{1,j+1} - a\alpha_j$ $= f_1$
                                   $- - o\ o\ o - -$
(25) $a\,W_{i-1,j} + b\,W_{i,j} + c\,W_{i+1,j} = (1-rk)W_{i,j+1}$ $= f_i$
                                   $- - o\ o\ o - -$
       $a\,W_{n-1,j} + b\,W_{n,j}$ $= (1-rk)W_{n,j+1} - c\beta_j$ $= f_n$

This system of equations may be written in matrix form as

(26)
$$\underline{A}\,\underline{W} = \underline{f}.$$

And by recursive solution of (26), knowing the values of $W_{i,j}$ at maturity, we generate the whole set of $W_{i,j}$ values. Note that since $\underline{A}$ is independent of j, the matrix must be inverted only once, so that each time step simply involves the multiplication of a vector by this matrix inverse. This is admittedly a more complex calculation than was required for the explicit solution: on the other hand, the implicit solution procedure is potentially more accurate.

Our objective is to demonstrate that the elements of this matrix inverse may be viewed as discounted probabilities, and that therefore the implicit solution procedure generates successively earlier values of $W_{i,j}$ by discounting the expected value at the end of the next time increment assuming risk neutral preferences.

The simple form of the matrix, A, suggests the use of Gaussian elimination to solve the equation system. We proceed by multiplying the second equation of (25) by (b/a) and subtracting from it the first equation to obtain a transformed second equation from which $W_{1,j}$ has been eliminated: we proceed in this way, multiplying each equation by (b/a) and subtracting from it its transformed predecessor, obtaining the transformed system of equations:

$$b_1^* W_{1,j} + c_1^* W_{2,j} = f_1^*$$
$$b_2^* W_{2,j} + c_2^* W_{3,j} = f_2^*$$
$$- - \circ \circ \circ - -$$

(27)
$$b_{n-1}^* W_{n-1,j} + c_{n-1}^* W_{n,j} = f_{n-1}^*$$
$$b_n^* W_{n,j} = f_n^*$$

In the first equation

$$b_1^* = b, \; c_1^* = c, \; f_1^* = f_1$$

and in general

(28)
$$b_i^* = (b/a) \, b_{i-1}^* - c_{i-1}^*$$

(29)
$$c_i^* = (c/a) \, b_{i-1}^*$$

(30)
$$f_i^* = (f_i/a) \, b_{i-1}^* - f_{i-1}^*.$$

Substituting for c_{i-1}^* in (28) from (29), we obtain the difference equation for b_i^*:

(31)
$$b_i^* = (b/a) \, b_{i-1}^* - (c/a) \, b_{i-2}^*.$$

467

The solution to this difference equation, given the initial conditions $b_1^* = b$, $c_1^* = c$ is:

(32)
$$b_i^* = (a^2/\sqrt{b^2-4ac})\,(\lambda_1^{i+1} - \lambda_2^{i+1})$$

where

(33)
$$\lambda_1 = (b + \sqrt{b^2-4ac})/2a$$

(34)
$$\lambda_2 = (b - \sqrt{b^2-4ac})/2a.$$

Then, substituting for b_{i-1}^* from (32) in (29), c_i^* may be written as:

(35)
$$c_i^* = (ac/\sqrt{b^2-4ac})\,(\lambda_1^i - \lambda_2^i).$$

The expression for f_i^* is obtained by substituting for b_i^* in (30) and solving recursively for f_2^*, f_3^* ... This yields

(36)
$$f_i^* = (a/\sqrt{b^2-4ac}) \sum_{j=1}^{i} L_j\, f_j\,(-1)^{(i-j)}$$

where
$$L_j = \lambda_1^j - \lambda_2^j.$$

The matrix inversion is completed by solving the system of equations (27) starting with the last equation. Define $Z_i = \sum_{j=1}^{i} L_j\, f_j\,(-1)^{(i-j)}$.
Then

$$W_{n,j} = f_n^*/b_n^* = Z_n/aL_n$$

$$W_{n-1,j} = \frac{Z_{n-1}}{aL_n} - \frac{c}{a^2}\frac{L_{n-1}\, Z_n}{L_n\, L_{n+1}}$$

$$- - \circ\circ\circ - -\,.$$

(37)
$$W_{n-q},j = \frac{L_{n-q}}{a}\left[\frac{Z_{n-q}}{L_{n-q}\, L_{n-q+1}} - \frac{c}{a}\frac{Z_{n-q+1}}{L_{n-q+1}\, L_{n-q+2}} \right.$$
$$+ \frac{c^2}{a^2}\frac{Z_{n-q+2}}{L_{n-q+2}L_{n-q+3}} + \cdots -$$
$$\left. + \left(\frac{-c}{a}\right)^q \frac{Z_n}{L_n\, L_{n+1}} \right]$$

$$- - \circ\circ\circ - -\,.$$

Set $(n-q) = i$ and collect coefficients of $W_{i,j+1}$ in (37), recalling that

$f_j = (1-rk)W_{i,j+1}$. Denoting the coefficient of $W_{i,j+1}$ by $(1-rk)p_i$, we have:

$$(38) \qquad p_i = \frac{L_i^2}{a} \sum_{j=i}^{n} (c/a)^{j-i} (1/L_j L_{j+1})$$

$$(39) \qquad p_{i-q} = (-1)^q \frac{L_i L_{i-q}}{a} \sum_{j=i}^{n} (c/a)^{j-i} (1/L_j L_{j+1})$$

$$(40) \qquad p_{i+q} = (-1)^q \frac{L_i L_{i+q}}{a} \sum_{j=i+q}^{n} (c/a)^{j-(i+q)} (1/L_j L_{j+1}).$$

The values of p_{i+q} ($q = 1-i, \ldots, -1, 0, +1, \ldots n-i$) are the elements of the ith row of $\underline{A}^{-1}$. We shall now show that as the boundaries become indefinitely remote p_{i+q} may be interpreted as the probability that the logarithm of the stock price will jump by qh. As the lower boundary becomes remote $i \to \infty$, while $(n-i) \to \infty$ as the upper boundary becomes remote.

First note that

$$(41) \qquad \frac{L_i}{L_{i+q}} = \frac{\lambda_1^i - \lambda_2^i}{\lambda_1^{i+q} - \lambda_2^{i+q}} = \frac{1}{\lambda_1^q} \frac{1 - (\lambda_2/\lambda_1)^i}{1 - (\lambda_2/\lambda_1)^{i+q}}$$

and that since $|\lambda_2/\lambda_1| < 1$

$$(42) \qquad \lim_{i \to \infty} \frac{L_i}{L_{i+q}} = \frac{1}{\lambda_1^q}.$$

Hence as $(n-i)$, $i \to \infty$,[2]

$$(43) \qquad \lim_{\substack{i \to \infty \\ n-i \to \infty}} p_i = p_0^* = \frac{1}{a} \left[\frac{1}{\lambda_1} + \frac{c}{a} \frac{1}{\lambda_1^3} + \frac{c^2}{a^2} \frac{1}{\lambda_1^5} \cdots \right]$$

$$= \lambda_1/(a\lambda_1^2 - c)$$

and from (38) and (39)

$$(44) \qquad \lim_{\substack{i \to \infty \\ n-i \to \infty}} p_{i-q} = p_{-q}^* = (-\frac{1}{\lambda_1})^q p_i^*, \text{ for } q = 1, \ldots, \infty$$

---

[2]Since λ_1 and λ_2 are the roots of the auxiliary equation of the difference equation (31), $\lambda_1 \lambda_2 = c/a$. Therefore, $|c/a\lambda_1^2| = |\lambda_2/\lambda_1| < 1$.

(45) $\lim\limits_{i\to\infty} p_{i+q} = p_q^* = (\frac{-c}{a\lambda_1})^q\, p_i^*$, for $q = 1, \ldots, \infty$.

Consider the sum of the p_q^* $(q = -\infty, \ldots, +\infty)$, S:

(46) $S = p_o^* \left[(1 - \frac{c}{a\lambda_1} + (\frac{c}{a\lambda_1})^2 - (\frac{c}{a\lambda_1})^3 \ldots) - \frac{1}{\lambda_1}(1 - \frac{1}{\lambda_1} + (\frac{1}{\lambda_1})^2 \ldots)\right]$

$= p_o^* \left[\dfrac{a\lambda_1}{a\lambda_1+c} - \dfrac{1}{1-\lambda_1}\right] = p_o^* \left[\dfrac{a\lambda_1^2-c}{(1+\lambda_1)(a\lambda_1+c)}\right]$

and, substituting for p_o^* from (43)

(47) $S = \dfrac{\lambda_1}{(1+\lambda_1)(a\lambda_1+c)}$.

But since λ_1 is a root of the auxiliary equation of (31) and $b = 1-(a+c)$,

$(1+\lambda_1)(a\lambda_1+c) = \lambda_1$ so that S=1. Thus the sum of the weights p_q^* $(q=-\infty, \ldots, +\infty)$

equals 1.

Moreover each element p_q^* is nonnegative so long as[3]

(48) $h^2 \leq \sigma^4/(r - \tfrac{1}{2}\sigma^2)^2$.

Thus since the p_q^* are nonnegative and sum to unity, they may be interpreted

as probabilities and we have

(49) $W_{i,j} = (1-rk) \sum\limits_{q=-\infty}^{\infty} p_q^*\ W_{i+q,j+1}$

$\simeq \dfrac{1}{1+rk} \sum\limits_{q=-\infty}^{\infty} p_q^*\ W_{i+q,j+1}.$

Again, the value of the contingent claim at time instant j may be regarded as given by the expected value of its value at (j+1) discounted at the
riskless rate, r. In this case the expected value of the claim at the next instant is obtained by assuming that y, the logarithm of the stock price, follows
the generalized jump process

$dy = $

_____

[3] For a proof see Appendix.

The locan mean and variance of this process are shown in the Appendix to be given by

(50)
$$E[dy] = (r - \frac{1}{2}\sigma^2)k$$

(51)
$$V[dy] = \sigma^2 k + (r - \frac{1}{2}\sigma^2)^2 k^2 .$$

Taking the diffusion limit as $k \to 0$, y again follows the stochastic differential equation (14) which again implies that the stochastic process for S is (15). Notice that for finite k the variance of the jump process approximation to the diffusion process is biased upwards by the square of the expected size of the jump. This suggests that the accuracy of the implicit method could be improved by adjusting the variance used in (19) by subtracting from the true variance the square of the expected change in the logarithm of the underlying asset value obtained under the assumption of risk neutrality.

Thus the implicit finite difference approximation to the log transform of the Black-Scholes differential equation (7) is also equivalent to approximating the diffusion process by a jump process. In this case the jump process is a generalized one which allows for the possibility that the stock price will jump to an infinity of possible future values rather than just three. It would appear that this "more realistic" approximation would result in more accurate determination of the value of the contingent claim, but this conjecture must wait upon detailed numerical analysis.

IV. Summary

In this paper we have established that the coefficients of the difference equation approximation to the Black-Scholes partial differential equation correspond to the probabilities of a jump process approximation to the underlying diffusion process. The simpler explicit finite difference approximation corresponds to a three-point jump process of the type discussed by Cox and Ross [6], while the more complex implicit finite difference approximation corresponds to a generalized jump process to an infinity of possible points.

APPENDIX

1. Condition for nonnegativity of weights in implicit solution.

(43) can also be written as

$$p^*_o = (b + \sqrt{b^2-4ac})/(b^2-4ac + b\sqrt{b^2-4ac})$$

but from (21) $b > 0$, and from (20), (21) and (22) $b^2-4ac > 0$. Therefore $p^*_o > 0$.

Then from (44) $p^*_{-q} > 0$, iff $\lambda_1 < 0$ which from (33) requires that $a < 0$. Then from (45), $p^*_q > 0$, also iff $c/a > 0$, so that c must also be negative. From (20) and (22), c and a are negative if and only if (48) is satisfied.

2. Mean and variance of the generalized Jump Process.

$$E(dy) = h \left[\sum_{q=1}^{\infty} q\, p^*_q - \sum_{q=1}^{\infty} q\, p^*_{-q} \right].$$

Substituting for p^*_q and p^*_{-q} from (44) and (45),

$$E(dy) = h \left[-\frac{c}{a\lambda_1}\left(1 - 2\frac{c}{a\lambda_1} + 3\left(\frac{c}{a\lambda_1}\right)^2 - \ldots\right) \right.$$
$$\left. + \frac{1}{\lambda_1}\left(1 - \frac{2}{\lambda_1} + \frac{3}{\lambda_1^2} - \ldots\right) \right] p^*_i.$$

Summing and using (43),

$$E(dy) = h \left[-\frac{ac\lambda_1}{(a\lambda_1+c)^2} + \frac{\lambda_1}{(1+\lambda_1)^2} \right] \frac{\lambda_1}{a\lambda_1^2-c}$$

$$E(dy) = (a-c)h = (r - \tfrac{1}{2}\sigma^2)k.$$

Q.E.D.

$$V(dy) = \sum_{q=0}^{\infty} p^*_{-q}(-qh - (a-c)h)^2 + \sum_{q=1}^{\infty} p^*_q (qh - (a-c)h)^2$$

$$= h^2 \left[\sum_{q=0}^{\infty} q^2\, p^*_{-q} + \sum_{q=1}^{\infty} q^2\, p^*_q - (a-c)^2 \right].$$

Summing the series and substituting for p^*_o as above we obtain:

$$V(dy) = h^2 \left[\left\{\frac{\lambda_1(1-\lambda_1)}{(1+\lambda_1)^3} - \frac{ac\lambda_1(a\lambda_1-c)}{(a\lambda_1+c)^3}\right\} \frac{\lambda_1}{a\lambda_1^2-c} - (a-c)^2 \right].$$

Simplifying yields:

$$V(dy) = -h^2[(a+c)b + 4ac]$$

and, substituting for a, b, and c, we obtain (51).   [473]

REFERENCES

[1] Black, F., and M. Scholes. "The Pricing of Options and Corporate Liabilities." *Journal of Political Economy*, Vol. 81 (1973), pp. 637-659.

[2] Boyle, P. "Options: A Monte Carlo Approach." *Journal of Financial Economics* (1976).

[3] Brennan, M., and E. Schwartz. "The Pricing of Equity-Linked Life Insurance Policies with an Asset Value Guarantee." *Journal of Financial Economics*, Vol. 3 (1976), pp. 195-214.

[4] _____. "Convertible Bonds: Valuation and Optimal Strategies for Call and Conversion." *Journal of Finance* (1976).

[5] _____. "The Valuation of American Put Options." *Journal of Finance* (1976).

[6] Cox, J. C., and S. A. Ross. "The Valuation of Options for Alternative Stochastic Processes." *Journal of Financial Economics*, Vol. 3 (1976), pp. 145-166.

[7] _____. "A Survey of Some New Results in Financial Option Pricing Theory." *Journal of Finance*, Vol. 31 (1976), pp. 383-402.

[8] Ingersoll, J. "A Theoretical and Empirical Investigation of the Dual Purpose Funds: An Application of Contingent Claims Analysis." *Journal of Financial Economics*, Vol. 3 (1976), pp. 83-124.

[9] _____. "A Contingent Claims Valuation of Convertible Bonds." Unpublished Manuscript, University of Chicago (1976).

[10] McCracken, D., and W. Dorn. "Numerical Methods and Fortran Programming." New York: John Wiley and Sons, Inc. (1969).

[11] Merton, R. C. "Theory of Rational Option Pricing." *Bell Journal of Economics and Management Science*, Vol. 4 (1973), pp. 141-183.

[12] _____. "On the Pricing of Corporate Debt: The Risk Structure of Interest Rates." *Journal of Finance*, Vol. 29 (1974), pp. 449-470.

[13] Parkinson, M. "Option Pricing: The American Put." *Journal of Business* (1976).

                                                                    [474]

Journal of Banking and Finance 3 (1979) 133–155. © North-Holland Publishing Company

A CONTINUOUS TIME APPROACH TO THE PRICING OF BONDS

Michael J. BRENNAN and Eduardo S. SCHWARTZ*

University of British Columbia, Vancouver, BC, Canada

This paper develops an arbitrage model of the term structure of interest rates based on the assumptions that the whole term structure at any point in time may be expressed as a function of the yields on the longest and shortest maturity default free instruments and that these two yields follow a Gauss–Wiener process. Arbitrage arguments are used to derive a partial differential equation which must be satisfied by the values of all default free bonds. The joint stochastic process for the two yields is estimated using Canadian data and the model is used to price a sample of Government of Canada bonds.

1. Introduction

A theory of the term structure of interest rates is intended to explain the relative pricing of default free bonds of different maturities. Complete theories of the term structure take as given the exogenous specifications of the economy: tastes, endowments, productive opportunities, and beliefs about possible future states of the world; then the prices of default free bonds of different maturities are derived from these exogenous specifications.[1] However, most extant theories of the term structure are partial equilibrium in nature and take as given beliefs about future realizations of the spot rate of interest, which are combined with simple assumptions about tastes to derive yields to maturity on discount bonds of different maturities.

The theory of the term structure has been cast traditionally in terms of the relationship between the forward rates which are inherent in the term structure and the corresponding expected future spot rates of interest. Thus the typical version of the pure expectations hypothesis asserts that forward rates are equal to expected future spot rates.[2] In contrast to the pure expectations hypothesis stands the liquidity premium hypothesis which

*The authors are grateful to Peter Madderom of the U.B.C. Computing Centre for extensive programming assistance, to R. Solanki for research assistance, and to M. Brenner for helpful comments. Earlier versions of the paper have been presented at seminars at Berkeley, U.C.L.A., the University of Washington and the meetings of the European Finance Association, Bad Homburg, 1977. The authors retain responsibility for remaining errors.

[1]For example, Stiglitz (1970), Rubinstein (1976), and Roll (1970).

[2]It is now realized that this assumption is incompatible with universal risk neutrality, the assumption on which this version of the pure expectations hypothesis is usually based. See Merton (1973), Brennan and Schwartz (1977), Cox, Ingersoll and Ross (1977).

asserts that forward rates always exceed the corresponding expected future spot rates by a liquidity premium, which is required to compensate investors for the greater capital risk inherent in longer-term bonds. The market segmentation hypothesis can be regarded as a modification of the liquidity premium hypothesis to allow for positive or negative liquidity premia on longer-term bonds: this hypothesis recognizes that long-term bonds are not necessarily more risky than short-term bonds for investors who have long-term horizons, so that the prices of bonds of different maturities are determined by the preferences of investors with different horizons, with the result that forward rates may bear no systematic relationship to expected future spot rates. A major limitation of both liquidity premium and market segmentation hypotheses is their lack of specificity: since the relationship of liquidity premium to maturity is not specified, there are as many undetermined parameters in the model as there are bond maturities considered.

More recently it has been recognized that, if assumptions are made about the stochastic evolution of the instantaneous rate of interest in a continuous time model, much richer theories of bond pricing can be derived, which constrain the relationship between the risk premia on bonds of different maturities. Thus Merton (1973), Brennan and Schwartz (1977), and Vasicek (1976) have all assumed that the instantaneous spot rate of interest follows a Gauss–Wiener process. Then the arbitrage arguments, which are familiar from the option pricing literature, may be adduced to show that the prices of riskless bonds of all maturities must obey the same partial differential equation which contains only a single utility-dependent function. Since the whole term structure may be derived by solution of this partial differential equation, it follows that the liquidity premia for all maturities must depend upon this single function.

A significant deficiency of this arbitrage model of the term structure is the unrealism of the assumption about the stochastic process for the interest rate. It is assumed that since the instantaneous interest rate follows a Markov process, all that is known about future interest rates is impounded in the current instantaneous interest rate, so that the value of a default free bond of any maturity may be written as a function of this instantaneous interest rate and time. This implies that, apart from deterministic shifts over time in tastes, the whole term structure of interest rates may be inferred from the current instantaneous interest rate. This is clearly at odds with reality.

In this paper we take a step towards a more realistic approach to the relative pricing of bonds of different maturities by allowing changes in the instantaneous interest rate to depend not only on its current value but also on the long-term rate of interest, so that the long-term rate and the instantaneous rate follow a joint Gauss–Markov process. This expansion of the state space from one rate of interest to two is intended to reflect the assumption, which is the basis of both the pure expectations hypothesis and the liquidity premium hypothesis, that the current long-term rate of interest contains information about future values of the spot rate of interest. It should be clear that the model developed here, viewed simply as a model of the term structure, is less ambitious than the single state variable models referred to above: where they derive the long-term rate of interest, we take it as exogenous and attempt to explain only the intermediate portion of the yield curve in terms of its extremities. On the other hand, we avoid the objectionable implication of the above models that the long rate is a deterministic function of the current instantaneous interest rate. It is anticipated that the major contribution of the model developed here will be for the pricing of interest dependent contingent claims which contain an option element, such as savings bonds, retractable bonds and callable bonds. Then, just as the original Black–Scholes (1973) model determines the price of a call option in terms of the price of the underlying stock, without considering how the price of the underlying stock itself is determined, this model will permit the pricing of interest dependent claims in terms of the two exogenously given interest rates. However, before advancing to the more ambitious task of pricing bonds with an option element, it is useful to evaluate the ability of the model to price straight bonds of different maturities and this is the major objective of this paper: a subsidiary task is the estimation of the utility dependent function in the partial differential equation.

In two contemporaneous papers Richard (1976), and Cox, Ingersoll and Ross (1977) have also developed models of the term structure which incorporate two state variables. While our model takes these as the instantaneous rate and the long-term rate, their models take the state variables as the instantaneous real rate of interest and the rate of inflation, changes in which are assumed to be independent: from these state variables they are able to derive the long-term rate of interest. The advantage of their models then lies in the endogeneity of the long-term rate of interest, but this is obtained at the cost of introducing two utility dependent functions into the partial differential equation for bond prices, which considerably complicates the problems of empirical estimation. Our model avoids the need for one of the utility dependent functions by taking as the second state variable the long-term rate of interest which is inversely proportional to an asset price, the price of the consol bond: the risk associated with this state variable may then be hedged away. Both Richard and Cox, Ingersoll and Ross avoid the estimation problems posed by the two utility dependent functions in the partial differential equation by making explicit assumptions about the tastes of the representative investor: Richard considers both linear and logarithmic utility functions while Cox, Ingersoll and Ross consider only the logarithmic case. We assume that the utility dependent functions are constants and estimate their values from the data at hand.

In the following section the partial differential equation which must be satisfied by the value of any default free discount bond is derived. In section 3 the parameters of the assumed stochastic process for interest rates are estimated using data on Canadian interest rates. Section 4 reports the results of using the model to price a sample of Government of Canada bonds.

2. The pricing equation for discount bonds

Letting r denote the instantaneous rate of interest and l the long-term rate of interest which is taken as the yield on a consol bond which pays coupons continuously, it is assumed that r and l follow a joint stochastic process of the general type,

$$dr = \beta_1(r, l, t)dt + \eta_1(r, l, t)dz_1,$$

$$dl = \beta_2(r, l, t)dt + \eta_2(r, l, t)dz_2, \qquad (1)$$

where t denotes calendar time and dz_1 and dz_2 are Wiener processes with $E[dz_1] = E[dz_2] = 0$, $dz_1^2 = dz_2^2 = dt$, $dz_1 dz_2 = \rho dt$. $\beta_1(.)$ and $\beta_2(.)$ are the expected instantaneous rates of change in the instantaneous and long-term rates of interest respectively, while $\eta_1^2(.)$ and $\eta_2^2(.)$ are the instantaneous variance rates of the changes in the two interest rates. ρ is the instantaneous correlation between the unanticipated changes in the two interest rates. Equation system (1) describes a situation in which changes in the instantaneous and long-term rates of interest are partially interdependent: both the expected change and the variance of the change in each interest rate may depend on the value of the other interest rate as well as on its own value. It is reasonable to suppose that the expected change in the instantaneous rate of interest will depend on the long-term rate of interest insofar as the long-term rate carries information about future values of the instantaneous rate; further, the expected change in the long rate must also depend on the current instantaneous rate if the expected rate of return on consol bonds is to be related to the rate of return on instantaneously riskless securities. In addition, (1) allows the unanticipated changes in the two interest rates to be correlated. While the degree of correlation is an empirical matter which will be addressed below, one may envisage the instantaneous rate changing as expectations of the instantaneous rate of inflation change, while the long rate responds to changing expectations about the long-run rate of inflation: it seems reasonable to suppose that changes in these expectations will be correlated but not perfectly so.

The price of a default free discount bond promising \$1 at maturity is assumed to be a function of the current values of the interest rates, r and l, and time to maturity, τ, which we write as $B(r, l, \tau)$. Applying Itô's Lemma, the stochastic process for the price of a discount bond is

$$dB/B = \mu(r, l, \tau)dt + s_1(r, l, \tau)dz_1 + s_2(r, l, \tau)dz_2,$$ (2)

where

$$\mu(r, l, \tau) = (B_1\beta_1 + B_2\beta_2 + \tfrac{1}{2}B_{11}\eta_1^2 + \tfrac{1}{2}B_{22}\eta_2^2 + B_{12}\rho\eta_1\eta_2 - B_3)/B,$$

$$s_1(r, l, \tau) = B_1\eta_1/B,$$

$$s_2(r, l, \tau) = B_2\eta_2/B,$$

and

$$B_1 = \partial B/\partial r, \quad B_2 = \partial B/\partial l, \quad B_3 = \partial B/\partial \tau \quad \text{etc.}$$

To derive the equilibrium relationship between expected returns on bonds of different maturities, consider forming a portfolio, P, by investing amounts x_1, x_2, x_3 in bonds of maturity τ_1, τ_2, τ_3 respectively. The rate of return on this portfolio is[3]

$$dP/P = [x_1\mu(\tau_1) + x_2\mu(\tau_2) + x_3\mu(\tau_3)]dt$$

$$+ [x_1s_1(\tau_1) + x_2s_1(\tau_2) + x_3s_1(\tau_3)]dz_1$$

$$+ [x_1s_2(\tau_1) + x_2s_2(\tau_2) + x_3s_2(\tau_3)]dz_2.$$ (3)

The rate of return on the portfolio will be non-stochastic if the portfolio proportions are chosen so that the coefficients of dz_1 and dz_2 in (3) are zero. That is, so that

$$x_1s_1(\tau_1) + x_2s_1(\tau_2) + x_3s_1(\tau_3) = 0,$$

$$x_1s_2(\tau_1) + x_2s_2(\tau_2) + x_3s_2(\tau_3) = 0.$$ (4)

Then, to avoid the possibility of arbitrage profits, it is necessary that the rate of return on this portfolio be equal to the instantaneous riskless rate of interest, r, so that

$$x_1(\mu(\tau_1) - r) + x_2(\mu(\tau_2) - r) + x_3(\mu(\tau_3) - r) = 0.$$ (5)

The zero risk conditions (4) and the no arbitrage condition (5) constitute a set of three linear homogeneous equations in the three portfolio proportions. They will possess a solution if and only if

$$\mu(\tau) - r = \lambda_1(r, l, t)s_1(\tau) + \lambda_2(r, l, t)s_2(\tau),$$ (6)

---

[3]The arguments, r and l, are omitted from the functions $\mu(\cdot)$, $s_1(\cdot)$ and $s_2(\cdot)$ for the sake of brevity: they are to be understood.

where the functions $\lambda_1(\cdot)$ and $\lambda_2(\cdot)$ are independent of maturity, τ. Eq. (6) is an equilibrium relationship which constrains the relative risk premia on bonds of different maturities. It expresses the instantaneous risk premium on a discount bond of any maturity as the sum of two elements: these are proportional to the partial covariances of the bond's rate of return with the unanticipated changes in the instantaneous and long term rates of interest, $s_1(\cdot)$ and $s_2(\cdot)$ respectively. $\lambda_1(\cdot)$ and $\lambda_2(\cdot)$ may then be regarded as the market prices of instantaneous and long term interest rate risk and will depend upon the utility functions of market participants. If the expressions for $\mu(\cdot)$, $s_1(\cdot)$ and $s_2(\cdot)$ are substituted in (6) the result will be a partial differential equation for the price of a discount bond, $B(r,l,\tau)$, which will contain the two utility dependent functions $\lambda_1(\cdot)$ and $\lambda_2(\cdot)$.[4] However, by making use of the fact that l is a function of the price of an asset which we assume to be traded, a consol bond, it can be shown[5] that $\lambda_2(\cdot)$ is given by

$$\lambda_2(r,l,t) = -\eta_2/l + (\beta_2 - l^2 + rl)/\eta_2. \tag{7}$$

Eq. (7) expresses $\lambda_2(\cdot)$ in terms of the two rates of interest and the parameters of the stochastic process for the long-term rate of interest. It therefore enables us to eliminate this utility dependent function from the partial differential equation for the price of a discount bond, so that substitution in the equilibrium relationship (6) of the expressions for $\mu(\tau)$, $s_1(\tau)$ and $s_2(\tau)$, and use of eq. (7) to eliminate $\lambda_2(\cdot)$, permits us to re-write the equilibrium relationship (6) as the partial differential equation

$$\tfrac{1}{2}B_{11}\eta_1^2 + B_{12}\rho\eta_1\eta_2 + \tfrac{1}{2}B_{22}\eta_2^2$$
$$+ B_1(\beta_1 - \lambda_1\eta_1) + B_2(\eta_2^2/l^2 + l^2 - rl) - B_3 - Br = 0. \tag{8}$$

Given the stochastic process (1) for the two interest rates r and l, (8) is the basic partial differential equation for the pricing of default free discount bonds. This equation, together with the boundary condition specifying the payment to be received at maturity, say $B(r,l,0)=1$, may be solved to yield the prices of discount bonds of all maturities from which the whole term structure of interest rates may be inferred. The term structure at any point in time will depend upon the current values of the state variables r and l, as well as upon the unknown function $\lambda_1(\cdot)$. The prices of regular coupon bonds may be obtained by treating them as portfolios of discount bonds; alternatively, if coupons are paid continuously at the rate c, then c should be added to the left-hand side of the partial differential eq. (8). In addition, this

---

[4]This would be identical to the partial differential equation obtained by Richard (1976) if the variable l is interpreted as the rate of inflation rather than as the long term rate of interest.

[5]See appendix.

equation is valid for all types of default free interest dependent claims, so that it may be applied for example to the pricing of saving bonds or callable bonds by the introduction of the appropriate boundary conditions defining the payoffs on the claims.

It is interesting to note that the partial differential equation is not only independent of $\lambda_2(\cdot)$, the market price of long-term interest rate risk, it is also independent of $\beta_2(\cdot)$, the drift parameter for the long term interest rate, so that the solution is independent of the expected rate of return on the consol bond. This result is analogous to the finding within the simple Black–Scholes (1973) model for the pricing of stock options that the function expressing the equilibrium price of the option in terms of the price of the underlying stock is independent of the expected rate of return on the underlying stock. The reason for the two results is the same: there exists an asset for which the partial derivatives of its value with respect to all of the state variables is known: in this case the consol bond, and in the Black–Scholes case the stock. It can be shown that in general the number of unknown utility dependent parameters left in the partial differential equation will be equal to the number of state variables, excluding time, less the number of assets for which the partial derivatives of the value function are known: in the Black–Scholes case this is zero and in the present case it is one. The time variable is excluded since the pure reward for the passage of time is equal to the interest rate. This proposition is illustrated more formally in the appendix.

The coefficients of the partial differential eq. (8) are the utility dependent function, $\lambda_1(\cdot)$, and the parameters of the underlying stochastic process for the two interest rates, (1). Empirical application of the model requires that the parameters of this stochastic process be estimated and this is taken up in the next section.

3. Estimation of the stochastic process

3.1. The form of the stochastic process

Estimation of the stochastic process for interest rates (1) presupposes some stronger assumptions about the form of the process than we have made hitherto. The first restriction comes from the requirement that the excess of the expected rate of return on the consol bond over the instantaneous rate of interest be commensurate with the degree of long-term interest rate risk of the consol. This requirement is expressed in eq. (7): solving this equation for $\beta_2(\cdot)$, we find

$$\beta_2(r, l, t) = l^2 - rl + \eta_2^2/l + \lambda_2\eta_2. \tag{9}$$

For empirical tractability it is assumed that $\lambda_2(\cdot)$, the market price of long-term interest rate risk, is constant.

The only other a priori restrictions which can be imposed on the stochastic process derive from the requirement that dominance by money be avoided, so that neither of the interest rates can be allowed to become negative. This possibility is avoided by assuming that

$$\eta_1(r,l,t)=r\sigma_1, \qquad \eta_2(r,l,t)=l\sigma_2, \tag{10}$$

and requiring that

$$\beta_1(r,l,t)\geq 0. \tag{11}$$

Eqs. (10) and (11) jointly imply that $\beta_2(r,l,t)\geq 0$. Eq. (10) specifies that the standard deviation of the instantaneous change in each interest rate is proportional to its current level.

To reflect the premise that the long-term rate contains information about future values of the instantaneous rate, it is assumed that the instantaneous rate stochastically regresses towards a function of the current long-term rate. This assumption and conditions (10) and (11) are satisfied by taking as the stochastic process for the logarithm of the instantaneous rate

$$\mathrm{d}\ln r=\alpha[\ln l-\ln p-\ln r]\mathrm{d}t+\sigma_1\mathrm{d}z_1, \tag{12}$$

which is equivalent to the assumptions that

$$\beta_1(r,l,t)=r[\alpha\ln(l/pr)+\tfrac{1}{2}\sigma_1^2], \tag{13}$$

$$\eta_1(r,l,t)=r\sigma_1. \tag{14}$$

The coefficient α represents the speed of adjustment of the logarithm of the instantaneous rate towards its current target value, $\ln(l/p)$, and p is a parameter relating the target value of $\ln r$ to the current value of $\ln l$.

Finally substituting for $\beta_2(\cdot)$ and $\eta_2(\cdot)$ from (9) and (10) in eq. (1), the stochastic process for the long-term rate of interest is

$$\mathrm{d}l=l[l-r+\sigma_2^2+\lambda_2\sigma_2]\mathrm{d}t+l\sigma_2\mathrm{d}z_2. \tag{15}$$

3.2. The linearized form of the stochastic process

Eqs. (12) and (15) constitute a non-linear system of stochastic differential equations governing the behaviour of the two interest rates. In order to estimate the system it is necessary first to linearize it, and to this end we approximate l and r by linear functions of $\ln l$ and $\ln r$. Thus, writing l and r

as functions of $\ln l$ and $\ln r$, and expanding in Taylor series about the mean sample values, $e^{\overline{\ln l}}$ and $e^{\overline{\ln r}}$,

$$l - r = e^{\overline{\ln l}} - e^{\overline{\ln r}}$$

$$\approx e^{\overline{\ln l}}(1 - \overline{\ln l}) - e^{\overline{\ln r}}(1 - \overline{\ln r}) + e^{\overline{\ln l}}\ln l - e^{\overline{\ln r}}\ln r. \tag{16}$$

Then using Itô's Lemma to obtain the stochastic process for $\ln l$ from (15), and substituting for $(l - r)$ from (16), the linearized stochastic differential equation for the logarithm of the long-term rate may be written as

$$d\ln l = [q - k_1 \ln r + k_2 \ln l]dt + \sigma_2 dz_2, \tag{17}$$

where

$$q = e^{\overline{\ln l}}(1 - \overline{\ln l}) - e^{\overline{\ln r}}(1 - \overline{\ln r}) + \tfrac{1}{2}\sigma_2^2 + \lambda_2\sigma_2,$$

while we may write the stochastic differential equation for the logarithm of the instantaneous rate as

$$d\ln r = \alpha[\ln l - \ln r - \ln p]dt + \sigma_1 dz_1. \tag{18}$$

This linearized system of stochastic differential equations for the logarithms of the two interest rates is written in matrix notation as

$$dy(t) = Ay(t)dt + b\,dt + d\xi(t), \tag{19}$$

where

$$y(t) = \begin{pmatrix} \ln r(t) \\ \ln l(t) \end{pmatrix}, \qquad d\xi(t) = \begin{pmatrix} \sigma_1 \, dz_1(t) \\ \sigma_2 \, dz_2(t) \end{pmatrix},$$

$$A = \begin{pmatrix} -\alpha & \alpha \\ -k_1 & k_2 \end{pmatrix}, \qquad b = \begin{pmatrix} -\alpha \ln p \\ q \end{pmatrix}.$$

3.3. The exact discrete model

While (19) is a system of linear stochastic differential equations, the data on interest rates which are required to estimate it are available only at discrete intervals. One approach to estimation when there are prior re-strictions on the parameters[6] has been proposed by Bergstrom (1966). This involves first substituting finite differences for differentials and averages of beginning and end of period values for the time dated vector $y(t)$, and then

---

[6]k_1 and k_2 are known and the coefficients of the two variables in the first equation are known to be equal in magnitude but opposite signs.

estimating the resulting linear equations by standard simultaneous equations methods. Unfortunately, as Phillips (1972) points out, the undesirable feature of this approach is the specification error which causes the resulting parameter estimates to be asymptotically biased. A more efficient and elegant procedure is to obtain the exact discrete model corresponding to (19) and to estimate the parameters from this model.

The exact discrete model corresponding to (19) is[7]

$$y(t) = e^A y(t-1) + A^{-1}[e^A - I]b + \zeta(t), \tag{20}$$

where

$$\zeta(t) = \int_{t-1}^{t} e^{(t-s)A} d\xi(s),$$

and the variance–covariance matrix of errors is

$$E[\zeta(t)\zeta'(t)] = \int_{0}^{1} e^{sA} \Sigma e^{sA'} ds, \tag{21}$$

where Σ is the instantaneous variance–covariance matrix with elements σ_1^2, σ_2^2, $\rho\sigma_1\sigma_2$.[8]

The matrix e^A is defined by

$$e^A \equiv T e^A T^{-1}, \tag{22}$$

where

$$e^A = \begin{pmatrix} e^{v_1} & 0 \\ 0 & e^{v_2} \end{pmatrix},$$

and v_1 and v_2 are the characteristic roots of the matrix A, while T is the matrix of characteristic vectors. In this case the characteristic roots are

$$v_1 = (k_2 - \alpha + \sqrt{(k_2 - \alpha)^2 - 4(k_1 - k_2)})/2,$$

$$v_2 = (k_2 - \alpha - \sqrt{(k_2 - \alpha)^2 - 4(k_1 - k_2)})/2, \tag{23}$$

and the matrix of characteristic vectors is

$$T \equiv \begin{pmatrix} 1 & 1 \\ \dfrac{k_1}{k_2 - v_1} & \dfrac{k_1}{k_2 - v_2} \end{pmatrix}. \tag{24}$$

---

[7]See Bergstrom (1966), Phillips (1972), Wymer (1972).

[8]It can be shown that $\int_0^1 e^{sA} \Sigma e^{sA'} ds \approx \Sigma$, so that the variance covariance matrix of errors from (20) provides good estimates of σ_1, σ_2 and $\sigma_{12} = \rho\sigma_1\sigma_2$.

Inverting A and carrying out the appropriate matrix multiplications in (20) the exact discrete model to be estimated is

$$y_1(t) = \frac{1}{v_1 - v_2} [e^{v_2}(k_2 - v_2) - e^{v_1}(k_2 - v_1)] y_1(t-1)$$

$$+ \frac{1}{k_1(v_1 - v_2)} [(k_2 - v_1)(k_2 - v_2)(e^{v_1} - e^{v_2})] y_2(t-1)$$

$$+ \frac{1}{(k_1 - k_2)(v_1 - v_2)} \{ \ln p[k_2[e^{v_1}(k_2 - v_1) - e^{v_2}(k_2 - v_2) + v_1 - v_2]$$

$$- \alpha k_1(e^{v_1} - e^{v_2})] + q[k_2(k_2 - v_1)(k_2 - v_2)(e^{v_1} - e^{v_2})/\alpha k_1$$

$$- e^{v_1}(k_2 - v_2) + e^{v_2}(k_2 - v_1) + v_1 - v_2] \} + \zeta_1(t). \tag{25}$$

$$y_2(t) = \frac{k_1}{v_1 - v_2}(e^{v_2} - e^{v_1}) y_1(t-1) + \frac{1}{v_1 - v_2} [e^{v_1}(k_2 - v_2) - e^{v_2}(k_2 - v_1)] y_2(t-1)$$

$$+ \frac{1}{(k_1 - k_2)(v_1 - v_2)} \{ \ln p[k_1[e^{v_1}(k_2 - v_1) - e^{v_2}(k_2 - v_2) + v_1 - v_2]$$

$$- \alpha k_1(e^{v_1} - e^{v_2})] + q[(k_2 - v_1)(k_2 - v_2)(e^{v_1} - e^{v_2})/\alpha$$

$$- e^{v_1}(k_2 - v_2) + e^{v_2}(k_2 - v_1) + v_1 - v_2] \} + \zeta_2(t). \tag{26}$$

Summarizing the analysis to this point, the system of stochastic differential equations (1) was first specialized by assuming that the standard deviation of the unanticipated instantaneous changes in each interest rate is proportional to the current level of that rate (10); by requiring that the instantaneous expected rate of return on a consol bond be commensurate with its degree of long-term interest rate risk (9), where $\lambda_2(\cdot)$, the market price of long-term interest rate risk, is taken as constant; and by requiring that the logarithm of the instantaneous interest rate stochastically regress towards a target value which depends on the current value of the long-term rate (12). The resulting system of stochastic differential equations, (12) and (15), was then linearized to yield the system (19), where $y_1(t)$ and $y_2(t)$ are the logarithms of the instantaneous rate and the long-term rate respectively. Finally, since the equation system is to be estimated using data on r and l at discrete time intervals, the exact discrete model, (25) and (26), corresponding to the linearized form (19) was found.

3.4. Empirical results

The three coefficients of the equation system (25), (26) to be estimated are α, $\ln p$ and q. In addition we require an estimate of the variance–covariance matrix Σ, since the elements of this matrix appear as coefficients in the partial differential eq. (8) for the value of a bond. The estimation was carried out using a non-linear procedure described by Malinvaud (1966) and employed by Phillips (1972) in a similar context. The data for the instantaneous rate of interest were the yields on 30-day Canadian Bankers' Acceptances converted to an equivalent continuously compounded annual rate of interest, while the long-term rate of interest was the continuously compounded equivalent of the average yields to maturity on Government of Canada bonds with maturities in excess of 10 years. Both interest rates series are mid-market closing rates on the last Wednesday of each month from January 1964 to December 1976.[9]

The estimated equation system is

$$d \ln r = 0.0701 [\ln l/r - 0.0599] dt + 0.0736 dz_1,$$
$$\quad (0.0050) \qquad (0.0050)$$

$$d \ln l = [0.0060 - 0.0051 \ln r + 0.0058 \ln l] dt + 0.0250 dz_2,$$
$$\quad (0.0020)$$

where the standard errors of the estimated coefficient are in parentheses and the coefficients of $-\ln r$ and $\ln l$ are the computed values of k_1 and k_2. The estimated correlation between the errors in the two equations, ρ, is 0.3747, and the adjustment coefficient of 0.0701 in the first equation implies that half of the adjustment in the instantaneous rate occurs within 10 months.

In terms of the coefficients of the basic partial differential eq. (8) for the pricing of discount bonds, the parameter estimates imply

$$\eta_1 \equiv r\sigma_1 = 0.0736\, r, \quad \eta_2 \equiv l\sigma_2 = 0.0250\, l, \quad \rho = 0.3747,$$

$$\beta_1(r, l, t) = r[\alpha \ln(l/pr) + \tfrac{1}{2}\sigma_1^2]$$

$$= r[0.0701(\ln l/r - 0.0599) + \tfrac{1}{2}(0.0736^2)].$$

4. Bond pricing and the term structure of interest rates

Re-writing the partial differential eq. (8) to take account of the specific stochastic process for r and l assumed in the previous section, we have, substituting for $\beta_1(\cdot)$, $\eta_1(\cdot)$ and $\eta_2(\cdot)$,

$$\tfrac{1}{2}B_{11}r^2\sigma_1^2 + B_{12}rl\rho\sigma_1\sigma_2 + \tfrac{1}{2}B_{22}l^2\sigma_2^2$$
$$+ B_1 r[\alpha \ln(l/pr) + \tfrac{1}{2}\sigma_1^2 - \lambda_1\sigma_1] + B_2 l[\sigma_2^2 + l - r] - B_3 - Br = 0. \tag{27}$$

[9]Taken from the Bank of Canada Review, Cansim Series 2560.33 and 2560.13.

Then the value of a discount bond promising \$1 at maturity, $\tau = 0$, is given by the solution to eq. (27) subject to the boundary condition

$$B(r, l, 0) = 1. \tag{28}$$

Using the values of α, $\ln p$, ρ, σ_1 and σ_2 estimated in section 3, eq. (27) with boundary condition (28) was solved[10] for values of λ_1, the market price of instantaneous interest rate risk, of -0.04, 0.0, 0.09. The resulting values of $B(r, l, \tau)$ are present value factors: for a given value of λ_1, $B(r, l, \tau)$ is the present value of \$1 payable with certainty in τ periods when the instantaneous and long-term rates of interest are r and l respectively.

A sample of 101 Government of Canada bonds was priced using the present value factors computed for each of the three values of λ_1. The bonds were priced on the last Wednesday of each quarter from January 1964 to January 1977 by applying the present value factors appropriate to the prevailing instantaneous and long-term rates of interest to the promised coupon and principal payments for each bond. The sample includes all Government of Canada bonds with maturities less than 10 years for which prices were available in the Bank of Canada Quarterly Review and which were neither callable nor exchangeable. The root mean square price prediction error was calculated for each of the three values of λ_1, and quadratic interpolation was used to estimate the value of λ_1 which minimizes the root mean square prediction error.[11] This estimated value of λ_1 was 0.0355 and the bonds were then priced for this value of λ_1.

In addition, for each of the four values of λ_1, yields to maturity were calculated based on the predicted bond values each quarter and these predicted yields to maturity were compared with the actual yields to maturity. The comparison of actual and predicted bond values and yields to maturity is reported, for each value of λ_1, in table 1: in this table all bonds are treated as having a par value of 100. Thus for the estimated value of $\lambda_1 = 0.0355$, the root mean square prediction error for bond prices is 1.56 and the mean error is -0.17. For the same value of λ_1, the root mean square prediction error for yields to maturity is 0.67% and the mean error is 0.24%. It is to be anticipated that the model will be less successful in predicting yields to maturity than in predicting bond prices, since a small error in the predicted bond price will cause a very large error in the predicted yield to maturity for short dated bonds.

---

[10]The solution procedure is described in the appendix.

[11]That is, a quadratic curve was fitted to the three pairs of RMSE and λ_1, and the RMSE minimizing value of λ_1 was computed. When the bonds were priced using this value of λ_1 the RMSE agreed with the interpolated value. This non-linear estimation procedure leads to a maximum likelihood estimator under the usual assumption of normal, independent, homoscedastic errors. A more efficient estimator which would allow for a generalized error structure was contemplated but ruled out on the basis of computational cost.

For both bond prices and yields to maturity, the actual values were regressed on the predicted values and the resulting regression statistics are reported in table 1 also. For unbiased predictions the intercept term (α) should be zero, and the slope coefficient (β) should be equal to unity. The actual slope coefficients for $\lambda_1 = 0.0355$ are 0.93 for bond prices and 0.79 for yields to maturity. While these regression results should be treated with caution since there is no assurance that the errors are either independent or normally distributed, it is encouraging to observe that there is a strong, though certainly not perfect, correspondence between the actual and predicted values.

Tables 2 and 3 report the results of predicting bond values and yields to maturity for the last Wednesday of each January from 1964 to 1977. These results are representative of those obtained for the other quarters for which predictions were made. While there is reasonable stability in the relationship between actual and predicted bond values, the relationship between actual and predicted yields to maturity is much more erratic. This reflects the greater difficulty in predicting this variable, referred to above, and also suggests that there are factors which are not encompassed in our model which determine the shape of the term structure.

Table 1

Predicted and actual bond prices and yields to maturity for alternative values of λ_1 (t-ratios in parentheses).

	Values of λ_1			
	−0.04	0.0	0.0355	0.09
Bond prices				
RMSE	1.95	1.65	1.56	1.74
Mean error	−1.05	−0.59	−0.17	0.41
α	13.44	10.01	7.28	4.12
	(21.44)	(15.40)	(10.46)	(5.04)
β	0.87	0.90	0.93	0.95
	(134.04)	(134.44)	(129.57)	(114.23)
R^2	0.93	0.93	0.93	0.91
Yields to maturity				
RMSE (%)	0.81	0.72	0.67	0.64
Mean error (%)	0.52	0.37	0.24	0.06
α (%)	1.12	1.15	1.18	1.25
	(18.40)	(18.24)	(18.23)	(18.40)
β	0.77	0.78	0.79	0.80
	(90.63)	(87.61)	(84.44)	(79.56)
R^2	0.86	0.86	0.85	0.83

Table 2

Predicted and actual bond prices by period for $\lambda_1 = 0.0355$ (α, β are the coefficients from the regression of actual values on predicted values).

Year (last Wednesday of January)	No. of observations	RMSE	Mean error (pred.–actual)	α (T-stat.)	β (T-stat.)	R^2	Instantaneous interest rate	Long-term interest rate
1964	17	1.09	0.61	4.62 (0.43)	0.95 (8.68)	0.82	3.69%	5.17%
1965	16	1.04	0.39	23.29 (2.91)	0.76 (9.59)	0.86	3.81	4.69
1966	20	2.15	1.63	37.75 (3.24)	0.61 (5.23)	0.59	4.00	5.41
1967	21	0.91	−0.58	9.49 (1.10)	0.91 (10.44)	0.84	5.85	5.60
1968	22	1.64	0.93	−37.57 (−4.60)	1.38 (16.38)	0.93	6.40	6.54
1969	28	0.97	0.46	−14.97 (−3.53)	1.15 (26.39)	0.96	6.60	7.16
1970	31	1.06	0.07	−10.98 (−5.52)	1.11 (53.39)	0.99	8.90	8.31
1971	30	2.01	−1.61	−0.45 (−0.10)	1.02 (22.66)	0.95	6.00	6.67
1972	32	1.36	0.43	−7.84 (−1.67)	1.07 (23.17)	0.95	3.95	6.73
1973	28	0.46	−0.06	−0.22 (−0.13)	1.00 (59.39)	0.99	4.75	7.16
1974	24	1.95	−1.84	2.42 (1.19)	0.99 (46.00)	0.99	8.75	7.75
1975	22	3.37	−2.84	17.04 (3.32)	0.85 (15.86)	0.92	7.00	8.30
1976	22	1.71	−1.44	5.32 (2.02)	0.96 (33.76)	0.98	9.00	9.29
1977	16	0.99	−0.94	3.70 (1.18)	0.97 (30.88)	0.98	8.33	9.09

Table 3

Predicted and actual yields to maturity by period for $\lambda_1 = 0.0355$ (α, β are the coefficients from regression of actual values on predicted values).

Year (last Wednesday of January)	No. of observations	RMSE	Mean error (pred.–actual)	α	(T-stat.)	β	(T-stat.)	R^2	Instantaneous interest rate	Long-term interest rate
1964	17	0.21%	−0.16%	−1.56	(−2.86)	1.40	(11.05)	0.88	3.69%	5.17%
1965	16	0.25	0.01	−5.26	(−6.13)	2.22	(11.15)	0.89	3.81	4.69
1966	20	0.53	−0.50	−1.52	(−2.06)	1.44	(9.02)	0.81	4.00	5.41
1967	21	0.64	0.50	13.93	(10.38)	−1.57	(−6.58)	0.68	5.85	5.60
1968	22	0.39	−0.12	35.38	(5.09)	−4.54	(−4.16)	0.45	6.40	6.54
1969	28	0.24	−0.06	−27.45	(−8.36)	5.05	(10.44)	0.80	6.60	7.16
1970	31	0.79	0.42	16.66	(11.44)	−1.00	(−5.88)	0.54	8.90	8.31
1971	30	0.85	0.76	−18.70	(−4.40)	3.86	(5.70)	0.53	6.00	6.67
1972	32	0.35	−0.04	−0.66	(−0.95)	1.13	(8.69)	0.71	3.95	6.73
1973	28	0.20	0.05	−0.48	(−1.24)	1.07	(16.64)	0.91	4.75	7.16
1974	24	1.20	1.04	11.04	(14.58)	−0.51	(−5.37)	0.56	8.75	7.75
1975	22	1.11	1.05	2.52	(0.98)	0.53	(1.57)	0.10	7.00	8.30
1976	22	0.75	0.68	6.80	(0.88)	0.17	(0.198)	0.00	9.00	9.29
1977	16	0.52	0.49	7.55	(1.35)	0.04	(0.06)	0.00	8.33	9.09

One factor which has been neglected in the model developed in this paper is the role of income taxes and their differential impact on coupon income and capital gains. To test whether income taxes cause the coupon stream of a bond to be valued less highly than the principal repayment at maturity, the predicted value of the principal payment was subtracted from the actual bond price and the difference was regressed on the predicted value of the coupon stream. If income taxes are important in the pricing of bonds, the resulting regression coefficient should be less than unity, the difference between unity and the estimated regression coefficient measuring the effective tax rate on coupon income. The regression results are reported in table 4 for the different values of λ_1. The evidence presented in this table suggests that the effect of income taxes is slight: for the estimated value of $\lambda_1 = 0.0355$, the estimated tax rate is only 4%, and even for $\lambda_1 = 0.09$ the estimated tax rate is only 8%.

Table 4

The influence of taxes on bond prices: (bond price − predicted value of principal) = $\alpha + \beta$ (predicted value of coupons).

	Values of λ_1			
	−0.04	0.0	0.0355	0.09
α	0.62	0.67	0.71	0.78
	(8.03)	(9.11)	(10.04)	(11.28)
β	1.03	0.99	0.96	0.92
	(249.33)	(254.09)	(256.38)	(256.24)
R^2	0.98	0.98	0.98	0.98

5. Conclusion

In this paper we have developed a theory of the term structure of interest rates based on the assumption that the value of all default free discount bonds may be written as a function of time and two interest rates, the instantaneous rate and the long-term rate, which follow a joint Markov process in continuous time. This assumption permitted us to derive in section 2 a partial differential equation which must be satisfied by the values of all default free discount bonds. The partial differential equation contains two utility dependent functions, $\lambda_1(\cdot)$ and $\lambda_2(\cdot)$, but $\lambda_2(\cdot)$ was eliminated by making use of the assumption that there exists a traded asset, a consol bond, which corresponds to one of the state variables, the long-term rate of interest.

In section 3 the stochastic process for the two interest rates was specialized and estimated using data on Canadian interest rates. The partial differential equation was then solved using the estimated parameters and selected values for the market price of instantaneous interest rate risk, λ_1, to find the value of λ_1 which minimized the price prediction errors for a sample of Canadian government bonds, and the predictive ability of the model was evaluated: the root mean square prediction error for bond prices was of the order of 1.5%.

It is anticipated that models of this type will have application in the management of bond portfolios and studies of the efficiency of bond markets. Perhaps the most interesting application is to the pricing of bonds which contain an option such as callable bonds and saving bonds. The latter are default free securities allowing the holder the right of redemption prior to maturity at a predetermined series of redemption prices. While instruments of this type are common in North America and several European countries, including France, Germany, Italy and the United Kingdom, they have received virtually no attention to date from financial economists. Work is currently in progress to apply the model developed in this paper to Canadian savings bonds.

This model should be seen as a first step in the application of a new approach to the term structure of interest rates and the pricing of default free securities. Further work is required on the specification and estimation of both the stochastic process for the interest rates and the market price of interest rate risk.

Appendix

A.1. The market price of long-term interest rate risk, $\lambda_2(r, l, t)$

It is shown here that if there exists a consol bond, the utility dependent market price of long-term interest rate risk may be expressed in terms of the two interest rates and the parameters of the stochastic process for the long-term rate of interest. Let $V(l)$ denote the price of a consol bond paying a continuous coupon at the rate of \$1 per period. Then the long-term rate of interest is defined by

$$V(l) = l^{-1},   \tag{29}$$

so that, applying Itô's Lemma, the stochastic process for the price of a consol bond is

$$dV/V = (\eta_2^2/l^2 - \beta_2/l)dt - (\eta_2/l)dz_2.   \tag{30}$$

Then, defining $s_1(\infty)$ and $s_2(\infty)$ as the partial covariances of the consol's bond's rate of return with the unanticipated changes in the two interest rates, it follows from eq. (30) that $s_1(\infty) = 0$, $s_2(\infty) = -\eta_2/l$. Further, defining $\mu(\infty)$

as the expected instantaneous rate of return on the consol bond including both the expected capital gain which is obtained from (30) and the rate of coupon payment per dollar of principal,

$$\mu(\infty) = \eta_2^2/l^2 - \beta_2/l + l. \tag{31}$$

Now the expected rate of return on the consol bond must also satisfy the equilibrium risk premium equation, (6), so that substituting in this equation for $\mu(\infty)$, $s_1(\infty)$ and $s_2(\infty)$ and solving for $\lambda_2(\cdot)$, we obtain

$$\lambda_2(r, l, t) = -\eta_2/l + (\beta_2 - l^2 + rl)/\eta_2, \tag{32}$$

which is eq. (7) of the text.

A.2. Asset prices and state variables

This section illustrates for eq. (6) that the number of utility dependent functions left in the partial differential equation is equal to the number of state variables, excluding time, less the number of assets for which the partial derivatives of the value functions are known. Substitute in the equilibrium condition (6) the expressions for $\mu(\cdot)$, $s_1(\cdot)$ and $s_2(\cdot)$ to obtain

$$B_1\beta_1 + B_2\beta_2 + \tfrac{1}{2}B_{11}\eta_1^2 + \tfrac{1}{2}B_{22}\eta_2^2 + B_{12}\rho\eta_1\eta_2 - B_3 - rB$$
$$= \lambda_1 B_1 \eta_1 + \lambda_2 B_2 \eta_2. \tag{33}$$

Now suppose that there exists an asset with value G, all of whose partial derivatives with respect to the state variables are known. The value of the asset must also satisfy the same partial differential equation,

$$G_1\beta_1 + G_2\beta_2 + \tfrac{1}{2}G_{11}\eta_1^2 G_{22}\eta_2^2 + G_{12}\rho\eta_1\eta_2 - G_3 - rG$$
$$= \lambda_1 G_1 \eta_1 + \lambda_2 G_2 \eta_2. \tag{34}$$

Then to eliminate λ_2 and β_2 eq. (34) is multiplied by B_2/G_2 and subtracted from (33) to yield

$$(B_1 - B_2 G_1/G_2)\beta_1 + \tfrac{1}{2}(B_{11} - B_2 G_{11}/G_2)\eta_1^2$$
$$+ \tfrac{1}{2}(B_{22} - B_2 G_{22}/G_2)\eta_2^2 + (B_{12} - B_2 G_{12}/G_2)\rho\eta_1\eta_2$$
$$- (B_3 - B_2 G_3/G_2) - r(B - B_2 G/G_2)$$
$$= \lambda_1(B_1 - B_2 G_1/G_2)\eta_1. \tag{35}$$

Since G and all of its partial derivatives are known functions, (35) contains only a single utility dependent function, $\lambda_1(\cdot)$, and the drift parameter for the corresponding state variable, β_1. If G is the consol bond, then substitution of the appropriate partial derivatives in (35) will yield our partial differential eq. (8). It should be clear that if G_1 were not zero, it would have been possible to eliminate λ_1 and β_1 instead of λ_2 and β_2, and that if a second distinct asset exists whose partial derivatives are known it will be possible to eliminate all four parameters.

A.3. Solution of the partial differential equation

Since there is no known analytic solution to the differential eq. (27) we apply a finite difference solution procedure. This requires that the equation be transformed to take advantage of the natural boundary conditions which occur as the interest rates approach zero and infinity.

To transform the equation, define the new state variables u_1 and u_2 where[12]

$$u_1 = 1/(1+nr), \quad u_2 = 1/(1+nl),$$

and let $B(r, l, \tau) \equiv b(u_1, u_2, \tau)$.

Writing the partial derivatives of $B(\cdot)$ in terms of those of $b(\cdot)$, we have

$$B_1 = -nu_1^2 b_1, \quad B_2 = -nu_2^2 b_2,$$
$$B_{11} = n^2 u_1^4 b_{11} + 2n^2 u_1^3 b_1, \quad B_{22} = n^2 u_2^4 b_{22} + 2n^2 u_2^3 b_2,$$
$$B_3 = b_3.$$

Substituting for r, l and the derivatives of $B(\cdot)$ in (27), we obtain the transformed equation

$$\tfrac{1}{2}b_{11}u_1^2(1-u_1^2)\sigma_1^2 + b_{12}u_1u_2(1-u_1)(1-u_2)\rho u_1u_2 + \tfrac{1}{2}b_{22}u_2^2(1-u_2^2)\sigma_2^2$$
$$+ b_1u_1(1-u_1)[\sigma_1^2(\tfrac{1}{2}-u_1) - \alpha(\ln u_1(1-u_2)/pu_2(1-u_1)) + \lambda_1\sigma_1]$$
$$+ b_2u_2(1-u_2)[-\sigma_2^2 u_2 - (1-u_2)/nu_2 + (1-u_1)/nu_1]$$
$$- b_3 - b(1-u_1)/nu_1 = 0. \tag{36}$$

The solution to this differential equation must satisfy the maturity boundary condition which is defined by assuming that the bond pays \$1 at maturity:

[12]The parameter n was chosen so that approximately one half of the range of u_1 and u_2 $(0, 1)$ relates to the relevant range of interest rates, 0–20%, in which solution accuracy is required, i.e. $n = 40$.

$$b(u_1, u_2, 0) = 1. \tag{37}$$

In addition we have the following natural boundaries obtained by letting u_1, u_2 approach zero and one[13] in the differential eq. (36):

(i)   For $r = \infty(u_1 = 0)$, $l = \infty(u_2 = 0)$.

Multiply (36) by nu_1 and let u_1 and u_2 approach zero to obtain

$$b(0, 0, \tau) = 0. \tag{38}$$

(ij)   For $r = \infty(u_1 = 0)$, $l \neq \infty$.

Multiply (36) by nu_1 and let u_1 approach zero to obtain the ordinary differential equation

$$b_2(0, u_2, \tau)u_2(1 - u_2) - b(0, u_2, \tau) = 0.$$

Solving this equation and imposing the requirement that $b(0, u_2, \tau) \leq 1$, we have

$$b(0, u_2, \tau) = 0. \tag{39}$$

(iii)   For $l = \infty(u_2 = 0)$, $r \neq \infty$.

Divide (36) by $\ln u_2$ and let u_2 approach zero to obtain

$$\alpha u_1(1 - u_1)b_1(u_1, 0, \tau) = 0,$$

and since $b(0, 0, \tau) = 0$ from (38), this implies that

$$b(u_1, 0, \tau) = 0. \tag{40}$$

The boundary conditions (38)–(40) state that if either interest rate is infinite, the value of the bond is zero.

(iv)   For $r = 0$ $(u_1 = 1)$, $l = 0$ $(u_2 = 1)$.

Setting u_1 and u_2 equal to unity in (36),

$$b_3(1, 1, \tau) = 0.$$

Combining this with the maturity value boundary, (37), we obtain

$$b(1, 1, \tau) = 1. \tag{41}$$

---

[13]This corresponds to letting the interest rates r and l approach infinity and zero respectively.

(v)   For $r=0$ $(u_1=1)$, $l\neq0$.

Taking the limit in (36) as $u_1\to1$,

$$\tfrac{1}{2}b_{22}u_2^2(1-u_2^2)\sigma_2^2+b_2u_2(1-u_2)[-\sigma_2^2u_2-(1-u_2)/nu_2]-b_2=0.$$

$$(42)$$

$b(1,u_2,\tau)$ is obtained as the solution to (42) subject to the boundary conditions (37), (40) and (41).

(vi)   For $l=0$ $(u_2=1)$, $r\neq0$.

Divide (36) by $\ln(1-u_2)$ and let $u_2\to1$ to obtain

$$\alpha u_1(1-u_1)b_1(u_1,1,\tau)=0.$$

$$(43)$$

The solution to (43) subject to the boundary (40) is

$$b(u_1,1,\tau)=1.$$

$$(44)$$

The finite difference approximation to (36) is obtained by defining $b(\cdot)$ at discrete intervals.

$$b(u_{1i},u_{2j},\tau_k)\equiv b(hi,hj,gk)$$

$$\equiv b_{i,j,k}, \qquad i,j=0,\ldots,m, \quad k=0,\ldots,K, \qquad (45)$$

where h and g are the step sizes for the interest rates and time to maturity respectively; since u_1 and u_2 are defined on the interval $(0,1)$, $hm=1$. Then writing finite differences in place of partial derivatives, (36) may be approximated by

$$c_1^{i,j}b_{i-1,j-1,k}+c_2^{i,j}b_{i-1,j,k}+c_3^{i,j}b_{i-1,j+1,k}$$

$$+c_4^{i,j}b_{i,j-1,k}+c_5^{i,j}b_{i,j,k}+c_6^{i,j}b_{i,j+1,k}$$

$$+c_7^{i,j}b_{i+1,j-1,k}+c_8^{i,j}b_{i+1,j,k}+c_9^{i,j}b_{i+1,j+1,k}$$

$$=b_{i,j,k-1}, \qquad i=1,\ldots,m-1, \quad j=1,\ldots,m-1, \qquad (46)$$

where $c_1^{i,j}$ etc. are coefficients derived from the parameters of the equation.

(46) is a system of $(m-1)^2$ equations in the $(m+1)^2$ unknowns $b_{i,j,k}$ $(i,j=0,1,\ldots,m)$; the remaining $4m$ equations are provided by the natural boundary conditions (i)–(vi) above.[14] The augmented system of equations may be solved recursively for the unknowns $b_{i,j,k}$ in terms of $b_{i,j,k-1}$, since the values

[14]Values of $b(1,u_2,\tau)$ are obtained by solving the finite difference approximation to (42).

$b_{i,j,0}$ are given by the maturity boundary condition (37). To take advantage of the structure of the coefficient matrix the equations were solved by the method of successive over-relaxation.[15]

[15]Westlake (1968).

References

Bergstrom, A.R., 1966, Non-recursive models as discrete approximations to systems of stochastic differential equations, Econometrica 34, 173–182.

Black, F. and M.J. Scholes, 1973, The pricing of options and corporate liabilities, Journal of Political Economy 81, 637–659.

Brennan, M.J. and E.S. Schwartz, 1977, Saving bonds, retractable bonds and callable bonds, Journal of Financial Economics 5, 67–88.

Cox, J. C., J. E. Ingersoll and S.A. Ross, 1977, Notes on a theory of the term structure of interest rates, Unpublished working paper.

Malinvaud, E., 1966, Statistical methods of econometrics (North-Holland, Amsterdam).

Merton, R.C., 1973, The theory of rational option pricing, Bell Journal of Economics and Management Science 4, 141–183.

Phillips, P.C.B., 1972, The structural estimation of a stochastic differential equation system, Econometrica 40, 1021–1041.

Richard, S.F., 1976, An analytical model of the term structure of interest rates, Working paper no. 1976–77 (Carnegie-Mellon University, Pittsburgh, PA).

Roll, R., 1970, The behaviour of interest rates (Basic Books, New York).

Rubinstein, M., 1976, The valuation of uncertain income streams and the pricing of options, The Bell Journal of Economics 7, 407–425.

Stiglitz, J.E., 1970, A consumption-oriented theory of the demand for financial assets and the term structure of interest rates, Review of Economic Studies.

Vasicek, O., 1976, An equilibrium characterization of the term structure, Unpublished manuscript.

Westlake, J.R., 1968, A handbook of numerical matrix inversion and solution of linear equations (Wiley, New York).

Wymer, C.R., 1972, Econometric estimation of stochastic differential equation systems, Econometrica 40, 565–577.

[13]

THE JOURNAL OF FINANCE • VOL XXIV, NO. 1 • MARCH 1979

The Pricing of Contingent Claims in Discrete Time Models

M. J. BRENNAN*

I

THE ESSENTIAL FEATURE OF modern option pricing theory is the derivation of risk neutral valuation relationships (RNVRs) for contingent claims. A contingent claim is an asset whose payoff depends upon the value of another "underlying" asset, the value of which is exogenously determined: a valuation relationship is a formula relating the value of the contingent claim, or its derivatives, to the value of the underlying asset and other exogenous parameters.[1] If the valuation relationship is risk-neutral, it is compatible with the assumption of risk neutral investor preferences, under which all securities have the same expected rate of return.

A risk neutral valuation relationship depends only upon potentially observable parameters and it is extremely significant that such a relationship can be derived from only weak assumptions about investor preferences, for, as Merton [10] has observed: "An exact formula for an asset price, based on observable variables only, is a rare finding in a general equilibrium model . . .". RNVRs have been derived from two quite different general classes of model: the first class places no restrictions on investor preferences beyond the assumption of non-satiety, but assumes that asset trading takes place continuously, while the second class of model places stronger restrictions on investor preferences but makes the more general assumption that asset trading takes place at discrete intervals.[2]

From the assumption of non-satiety alone, the only results which can be obtained are those which depend upon the absence of riskless arbitrage opportunities. In the case in which trading takes place continuously, both the underlying asset and the contingent claim are traded assets and at least one of them is infinitely divisible, and the price dynamics of the underlying asset can be de-

* The University of British Columbia

This paper was completed while the author was visiting the Manchester Business School. Financial assistance from the Canada Council is gratefully acknowledged. The author thanks Mark Rubinstein for comments on an earlier draft, Gordon Sick for assistance with one of the proofs, and Tom Ho of the Journal for useful suggestions. Any remaining errors or obscurities are the responsibility of the author.

[1] The relationship may be an equation relating the value of the contingent claim to the value of the underlying asset as, for example, the Black-Scholes (2) formula, or it may be a differential equation relating the two asset values for which no general solution is known.

[2] Rubinstein (15) remarks that "since the time interval between dates can be made arbitrarily small in discrete time models, they are in this respect of greater generality," (than continuous time models).

A third class of model developed by Rubinstein (16) in a forthcoming book dispenses with the need for stronger restrictions on investor preferences in a discrete time context by assuming that the value of the underlying asset follows a two-state jump process.

scribed by an *Itô* process, this no-arbitrage condition can be shown to imply a partial differential equation relating the value of the contingent claim to the value of the underlying asset, and this partial differential equation does not involve investor preferences. The solution of this differential equation subject to the appropriate boundary conditions is also preference free and therefore provides a valuation relationship which is consistent with risk neutral preferences—a RNVR. The prototype of this kind of analysis is the Black-Scholes [2], Merton [10] formula for the value of dividend protected, European call and put option contracts. Subsequent research (Merton [11], Ingersoll [9], Brennan and Schwartz [4], Emanuel [6], *et. al.*) has provided RNVRs for contingent claims with different boundary conditions (risky corporate debt, convertible bonds, put options, preferred shares, etc.), and for contingent claims on assets whose price dynamics follow different stochastic processes (Cox and Ross [5]). In summarizing this mode of analysis, Cox and Ross [5] have argued that whenever a portfolio can be constructed which includes the contingent claim and the underlying asset in such proportions that the instantaneous return on the portfolio is non-stochastic, the resulting valuation relationship is risk neutral.

In a model in which trading takes place only at discrete intervals, it is in general not possible to construct a portfolio containing the contingent claim and the underlying asset in such proportions that the resulting portfolio return is non-stochastic.[3] Therefore no useful results can be obtained simply by imposing non-satiety on investor preferences: further restrictions are required. Thus Merton (10) has stated that the Black-Scholes (2) formula for the value of a European call option may be obtained in a discrete time model if:

(i) there is a single investor whose utility function exhibits constant proportional risk aversion,

(ii) returns on the underlying asset follow a lognormal distribution, and

(iii) the underlying asset is aggregate national wealth.

More recently, Rubinstein (14) has generalized the conditions under which the Black-Scholes formula may be obtained within a discrete time trading model. The assumption of a single investor is replaced by the requirement that the conditions for aggregation are met so that securities are priced as though all investors had the same characteristics as a representative investor: as in Merton (10), the representative investor is assumed to exhibit constant proportional risk aversion. The assumption that the underlying asset is aggregate national wealth is relaxed to the requirement that the return on the underlying asset and the return on aggregate wealth (or, equivalently, the rate of growth of aggregate consumption) follow an arbitrary bivariate lognormal distribution.

In addition to the greater generality of discrete time models referred to above, the chief advantage of the discrete time approach to the pricing of contingent claims is that the restriction of investor preferences eliminates the requirement of the continuous time approach that an instantaneously riskless portfolio may

---

[3] There are two cases in which it is possible to create such a portfolio with a non-stochastic return in a discrete time context. The first is when the value of the contingent claim is a linear function of the value of the underlying asset: examples include the perpetual callable warrant (Merton (10)) and the cumulative preferred share (Emanuel (6)). The second is when the value of the underlying asset follows a two state jump process. (See footnote 2.)

be constructed which includes both the contingent claim and the underlying asset. Such a portfolio can be constructed only under special assumptions: these require restrictions on the stochastic process for the value of the underlying asset, and that the underlying asset and the contingent claim be not only traded assets but may be purchased and sold continuously in any proportions. The discrete time model, on the other hand, imposes no such requirements and hence extends the scope of option pricing principles to the relative valuation of a broad class of assets for which one or other of these assumptions is not satisfied. For example, certain kinds of tax liability may be regarded as contingent claims whose value depends upon the accounting income of the firm—in this case neither the contingent claim nor the "underlying asset" is a traded asset; the value of income bonds will similarly depend upon accounting profits—a non-traded asset. Costs which will be paid only in the event of bankruptcy also represent a non-traded contingent claim. The option to purchase physical assets at the expiration of a lease contract is a contingent claim which can only be traded in fixed amounts. The opportunity of a firm to make profitable investments in the future, if that should prove profitable[4], is a contingent claim which is not traded. In all of these examples the contingent claims involved cannot be priced on the basis of the arbitrage principles alone, so that further restrictions on preferences must be introduced if these claims are to be valued.

A further potential advantage of the discrete time approach is that it permits the introduction of heterogeneous probability assessments across investors and even individual uncertainty as to the parameters of the underlying probability distributions, thus removing the most restrictive feature of the continuous time model which is the assumption that the parameters of the underlying stochastic process are known with certainty and agreed upon by all investors.

More generally, a sufficient reason for wishing to explore the pricing of contingent claims in a discrete time framework is that this is the major competing paradigm to the continuous time framework: neither framework is satisfactory in all respects, and it remains to be seen which will ultimately prove the more fruitful. In this paper we examine the pricing of contingent claims in discrete time models in the context of a capital market in which the aggregation problem has been solved so that security prices are determined "as if there exist only identical individuals whose resources, beliefs and tastes are a composite of the actual individuals in the economy."[5] Making specific assumptions about the bivariate distribution of returns on the underlying asset and on aggregate wealth, we seek the conditions on the tastes of the representative investor which are necessary for a risk neutral valuation relationship to obtain. Although we restrict our attention to the bivariate normal and lognormal distributions, the techniques of the paper may be applied to any other probability distribution for which the relevant density functions exist. Our results for the lognormal distribution show that a necessary and sufficient condition for a RNVR to hold for arbitrary bivariate lognormal distributions is that the representative investor exhibit constant proportional risk aversion: Rubinstein [14] has previously shown that the Black-Scholes formula, a special case of a RNVR, obtains in this case. Our results

[4] See Myers and Turnbull (12).
[5] Rubinstein (13).

are more general than his in applying to any RNVR and it is hoped that our proofs are more transparent. We also show that a necessary and sufficient condition for a RNVR to hold for arbitrary bivariate normal distributions is that the representative investor exhibit constant absolute risk aversion. Our results for normal distributions overcome the chief objections to the single period capital asset pricing model: that it must rest either upon quadratic utility functions or unlimited liability. We are able to value limited liability securities within the framework of a capital asset pricing model based on exponential utility or constant absolute risk aversion.

   In Section II, we describe the single period model of market equilibrium which is the basis of our subsequent analysis. In Section III, our major results are presented in a single period framework and in Section IV, we show how they may be extended to a multi-period framework within two extant models of multi-period capital market equilibrium.

II

In a one period economy in which the aggregation problem has been solved[6], security prices are determined as though there existed only identical representative investors. The decision problem of such an investor may be written as

$$\underset{\{c_o, x_j\}}{\text{Max}} \left[U(c_o) + E\{ V[(w_o - c_o)r_f + \sum_{j=1}^{n} x_j (p_{j1} - p_{jo} r_f)]\} \right] \tag{1}$$

where w_o — the initial wealth of a representative investor,
       c_o — the initial consumption of a representative investor,
       $U(\cdot)$ — utility function defined over initial consumption, c_o,
       $V(\cdot)$ — utility function defined over end of period wealth,

$$w_1 = (w_o - c_o)r_f + \sum_{j=1}^{n} x_j(p_{j1} - p_{jo}r_f),$$

       r_f — one plus the riskless interest rate,
       p_{j1} — the end of period price of risky security j ($j = 1, \ldots, n$),
       p_{jo} — the initial price of risky security j,
       x_j — the number of units of risky security j purchased,
       $E\{\cdot\}$ — the expectations operator.

   Assuming a maximum in (1), the first order conditions are

$$U'(c_o) - r_f E[V'(w_1)] = 0 \tag{2}$$

$$E[V'(w_1)p_{j1}] - p_{jo} r_f E[V'(w_1)] = 0 \quad (j = 1, \ldots, n) \tag{3}$$

where the primes denote differentiation. It follows from the market clearing conditions and the identical characteristics of the representative investors that $c_o = C_o/m$ and $w_1 = W_1/m$ where C_o and W_1 represent the exogenously determined

---

[6] The aggregation problem is solved if security prices are independent of the allocation of wealth across investors. Rubinstein (13) derived sufficient conditions for aggregation which were subsequently shown by Brennan and Kraus (3) to be also necessary. These conditions are that either all investors have identical cautiousness and beliefs or all investors have exponential utility functions.

The Pricing of Contingent Claims   57

aggregates of initial consumption and end of period wealth respectively, and m is the total number of investors. Using these market clearing conditions, equations (2) and (3) suffice to determine the return on the riskless security, r_f, and the initial prices, p_{jo}, of each of the n risky securities.

Dropping the subscript j, the initial price of any security, p_o, is given by

$$p_o = r_f^{-1} E[yp_1] \tag{4}$$

where $y \equiv V'(w_1)/E[V'(w_1)]$ is the "relative marginal utility of wealth" of the representative investor.

Rewriting equation (4) as:

$$p_o = r_f^{-1} E[E(yp_1|p_1)] = r_f^{-1} E[p_1 E(y|p_1)]$$

We obtain:

$$p_o = r_f^{-1} E[z(p_1)p_1] \tag{5}$$

where $z(p_1) \equiv E[y|p_1]$ is the conditional expected relative marginal utility function: we shall refer to $z(p_1)$ as the conditional marginal utility function. Equation (5) states that the price of any security may be expressed as the expected value of the end of period price weighted by its conditional marginal utility and discounted at the riskless interest rate. This is the basic valuation equation we shall employ in the following section.

III

Let $g(p_1)$ denote the end of period payoff on the contingent claim as a function of the end of period value of the underlying asset, p_1, and let $f(p_1|p_o)$ denote the density function of the end of period asset price conditional on its initial price, p_o. Define $\hat{f}(p_1|p_o)$ as a density function whose location parameter is chosen so that the mean of the distribution is $p_o r_f$, while the other parameters of the distribution are identical to those of $f(p_1|p_o)$. Then a RNVR is said to exist if the value of the contingent claim at the beginning of the period may be written as a function of the value of the underlying asset $W(p_o)$, where

$$W(p_o) = r_f^{-1} \int_{-\infty}^{\infty} g(p_1)\hat{f}(p_1|p_o) dp_1 \tag{6}$$

Thus, if a RNVR exists, the contingent claim may be valued as though investor preferences were risk neutral: under risk neutrality, the appropriate distribution of p_1 will be $\hat{f}(p_1|p_o)$, and the contingent claim may be valued by discounting its expected terminal value at the riskless rate r_f, as in equation (6).

In this section we consider, for two particular assumptions about the bivariate distribution of returns on aggregate wealth and the underlying asset, the conditions under which a RNVR will obtain.

1. The Bivariate Lognormal Distribution

The original Black-Scholes formula for the value of a call option on a common stock and most of the subsequent continuous time models for the pricing of contingent claims have been based on the assumption that the return on the underlying asset follows a lognormal distribution. Moreover, Rubinstein [14] has shown that the assumption of constant proportional risk aversion together with bivariate lognormality is sufficient to obtain the Black-Scholes formula in a discrete time model. In addition, the lognormal distribution appears to describe fairly well the empirical distribution of returns on common stocks. It is therefore of interest to enquire how general are the assumptions about the preferences of the representative investor which will lead to a RNVR in a discrete time model in which the return on the underlying asset and the return on aggregate wealth follow an arbitrary bivariate lognormal distribution.

If the return on the underlying asset follows a lognormal distribution, then

$$f(p_1|p_o) = (p_1 \, \sigma\sqrt{2\pi})^{-1} \quad \exp \quad \frac{-1}{2\sigma^2} \{\ell n p_1 - \mu - \ell n p_o\}^2 \tag{7}$$

$$E[p_1|p_o] = p_o \exp\{\mu + \tfrac{1}{2}\sigma^2\} \tag{8}$$

where μ and σ are respectively the location and scale parameters of the lognormal distribution of price relatives on the underlying asset. The location parameter of $\hat{f}(p_1|p_o)$, $\hat{\mu}$, is chosen so that

$$p_o\exp\{\hat{\mu} + \tfrac{1}{2}\sigma^2\} = p_o r_f \tag{9}$$

so that $\hat{\mu} = \ln r_f - \tfrac{1}{2}\sigma^2$. Hence, if a RNVR exists under the lognormal assumption, the value of a contingent claim may be written from (6) and (7) as:

$$W(p_0) = r_f^{-1} \int_{-\infty}^{\infty} g(p_1)(p_1 \, \sigma\sqrt{2\pi})^{-1}\exp\frac{-1}{2\sigma^2}\left\{\ln(p_1/p_0) - \ln r_f + \frac{1}{2}\sigma^2\right\}^2 dp_1 \tag{10}$$

However, using the basic valuation equation (5), the value of the contingent claim is

$$W(p_0) = r_f^{-1} E[z(p_1)g(p_1)]$$

$$= r_f^{-1} \int_{-\infty}^{\infty} g(p_1)z)(p_1 \, \sigma\sqrt{2\pi})^{-1}\exp\frac{-1}{2\sigma^2}\{\ln(p_1/p_0) - \mu\}^2 dp_1 \tag{11}$$

Thus a RNVR exists under the lognormal assumption only if the two expressions for the value of the contingent claim (10) and (11) are equivalent for all possible bivariate lognormal distributions of the end of period price of the underlying asset, p_1, and aggregate wealth, W_1: (10) is a RNVR, while (11) is the valuation expression derived from the equilibrium model of Section II. This gives rise to the following theorem.

THEOREM 1: *A necessary condition for a RNVR to exist under the assumption of an arbitrary bivariate lognormal distribution of the price of the underlying asset and aggregate wealth (the lognormal assumption) is that the conditional marginal utility function $z(p_1)$ be of the form $K(p_1/p_0)^\beta$, where K and β are appropriately defined constants.*

Proof: If a RNVR exists, then the two expressions (10) and (11) are equivalent for all functions $g(p_1)$. Hence

$$z(p_1)(p_1\sigma\sqrt{2\pi})^{-1}\exp\frac{-1}{2\sigma^2}\{\ln(p_1/p_0) - \mu\}^2$$

$$= (p_1\sigma\sqrt{2\pi})^{-1}\exp\frac{-1}{2\sigma^2}\left\{\ln(p_1/p_0) - \ln r_f + \frac{1}{2}\sigma^2\right\}^2 \quad (12)$$

or

$$z(p_1) = K(p_1/p_0)^{-\eta/\sigma^2} \quad (13)$$

where

$$K = \exp\{\eta(\mu + \ln r_f - \tfrac{1}{2}\sigma^2)/2\sigma^2\}, \quad \text{and} \quad \eta = \mu - \ln r_f + \tfrac{1}{2}\sigma^2$$

This establishes that the conditional marginal utility function is of the form specified in the theorem.

In the next theorem we establish that $z(p_1)$ will be a power function as specified in theorem 1 only if the marginal utility function of the representative investor is also a power function, in which case the utility function of the representative investor exhibits constant proportional risk aversion being either a power or a logarithmic function. These are the two utility functions for which Rubinstein was able to obtain the Black-Scholes formula for the value of a call option in a discrete time model with bivariate lognormality.

THEOREM 2: *A necessary condition for the conditional marginal utility function, $z(p_1)$, to be of the form (13) under the assumption of an arbitrary bivariate lognormal distribution of the price of the underlying asset and aggregate wealth (the lognormal assumption) is that the marginal utility function of the representative investor, $V'(w_1)$, is of the form w_1^a.*

Proof: By definition,

$$z(p_1) = E[V'(w_1)|p_1]/E[V'(w_1)] \quad (14)$$

Since w_1 and p_1 are bivariate lognormal, $\ln w_1$ ($= \ln W_1 - \ln m$) and $\ln p_1$ are bivariate normal, so that the conditional distribution of $\ln w_1$, given $\ln p_1$ is normal with mean and standard deviation, $\mu_w + \rho\frac{\sigma_w}{\sigma}[\ln(p_1/p_0) - \mu]$, and $\sqrt{1-\rho^2}\,\sigma_w$ respectively, where μ_w and σ_w are the mean and standard deviation of the unconditional distribution of $\ln w_1$, and ρ is the correlation between $\ln w_1$ and $\ln p_1$.

If $z(p_1)$ is to be of the form (13) for arbitrary bivariate lognormal distributions, it must be of this form when $\rho = 1$. Then[7]

$$E[V'(w_1)|p_1] = V'(E[w_1|p_1]) = V'\left(\exp\left\{\mu_w + \frac{\sigma_w}{\sigma}(\ln(p_1/p_0) - \mu)\right\}\right) \quad (15)$$

and, using (13), (14) and (15),

$$z(p_1) = K(p_1/p_0)^{-\eta/\sigma^2} = V'\left(\exp\left\{\mu_w + \frac{\sigma_w}{\sigma}(\ln(p_1/p_0) - \mu)\right\}\right)/E[V'(w_1)] \quad (16)$$

[7] See Aitchison and Brown (1) for the expression for the mean of a lognormal variable.

Writing the argument of $V'(\cdot)$ in (16) as x and eliminating (p_1/p_0), it follows that $V'(\cdot)$ is a power function.

We next show, generalizing Rubinstein's [14] result, that the assumption of a power marginal utility function is sufficient, given bivariate lognormality, for a RNVR to obtain.

THEOREM 3 (*Rubinstein*): *A sufficient condition for a RNVR to obtain under the assumption of bivariate lognormality is that the marginal utility function of the representative investor is a power function; the utility function exhibits constant proportional risk aversion.*

Proof: Suppose $V'(w_1) = w_1^\alpha$. Then, using the definition of $z(p_1)$, (14), and noting that the conditional and marginal distributions of w_1^α are also lognormal, we obtain

$$z(p_1) = \exp - \{\alpha\rho\ \sigma_w\ \mu/\sigma + \tfrac{1}{2}\alpha^2\ \rho^2\ \sigma_w^2\}(p_1/p_0)^{\alpha\rho\sigma_w/\sigma} \tag{17}$$

But from the basic valuation equation (5),

$$r_f = E[z(p_1)(p_1/p_0)] \tag{18}$$

Substituting for $z(p_1)$ from (17) and using the expression for the expectation of a lognormal variable, (18) may be rewritten as

$$r_f = \exp - \{\alpha\rho\sigma_w\mu/\sigma + \tfrac{1}{2}\alpha^2\rho^2\sigma_w^2\}\ E[(p_1/p_0)^{1+\alpha\rho\sigma_w/\sigma}]$$

$$= \exp\{-\alpha\rho\mu\sigma_w/\sigma - \tfrac{1}{2}\alpha^2\rho^2\sigma_w^2 + (1 + \alpha\rho\sigma_w/\sigma)\ \mu + \tfrac{1}{2}(1 + \alpha\rho\sigma_w/\sigma)^2\sigma^2\} \tag{19}$$

Simplifying (19), we obtain the market equilibrium relationship:

$$\mu + \tfrac{1}{2}\sigma^2 - \ln r_f = -\alpha\rho\ \sigma\ \sigma_w^{\ 8} \tag{20}$$

Using the basic valuation equation (5) for the value of the contingent claim,

$$W(p_0) = r_f^{-1} \int_0^\infty g(p_1)z(p_1)(\sigma\ p_1\sqrt{2\pi})^{-1}\exp\frac{-1}{2\sigma^2}\ \{\ln(p_1/p_0) - \mu\}^2\ dp_1 \tag{21}$$

After substituting for $z(p_1)$ from (17), (21) becomes

$$W(p_0) = r_f^{-1} \int_0^\infty g(p_1)(\sigma\ p_1\sqrt{2\pi})^{-1}\exp\frac{-1}{2\sigma^2}\ \{\ln(p_1/p_0)$$

$$-(\mu + \alpha\rho\ \sigma_w\ \sigma)\}^2\ dp_1 \tag{22}$$

Finally, using the market equilibrium relationship (20) to eliminate μ and α in

---

[8] We note in passing that equation (20) implies that those securities whose returns are bivariate lognormal with aggregate wealth have equilibrium returns consistent with a continuous time model of market equilibrium. A similar observation is made by Rubinstein (14).

(22) we obtain the following RNVR:

$$W(p_0) = r_f^{-1} \int_0^\infty g(p_1)(\sigma\, p_1\sqrt{2\pi})^{-1}\exp\frac{-1}{2\sigma^2}\left\{\ln(p_1/p_0)\right.$$

$$\left. -\left(\ln r_f - \frac{1}{2}\sigma^2\right)\right\}^2 dp_1 \quad (23)$$

But equation (23) is identical to equation (10), the definition of a RNVR under the assumption of lognormal returns.

If $g(p_1) = \max[p_1 - E, 0]$, then substitution for $g(p_1)$ in equation (23) yields the familiar Black-Scholes equation for the value of a call option when there is one period left to expiration. Note however that equation (23) applies to any type of contingent claim whose value depends only on the terminal price of the underlying asset including put options, risky corporate debt, convertible bonds or even options on options.[9] While the results in this section relate to only a single period model we shall show in Section IV that they may be generalized to a multi-period situation.

2. *The Bivariate Normal Distribution*

The assumption of normal distributions has a long lineage in models of security market equilibrium, and there may be good reasons for preferring this assumption to that of lognormality when the underlying asset is not an equity security but the right to a cash flow which may take on negative values. In the following three theorems we show that constant absolute risk aversion plays the same role in the derivation of RNVRs with normal distributions as constant relative risk aversion plays with lognormal distributions. Under the assumption of normality $f(p_1|p_0)$ is given by

$$f(p_1|p_0) = (\sigma\sqrt{2\pi})^{-1}\exp\frac{-1}{2\sigma^2}\{p_1 - \mu p_0\}^2 \quad \text{and} \quad E[p_1|p_0] = \mu p_0 \quad (24)$$

where μ and σ are the mean and standard deviation respectively of the normal distribution of price relatives. The location parameter of $\hat{f}(p_1|p_0)$, $\hat{\mu}$, is equal to $p_0 r_f$, so that if a RNVR exists, the value of a contingent claim may be written as

$$W(p_0) = r_f^{-1} \int_{-\infty}^\infty g(p_1)(\sigma\sqrt{2\pi})^{-1}\exp\frac{-1}{2\sigma^2}(p_1 - r_f p_0)^2 dp_1 \quad (25)$$

However, using the basic valuation equation (5), the value of the contingent claim is

$$W(p_0) = r_f^{-1} \int_{-\infty}^\infty g(p_1)z(p_1)(\sigma\sqrt{2\pi})^{-1}\exp\frac{-1}{2\sigma^2}(p_1 - \mu p_0)^2 dp_1 \quad (26)$$

[9] These have been dealt with in a similar context by Geske (7).

If a RNVR exists (25) and (26) must be equivalent, which gives rise to the following theorem which is the counterpart of Theorem 1 for normal distributions.

THEOREM 4: *A necessary condition for a RNVR to exist under the assumption of an arbitrary bivariate normal distribution of the price of the underlying asset and aggregate wealth (the normal assumption) is that the conditional marginal utility function, $z(p_1)$, be of the form* exp (βp_1).

Proof: Proceeding as in the proof of Theorem 1, a necessary condition for a RNVR to exist is that

$$z(p_1)\exp\frac{-1}{2\sigma^2}\{p_1 - \mu p_0\}^2 = \exp\frac{-1}{2\sigma^2}\{p_1 - r_f p_0\}^2 \tag{27}$$

or

$$z(p_1) = \exp\{(p_0(r_f - \mu)/\sigma^2)p_1\}\exp\frac{-1}{2\sigma^2}\{p_0^2(r_f^2 - \mu^2)\} \tag{28}$$

which is equivalent as a (marginal) utility function to $\exp(\beta p_1)$, where $\beta = p_0(r_f - \mu)/\sigma^2$.

In Theorem 5, which is the analogue of Theorem 2, we show that the conditional marginal utility function can be exponential only if the marginal utility function of the representative investor is also exponential. This implies that the representative investor has constant absolute risk aversion.

THEOREM 5: *A necessary condition for the conditional marginal utility function to be of the form* (28) *under the assumption of an arbitrary bivariate normal distribution of the price of the underlying asset and aggregate wealth (the normal assumption) is that the marginal utility function of the representative investor, $V'(w_1)$, be of the form* exp $(-\alpha w_1)$.

Proof: By definition,

$$z(p_1) \equiv E[V'(w_1)|p_1]/E[V'(w_1)] \tag{29}$$

The conditional distribution of w_1 given p_1 is normal with mean $\mu_w + (\rho\sigma_w/\sigma)(p_1 - \mu p_0)$ and variance $(1 - \rho^2)\sigma_w^2$, where μ_w and σ_w^2 are respectively the unconditional mean and variance of w_1, and ρ is the correlation between w_1 and p_1. If $z(p_1)$ is to be of the form (28) for arbitrary bivariate normal distributions, it must be of this form when $\rho = 1$. Then (28) and (29) together imply that

$$z(p_1) = \exp\{(p_0(r_f - \mu)/\sigma^2)p_1\}\exp\frac{-1}{2\sigma^2}\{p_0^2(r_f^2 - \mu^2)\}$$

$$= V'[\mu_w + (\sigma_w/\sigma)(p_1 - \mu p_0)]/E[V'(w_1)] \tag{30}$$

Writing the argument of $V'(\cdot)$ in (30) as x, and eliminating p_1, it follows that $V'(\cdot)$ is an exponential function.

Finally, we show that exponential utility is sufficient to derive a RNVR under the assumption of bivariate normality.

The Pricing of Contingent Claims 63

THEOREM 6: *A sufficient condition for a RNVR to obtain under the normal assumption is that the (marginal) utility function of the representative investor be exponential. In this case the utility function is characterized by constant absolute risk aversion.*

Proof: Suppose $V'(w_1) = \exp(\alpha w_1)$. Then, using the definition of the conditional marginal utility function (29), and the assumed normality of w_1,

$$z(p_1) = \exp\{(\alpha\rho\sigma_w/\sigma)(p_1 - \mu p_0) - \tfrac{1}{2}\alpha^2\rho^2\sigma_w^2\} \tag{31}$$

Then, substituting for $z(p_1)$ from (31) in the basic valuation equation (5), and recalling that p_1 has a normal density function,

$$p_0 r_f = E[p_1 z(p_1)] = \int_{-\infty}^{\infty} p_1(\sigma\sqrt{2\pi})^{-1}\exp\frac{-1}{2\sigma^2}\{-2\alpha\rho\sigma\sigma_w(p_1 - \mu p_0)$$

$$+ \alpha^2\rho^2\sigma^2\sigma_w^2 + (p_1 - \mu p_0)^2\}\,dp_1$$

$$= \int_{-\infty}^{\infty} p_1(\sigma\sqrt{2\pi})^{-1}\exp\frac{-1}{2\sigma^2}\{p_1 - (\mu p_0 - \alpha\rho\sigma\sigma_w)\}^2 dp_1 \tag{32}$$

$$p_0 r_f = \mu p_0 - \alpha\rho\sigma\sigma_w \tag{33}$$

Equation (33) is the standard capital asset pricing model market equilibrium condition.

Next, applying the basic valuation equation (5) to the value of the contingent claim, we have

$$W(p_0) = r_f^{-1}\int_{-\infty}^{\infty} g(p_1)z(p_1)(\sigma\sqrt{2\pi})^{-1}\exp\frac{-1}{2\sigma^2}\{p_1 - \mu p_0\}^2 dp_1 \tag{34}$$

After substituting for $z(p_1)$ from (31), (34) becomes

$$W(p_0) = r_f^{-1}\int_{-\infty}^{\infty} g(p_1)(\sigma\sqrt{2\pi})^{-1}\exp\frac{-1}{2\sigma^2}\{p_1 - (\mu p_0 - \alpha\rho\sigma\sigma_w)\}^2 dp_1 \tag{35}$$

Finally, using the market equilibrium condition (33), (35) reduces to

$$W(p_0) = \int_{-\infty}^{\infty} g(p_1)(\sigma\sqrt{2\pi})^{-1}\exp\frac{-1}{2\sigma^2}\{p_1 - p_0 r_f\}^2 dp_1 \tag{36}$$

and equation (36) is a RNVR, identical to equation (25).

It is interesting to observe therefore that the twin assumptions of constant absolute risk aversion and multivariate normality suffice to permit the derivation of RNVRs within the traditional framework of the capital asset pricing model. For example, suppose that the contingent claim is a call option so that $g(p_1) =$

max$[p_1 - E, 0]$. Then equation (36) reduces to

$$W(p_0) = r_f^{-1} \int_E^\infty (p_1 - E)(\sigma \sqrt{2\pi})^{-1} \exp \frac{-1}{2\sigma^2} \{p_1 - p_0 r_f\}^2 dp_1 \qquad (37)$$

and employing a change of variable, this may be written as

$$W(p_0) = (p_0 - E r_f^{-1}) \int_{(E-p_0 r_f)/\sigma}^\infty (\sqrt{2\pi})^{-1} \exp\{-\tfrac{1}{2}z^2\} dz$$

$$+ r_f^{-1}\sigma \int_{(E-p_0 r_f)/\sigma}^\infty z(\sqrt{2\pi})^{-1} \exp\{-\tfrac{1}{2}z^2\} dz \qquad (38)$$

$$W(p_0) = (p_0 - E r_f^{-1})N\left(\frac{p_0 r_f - E}{\sigma}\right) + r_f^{-1}\sigma n\left(\frac{E - p_0 r_f}{\sigma}\right) \qquad (39)$$

where $N(\cdot)$ is the cumulative standard normal density function, and $n(\cdot)$ is the standard normal density function.

Equation (39) is the analogue within the single period capital asset pricing model of the Black-Scholes formula for the value of a call option. Perhaps the most useful application of this result is that it enables us to value limited liability securities within this capital asset pricing model framework. Since the traditional capital asset pricing model depends either upon multivariate normality or quadratic utility and limited liability securities do not follow a normal distribution, this has hitherto been possible only under the assumption of quadratic utility functions, an assumption which has been shown to lead to absurd results in this context.[10]

Thus consider an all equity financed firm and suppose that the end of period value of the firm, v_1, is normally distributed. v_1 should be regarded as the end of period value of the firm's securities if there were no limited liability, and clearly this may be negative. The initial value of the firm, v_0, may be determined from our basic valuation equation (5), which, given the assumptions of bivariate normality and exponential utility was shown to imply equation (33). Recognizing that $\mu v_0 = E[v_1]$, equation (33) implies that the initial value of the firm is

$$v_0 = r_f^{-1}\{E[v_1] - \alpha \rho \sigma \sigma_w\} \qquad (40)$$

Given limited liability for the equity shareholders, "ownership rights" to the firm are shared between the shareholders and those who stand to lose should the end of period value of the firm turn out to be negative. The shareholders may then be thought of as possessing a call option to purchase the firm at the end of the period for an exercise price of zero. The value of this call option, the shareholders equity, e_0, may then be expressed in terms of the aggregate value of the firm v_0, which is given by equation (40), by substituting v_0 for p_0 in equation

[10] See Gonzales *et al.* (8).

(39) and setting $E = 0$. This yields

$$e_0 = r_f^{-1} N\left(\frac{v_0 r_f}{\sigma}\right) - r_f^{-1} \sigma n\left(\frac{v_0 r_f}{\sigma}\right) \tag{41}$$

We can readily show that $e_0 > v_0$ if $\sigma > 0$. First set $E = 0$ and make the appropriate substitutions in equation (38) to obtain

$$e_0 = v_0 \int_{-v_0 r_f/\sigma}^{\infty} (\sqrt{2\pi})^{-1} \exp\{-\tfrac12 z^2\}\, dz + r_f^{-1}\sigma \int_{-v_0 r_f/\sigma}^{\infty} (\sqrt{2\pi})^{-1} z \exp\{-\tfrac12 z^2\}\, dz$$

$$= v_0\left(1 - \int_{-\infty}^{-v_0 r_f/\sigma} (\sqrt{2\pi})^{-1} \exp\{-\tfrac12 z^2\}\, dz\right) - r_f^{-1}\sigma \int_{-v_0 r_f/\sigma}^{\infty} (\sqrt{2\pi})^{-1} z$$

$$\cdot \exp\{-\tfrac12 z^2\}\, dz \tag{42}$$

$$e_0 = v_0 - r_f^{-1} \int_{-\infty}^{-v_0 r_f/\sigma} (\sqrt{2\pi})^{-1} (v_0 r_f + \sigma z) \exp\{-\tfrac12 z^2\}\, dz \tag{43}$$

Then making the change of variable $v_1 = v_0 r_f + \sigma z$, (43) reduces to

$$e_0 = v_0 - r_f^{-1} \int_{-\infty}^{0} (\sqrt{2\pi})^{-1} v_1 \exp\left\{\frac{-1}{2\sigma^2}(v_1 - v_0 r_f)^2\right\} dv_1 \tag{44}$$

and since the integral in (44) is negative, $e_0 > v_0$. This result of course depends upon the assumption that the providers of limited liability do so at no cost. If a charge is made, then in equilibrium it will be such that $e_0 - v_0$: the shareholders will simply exchange a set of unlimited liability claims for a set of limited liability claims of equal value. If the charge C, for limited liability is made at the beginning of the period then from (44) it will be given by

$$C = - r_f^{-1} \int_{-\infty}^{0} (\sigma \sqrt{2\pi})^{-1} v_1 \exp\left\{\frac{-1}{2\sigma^2}(v_1 - v_0 r_f)^2\right\} dv_1 \tag{45}$$

Simplifying,

$$C = r_f^{-1} n\left(\frac{v_0 r_f}{\sigma}\right) - v_0 \tag{46}$$

Alternatively, the charge for the provision of limited liability may be made by setting the exercise price of the shareholders' call option sufficiently high that $e_0 = v_0$. Equations (40), (41) and (46) constitute an integrated theory of the pricing of limited liability claims under the assumption of multivariate normality for the underlying assets. Further, by appropriate specification of the payoff on the contingent claim it is possible to analyze problems arising from default risk and the tax-deductibility of corporate interest payments within a traditional capital asset pricing framework.

IV

In this section we show that the single period results obtained so far generalize in a natural way to a multi-period setting if the multi-period model of capital market equilibrium is such a RNVR obtains in each period. There exist two multi-period models of capital market equilibrium, corresponding to the assumptions of lognormal and normal returns respectively, which are such that a RNVR obtains on a period by period basis.

First, Rubinstein [14] has shown that if investors possess time additive utility functions with constant proportional risk aversion and aggregate consumption follows a random walk,[11] then the period by period market equilibrium is indistinguishable from that of a single period model in which investors have a utility function for terminal wealth which exhibits constant proportional risk aversion. Hence by Theorem 3 a RNVR exists on a period by period basis under the assumptions of this model, if in addition it is assumed that the bivariate distribution of returns on the underlying asset and aggregate wealth (or, equivalently, aggregate consumption) is lognormal.

Secondly, Stapleton and Subrahmanyam [17] (SS) have shown that if the underlying cash flows in the economy follow a multivariate normal distribution and investors possess time-additive exponential utility functions then the single period returns on securities representing the rights to these cash flows are also normally distributed, and the period by period market equilibrium is indistinguishable from that of a single period model in which investors have utility functions for terminal wealth which exhibit constant absolute risk aversion and returns are multivariate normal. Hence by Theorem 6 a RNVR exists on a period by period basis under the assumptions of the SS model. The nature of the multi-period relationship for pricing contingent claims within these two paradigms is described in the following two theorems.

Define:

$W(p, \tau)$ — the value of a contingent claim exercisable only at maturity when there are τ periods to maturity and the price of the underlying asset is p.

r_{fi} — one plus the one period riskless rate of interest when there are i periods to maturity

$R_{f\tau}$ $\equiv \prod_{i=1}^{\tau} r_{fi}$

THEOREM 7 (Rubinstein): *Under the assumptions of the Rubinstein model with bivariate lognormality, the value of a contingent claim when there are τ periods to maturity may be written as*

$$W(p, \tau) = R_{f\tau}^{-1} \int_0^\infty g(s) \left(s \sum_\tau \sqrt{2\pi} \right)^{-3} \exp \frac{-1}{2\Sigma_\tau^2}$$

$$\left\{ \ln s - \ln p - \ln R_{f\tau} + \frac{1}{2} \Sigma_\tau^2 \right\}^2 ds \quad (47)$$

[11] The assumption that aggregate consumption follows a random walk is unnecessary if the utility function is logarithmic.

where $\sum_\tau^2 = \sum_{i=1}^\tau \sigma_i^2$, and σ_i^2 is the variance of the logarithm of the price relative of the underlying asset when there are i periods to maturity.

Proof: Since under the conditions of the theorem a RNVR exists each period we may write, using equation (23),

$$W(x, 1) = r_{f1}^{-1} \int_0^\infty g(s)(s\,\sigma_1\,\sqrt{2\pi})^{-1}\exp\frac{-1}{2\sigma_1^2}\left\{\ln s - \ln x - \ln r_{f1} + \frac{1}{2}\sigma_1^2\right\} ds \quad (48)$$

and

$$W(p, 2) = r_{f2}^{-1} \int_0^\infty W(x, 1)(x\,\sigma_2\,\sqrt{2\pi})^{-1}$$

$$\cdot \exp\frac{-1}{2\sigma_2^2}\left\{\ln x - \ln p - \ln r_{f2} + \frac{1}{2}\sigma_2^2\right\} dx \quad (49)$$

Then substituting (48) into (49) and integrating over x, the value of the underlying asset when there is one period to maturity, we obtain

$$W(p, 2) = r_{f1}^{-1} r_{f2}^{-1} \int_0^\infty g(s)(s^2\,2\pi(\sigma_1^2 + \sigma_2^2))^{-1/2}$$

$$\cdot \exp\frac{-1}{2(\sigma_1^2 + \sigma_2^2)}\left\{\ln s - \ln p - \ln r_{f1}r_{f2} + \frac{1}{2}(\sigma_1^2 + \sigma_2^2)\right\}^2 ds \quad (50)$$

and, proceeding recursively, we obtain (47).

THEOREM 8: *Under the assumptions of the SS model (multivariate normality and constant absolute risk aversion), the value of a contingent claim when there are τ periods to expiration may be written as*

$$W(p, \tau) = R_{f\tau}^{-1} \int_{-\infty}^\infty g(s)\left(\sum_\tau \sqrt{2\pi}\right)^{-1}\exp\frac{-1}{2\sum_\tau^2}(s - R_{f\tau}\,p)^2\, ds \quad (51)$$

where

$$\sum_\tau^2 = \sigma_1^2 + r_{f1}^2\sigma_2^2 + r_{f1}^2 r_{f2}^2\sigma_3^2 + \cdots \, r_{f1}^2 r_{f2}^2 \cdots r_{f\tau-1}^2\sigma_\tau^2$$

and σ_i^2 is the variance of the price of the underlying asset when there are i periods to expiration, conditioned on the information available one period earlier.

Proof: Since under the conditions of the theorem a RNVR exists each period we may write, using equation (25),

$$W(x, 1) = r_{f1}^{-1} \int_{-\infty}^\infty g(s)(\sigma_1\,\sqrt{2\pi})^{-1}\exp\frac{-1}{2\sigma_1^2}\{\ln s - \ln x\}^2\, ds \quad (52)$$

and

$$W(p, 2) = r_{f2}^{-1} \int_{-\infty}^\infty W(x, 1)(\sigma_2\,\sqrt{2\pi})^{-1}\exp\frac{1}{2\sigma_2^2}\{\ln x - \ln p\}^2\, dx \quad (53)$$

Then, substituting (52) into (53) and integrating over x we obtain

$$W(p, 2) = r_{f1}^{-1} r_{f2}^{-1} \int_{-\infty}^{\infty} g(s)(2\pi(\sigma_1^2 + r_{f1}^2 \sigma_2^2))^{-1/2}$$

$$\cdot \exp \frac{-1}{2(\sigma_1^2 + r_{f1}^2 \sigma_2^2)} \{s - r_{f1}r_{f2}\, p\}^2\, ds \quad (54)$$

Proceeding recursively we obtain (51).

While the theorems in this section relate solely to options exercisable at maturity on assets which have no payouts, extension to American type options on assets which do have payouts is straightforward and analogous to the analysis in continuous time models.

REFERENCES

1. J. Aitchison, and J. M. C. Brown. *The Lognormal Distribution* (Cambridge University Press, Cambridge, 1963).
2. F. Black, and M. Scholes. "The Pricing of Options and Corporate Liabilities." *Journal of Political Economy 81* (1973).
3. M. J. Brennan, and A. Kraus. "Necessary Conditions for Aggregation in Securities Markets." *Journal of Financial and Quantitative Analysis* (forthcoming).
4. M. J. Brennan, and E. S. Schwartz. "The Valuation of American Put Options." *Journal of Finances, 32* (1977).
5. J. C. Cox, and S. A. Ross. "The Valuation of Options for Alternative Stochastic Processes." *Journal of Financial Economics 3* (1976).
6. D. Emanuel. "Valuing Preferred Stock and Other Perpetual Claims." (University of British Columbia Working Paper, No. 498, 1977).
7. R. Geske. "The Valuation of Compound Options." (unpublished manuscript, University of California, Berkeley, 1976).
8. N. Gonzales, R. Litzenberger, and J. Rolfo. "On Mean Variance Models of Capital Structure and the Absurdity of Their Predictions." *Journal of Financial and Quantitative Analysis 12* (1977).
9. J. E. Ingersoll. "A Contingent-Claims Valuation of Convertible Securities." *Journal of Financial Economics 4* (1977).
10. R. C. Merton. "Theory of Rational Option Pricing." *Bell Journal of Economics and Management Science 4* (1973).
11. R. C. Merton. "On the Pricing of Corporate Debt: The Risk Structure of Interest Rates." *Journal of Finance, 29* (1974).
12. S. C. Myers, and S. Turnbull. "Capital Budgeting and the Capital Asset Pricing Model: Good News and Bad News." *Journal of Finance 32* (1977).
13. M. Rubinstein. "An Aggregation Theorem for Securities Markets." *Journal of Financial Economics, 1* (1974).
14. M. Rubinstein. "The Valuation of Uncertain Income Streams and the Pricing of Options." *Bell Journal of Economics and Management Science 7* (1976a).
15. M. Rubinstein. "The Strong Case for the Generalized Logarithmic Utility Model as the Premier Model of Financial Markets." *Journal of Finance 31* (1976b).
16. M. Rubinstein. "Option Markets." (unpublished manuscript).
17. R. C. Stapleton, and M. G. Subrahmanyam. "A Multi-Period Equilibrium Asset Pricing Model." (unpublished manuscript).

[14]

JOURNAL OF FINANCIAL AND QUANTITATIVE ANALYSIS
Volume XVI, No. 3, September 1981

OPTIMAL PORTFOLIO INSURANCE

*M.J. Brennan and R. Solanki**

The form of the Pareto optimal general insurance contract has been investigated by Borch [5], Arrow [3], and Raviv [16]. This paper extends their work to the consideration of the optimal investment portfolio insurance contract. This is a contract whose payoff depends upon the investment performance of some specified portfolio of common stocks. Portfolio insurance differs from general insurance in two important ways. First, investment portfolio insurance lacks the property of stochastic independence between losses on different contracts which is characteristic of general insurance, and this has led some actuaries to question whether portfolio insurance contracts should be sold in view of the risks they pose for the solvency of insurance companies. Recent developments in the theory of option pricing suggest, however, that under certain assumptions an insurance company will be able to eliminate the risks associated with portfolio insurance contracts by following an appropriately defined investment strategy. Secondly, there exists a market for the pricing of investment risks, the securities market; and, under appropriate assumptions, the equilibrium price of portfolio insurance contracts may be determined without specification of the preferences of insurance companies. This permits consideration of insurance company preference functions to be dispensed with, in marked contrast to the earlier literature concerned with general insurance, which treats insurance company preferences symmetrically with those of the insurance purchaser. In addition, since the characteristics of the insured portfolio are known to the insurer, and the performance of the portfolio is beyond the control of the insured, portfolio insurance is not prone to the problems of adverse selection and moral hazard which are liable to arise in general insurance.[1]

A portfolio insurance contract provides for a benefit payable at maturity which is a function of the value at maturity of some specified portfolio of common stocks: the insured or reference portfolio. The insured mutual fund

---

Both authors, University of British Columbia. The comments and assistance of A. Kraus, V. Hausmann, and K. Ramaswamy, and the helpful suggestions of a referee of this journal are gratefully acknowledged.

[1]Rothschild and Stiglitz [17], Spence and Zeckhauser [19].

redemption value program offered by some insurance companies in the United States is an example of a pure portfolio insurance contract. This program, offered to investors in specified mutual funds, provides a benefit payable at maturity which is equal to the greater of zero and the difference between a guaranteed amount and the value at maturity of the proceeds yielded by a specified program of investments in the mutual fund. The mutual fund investor who purchases such a contract is thereby assured that his total return from the mutual fund investment and the insurance contract will not be less than the guaranteed amount.

Other insurance contracts combine pure portfolio insurance with mortality or life insurance. For example, one type of equity linked life insurance contract which is issued in both Canada and the United Kingdom provides that the benefit payable at contract expiration, whether at maturity or at prior death, will be equal to the greater of the value of some reference portfolio of common stocks and a guaranteed amount.[2] Under this contract the insurance company is providing life insurance since the date of the contract expiration is uncertain: it is also providing portfolio insurance through the medium of the guarantee. Similar in concept is the variable life insurance contract issued in the United States. This is a whole life contract under which the insured receives a benefit at death which is proportional to the value of a reference portfolio of common stocks: since the benefit is subject to a minimum guarantee, this contract also contains an element of portfolio insurance.

In all three of the above types of contract the portfolio insurance takes the form of a simple guarantee with or without an accompanying investment in the underlying portfolio. This guarantee relieves the individual entirely of the risk that the value of his investment will fall below the guaranteed amount; there is in effect no co-insurance clause in such contracts. It seems intuitively improbable that these contracts would be optimal for investors with different attitudes towards risk, and indeed it is shown below that a simple guarantee contract, priced according to the assumptions of this paper, will almost never be optimal for an investor. This paper is concerned with deriving the optimal portfolio insurance contract for an investor who is assumed to invest the whole of his wealth in the one contract. Insofar as investors might be induced to follow such a policy, this strong assumption offers some insight into the types of contract which would be most likely to appeal to them.

Ignoring mortality considerations, the problem is formally equivalent to the design of the optimal mutual fund redemption value insurance contract. The optimal contract for a particular investor depends upon both his tastes and his

---

[2]This type of contract has been analyzed extensively by Brennan and Schwartz [8].

opportunities. The former are represented by a von Neumann Morgenstern utility
function defined over the possible contract payoffs. His opportunities are defined by his wealth and the prices of alternative insurance contracts: the wealth
available for investment is taken as exogenous; the prices of alternative contracts are derived by assuming that the return on the portfolio over any finite
interval of time is lognormally distributed, and that there exists a risk neutral
valuation relationship between the value or price of the insurance contract and
the value of the underlying stock portfolio. A risk neutral valuation relationship exists if the relationship between the value of the contract and the value
of reference portfolio is the same as would exist if all market participants
were risk neutral. The important contribution of the option pricing literature
has been to show that risk neutral valuation relationships may exist even when
market participants are not actually risk neutral. Thus, Black-Scholes [4] and
Merton [15] have shown that sufficient conditions for a risk neutral valuation
relationship under the lognormal assumption stated above are that the riskless
interest rate be known, the value of the reference portfolio follow a Gauss-
Wiener process,[3] and that continuous trading in frictionless markets be possible
for either the insurance contract or the reference portfolio. Rubinstein [18],
Breeden and Litzenberger [6], and Brennan [7] have also established that a necessary and sufficient condition for a risk neutral valuation relationship in a discrete time model with lognormal returns is that the representative investor in
the economy possess a utility function belonging to the iso-elastic class.
Heaney [11] has recently provided an integration of the continuous trading and
preference based approaches to the derivation of risk neutral valuation relationships in terms of the quotient kernel of an arbitrage-free economy with exogenously specified asset price dynamics.

The results derived below for optimal portfolio insurance contracts correspond to those which would be obtained by analyzing the optimal portfolio strategy of an investor in a continuous time model.[4] This correspondence is not for-
tuitous since the assumption of a risk neutral valuation relationship for the
insurance contract enables the investor to obtain the same distribution of wealth
outcomes as he could obtain by trading on his own account in a continuous time
framework. Indeed, the risk-eliminating investment strategy for an insurance
company selling such a contract[5] will be shown to be identical to the optimal

---

[3]Perhaps with deterministic discrete jumps.

[4]See, for example, Merton [14].

[5]Assuming that continuous trading is permitted.

strategy of the investor who invests directly on his own account. Despite this correspondence, the assumption of a risk neutral valuation relationship is weaker than the assumption of continuous trading since, as mentioned above, the former can be derived without the latter by appropriate restriction of the preferences of the representative investor. Moreover, the analysis here differs from that of the optimal portfolio strategy literature in its emphasis on the optimal contract payoff function and the associated probability distribution of payoffs. The associated risk-eliminating investment strategy, if continuous trading is permitted, is of only secondary interest.

The analysis is developed in terms of the optimal contract payoff function which expresses the total benefit received as a function of the value of the underlying insured or reference portfolio. This is a natural generalization of the common notion of insurance under which the contract payoff is not required to correspond to any definition of loss incurred by the insured party; instead, the contract is treated as a pure contingent claim. This is in contrast to the approach followed by Leland [13] in a recent paper which is also concerned with portfolio insurance. Leland restricts the definition of portfolio insurance to contracts whose payoffs may be represented as convex functions of the return on the market portfolio. He then analyzes the conditions on individual and market preferences and beliefs under which an individual will demand such a contract. In this paper, on the other hand, the underlying portfolio is arbitrary, and market preferences and beliefs are not introduced.[6] Instead, the investor is assumed to be able to purchase arbitrary insurance contracts at prices exogenously determined by the risk neutral valuation relationship discussed above, and the concern is with the determination of the optimal contract for an investor with given beliefs, tastes, and wealth.

While this paper shares much in common with Leland [13], the focus of the two papers is somewhat different. Leland is concerned with the central planner's problem of characterizing the class of Pareto optimal risk sharing contracts between an individual investor and the hypothetical representative investor who supports market prices. We, on the other hand, consider the problem faced by the individual investor who is concerned only with maximizing his own expected utility. Of course, given the market completeness implicit in the availability of different contracts, and competitive behavior by the individual investor, the contract which is optimal for him will belong to the central planner's class of

---

[6]More specifically, only the individual's beliefs about the expected rate of return on the reference portfolio enter the optimal contract payoff function. All market participants, however, are assumed to agree on the variance of the rate of return.

Pareto optimal risk sharing arrangements between the individual investor and the representative investor who supports market prices. By introducing a contract pricing function, however, we are able to determine explicitly the member of the Pareto optimal class which will be chosen optimally by an investor with given wealth.

In Section I the necessary and sufficient conditions for contract optimality are characterized for arbitrary utility functions, return distributions, and pricing functions. In Section II the single premium portfolio insurance contract is analyzed under the assumptions of lognormal returns and risk neutral valuation relationships. In Section III two types of periodic premium contract are considered; only that one which is equivalent to the single premium contract is found to be efficient. Section IV describes an investment strategy which can be followed by the insurance company to eliminate the risks associated with the sale of portfolio insurance. Optimal contracts for HARA class utility functions are calculated in Section V and the paper concludes with a brief discussion of mortality considerations.

I. Necessary and Sufficient Conditions for Contract Optimality

The optimal contract is defined as that which maximizes the expected utility of the investor given his available wealth, and the contract pricing function. Thus define:

X_τ the value of the reference portfolio at time τ, where the contract is initiated at $\tau = 0$, and matures at $\tau = T$.

$g(X_T)$ the contract payoff function: this is the amount that the investor receives at maturity as a function of the value of the reference portfolio at that time.

$U(\cdot)$ the investor's von Neumann Morgenstern utility function defined over the contract payoff, assumed to be monotone, increasing, and strictly concave.

$f(X_T;X_\tau)$ the probability density function for the value of the portfolio at time T conditioned on its value at time τ as assessed by the investor.

$p(X_T;X_\tau)$ the pricing function at time τ for claims payable at time T contingent on the value of the reference portfolio at that time.

W the investor's wealth available for investment in the contract.

Since the whole of the investor's wealth is assumed to be invested in the contract, the optimal contract payoff function is the solution to the problem:

(1) $$\underset{g(\cdot)}{\text{Maximize}} \int_0^\infty U[g(X_T)] \; f(X_T;X_0) \; dX_T$$

283

subject to the budget constraint

(2)
$$\int_0^\infty g(X_T) \ p(X_T;X_0) \ dX_T \leq W.$$

It is shown in the Appendix (A) that the solution to this problem satisfies

(3)
$$U'[g(X_T)] = \lambda \ p(X_T;X_0)/f(X_T;X_0)$$

which is the continuous state space analogue of the standard optimality condition that the price of a security be proportional to the expected marginal utility of its payoff. In this equation λ is a multiplier which is determined from the budget constraint.

From (3) the optimal contract payoff function is given by

(4)
$$g(X_T) = U'^{-1} [\lambda \ p(X_T;X_0)/f(X_T;X_0)].$$

Thus, the optimal contract is determined once the utility, pricing, and density functions are specified. To this end we assume:

A1. Portfolio Returns: the rate of return on the reference portfolio follows a lognormal distribution.

A2. Partial Agreement: the representative investor who supports the market equilibrium and the individual investor who is purchasing the contract agree on the variance of the lognormal distribution.

A3. Risk Neutral Valuation: the pricing function is consistent with risk neutral preferences.

In addition, we shall assume that the continuously compounded riskless interest rate, r, is known and constant.

In a discrete time context, assumptions A1 and A2 are consistent with the individual and the representative investor disagreeing about the mean logarithmic rate of return on the reference portfolio, and the representative investor's assessment of this parameter may change from period to period. In continuous time, these assumptions are consistent with the reference portfolio following a Gauss-Wiener process whose drift parameter may be assessed as varying stochastically by all market participants except the individual investor under consideration. Assumptions A1 and A2 are consistent with the risk neutral valuation relationship assumption, A3.

If prices are assumed to be supported by a representative investor, then the pricing function can be written as the product of his density function and his conditional expected marginal utility of wealth function (up to a constant of proportionality):

$$p(X_T;X_\tau) \propto h(X_T;X_\tau) \; V(X_T)^7$$

where $h(\cdot)$ and $V(\cdot)$ are the density function and the conditional expected marginal utility function of the representative investor respectively.

In this paper our assumptions are directly about the form of $p(\cdot)$ and $h(\cdot)$; Leland's assumptions are about the forms of $h(\cdot)$ and $V(\cdot)$. Where one chooses to start is largely a matter of taste and convenience. As we have already remarked, our pricing function may be justified either by the classical continuous time arbitrage argument or by the assumption of a representative investor with power utility and lognormal probability assessments. Given the concern of this paper with the optimal decisions of the individual investor we take the pricing function as primitive.

II. The Single Premium Contract

Under a single premium portfolio insurance contract, the reference portfolio is defined by the deemed investment of an amount X_o in the reference portfolio at the initiation of the contract, no further contributions or withdrawals occurring thereafter. Note that it is not necessary that this deemed investment actually be made, the reference portfolio serving only as a benchmark.

Then, under assumption A1 the conditional density function of the value of the reference portfolio at maturity, X_T, as assessed by the investor, is

$$(5) \qquad f(X_T;X_o) \equiv f(X_T/X_o) \equiv f(Z_{oT})$$

where Z_{oT} is one plus the return on the reference portfolio over the life of the contract and

$$(6) \qquad f(Z_{oT}) = \frac{1}{Z_{oT}\sigma\sqrt{2\pi T}} \; \exp \frac{-1}{2T\sigma^2} \; [\ln Z_{oT} - \mu T]^2$$

where μ and σ^2 are respectively the mean and variance of one plus the rate of return on the underlying portfolio as assessed by the investor.

Furthermore, assumptions A2 and A3 imply that the contract pricing function is given by

---

[7] See equation (5) of Leland [13].

(7) $$p(X_T; X_o) \equiv p(X_T/X_o) \equiv p(Z_{oT})$$

$$= \frac{e^{-rT}}{Z_{oT}\sigma\sqrt{2\pi T}} \exp \frac{-1}{2T\sigma^2} [\ln Z_{oT} - (r - \tfrac{1}{2}\sigma^2)T].$$

The intuition behind this pricing function is that if market participants had risk neutral preferences, the instantaneous expected rate of return on the reference portfolio, $(\mu + \tfrac{1}{2}\sigma^2)$, would be equal to r, and the present value of the contract would be obtained by discounting its expected value at time T at the riskless rate, r. As pointed out in the Introduction, such a risk neutral valuation relationship may exist even though market participants are not actually risk neutral.[8]

Substituting the density and pricing functions (6) and (7) into equation (4), the optimal contract payoff function is of the form

(8) $$g(X_T) = g(X_o Z_{oT}) = U'^{-1}[k \ Z_{oT}^{-a/\sigma^2}] = U'^{-1}[KX_T^{-a/\sigma^2}]$$

where $K = kX_o^{a/\sigma^2}$, $k = \lambda \exp[-(r\sigma^2 + a(a - 2\mu)/2)T/\sigma^2]$ and $a = \mu + \tfrac{1}{2}\sigma^2 - r$ is the continuously compounded risk premium on the reference portfolio as assessed by the investor. Since K contains the multiplier from the budget constraint, it may be regarded as a constant to be determined by the investor's wealth.

Assuming that the risk premium assessed by the investor is positive, so that a > 0, the following general properties of the payoff function may be inferred from equation (8):

(i) The optimal payoff function is a strictly increasing function of the return on the reference portfolio. Differentiating (8) with respect to X_T for a given X_o, it follows that $g'(\cdot) > 0$ since $U''(\cdot) < 0$.

(ii) The optimally chosen reference portfolio will have the highest value of μ for a given value of σ^2 and will, therefore, lie on the efficient frontier. This follows from first degree stochastic dominance since $g'(\cdot) > 0$, and μ does not enter the budget constraint (2) under assumption A3.

(iii) The investor is indifferent between any two reference portfolios which have the same reward to variability ratio, a/σ. This proposition is established in the Appendix (B).

(iv) It follows from (ii) and (iii) that the optimal reference portfolio

---

[8]See Cox and Ross [9].

for the investor is the one who maximizes the reward to variability ratio.

(v)   The optimal payoff function is concave or convex in X_T at a point, according to whether the derivative of the investor's risk tolerance function evaluated at the optimal payoff for that value of X_T is less than or greater than the ratio of the variance rate to the risk premium of the reference portfolio:

(9) $$g''(X_T) \overset{<}{>} 0 \quad \text{as} \quad \frac{dT[g(X_T)]}{d \, g(X_T)} \overset{<}{>} \frac{\sigma^2}{a}$$

where $T(g) = -U'(g)/U''(g)$ is the risk tolerance function of the investor. This result follows from differentiating equation (8) twice with respect to X_T and using the definition of the risk tolerance function.

In the case in which the reference portfolio is the market portfolio and the representative investor's assessment of μ agrees with that of the individual investor under consideration, this condition corresponds to Leland's [13] Proposition II which states that the optimal payoff function is convex if the individual's risk tolerance is increasing more rapidly with g than the representative investor's risk tolerance is increasing with X_T. This correspondence derives from the fact that lognormal market returns are consistent only with isoelastic derived utility for wealth for the representative investor. Then σ^2/a is equal to the cautiousness of the representative investor which is the (constant) derivative of his risk tolerance with respect to wealth.

(vi)   The optimal payoff function is linear in the value of the reference portfolio if and only if the risk tolerance function is linear in wealth with cautiousness σ^2/a. This follows from condition (8) and under Leland's conditions corresponds to the situation in which the individual investor has the same constant risk tolerance as does the representative investor.

Since the only extant portfolio insurance contracts are of the simple guarantee type in which the individual receives the value of the reference portfolio if this exceeds the guaranteed amount and otherwise receives the guaranteed amount, it is of interest to examine the conditions under which this type of contract would be optimal for an investor. The payoff on such a contract may be written for some guaranteed amount, G, as:

(10) $$g(X_T) = \begin{cases} G & \text{if } X_T \leq G \\ X_T & \text{if } X_T > G. \end{cases}$$

Substituting the expression for the optimal payoff function (8) in (10), the guarantee type contract will be optimal if and only if

(11) $$U'(G) = K \, X_T^{-a/\sigma^2} \quad \text{for } X_T \leqslant G$$

(12) $$U'(X_T) = K \, X_T^{-a/\sigma^2} \quad \text{for } X_T > G.$$

Condition (11) requires that the risk premium on the reference portfolio, a, be equal to zero, and then condition (12) requires that the utility function be linear in wealth for wealth levels in excess of G. Given the stringency of these conditions, it is not surprising that such contracts have found limited success in North America and have thrived only in the United Kingdom where they offer special tax advantages.

III.   The Periodic Premium Contract

Under most portfolio insurance contracts which provide for payments by the insured investor to be made periodically over the life of the contract, the reference portfolio is defined by the periodic investment of a specified component of the periodic payment in a specified fund of common stocks; the value of the reference portfolio then changes over time in response to both the realized returns on the underlying common stocks and the periodic deemed investments. We shall refer to this as a Type I periodic premium contract. Under a Type II contract, on the other hand, while the payments by the insured investor are made periodically, the reference portfolio is defined by a single deemed investment at contract initiation as was the case with the single premium contract. There exists a potential problem with the Type II contract in that if the early investment experience on the reference portfolio is sufficiently unfavorable, the insured investor may have an incentive to cease making payments and abandon the contract. This will occur whenever the present value of the payoff given the current value of the reference portfolio falls short of the present value of the remaining payments to be made. The problem may be avoided, however, if the contract is structured so that the insurance company lends the individual the money to purchase the contract, with the subsequent payments by the individual being used to repay the loan. The individual is then no longer free to abandon the contract, which is essentially a single premium contract as discussed in the preceding section, financed by a loan. Such a loan financed single premium contract is the Category C policy discussed by Grant and Kingsnorth [10] in their survey of equity linked insurance. Since the Type II contract is equivalent to the single premium contract, it remains only to discuss the Type I contract.

The condition for the optimality of a Type I contract whose payoff depends on the terminal value of a periodic investment reference portfolio is still given by equation (4), where λ is chosen to satisfy the budget constraint (2), and W is now interpreted as the present value of the payments to be made. Under assumption A1, that the rate of return on the reference portfolio is lognormally distributed, the terminal value of the portfolio will be given by a sum of lognormal random variables. Consequently, there exists no simple form for $f(X_T; X_O)$ or $p(X_T; X_O)$ and no analytic results are available.

It will be shown, however, that the Type I contract is always inefficient relative to the Type II or the single premium contract; that is, efficiency demands that the reference portfolio be defined by a single deemed investment in common stocks at the time the contract is initiated. Thus, consider a two period Type I contract in which the reference portfolio is defined by an investment of m at the beginning of the first and second periods, and let Z_1 and Z_2 be the lognormally distributed one plus rates of return in the two periods. The value of the reference portfolio at the expiration of the contract will then be $X_2 = m (Z_1 Z_2 + Z_2)$.

The efficient, expected utility maximizing, contract payoff will be a function of Z_1 and Z_2 which we write as $S(Z_1, Z_2)$. The Type I contract whose payoff is a function of X_2 will be efficient if and only if $S(Z_1, Z_2)$ can be written as a function of X_2 alone. That is, if and only if

$$(13) \qquad S(Z_1, Z_2) \equiv g(X_2) \equiv g\{m(Z_1 Z_2 + Z_2)\}$$

for some function $g(\cdot)$. We shall show that (13) does not hold.

$S(Z_1, Z_2)$ is determined as the solution to

$$(14) \qquad \underset{S(Z_1, Z_2)}{\text{Max}} \int_0^\infty \int_0^\infty U [S(Z_1, Z_2)] f(Z_1) f(Z_2) \, dZ_1 \, dZ_2$$

subject to the budget constraint

$$(15) \qquad \int_0^\infty \int_0^\infty S(Z_1, Z_2) \, p(Z_1, Z_2) \, dZ_1 \, dZ_2 = W$$

where $f(Z_i) = (\sigma Z_i \sqrt{2\pi})^{-1} \exp \dfrac{-1}{2\sigma^2} [\ln Z_i - \mu]^2$ is the density function of the one period rate of return on the reference portfolio and W is the present value of the payments to be made under the contract. $p(Z_1, Z_2)$, the pricing function for one dollar to be delivered in two periods contingent on the realized portfolio returns, is, under the risk neutral valuation assumption A3, given by

$$(16) \qquad p(Z_1, Z_2) = \exp(-2r) \prod_{i=1}^{2} \frac{1}{\sigma Z_i \sqrt{2\pi}} \exp - \frac{1}{2\sigma^2} \{\ln Z_i - (r - \tfrac{1}{2}\sigma^2)\}^2.$$

Proceeding as in Section I, the efficient payoff function is given by

(17)
$$S(Z_1, Z_2) = U'^{-1} \left[\frac{\lambda \, p(Z_1, Z_2)}{f(Z_1) f(Z_2)} \right].$$

Then substituting for $p(Z_1, Z_2)$ and $f(Z_i)$

(18)
$$S(Z_1, Z_2) = U'^{-1} \{\lambda \exp(-2r) \, \exp \frac{-1}{\sigma 2} [a \, \ell n \, Z_1 Z_2 + Q])\}$$

$$S \equiv \hat{S}(Z_1 Z_2)$$

where Q is a constant independent of Z_1 and Z_2.

Equation (18) states that the payoff on an efficient contract is a function of the value of a reference portfolio constructed by investing an arbitrary amount in the reference portfolio at contract initiation. It is apparent that the efficient payoff function does not satisfy condition (13) so that the Type I contract is indeed inefficient.

It is interesting to note that the preceding argument constitutes a proof of the non-optimality of a dollar cost averaging policy for an expected utility of terminal wealth maximizing investor under the distributional assumptions made in this paper, if continuous trading is permitted. With continuous trading the risk neutral valuation relationship holds, and the optimal terminal wealth allocation satisfies (18). Under dollar cost averaging, the terminal wealth is X_2 and this does not satisfy (18).

IV.   Insurance Company Investment Strategies

The assumption of exogenously given insurance contract prices provided by the risk neutral valuation relationship has enabled us to dispense with consideration of insurance company preferences in deriving the optimal contract. Nevertheless, an insurance company which has sold a portfolio insurance contract has a liability whose value at maturity depends, in a (generally) non-linear fashion, upon the value of the reference portfolio at that time. The sale of many such contracts whose payoffs are contingent upon the investment performance of the same reference portfolio may pose a threat to insurance company solvency which would not only render the sale of such contracts unattractive, but would also vitiate the preceding analysis by rendering some contract payoff functions unattainable.

If continuous trading in the underlying porfolios is permitted, however, then there exists an investment strategy for the insurance company to follow which will eliminate the risk of the liability in the sense that if the contract is priced according to the risk neutral valuation relationship, and if the insurance company follows the prescribed investment strategy, it will make zero profit for any contract payoff function, whatever the value of the reference portfolio at contract maturity; hence, the possibility of bankruptcy is eliminated. The basis of the argument is the hedging strategy familiar from the option pricing literature[9]: its application to companies selling portfolio insurance contracts of the simple guarantee type has already been described by Brennan and Schwartz [8].

Under the lognormal assumption the instantaneous change in the value of the reference portfolio is given by[10]

$$(19) \qquad \frac{dX}{X} = \mu dt + \sigma dZ$$

when dZ is a Gauss-Wiener process with $dZ^2 = dt$ and $E[dZ] = 0$. Using Ito's Lemma, the instantaneous change in the value of a particular contract, $V(X,\tau)$ is

$$(20) \qquad dV = [V_x \mu X + V_\tau + \tfrac{1}{2}V_{xx} \sigma^2 X^2]d\tau + V_x \sigma X\, dZ$$

where subscripts denote partial derivatives. Suppose that corresponding to this contract the insurance company holds assets M $(=V)$[11] and invests an amount q in the reference portfolio, leaving $(V-q)$ to be invested in the riskless security. The instantaneous change in the value of the assets is then

$$(21) \qquad dM = [q\mu + (V-q)r]\, d\tau + q\sigma\, dZ.$$

If the insurance company chooses the investment strategy of setting $q = XV_x$, its instantaneous profit is

$$(22) \qquad dM - dV = [rV - rXV_x - V_\tau - \tfrac{1}{2}\sigma^2 X^2 V_{xx}]d\tau.$$

This instantaneous profit will be zero if the value of the contract satisfies the partial differential equation obtained by setting the expression in

---

[9] See Black and Scholes [4], and Merton [15].

[10] In the case of the Type I periodic premium contract, the value of the portfolio will jump by a deterministic amount on the date of a deemed investment in the reference portfolio. Since these jumps are fully anticipated, however, they do not affect the value of the contract and equation (20) remains valid even on such dates.

[11] In the case of the periodic premium contract these assets include the present value of the payments receivable by the company.

parenthesis equal to zero. It is well known,[12] however, that under the risk neutral valuation relationship assumption A3, the value of the contract does satisfy this equation. Therefore, if the insurance company charges $V(X_o,0)$ for the contract, it will make zero profit independently of the value of the reference portfolio at contract maturity.

It should be recognized that, in principle, the role of the insurance company is redundant if continuous trading is permitted. It was shown in the previous section that the optimal payoff will be a function of the value of a single deemed investment reference portfolio. Having determined this payoff function, the investor could follow the investment policy described here for the insurance company and thereby achieve that payoff function. Thus, this investment policy corresponds to that which would be followed by an expected utility of terminal wealth maximizing the investor who was free to trade continuously. While previous analyses have derived this investment strategy directly by a stochastic dynamic programming approach,[13] it is derived here as a byproduct of the optimal payoff function. In practice, of course, economies of scale in transactions provide a role for the insurance company, a role which is enhanced by the joint provision of mortality and portfolio insurance by the insurance company.[14]

V. Optimal Contracts for HARA Utility

All members of the hyperbolic risk aversion class of utility functions may be expressed as

$$(23) \qquad U(Y) = \frac{1-\gamma}{\gamma} \left[\frac{Y}{1-\gamma} + \eta \right]^{\gamma}$$

by appropriate specification of the parameters β, γ, and η. The utility function is monotone, increasing, and strictly concave for all non-negative Y if $\beta > 0$; $\gamma \leqslant 1$; $\eta \geqslant 0$.[15]

For a member of this class the inverse marginal utility function is

$$(24) \qquad U'^{-1}(y) = (1-\gamma) \, [y^{1/\gamma-1} - \eta].$$

---

[12] See Cox and Ross [9].

[13] See, for example, Merton [14].

[14] See Section VI.

[15] See Merton [14].

Substituting from equation (24) in equation (8), the optimal contract pay-off function is

$$(25) \qquad g(X_T) = A + B \, X_T^{a/\sigma^2(1-\gamma)}$$

when $A = \eta(\gamma-1)$, $B = (1-\gamma)K^{1/(1-\gamma)}$, and K is determined from the budget constraint.[16]

Inspection of the optimal payoff function (25) reveals that for $\gamma \neq -\infty$ the minimum payoff depends only on the properties of the utility function and, assuming $a > 0$, the optimal payoff is a convex (concave) function of the value of the reference portfolio if a is greater (less) than $\sigma^2(1-\gamma)$.

The value of B in equation (25) is determined by setting the value of the contract at initiation equal to the investor's wealth, W, using the pricing function (7). Then the optimal payoff function may be written in terms of the investor's wealth as

$$(26) \quad g(X_T) = A + (We^{rT} - A) \, \exp\left\{ -\left(\frac{a(r-\tfrac{1}{2}\sigma^2)}{\sigma^2(1-\gamma)} + \frac{a^2}{2\sigma^2(1-\gamma)^2} \right) T \right\} (X_T/X_o)^{a/\sigma^2(1-\gamma)}.$$

Since (X_T/X_o) follows a lognormal distribution, equation (26) implies that the payoff $g(X_T)$ follows a three parameter lognormal distribution $\Lambda(\tau, m, s)$ where τ is the threshold parameter,[17] and

$$\tau = A,$$

$$m = \ln(We^{rT} - A) + \frac{a^2 T}{\sigma^2(1-\gamma)} \left(1 - \frac{1}{2(1-\gamma)} \right), \text{ and}$$

$$s^2 = a^2 T/\sigma^2(1-\gamma)^2.$$

In the exponential case $g(X_T)$ follows a normal distribution with mean $We^{rT} + a^2 \eta/\sigma^2$ and variance $a^2\eta^2/\sigma^2$.

To illustrate the nature of the solutions obtained, the optimal payoff functions and associated density functions were computed for three members of the HARA class. In these examples it is assumed that the contract premium is $10,000 and the contract term is 10 years. The riskless rate is taken as 6 percent, and the mean and variance of the lognormal distribution of reference fund returns as 8 percent and 4 percent per annum respectively: these latter figures

---

[16]When the utility function is exponential ($\gamma = -\infty$), equation (24) reduces to $U'^{-1}(y) = -\eta\ln\eta y$, and in (25) $A = -\eta\ln\eta K$, and $B = a\eta/\sigma^2$.

[17]Aitchison and Brown [1].

Figure 1
DENSITY FUNCTION OF PAYOFF AND OPTIMAL PAYOFF FUNCTION
FOR ALTERNATIVE HARA CLASS UTILITY FUNCTIONS

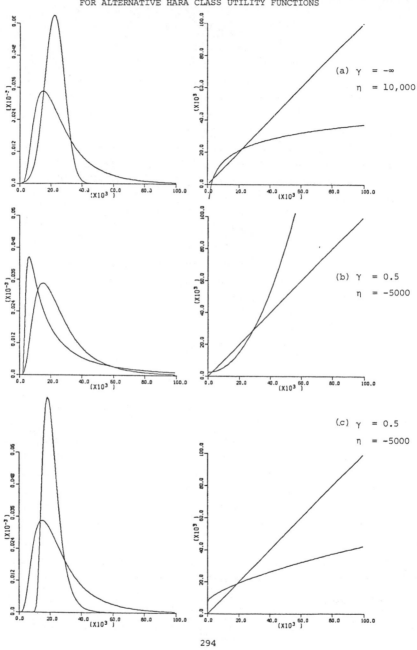

(a) $\gamma = -\infty$
 $\eta = 10,000$

(b) $\gamma = 0.5$
 $\eta = -5000$

(c) $\gamma = 0.5$
 $\eta = -5000$

294

correspond approximately to the returns reported by Ibbotson and Sinquefield [12] for the Standard and Poor's Index for the period 1926-1974.

Figure 1(a) shows the payoff and associated density for an exponential utility function. For this class of utility function the payoff function is always concave and the density function is normal. As the coefficient of absolute risk aversion is decreased, the mean and variance of the normal density increase.

Figures 1(b) and 1(c) refer to two extended power utility functions. For the more risk averse utility function the payoff function is concave and for the less risk averse convex. Decreases in η increase the intercept of the payoff function and decrease the slope at all points proportionally.

It is apparent that even from the restricted class of HARA utility functions a rich class of payoff functions and associated terminal wealth density functions may be generated. Furthermore, from a practical point of view in the design of optimal portfolio strategies of expected utility of terminal wealth maximizing investors, it may well prove easier for the investor to choose directly his optimal payoff function or density function than it would be for him to communicate his utility function to a portfolio manager.

VI. Mortality

Extension of the above analysis to allow for mortality and the probability that the contract will expire before maturity is straightforward and will only be sketched here. Assuming a periodic premium contract in which the reference portfolio is defined by a single deemed investment in the reference fund at contract initiation, X_0, the optimal contract, is found by choosing the payoff functions, $g_\tau(\cdot)$, to maximize.

$$(27) \qquad \sum_{\tau=1}^{T} \pi_\tau U_\tau[g_\tau(X_\tau)] f(X_\tau; X_0) \, dX_\tau$$

subject to the budget constraint

$$(28) \qquad \sum_{\tau=1}^{T} \pi_\tau g_\tau(X_\tau) p(X_\tau; X_0) \, dX_\tau = W$$

where $\pi_\tau (\tau = 1, \ldots, T-1)$ is the probability that the individual will die in period τ of the contract, and π_T is the probability that he will survive to maturity. $U_\tau(\cdot)$ is the utility function defined over the benefit payable in period τ, $g_\tau(X_\tau)$. The budget constraint assumes that mortality risk is ignored in determining the contract premium; W is the present value of the expected premiums to be paid; i.e., $W = P + P \sum_{\tau=1}^{T-1} e^{-r\tau}(1 - \sum_{i=1}^{\tau} \pi_i)$ where P is the periodic annual premium.

The optimal payoff functions then satisfy

$$(29) \qquad g_\tau(X_\tau) = U_\tau'^{-1} [\lambda p(X_\tau; X_o) / \pi_\tau f(X_\tau; X_o)] \qquad (\tau = 1, \ldots, T)$$

and the budget constraint (28). Determination of the optimal payoff functions will typically involve the solution of a non-linear equation for λ. Given λ, however, the optimal payoff functions for general time-dependent utility functions of the HARA class are

$$(30) \qquad g_\tau(X_\tau) = \eta_\tau(\gamma_\tau - 1) + (1 - \gamma_\tau) \left(\frac{\lambda}{\pi_\tau}\right)^{1/(\gamma_\tau - 1)}$$

$$\exp\{-(r\sigma^2 + a(a - 2\mu)/2)\tau/\sigma^2(\gamma_\tau - 1)\} X_\tau^{-a/\sigma^2} \qquad (\tau = 1, \ldots, T).$$

APPENDIX

A. To solve the control theory problem of determining the optimal payoff func-
    tion define $t = F(X_T)$ where $X_T > 0$ and $F(\cdot)$ is the cumulative density func-
    tion of X_T. Then $X_T = F^{-1}(t) \equiv h(t)$. Substituting for X_T in expressions
    (1) and (2) of the text and noting that the budget constraint will be bind-
    ing at the optimum yields the following equivalent control theory problem

(A1)
$$\underset{g\{\cdot\}}{\text{Max}} \int_0^1 U[g\{h(t)\}]\, dt$$

subject to

(A2)
$$\dot{w} = g\{h(t)\}\ p\{h(t);\ X_o\}/f\{h(t);\ X_o\}$$

(A3)
$$w(0) = 0$$

(A4)
$$w(1) = W.$$

The necessary conditions for an optimum are the Euler equations.

(A5)
$$U'[g\{h(t)\}] = \lambda(t)p\{h(t);X_o\}/f\{h(t);X_o\}$$

(A6)
$$\frac{d\lambda(t)}{dt} = 0$$

and conditions (A2) (A3) and (A4) which correspond to the budget constraint
(2).

The second order conditions for an optimum are satisfied since the maximand
and the constraint (A2) are concave in W and $g\{\cdot\}$ taken together.[18]

B. To establish proposition (iii), the indifference of an investor between two
    candidate reference portfolios having the same reward to variability ratios,
    it is convenient to parameterize on λ, the multiplier from the budget con-
    straint. Thus define $V(\lambda;\mu,\sigma^2)$ as the expected utility from the optimal
    contract given λ and the characteristics of the reference portfolio. Simi-
    larly define $W(\lambda;\mu,\sigma^2)$ as the cost of the contract. It suffices then to
    show that

---

[18] Arrow and Kurz [2, Chapter 2].

$$
\left.\begin{array}{l}
W(\lambda;\mu_1,\sigma_1^2) = W(\lambda;\mu_2,\sigma_2^2) \\[2mm]
V(\lambda;\mu_1,\sigma_1^2) = V(\lambda;\mu_2,\sigma_2^2)
\end{array}\right\} \quad \text{if} \quad \frac{\mu_1+\frac{1}{2}\sigma_1^2-r}{\sigma_1} = \frac{\mu_2+\frac{1}{2}\sigma_2^2-r}{\sigma_2} .
$$

Using (8) and the definition of V

$$
V(\lambda,\mu,\sigma^2) = \int_0^\infty U[U'^{-1}[q(Z)]] (Z\sigma\sqrt{2\pi T})^{-1} \exp\frac{-1}{2T\sigma^2} [\ln Z - \mu T]^2 dZ
$$

where $q(Z) = \lambda \exp[-(r\sigma^2 + a(a - 2\mu)/2) T/\sigma^2] Z^{-a/\sigma^2}$.

Changing the variable of integration from Z to q,

$$
V(\lambda,\mu,\sigma^2) = \int_0^\infty U[U'^{-1}(q)] (q\sigma\sqrt{2\pi T})^{-1} \exp\frac{-\sigma^2}{2a^2 T} [\ln q - \ln\lambda + rT + \frac{Ta^2}{2\sigma^2}]^2 dq
$$

so that the expected utility of the optimal contract depends on the characteristics of the reference portfolio only through the ratio a/σ. It may be
shown similarly that $W(\lambda;\mu,\sigma^2)$ depends on the characteristics of the reference portfolio only through a/σ which establishes the result.

REFERENCES

[1] Aitchison, J., and J.M.C. Brown. *The Lognormal Distribution*. Cambridge University Press (1963).

[2] Arrow, Kenneth J., and Mordecai Kurz. *Public Investment, The Rate of Return and Optimal Fiscal Policy*. Baltimore: Johns Hopkins Press (1970).

[3] Arrow, Kenneth J. *Essays in the Theory of Risk Bearing*. Chicago (1971).

[4] Black, F., and M. Scholes. "The Pricing of Options and Corporate Liabilities." *Journal of Political Economy*, Vol. 81 (May-June 1973), pp. 637-654.

[5] Borch, K. "The Safety Loading of Insurance Premiums." *Skandinavisk Aktuarietidskrift,* Vol. 43 (1960), pp. 163-184.

[6] Breeden, D.T., and R. H. Litzenberger. "Prices of State Contingent Claims Implicit in Option Prices." *Journal of Business*, Vol. 51 (October 1978), pp. 621-652.

[7] Brennan, M.J. "The Pricing of Contingent Claims in Discrete Time Models." *Journal of Finance*, Vol. 34 (March 1979), pp. 63-68.

[8] Brennan, M.J., and E.S. Schwartz. "The Pricing of Equity Linked Insurance Policies with an Asset Value Guarantee." *Journal of Financial Economics,* Vol. 3 (June 1978), pp. 195-213.

[9] Cox, J.C., and S.A. Ross. "The Valuation of Options for Alternative Stochastic Processes." *Journal of Financial Economics,* Vol. 3 (January/March 1976), pp. 145-166.

[10] Grant, A.T., and G.A. Kingsnorth. "Unit Trusts and Equity Linked Endowment Insurance." *Institute of Actuaries Journal*, Vol. 93 (1967), pp. 387-421.

[11] Heaney, W.J. "The Equilibrium Valuation Operator and Financial Market Efficiency." Unpublished dissertation, Simon Fraser University (1979).

[12] Ibbotson, R., and R. Sinquefield. "Stocks, Bonds, Bills, and Inflation: Year by Year Historical Returns." *Journal of Business*, Vol. 49 (1976), pp. 11-47.

[13] Leland, Hayne E. "Who Should Buy Portfolio Insurance?" *Journal of Finance,* Vol. 35 (1980).

[14] Merton, R.C. "Optimum Consumption and Portfolio Rules in a Continuous Time Model." *Journal of Economic Theory*, Vol. 3 (December 1971), pp. 373-413.

[15] _____. "Theory of Rational Option Pricing." *Bell Journal of Economics and Management Science,* Vol. 4 (Spring 1973), pp. 141-183.

[16] Raviv, A. "The Design of an Optimal Insurance Policy." *American Economic Review,* Vol. 69 (March 1979), pp. 84-96.

[17] Rothschild, M., and J. Stiglitz. "Equilibrium in Imperfect Insurance Markets: An Essay in the Economics of Imperfect Information." *Quarterly Journal of Economics* , Vol. 90 (1976), pp. 629-650.

[18] Rubinstein, M. "The Valuation of Uncertain Income Streams and the Pricing of Options." *Bell Journal of Economics and Management Science,* Vol. 7 (Autumn 1976), pp. 407-425.

[299]

[19] Spence, M., and R. Zeckhauser. "Insurance, Information and Individual Action." *American Economic Review,* Vol. 61 (1971), pp. 380-387.

[15]

THE JOURNAL OF FINANCE • VOL. XLIII, NO. 2 • JUNE 1988

Time-Invariant Portfolio Insurance Strategies

MICHAEL J. BRENNAN and EDUARDO S. SCHWARTZ*

ABSTRACT

This paper characterizes the complete class of time-invariant portfolio insurance strategies and derives the corresponding value functions that relate the wealth accumulated under the strategy to the value of the underlying insured portfolio. Time-invariant strategies are shown to correspond to the long-run policies for a broad class of portfolio insurance payoff functions.

THE LINK BETWEEN PORTFOLIO insurance and investment strategy was first noted by Brennan and Schwartz [5], who pointed out that insurance companies that had guaranteed the minimum payments they would make under equity-linked life insurance policies could hedge the resulting liability by following an investment strategy derived from the Black-Scholes [4] option-pricing model. Pure portfolio insurance without any element of mortality insurance appears to have been offered first by the Harleysville Mutual Insurance Company in 1971; however, a lack of public interest in this product led to its withdrawal by 1979.[1] Despite this initial lack of success, there has been, in recent years, an explosive growth in the sale of portfolio insurance strategies to institutional portfolio managers.[2]

Under ideal conditions, a simple portfolio insurance strategy ensures that the value of the insured portfolio, at some specified date, will not fall below some specified level. This property may be of considerable significance to portfolio managers if their investment performance is monitored on a periodic basis and if poor performance is heavily penalized; it may also be of significance to the owner of an investment portfolio that is held to meet some known set of future liabilities. However, there are at least two difficulties with this simple type of portfolio insurance. First, under almost all circumstances, a simple portfolio insurance strategy is inconsistent with expected-utility maximization.[3] Second, in many circumstances, the specification of the precise date on which the insurance is to be effective is arbitrary because institutional investment portfolios typically have no predetermined final date. Moreover, the specification of the

* Both authors from Anderson Graduate School of Management, University of California, Los Angeles. We would like to thank Fischer Black, an anonymous referee, and the participants in the Finance Workshops at U.C. Berkeley and the University of British Columbia and the European Finance Association Meetings in Madrid for their helpful comments on this paper. This research was supported in part by a grant from Leland, O'Brien, Rubinstein Associates.

[1] See Gatto et al. [9].

[2] The pioneers in the sale of portfolio insurance strategies were Leland, O'Brien, Rubinstein Associates.

[3] See Brennan and Solanki [6] and Benninga and Blume [2].

effective date of the insurance induces an investment strategy that is strongly time dependent.

Leland [14] and Brennan and Solanki [6] have generalized the concept of portfolio insurance to payoffs that are arbitrary functions of the value of some reference portfolio and have analyzed the types of function that will be optimal for individuals with different tastes and expectations. More recently, Perold [19] and Black and Jones [3] have popularized one of these functions and the associated investment strategy; this is the function that is appropriate for an individual with constant proportional risk aversion if the investment opportunity set is stationary; as Merton [15] and Hakansson [10] had shown earlier, if the investment opportunity set is constant, such an investor keeps a constant proportion of his or her wealth in risky assets. Besides its obvious simplicity, this constant-proportion investment strategy has the advantage over the simple portfolio insurance strategy of being time independent.

It is known from the work of Mossin [18], Leland [13], Hakansson [11],[4] and others that, for broad classes of utility functions defined over terminal wealth, the optimal investment strategy becomes constant as the horizon recedes. Given the indefinite horizons of most institutional investment portfolios, it is therefore of interest to consider the class of investment strategies under which the fraction of wealth allocated to risky assets is independent of time. The constant-proportion strategy is, of course, one member of this class, while, for a finite horizon, the simple portfolio insurance strategy mentioned above is not.

In this paper, we offer a complete characterization of the class of time-invariant insurance investment policies and their associated payoff functions and present some particular examples. The setting is one in which there is a single risky portfolio and a riskless security. The return on the risky portfolio is assumed to follow an Itô process with a constant variance rate, and the return on the riskless security is assumed to be an intertemporal constant. Although there exists a broad class of time-invariant portfolio insurance strategies that are optimal for some risk-averse expected-utility maximizer as the investment horizon recedes, we consider the whole class of time-invariant strategies and ignore the issue of an appropriate objective function for an institutional portfolio manager.[5]

Section I provides a formal definition of time invariance and derives the main results. The value functions yielded by the time-invariant investment strategies are characterized in Section II. Section III concludes the paper.

I. Time-Invariant Strategies

We assume that P, the value of the underlying risky-asset portfolio (the insured or "reference" portfolio), follows a continuous stochastic process of the general

---

[4] Mossin [18] showed that, if the utility function is of the extended power class, the optimal investment strategy tends asymptotically to the constant-proportions policy. These results were extended by Leland [13], who examined the class of utility functions for which the measure of constant relative risk aversion converges as wealth approaches infinity. Hakansson [11] offers bounds on the utility function that are sufficient to yield the constant-proportions investment policy asymptotically.

[5] Indirect evidence that institutional portfolio managers are not concerned with expected utility maximization is to be found in the popularity of simple portfolio insurance.

type:

$$\frac{dP}{P} = \mu dt + \sigma dz, \tag{1}$$

where dz is the increment to a standard Gauss-Wiener process and μ is the (possibly stochastic) instantaneous expected rate of return on the portfolio.

Let $V(P, t)$ denote the value at time t of the funds accumulated under a particular investment strategy, the "value of the strategy". We shall be concerned with investment strategies under which

(i) the fraction of the reference portfolio held can be written as a right-continuous function of, at most, the current value of the portfolio and time, $z(P, t)$;

(ii) the balance of the funds invested under the strategy, $V(P, t) - z(P, t)P$, is held in the riskless security, which earns at the continuously compounded rate, r;

(iii) no funds are added or withdrawn so that the strategy is "self-financing" (we shall refer to such investment strategies as "(generalized) portfolio insurance (investment) strategies").[6]

The basis of the Black-Scholes [4], Merton [16] option-pricing model is that any terminal payoff function of the form $y(P)$ can be achieved by following an investment strategy of the type we describe and that the value of the funds held under the strategy, $V(P, t)$, $t \le T$, where T is the payoff date, satisfies a certain partial-differential equation. The following lemma, which is related to a result of Merton [17],[7] states that the value function under any investment strategy of this type is a function only of P and t and that it satisfies the Black-Scholes partial-differential equation.

LEMMA: *Consider a self-financing investment strategy in which an amount $z(P, t)P$ is invested in a reference portfolio with a value that follows the stochastic process (1) and the balance is invested in riskless securities. Then the value of the wealth accumulated under the strategy may be written as $V(P, t)$, where*

(i) *the value function $V(P, t)$ satisfies the Black-Scholes equation:*

$$\tfrac{1}{2}\sigma^2 P^2 V_{pp} + rPV_p + V_t - rV = 0 \tag{2}$$

and

(ii) $$z(P, t) = V_p(P, t). \tag{3}$$

Proof: Let $H(\omega, t)$ denote the value function for the self-financing strategy $z(P, t)$ at time t, where $\omega \in \Omega$ is the state at time t. Then

$$H(\omega, t) = z(P, t)P + B(\omega, t), \tag{4}$$

---

[6] Cox and Leland [7] describe such investment strategies as "path independent" and show that these are the only efficient investment strategies for an expected-utility maximizer if the investment opportunity set is constant.

[7] See also Cox and Leland [7].

where $B(\omega, t)$ is the amount of funds held in the riskless security. Since the strategy is self-financing,

$$dH = zdP + rBdt. \tag{5}$$

Consider the value function $V(P, t)$. Itô's Lemma implies that

$$dV = V_p dP + [V_t + \tfrac{1}{2}\sigma^2 P^2 V_{pp}]dt. \tag{6}$$

Comparing coefficients in (5) and (6), it is apparent that $dV = dH$ if the value function $V(P, t)$ is such that

$$V_p(P, t) = z(P, t) \tag{3}$$

and

$$V_t + \tfrac{1}{2}\sigma^2 P^2 V_{pp} = rB. \tag{7}$$

Then, if $H(\omega, t_0) = V(P, t_0)$, $H(\omega, t) = V(P, t)$, so that the value of the wealth accumulated under the strategy depends only on the current value of P and t. Substitution for B from (4) into (7) yields (2).   Q.E.D.

We are concerned with the characteristics of time-invariant investment strategies, which are defined as follows.

Definition: A portfolio insurance investment strategy is time invariant if the fraction of wealth under the strategy that is allocated to the reference portfolio is at most a function of the current value of the portfolio, P:

$$\frac{PV_p}{V} = f(P). \tag{8}$$

As shown in the Lemma, the wealth accumulated under a generalized portfolio insurance investment strategy at time T may be written as $V(P, T) = y(P)$, where $y(P)$ is the terminal payoff function. Given the long investment horizons of many institutional investors, it is of interest to characterize the class of payoff functions, $y(P)$, for which the associated investment strategy becomes time invariant as the horizon recedes. This class is described by the following turnpike theorem.

THEOREM 1: *A necessary and sufficient condition for the investment strategy that yields the payoff function* $y(P)$ *to be asymptotically time invariant is that*

$$\lim_{T\to\infty} \frac{E^*[y'(P(T))P(T)]}{E^*[y(P(T))]} = h(P(0)), \tag{9}$$

where $P(t)$ is the value of the reference portfolio at time t and $E^*[\cdot]$ denotes the expectation with respect to the "risk-adjusted" stochastic process[8] or the "equivalent martingale measure".[9]

Proof: $V(P, t)$ satisfies equation (2) subject to the boundary condition

---

[8] See Cox and Ross [8].
[9] See Harrison and Kreps [12].

$V(P, T) = y(P)$. The solution may be written, for $t = 0$, as

$$V(P, 0) = e^{-rT} \int_0^\infty y(x) \times \phi(x, T) \, dx, \tag{10}$$

where

$$\phi(x, T) = \frac{1}{x\sigma\sqrt{2\pi T}} e^{-\frac{1}{2T\sigma^2}\left[\ln\frac{x}{P} - \left(r - \frac{1}{2}\sigma^2\right)T\right]^2}$$

is the risk-adjusted lognormal density.

Differentiating (10) with respect to P yields, after some manipulation,

$$\frac{V_p \times P}{V} = -\frac{\ln P}{T\sigma^2} - \frac{r - \frac{1}{2}\sigma^2}{\sigma^2} + \frac{1}{T\sigma^2} \frac{\int_0^\infty y(x) \times \ln x \times \phi(x, T) \, dx}{\int_0^\infty y(x) \times \phi(x, T) \, dx}. \tag{11}$$

Using Stein's Lemma,[10] (11) may be written as

$$\frac{V_p \times P}{V} = \frac{E^*[y'(P(T)) \times P(T)]}{E^*[y(P(T))]}.$$

Hence,

$$\lim_{T \to \infty} \frac{V_p \times P}{V} = f(P)$$

if and only if condition (9) holds.   Q.E.D.

We state without proof the following theorem, which characterizes a class of payoff functions that induce asymptotically time-invariant investment strategies.

THEOREM 2: *A sufficient condition for the portfolio insurance investment strategy to become time invariant as the horizon recedes is that the payoff function $y(P)$ be given by*

(i) $y(P) = \max(P, k) + \eta(P),$

(ii) $y(P) = \sum_i a_i P^{\beta i} + \eta(P),$

where $\eta(P)$ is the payoff on any contingent claim with present value that approaches zero as the date of the contingent payment recedes (i.e., $|\eta(P)| < a + bP^\beta$ for some $\beta < 1$).

Since any monotone increasing payoff function is optimal for some risk-averse utility function,[11] the above theorem extends the portfolio turnpike results of Hakansson [11] and Ross [20] to the class of utility functions for which the above payoff functions are optimal.

The following two theorems characterize the whole class of value functions and investment strategies that are permissible if the investment strategy is time invariant.

---

[10] See Rubinstein [21].
[11] See Brennan and Solanki [6].

THEOREM 3: *Under a time-invariant investment strategy, the value function,*
$V(P, t)$, *is of the form*

$$V(P, t) = e^{\gamma t}[C_1 P^{\alpha_1} + C_2 P^{\alpha_2}], \tag{12}$$

*where C_1, C_2, and γ are constants that are chosen to satisfy the initial budget
constraint, $\gamma \leq (r + \frac{1}{2}\sigma^2)/2\sigma^2$, and*

$$\alpha_1 = \frac{-(r - \frac{1}{2}\sigma^2) + \sqrt{(r + \frac{1}{2}\sigma^2)^2 - 2\gamma\sigma^2}}{\sigma^2},$$

$$\alpha_2 = \frac{-(r - \frac{1}{2}\sigma^2) - \sqrt{(r + \frac{1}{2}\sigma^2)^2 - 2\gamma\sigma^2}}{\sigma^2}.$$

Proof: Integrating (8), the condition for time invariance, we obtain

$$V(P, t) = k(t)g(P), \tag{13}$$

where $k(t)$ is a constant of integration and

$$g(P) = \exp\left[\int_0^P f(x)/x \, dx\right]. \tag{14}$$

Since $V(P, t)$ satisfies the partial-differential equation (2), (13) implies for
$g'(\cdot) \neq 0$ and $k(\cdot) \neq 0$ that

$$\tfrac{1}{2}\sigma^2 P^2 g'' + rPg' - (r - k'/k)g = 0. \tag{15}$$

Since $g(\cdot)$ is a function only of P, $k'/k = \gamma$, a constant, so that $k(t) = k_0 e^{\gamma t}$.
Then, substituting the solution to (15) in (13) and using the definition of $k(t)$
yield (12).   Q.E.D.

THEOREM 4: *Under a time-invariant investment strategy $f(P)$, the fraction of
wealth allocated to the reference portfolio is given by*

$$f(P) = w(P)\alpha_1 + (1 - w(P))\alpha_2, \tag{16}$$

where

$$w(P) = C_1 P^{\alpha_1}/(C_1 P^{\alpha_1} + C_2 P^{\alpha_2}). \tag{17}$$

Proof: This follows immediately from (8) and (12).   Q.E.D.

The value function (12) is multiplicatively separable in a function of time and
a function of the value of the reference portfolio. The parameter γ is a "growth
parameter"; it is the rate at which the value function grows for a given value of
the reference portfolio. As we shall see below, it is possible to construct value
functions with a minimum, in which case γ is the guaranteed minimum long-run
rate of return. For a given value of the parameter γ, the constants of integration
C_1 and C_2 must be chosen to satisfy the constraint that the initial value of the
strategy be equal to the funds available for investment; therefore, for any value
of γ, there exists a one-parameter family of value functions and investment
strategies.

    Two simple cases correspond to one hundred percent investment in the reference portfolio, $f(P) = 1$, and one hundred percent investment in riskless securities, $f(P) = 0$. It may be verified that these strategies correspond to the value functions $V(P, t) = C_1 \times P$ and $V(P, t) = C_1 e^{rt}$, respectively.

While the investment strategy characterized above is time invariant, the joint distribution of the rate of return earned under this strategy and the rate of return on the reference portfolio in general will be nonconstant, even if the distribution of the return on the reference portfolio is constant. An institutional portfolio manager is most often evaluated on the basis of the realized distribution of returns on his or her portfolio. If the evaluation rule is constant, he or she is likely to choose a strategy with a *return distribution* that is constant. The class of such strategies is characterized by the following theorem.

THEOREM 5: *A necessary and sufficient condition for the rate of return under a portfolio insurance investment strategy to follow a constant stochastic process (independent of P and t), if the return on the reference portfolio follows a constant stochastic process, is that C_1 or C_2 in equation (12) be equal to zero or, equivalently, that $w(P)$ in equation (16) be equal to zero or one.*
    Then

$$V(P, t) = C_1 e^{\gamma t} P^{\alpha_1} \tag{18}$$

or

$$V(P, t) = C_2 e^{\gamma t} P^{\alpha_2}. \tag{19}$$

Proof: (i) Sufficiency: Under this strategy, the fraction of wealth allocated to the reference portfolio is constant, which implies that the instantaneous return on the strategy is a fixed linear function of the return on the reference portfolio. (ii) Necessity: Since the rate of return under the policy is a linear combination of the riskless interest rate and the risky return on the reference portfolio, its stochastic process can be constant only if the portfolio weight $f(P)$ is a constant. However, this implies that $w(P)$ is constant, so that, from (17), $C_1 = 0$ or $C_2 = 0$.   Q.E.D.

This investment policy has been previously recognized as the optimal portfolio insurance strategy for an investor with constant proportional risk aversion when the opportunity set is time invariant by Brennan and Solanki [6]; a related strategy has been recently popularized by Black and Jones [3], who limit the fraction of wealth allocated to the reference portfolio to unity.

An alternative notion of time invariance is that the *value function* $V(P, t)$ is time invariant. If this condition is satisfied, then the relative performance of the strategy and the reference portfolio will also be time invariant. Investment strategies yielding time-invariant value functions are characterized by the following theorem.

THEOREM 6: *The necessary and sufficient condition for the value function $V(P, t)$ to be time invariant (independent of t) is that the fraction of wealth allocated to the reference portfolio be given by*

$$f(P) = w(P) - (1 - w(P))2r/\sigma^2, \tag{20}$$

where

$$w(P) = C_1 P / (C_1 P + C_2 P^{(-2r/\sigma^2)}). \qquad (21)$$

Then the value function $V(P)$ is

$$V(P) = C_1 P + C_2 P^{(-2r/\sigma^2)}. \qquad (22)$$

Proof: For a time-invariant value function, $V_t = 0$. Then (22) is the complete solution to the ordinary differential equation obtained from (2). The investment strategy (20)–(21) follows immediately from (8) and (22).

Comparing (12) with (22), it is apparent that the time-invariant value function (22) follows from the time-invariant investment strategy in which $\gamma = 0$.   Q.E.D.

II. Characterizing the Value Functions

To illustrate the possible types of value function that are attainable under time-invariant portfolio insurance investment strategies, Figures 1 through 6 depict some representative value functions for different assumptions about γ and for a fixed pair of environmental parameters ($r = 0.07$ and $\sigma^2 = 0.04$). In constructing

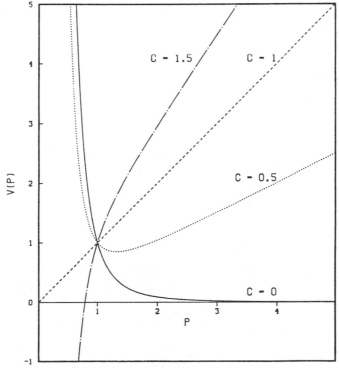

Figure 1. Value Functions for Time-Invariant Portfolio Insurance Policies When $\gamma = 0.0$.

($r = 0.07$; $\sigma^2 = 0.04$)

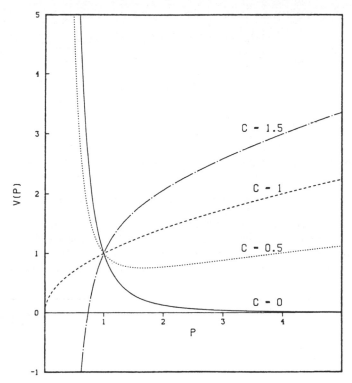

Figure 2. Value Functions for Time-Invariant Portfolio Insurance Policies at $t = 0$ When $0 < \gamma < r$.

$$(r = 0.07; \quad \sigma^2 = 0.04; \quad \gamma = 0.04)$$

these figures, the reference portfolio is standardized so that $V(1, 0) = 1$ and the value functions are shown for $t = 0$. The standardization implies that the value function (9) may be written as

$$V(P, t) = e^{\gamma t}[cP^{\alpha_1} + (1 - c)P^{\alpha_2}] \tag{12'}$$

or, for $\gamma = 0$, as

$$V(P) = cP + (1 - c)P^{-2r/\sigma^2}. \tag{22'}$$

We shall refer to the value functions corresponding to $c = 0$ or $c = 1$ as the "basic" value functions since all value functions may be constructed as weighted combinations of these.

A. Zero Growth Rate: $\gamma = 0$

Figure 1 shows the time-invariant value functions that are obtained when $\gamma = 0$. Since $\alpha_1 = 1$, the basic value function for $c = 1$ is linear and corresponds to a policy of investing one hundred percent of wealth in the reference portfolio. The negatively sloped basic value function $c = 0$ follows from a policy of shorting

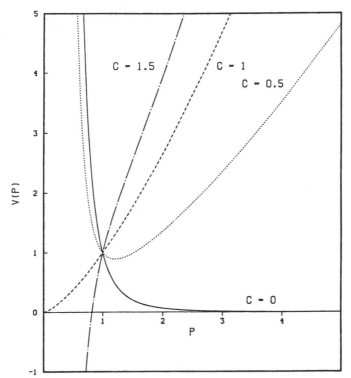

Figure 3. Value Functions for Time-Invariant Portfolio Insurance Policies at $t = 0$ When $\gamma < 0$.

$$(r = 0.07; \quad \sigma^2 = 0.04; \quad \gamma = -0.04)$$

the reference portfolio by a constant fraction of wealth α_2. Monotonically increasing and strictly concave value functions are obtained by choosing values of the mixing parameter $c > 1$. However, by choosing convex combinations of the two basic value functions (e.g., $c = \frac{1}{2}$), it is possible to obtain a value function with a minimum or "guaranteed" value. Moreover, in contrast to traditional portfolio insurance strategies,[12] the minimum value is realized on a set of measure zero. However, like traditional portfolio insurance strategies, nonmonotone value functions are unlikely to be optimal for expected utility maximizers.[13]

The value function is completely determined by the mixing parameter c, and, for $0 < c < 1$, it has a natural interpretation in terms of the "cost" of insurance. Thus, define $\rho(P; c)$, the *relative* value function, as the ratio of the wealth realized under a particular portfolio insurance strategy to the value of the reference portfolio:

$$\rho(P; c) \equiv \frac{V(P)}{P} = c + (1 - c)P^{-1-2r/\sigma^2}. \tag{23}$$

[12] Cf. Brennan and Schwartz [5] and Rubinstein [22].
[13] See Arrow [1].

Time-Invariant Portfolio Insurance Strategies   293

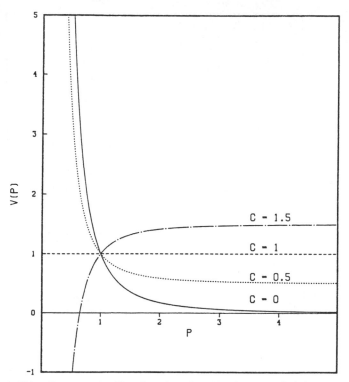

Figure 4. Value Functions for Time-Invariant Portfolio Insurance Policies at $t = 0$ When $\gamma = r = 0.07$.

$$(\sigma^2 = 0.04)$$

Then

$$\lim_{P \to \infty} \rho(P; c) = c. \tag{24}$$

Therefore, $(1 - c)$ may be interpreted as the proportional cost of the insurance strategy under favorable outcomes. The benefit of the insurance strategy depends on the minimum of the value function. Differentiating the value function $(22')$, it can be seen that the value function is minimized[14] at

$$P^* = \left[\frac{2r(1 - c)}{\sigma^2 c}\right]^{(\sigma^2/\sigma^2 + 2r)} \tag{25}$$

The minimum value is obtained by substituting from (25) in $(22')$. Table I gives the minimum values for different values of the mixing parameter c. For example, $c = 0.95$ guarantees that the value function will never fall below 0.84 and that this minimum is not attained until the reference portfolio value falls to 0.69. The implied "insurance cost" as measured by the value of the strategy relative to the

---

[14] The second-order condition is satisfied if $0 < c < 1$.

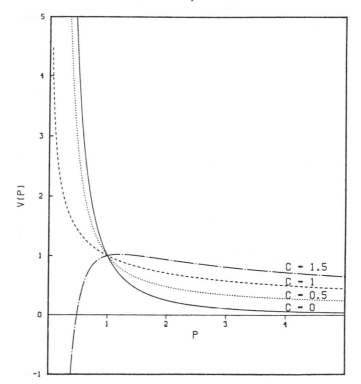

Figure 5. Value Functions for Time-Invariant Portfolio Insurance Policies at $t = 0$ When $\gamma > r$ and $\sigma^2 < 2r$.

$$(r = 0.07; \quad \sigma^2 = 0.04; \quad \gamma = 0.09)$$

value of the reference portfolio for high values of the reference portfolio is $1 - 0.95 =$ five percent. Similarly, an "insurance cost" of about twenty percent guarantees that the value function never falls below its initial value of unity. Under this strategy, the guaranteed minimum rate of return for any horizon is zero.

B. Growth Rate below the Interest Rate: $\gamma < r$ and $\gamma \neq 0$

Figures 2 and 3 depict the value functions obtained when $0 < \gamma < r$ and $\gamma < 0$, respectively. The basic value function $c = 1$, which is linear when $\gamma = 0$, becomes increasing concave for $\gamma > 0$ and increasing convex for $\gamma < 0$. The basic value function $c = 0$ remains decreasing convex for all values of γ, the convexity decreasing in γ.

Note that, when $\gamma \neq 0$, the value functions are no longer time invariant but shift up at the (possibly negative) rate γ.

The investment strategies discussed by Black and Jones [3] and by Perold [19] correspond to the basic value function $c = 1$, which results from investing a constant fraction of wealth in the reference portfolio. The richer class of time-

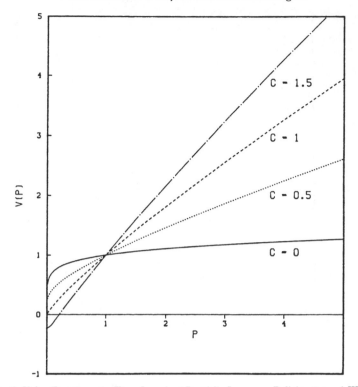

Figure 6. Value Functions for Time-Invariant Portfolio Insurance Policies at $t = 0$ When $\gamma > r$ and $\sigma^2 > 2r$.

Table I

Minima of the Value Function When γ = 0 for Alternative Values of the Mixing Parameter c[a]

c	P^*	$V(P^*)$
0.80	0.97	1.00
0.90	0.81	0.94
0.95	0.69	0.84
0.97	0.61	0.76
0.99	0.48	0.61

[a] $r = 0.07$; $\sigma^2 = 0.04$.

invariant investment strategies described in Theorem 4 yields arbitrary linear combinations of the two basic value functions as shown in equation (12′). Moreover, for convex combinations ($0 < c < 1$), the value function attains a minimum that rises over time at the rate γ. These value functions yield guaranteed minimum or "insured" long-run rates of return equal to γ. Differentiating

Table II

Minima of the Value Function at $t = 0$
for Alternative Values of γ and the
Mixing Parameter c^a

	$\gamma = -0.04$	
c	P^*	$V(P^*, 0)$
0.80	0.93	0.99
0.90	0.80	0.90
0.95	0.70	0.78
0.97	0.63	0.69
0.99	0.51	0.52

	$\gamma = 0.04$	
c	P^*	$V(P^*, 0)$
0.80	1.12	0.99
0.90	0.89	0.99
0.95	0.72	0.94
0.97	0.62	0.89
0.99	0.45	0.77

$^a r = 0.07; \sigma^2 = 0.04.$

(12′) with respect to P, it is seen that this minimum is attained at

$$P^* = \left[-\frac{(1 - c)\alpha_2}{c\alpha_1} \right]^{(1/\alpha_1 - \alpha_2)}, \tag{26}$$

and the guaranteed minimum value for any time t is obtained by substituting (26) into (12′).

Table II gives values of P^* and the initial guaranteed minimum value, $V(P^*, 0)$, for different values of the guaranteed growth rate γ and the mixing parameter c.

C. Growth at the Interest Rate: $\gamma = r$

Figure 4 shows that, when $\gamma = r$, the basic value function $c = 1$ becomes a horizontal line rising at the interest rate as the investment strategy consists of investing everything in the riskless asset. Values of $c > 1$ yield monotonically increasing, strictly concave value functions, but there exist no value functions with a minimum.

D. Growth above the Interest Rate: $r < \gamma \leq (r + \frac{1}{2}\sigma^2)^2/2\sigma^2$ [15]

In this case, both basic value functions slope down and approach zero for large values of P as long as $\sigma^2 < 2r$. Then all value functions either are monotonically decreasing or contain an interior maximum. Figure 5 illustrates this case.

When $\sigma^2 > 2r$, both basic value functions are positive, monotonically increas-

---

[15] The upper bound is the maximum value of γ for which the value function is defined. At this bound, the basic value functions are coincident.

ing, and strictly concave so that all convex-combination value functions share this property. Figure 6 depicts an example of this case.

E. Switching Strategies

As we have already mentioned, the time-invariant portfolio insurance strategies we have described that offer a minimum guaranteed rate of return when $\gamma < r$ possess nonmonotone value functions that imply short positions in the reference portfolio over the negatively sloped range. A feasible policy that avoids this problem while retaining most of the properties we have discussed[16] involves switching between two time-invariant strategies according to $P \gtrless P^*$.

Consider the policy of switching between the two classes of stationary strategies described in Theorem 2:

$$f(P) = w(P)\alpha_1 + (1 - w(P))\alpha_2 \quad \text{if} \quad P > P^*$$

$$= 0 \quad \text{if} \quad P \le P^*,$$

where

$$P^* = \left[\frac{-\alpha_2(1 - c)}{\alpha_1 c}\right]^{(1/\alpha_1 - \alpha_2)}. \tag{27}$$

Under this hybrid policy, which is depicted in Figure 7, wealth increases at the riskless interest rate (and the whole value function shifts up at the same rate) if $P \le P^*$. If $P > P^*$, the whole value function shifts up at the rate γ.

Thus, the value function may be written as

$$\tilde{V}(P, t) = e^{\tilde{\delta}t}[cP^{\alpha_1} + (1 - c)P^{\alpha_2}] \quad \text{for} \quad P > P^*$$

$$= e^{\tilde{\delta}t} \quad \text{for} \quad P \le P^*, \tag{28}$$

where

$$\tilde{\delta} = \tilde{q}\gamma + (1 - \tilde{q})r$$

and $\tilde{q}$ is the fraction of the time since $t = 0$ for which $P > P^*$.

It is apparent that this policy guarantees a minimum rate of return of γ.

III. Conclusion

We have analyzed a class of time-independent portfolio insurance strategies in a simplified setting in which the interest rate and the risk of the underlying portfolio are known constants. To each strategy there corresponds a value function relating the value of the funds accumulated under the strategy to the value of the underlying reference portfolio. These value functions shift up at the rate γ. Indeed, they are the only class of constant-growth-rate value functions. A natural generalization is to consider value functions that shift up at the rate γ and shift to the right at a different rate π.[17] This class of value functions is attainable by allocating to the reference portfolio at time t a fraction of wealth

---

[16] The proposed policy, however, is not path independent.
[17] π may be thought of as the long-run rate of inflation.

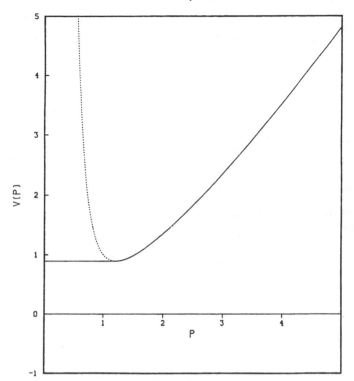

Figure 7. Value Functions for a Strategy of Switching between Two Time-Invariant Policies as $P \gtreqless P^*$. (The functions shift up at a rate γ when $P > P^*$ and at a rate r when $P < P^*$.)

$$(r = 0.07; \quad \sigma^2 = 0.04; \quad \gamma = -0.04; \quad c = 0.5)$$

equal to some function of the "discounted" value of the reference portfolio, $f(Pe^{-\pi t})$. While such policies are not time independent, they may be of interest in their own right and correspond to time-invariant strategies if the reference portfolio is defined in real terms and the rate of inflation is a constant π.

Time-independent investment strategies were shown to be the appropriate long-run portfolio insurance strategies for a broad class of insurance payoff functions. Since all monotone increasing payoff functions may be supported by some risk-averse utility function, our results extend earlier turnpike theorems.

We have not attempted to deal with the issue of an appropriate objective function for institutionally managed portfolios. A complete theory must deal with the problems created by the agency relationship between the portfolio sponsor and the portfolio manager, as well as taking account of transaction costs and uncertainty regarding the interest rate and risk parameters.

REFERENCES

1. K. J. Arrow. *Essays in the Theory of Risk-Bearing*. Chicago: Markham Publishing Co., 1971.
2. S. Benninga and M. Blume. "On the Optimality of Portfolio Insurance." *Journal of Finance* 40 (December 1985), 1341–52.

3. F. Black and R. Jones. "Simplifying Portfolio Insurance." Goldman Sachs Research—Portfolio Strategy, August 1986.

4. F. Black and M. J. Scholes. "The Pricing of Options and Corporate Liabilities." *Journal of Political Economy* 81 (1973), 637–59.

5. M. J. Brennan and E. S. Schwartz. "The Pricing of Equity-Linked Life Insurance Policies with an Asset Value Guarantee." *Journal of Financial Economics* 3 (1976), 195–213.

6. M. J. Brennan and R. Solanki. "Optimal Portfolio Insurance." *Journal of Financial and Quantitative Analysis* 16 (1981), 279–300.

7. J. Cox and H. E. Leland. "Notes on Intertemporal Investment Policies." Working paper, University of California, Berkeley, August 1982.

8. J. Cox and S. Ross. "The Valuation of Options for Alternative Stochastic Processes." *Journal of Financial Economics* 3 (1976), 145–66.

9. M. A. Gatto, R. Geske, R. Litzenberger, and H. Sosin. "Mutual Fund Insurance." *Journal of Financial Economics* 8 (1980), 283–317.

10. N. H. Hakansson. "Optimal Investment and Consumption Strategies under Risk for a Class of Utility Functions." *Econometrica* 38 (1970), 587–607.

11. ———. "Convergence to Isoelastic Utility and Policy in Multiperiod Portfolio Choice." *Journal of Financial Economics* 1 (1974), 201–24.

12. M. Harrison and D. Kreps. "Martingales and Arbitrage in Multiperiod Securities Markets." *Journal of Economic Theory* 20 (1979), 381–408.

13. H. E. Leland. "On Turnpike Portfolios." In G. P. Szego and K. Shell (eds.), *Mathematical Methods in Investment and Finance. Proceedings of an International Symposium [15 September 1971, Venice, Italy].*

14. ———. "Who Should Buy Portfolio Insurance." *Journal of Finance* 35 (1980), 581–94.

15. R. C. Merton. "Optimum Consumption and Portfolio Rules in a Continuous-Time Model." *Journal of Economic Theory* 3 (1971), 374–413.

16. ———. "Theory of Rational Option Pricing." *Bell Journal of Economics and Management Science* 4 (1973), 141–83.

17. ———. "On the Pricing of Contingent Claims and the Modigliani-Miller Theorem." *Journal of Financial Economics* 5 (1977), 241–50.

18. J. Mossin. "Optimal Multiperiod Portfolio Policies." *Journal of Business* 41 (1968), 215–29.

19. A. F. Perold. "Constant Proportion Portfolio Insurance." Working paper, Harvard Business School, August 1986.

20. S. Ross. "Portfolio Turnpike Theorems for Constant Policies." *Journal of Financial Economics* 1 (1974), 171–98.

21. M. Rubinstein. "The Value of Uncertain Income Streams and the Pricing of Options." *Bell Journal of Economics* 7 (1976), 407–25.

22. ———. "Alternative Paths to Portfolio Insurance." *Financial Analysts Journal* 41 (1985), 42–52.

Michael J. Brennan
Eduardo S. Schwartz
University of California, Los Angeles

Portfolio Insurance and Financial Market Equilibrium

I. Introduction

The explosive growth in the popularity of portfolio insurance investment programs that has taken place over the last few years and the events of October 1987 have created concern that the simultaneous use of such strategies by a large number of market participants may have the effect of substantially increasing the volatility of stock market prices,[1] with adverse consequences for both the stability of the financial system and the cost of funds raised by private sector corporations.[2]

Portfolio insurance is most conveniently defined as an investment strategy whose object is to ensure that the value of the funds under management is a convex function of the value of

This article compares a capital market in which prices are set by a single expected utility maximizing investor with a market in which the expected utility maximizing investor owns only a part of the wealth, the balance being held by an investor who follows a portfolio insurance strategy. Comparative values for the market risk premium, the cost of insurance, the market volatility, and the level of interest rates are computed for different levels of portfolio insurance.

1. Industry sources suggest that between 50 and 100 billion dollars of funds are currently managed under portfolio insurance programs. This is about 2%–4% of the total equity market capitalization of approximately 2,250 billion dollars.

2. See "Is Prudence to Blame for a More Volatile Market?" *New York Times* (February 1, 1987). "The market's volatility makes portfolio insurance more attractive, and as money managers flock to that approach, their activities in the futures markets, provide more room for program trading—thus laying the groundwork for bigger swings in stock prices." The possible negative effects of portfolio insurance have received widespread attention in the aftermath of the 1987 stock market crash. As Hart and Kreps (1986) have pointed out, increased variability in speculative prices is not necessarily welfare decreasing.

(*Journal of Business*, 1989, vol. 62, no. 4)

some underlying insured or reference portfolio.[3] It has been shown that, under standard assumptions of stationarity, the optimal reference portfolio is the mean variance efficient portfolio which, according to the capital asset pricing model (CAPM), is the market portfolio of all risky assets;[4] and, in fact, a large proportion of existing portfolio insurance programs are based on Standard and Poor's 500 (S&P 500) or some other such proxy for the market portfolio. A portfolio strategy that is designed to give a convex payoff function will require that units of the reference portfolio be sold after its price has declined and be bought after its price has risen. It is this aspect of portfolio insurance that has met with criticism, for, it is argued, such selling on market weakness will give rise to further price declines, and purchases on market strengths will accentuate the price increases. Thus, it is argued, portfolio insurance strategies increase market volatility.[5]

Portfolio insurance and related dynamic investment strategies have become commercially feasible only as a result of the dramatic reduction in the costs of trading portfolios brought about by the development of stock index futures contracts. As Duffie and Huang (1985) emphasize, the ability to engage in continuous dynamic trading strategies may serve to complete an otherwise incomplete securities market if a Radner equilibrium of plans, prices, and price expectations is achieved. Neglecting endowment effects, this will represent a welfare improvement. However, if investor plans are not coordinated, then it is possible that the trading induced by portfolio insurance may cause liquidity problems of the type described by Grossman (1987) and Leland (1987). Even if such coordination problems do not arise, portfolio insurance will affect the properties of the financial market equilibrium such as the level and volatility of security prices. In this article we analyze the potential effects of portfolio insurance on financial markets abstracting from the possible liquidity problems that may be caused by a lack of coordination between investors or by institutional frictions.

Since dynamic investment strategies are known to be optimal for a wide class of investment strategies,[6] it seems that the case against portfolio insurance must be made on grounds other than that it gives rise to an increase in the amount of trading in response to price changes or that portfolio insurance increases volatility. One possibility is that portfolio insurance strategies are employed, not to maximize the welfare of the investor, but to protect the interests of an agent who is

---

3. See Leland (1980). Also see Brennan and Schwartz (1976).
4. See Brennan and Solanki (1981).
5. Grossman (1987) makes the somewhat different point that the creation of synthetic securities by dynamic investment strategies may reduce the information available to investors from market prices, thereby creating coordination problems in the implementation of the strategies.
6. See, e.g., Merton (1971).

delegated the task of managing a portfolio; such an agent may have no interest in the return on the portfolio, per se, but only insofar as it affects his wage. If agents' incentive schemes are inappropriately defined, then dynamic investment strategies may enable them to game the reward scheme and perhaps to have adverse consequences for market volatility in the process.

Thus the strongest case against the likely consequences of portfolio insurance can be made if it is assumed that the investors who follow such strategies are not expected utility maximizing individuals but automata who blindly follow the investment rule required by the strategy whatever its consequences for the distribution of their final portfolio payoffs. In this article we adopt this extreme viewpoint and compare a capital market in which prices are set by a single expected utility maximizing investor[7] with a market in which the expected utility maximizing investor owns only a part of the wealth, the balance being held by an investor who follows a simple portfolio insurance strategy.

In Section II we introduce the basic valuation framework and describe the information structure that determines the stochastic evolution of market prices. In Section III we specialize this framework to an economy with isoelastic utility; this is used in Section IV to provide quantitative estimates of the effects of portfolio insurance on financial markets. Section V concludes the article.

II. The Valuation Framework

Consider a pure exchange economy that lasts for a single period. Consumption takes place at the beginning and end of, but not during, the period. However, trading is continuous. Prices are set by a single representative risk-averse investor who takes prices as given and whose utility function may be written as

$$U(C_{0r}) + \rho\, U(W_r),\qquad(1)$$

where C_{0r} denotes his consumption at the beginning of the period, and W_r is his wealth at the end of the period, wealth which is available for consumption. Market clearing implies that the initial consumption and terminal wealth of the representative investor be equal to the aggregate supplies C_0 and W.

The information structure of the economy known to all agents is represented by a geometric Brownian motion y:

$$\frac{dy}{y} = \eta dz,\qquad(2)$$

---

7. It is well known that if markets are Pareto efficient, prices are set as though there exists a single representative investor; see, e.g., Constantinides (1982).

where dz is the increment to a Wiener process. The end-of-period aggregate wealth is determined by $y(1)$, the value of y at the end of the period, and we adopt the normalization $W = y(1)$, so that for any time $t, 0 > t > 1$,

$$E[W|y(t)] = y(t). \tag{3}$$

Conditional on $y(t)$, the information available at time t, aggregate terminal wealth, W, is lognormally distributed with parameters $[y(t) - \frac{1}{2}\eta^2(1 - t), \eta^2(1 - t)]$ so that the uncertainty about terminal wealth is resolved at a constant rate over the period. Moreover, the information structure implies that asset prices follow continuous sample paths, so that any contingent claim on the market portfolio can be constructed by an appropriate dynamic strategy involving the market portfolio and the riskless asset.[8]

The first-order condition for the portfolio problem of the representative investor implies that $P_j(y(0),0)$, the price at the beginning of the period of asset j whose risky terminal payoff is X_j, is given by

$$P_j(y(0),0) = E[U'(W) \cdot X_j|y(0)]/(E[U'(W)|y(0)] \cdot R_F), \tag{4}$$

where

$$R_F \equiv U'(C_0)/\rho E[U'(W)|y(0)], \tag{5}$$

and R_F is the gross, riskless interest rate for the period.

Since the interest rate is undefined for $t > 0$, it is convenient to use the riskless asset as a numeraire and define the normalized prices:

$$p_j(y(t),t) = E[U'(W) \cdot X_j|y(t)]/E[U'(W)|y(t)] \quad \text{for } 0 \le t \le 1. \tag{6}$$

This completes the description of the base economy into which we now introduce portfolio insurance. The representative portfolio insurer is assumed to be a pure automaton who follows a portfolio strategy that yields an insured position in the market portfolio.[9] His terminal wealth, W_I, is given by

$$W_I = g(W), \tag{7}$$

where $g(W)$ is a convex terminal payoff function. The strategy of the portfolio insurer and his resulting payoff function are known to all market participants.[10] However, the representative investor is now representative of the expected utility maximizing investors, but not of the portfolio insurers. Thus, introduction of the representative insurer corresponds to an assumed change in the behavior of some of the investors, from expected utility maximization to automaton-like port-

---

8. See Huang (1985) for a formal analysis.
9. By portfolio insurer we mean the individual or institution that follows a portfolio insurance strategy. This usage, while standard in this context, contrasts with that in the traditional insurance literature.
10. The implications of relaxing this assumption are the focus of Grossman's (1987) analysis.

folio insurance. When we move from the base economy to the corresponding economy with portfolio insurance we do not change the risk aversion of the representative investor. This is tantamount to assuming that the investors who become portfolio insurers are also representative. The effect of introducing portfolio insurance estimated in this way is an upper bound on the effects likely to be observed in practice since in practice portfolio insurers are likely to be drawn from the more risk-averse participants in the market.

The terminal wealth of the representative investor is equal to the difference between aggregate wealth and the wealth of the representative portfolio insurer:

$$W_r = W - g(W). \tag{8}$$

Prices of risky claims are now determined by the optimizing decisions of the representative investor so that, corresponding to (6), the normalized price of claim j is given by

$$p_j^I(y(t),t) = E[U'(W - g(W)) \cdot X_j | y(t)]/E[U'(W - g(W))|y(t)], \tag{9}$$

where the superscript I distinguishes the prices that prevail in the market with portfolio insurance. In what follows we shall be interested in the behavior of $p_M(y(t),t)$ and $p_M^I(y(t),t)$, the values of the market portfolio in the base economy and the economy with portfolio insurance, respectively. These are obtained by substituting W for X_j in (6) and (9).

It follows from Ito's lemma and the assumed information structure (2) that the instantaneous standard deviation of return on the market portfolio is given by[11]

$$\sigma(y(t),t) = \frac{y}{p_M^I} \cdot \frac{\partial p_M^I}{\partial y} \cdot \eta. \tag{10}$$

Thus, to determine the effect of portfolio insurance on market volatility it is necessary only to specify the insurance payoff function, $g(W)$, the utility function of the representative investor, and the underlying risk of the economy that is represented by η. Then the market volatility, $\sigma(y,t)$, may be found from equations (9) and (10) and the stochastic process for y, equation (2).

III. An Economy with Isoelastic Utility

Suppose now that the utility function of the representative investor can be written as

$$U(C_{0r},W_r) = \frac{1}{1-\gamma} [C_{0r}^{1-\gamma} + \rho W_r^{1-\gamma}], \tag{11}$$

with $\gamma \geq 0$.

11. Returns are defined using the riskless asset as a numeraire.

Setting X_j equal to W in equation (6) and evaluating the expectations using (11) and the properties of the log-normal density, we obtain the following expression for the value of the market portfolio in the base economy for $0 \le t \le 1$:

$$p_M(y,t) = y \cdot e^{-\gamma \eta^2 (1-t)}. \tag{12}$$

Similarly from (5) the interest rate at the beginning of the period rate is given by

$$R_F = y^\gamma \cdot e^{-1/2\gamma(\gamma+1)\eta^2} \cdot \frac{U'(C_0)}{\rho}. \tag{13}$$

Substituting for p_M and $\partial p_M/\partial y$ from (12) in (10), it is immediate that

$$\sigma(y,t) = \eta, \tag{14}$$

so that, in the absence of portfolio insurance, the market volatility is a constant equal to the underlying risk parameter η. Note that, while the degree of risk aversion affects the value of the market portfolio and the interest rate, it does not affect the volatility of the market portfolio.

IV.   The Effects of Portfolio Insurance

We consider a simple portfolio insurance payoff function:

$$g(W) = \max [\alpha W, \beta], \tag{15}$$

where β is the minimum guaranteed return and α is the fraction of the market portfolio that is subject to portfolio insurance.

We define the units for wealth so that $\beta = \alpha$; then $W = 1$ corresponds to the level of aggregate wealth (return on the market portfolio) at which the guarantee becomes effective. Then, for an economy in which a fraction α of the market portfolio is insured, the normalized value of the insured portfolio is written $p_I^\alpha(y,t)$, the normalized value of the market portfolio is written as $p_M^\alpha(y,t)$, and the interest rate is $R_F^\alpha(y,t)$.

The guarantee that is offered by portfolio insurance cannot, even under idealized conditions, be unconditional, for the existence of limited liability implies that the payoff to portfolio insurers cannot exceed aggregate wealth W. Therefore, the payoff function after normalization must be modified to

$$g_\alpha(W) = \min [W, \max (\alpha W, \alpha)]. \tag{16}$$

The critical parameters in the analysis are the relative risk aversion of the representative investor and the underlying risk parameter η. For the latter we use 0.2 per year, which roughly corresponds to the average volatility of common stocks over the period 1926–81 as reported by Ibbotson and Sinquefield (1982).

Estimates of aggregate, relative risk aversion have been obtained both from cross-sectional data on asset holdings and from time-series data on asset returns. Using the former approach, Friend and Blume (1975) obtain an estimate of approximately 2. Estimates obtained from time-series data on asset returns include Grossman and Shiller (1981) with an estimate of about 4, Hansen and Singleton (1983) with a range of 0.07–0.62, Ferson (1982) with a range of -1.4–5.4, and Brown and Gibbons (1985) with an estimate of about 2. To provide an indication of the sensitivity of our results to the precise measure of risk aversion, we report results for risk-aversion parameters of 2 and 4.

Portfolio insurance changes the allocation of risk-bearing across market participants and, in principle, will affect the prices of all financial assets as well as the interest rate. In what follows we shall consider first the effect of the amount of portfolio insurance on the risk premium on the market portfolio and the cost of insurance, using the riskless bond as a numeraire. Since portfolio insurance is not, in general, an optimal policy for an expected utility maximizer investor (see Brennan and Solanki 1981) we shall also consider the opportunity cost of following the insurance strategy relative to the expected utility maximizing strategy. Second, we consider the effects of the amount of portfolio insurance on market volatility, as measured both by the instantaneous standard deviation of return on the market portfolio and the volatility implied by the cost of insurance using the Black-Scholes approach to valuation. Finally, we shall assess the effect of the amount of portfolio insurance on the level of interest rates in our simple economy.

The Market Risk Premium

Since y is the expected terminal value of the market portfolio and P_M^α $(y,0)$ is the beginning of period value,

$$y/P_M^\alpha(y,0) = 1 + \bar{r}_M,$$

where $\bar{r}_M$ is the expected rate of return on the market portfolio.
   Then, using relations (4), (5), and (6):

$$\frac{y}{P_M^\alpha(y,0)} - 1 \equiv \frac{1}{R_F^\alpha(y,0)} \cdot \frac{y}{P_M^\alpha(y,0)} - 1$$

$$\equiv \frac{1 + \bar{r}_M}{1 + r_f} - 1 \tag{17}$$

$$\approx \bar{r}_M - r_f,$$

where r_f is the 1-year riskless interest rate and $\bar{r}_m - r_f$ is the market risk premium.
   In the absence of portfolio insurance, $p_M^\alpha(y,0)$ is obtained from ex-

TABLE 1   **Market Risk Premium for Alernative Amounts of Portfolio Insurance**

y	$\alpha - 0\%$	$\alpha = 1\%$	$\alpha = 5\%$	$\alpha - 10\%$	$\alpha = 20\%$
$\gamma = 2$:					
.80	8.32	8.45	8.95	9.71	11.84
.90	8.32	8.42	8.83	9.43	11.05
1.00	8.32	8.40	8.70	9.15	10.32
1.10	8.32	8.38	8.59	8.89	9.68
1.20	8.32	8.36	8.49	8.68	9.17
$\gamma = 4$:					
.80	17.35	17.63	18.88	20.81	27.10
.90	17.35	17.59	18.64	20.23	25.00
1.00	17.35	17.54	18.39	19.65	23.30
1.10	17.35	17.50	18.13	19.08	21.76
1.20	17.35	17.45	17.90	18.56	20.40

NOTE.—γ = coefficient of relative risk aversion; y = expected terminal value of market portfolio; α = fraction of market portfolio insured. Nos. in table indicate percentages.

pression (6) with $X_j = W$. When there is portfolio insurance, the normalized value of the market portfolio, $p_M^\alpha(y,0)$ is given by expression (9) with $X_j = W$.

For the economy with isoelastic utility the market risk premium in the absence of portfolio insurance is $[\exp(\gamma\eta^2) - 1]$, as seen from equation (12). In order to estimate the effect of portfolio insurance on the market-risk premium, expression (9) with $X_j = W$ was integrated numerically using the lognormal density for W and the power utility assumption.[12]

The results are reported in table 1. In interpreting this and the subsequent tables, it is useful to remember that the guarantee becomes effective for $W \leq 1$ and that y is the expected value of W. The central row of the table ($y = 1.0$) corresponds to the situation in which the expected terminal value of the market portfolio is precisely "at the money" as illustrated in figure 1. The columns of the tables correspond to different assumptions about the fraction of the market portfolio which is subject to portfolio insurance.

When the coefficient of relative risk aversion is 2, the market-risk premium in the absence of portfolio insurance is 8.32%, which corresponds closely with the historical average risk premium. The effect of portfolio insurance is to increase the market risk premium. When y is at the money and the proportion insured is 5% the effect is to increase the

12. As the referee has pointed out, the expectations in (9) are not defined for power utility if there is positive probability that the representative investor has wealth. To resolve this technicality the payoff function (16) was modified to

$$\min\left[W - \epsilon, \max(\alpha W, \alpha)\right] \quad \text{for } \epsilon > 0.$$

The value of ϵ was set at 1% of the level of aggregate wealth at which the guarantee becomes effective. The results were insensitive to the choice of ϵ since, even for $\alpha = .20$, a return eight standard deviations below the mean is required before ϵ affects the payoff.

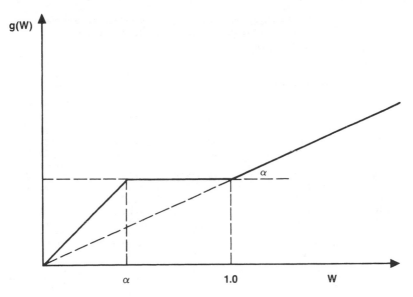

FIG. 1.—The aggregate payoff on insured portfolios when a fraction of the market is insured.

risk premium by 0.38%.[13] The effect becomes less pronounced when y is in the money, for then the dynamic strategy of portfolio insurers requires them to hold a higher proportion of equities, leaving less risk to be borne by the price-setting representative investor. The reverse is true when y is out of the money. As y decreases, the portfolio insurers invest almost entirely in bonds supplied by the representative investors so that the risk premium rises. As one would expect, the effect on the risk premium is increasing in the proportion of the market portfolio under portfolio insurance.

The lower part of the table reports analogous results when the coefficient of risk aversion is equal to 4. In this case the risk premium, even without portfolio insurance, is 17.35%, which is implausibly high. However, we include this result to emphasize the importance of the risk-aversion assumption.

The Cost of Insurance

It is to be expected that, since portfolio insurance is supplied willingly by the optimizing representative investors, its cost will increase as the number of investors demanding insurance increases. We consider two measures of cost. The first is the value of the insured portfolio payoff

---

13. This fraction is of the same order as the fraction of aggregate equity values subject to portfolio insurance prior to the events of October 1987.

TABLE 2   **Value of the Insurance Payoff as a Fraction of the Value of the Market Portfolio for Alternative Amounts of Portfolio Insurance:**
$P_I^\alpha(y,0)/P_M^\alpha(y,0)$

y	$\alpha = 1\%$	$\alpha = 5\%$	$\alpha = 10\%$	$\alpha = 20\%$
$\gamma = 2$:				
.80	1.36	6.84	13.77	28.07
.90	1.23	6.15	12.36	25.05
1.00	1.13	5.67	11.38	22.95
1.10	1.07	5.37	10.75	21.61
1.20	1.04	5.19	10.39	20.82
$\gamma = 4$:				
.80	1.47	7.44	15.12	31.80
.90	1.32	6.64	13.44	27.91
1.00	1.20	6.04	12.20	25.07
1.10	1.12	5.63	11.33	23.06
1.20	1.07	5.36	10.75	21.73

NOTE.—γ = coefficient of relative risk aversion; y = expected terminal value of market portfolio; α = fraction of market portfolio insured. Nos. in table are percentages.

relative to the value of the corresponding uninsured (market) portfolio. The (normalized) value of the insured portfolio is obtained from equation (9) with $X_j = g_\alpha(W)$. The (normalized) cost of the uninsured market portfolio is also obtained from (9) with $X_j = W$. Both expressions are evaluated numerically using the log-normal density and the power-utility assumption.

Table 2 reports the value of the fraction of current aggregate wealth accounted for by the insured portfolio payoff, given the fraction of terminal wealth that is insured. Thus, in the upper half of the table, when α equals 5% and y equals 1.0, the value of the insured portfolio payoff is 5.67% of aggregate wealth, so that the cost of insuring a 5% share of terminal wealth is 0.67% of the value of current wealth, or 13.4% of the value of the insured portfolio.

The cost of insurance rises more than proportionately to the amount insured, so that, when α equals 20%, the cost of insurance is 2.95%, which is 4.40 times the cost when α equals 5%. The nonlinearity becomes more pronounced in the extreme case when the coefficient of risk aversion is 4.

A different measure of the cost of portfolio insurance is the opportunity cost to a representative investor of switching from the expected utility maximizing investment strategy to the portfolio insurance strategy. The certainty equivalent per normalized dollar of initial wealth for a representative investor who follows the optimal strategy, given that a fraction α of aggregate wealth is insured, may be written as $\omega^r(y,\alpha)$, where y is the initial value of the expectations index. This certainty

TABLE 3   Difference between Certainty Equivalents for Optimizing Investors and
               for Portfolio Insurers: Cents per Dollar of Investment

y	$\alpha = 1\%$	$\alpha = 5\%$	$\alpha = 10\%$	$\alpha = 20\%$
$\gamma = 2$:				
.80	3.67	4.16	4.94	7.49
.90	2.91	3.27	3.84	5.61
1.00	1.98	2.22	2.59	3.70
1.10	1.17	1.31	1.52	2.13
1.20	.61	.68	.78	1.09
$\gamma = 4$:				
.80	7.89	9.08	11.07	18.78
.90	6.72	7.68	9.24	14.69
1.00	5.10	5.81	6.96	10.75
1.10	3.42	3.90	4.65	7.08
1.20	2.05	2.33	2.77	4.17

NOTE.—γ = coefficient of relative risk aversion; y − expected terminal value of market portfolio; α = fraction of market portfolio insured.

equivalent is defined by[14]

$$\omega^r(y,\alpha) = \frac{\{E[(W - g_\alpha(W))^{(1-\gamma)}|y]\}^{\frac{1}{1-\gamma}}}{p_M^\alpha(y,0) - p_I^\alpha(y,0)}. \tag{18}$$

Similarly, the certainty equivalent per normalized dollar invested for a representative investor following the insurance strategy, $\omega^i(y,\alpha)$, is

$$\omega^i(y,\alpha) = \frac{\{E[g_\alpha(W)^{1-\gamma}|y]\}^{\frac{1}{1-\gamma}}}{p_I^\alpha(y,0)}. \tag{19}$$

Then $\delta(y,\alpha) = \omega^r(y,\alpha) - \omega^i(y,\alpha)$ is the opportunity cost to a representative investor of switching to the insurance strategy. Table 3 reports these opportunity costs.

It is seen that when $y = 1.0$ and $\alpha = 5\%$ the opportunity cost for a representative investor of switching to the insurance strategy is 2.22 cents per dollar, or 2.22%. This means that an investor with representative tastes who follows the insurance strategy is effectively throwing away 2.22% of his wealth each year. Of course, this cost is relevant only for investors with representative tastes. Nevertheless, the fact that this opportunity cost rises as the fraction of wealth insured increases suggests that the higher is the proportion of investors following insurance strategies, the greater is the disincentive for new investors to join them. The increase in the opportunity costs is the result of both an

14. This certainty equivalent is calculated by noting that the representative investor's payoff is given by expression (8), while his initial investment is given by the denominator of expression (18).

TABLE 4   **Instantaneous Market Volatility Relative to Market Volatility in the Absence of Portfolio Insurance**

y	$\alpha = 1\%$	$\alpha = 5\%$	$\alpha = 10\%$	$\alpha = 20\%$
$\gamma = 2$:				
.80	1.00	1.01	1.02	1.06
.90	1.00	1.01	1.02	1.06
1.00	1.00	1.01	1.03	1.06
1.10	1.00	1.01	1.02	1.06
1.20	1.00	1.01	1.02	1.05
$\gamma = 4$:				
.80	1.00	1.02	1.04	1.16
.90	1.00	1.02	1.04	1.13
1.00	1.00	1.02	1.05	1.13
1.10	1.00	1.02	1.05	1.13
1.20	1.00	1.02	1.05	1.12

NOTE.—γ = coefficient of relative risk aversion; y = expected terminal value of market portfolio; α = fraction of market portfolio insured.

increase in the certainty equivalent for the optimizing investor and a decrease of the certainty equivalent of the insurer.

Market Volatility

Market volatility is measured in two ways. First, the instantaneous standard deviation of the return on the market portfolio at the beginning of the period is computed using equation (10). The ratio of the market volatility to its value when there is no portfolio insurance is reported in table 4.

The effect of portfolio insurance on instantaneous market volatility increases more than proportionately with the proportion of the market subject to insurance. However, for a coefficient of risk aversion of 2 the effects are modest when $\alpha \leq 20\%$.

Our second measure of market volatility is based on the Black-Scholes approach to the valuation of contingent claims. The basic assumption of the Black-Scholes model is that the price of the underlying asset follows a diffusion process with a nonstochastic variance rate. Under the stronger assumption that the variance rate is a constant, it is straightforward to invert the Black-Scholes formula for the variance rate implied by observed prices. In the current context the underlying asset is the market portfolio, and in the presence of portfolio insurance the instaneous variance rate will depend upon the state variable y, as seen in table 4.

Nevertheless, the risk-neutral pricing principle that underlies the Black-Scholes model will continue to hold since both the asset price (the value of the market portfolio) and its instantaneous variance rate depend on the single-state variable y. Therefore, we use the risk-neutral valuation principle to infer the implied volatility corresponding to the value of the portfolio insurance contract and the value of the

TABLE 5   Implied Market Volatility Relative to Market Volatility in the Absence of Portfolio Insurance

y	$\alpha = 1\%$	$\alpha = 5\%$	$\alpha = 10\%$	$\alpha = 20\%$
$\gamma = 2$:				
.80	1.00	1.01	1.01	1.03
.90	1.00	1.01	1.01	1.03
1.00	1.00	1.00	1.01	1.03
1.10	1.00	1.01	1.01	1.03
1.20	1.00	1.01	1.01	1.03
$\gamma = 4$:				
.80	1.00	1.01	1.02	1.07
.90	1.00	1.01	1.03	1.07
1.00	1.00	1.01	1.03	1.07
1.10	1.00	1.01	1.03	1.07
1.20	1.00	1.01	1.03	1.07

NOTE.—γ = coefficient of relative risk aversion; y = expected terminal value of market portfolio; α = fraction of market portfolio insured.

market portfolio. This implied volatility provides a measure of the average volatility over the remaining life of the contract.[15]

The implied volatility is defined as the instantaneous standard deviation of return on the market portfolio that would account for the observed relation between the normalized prices of the market portfolio and the insurance contract on the assumption that the return on the market portfolio is lognormally distributed and its expected value is equal to zero.[16]

Specifically, the implied volatility $\hat{\sigma}$ is given by the solution to

$$p_T^\alpha(y,0) = \int g_\alpha(W) \cdot \frac{1}{W\hat{\sigma}\sqrt{2\pi}} \exp\left[-\frac{1}{2}\left(\ln\frac{W}{p_M^\alpha(y,0)} + \frac{1}{2}\hat{\sigma}^2\right)\Big/\hat{\sigma}^2\right]dW.$$

(20)

In this equation, $g_\alpha(W)$ is the payoff on the insured portfolio given by equation (15). Values $p_T^\alpha(y,0)$ and $p_M^\alpha(y,0)$ are the normalized values of the insured portfolio and the market portfolio, respectively. These are computed as before, using equation (9).

Relative values of the implied volatility are reported in table 5. As with the instantaneous market volatility, the effect of portfolio insurance on the implied market volatility is modest. For example, if the risk-aversion coefficient is 2, the implied volatility increases by only 3% when the fraction of the market insured is 20%, and even when the risk-aversion coefficient is 4, the effect is still only 7%.

15. Although use of the implied volatility cannot be rigorously justified in this context, the implied volatility has the advantage of being widely used in practice.

16. The zero expected return arises in this context because both the price of the underlying asset and the claim price are expressed in terms of the price of end-of-period units.

TABLE 6   **Proportion of the Market Portfolio Held by Portfolio Insurers for Alternative Amounts of Portfolio Insurance**

y	α = 1%	α = 5%	α = 10%	α = 20%
γ = 2:				
.80	.08	.38	.73	1.29
.90	.20	1.00	1.94	3.62
1.00	.38	1.88	3.71	7.09
1.10	.57	2.83	5.59	10.89
1.20	.73	3.63	7.21	14.20
γ = 4:				
.80	.03	.16	.24	.39
.90	.11	.52	.96	1.52
1.00	.24	1.16	2.21	3.84
1.10	.41	2.00	3.88	7.11
1.20	.58	2.87	5.62	10.63

NOTE.—γ = coefficient of relative risk aversion; y = expected terminal value of market portfolio; α = fraction of market portfolio insured. Nos. in table are percentages.

These findings with respect to market volatility suggest that portfolio insurance is likely to have small effects on the variability of stock prices, at least in perfect markets in which the activities of portfolio insurers are fully anticipated.

Trading Volume

Portfolio insurance is implemented by a dynamic strategy of moving funds between equities and a riskless asset. The effect of this is to reallocate the burden of risk bearing between portfolio insurers and the optimizing representative investors. Thus, after a decline in stock prices, portfolio insurers will sell stock, increasing the share of risk borne by the rest of the market. Since, in less-than-perfect markets, there may be some limits to the ability of the rest of the market to absorb sudden increases in risk, it is important to gain some idea of the magnitude of the risk transfers that portfolio insurance is likely to involve in practice. This can be measured by the volume of trading induced by portfolio insurance strategies. To estimate portfolio-insurance-induced trading volume, the fraction of the market portfolio held by portfolio insurers was computed for different values of the expectational variable y. It is well known that this fraction is equal to the "hedge ratio" or partial derivative of the value of the insured portfolio with respect to the value of the market portfolio:

$$\partial p_I^\alpha / \partial p_M^\alpha \equiv \frac{\partial p_I^\alpha(y,0)/\partial y}{\partial p_M^\alpha(y,0)/\partial y}. \tag{21}$$

The hedge ratios, which were calculated numerically using equation (9), are reported in table 6. For the range of parameters values considered, the value of the market portfolio $P_M^\alpha(y,0)$ is approximately proportional to the information variable y. Therefore, it is possible to gauge approximately the amount of portfolio-insurance-associated trading that will be induced by a given change in the level of stock prices. If the fraction of the market portfolio subject to portfolio insurance is 5% and the risk aversion parameter is 2, then a change in y from 1.00 to 1.10 induces portfolio insurers to purchase an additional 2.83% $-$ 1.88% = 0.95% of the market portfolio. Thus each 1% change in stock prices induces portfolio-insurance-related trading equal in value to approximately 0.1% of the value of the market portfolio. Trading effects are roughly twice as large when the fraction of the market subject to insurance is 10%. By way of comparison, average daily turnover in the New York Stock Exchange in 1986 was 0.3% and an additional 0.5% was traded in the S&P 500 futures contracts. On October 19, 1987, when the market dropped by more than 20%, the combined trading in these two markets was of the order of 2% of the value of the underlying stocks.

It seems, therefore, that under current institutional arrangements even modest levels of portfolio insurance may impose major strains on the liquidity of the markets in the event of large changes in expectations.

Interest Rates

Thus far we have not considered the possible effects of portfolio insurance on the level of interest rates. In the absence of portfolio insurance, the gross interest rate is given by equation (5), which, under the joint assumptions of lognormality and power utility, implies that

$$R_F = \frac{C_0^{-\gamma}}{\rho} y^\gamma \exp\left[-\tfrac{1}{2}\gamma\eta^2(1+\gamma)\right]. \tag{22}$$

In order to estimate the effect of portfolio insurance on the interest rate we assume that portfolio insurers represent a fraction f of all investors, that all investors have the same initial wealth, and that initial consumption is the same for portfolio insurers and the other (representative) investors.

The fraction of investors who are designated as portfolio insurers is $P_I^\alpha(y,0)/P_M^\alpha(y,0)$. This is the fraction of the original identical investors who have exchanged their claims to the market portfolio for the insured claim. Then, the initial consumption of the (price-setting) representative investor is $(1-f)C_0$ so that the gross interest rate is

$$R_F^\alpha(y,0) = \frac{(1-f)^{-\gamma}(C_0)^{-\gamma}}{\rho E[[W-g_\alpha(W)]^{-\gamma}|y]}. \tag{23}$$

The results reported in table 7 assume that the expected growth rate in aggregate consumption is a constant m so that $C_0 = y/m$. In particu-

TABLE 7   Riskless Interest Rate for Alternative Amounts of Portfolio Insurance

y	α = 0%	α = 1%	α = 5%	α = 10%	α = 20%
γ = 2:					
.80	2.92	2.82	2.36	1.74	.31
.90	2.92	2.84	2.47	1.96	.79
1.00	2.92	2.86	2.58	2.20	1.29
1.10	2.92	2.88	2.69	2.42	1.78
1.20	2.92	2.90	2.78	2.61	2.20
γ = 4:					
.80	− 14.23	− 14.43	− 15.21	− 16.05	− 16.18
.90	− 14.23	− 14.40	− 15.07	− 15.83	− 16.52
1.00	− 14.23	− 14.37	− 14.92	− 15.58	− 16.48
1.10	− 14.23	− 14.34	− 14.76	− 15.29	− 16.20
1.20	− 14.23	− 14.31	− 14.61	− 15.00	− 15.77

NOTE.—γ = coefficient of relative risk aversion; y = expected terminal value of market portfolio; α fraction of market portfolio insured. Nos. in table are percentages.

lar, we assume that $m = 1.05$ and that the impatience parameter ρ is equal to 0.95.

As seen in the table, the effect of portfolio insurance is to reduce the net interest rate, and the effect is more pronounced the lower the expectational variable y. Thus when y is at the money the effect of 5% portfolio insurance is to reduce the real interest rate from 2.92% to 2.58%, when γ equals 2. When γ equals 4 the effect is roughly twice as large. The reason for the reduction is that the portfolio insurers increase demand for the riskless asset while reducing their demand for shares in the market portfolio.

Time Horizon

We have arbitrarily set the length of the single period at 1 year. The effect on the market risk premium and volatility of changing the length of the period is identical to that of changing the exogenous variance η^2. A doubling of the variance corresponds to a doubling of the time horizon. Simulations in which the variance rate was increased by a factor of 4 had no significant effect on the market-risk premium and volatility reported above when interpreted on a yearly basis.

V. Conclusion

In this article we have presented estimates of the effects of portfolio insurance in a frictionless economy characterized by a single representative agent with power utility and rational expectations. Portfolio insurance was introduced by assuming that a fraction of agents were able to purchase claims on the end-of-period market portfolio with characteristics similar to those promised by portfolio insurance strategies.

These claims and the market portfolio itself were assumed to be priced by the remaining expected utility maximizing representative investors.

In this context, the effect of portfolio insurance on market volatility was found to be slight for reasonable parameter values. Moreover, the more widely followed the portfolio insurance strategy is, the more costly it becomes, both when the cost is measured by the value of the implicit put option and when it is measured by the difference in certainty equivalents achieved by optimizing portfolio insurance investors with the same utility function. The increasing cost of portfolio insurance suggests that the popularity of such strategies will be self-limiting. On the other hand, even modest levels of portfolio insurance potentially involve trading volume that is large relative to current turnover rates. This suggests that there may exist additional liquidity-related costs to following portfolio insurance strategies under current institutional arrangements.

An important assumption of the analysis is that a Radner equilibrium of plans, prices, and price expectations is achieved, that is to say, that individual investors are able to take into account the strategies of other investors in formulating their own investment strategies. In this context the assumption implies that optimizing investors are aware of the extent of portfolio insurance strategies. This seems to be a reasonable assumption for analyzing the effects of portfolio insurance in the long run. However, to the extent that the assumption is violated, the effect of portfolio insurance on market volatility may be greater than our calculations suggest because of liquidity problems of the type discussed by Grossman (1987) or possible misinterpretation of the information content of portfolio-insurance-induced transactions.

References

Brennan, M. J., and Schwartz, E. S. 1976. The pricing of equity linked life insurance policies with an asset value guarantee. *Journal of Financial Economics* 3:195–213.
Brennan, M. J., and Solanki, R. 1981. Optimal portfolio insurance. *Journal of Financial and Quantitative Analysis* 16, no. 3:279–300.
Brown, D. P., and Gibbons, M. R. 1985. A simple econometric approach for utility-based asset pricing models. *Journal of Finance* 40, no. 2:359–82.
Constantinides, G. M. 1982. Intertemporal asset pricing with heterogeneous consumers and without demand aggregation. *Journal of Business* 55:253–67.
Duffie, D., and Huang, C. 1985. Implementing Arrow-Debreu equilibria by continuous trading of few long-lived securities. *Econometrica* 53, no. 6:1337–56.
Ferson, W. 1982. Expected real interest rates and consumption in efficient financial markets. Ph.D. dissertation, Stanford University.
Friend, I., and Blume, M. 1975. The demand for risky assets. *American Economic Review* 65:900–922.
Grossman, S. J. 1987. An analysis of the implications for stock and futures price volatility of program trading and dynamic hedging strategies. Princeton University Financial Research Center Memorandum no. 82.
Grossman, S. J., and Shiller, R. 1981. The determinants of variability of stock market prices. *American Economic Review* 71:222–27.

Hansen, L., and Singleton, K. 1983. Stochastic consumption, risk aversion, and the temporal behavior of asset returns. *Journal of Political Economy* 91:249–65.

Hart, O. D., and Kreps, D. M. 1980. Price destabilizing speculation. *Journal of Political Economy* 94 (October): 927–52.

Huang, C. 1985. Information structure and viable price systems. *Journal of Mathematical Economics* 14:215–240.

Ibbotson, R., and Sinquefield, R. 1982. *Stocks, Bonds, Bills and Inflation: Historical Returns*. Chicago: Financial Analysts Research Foundation.

Leland, H. E. 1980. Who should buy portfolio insurance. *Journal of Finance* 35, no. 2:581–94.

Leland, H. E. 1987. On the stock market crash and portfolio insurance. Unpublished manuscript. Berkeley: University of California.

Merton, R. C. 1971. Optimum consumption and portfolio rules in a continuous-time model. *Journal of Economic Theory* 3:373–413.

[17]

Information, Trade, and Derivative Securities

Michael J. Brennan
University of California, Los Angeles,
and London Business School

H. Henry Cao
University of California, Los Angeles

Hellwig's (1980) model is used to analyze the value of improving trading opportunities by more frequent trading in the underlying asset, or by trading in a derivative asset. With multiple trading sessions, uninformed investors behave as rational trend followers, while more informed investors follow a contrarian strategy. As trading becomes continuous, Pareto efficiency is achieved. With trading in an appropriate derivative security, Pareto efficiency may be achieved in only a single round of trading. All derivative claims are then priced on Black and Scholes (1973) principles and, in the absence of further supply shocks, no trading will take place in subsequent trading rounds.

It is common for securities markets to develop initially as periodic call markets and only later to offer the opportunity for continuous trading through the day.[1] Most recently, we have witnessed the development of

---

We thank Anat Admati and Lesley Sun for helpful comments, and Alex Dontoh, Joshua Ronen, and Bharat Sarath for pointing out an error in an earlier draft. The article has been improved by the comments of participants at seminars at the University of British Columbia, University of Lausanne, Duke University, Norwegian School of Economics, and the University of Vienna. We thank the editor, Franklin Allen, and an anonymous reviewer for suggestions that have improved the clarity of the exposition. Correspondence should be addressed to M. J. Brennan, Anderson Graduate School of Management, UCLA, Los Angeles, CA 90024.

[1] Trading frequency still differs considerably across security markets. Ghana's bourse trades for only 2 days a week and Morocco's for only $1\frac{1}{2}$ hours a day. *Economist*, June 11, 1994.

The Review of Financial Studies Spring 1996 Vol. 9, No. 1, pp. 163–208
© 1996 The Review of Financial Studies 0893-9454/96/$1.50

The Review of Financial Studies / v 9 n 1 1996

after-hours and even round-the-clock trading in some securities, as well as the concomitant introduction of an extensive array of derivative assets. Since the maintenance of markets is costly, it is useful to analyze the magnitude of the benefits conferred by the introduction of new markets, either by the more frequent opening of existing markets, or by the opening of new markets in derivative securities. In this article we address these issues in the context of a noisy rational expectations model of the type of Hellwig (1980), by assuming that knowledge about final asset payoffs emerges gradually over time and then considering the effect of allowing investors to trade more frequently. The welfare gain for an individual investor from more frequent trading is shown to be an increasing function of the absolute value of the difference between the precision of his prior information and the risk tolerance weighted average precision of all investors; it is also (and equivalently) an increasing function of the volume of trade of the investor.

We also demonstrate that, for a given number of market sessions, welfare is maximized when information is released in such a way that the variance of price change between successive market sessions is constant over time. This result provides a social justification for disclosure laws that require firms to disclose material new information immediately, rather than saving the disclosure for the periodic financial statement dates.[2] The model also casts light on trading behavior in markets with disparately informed agents.[3] We show that poorly informed agents tend to be "trend-chasers," purchasing more of the risky security when its price rises and selling when its price falls, while better informed agents act as contrarians, selling on a price rise and buying on a fall.[4] Some authors have suggested that the observed increase in purchases of mutual funds when the market has risen is evidence of irrational "barn door closing behavior" [Patel, Zeckhauser, and Hendricks (1991)] — our model suggests rather that such behavior is rational for poorly informed investors who are the ones most likely to purchase mutual funds.[5]

We also show that, for a given number of market sessions, the total

---

[2] Diamond (1985) provides an alternative explanation for why firms wish to release information early.

[3] Previous authors have used the noisy rational expectations model to analyze the effect of public information announcements on the volume of trade. [see, e.g., Grundy and McNicholls (1989), He and Wang (1993), and Kim and Verrecchia (1991a, b)].

[4] This is similar to the result of DeLong et al. (1990) although their result depends on nonrational beliefs on the part of investors, while ours requires only an assumption of information asymmetry.

[5] The behavior of poorly informed investors in our model should be distinguished from that of the positive feedback traders in DeLong et al. (1990) whose demand for the risky security depends on its lagged price change.

volume of trade is maximized when the arrival of new information is smooth, in the sense that the variance of price changes between successive market sessions is constant over time: the volume of trade is proportional to the square root of the number of market openings when the number is large, and approaches infinity as the limit of continuous trading is reached. Thus, the model is able to account for the high volume of trading that is observed in extant securities markets in terms of the portfolio adjustments to new information of investors endowed with information of differential precision:[6] only an infinitesimal level of supply noise is necessary to generate an infinite volume of trading if the market is open continuously and information arrives smoothly.

When the number of market openings increases without limit, the limiting payoff allocation is Pareto efficient,[7] provided that the information flow satisfies a technical smoothness condition. The intuition for this result is that the price process approaches a diffusion, so that the market becomes dynamically complete. In this model in which investors have exponential utility and returns are normally distributed, the Pareto efficient allocation is such that the payoffs of individual investors are quadratic functions of the aggregate payoff — the better informed investors choose trading strategies that yield payoff functions that are concave, while the less well informed synthesize convex payoff functions. The former are analogous to the payoff on a "covered call" strategy, while the latter are similar to a "protective put" strategy. Such strategies have been shown to be optimal for investors whose risk tolerance increases with wealth more or less rapidly than the average, or who have average risk tolerance but are more or less optimistic than the average about the expected return on the security [see Brennan and Solanki (1981) and Leland (1980)]. Our analysis extends the justification of portfolio insurance like payoffs to include differences in the precision of private information when investors have constant (but different) risk tolerance; in interesting contrast to Leland (1980), whether an investor chooses to synthesize a convex or a concave payoff function is independent of the degree of relative optimism, depending only on the precision of the private information signal. The Pareto efficiency of the limiting economy implies that in this economy the prices of derivative claims on the underlying asset satisfy the risk neutral pricing property of the Black and Scholes (1973) model, and are priced using a market consensus volatility.

---

[6] The total volume of trading depends not only on the aggregate supply noise but also on the dispersion of the precisions of the investors' private information.

[7] See also Duffie and Huang (1985) for an analysis of how multiplicity of trading opportunities can substitue for numbers of securities in achieving Pareto efficiency.

Since the Pareto efficient allocation in this model is a quadratic function of the aggregate payoff on the risky security, it can be achieved by the introduction of a derivative claim whose payoff is equal to the square of the difference between the initial security price and its final payoff. The introduction of this derivative claim has no effect on the equilibrium price of the risky security.[8] However, since the resulting equilibrium is Pareto efficient, the no-trade result of Milgrom and Stokey (1982) applies, and no further trade takes place as new public information about the security payoff becomes available. Thus, in this case, the opening of a single derivative security market makes redundant any market opening after time 0, and is a complete substitute for a continuous market in the underlying risky asset.[9]

This article is organized as follows. In Section 1 the basic single trading period model of Hellwig (1980) is presented for reference. Section 2 analyzes the welfare effects of increasing the number of trading sessions, and discusses trading strategies and the volume of trade. Section 3 shows that as the number of trading sessions increases, the payoff allocation approaches Pareto efficiency, subject to a smoothness condition on the public information flow. Section 4 shows that the Pareto efficient allocation can be achieved with a single round of trading if a particular derivative asset is introduced. Section 5 relaxes the assumption that there is only a single supply shock at time 0 and allows for the effects of supply shocks at each trading session. Section 6 concludes the article.

1. The Basic Single-Period Model

Following Hellwig (1980), the market is assumed to consist of a continuum of investors, each indexed by i where $i \in [0, 1]$. At time 0 each investor is endowed with x_i units of the risky asset and, to avoid unnecessary notation, we assume that individual endowments of the riskless asset are zero; without loss of generality, the riskless interest rate is taken as zero. The risky asset pays off at time 1 an amount $\tilde{u}$, where $\tilde{u}$ is normally distributed with mean $\bar{u}$ and precision h. The per capita supply of risky assets, $\tilde{x}$, is normally distributed with mean 0 and precision p. Before trading at time 0 each investor receives a

---

[8] The reason for this is that exponential utility prices are the same as if there existed a single representative investor with characteristics independent of the initial wealth distribution [see Breenan and Kraus (1978) and Rubinstein (1974)]. Since the representative investor does not trade, the prices she supports are independent of the available trading opportunities and securities.

[9] If there are additional supply shocks after time 0, then there will still be trade when the derivative security is introduced.

private signal about the risky asset payoff,

$$\tilde{z}_i = \tilde{u} + \tilde{\epsilon}_i, \tag{1}$$

where $\tilde{\epsilon}_i$ is normally and independently distributed with mean 0 and precision s_i.[10] Investor i has a negative exponential utility function defined over time 1 wealth, $U(w_i) = -\exp(-w_i/r_i)$, where the risk tolerance r_i is assumed to be uniformly bounded.

Let P_0 be the price of the risky asset, D_{0i} be the demand of investor i for the risky asset, $\tilde{F}_{0i}$ denote the information set of investor i, and $\tilde{F}_0$ denote the public information set, including the price at time 0. Investor i's time 1 wealth is given by $w_i = P_0 x_i + (\tilde{u} - P_0)\tilde{D}_{0i}$. It is well known that in this setting [Hellwig (1980)] a linear equilibrium exists in which

$$P_0 = K_0^{-1}[(K_0 - s)\tilde{\mu}_0 + s\tilde{u} - \tilde{x}/r], \tag{2}$$

$$\tilde{D}_{0i} = r_i K_{0i}[\tilde{\mu}_{0i} - P_0] = r_i[s_i \tilde{z}_i - s\tilde{u} + \tilde{x}/r - (s_i - s)P_0], \tag{3}$$

where

$$\tilde{\mu}_0 \equiv E(\tilde{u} \mid \tilde{F}_0) = \frac{b\tilde{u} + r^2 s^2 p\tilde{q}}{b + r^2 s^2 p},$$

$$\tilde{\mu}_{0i} \equiv E(\tilde{u} \mid \tilde{F}_{0i}) = \frac{(K_0 - s)\tilde{\mu}_0 + s_i \tilde{z}_i}{K_{0i}} = \frac{b\tilde{u} + s_i \tilde{z}_i + r^2 s^2 p\tilde{q}}{b + s_i + r^2 s^2 p},$$

$$\tilde{q} = \tilde{u} - \tilde{x}/rs,$$

$$r \equiv \int_0^1 r_i \, di, \quad s \equiv \frac{1}{r}\int_0^1 r_i s_i \, di,$$

$$K_{0i} \equiv \mathrm{var}^{-1}(\tilde{u} \mid \tilde{F}_{0i}) = b + s_i + r^2 s^2 p,$$

$$K_0 \equiv \int_0^1 \frac{r_i}{r} K_{0i} \, di = b + s + r^2 s^2 p.$$

Equation (2) expresses the equilibrium price as a precision weighted average of $\tilde{\mu}_0$, the expected payoff conditional on all public information, and $\tilde{u}$, the average value of the private information signals, less a risk premium that depends on the realized per capita asset supply,

---

[10] Note that we are assuming that investor signal errors are independent. If signal errors are correlated, the equilibrium is qualitatively similar to that described below, except that the coefficients of the linear pricing function in Equation (2) must be derived from the roots of a cubic equation [see Grundy and McNicholls (1989)]; the simplifying assumption made here permits direct calculation of these coefficients.

The Review of Financial Studies / v 9 n 1 1996

$\tilde{x}$. The expected utility of investor i conditional on his endowment, but before receipt of the private information signal, is

$$EU_i = \frac{-1}{\sqrt{L_0 K_{0i}}} \exp\left[\frac{-\bar{u} x_i}{r_i} + \left(\frac{1}{b} - \frac{1}{K_0^2 L_0} \right) \frac{x_i^2}{2r_i^2} \right] \qquad (4)$$

where

$$L_0 \equiv \mathrm{var}(\tilde{u} - \tilde{P}_0) = K_0^{-2}(K_0 + s + r^{-2} p^{-1}).$$

Note that expected utility is decreasing in s: since the informativeness of the price signal, $\tilde{q}$, is increasing in the (weighted) average signal precision, s, this corresponds to the Hirshleifer (1972) finding that an increase in public information can have adverse welfare consequences by reducing risk sharing opportunities. Investor i's wealth at time 1, w_i, is a linear function of the risky asset payoff, $\bar{u}$, and may be written as

$$w_i(\tilde{u}) = P_0 x_i + r_i(\tilde{u} - P_0)\left[s_i(\tilde{z}_i - P_0) + \frac{b(\tilde{u} - P_0)}{1 + r^2 s p} \right]. \qquad (5)$$

The marginal rate of substitution for investor i between wealth contingent on $u = u_l$ and $u = u_k$ is given by

$$\begin{aligned} M_{kl}^i &= \frac{\exp\{-K_{0i}(u_k - \mu_{0i})^2/2 - w_i(u_k)/r_i\}}{\exp\{-K_{0i}(u_l - \mu_{0i})^2/2 - w_i(u_l)/r_i\}} \\ &= \exp\left\{ -\frac{1}{2} K_{0i}(u_k - u_l)(u_k + u_l - 2P_0) \right\}. \end{aligned} \qquad (6)$$

Since the marginal rate of substitution is investor specific through K_{0i}, the precision of the investor's posterior beliefs, this equilibrium in which allocations are constrained to be linear fuctions of the asset payoff is not Pareto efficient.[11]

2. Addtional Market Sessions

In this section we extend the model of the previous section to allow for additional market sessions between time 0 and the asset payoff at time 1. Immediately before each market session there is assumed to be a public signal about the asset payoff, so that the precision of public information about the payoff increases through time. In Section 2.1 we consider the welfare gains from improved risk sharing made possible by the increased trading opportunites. In Section 2.2

---

[11] The notion of Pareto efficiency that we use here and throughout this article is that of ex post conditional Pareto efficiency; that is, Pareto efficiency conditional on P_0 and realized endowments x_i, where expected utility is evaluated using each investor's posterior beliefs.

we analyze the trading strategies of investors in this multisession setting. Section 2.3 is concerned with the volume of trade. Section 2.4 shows that Pareto efficiency is achieved as the number of trading sessions is increased without limit, provided that the information flow is sufficiently smooth. Section 2.5 derives the stochastic process for the asset price as trading becomes continuous.

2.1 Value of additional market sessions

Since the one-period equilibrium is not Pareto efficient, there remain unexploited gains from trade; these could be realized by opening additional (derivative) asset markets, but we consider first the gains from additional openings of the market in the single risky asset, as new information about the final asset payoff becomes publicly available. Specifically, consider a setting in which information about the final payoff $\tilde{u}$ is made available gradually by a series of public signals $\tilde{y}_t = \tilde{u} + \tilde{\eta}_t$ at time $\tau_t = t/T$, $t = 1, \ldots, T-1$, where $\tilde{\eta}_t$ is independently and normally distributed with mean 0 and precision n_t.[12] After each signal the market opens for trading, and at time 1, the return of the risky asset is realized and consumption occurs.[13]

Let P_t denote the price of the risky asset at time τ_t. In a rational expectations equilibrium investors realize that at time τ_t the previous and current prices for the risky security, $\tilde{P}_j$, $j = 0, \ldots, t$, reflect the information held by other traders, and their conjectures about the relation of the price and traders information are self-fulfilling.

Trader i's optimal demand for the risky asset at time τ_t, $\tilde{D}_{ti}$, is required to be $\tilde{F}_{ti}$ measurable, where $\tilde{F}_{ti}$ denotes the subsigma field generated by $\{\tilde{z}_i, \tilde{y}_j, \tilde{P}_j, j = 0, \ldots, t\}$. The subsigma field generated by $\{\tilde{y}_j, \tilde{P}_j, j = 1, \ldots, t\}$ is denoted by $\tilde{F}_t$.

Let a linear conjecture of $\tilde{P}_t$ be written as

$$\tilde{P}_t = \alpha_t \bar{u} + \beta_t \tilde{u} - \gamma_t \tilde{x} + \sum_{j=0}^{t} \theta_{tj} \tilde{y}_j. \tag{7}$$

Then the signal about $\tilde{u}$ derivable from $\tilde{P}_t$ can be written as

$$\tilde{q}_t = \frac{\tilde{P}_t - \alpha_t \bar{u} - \sum_{j=0}^{t} \theta_{tj} \tilde{y}_j}{\beta_t} = \tilde{u} - \frac{\gamma_t}{\beta_t} \tilde{x}. \tag{8}$$

---

[12] The model can be extended to include new random supply shocks of the risky asset, new private information acquisition, and common errors in their private information. For the ease of exposition, we restrict our model to the present setting. Section 6 considers some of these generalizations.

[13] We set $\eta_T = 0$, $n_T = \infty$ to reflect the assumption that risky asset payoff is realized at time 1.

The Review of Financial Studies / v 9 n 1 1996

There are two types of equilibria in this model.[14] In the first type, prices fully reveal private information at the first trading session t, for which $\frac{\gamma_1}{\beta_1} \neq \frac{\gamma_t}{\beta_t}$. For example, if $\frac{\gamma_1}{\beta_1} \neq \frac{\gamma_2}{\beta_2}$ the payoff of the risky asset is revealed at time τ_2 and is equal to

$$\frac{\frac{\beta_1}{\gamma_1}\tilde{q}_1 - \frac{\beta_2}{\gamma_2}\tilde{q}_2}{\frac{\beta_1}{\gamma_1} - \frac{\beta_2}{\gamma_2}}.$$

The price at time τ_2 is equal to the final payoff and individual investor demands are indeterminate. In the second type of equilibrium, the prices only partially reveal the private information; this implies that all the prices contain the same information, so that $\tilde{q}_t = \tilde{q}$ for $t = 0, \ldots, T - 1$. The fully revealing equilibrium lacks intuitive appeal since it requires that $\beta_2 = 1$ and $\gamma_2 = 0$, and investors' demands depend on neither price nor private information; therefore we focus on the partially revealing equilibrium in the remainder of this article.

The rational expectations partially revealing equilibrium is described in the following theorem. All proofs are in the Appendix.[15]

Theorem 1. *In an economy with T trading sessions, there exists a partially revealing rational expectations equilibrium in which prices, and demands for the risky asset, are given by*

$$\tilde{P}_t = K_t^{-1}[(K_t - s)\tilde{\mu}_t + s\tilde{u} - \tilde{x}/r], \tag{9}$$

$$\tilde{D}_{ti} = r_i K_{ti}[\tilde{\mu}_{ti} - \tilde{P}_t] = r_i[s_i\tilde{z}_i - s\tilde{u} + \tilde{x}/r - (s_i - s)\tilde{P}_t], \tag{10}$$

where

$$\tilde{\mu}_t \equiv E(\tilde{u} \mid \tilde{F}_t) = \frac{b\tilde{u} + \sum_{j=0}^{t} n_j\tilde{y}_j + r^2 s^2 p\tilde{q}}{b + \sum_{j=0}^{t} n_j + r^2 s^2 p},$$

$$\tilde{\mu}_{t_i} \equiv E(\tilde{u} \mid \tilde{F}_{ti}) = \frac{(K_t - s_i)\tilde{\mu}_t + s_i\tilde{z}_i}{K_{ti}}$$

$$= \frac{b\tilde{u} + \sum_{j=0}^{t} n_j\tilde{y}_j + s_i\tilde{z}_i + r^2 s^2 p\tilde{q}}{b + \sum_{j=0}^{t} n_j + s_i + r^2 s^2 p},$$

$$\tilde{q} = \tilde{u} - \tilde{x}/rs,$$

---

[14] The fully revealing equilibrium is also discussed in Grundy and McNichols (1989).

[15] Since there is no public information release in the first trading period, for notational simplicity we define $n_0 = 0$, $\tilde{y}_0 = 0$. This model can be easily extended to the case where there is public information in the first period and all the conslusions derived here hold.

$$K_{ti} \equiv var^{-1}(\tilde{u} \mid \tilde{F}_{ti}) = b + s_i + \sum_{j=0}^{t} n_j + r^2 s^2 p,$$

$$K_t \equiv \int_0^1 \frac{r_i}{r} K_{ti} di = b + s + \sum_{j=0}^{t} n_j + r^2 s^2 p.$$

Notice that in this equilibrium the signal from the price is the same in each period since $\frac{Y_t}{\beta_t} = \frac{1}{rs}$ is independent of t, that is, $\tilde{q}_t = \tilde{u} - \bar{x}/rs = \tilde{q}$. Moreover, since P_0 and $\tilde{P}_t$ jointly reveal $\sum_{j=0}^{t} n_j \tilde{y}_j$, the time τ_t price $\tilde{P}_t$ is a sufficient statistic for all the public information flow up to time τ_t. An interesting feature of the equilibrium is that the allocation of securities at time τ_t is not affected by the anticipation of future public announcements.

In the following lemma the expected utility of investor i, conditional on his endowment but before receipt of the private information signal, EU_i, is expressed as a function of his individual, and the market average, precisions in each of the T market sessions.

Lemma 1.

$$EU_i = \prod_{t=1}^{T-1} \sqrt{\frac{K_{(t-1)i}}{K_{(t-1)i} + n_t(s_i - s)^2/K_t^2}}$$

$$\times \frac{-1}{\sqrt{L_0 K_{0i}}} \exp\left[\frac{-\tilde{u} x_i}{r_i} + \left(\frac{1}{b} - \frac{1}{K_0^2 I_0}\right)\frac{x_i^2}{2 r_i^2}\right]. \tag{11}$$

As Kim and Verrecchia (1991a) point out, an investor's expected utility in this type of model can be expressed as the product of the expected utility without any future trade, and a term that corresponds to the utility gain from future trading opportunities. This permits a simple calculation of the monetary value of trading opportunities. Thus define $\gamma_i(T)$ as the (monetary) value of T market sessions for investor i; it is the maximum amount the investor would be willing to pay to have T trading sessions rather than simply one session at time 0. Comparing the expression for expected utility in the single trading session economy of Section 2 with that for the T session economy in Lemma 1, $\gamma_i(T)$ is given by

$$\gamma_i(T) = \frac{r_i}{2} \sum_{t=1}^{T-1} \ln\left(1 + \frac{n_t(s_i - s)^2}{K_t^2 K_{(t-1)i}}\right). \tag{12}$$

Equation (12) implies that the gain from additional market sessions is positive for all investors except those whose private signal precision is equal to the risk tolerance weighted average precision. Contrary to

171

The Review of Financial Studies / v 9 n 1 1996

the effect of an increase in public information before trading, which reduces welfare, the effect of increased public information flow after the initial trading session, combined with the additional trading sessions, is to increase welfare for all investors by improving risk sharing opportunites.[16] The magnitude of the welfare gain depends on the rate at which the individual and the market average posterior precisions, K_t and K_{ti}, change between market sessions, as well as the time pattern of the public signal precisions, n_t. This is intuitive, since if, for example, the first public signal were perfectly precise then there would be no trade in subsequent market sessions, and the number of sessions would then be irrelevant. A reasonable conjecture is that the gains from improved risk sharing through additional trading sessions will be maximized when the variance of price changes between sessions is constant. This conjecture is verified in the following lemma. Define $\nabla \tilde{P}_t \equiv \tilde{P}_t - \tilde{P}_{t-1}$. Then

Lemma 2. $\gamma_i(T)$, *the value of T market sessions for investor i, is maximized when n_t, the precision of the public information signals, is given by*

$$n_t = \frac{TK_0}{(T - t)(T - t + 1)}. \tag{13}$$

This time path of precisions implies that var[∇P_t] is constant. The maximized value of $\gamma_i(T)$ is

$$\gamma_i^*(T) = \frac{r_i}{2}\left[T \ln\left(1 + \frac{s_i - s}{TK_0}\right) - \ln\frac{K_{0i}}{K_0}\right]. \tag{14}$$

The lemma implies that welfare is maximized for all investors when information about the asset payoff is released smoothly over time so that the variance of price changes between market sessions is equal. Additional market openings allow traders to take linear positions in a finer partition of the aggregate price change $\tilde{u} - P_0$. As will be shown in Section 3, in a continuous-time economy it is optimal for investors to synthesize by a dynamic trading strategy a payoff that is a quadratic function of the asset payoff; equalizing the variance of price changes between sessions allows traders to minimize the certainty equivalent cost of "hedging errors" given their exponential utility functions.

The lemma suggests that if the firm receives information smoothly then a policy of immediate disclosure is optimal. On the other hand, if information is received by the firm in a lumpy fashion, then the lemma suggests that risk sharing could be improved if the public release of

---

[16] In this setting there is no endowment effect associated with the increased trading sessions since P_0 remains unchanged.

Table 1
The value of additional market sessions for an investor, as a function of his relative signal precision $(s_i - s)$.

σ_{0i}	$s_i - s$	2	4	8	16	T 32	64	128	256	512	8192
0.05	300	558	1065	1452	1704	1852	1932	1974	1995	2006	2016
0.06	178	451	809	1051	1195	1275	1317	1339	1350	1355	1361
0.07	104	305	519	650	723	762	782	792	797	800	802
0.08	56	158	256	311	341	356	364	368	370	371	372
0.09	23	45	70	83	90	93	95	96	96	96	97
0.11	−17	55	80	92	98	100	102	103	103	103	103
0.12	−31	238	337	382	404	415	420	423	424	425	425
0.13	−41	575	795	893	939	962	973	978	981	983	984
0.14	−49	1089	1475	1642	1720	1758	1776	1786	1790	1793	1795

σ_{0i} is the standard deviation of the investor's posterior distribution over the asset payoff. T is the number of trading sessions per period. The example is constructed so that the risky asset has an expected return of about 10 percent per period, and the investor invests about $100,000 in the risky asset. The values in the table are in dollars.

the information could be smoothed out; there are obvious practical difficulties in implementing such a policy. To illustrate the effect on welfare gains of the number of trading sessions and the degree of information asymmetry, we consider an example in which the time period is 1 year, $\bar{u} = 1.1$, $K_0 = 100$, and the average per capita supply is such that on average $P_0 = 1$; this corresponds roughly to a situation in which the expected return per year on the risky asset is 10 percent of the average price, and the standard deviation of the (conditional) annual return is also 10 percent. Thus the example is intended to represent the value of more than one trading session per year. In Table 1 we report the values of $\gamma_i^*(T)$ for individual i whose risk tolerance, r_i, is chosen so that $\tilde{D}_{ti}$ is equal to $\$100,000$ when $\tilde{\mu}_{0i} = \bar{u}$. On average, such an investor will invest approximately $100,000 in the risky asset. In the table $\sigma_{0i} = \sqrt{1/K_{0i}}$ denotes the standard deviation of investor i's posterior distribution of the risky asset return, given the price P_0 and investor i's private signal.

The table shows that the potential welfare gains for both the well informed and the poorly informed are substantial; for example, for an investor with no private information ($s_i = 0$, so that $s_i - s = -49$), the value of additional trading sessions is as much as 1.8 percent of his investment in the risky security, or 18 percent of the expected return on the risky asset. For a well-informed investor ($s_i - s = 300$) the value of the additional trading opportunities is about 2.0 percent of his investment in the risky security. However, it is notable that the bulk of the welfare gain is realized with about 16 trading sessions per year. Thus the model suggests that the welfare gains from introducing round-the-clock trading are likely to be modest. Nevertheless, it is interesting to note that for an investor with about $100,000 invested in

The Review of Financial Studies / v 9 n 1 1996

the risky asset, the better informed he is, the more he is willing to pay for near continuous trading. For example, the best informed investor represented in the table would be willing to pay $21 to increase the number of trading sessions from 256 per year, or roughly daily, to 8,192, or roughly 32 times per day; the uninformed investor on the other hand would be willing to pay only $5 for the same increase in trading sessions.

2.2 Trading strategies and price behavior

In order to characterize investors' trading strategies we consider the change in the demand of investor i for the risky asset between successive market sessions:[17] using Equations (9) and (10), we have

$$\tilde{D}_{(t+1)i} - \tilde{D}_{ti} = -r_i(s_i - s)(\tilde{P}_{t+1} - \tilde{P}_t). \tag{15}$$

The following corollaries characterize the relation between price moves and the trades of investors.

Corollary 1.
   (i) *The trades of the well-informed investors ($s_i > s$) at time τ_t are negatively correlated with the price change at time τ_t.*
   (ii) *The trades of the poorly informed investors ($s_i < s$) in each trading session t are positively correlated with the price change at time τ_t;*
   (iii) *The trades of the poorly informed investors at time τ_t are negatively correlated with those of the well-informed investors at time τ_{t-1}.*
   (iv) *The averagely informed investors ($s_i = s$) will not trade.*
   (v) *Trades exhibit positive autocorrelation for all investors.*

Corollary 2. *The price change at time τ_{t+1} is negatively correlated with the price and is positively correlated with the price change at time τ_t, that is,*

$$cov(\tilde{P}_{t+1} - \tilde{P}_t, \tilde{P}_t) < 0, \tag{16}$$

$$cov(\tilde{P}_{t+1} - \tilde{P}_t, \tilde{P}_t - \tilde{P}_{t-1}) > 0. \tag{17}$$

The intuition for these two corollaries is that well-informed investors sell when the price is high and buy when the price is low, since they have more precise information about the risky asset payoff than the average investor. Less-informed investors rely more on the signal revealed by the price, and therefore buy when the price is high and sell when it is low. Corollary 1 shows that positive correlation

---

[17] Kim and Verrecchia (1991b) analyze trades and trading volume in a two trading session economy with two public signals.

between mutual fund sales and market returns does not necessarily imply irrational "barn-door closing" behavior on the part of the small investors who purchase these funds; rather, it is fully consistent with rational behavior for investors who are less well informed. Warther (1994) reports that security returns are strongly related to contemporaneous cash flows into mutual funds: there is no lagged relation such as would be predicted by trend following behavior, and he is unable to explain the phenomenon in terms of price pressure. However, it is quite consistent with the predictions of Corollary 1 if mutual fund investors are less well informed than average, and therefore place greater weight on new public information signals than the market as a whole.[18] The aggressiveness of traders is proportional to their risk tolerance. In addition, when the proportion of uninformed traders increases (s decreases), informed traders trade more aggressively.

2.3 Volume of trade
The sources of price volatility and trading volume and their interrelation are topics of enduring interest in financial economics. The numerous empirical studies that have examined the contemporaneous behavior of volume and absolute price changes have found a positive correlation between the two [Karpoff (1987)]. Since the dynamics of price volatility and trading volume can only be studied in a multiple trading session economy, in this section we extend the results of Kim and Verrecchia (1991b) to a T session economy, and present new results on the autocorrelation properties of trading volume and the relation between trading volume and the frequency of trading.

Let $\nabla \tilde{P}_t = P_t - \tilde{P}_{t-1}$, $t = 1, \ldots, T - 1$ denote the price change at time τ_t. Let trading volume at time τ_t, V_t, be defined as one-half the sum of all purchases and sales,[19] that is,

$$V_t = \frac{1}{2} \int_0^1 |\tilde{D}_{ti} - \tilde{D}_{(t-1)i}| \, di = \frac{1}{2} \int_0^1 r_i |s_i - s| \, di |\nabla \tilde{P}_t|. \tag{18}$$

In our model there is no hedging demand for the risky asset, and all trading is informationally based. As a result we obtain the simple result that the trading volume in each period is proportional to the product of the absolute price change and the dispersion of investors' private information precisions.[20] Expected volume at time τ_t, $E[V_t]$, is

---

[18] Capon, Fitzsimons, and Prince (1993) cite evidence of lack of sophistication among mutual fund investors.

[19] Note that D_{Ti} is not well defined since the risky asset becomes riskless at time 1. Nevertheless, we can define $\tilde{D}_{Ti} = r_i(s_i \tilde{z}_i - s\tilde{q} + (s - s_i)\tilde{u})$ to preserve the relation between demands and prices expressed in Equation (10).

[20] A similar result is obtained by Harris and Raviv (1993) in a model in which investors have different

The Review of Financial Studies / v 9 n 1 1996

obtained from Equation (18) by noting that $E[\nabla \tilde{P}_t] = 0$ and using an elementary property of the normal distribution:

$$E[V_t] = \sqrt{\frac{\text{var}[\nabla \tilde{P}_t]}{2\pi}} \int_0^1 r_i |s_i - s| \, di.$$

Since

$$\text{var}[\nabla \tilde{P}_t] = \frac{n_t}{K_{t-1} K_t} + \frac{n_t^2}{K_{t-1}^2 K_t^2} \left(s + \frac{1}{r^2 p} \right),$$

it is straightforward to show that the expected volume at time τ_t is increasing in the precision of the public information signal at time τ_t, n_t, and decreasing in the prior average precision, K_{t-1}.

In Corollary 2, we have shown that price changes are negatively serially correlated. Since the correlation coefficient between the absolute values of two normally distributed variables $\tilde{x}$ and $\tilde{y}$ with correlation $r(\tilde{x}, \tilde{y})$ and means equal to zero is given by

$$corr(|\tilde{x}|, |\tilde{y}|) = \frac{2}{\pi - 2} \int_0^{r(\tilde{x}, \tilde{y})} \arcsin t \, dt > 0.$$

The following lemma is immediate.

Lemma 3. *The absolute price change and the volume of trade are positively serially correlated.*

The lemma is consistent with the empirical evidence of Harris (1987) on the autocorrelation of trading volume and squared price changes [see also Harris and Raviv (1993)].

We saw in Lemma 2 that welfare is maximized when the variance of price changes between market sessions is equalized. In the following lemma, we show that the expected volume of trade is also maximized when the variance of price changes between market sessions is equalized.

The total volume of trade in an economy with T trading sessions is given by

$$Volume = \sum_{t=1}^{T} V_t.$$

Using Equation (18) for V_t we get

Lemma 4.

(i) The expected total volume of trade in a T trading session economy

---

opinions and so ignore the information in price.

is maximized when the variance of the price change at time τ_t is the same for all $t = 1, \ldots, T - 1$.

(ii) When T is large the expected trading volume is proportional to the square root of T, that is,

$$E[Volume] = Q\sqrt{\frac{1}{2\pi}}\sqrt{\frac{K_0 T + s + r^{-2}p^{-1}}{K_0^2}} = Q\sqrt{\frac{T}{2\pi K_0}} + O\left(\sqrt{\frac{1}{T}}\right),$$

where $Q \equiv \int \frac{1}{2}r_i|s_i - s|\,di$ measures information asymmetry and $O(\sqrt{\frac{1}{T}})$ means of order $\sqrt{\frac{1}{T}}$.

The lemma implies that if information arrives smoothly so that price volatility is constant, then the small amount of supply noise or noise trading in the first trading session necessary to prevent the price from being fully revealing can give rise to an unlimited amount of rational trading volume as the number of market sessions increases without limit. The lemma implies that for large T the expected volume per session is proportional to $\sqrt{1/T}$.

3. Convergence to a Continuous-Time Economy

In Section 3.1 we demonstrate formally that as the number of trading sessions increases without limit the wealth allocation converges to the Pareto efficient allocation, provided that the information flow is sufficiently smooth. The intuition for this result is that the multiplication of trading opportunities made possible by a large number of trading sessions makes the market essentially complete with only two securities, the riskless asset and the risky security. We also show that the Pareto efficiency of the limiting economy implies that derivative securities (which are of course redundant) are priced according to Black and Scholes (1973) principles and that the volatility used to price derivative assets is the inverse of the risk tolerance weighted average of the posterior precisions of the individual investors, K_0^{-1}. In Section 3.2 we present a heuristic continuous time model which shows that, despite their different information sets, investors agree on the variation of the price process, and this agreement is of course necessary if they are to agree on the prices of derivative assets.

3.1 Pareto efficiency in the limiting economy

It was shown in Section 1 that the allocation of wealth achieved with a single trading session is not Pareto efficient, and it is straightforward to extend this result to a setting with multiple trading sessions. However, as we have seen, investor welfare is an increasing function of the number of trading sessions, and it is natural to conjecture that Pareto efficiency will be achieved as the number of trading sessions increases without limit. In this section we show that as the number of trading sessions is increased, the equilibrium wealth allocation converges in probability to the Pareto optimal allocation.

As we increase the number of trading sessions we impose the requirement that the public information flow is sufficiently smooth that the variance of the price changes between trading sessions tends to zero. Formally, we assume **Condition A**:

$$\max_t \operatorname{var}[\nabla \tilde{P}_t] = O(\nabla t). \tag{19}$$

The following lemma, which is used in the proof of Theorem 2, gives the limiting vlaue of $\gamma_i(T)$ and the expected utility of the investor as the number of trading sessions approaches infinity.

Lemma 5. *If the information structure satisfies Condition A, then as* $T \to \infty$: *(i)* $\gamma_i(T)$, *the value of the additional trading opportunities for investor i converges to*

$$\gamma_i^*(T) = \frac{r_i}{2}[(K_{0i} - K_0)/K_0 - \ln(K_{0i}/K_0)]; \tag{20}$$

(ii) His ex ante utility converges to

$$EU_i^* = \frac{-1}{\sqrt{L_0 K_0}} \exp\left[\frac{-\bar{u}x_i}{r_i} - \frac{s_i - s}{2K_0} + \left(\frac{1}{b} - \frac{1}{K_0^2 L_0}\right) \frac{x_i^2}{2r_i^2}\right]. \tag{21}$$

Thus, as the frequency of trading opportunities increases, the utility of the investor no longer depends on the time path of the public information signal precision as it does in the finite trading session economy as shown in Lemma 1. The following theorem shows that in the limit, each investor's wealth converges in probability to the expost conditional Pareto efficient wealth allocation.

Theorem 2.

(i) The wealth of investor i at period 1 converges in probability to $w_i^e(\tilde{u})$ *as* $T \to \infty$, *where* $w_i^e(\tilde{u})$ *is given by*

$$w_i^e(\tilde{u}) = P_0 x_i + (\tilde{u} - P_0)\tilde{D}_{0i} + \frac{1}{2}r_i(s - s_i)[(\tilde{u} - P_0)^2 - K_0^{-1}], \tag{22}$$

and D_{0i} *is as given in Equation (3).*

(ii) The allocation $w_i^e(\tilde{u})$ *is Pareto optimal, given the period 0 information and initial endowments, and the expected utility of each*

investor converges to that yielded by the Pareto efficient allocation $w_i^e(\tilde{u})$, as $T \to \infty$.

Thus, while partially revealing rational expectations models of markets in which there are only two securities and investors have information of different precisions yield equilibria that are Pareto inefficient, the introduction of continuous trading opportunities effectively makes the market complete, yielding a Pareto efficient allocation.[21] We note from Equation (22) that the Pareto optimal payoff for investor i is a quadratic function of the risky asset payoff, $\tilde{u}$, which is concave (convex) if the investor's private information is more (less) precise than that of the risk tolerance weighted average. Moreover, while the payoff depends on the investor's private information signal, $\tilde{z}_i$, through $\tilde{D}_{0i}$, it does not depend on the public information signals, $\tilde{y}_j$.[22]

Lemma 6. *As the limiting economy is Pareto efficient, it follows from the results of Brennan and Kraus (1978) and Rubinstein (1974) that, in the limiting economy, security prices are as if there existed a single representative investor with risk tolerance r, and beliefs $N(\mu_R, K_0^{-1})$, where $\mu_R = K_0^{-1}[b\tilde{u} + (s + r^2 s^2 p)\tilde{u} - rsp\tilde{x}]$.*

Given that prices are supported by a representative investor with constant absolute risk aversion, and that from his perspective the return on the single risky asset is normally distributed with parameters $N(\mu_R, K_0^{-1})$, it follows from the results of Brennan (1979) that all contingent claims on the risky asset are priced in accord with Black and Scholes (1973) principles, that is, as though the return on the risky asset were distributed normally with mean P_0 and variance K_0^{-1}.[23] In particular, the price of a call option on the underlying risky asset with exercise price E, $C'(P_0; E)$ is given by

$$C(P_0; E) = N\left(\frac{P_0 - E}{\sigma}\right) + \sigma n\left(\frac{E - P_0}{\sigma}\right), \tag{23}$$

where $n(\cdot)$ and $N(\cdot)$ are the standard normal density and standard normal distribution functions, respectively, and $\sigma = \sqrt{1/K_0}$. Equation (23) shows that in this noisy rational expectations equilibrium with hetero-

---

[21] Duffie and Huang (1985) have shown that when information is homogeneous a Pareto efficient allocation can be achieved by dynamic trading in a market with a few long-lived securities, provided that the martingale multiplicity of the information structure is not greater than one less than the number of securities. Their martingale multiplicity condition plays the same role as our Condition A.

[22] Laffont (1985) presents an example in which the allocation achievable by a linear rational expectations equilibrium is Pareto dominated by an incentive compatible mechanism in which the allocation is allowed to be nonlinear in the *private* information.

[23] If the gross interest factor is R then the mean is $P_0 R$.

The Review of Financial Studies / v 9 n 1 1996

geneous private information precision and continuous trading, not only does the price of the risky asset aggregate the private information about the mean of the asset payoffs, but the prices of derivative assets aggregate the posterior precisions of the individual investors. Note that in this model investors are able to agree on the price of the derivative asset despite having different assessments of the variance of the asset payoff, K_{0i}^{-1}.[24] We shall see in the next section, however, that investors do agree on the instantaneous volatility of the price process.

3.2 A heuristic continuous-time model

To analyze the trading of investors in a continuous-time model, it is convenient to assume that the public information at time τ can be summarized by the sufficient statistic $\tilde{Y}_\tau = \tilde{u} + \tilde{\zeta}_\tau$,[25] where ζ_τ follows the stochastic process

$$d\zeta_\tau = -\frac{n_\tau}{K_\tau - K_0}\zeta_\tau d\tau + \frac{\sqrt{n_\tau}}{K_\tau - K_0}dz, \qquad (24)$$

where $K_\tau - K_0 = \int_0^\tau n_t\, dt$ and $\int_0^t n_\tau\, d\tau \overset{t \to 1}{\longrightarrow} \infty$ to ensure that the public information eventually reveals the risky asset payoff $\tilde{u}$ at time 1. Let $\tilde{P}_\tau$ denote the price and $\tilde{D}_{\tau i}$ denote the demand of investor i for the risky asset at time τ. Let $\tilde{F}_{\tau i}$ denote the filtration generated by $\{\tilde{P}_t, \tilde{y}_t, 0 \le t \le \tau, \tilde{z}_i\}$ and $\tilde{F}_\tau$ denote the filtration generated by $\{\tilde{P}_t, \tilde{y}_t, 0 \le t \le \tau\}$. It follows from our previous results that in this economy there exists an equilibrium as described in the following theorem.

Theorem 3. *There exists a partially revealing rational expectations equilibrium in which prices and demands for the risky asset are given by*

$$\tilde{P}_\tau = K_\tau^{-1}[(K_\tau - s)\tilde{\mu}_\tau + s\tilde{u} - \tilde{x}/r], \qquad (25)$$

$$\tilde{D}_{\tau i} = r_i K_{\tau i}[\tilde{\mu}_{\tau i} - \tilde{P}_\tau] = r_i[s_i\tilde{z}_i - s\tilde{u} + \tilde{x}/r - (s_i - s)\tilde{P}_\tau], \qquad (26)$$

where

$$\tilde{\mu}_{\tau i} \equiv E(\tilde{u} \mid \tilde{F}_{\tau i}) = \frac{b\tilde{u} + s_i\tilde{z}_i + (K_\tau - K_0)\tilde{Y}_\tau + r^2 s^2 p\tilde{q}}{K_{\tau i}},$$

$$\tilde{q} = \tilde{u} - \tilde{x}/rs,$$

---

[24] This result extends also to a multiasset version of the noisy rational expectations economy.

[25] In discrete time, the sufficient statistic is given by $\tilde{Y}_{\tau_t} \equiv \sum_{j=0}^t n_j\tilde{y}_j/\sum_{j=0}^t n_j$, so that $\tilde{\zeta}_{\tau_t} \equiv \tilde{Y}_{\tau_t} - \tilde{u} = \sum_{j=0}^t n_j\tilde{\eta}_j/\sum_{j=0}^t n_j$ and $\nabla\tilde{\zeta}_{\tau_t} \equiv \tilde{\zeta}_{\tau_t} - \tilde{\zeta}_{\tau_{t-1}} = -n_t\tilde{\zeta}_{\tau_{t-1}}/\sum_{j=0}^t n_j + n_t\tilde{\eta}_t/\sum_{j=0}^t n_j$.

$$K_{\tau i} \equiv var^{-1}(\tilde{u} \mid \tilde{F}_{\tau i}) = K_\tau + s_i - s,$$

$$K_\tau \equiv \int_0^1 \frac{r_i}{r} K_{\tau i} \, di = b + s + \int_0^\tau n_t \, dt + r^2 s^2 p.$$

The price process conditional on $\tilde{u}$ is obtained by applying Ito's Lemma to Equation (25):

$$d\tilde{P}_\tau = \frac{n_\tau}{K_\tau}(\tilde{u} - \tilde{P}_\tau)d\tau + \frac{\sqrt{n_\tau}}{K_\tau} dz, \tag{27}$$

where dz is the increment to a standard Wiener process.

However, investors have only imperfect information about $\tilde{u}$, and the price process adapted to the filtration $\tilde{F}_{\tau i}$ is obtained by noting that conditional on the filtration $\tilde{F}_{\tau i}$ the public signal follows a stochastic process of the form

$$d\tilde{Y}_\tau = -\frac{n_\tau}{K_\tau - K_0}(\tilde{\mu}_{\tau i} - \tilde{Y}_\tau) + \frac{\sqrt{n_\tau}}{K_\tau - K_0} dz_i. \tag{28}$$

This yields the adapted price process:

$$d\tilde{P}_\tau = \frac{n_\tau}{K_\tau}(\tilde{\mu}_{\tau i} - \tilde{P}_\tau)d\tau + \frac{\sqrt{n_\tau}}{K_\tau} dz_i. \tag{29}$$

Notice that although different investors have different estimates about the drift of the price, they agree on the variation process of the price. This conforms with the no arbitrage requirement in Duffie and Huang (1986) that the variation process should be the same for all individuals even when there is differential information. The variation process of $\tilde{P}$, $[\tilde{P}, \tilde{P}]_\tau$ is given by $P_0^2 + \int_0^\tau \frac{n_t}{K_t^2} \, dt = P_0^2 + \frac{1}{K_0} - \frac{1}{K_\tau}$.

The final wealth for investor i in this continuous-time model is found from Equations (25) and (26):

$$
\begin{aligned}
w_i(\tilde{u}) &= P_0 x_i + \int_0^1 \tilde{D}(t) \, d\tilde{P}(t) \\
&= P_0 x_i + (\tilde{u} - P_0)\tilde{D}_{0i} + r_i(s - s_i) \int_0^1 (\tilde{P} - P_0) \, d\tilde{P} \\
&= P_0 x_i + (\tilde{u} - P_0)\tilde{D}_{0i} + \frac{r_i}{2}(s - s_i)(\tilde{u} - P_0)^2 \\
&\quad - \frac{r_i}{2}(s - s_i)[\tilde{P} - P_0, \tilde{P} - P_0]_1 \\
&= P_0 x_i + (\tilde{u} - P_0)\tilde{D}_{0i} + \frac{r_i}{2}(s - s_i)[(\tilde{u} - P_0)^2 - K_0^{-1})]. \tag{30}
\end{aligned}
$$

Comparing Equations (22) and (30), the final wealth of each investor in the continuous-time economy is identical to that in the limiting discrete-time economy; since we saw that the Black and Scholes (1973) option pricing result obtained in the limiting economy, it holds also in this continuous-time economy. This is in contrast to the result of Back (1993) who also analyzes option pricing in a continuous-time economy with differentially informed investors and finds that the Black and Scholes (1973) result does not hold — the major differences between his model and ours is that he assumes that there is net supply noise in the options market and that there is only one informed investor who behaves monopolistically; the results of Holden and Subrahmanyam (1992) suggest that this assumption is critical in preventing the private information from being instantaneously revealed.

4. Pareto Efficiency with a Single Round of Trading and a Quadratic Option

Since in this model with exponential utility and normal payoff distribution, the Pareto efficient allocation of wealth $w_i^e(\tilde{u})$ given in Equation (22) is a quadratic function of the final payoff of the risky asset $\tilde{u}$, the Pareto efficient allocation can be achieved in only a single round of trading if the set of available securities is extended to include a derivative asset with a payoff that is a quadratic function of $\tilde{u}$.[26] In this section we introduce into the market at time 0 a derivative asset whose payoff at time 1 is $C(\tilde{u}) = (\tilde{u} - P_0)^2$.[27] The derivative asset or option is in zero net supply. Theorem 4 establishes that there exists an equilibrium in which the Pareto efficient allocation is achieved in one round of trading, and the price of the risky asset is the same as in the basic single-period model.

Theorem 4. *Let P_C denote the price of the option and D_{C0i} denote the demand for the option by investor i in the first period. Then there exists a rational expectations partially revealing equilibrium in the economy with the option in which*

$$P_0 = K_0^{-1}[b\bar{u} + (s + r^2 s^2 p)\tilde{u} - (r^{-1} + rsp)\tilde{x}], \qquad (31)$$

$$\tilde{D}_{0i} = r_i K_{0i}[\tilde{\mu}_{0i} - P_0] = r_i[s_i\tilde{z}_i - s_i\tilde{u} + \tilde{x}/r - (s_i - s)P_0], \qquad (32)$$

$$P_C = K_0^{-1}, \qquad (33)$$

---

[26] Nau and McCardle (1991), who have also recognized the role of a quadratic payoff in achieving a Pareto efficient allocation in a model with exponential utility and normal distributions when investors' posterior beliefs have different precisions, point out that such a payoff can be achieved by purchasing "straddles" composed of uniform distributions of call and put options at all exercise prices.

[27] Similar results obtain if the derivative asset has a general quadratic payoff.

$$D_{C0i} = \frac{r_i}{2}(P_C^{-1} - K_{0i}) = \frac{r_i}{2}(s - s_i). \tag{34}$$

It is straightforward to show that the wealth allocation in this economy is the Pareto efficient allocation $w_i^e(\tilde{u})$. In this equilibrium, the
less-informed investors ($s_i < s$) take long positions in the option,
while the well-informed ($s_i > s$) investors take short positions. Let
trading volume in the option be defined as the gross long position,

$$Volume(C) \equiv \frac{1}{2}\int_0^1 |D_{Ci}|\, di.$$

Then we have

$$Volume(C) = Q/2,$$

where

$$Q \equiv \int_0^1 \frac{1}{2}r_i|s_i - s|\, di.$$

The volume of trade in the option is equal to half of the asymmetric
information measure Q, and the demand for the option arises because
of the differences in the precision of investors' private information,
so that if every investor had the same precision of information, the
demand for the option would be zero. Thus the Pareto inefficiency in
the one trading session economy with only one risky asset is due to
the differences in the precision of the private information of investors.

Theorem 4 shows that the introduction of a new option achieves
the same goal as continuous market sessions in improving social welfare. However, the continuous trading economy requires an infinite
volume of trading as we saw in Section 2.3. It is apparent that if there
is any social cost to trading then the introduction of a derivative asset
is more efficient than the introduction of continuous trading in promoting investor welfare. The option would be redundant in an infinite
trading session economy since it can be replicated by dynamic trading
strategies in equilibrium. Nevertheless, if the option is introduced in
the first trading session, investors will trade in it and arrive at a Pareto
optimal allocation wealth. Then, according to the Milgrom and Stokey
(1982) theorem, there will be no further trade as additional public or
private information arrives.

While there will be no trade following public information arrivals, it
is easy to show that the shadow price of the risky asset at time τ_1 will
still be $\tilde{P}_1$. The shadow price of the option at time τ_1 will be changed
to $P_{C1} = K_1^{-1} + (\tilde{P}_1 - P_0)^2 = P_{C0} + \{(\tilde{P}_1 - P_0)^2 - E_{\tau 0}[(\tilde{P}_1 - P_0)^2]\}$,
where $E_{\tau 0}[\cdot]$ denotes expectations of a representative investor (who
has signal precision s and takes no position in the risky asset or the
option) at time 0. Thus the shadow price of the option increases with

The Review of Financial Studies / v 9 n 1 1996

realized price volatility. However, since everybody now wants to hold more of the option, there is no further trade in it.

If new private information arrives after the first round of trading, the final asset payoff will be fully revealed and the volume of trade is not well defined since the risky asset becomes riskless.

5. Further Results for an Economy with Options

In this section we extend our analysis of the economy with quadratic options. In Section 5.1 we consider an economy with two trading sessions and a second supply shock in the second session; the equilibrium is analyzed both with and without a quadratic option. In Section 5.2 we consider the effect on trade of additional private signals prior to the later trading sessions. In Section 5.3 we compare the measure of investors who have no private information with the market maker of the Kyle (1985) model, by analyzing the relation between the trades of the uninformed measure of investors and the price change and comparing it with the relation between price change and order flow in the Kyle model. In Section 5.4 we analyze an economy with only short-term options and consider the dynamic trading strategies that this entails.

5.1 The effect of additional supply shocks in an economy with options

We have seen in Section 4 that there will be no trade after a public signal if a quadratic option is traded in an earlier market session, since the option is sufficient to ensure that the resulting equilibrium is Pareto efficient. However, that result was predicated on there being no further supply shocks. Now we assume that new liquidity traders enter the market in the second trading session with exogenously determined per capita supply $\tilde{x}_1$, which is distributed normally with mean 0 and precision p_1. Then there exists an equilibrium described in the following theorem in which the price in the second session adjusts to reflect the new public signal and the supply shock, but does not reveal any further private information.

Theorem 5.
(i) *In an economy with two trading sessions, a single risky asset, and a new supply shock in the second trading session, there exists a partially revealing rational expectations equilibrium in which prices and demands for the risky asset are given by*

$$P_0 = K_0^{-1}[(K_0 - s)\tilde{\mu}_0 + s\tilde{u} - \tilde{x}/r], \qquad (35)$$

$$\tilde{D}_{0i} = r_i K_{0i}[\tilde{\mu}_{0i} - P_0] = r_i[s_i\tilde{z}_i - s\tilde{u} + \tilde{x}/r - (s_i - s)P_0], \qquad (36)$$

$$\tilde{P}_1 = K_1^{-1}[(K_1 - s)\tilde{\mu}_1 + s\tilde{u} - (\tilde{x} + \tilde{x}_1)/r], \qquad (37)$$

$$\tilde{D}_{1i} = r_i K_{1i}[\tilde{\mu}_{1i} - \tilde{P}_1] = \tilde{D}_{0i} + r_i(s - s_i)(\tilde{P}_1 - \tilde{P}_0) + \frac{r_i\tilde{x}_1}{r}. \qquad (38)$$

(ii) If a quadratic option with payoff $(\tilde{u} - P_0)^2$ is introduced into the market in the first trading session, then there exists the following equilibrium:

$$P_0 = K_0^{-1}[(K_0 - s)\tilde{\mu}_0 + s\tilde{u} - \tilde{x}/r], \qquad (39)$$

$$\tilde{D}_{0i} = r_i K_{0i}[\tilde{\mu}_{0i} - P_0] = r_i[s_i\tilde{z}_i - s\tilde{u} + \tilde{x}/r - (s_i - s)P_0], \qquad (40)$$

$$\tilde{P}_1 = K_1^{-1}[(K_1 - s)\tilde{\mu}_1 + s\tilde{u} - (\tilde{x} + \tilde{x}_1)/r], \qquad (41)$$

$$\tilde{D}_{1i} = \tilde{D}_{0i} + \frac{r_i\tilde{x}_1}{r}, \qquad (42)$$

$$P_{C0} = K_0^{-1} + [K_1(1 + K_1 r^2 p_1)]^{-1}, \quad \tilde{P}_{C1} = (\tilde{P}_1 - P_0)^2 + K_1^{-1}, \qquad (43)$$

$$D_{C0i} = \frac{r_i}{2}\left(\frac{1}{P_{C0} - [K_1(1 + K_1 r^2 p_1)]^{-1}} - K_{0i}\right) = \frac{r_i}{2}(s - s_i), \qquad (44)$$

$$D_{C1i} = \frac{r_i}{2}\left(\frac{1}{\tilde{P}_{C1} - (\tilde{P}_1 - P_0)^2} - K_{1i}\right) = \frac{r_i}{2}(s - s_i). \qquad (45)$$

The only effect of the second session supply noise is to shift the second period risky asset price by an amount that is proportional to the noise realization.

When there is no option, the trade of investor i in the second market session is given by

$$\nabla \tilde{D}_{1i} \equiv \tilde{D}_{1i} - \tilde{D}_{0i} = \frac{r_i\tilde{x}_1}{r} + r_i(s - s_i)(\tilde{P}_1 - \tilde{P}_0).$$

The first component of the trade, $r_i\tilde{x}/r$, is investor i's share of the increased supply made available by liquidity traders. The second component is the informational trade generated by the differential responses of investors with different prior precisions to the public signal. However, as Equation (42) shows, introduction of the quadratic option eliminates the second motive for trade, so that in equilibrium there are only liquidity trades, and it can be shown that the net result is a decrease in the volume of trading in the risky asset.[28]

---

[28] In contrast Skinner (1989) finds an adjusted increase of 4 percent in the volume of trading in the underlying security following the introduction of options trading. However, see the discussion following Theorem 6.

The Review of Financial Studies / v 9 n 1 1996

A striking feature of the equilibria described in Theorem 5 is that the price of the underlying risky asset is in no way affected by the introduction of trading in the option. This contrasts with the theoretical results of Detemple and Selden (1991) who find that in an incomplete markets economy with quadratic utility and a particular type of difference of opinion, the introduction of options trading raises the price of the underlying asset. It also conflicts with the bulk of the empirical evidence on the effects of the introduction of option trading, which finds a positive effect on the underlying asset price.[29] However, Figlewski and Webb (1993) provide a possible explanation by showing that one effect of options trading is to relax constraints on short sales which, while assumed away in our model, may be important in practice. In addition, we have ignored any effect of option introduction on incentives to collect information [see Cao (1994)]. Several authors have suggested that options are a more attractive investment for informed investors than the underlying stock,[30] and Easley, O'Hara, and Srinivas (1993) construct a sequential trade model in which informed traders prefer to trade in the options. They, as well as Amin and Lee (1993), find evidence of informed trading in the options market. However, in our model it is the investors with the less precise signals who have the greatest demand for the option, and the demand for the option depends only on the private signal precision and not the signal realization: thus in our model trading in the option conveys no information about the asset payoff. Empirical evidence on lead-lag relations between stock and options markets remains inconclusive, despite earlier claims that options lead stocks [e.g., Manaster and Rendleman (1982)]; our model is consistent with the recent findings of Chan, Chung, and Johnson (1993) who conclude that neither market leads the other.

In the economy with the option, the final wealth of investor i is given by

$$w_i(\tilde{u}, \tilde{x}_1) = P_0 x_i + \tilde{D}_{0i}(\tilde{u} - \tilde{P}_0) + \frac{r_i \tilde{x}_1}{r}(\tilde{u} - P_0)$$

$$+ \frac{r_i}{2}(s - s_i)[(\tilde{u} - P_0)^2 - P_{C0}],$$

---

[29] Jennings and Starks (1986) and Skinner (1990) find evidence that the introduction of option trading causes the underlying risky asset to be priced more efficiently. Conrad (1989) reports that the introduction of option trading is accompanied by an increase in the price of the underlying asset and a reduction in its volatility. Similar results are reported by Detemple and Jorion (1990), who also find that the introduction of options trading on an individual stock is associated with an increase in the level of the industry and overall market prices. On the other hand, Lamoureaux (1991) finds that the introduction of options has no effect on the price volatility of the underlying asset.

[30] Skinner (1989) quotes Black (1975), Cox and Rubinstein (1985), and Manaster and Rendleman (1982) to this effect.

and the marginal rate of substitution for individual i across states $(\tilde{u} = u_k, \tilde{x}_1 = x_l)$ and $(\tilde{u} = u_m, \tilde{x}_1 = x_n)$, M^i_{klmn}, is independent of i:

$$
\begin{aligned}
M^i_{klmn} &= \frac{\exp\{-p_1 \tilde{x}_1^2/2\} \exp\{-K_{0i}(u_k - \tilde{\mu}_{0i})^2/2\} \exp\{-w_i(u_k, x_l)/r_i\}}{\exp\{-p_1 x_n^2/2\} \exp\{-K_{0i}(u_l - \tilde{\mu}_{0i})^2/2\} \exp\{-w_i(u_m, x_n)/r_i\}} \\
&= \frac{\exp\{-K_0(u_k - P_0)^2/2 - p_1 x_l^2/2 - x_l(u_k - P_1)/r\}}{\exp\{-K_0(u_m - P_0)^2/2 - p_1 x_n^2/2 - x_n(u_m - P_1)/r\}}.
\end{aligned} \quad (46)
$$

Thus the option contracts allow the market to achieve Pareto efficient risk sharing with respect to both the asset payoff, $\tilde{u}$, and the second period supply noise, $\tilde{x}_1$. Despite the Pareto efficiency of the equilibrium, we note that the option price in the first trading session does not satisfy the Black and Scholes (1973) pricing principle. The reason for this is that the final wealth of the representative investor is no longer normally distributed on account of the supply shocks. However, conditional on the second-period supply shock, the final wealth is normally distributed, and consequently the option price in the second[31] trading session does satisfy the Black and Scholes (1973) principle.

Comparing Theorem 4 with Theorem 5, it is apparent that the supply noise introduced in the second trading session has no effect on the investors' demands for the option. On the other hand, the price of the option is increasing in the variance of the supply shock in the second session, which increases the variance of the price of the risky asset in the second session.

5.2 Informational trade with new private information

We now extend the model to incorporate private information acquisition after the first trading session. In particular, we assume that before each trading session, $t = 1, \ldots, T$, investor i receives a private signal $\tilde{z}_{ti} = \tilde{u} + \tilde{\eta}_{ti}$ of precision s_{ti}. We also assume that in each trading session, $t = 1, \ldots, T$, there is a new per capita supply shock caused by liquidity traders, $\tilde{x}_t$, which is normally and independently distributed with mean 0 and precision p_t. Public information signals are received as described above. In addition, let $\tilde{F}_{ti}$ denote the subsigma field generated by investor i's information set and $\tilde{F}_t$ denote the subsigma field generated by public information set up to include session t. The following theorem describes the equilibria that obtain with and without the introduction of quadratic options.

---

[31] More generally, the last.

The Review of Financial Studies / v 9 n 1 1996

Theorem 6. *In an economy with T trading sessions, a single risky asset, and, before each trading session, a supply shock, a public information signal, and new private information signals, there exists a partially revealing rational expectations equilibrium in which prices and demands for the risky asset are given by*

$$\tilde{P}_t = K_t^{-1}\left[\left(K_t - \sum_{j=0}^{t} s_j\right)\tilde{\mu}_t + \sum_{j=0}^{t}\{s_j\tilde{u} - \tilde{x}_j/r\}\right], \tag{47}$$

$$\tilde{D}_{ti} = r_i K_{ti}[\tilde{\mu}_{ti} - \tilde{P}_t] = r_i\left[\sum_{j=0}^{t}\{s_{ji}\tilde{z}_{ji} - s_j\tilde{u} + \tilde{x}_j/r - (s_{ji} - s_j)\tilde{P}_t\}\right], \tag{48}$$

$$s_t \equiv \frac{1}{r}\int_0^1 r_i s_{ti}\, di,$$

$$\tilde{\mu}_t \equiv E(\tilde{u}\mid \tilde{F}_t) = \frac{b\bar{u} + \sum_{j=0}^{t}\{n_j\tilde{y}_j + r^2 s_j^2 p_j \tilde{q}_j\}}{b + \sum_{j=0}^{t}\{n_j + r^2 s_j^2 p_j\}},$$

$$\tilde{\mu}_{t_i} \equiv E(\tilde{u}\mid \tilde{F}_{ti}) = \frac{(K_t - \sum_{j=0}^{t} s_j)\tilde{\mu}_t + \sum_{j=0}^{t} s_j\tilde{z}_{ji}}{K_{ti}}$$

$$= \frac{b\bar{u} + \sum_{j=0}^{t}\{n_j\tilde{y}_j + s_{ji}\tilde{z}_{ji} + r^2 s_j^2 p_j \tilde{q}_j\}}{b + \sum_{j=0}^{t}\{n_j + s_{ji} + r^2 s_j^2 p_j\}},$$

$$\tilde{q}_t = \tilde{u} - \tilde{x}_t/rs_t,$$

$$K_{ti} \equiv var^{-1}(\tilde{u}\mid \tilde{F}_{ti}) = b + \sum_{j=0}^{t}\{n_j + s_{ji} + r^2 s_j^2 p_j\},$$

$$K_t \equiv \int_0^1 \frac{r_i}{r}K_{ti}\, di = b + \sum_{j=0}^{t}\{n_j + s_j + r^2 s_j^2 p_j\}.$$

(ii) Suppose that T − 1 quadratic options $\tilde{C}_t$, t = 1, ..., T − 1, with payoffs at time 1 of $(\tilde{u} - \tilde{P}_t)^2$, are available for trade in the first trading session. Let $P_{\tilde{C},j}$ denote the price of $\tilde{C}_t$ at trading session j, and $D_{\tilde{C},ji}$ denote the demand of individual i for option $\tilde{C}_t$ at trading session j.

Then there exists the following equilibrium.[32]

$$\tilde{P}_t = K_t^{-1}\left[\left(K_t - \sum_{j=0}^{t} s_j\right)\tilde{\mu}_t + \sum_{j=0}^{t}\{s_j\tilde{u} - \tilde{x}_j/r\}\right], \tag{49}$$

$$\tilde{D}_{ti} = r_i\left[\sum_{j=0}^{t}\{s_{ji}\tilde{z}_{ji} - s_j\tilde{u} + \tilde{x}_j/r - (s_{ji} - s_j)\tilde{P}_j\}\right], \tag{50}$$

$$P_{\tilde{C},0} = \sum_{j=t+1}^{T}\left[K_{j-1}^{-1} - \left(K_j + s_j + \frac{1}{r^2 p_j}\right)^{-1} + K_j^{-1}\right], \tag{51}$$

$$P_{\tilde{C},j} = P_{\tilde{C},0}I_{\{j\le t\}} + [P_{\tilde{C},0} + (\tilde{P}_j - \tilde{P}_t)^2]I_{\{j>t\}}, \tag{52}$$ [33]

$$D_{\tilde{C},ji} = D_{\tilde{C},0i}$$

$$= \frac{r_i}{2}\left(\frac{1}{P_{\tilde{C},0} + \sum_{j>t}[(K_j + s_j + \frac{1}{r^2 p_j})^{-1} - 2K_j^{-1}]} - K_{ti} - \sum_{j<t} D_{\tilde{C},0i}\right)$$

$$= \frac{r_i}{2}(s_t - s_{ti}). \tag{53}$$

Without the options, the trade for investor i in the risky asset in session t is given by

$$\nabla\tilde{D}_{ti} \equiv \tilde{D}_{ti} - \tilde{D}_{(t-1)i} \tag{54}$$

$$= r_i\left[s_{ti}\tilde{z}_{ti} - s_t\tilde{u} + \frac{\tilde{x}_t}{r} + \sum_{j=0}^{t-1}(s_j - s_{ji})(\tilde{P}_t - \tilde{P}_{t-1}) + (s_t - s_{ti})\tilde{P}_t\right].$$

It is clear from this expression that the precision of the private information received prior to t affects the volume of trade in session t. With the options, the trade for investor i is given by

$$\nabla\tilde{D}_{ti} = r_i\left[s_{ti}\tilde{z}_{ti} - s_t\tilde{u} + \frac{\tilde{x}_t}{r} + (s_t - s_{ti})\tilde{P}_t\right]. \tag{55}$$

Thus with the quadratic options, private information causes trading only in the session in which it is received. The intuition is that the options allow investors to trade to a Pareto efficient allocation with respect to their current information, and this eliminates the need for further trading based on that information. However, the net effect of

---

[32] As the cases before, we define $K_T = \infty$, $p_T = \infty$ for simplicity of notation.

[33] I_A is the indicator function of event A.

The Review of Financial Studies / v 9 n 1 1996

the introduction of options on the total volume of trade is indeterminate. Note that, even with the introduction of new liquidity traders and new private information, the options still do not affect the price process for the underlying risky asset. However, the prices of the options are affected by the acquisition of new private information.

5.3 Market depth and a comparison with the Kyle model

Subrahmanyam (1991) has extended the classic Kyle (1985) model of a security market with private information to allow for risk aversion in both the competitive market maker and the risk averse informed traders. If we think of the subset of traders in our model who receive no private information as uninformed market makers, then our model is isomorphic to that of the Subrahmanyam version of the Kyle model, except that informed traders in our model behave competitively rather than strategically, and place limit rather than market orders. Thus denote the subset of investors for whom $s_t = s = 0$ by M for market maker, and define the risk tolerance of the market maker by $r_M = \int_M r_i \, di$. Then in the economy without options, the order flow absorbed by the market maker is given from Equation (54) by

$$
\nabla \tilde{D}_{Mt} = r_M \left[s_t(\tilde{P}_t - \tilde{u}) + \tilde{x}_t / r + \sum_{j=0}^{t-1} s_j \nabla P_t \right]
$$

$$
= - \frac{r_M}{1 + r^2 s_t p_t} \left[K_{t-1}(\tilde{P}_t - \tilde{P}_{t-1}) + n_t(\tilde{y}_t - \tilde{P}_t) + \sum_{j=0}^{t-1} s_j \nabla P_t \right].
$$

In the economy with options, on the other hand, the order flow absorbed by the market maker is given by

$$
\nabla \tilde{D}_{Mt} = r_M[s_t(\tilde{P}_t - \tilde{u}) + \tilde{x}_t / r]
$$

$$
= - \frac{r_M}{1 + r^2 s_t p_t} [K_{t-1}(\tilde{P}_t - \tilde{P}_{t-1}) + n_t(\tilde{y}_t - \tilde{P}_t)]. \quad (56)
$$

To facilitate comparison with Kyle type models, we further assume that there are no public announcements, so that $n_t = 0$, and define $\tilde{X}_t \equiv -\nabla \tilde{D}_{Mt}$ as the order flow received by the market maker.[34] Then the price change is related to the order flow as follows: in the market

---

[34] With this convention a positive order flow corresponds to purchases.

without options

$$\nabla \tilde{P}_t = r_M^{-1} \left[\frac{K_{t-1}}{1 + r^2 s_t p_t} - \sum_{j=0}^{t-1} s_j \right]^{-1} \tilde{X}_t. \tag{57}$$

The corresponding equation for the economy with options is

$$\nabla \tilde{P}_t = r_M^{-1} \left[\frac{K_{t-1}}{1 + r^2 s_t p_t} \right]^{-1} \tilde{X}_t. \tag{58}$$

Following common usage, we define the market depth as $1/\lambda$, the coefficient of $\tilde{X}_t$ in these equations. Then the market depth in the economy with options, $1/\lambda^*$, is given by

$$1/\lambda^* = \frac{r_M K_{t-1}}{1 + r^2 s_t p_t}. \tag{59}$$

The market depth in the economy without options, $1/\lambda^0$, is

$$1/\lambda^0 = 1/\lambda^* - r_M \sum_{j=0}^{t-1} s_j. \tag{60}$$

In the market with options, market depth is increasing in the risk tolerance of the market makers and in the average posterior precision of the market, K_t; it is decreasing in the market risk tolerance, r, and the average precision of the current private signal, s_t, which jointly determine the aggressiveness of informed trading; it is also decreasing in the precision of noise trading in the current session, p_t. These results are consistent with the single trading session model of Subrahmanyam (1991) in which market depth increases with both the risk tolerance of the market maker and the variance of supply noise.

We see from Equation (58) that market depth is less in the economy without options. We state this result as

Theorem 7. *The introduction of options trading in a security leads to an increase in market depth.*

The intuition for the reduced market depth in the economy without options[35] is that in the absence of options less-informed traders (including market makers) tend to be trend followers as the result of prior information disadvantages, as we saw in Corollary 1. This creates a tendency for market makers to trade in the same direction as the price

---

[35] Fedenia and Grammatikos (1992) find that the bid-ask spread decreases for NYSE stocks following the introduction of options, while the opposite result is found for OTC stocks.

The Review of Financial Studies / v 9 n 1 1996

change, the strength of this tendency being directly proportional to the accumulated information disadvantage, $\sum_{j=0}^{t-1} s_j$; if this information disadvantage is sufficiently large market depth may be zero or even negative. In Kyle's (1989) single trading session model, risk averse informed and uninformed investors and noise traders submit demand functions to an auctioneer; whereas in our model, all participants behave competitively. When the numbers of informed and un-informed investors go to infinity, Kyle's (1989) model converges to the Hellwig (1980) model. Therefore a natural conjecture is that if Kyle's (1989) model is extended to many trading sessions then, as the number of informed and un-informed investors goes to infinity, it will converge to our model. Unfortunately, the multiple trading session version of Kyle's (1989) model is extremely difficult to analyze.

5.4 Trading behavior with short-term quadratic options
In section 5.2 it was shown that the introduction of quadratic options would lead to a reduction in the volume of trade based on private information. However, this result is sensitive to the type of options available for trade. We show in this section that when only short-term quadratic options are available, investors have the same ex ante utility although their trading behavior is affected. For simplicity, we discuss the two trading session economy.

Theorem 8. *When options $\tilde{O}_0(\tilde{P}_1) \equiv (\tilde{P}_1 - P_0)^2$, $\tilde{O}_1(\tilde{P}_1, \tilde{u}) \equiv (\tilde{u} - \tilde{P}_1)^2$, are introduced into the economy of section 5.2 with $T = 2$, the prices and demands for the risky assets are the same as in the market without options. Let $P_{\tilde{O}_0}$ be the price of $\tilde{O}_0$ at time 0, $D_{\tilde{O}_0 i}$ be the demand of individual i at time 0. The prices and demands for the options are given by*

$$P_{\tilde{O}_0} = K_0^{-1} - \left[K_1 + s_1 + \frac{1}{r^2 p_1}\right]^{-1},$$

$$P_{\tilde{O}_1} = K_1^{-1},$$

$$D_{\tilde{O}_0 i} = \frac{r_i}{2}(s_0 - s_{0i}),$$

$$D_{\tilde{O}_0 0 i} = D_{\tilde{O}_1 1 i} = \frac{r_i}{2}[(s_0 - s_{0i}) + (s_1 + s_{1i})].$$

The intuition for this result can be understood as follows. The identity,

$$(\tilde{u} - P_0)^2 = (\tilde{P}_1 - P_0)^2 + 2(\tilde{P}_1 - P_0)(\tilde{u} - \tilde{P}_1) + (\tilde{u} - \tilde{P}_1)^2,$$

implies that the payoff on the holding of $\frac{r_i}{2}(s_0 - s_{0i})$ units of the option $\tilde{C}_0$ of Theorem 6 with payoff $\frac{r_i}{2}(s_0 - s_{0i})(\tilde{u} - P_0)^2$ can be replicated in the economy of this section by the following strategy: purchase $\frac{r_i}{2}(s_0 - s_{0i})$ units of option $\tilde{O}_0$ in the first trading session, and in the second trading session purchase $r_i(s_0 - s_{0i})(\tilde{P}_1 - P_0)$ units of the risky asset and $\frac{r_i}{2}(s_0 - s_{0i})$ units of the option $\tilde{O}_1$. Notice that $r_i(s_0 - s_{0i})(\tilde{P}_1 - P_0)$ units of the risky asset is exactly the amount of informational trades eliminated by the introduction of the options $\tilde{C}_0$, $\tilde{C}_1$. This gives the result that when only the short-term options $\tilde{O}_0$, $\tilde{O}_1$ are available, the volume of trading in the risky security is the same as in the economy without options. However, since the short-term options $\tilde{O}_0$, $\tilde{O}_1$ and the underlying risky asset can replicate the payoff of the long-term option $\tilde{C}_1$, the welfare of investors is the same as in the economy with long-term options.

This example shows that the trading behavior of investors depends crucially upon the nature of the derivative assets available in the market as well as upon differences in the tastes and information of investors.

6. Conclusion

In this article we developed a noisy rational expectations model of the type of Hellwig (1980) in order to consider the effect of allowing investors to trade more frequently when public information about the asset payoff emerges gradually over time. For representative parameter values we find that there are significant welfare gains to both the well informed and the poorly informed from trading more frequently than once a year — only the averagely informed fail to gain. Well-informed traders tend to sell on a price rise, while the relatively poorly informed buy on a rise and, as the limit of continuous trading is reached, the well-informed synthesize by a dynamic strategy a payoff that is a concave function of the risky asset payoff, while the poorly informed synthesize a convex payoff function. This provides a new rationale for portfolio insurance type payoff functions based on differences in the quality of private information. The limiting continuous time economy is shown to achieve a Pareto efficient allocation, provided that a smoothness condition on the arrival of public information is satisfied.

Pareto efficiency may also be achieved in a single round of trading if there exists an option type contract whose payoff is a quadratic function of the payoff on the underlying risky asset; as a result there is no trading in response to new public information in such an economy. This points to the need to give attention to the array of available securities in making predictions about trading volume.

The Review of Financial Studies / v 9 n 1 1996

When the market achieves Pareto efficiency, either through conti-
nous trading or through trading in options, there exists a representative investor and option contracts are priced in accordance with the
martingale principles of Black and Scholes (1973). Despite the differences in the precisions of investors' assessments of the final asset
payoff, they agree on the volatility for pricing options.

The foregoing results were developed for an economy with only a
single supply shock and set of private information signals at time 0.
It is shown that the introduction of new supply shocks and new private information signals prior to each trading session restores trading
volume in all trading sessions, even if quadratic options are traded.
However, in the economy with options, trading is induced only by the
need for each investor to take up the appropriate share of the supply
shock.

It is argued that investors who receive no private information may
be regarded as Kyle (1985) type market makers in a model in which
all participants are risk averse, behave competitively, and submit limit
orders. An expression for market depth is derived and compared with
that of Subrahmanyam (1991); it is found that the introduction of option contracts leads to an increase in market depth, by eliminating the
tendency of the uninformed market makers to trade as trend followers
on account of their cumulative information disadvantage. In a subsequent article we extend the results on market making to a competitive
risk averse economy in which investors may place market orders as
well as limit orders. Further directions for research include extending the model to incorporate many risky assets and endogenizing the
acquisition of private information.

Appendix

Throughout the Appendix we set $x_i = 0$ without loss of generality,
unless otherwise stated.

Proof of Theorem 1. It is straightforward to verify that in the proposed
equilibrium aggregate asset demand is equal to supply in each period.
It remains only to show that, given the conjectured equilibrium, the
optimal demand for the risky asset by investor i, $\tilde{d}_{ti}^*$ is equal to $\tilde{D}_{ti}$,
the conjectured equilibrium demand given in Equation (10). Let $E_{ti}[\cdot]$
denote the expectation with respect to the information set $\tilde{F}_{ti}$, let
$\tilde{w}_{ti} \equiv \sum_{j=1}^{t}(\tilde{P}_j - \tilde{P}_{j-1})\tilde{D}_{(j-1)i}$ be the wealth of investor i at time τ_t, and
let $V_{it}^T(w)$ be the expected utility of trader i at time τ_t in a T trading
session economy under the optimal policy. Then at the beginning of

the last trading session,

$$V_{i(T-1)}^T(w) = \max_{d_{(T-1)i}} E_{(T-1)i} \left[-\exp \left\{ -\left[\frac{w}{r_i} + (\tilde{u} - \tilde{P}_{T-1}) \frac{d_{(T-1)i}}{r_i} \right] \right\} \right].$$

(61)

This problem is identical to that in the single-session economy discussed in Section 2, and the optimal asset demand, $\tilde{d}_{(T-1)i}^*$ is given by

$$\tilde{d}_{(T-1)i}^* = r_i K_{(T-1)i} (\tilde{\mu}_{(T-1)i} - \tilde{P}_{T-1})$$

$$= r_i (s_i z_i - s\tilde{u} + \tilde{x}/r - (s_i - s)\tilde{P}_{T-1}).$$

(62)

Comparing Equation (62) with Equation (10), it is apparent that $\tilde{d}_{(T-1)i}^* = \tilde{D}_{(T-1)i}$ and the conjectured equilibrium is confirmed for the final trading session. Then the expected utility of investor i under the optimal policy at the beginning of the final trading session, $V_{(T-1)i}^T(w)$, is

$$V_{(T-1)i}^T(w) = E_{(T-1)i} \left[-\exp \left\{ \left[\frac{w}{r_i} + (\tilde{u} - \tilde{P}_{T-1}) \frac{\tilde{D}_{(T-1)i}}{r_i} \right] \right\} \right]$$

$$= -\exp \left\{ -\left[\frac{w}{r_i} + \frac{(\tilde{D}_{(T-1)i}/r_i)^2}{2K_{(T-1)i}} \right] \right\}.$$

Define $\nabla \tilde{D}_{(T-1)i} \equiv \tilde{D}_{(T-1)i} - \tilde{D}_{(T-2)i}$, the change in demand for the risky asset under the conjectured optimal strategy. The mean and variance of this change in demand are given by

$$E[\nabla \tilde{D}_{(T-1)i}/r_i \mid \tilde{F}_{(T-2)i}] = \frac{n_{T-1}(s - s_i)}{K_{T-1}K_{(T-1)i}} D_{(T-2)i},$$

(63)

$$\text{var}[\nabla \tilde{D}_{(T-1)i} \mid \tilde{F}_{(T-2)i}] = \frac{(s - s_i)^2 n_{T-1} K_{(T-1)i}}{K_{(T-2)i} K_{T-1}^2}.$$

(64)

Armed with these expressions, we can calculate the expected utility at time $T - 2$ as a function of wealth at $T - 2$, $w_{(T-2)i}$, and the number of units of the risky asset purchased, $d_{(T-1)i}$.

$$E_{(T-2)i}[V_{(T-1)i}^T(\tilde{w}_{(T-1)i} \mid w_{T-2} = w, d_{(T-2)i}]$$

(65)

$$= E_{(T-2)i} \left[-\exp \left\{ -\left[\frac{w}{r_i} + (\tilde{P}_{T-1} - \tilde{P}_{T-2}) \frac{d_{(T-2)i}}{r_i} \right. \right. \right.$$

$$\left. \left. \left. + \frac{(\tilde{D}_{(T-1)i}/r_i)^2}{2K_{(T-1)i}} \right] \right\} \right]$$

The Review of Financial Studies / v 9 n 1 1996

$$= -\sqrt{\frac{K_{(T-2)i}K_{T-1}^2}{2\pi(s-s_i)^2 n_{T-1}K_{(T-1)i}}}$$

$$\int \exp\left\{-\left[\frac{w}{r_i} + \frac{\tilde{D}_{(T-1)i}}{r_i}\frac{d_{(T-2)i}/r_i}{s-s_i}\right.\right.$$

$$+ \frac{(\nabla\tilde{D}_{(T-1)i}/r_i + D_{(T-2)i}/r_i)^2}{2K_{(T-1)i}}$$

$$\left.\left.+ \frac{(\nabla\tilde{D}_{(T-1)i} - E_{(T-2)i}[\nabla\tilde{D}_{(T-1)i}])^2}{2\,\text{var}_{(T-2)i}[\nabla\tilde{D}_{(T-1)i}]}\right]\right\}\,d\nabla\tilde{D}_{(T-1)i}$$

$$= -\sqrt{\frac{K_{(T-2)i}}{K_{(T-2)i} + n_{T-1}((s_i - s)/K_{T-1})^2}}$$

$$\exp\left\{-\left[\frac{w}{r_i} + \frac{[(d_{(T-2)i} - D_{(T-2)i})/r_i]^2}{2(s_i - s + K_{T-2}K_{T-1}/n_{T-1})}\right.\right.$$

$$\left.\left.\frac{(D_{(T-2)i}/r_i)^2}{2K_{(T-2)i}}\right]\right\}. \tag{66}$$

Maximizing with respect to $d_{(T-2)i}$ at time τ_{T-2} we find $d^*_{(T-2)i} = D_{(T-2)i}$. Therefore, the investor's expected utility at the beginning of session $T-2$ under the optimal policy, $V^T_{(T-2)i}(w)$, is given by

$$V^T_{(T-2)i}(w) = -\sqrt{\frac{K_{(T-2)i}}{K_{(T-2)i} + n_{T-1}((s_i - s)/K_{T-1})^2}}\, V^{T-1}_{(T-2)i}(w). \tag{67}$$

Proceeding recursively, Equation (67) implies that the investor behaves myopically in each trading session, so his demand for the risky security is given by Equation (10). This completes the proof. ∎

Proof of Lemma 1. Taking account of the investor's initial endowment, x_i, the ex ante utility of investor i in a one trading session economy is given in Verrecchia (1982):

$$V^1_{0i}(w) = \frac{-1}{\sqrt{L_0 K_{0i}}}\exp\left[\frac{-\bar{u}x_i}{r_i} + \left(\frac{1}{b} - \frac{1}{K_0^2 L_0}\right)\frac{x_i^2}{2r_i^2}\right].$$

Applying Equation (67) recursively yields the result of the lemma. ∎

Proof of Lemma 2. Let $\delta_t \equiv \frac{1}{K_{t-1}} - \frac{1}{K_t}$, then $\sum_{t=1}^{T} \delta_t = \frac{1}{K_0}$. Equation (12) can be simplified to get

$$\gamma_i(T) = \frac{r_i}{2}\left[\sum_{t=1}^{T} \ln(1 + (s_i - s)\delta_t) - \ln\frac{K_{0i}}{K_0}\right].$$

Since $\ln(1 + (s_i - s)\delta_t)$ is a concave function, it follows from Jensen's inequality that $\gamma_i(T)$ is maximized by setting δ_t constant. But, direct calculation from Equation (9) gives

$$\text{var}[\nabla \tilde{P}_t] = \delta_t + \delta_t^2\left(s + \frac{1}{r^2 p}\right). \tag{68}$$

This finishes the first part of Lemma 2. Direct calculation gives the second part. ∎

Proof of Corollary 1. Follows immediately from Equation (15) and Corollary 2. ∎

Proof of Corollary 2. Equation (9) implies that

$$\text{cov}(\nabla \tilde{P}_{t+1}, \tilde{P}_t) = -\frac{n_{t+1}1 + r^2 sp}{K_t^2 K_{t+1} r^2 p}\text{cov}(\nabla \tilde{P}_{t+1}, \nabla \tilde{P}_t)$$

$$= \frac{n_{t+1} n_t (1 + r^2 sp)}{K_{t-1} K_t^2 K_{t+1} r^2 p}. \tag{69}$$

∎

Proof of Lemma 4. From Lemma 2, $\text{var}[\nabla \tilde{P}_t] = \delta_t + \delta_t^2(s + \frac{1}{r^2 p})$. Then using the elementary fact that $E[|x|] = \sqrt{2\sigma^2/\pi}$, for a normal distribution with mean 0 and variance σ^2, we have

$$E[Volume] = Q\sqrt{\frac{1}{2\pi}}\sum_{t=1}^{T}\sqrt{\delta_t + \delta_t^2\left(s + \frac{1}{r^2 p}\right)}. \tag{70}$$

Since $\sqrt{\delta_t + \delta_t^2(s + \frac{1}{r^2 p})}$ is a concave function of δ_t, and $\sum_{t=1}^{T}\delta_t = \frac{1}{K_0}$ from the proof of Lemma 2, it follows from Jensen's inequality that total expected volume is maximized when δ_t is constant for all t, and then we have

$$E[Volume] = Q\sqrt{\frac{1}{2\pi}}\sqrt{\frac{T}{K_0} + \frac{1 + r^2 sp}{K_0^2 r^2 p}}. \tag{71}$$

∎

The Review of Financial Studies / v 9 n 1 1996

Proof of Lemma 5. Let $\gamma_i(T) \equiv \frac{r_i}{2} \sum_{t=1}^{T-1} \ln(1 + \frac{n_t(s_i - s)^2}{K_t^2 K_{(t-1)i}}) \equiv \sum_{t=1}^{T} \ln(1 + \sigma_i(t, T))$. Then, defining $\bar{\delta} \equiv \max_t[\delta_t]$, since $\text{var}[\nabla P_{t+1}] = \delta_{t+1} + \delta_{t+1}^2(s + \frac{1}{r^2 p})$, regularity Condition A becomes $\lim_{T \to \infty} \bar{\delta}(T) = 0$.

Now we define

$$
\begin{aligned}
\bar{\gamma}_t(T) &\equiv \frac{r_i}{2} \sum_{t=1}^{T} \sigma_i(t, T) = \frac{r_i}{2} \sum_{t=1}^{T-1} \frac{n_t(s_i - s)^2}{K_t^2 K_{(t-1)i}} \\
&= \frac{r_i}{2} \sum_{t=0}^{T-2} \left(\frac{1}{K_t} - \frac{1}{K_{t+1}} \right) \frac{(s_i - s)^2 / K_t}{1 + (s_i - s)/K_t} \\
&\quad - \left(\frac{1}{K_t} - \frac{1}{K_{t+1}} \right)^2 \frac{(s_i - s)^2}{1 + (s_i - s)/K_t}.
\end{aligned}
\tag{72}
$$

∎

Obviously the second term converges to 0 and the first term converges to the integral

$$
\frac{r_i}{2} \int_0^{\frac{1}{K_0}} \frac{(s_i - s)^2 t}{1 + (s_i - s)t} \, dt = \frac{r_i}{2} \left[\frac{s_i - s}{K_0} - \ln\left(1 + \frac{s_i - s}{K_0}\right) \right].
$$

Using the elementary fact that $x/(1 + x) \leq \ln(1 + x) \leq x$, we have

$$
\frac{r_i}{2} \sum_{t=1}^{T-1} \frac{\sigma_i(t, T)}{1 + \sigma_i(t, T)} \leq \frac{r_i}{2} \sum_{t=1}^{T-1} \ln(1 + \sigma_i(t, T))
$$

$$
= \gamma_i(T) \leq \frac{r_i}{2} \sum_{t=1}^{T-1} \sigma_i(t, T) = \bar{\gamma}_i(T).
$$

Since

$$
\begin{aligned}
\sigma_i(t, T) &\equiv \frac{n_t(s_i - s)^2}{K_t^2 K_{(t-1)i}} = \frac{n_t}{K_{t-1} K_t} \frac{(s - s_i)^2}{K_{(t-1)i}} \\
&\leq \frac{(s - s_i)^2}{K_{(t-1)i}} \bar{\delta}(T) \leq \left[\frac{(s - s_i)^2}{K_{0i}} \right] \bar{\delta}(T),
\end{aligned}
$$

we get

$$
\frac{\bar{\gamma}_i(T)}{1 + \bar{\delta}(T)(s - s_i)^2 / K_{0i}} \leq \gamma_i(T) \leq \bar{\gamma}_i(T),
$$

which implies that

$$
\lim_{T \to \infty} \gamma_i(T) = \lim_{T \to \infty} \bar{\gamma}_i(T) = \frac{r_i}{2} \left[\frac{s_i - s}{K_0} - \ln\left(1 + \frac{s_i - s}{K_0}\right) \right].
$$

The expected utility at trading session 0 is

$$\lim_{T \to \infty} V_{0i}^T(w) = \sqrt{\frac{K_{0i}}{K_0}} \exp\left[\frac{s - s_i}{2K_0}\right] V_{0i}^1(w). \tag{73}$$

■

Proof of Theorem 2. The final wealth of investor i is

$$\tilde{w}_i = \sum_{t=0}^{T-1} (\tilde{P}_{t+1} - \tilde{P}_t)\tilde{D}_{ti} = (\tilde{u} - P_0)\tilde{D}_{0i} + \sum_{t=0}^{T-1} (\tilde{P}_{t+1} - \tilde{P}_t)(\tilde{D}_{ti} - \tilde{D}_{0i})$$

$$= (\tilde{u} - P_0)\tilde{D}_{0i} + r_i(s - s_i)\sum_{t=0}^{T-1} (\tilde{P}_{t+1} - \tilde{P}_t)(\tilde{P}_t - P_0)$$

$$= (\tilde{u} - P_0)\tilde{D}_{0i} + \frac{r_i}{2}(s - s_i)[(\tilde{u} - P_0)^2 - \sum_{t=0}^{T-1} (\tilde{P}_{t+1} - \tilde{P}_t)^2]$$

$$= (\tilde{u} - P_0)(\tilde{D}_{0i} - r_i\tilde{b}_i(T)) + \frac{r_i}{2}(s - s_i - a_i(T))(\tilde{u} - \tilde{P}_0)^2$$

$$\quad - \frac{r_i(s - s_i)}{2K_0} - r_i\tilde{c}_i(T)$$

$$= w_i^e(\tilde{u}) - \frac{r_i}{2}a_i(T)(\tilde{u} - P_0)^2 - r_i\tilde{b}_i(T)(\tilde{u} - P_0) - r_i\tilde{c}_i(T),$$

where

$$a_i(T) = (s - s_i)\sum_{t=0}^{T-1} \frac{n_{t+1}^2}{K_t^2 K_{t+1}^2},$$

$$\tilde{b}_i(T) = (s - s_i)\sum_{t=1}^{T-1} \left(\frac{1}{K_{t-1}} - \frac{2}{K_t} + \frac{1}{K_{t+1}}\right)\frac{\sum_{j=0}^{t} n_j\tilde{\eta}_j}{K_t},$$

$$\tilde{c}_i(T) = -(s - s_i)\sum_{t=0}^{T-1} \left[\left(\tilde{\eta}_{t+1} - K_t^{-1}\sum_{j=0}^{t} n_j\tilde{\eta}_j\right)K_t^{-1}\sum_{j=0}^{t} n_j\tilde{\eta}_j + \frac{1}{2K_0}\right],$$

and $w_i^e(\tilde{u})$ is given by

$$w_i^e(\tilde{u}) = (\tilde{u} - P_0)\tilde{D}_{0i} + \frac{1}{2}r_i(s - s_i)((\tilde{u} - P_0)^2 - K_0^{-1}). \tag{74}$$

For notational simplicity we use $n_T/K_t = 1$, $\eta_T = 0$ to denote the fact that the risky asset payoff realized at time $\tau_T = 1$. Condition A

The Review of Financial Studies / v 9 n 1 1996

implies that $\lim_{T\to\infty} a_i(T) = 0$, and that

$$
\lim_{T\to\infty} E[\tilde{c}_i(T)] = \lim_{T\to\infty} -(s - s_i)\left[-\sum_{t=0}^{T-1}\frac{n_{t+1}}{K_{t+1}K_t^2}\sum_{j=0}^{t}n_j + \frac{1}{2K_0}\right]
$$

$$
= (s - s_i)\lim_{T\to\infty}\left[\sum_{t=0}^{T-1}\left(\frac{1}{K_t} - \frac{1}{K_{t+1}}\right)\left(1 - \frac{K_0}{K_t}\right) - \frac{1}{2K_0}\right]
$$

$$
= 0.
$$

The final equality follows since the first term of the previous line is the Riemann representation of the integral $\int_0^{1/K_0}[1 - K_0 t]\,dt = \frac{1}{2K_0}$ given Condition A.

Let $\tilde{\eta}$ denote the vector $(\tilde{\eta}_1, \ldots, \tilde{\eta}_{T-1})$. Direct calculation of the expected utility of final wealth conditional on $\tilde{\eta}$ gives

$$
E\left[-\exp\left\{\frac{\tilde{w}_i}{r_i}\right\} \mid \tilde{\eta}\right] = E\left[-\exp\left\{-(\tilde{u} - P_0)\left(\frac{\tilde{D}_{0i}}{r_i} - \tilde{b}_i(T)\right)\right.\right.
$$

$$
- \frac{s - s_i - a_i(T)}{2}(\tilde{u} - P_0)^2
$$

$$
\left.\left. + \frac{s - s_i}{2K_0} + \tilde{c}_i(T)\right\} \mid \tilde{F}_{0i}, \tilde{\eta}\right]
$$

$$
= -\sqrt{\frac{K_{0i}}{2\pi}}\exp\left[\frac{s - s_i}{2K_0}\right]
$$

$$
\times \int \exp\left\{-(\tilde{u} - P_0)\left(\frac{\tilde{D}_{0i}}{r_i} - \tilde{b}_i(T)\right)\right.
$$

$$
- \frac{s - s_i - a_i(T)}{2}(\tilde{u} - P_0)^2
$$

$$
\left. + \tilde{c}_i(T) - \frac{K_{0i}}{2}(\tilde{u} - \tilde{\mu}_{0i})^2\right\}\,d\tilde{u}
$$

$$
= -\sqrt{\frac{K_{0i}}{2\pi}}\exp\left[\frac{s - s_i}{2K_0}\right]
$$

$$
\times \int \exp\left\{(\tilde{u} - P_0)\tilde{b}_i(T)\right.
$$

$$
\left. - \frac{K_0 - a_i(T)}{2}(\tilde{u} - P_0)^2 + \tilde{c}_i(T)\right.
$$

$$-\frac{K_{0i}}{2}(\tilde{\mu}_{0i} - P_0)^2\right\} d\tilde{u}$$

$$= -\sqrt{\frac{K_{0i}}{K_0 - a_i(T)}}\, \exp\left[\frac{s - s_i}{2K_0}\right]$$

$$\times \exp\left\{-\frac{\tilde{D}_{0i}^2}{2r_i^2 K_{0i}} + \frac{\tilde{b}_i^2(T)}{2[K_0 - a_i(T)]} + \tilde{c}_i(T)\right\}$$

$$= -\sqrt{\frac{K_{0i}}{K_0 - a_i(T)}}\, \exp\left[\frac{s - s_i}{2K_0}\right]$$

$$\times \exp\left\{\frac{\tilde{b}_i^2(T)}{2[K_0 - a_i(T)]} + \tilde{c}_i(T)\right\} V_{0i}^1(0).$$

Taking the expectation over $\tilde{\eta}$ we have

$$V_{0i}^T(0) = -\sqrt{\frac{K_{0i}}{K_0 - a_i(T)}}\, \exp\left[\frac{s - s_i}{2K_0}\right]$$

$$\times E\left[\exp\left(\frac{\tilde{b}_i^2(T)}{2[K_0 - a_i(T)]} + \tilde{c}_i(T)\right)\right] V_{0i}^1(0) \qquad (75)$$

However, from Lemma 5, we have

$$\lim_{T\to\infty} V_{0i}^T(0) = \sqrt{\frac{K_{0i}}{K_0}}\, \exp\left[\frac{s - s_i}{2K_0}\right] V_{0i}^1(0). \qquad (76)$$

Equating the limit of Equation (75) to Equation (76), and recalling that $\lim_{T\to\infty} a_i(T) = 0$, implies that

$$\lim_{T\to\infty} E\left[\exp\left\{\frac{\tilde{b}_i^2(T)}{2[K_0 - a_i(T)]} + \tilde{c}_i(T)\right\}\right] = 1.$$

However, since $\exp(\cdot)$ is convex Jensen's inequality implies that

$$1 = \lim_{T\to\infty} E\left[\exp\frac{\tilde{b}_i(T)^2}{2[K_0 - a_i(T)]} + \tilde{c}_i(T))\right] \geq \lim_{T\to\infty} E[\exp(\tilde{c}_i(T))]$$

$$\geq \lim_{T\to\infty} \exp(E[\tilde{c}_i(T)]) = \exp(\lim_{T\to\infty} E[\tilde{c}_i(T)]) = 1,$$

which implies that $\tilde{c}_i(T)$ converges to 0 in probability. To show that $\tilde{b}_i(T)$ also converges to zero in probability note that Jensen's inequal-

The Review of Financial Studies / v 9 n 1 1996

ity also implies that

$$
\begin{aligned}
1 &= \lim_{T \to \infty} E\left[\exp\left(\frac{[\tilde{b}_i(T)]^2}{2[K_0 - a_i(T)]} + \tilde{c}_i(T) \right) \right] \\
&\geq \lim_{T \to \infty} \exp\left(E\left[\frac{\tilde{b}_i(T)^2}{2[K_0 - a_i(T)]} + \tilde{c}_i(T) \right] \right) \\
&= \exp\left(\lim_{T \to \infty} E\left[\frac{\tilde{b}_i(T)^2}{2[K_0 - a_i(T)]} + \tilde{c}_i(T) \right] \right) \\
&= \exp\left(\lim_{T \to \infty} E\left[\frac{\tilde{b}_i(T)^2}{2[K_0 - a_i(T)]} \right] \right) \geq 1.
\end{aligned}
$$

Therefore, $\lim_{T \to \infty} E[\tilde{b}_i(T)^2 / 2[K_0 - a_i(T)]] = 0$, which implies that $\tilde{b}_i(T)$ converges to 0 in probability. In summary, we have shown that the wealth of investor i converges to $\tilde{w}_i^e(\tilde{u})$ as $T \to \infty$. To show that the limiting wealth allocation $w_i^e(\tilde{u})$ is Pareto optimal, we need to show that the marginal rate of substitution between state $\tilde{u} = u_k$, u_l is the same for all investors. The marginal rate of substitution between state k and l for investor i is

$$
\begin{aligned}
M_{kl}^i &= \frac{\exp\{-K_{0i}(u_k - \tilde{\mu}_{0i})^2/2 - w_i^e(u_k)/r_i\}}{\exp\{-K_{0i}(u_l - \tilde{\mu}_{0i})^2/2 - w_i^e(u_l)/r_i\}} \\
&= \exp\{K_0(u_l - u_k)(u_l + 2P_0 + 2u_k)\},
\end{aligned}
$$

which is independent of i. ∎

Proof of Theorem 4. Substituting for the investor's terminal wealth in the utility function, using the conjectured equilibrium price of the option, and taking expectations, investor i's portfolio problem may be written as

$$
\max_{d_{C0i}, d_{0i}} EU_i \equiv -\sqrt{\frac{1}{1 + \frac{2d_{C0i}}{r_i K_{0i}}}}
$$
$$
\times \exp\left\{ \frac{[\frac{d_{0i}}{r_i} - K_{0i}(\mu_{0i} - P_0)]^2}{K_{0i} + \frac{2d_{C0i}}{r_i}} + \frac{d_{C0i}}{K_0 r_i} - \frac{K_{0i}}{2}(\mu_{0i} - P_0)^2 \right\},
$$

where d_{C0i} and d_{0i} are the number of units of the option and the risky asset purchased by the investor. The optimal portfolio is given by

$$
d_{0i}^* = r_i K_{0i}(\mu_{0i} - P_0), \quad d_{C0i}^* = r_i(s - s_i)/2.
$$

The optimal portfolio is identical to the equilibrium portfolio of the theorem: market clearing for the risky asset follows from our previous results and is immediate for the option. ∎

Proof of Theorem 5. See proof of Theorem 6. ∎

Proof of Theorem 6.

(i) For simplicity of exposition, we provide the proof for the case of two trading sessions: the extension to a multiple-period model is straightforward. It is immediate that the conjectured price functions are consistent with market clearing given the conjectured demand functions. It remains to show that the conjectured demand function is optimal. Let $V_{1i}(w)$ be the derived utility of individual i in the final trading session:

$$V_{1i}(\tilde{w}) \equiv \max_{d_{1i}} E\left[-\exp\left\{\frac{-1}{r_i}\left[\tilde{w} + (\tilde{u} - P_1)\, d_{1i}\right]\right\} \mid \tilde{F}_{1i}\right], \qquad (77)$$

where $\tilde{w} = (\tilde{P}_1 - P_0)D_{0i}$. It follows from our previous results that

$$V_{1i}(\tilde{w}) = -\exp\left\{\frac{-1}{r_i}\left[(\tilde{P}_1 - P_0)\tilde{D}_{0i} + \frac{r_i K_{1i}}{2}(\tilde{\mu}_{1i} - \tilde{P}_1)^2\right]\right\}, \qquad (78)$$

$$\tilde{D}_{1i} = r_i K_{1i}(\tilde{\mu}_{1i} - \tilde{P}_1) = r_i \sum_{j=0}^{1}\{s_{ji}z_{ji} - s_{ji}\tilde{u} + \tilde{x}_j/r - (s_{ji} - s_j)\tilde{P}_1\}. \qquad (79)$$

Define $A_i \equiv \tilde{\mu}_{1i} - \tilde{P}_1$, $B \equiv \tilde{P}_1 - \tilde{P}_0$, $G_i \equiv (K_{1i}E[A_i \mid F_{0i}],\ d_{0i}/r_i)'$, $I_i \equiv E[(A_i, B)' \mid F_{0i}]$, $\Sigma_i \equiv \text{var}[(A_i, B) \mid F_{0i}]$, and

$$\Phi_i \equiv \frac{1}{|\Sigma_i|}\begin{pmatrix} \Sigma_{22i} + K_{1i}|\Sigma_i| & -\Sigma_{21i} \\ -\Sigma_{12i} & \Sigma_{11i} \end{pmatrix}.$$

Then the objective function for the first trading session may be written as

$$E[V_{1i}(\tilde{w} \mid F_{0i}] = -\sqrt{\frac{1}{1 + K_{1i}\Sigma_{11i}}}\, \exp\{G_i'\Phi_i^{-1}G_i/2 - G_i'I_i\}. \qquad (80)$$

The first-order condition is

$$G_i'\Phi_i^{-1}\frac{dG_i}{dd_{0i}} = I'\frac{dG_i}{dd_{0i}}.$$

Simplifying we obtain the optimal first-session demand for the risky asset:

$$d_{0i}^* = r_i\frac{(1 + K_{1i}\Sigma_{11i})E[B \mid F_{0i}] - K_{1i}\Sigma_{12i}E[A_i \mid F_{0i}]}{\Sigma_{22i} + K_{1i}|\Sigma_i|};$$

The Review of Financial Studies / v 9 n 1 1996

where

$$E[A_i \mid F_{0i}] = \frac{K_0}{K_1}[\mu_{0i} - P_0], \ E[B \mid F_{0i}] = \frac{K_1 - K_0}{K_1}[\mu_{0i} - P_0],$$

$$\Sigma_{22i} = \frac{1}{K_1^2}\left[\frac{(K_1 - K_0)(K_{1i} + s_1 - s_{1i})}{K_{0i}} + s_1 + 1/r^2 p_1\right],$$

$$K_{1i}|\Sigma_i| = \frac{1}{K_1^2}\left[\frac{(1 + r^2 s_1 p_1)(K_{1i} - K_{0i})}{K_{0i} r^2 p_1} + \frac{(s_{1i} - s_1)(K_1 - K_0)}{K_{0i}}\right],$$

$$1 + K_{1i}\Sigma_{11i} = \frac{K_{1i}}{K_1^2 K_{0i}}[K_0^2 + K_{0i}(K_1 - K_0 + s_1 + 1/r^2 p_1)],$$

$$\Sigma_{12i} = \frac{1}{K_1^2}\left[\frac{(K_1 - K_0)(K_0 - K_{0i})}{K_{0i}} - s_1 - 1/r^2 p)\right].$$

Simple algebra yields

$$d_{0i}^* = r_i K_{0i}[\tilde{\mu}_{0i} - P_0],$$

which is identical to the conjectured demand, D_{0i}.

(ii) Follows from Theorem 8 and the following discussion which shows the equivalence of the options analyzed in Theorems 6 and 8. ∎

Proof of Theorem 8. With the options $\tilde{O}_0 \equiv (\tilde{P}_1 - P_0)^2$, $\tilde{O}_1 \equiv (\tilde{u} - \tilde{P}_1)^2$, the price for $\tilde{O}_1$ can be determined in the second trading session and is given by $P_{\tilde{O}_1} = K_1^{-1}$. Since $P_{\tilde{O}_1}$ is a nonrandom, it follows that the price for $\tilde{O}_1$ in the first period is also the same.

The following expression for the derived utility at the last trading session is obtained by substituting the equilibrium portfolio demands into the objective function stated in the proof of Theorem 4:

$$V_{1i}(w) = -\sqrt{\frac{K_{1i}}{K_{1i} + 2D_{\tilde{O}_1 i}/r_i}}\exp\left[-\frac{w}{r_i} + \frac{D_{\tilde{O}_1 i}}{r_i K_1} - \frac{K_{1i}}{2}(\tilde{\mu}_{1i} - \tilde{P}_1)^2\right],$$

where $w = (P_1 - P_0)D_{0i} + D_{\tilde{O}_1 i}((P_1 - P_0)^2 - P_{\tilde{O}_1})$. Dropping the non-random terms in $V_{i1}(w)$, investor i's optimization problem in the first trading session is to maximize the expected value of $\tilde{U}_{i1}(d_{0i}, d_{\tilde{O}_1 i})$ by the portfolio choice d_{0i}, $d_{\tilde{O}_b i}$, where

$$
\tilde{U}_{1i}(d_{0i}, d_{\tilde{O}_b i}) \equiv \exp\left[-\frac{(P_1 - P_0)d_{0i} + d_{\tilde{O}_b i}((P_1 - P_0)^2 - P_{\tilde{O}_b})}{r_i} \right.
$$
$$
\left. -\frac{K_{1i}}{2}(\tilde{\mu}_{1i} - \tilde{P}_1)^2 \right]. \tag{81}
$$

Defining $A_i \equiv \mu_{1i} - \tilde{P}_1$, $B \equiv \tilde{P}_1 - P_0$, $G_i \equiv (K_{1i}E[A_i \mid F_{0i}], D_{0i}/r_i)'$, $I_i \equiv E[(A_i, B)' \mid F_{0i}]$, $\Sigma_i \equiv \mathrm{var}[(A_i, B) \mid F_{0i}]$, and taking the expectation in Equation (81), we get

$$
E[\tilde{U}_{1i}(d_{0i}, d_{\tilde{O}_b i}) \mid F_{0i}] = -\sqrt{\frac{1}{1 + K_{1i}\Sigma_{11i} + 2D_{\tilde{O}_b i}(\Sigma_{22i} + K_{1i}|\Sigma_i|)/r_i}}
$$
$$
\times \exp\left\{ \frac{\tilde{P}_{\tilde{O}_b} D_{\tilde{O}_b i}}{r_i} + G_i'\Phi_i^{-1}G_i/2 - G_i'I_i \right\}, \tag{82}
$$

where

$$
\Phi_i = \frac{1}{|\Sigma_i|}\begin{pmatrix} \Sigma_{22i} + K_{1i}|\Sigma_i| & -\Sigma_{21i} \\ -\Sigma_{12i} & \Sigma_{11i} + 2D_{\tilde{O}_b i}|\Sigma_i| \end{pmatrix}.
$$

The first-order condition for the optimal holding of the options, $d^*_{\tilde{O}_b i}$, is given by

$$
\frac{\Sigma_{22i} + K_{1i}|\Sigma_i|}{1 + K_{1i}\Sigma_{11i} + 2d^*_{\tilde{O}_b i}(\Sigma_{22i} + K_{1i}|\Sigma_i|)/r_i} = P_{\tilde{O}_b},
$$

which simplifies to

$$
\left[\frac{1}{K_0} - \frac{1}{K_1 + s_1 + 1/r^2 p_1}\right]^{-1} + s_{0i} - s_0 + 2d^*_{\tilde{O}_b i}/r_i = P_{\tilde{O}_b}^{-1}.
$$

Equating the aggregate demand for the option to zero yields the equilibrium price of the option

$$
P_{\tilde{O}_b} = \frac{1}{K_0} - \frac{1}{K_1 + s_1 + 1/r^2 p_1},
$$

and the equilibrium holding of the option, $d_{O_b i}$, is obtained by substituting the expression for the price into the previous equation:

$$
d^*_{\tilde{O}_b i} = \frac{r_i}{2}(s_0 - s_{0i}) \equiv D^*_{\tilde{O}_b i}.
$$

The Review of Financial Studies / v 9 n 1 1996

The first-order condition for the equilibrium holding of the risky asset, d_{0i}, is

$$G_i' \Phi_i^{-1} \frac{dG_i}{dd_{0i}} = I' \frac{dG_i}{dd_{0i}},$$

which may be written as

$$(2d_{\tilde{Q}_0 i} E[B \mid F_{0i}] + d_{0i}/r_i)(\Sigma_{22i} + K_{1i}|\Sigma_i|) + K_{1i}\Sigma_{12i}E[A_i \mid F_{0i}]$$
$$= (1 + K_{1i}\Sigma_{11i} + 2d_{\tilde{Q}_0 i}\Sigma_{22i} + 2d_{\tilde{Q}_0 i}K_{1i}|\Sigma_i|)E[B \mid F_{0i}],$$

and simplifies to

$$d_{0i}^* = r_i \frac{(1 + K_{1i}\Sigma_{11i})E[B \mid F_{0i}] - K_{1i}\Sigma_{12i}E[A_i \mid F_{0i}]}{\Sigma_{22i} + K_{1i}|\Sigma_i|}$$

This is the same as the expression for d_{0i}^* in the proof of Theorem 6, which implies that the equilibrium demand for the risky asset is the same with or without the option. ∎

References

Amin, K., and M. C. Lee, 1993, "Option Trading and Earnings News Dissemination," working paper, University of Michigan.

Back, K., 1993, "Asymmetric Information and Options," *Review of Financial Studies*, 6, 435–472.

Bhushan, R., 1989, "Firm Characteristics and Analyst Following," *Journal of Accounting and Economics*, 11, 255–274.

Black, F., 1975, "Fact and Fantasy in the Use of Options," *Financial Analysts Journal*, 31, 36–41, 61–72.

Black, F., and M. S. Scholes, 1973, "The Pricing of Options and Corporate Liabilities," *Journal of Political Economy*, 81, 637–654.

Brennan, M. J., 1979, "The Pricing of Contingent Claims in Discrete Time Models," *Journal of Finance*, 34, 53–68.

Brennan, M. J., and Kraus, A., 1978, "Necessary Conditions for Aggregation in Security Markets," *Journal of Financial and Quantitative Analysis*, 40, 7–18.

Brennan, M. J., and R. Solanki, 1981, "Optimal Portfolio Insurance," *Journal of Financial and Quantiative Analysis*, 16, 279–300.

Cao, H. H., 1994, "The Effect of Derivative Assets on Endogenous Information Acquisition and Price Behavior in a Rational Expectations Economy," working paper, University of California, Los Angeles.

Capon, N., G. J. Fitzsimons, and R. A. Prince, 1993, "An Individual Level Analysis of the Mutual Fund Investment Decision," working paper, Columbia University.

Chan, K., Y. P. Chung, and H. Johnson, 1993, "Why Option Prices Lag Stock Prices: A Trading-Based Explanation," *Journal of Finance*, 48, 1957–1968.

Conrad, J., 1989, "The Price Effect of Option Introduction," *Journal of Finance*, 44, 487–498.

Cox, J., and M. Rubinstein, 1985, *Options Markets*, Prentice-Hall, Englewood Cliffs, N.J.

DeLong, J. B., A. Shleifer, L. Summers, and R. J. Waldman, 1990, "Positive Feedback Investment Strategies and Destabilizing Rational Speculation," *Journal of Finance*, 45, 379–395.

Detemple, J., and P. Jorion, 1990, "Option Listing and Stock Returns," *Journal of Banking and Finance*, 14, 781–801.

Detemple, J., and L. Selden, 1991, "A General Equilibrium Analysis of Options and Stock Market Interactions," *International Economic Review*, 32, 279–303.

Diamond, D. W., 1985, "Optimal Release of Information by Firms," *Journal of Finance*, 40, 1071–1094.

Duffie, D., and C.-F. Huang, 1985, "Implementing Arrow-Debreu Equilibrium by Continuous Trading of Few Long-Lived Securities," *Econometrica*, 53, 1337–1356.

Duffie, D., and C.-F. Huang, 1986, "Multi-period Security Markets with Differential Information: Martingales and Resolution Times," *Journal of Mathematical Economics*, 15, 283–303.

Easley, D., M. O'Hara, and P. S. Srinivas, 1993, "Option Volume and Stock Prices: Evidence on Where Informed Traders Trade," working paper, Cornell University.

Fedenia, M., and T. Grammatikos, 1992, "Options Trading and the Bid-Ask Spread on the Underlying Stocks," *Journal of Business*, 65, 335–351.

Figlewski, S., and G. P. Webb, 1993, "Options, Short Sales and Market Completeness," *Journal of Finance*, 48, 761–777.

Grundy, B. D., and M. McNichols, 1989, "Trade and the Revelation of Information through Prices and Direct Disclosure," *Review of Financial Studies*, 2, 495–526.

Harris, L., 1987, "Transaction Data Tests of the Mixture of Distributions Hypothesis," *Journal of Financial and Quantitative Analysis*, 22, 127–141.

Harris, M., and A. Raviv, 1993, "Differences of Opinion Make a Horse Race," *Review of Financial Studies*, 6, 473–506.

He, H., and J. Wang, 1993, "Differential Information and Dynamic Behavior of Stock Trading Volume," working paper, Massachusetts Institute of Technology.

Hellwig, M. F., 1980, "On the Aggregation of Information in Competitive Markets," *Journal of Economic Theory*, 22, 477–498.

Hirshleifer, J., 1972, "The Private and Social Value of Information and the Reward to Inventive Activity," *American Economic Review*, 62, 561–574.

Holden, C. W., and A. Subrahmanyam, 1992, "Long-lived Private Information and Imperfect Competition," *Journal of Finance*, 47, 247–270.

Jennings, R., and L. Starks, 1986, "Earnings Announcements, Stock Price Adjustment, and the Existence of Option Markets," *Journal of Finance*, 41, 107–125.

Karpoff, J. M., 1986, "A Theory of Trading Volume," *Journal of Finance*, 41, 1069–1087.

Karpoff, J. M., 1987, "The Relation between Price Changes and Trading Volume: A Survey," *Journal of Financial and Quantiative Analysis*, 22, 109–126.

Kim, O., and Robert E. Verrecchia, 1991a, "Market Reaction to Anticipated Announcements," *Journal of Financial Economics*, 30, 273–309.

207

The Review of Financial Studies / v 9 n 1 1996

Kim, O., and R. E. Verrecchia, 1991b, "Trading Volume and Price Reactions To Public Announcements," *Journal of Accounting Research*, 29, 302–321.

Kyle, A. S., 1985, "Continuous Auctions and Insider Trading," *Econometrica*, 53, 1315–1335.

Kyle, A. S., 1989, "Informed Speculation with Imperfect Competition," *Review of Economic Studies*, 56, 317–356.

Laffont, J.-J., 1985, "On the Welfare Analysis of Rational Expectations Equilibria with Asymmetric Information," *Econometrica*, 53, 1–29.

Lamoreaux, C., 1991, "Option Listing Does not Affect the Variance of the Underlying Stock: A Cautionary Tale," working paper, Washington University.

Lauterbach, B., and M. Ungar, 1993, "Switching to More Frequent Trading and Its Impact on Return Behavior and Volume of Trade," working paper, Bar Ilan University.

Leland, H. E., 1980, "Who Should Buy Portfolio Insurance?" *Journal of Finance*, 35, 581–594.

Manaster, S., and R. J. Rendleman, 1982, "Option Prices as Predictors of Equilibrium Stock Prices," *Journal of Finance*, 37, 1043–1057.

Milgrom, P., and N. Stokey, 1982, "Information, Trade and Common Knowledge," *Journal of Economic Theory*, 26, 17–27.

Nau, R. F., and K. F. McCardle, 1991, "Arbitrage, Rationality and Equilibrium," *Theory and Decision*, 31, 199–240.

Patel, J., R. Zeckhauser, and D. Hendricks, 1991, "The Rationality Struggle: Illustrations from Financial Markets," *American Economic Review*, 81, 232–236.

Rubinstein, M., 1974, "An Aggregation Theorem for Securities Markets," *Journal of Financial Economics*, 1, 225–244.

Skinner, D. J., 1989, "Options Markets and Stock Return Variability," *Journal of Financial Economics*, 23, 61–78.

Skinner, D. J., 1990, "Options Markets and the Information Content of Accounting Earnings Releases," *Journal of Accounting and Economics*, 13, 191–211.

Subrahmanyam, A., 1991, "Risk Aversion, Market Liquidity and Price Efficiency," *Review of Financial Studies*, 4, 417–441.

Verrecchia, R. E., 1982, "Information Acquisition in a Noisy Rational Expectations Economy," *Econometrica*, 50, 1415–1430.

Warther, V. A., 1994, "Aggregate Mutual Fund Flows and Security Returns," working paper, University of Southern California.

[18]

Stripping the S&P 500 Index

Michael J. Brennan

A new market in S&P 500 Index dividend strips, which are claims to a year's dividend on the index, would not only improve risk sharing but, more importantly, would also serve to focus investor attention on the fundamentals that determine the value of the index rather than simply on the future resale value of the index. Such a market would also reveal the market assessment of certainty-equivalent growth rates in dividends and thus help to promote rational pricing. Calculations are presented to illustrate the prices at which the index strips might trade, the associated certainty-equivalent growth rates, and the expected returns for given expected dividend growth rates.

———————◆———————

s doubts grow about the solvency of social security systems worldwide, and as corporations draw back from underwriting retirement income through defined-benefit pension plans, individuals are increasingly thrown back on their own resources to provide for their old age. Imagine, then, a world in which, perhaps like the old Eastern bloc countries, the only choice available to investors for a store of value is either a fixed-income security or valuable collectibles, such as gold, art, first editions, old clothes of the rich and famous, and so on. It is obvious that such an economic system would expose men and women attempting to provide for their retirement to tremendous and unnecessary risks because, unless they chose the fixed-income security, their future wealth would be dependent on how society valued the collectible items when the time came for them to sell and use the proceeds for retirement. Yet, our own system, in which investors choose between bonds and stocks, is not so very different. The return from owning stocks depends in large part on the level of stock prices when they are bought relative to the level when they are sold; but those price levels, like the prices of gold and collectibles, will depend heavily on the state of confidence, or long-term expectation, and may bear little relation to the *current* cash flow provided by the underlying assets. Figure 1 shows the variation in the price paid per dollar of annual dividends for the S&P 500 Index for the 1951–96

period. The price ranges from $15.04 to $41.24. Thus, the prices at which stocks trade show enormous variation relative to dividends, which are the *current* fundamentals. On the other hand, as shown in Figure 2, dividends themselves grow relatively smoothly. One need not claim, as some authors have, that stock prices move too much to be justified by fundamentals to recognize that there is considerably less risk associated with the dividends on the S&P 500 in any given year than is associated with the index itself. Yet, many investors are basing their retirement plans on the prices at which they expect to sell stocks in the future; they must be hoping that the price that the market is willing to pay for a dollar of dividends when the time comes to liquidate will be as high as (or even higher than) it is today.

But, after several years of extraordinary returns on U.S. stock market indexes, there can be few investors in the U.S. equity markets who are not wondering whether the market is currently "too high." I well remember asking a Japanese investment banker in 1988 how the dividend yield on the Tokyo market at that time could be so low (less than 1 percent). His reply was revealing. He said that the reason was that the "Japanese people do not like dividends very much." He obviously thought that the current prices of stocks, like the prices of collectibles, could be justified mainly by reference to their expected future prices, without regard to the dividend flow. This "greater fool" approach to valuation, once embraced by investors en masse, creates an inherently unstable situation, as the subsequent history of the Tokyo market was to demonstrate. A stock market in which prices depend almost entirely on hopes of future resale

Michael J. Brennan is the Goldyne and Irwin Hearsh Professor of Banking and Finance at the University of California at Los Angeles and a professor of finance at London Business School.

Figure 1.   Price–Dividend Ratio for the S&P 500, 1951–96

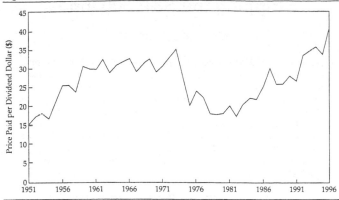

Note: The price is the January value of the S&P 500 to the value of the dividends paid on the S&P 500 portfolio during the calendar year.
Source: Based on Shiller (1989).

Figure 2.   Logarithm of Annual Dividends for the S&P 500, 1951–96

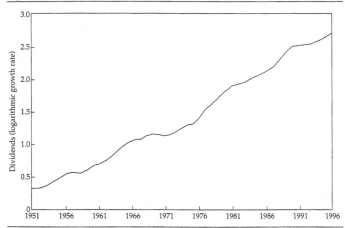

Note: The logarithm is the natural logarithm of the annual dividends paid on the S&P 500 portfolio.
Source: Based on Shiller (1989).

values is like a pyramid poised on its apex: Lacking sound foundations, it is likely to topple at the slightest disturbance that raises doubts about the future purchasers, whose future assumed behavior is underpinning the current level of prices.

No one knows whether the current level of prices in the United States is in fact "too high" or "too low." Indeed, it is not possible to know this without knowing what future growth rate of dividends the market is assuming and what risk premium or expected rate of return the market is requiring, since it is the relation between these two variables that determines whether the pricing is rational. This is illustrated by the simple Gordon growth model, in which the rational price is equal to the current dividend divided by the difference between the expected rate of return and the expected dividend growth rate. Prices may be high, for example, because expectations about future dividends are optimistic, or risk premiums are low, or because investors are simply extrapolating past returns, or because the demand for stocks by Baby Boomers saving for retirement is high (Bakshi and Chen 1994). We cannot tell the extent to which these different factors are important, because we currently cannot observe the value that the market is placing on what it is that stocks produce, namely dividends or, equivalently, the growth rate of dividends the market is implicitly discounting. But without being able to tell the dividend growth rate that the market is building into the current level of prices, investors cannot pit their estimates against those of the market. As a result, the level of the market may become disconnected from rational expectations about future dividend growth. This is what seems to have happened in Japan in the 1980s.

Is there anything that we can do to reduce the exposure of long-term stock market investors to the risks imposed by the need for them to sell their holdings in order to realize cash for consumption? Is there anything that we can do to clarify and expose the assumptions about fundamentals that the market is implicitly making in valuing stocks? I believe that there is. It is to have a market in S&P 500 strips, just as we already have a market in Treasury strips. The market in S&P 500 strips would trade the rights to the dividends paid on the S&P 500 portfolio for different calendar years.[1] The introduction of such a market would not only improve the allocation of risk in the economy by reducing the exposure of investors to the vagaries of the resale market for stocks, but it would also enhance the ability of markets to aggregate and transmit information—in this case about expected dividend growth rates. The development of markets in which future dividends, the fundamentals for valuation, are traded would also provide an incentive for analysts to concentrate on forecasting those fundamentals (in the jargon, "gathering costly information about future dividend growth rates"), rather than to concentrate on simply forecasting the level of the market itself.[2] In addition, since the level of the market index must be consistent with the prices of the future dividend flows, the relation between these will serve to reveal the implicit assumptions that the market is making in arriving at its valuation. These assumptions will then be the focus of analysis and debate.

A Market for Strips

To understand how a market in S&P 500 strips

would work, consider first how the market in Treasury strips works. This market, whose prices for a representative day are shown in Table 1, is a market for fixed dollar payments at a specified future date. For example, the price of $100 to be received in August 2000 is $83:28/32 and, as the last column of Table 1 reports, this represents a rate of return of 6.13 percent. The future payments that are traded in the Treasury strips market are the individual coupon and principal payments on Treasury bonds.

Table 1. U.S. Treasury Strip Prices and Yields, September 11, 1997

Year	Ask Price (32nds)	Ask Yield
1998	$94:29	5.78%
1999	89:10	5.98
2000	83:28	6.13
2001	78:21	6.22
2002	73:28	6.26
2003	69:06	6.33
2004	64:21	6.41
2005	60:10	6.49
2006	56:10	6.54
2007	52:18	6.59
2008	49:01	6.64
2009	45:21	6.69
2010	42:17	6.73
2011	39:20	6.77
2012	36:29	6.80
2013	34:12	6.82
2014	32:01	6.84
2015	29:29	6.86
2016	28:28	6.87
2017	26:00	6.88
2018	24:08	6.89
2019	22:22	6.89
2020	21:05	6.89

Source: Wall Street Journal, September 12, 1997.

Unlike the coupon and principal on Treasury bonds, which are fixed in advance, the dividends on stocks vary from year to year. Table 2 reports the aggregate dividend paid on the S&P 500 Index each year and the index level at the beginning of each year from 1960 to 1997.[3] The index corresponds to the value of a value-weighted portfolio of 500 stocks whose membership is subject to change. The dividends on the portfolio are assumed to be paid out (rather than re-invested). The portfolio, which was worth 614.42 at the beginning of 1996, paid a dividend of 14.90 during 1996. Define for convenience the *prospective dividend yield* as the dividend for the year divided by the price at the beginning of the year.[4] So the dividend yield for 1996, shown in the fourth column of Table 2, is 14.90/614.42 = 2.43

Table 2. S&P 500 Index Levels, Dividends, and Prospective Dividend Yields

Year	Index	Dividend	Dividend Yield
1960	58.03	1.95	3.36%
1961	59.72	2.02	3.38
1962	69.07	2.13	3.08
1963	65.06	2.28	3.50
1964	76.45	2.50	3.27
1965	86.12	2.72	3.16
1966	93.32	2.87	3.08
1967	84.45	2.92	3.46
1968	95.04	3.07	3.23
1969	102.04	3.16	3.10
1970	90.31	3.14	3.48
1971	93.49	3.07	3.28
1972	103.30	3.15	3.05
1973	118.42	3.38	2.85
1974	96.11	3.60	3.75
1975	72.56	3.68	5.07
1976	96.86	4.05	4.18
1977	103.81	4.67	4.50
1978	90.25	5.07	5.62
1979	99.71	5.65	5.67
1980	110.87	6.16	5.56
1981	132.97	6.63	4.99
1982	117.28	6.87	5.86
1983	144.27	7.09	4.91
1984	166.39	7.53	4.53
1985	171.61	7.90	4.60
1986	208.19	8.28	3.98
1987	264.51	8.81	3.33
1988	250.48	9.73	3.88
1989	285.41	11.05	3.87
1990	339.97	12.10	3.56
1991	325.50	12.20	3.75
1992	416.08	12.38	2.98
1993	435.23	12.58	2.86
1994	472.99	13.18	2.79
1995	465.25	13.79	2.96
1996	614.42	14.90	2.43
1997	766.22		

Note: Index level is for the beginning of the year.

percent. The table confirms the well-known fact that dividend yields have declined drastically in the past 20 years. It is this decline that has, in part, given rise to questions about the sustainablity of the current level of prices. The portfolio was worth 766.22 in January 1997 and is currently trading at 923.91. The dividends for 1997 are not yet known but, for the sake of argument, suppose that 1997 dividends grow by 10 percent over 1996 dividends; they will then be 16.39. The *realized* dividend yield for 1997 will then be 16.39/766.22 = 2.14 percent.

Now, suppose that an investment bank invested $923.91 million in an S&P 500 index fund on January 1, 1998, when the index was (still) trading at 923.91. The bank would then be able to sell

off strips entitling the holder to a given year's dividends on the index portfolio. A natural contract would be for $500 times the index dividends. Since the bank has invested $1 million times the index, it would be able to sell off $1,000,000/500 = 2,000 contracts for each year's dividends. For example, if the dividends on the index grew to 22.80 in 2003, then the holder of a single contract for the year 2003 would receive $500 × 22.80 = $11,400 in the year 2003. Suppose, for example, that the bank sold off all the dividends up to and including the dividend in 2019; then the bank would still own the rights to all dividends from 2020 on. This residual security would be the "2020 stripped (S&P 500) index." There is no reason why contracts for the stripped index should not also be traded: They would be attractive to individuals whose planned accumulations were such that they did not expect to consume any income from their portfolios before 2020. The dividend strips, on the other hand, would be attractive to individuals who expected to be consuming part of their portfolios over the intervening years. We shall have more to say below about the risk-sharing advantages of a market in dividend strips.

The market prices of the dividend strips, which reveal the market's valuation of dividends in each of the years, will reflect the market's (risk-adjusted) expectations about future dividend growth from year to year (more about this in the next section). Insofar as these growth rates converge to a constant for the distant years, this constant growth rate can be used in the standard Gordon growth formula (see Gordon and Shapiro 1956) to determine the market's implied dividend yield at the horizon. Then, with the dividend yield at the horizon and the price of the horizon year's dividend known, the price of the stripped index at the horizon can be constructed as the price of the horizon year dividend divided by the dividend yield. Thus, by focusing on the prices of the dividend strips for the next T years, one can arrive at a valuation for the market that rationally reflects the market's expectations of fundamentals, that is, the future dividend flows.

The Prices of Strips

At what prices might the dividend strips, the claims to these year-by-year dividends, trade? The first thing to note, of course, is that, if there are T strips, the prices of the T strips plus the price of the right to the index at the end of year T (the stripped index) will add up to the current level of the index. But, this is as far as one can go using only first principles, which is why the market prices of the strips would provide additional information about market expectations.

Therefore, to provide an illustration, the price

of the index will be allocated between the dividends of the different years and the residual "stripped index," by assuming that the future dividend yield on the index is a known constant. In particular, following Ross (1978), if S_0 is the current value of the index, and the dividends paid in year t are δS_{t-1}, so that the *prospective* dividend yield on the index portfolio, δ, is constant over time, then the present value at time zero of the dividends to be paid during year t is given by[5]

$$V_0(D_t) = \delta(1 - \delta)^{(t-1)} S_0,$$

and the value of the stripped index at the end of year T is equal to

$$V_0(S_T) = (1 - \delta)^T S_0.$$

Therefore, *as an example* of what a market for dividend strips might look like, the second column of Table 3 gives the present value, or imputed price, of each year's dividend strip up to 2019, under the assumption that the prospective yield on the index remains constant at 2.14 percent, which is equal to

the 1997 dividend of 16.39 (assuming 10 percent growth over 1996) divided by 766.22, the index level at the beginning of 1997.[6] Notice that the assumption that the dividend yield on the index portfolio is constant over time is not the same as assuming that the future dividends are known. It is the assumption that the dividend payment will fluctuate as much as the index itself. This assumption probably overstates the risk of dividends, particularly in the short run. Nevertheless, this approach provides a simple formula for allocating the total value of the index across the different dividend strips and the residual stripped index.

Under the constant dividend yield formula, the imputed values of each future year's dividends decline from year to year by a factor of $(1 - 0.0214) = 0.9786$. The formula attributes 574.04, or around 62 percent of the current index value, to the dividends after the year 2019, which are impounded in the value of the year 2020 stripped index. Note that, although individual value assignments are disput-

Table 3. Imputed Prices of Dividend Strips and Implied Certainty-Equivalent Growth Rates

Year	Imputed Price of Dividend Strip	Treasury Yield	Certainty-Equivalent Dividend Growth Rate	Certainty-Equivalent Forward Growth Rate
1998	19.77	5.84%	27.68%	28.68%
1999	19.35	5.98	15.15	3.85
2000	18.93	6.13	11.36	4.15
2001	18.53	6.22	9.53	4.21
2002	18.13	6.26	8.43	4.14
2003	17.74	6.33	7.75	4.40
2004	17.36	6.41	7.29	4.60
2005	16.99	6.49	6.97	4.76
2006	16.63	6.54	6.71	4.63
2007	16.27	6.59	6.51	4.75
2008	15.93	6.64	6.36	4.85
2009	15.58	6.69	6.24	4.95
2010	15.25	6.73	6.14	4.92
2011	14.92	6.77	6.06	5.00
2012	14.61	6.80	5.98	4.93
2013	14.29	6.82	5.91	4.83
2014	13.99	6.84	5.85	4.87
2015	13.69	6.86	5.80	4.91
2016	13.39	6.87	5.74	4.76
2017	13.11	6.88	5.69	4.78
2018	12.83	6.89	5.65	4.80
2019	12.55	6.89	5.60	4.60
Stripped 2020 index	574.04			
Sum	923.91			
1997 dividend	16.39			
January 1998 index value	923.91			
Prospective dividend yield	2.14%			

able and reflect the special assumption of the constant dividend yield formula, the overall value assignment adds up to the (then) current value of the index of 923.91.

Improvements in Risk Sharing

Stock prices are much more unpredictable than dividends, and the need to sell shares to meet consumption requirements imposes risks that individuals saving for retirement would avoid if they could purchase a finite stream of dividends directly. Indeed, economic theory suggests that from a risk-sharing perspective, it is efficient for individuals to condition their consumption in a given period on the aggregate consumption flow (Huang and Litzenberger 1988, Chapter 5). Therefore, to the extent that the growth in the aggregate dividend on the index is more closely related to the growth of aggregate consumption than is the return on the index, it is inefficient for investors who need to make near-term withdrawals from their portfolios to meet current consumption to be holding the market index rather than an appropriately weighted portfolio of dividend strips. It is reasonable to expect that dividend growth will be more closely related to the change in consumption than will the return on a stock market index, because even in an efficient market, the return on the index will reflect changes in the expectations at that date about *future* dividends.

Table 4 provides some summary statistics that seem to confirm this intuition. Although the correlations between the growth rate of real consumption and the growth rates in real dividends and real stock prices are similar, the table shows that the standard deviations of the growth rates in real stock prices have exceeded the standard deviations

in growth rates of real dividends by a factor of three in the post-World War II era. As a result, the standard deviation of the difference between the growth rate of consumption and the growth rate of real dividends is only 3.81 percent, compared with the standard deviation of the difference between the growth rate of consumption and the growth rate of stock prices of 14.77 percent. This suggests that there would be significant demand for dividend strips and that major improvements in risk sharing could be facilitated by introducing trading in such securities.

Almost 20 years ago, Hakansson (1978) proposed dividing up the market index into "supershares" in order to improve risk-sharing.[7] Although both proposals divide up the market index into different claims, Hakansson's program (which has largely been completed through the trading of index options, index-linked Certificates of Deposit, the failed Superfund, and so on) proposed to divide it into sub-claims whose payoffs would be contemporaneous, a key feature of the dividend strips is that their payoffs would be realized in different years.

Extracting Expectations from the Strip Prices

The second benefit of a market in dividend strips is that it would reveal the assumptions that the market is implicitly making in valuing stocks. As Hayek (1945) and Grossman (1989) have stressed, an important function of market prices is to aggregate and transmit information in the economy. The prices of dividend strips would perform this role for information about the expected rates of growth of divi-

---

Table 4. Measures of Association between Consumption Growth and Growth in Real Dividends and Stock Prices

Period	Dividends	Stock Prices
Correlations between annual growth rates in real dividends and consumption and real stock prices and consumption		
1890–1985	0.36	0.50
1951–1985	0.50	0.50
Standard deviations of annual growth rates in real dividends and real stock prices		
1890–1985	11.79%	17.52%
1951–1985	4.26	15.27
Standard deviations of differences in annual growth rates between real consumption and real dividends and between real consumption and real stock prices		
1890–1985	11.02%	16.07%
1951–1985	3.81	14.77

Source: Shiller (1989).

dends, which is the primary determinant of rational stock prices. In this section, the assumed prices of the dividend strips are used first to calculate the implicit risk-adjusted expected growth rates of dividends. Then, the long run risk-adjusted growth rate of dividends is used in conjunction with the price of a distant year's dividend to infer the value of the dividend-stripped value of the index. Finally, some illustrative calculations show how forecasts of dividend growth rates may be used to estimate the expected rates of return on the dividend strips as well as on the dividend-stripped index.

Expected Dividend Growth Rates. The third column of Table 3 reported the yields on Treasury strips maturing in August of each year as quoted in the *Wall Street Journal* of September 12, 1997. Given the imputed prices of the dividend strips, the dividend of 16.39 in 1997, and the Treasury yields, there exists for each year an implicit constant rate of growth in dividends from 1997 forward that will give the purchaser of the dividend strip the same rate of return as would be earned from buying the Treasury strip.[8] These *certainty-equivalent* growth rates were shown in the fourth column of Table 3. They are calculated under the assumption that the whole of the dividend is paid on the last day of the year.[9] These growth rates do not allow for the investor to earn any risk premium for the greater risks associated with investment in the equity market. The certainty-equivalent forward growth rates reported in the fourth column of the table were calculated in the same manner as forward interest rates. For comparison, note that the (arithmetic) average growth rate in dividends on the S&P 500 was 5.9 percent between 1960 and 1996 and 5.92 percent between 1960 and 1996—not much above the implied certainty equivalent growth rates for the longer-maturity dividend strips and well below the implied growth rates for the short-maturity strips.

Valuing the Stripped Index. How reasonable is the value of 574.04 assigned to the 2020 stripped index in Table 3? If one observed this market price for the stripped index, would it seem reasonable relative to the value of 12.55 assigned to the 2019 dividend? Consider the Treasury yield curve and the estimated long-run certainty-equivalent growth rates for dividends. If the long-run certainty-equivalent growth rate, g, is taken from the forward rate curve, a value of about 4.8 percent seems appropriate. Similarly, a value of around 7 percent seems appropriate for a long-term forward interest rate in 2020. Used in the Gordon growth formula, these rates imply that the index

level in 2020 would be related to the 2019 dividend, D_{2019}, as follows:

$$P_{2020} = \frac{D_{2019} \times 1.048}{0.07 - 0.048} = 47.64 \times D_{2019}.$$

Because the price assigned to the 2019 dividend is 12.55, this equation would imply a value for the 2020 stripped index of $12.55 \times 47.64 = 597.88$, which is not far from the market value imputed to the stripped index, 574.04.

The point of this illustration is that the long-run certainty-equivalent dividend growth rates and Treasury yields would have to be consistent with the relation between the market value of the stripped index and the market value of the longest dividend strip. Therefore, opening markets for the dividend strips would provide additional information relevant to assigning a value to the stripped index and thus to the value of the index today, because the value of the stripped index is a large component of the value of today's index.

Estimating Expected Rates of Return. Instead of using the prices of the dividend strips to calculate the implied certainty-equivalent growth rates as in Table 3, one could make one's own dividend growth forecasts and ask what the expected rate of return on each dividend strip and the 2020 stripped index would be. Table 5 contains the forecasts for the dividends under the assumption of a growth rate of 6 percent from 1997 forward and presents a comparison of these forecasts with the prices assigned to the dividend strips. Note first that the value assigned to the near-term dividends is too generous in relation to the 6 percent dividend growth assumption; the expected returns are negative for the near-term strips. Even for the longer-term strips, whose value assignments must be too low, under the assumption of a constant prospective dividend yield and a dividend growth rate about equal to the rate realized over the past 36 years, the expected rate of return on the strips and the stripped index is about 7 percent, barely above the corresponding Treasury yields. The expected value of the index in 2020 (2,925.50) is calculated by applying the prospective dividend yield of 2.14 percent to the year 2020 dividend, which is calculated from the 2019 dividend and the assumed growth rate.

Table 6 repeats the analysis but with a 7 percent growth rate. Now, the expected returns on the more distant dividend strips rise to somewhat above 8, or about 1.5 percent above the corresponding Treasury yields.

Finally, Table 7 repeats the analysis under the assumption that the 1998 dividend will grow by 45

Table 5. Calculation of Expected Returns on Dividend Strips for Dividend Growth Rate of 6 Percent

Year	Expected Dividend	Imputed Price of Dividend Strip	Expected Return	Treasury Yield
1998	17.37	19.77	−12.13%	5.84%
1999	18.42	19.35	−2.44	5.98
2000	19.52	18.93	1.02	6.13
2001	20.69	18.53	2.80	6.22
2002	21.93	18.13	3.88	6.26
2003	23.25	17.74	4.61	6.33
2004	24.64	17.36	5.13	6.41
2005	26.12	16.99	5.52	6.49
2006	27.69	16.63	5.83	6.54
2007	29.35	16.27	6.08	6.59
2008	31.11	15.93	6.28	6.64
2009	32.98	15.58	6.45	6.69
2010	34.96	15.25	6.59	6.73
2011	37.06	14.92	6.71	6.77
2012	39.28	14.61	6.82	6.80
2013	41.64	14.29	6.91	6.82
2014	44.13	13.99	6.99	6.84
2015	46.78	13.69	7.07	6.86
2016	49.59	13.39	7.13	6.87
2017	52.56	13.11	7.19	6.88
2018	55.72	12.83	7.24	6.89
2019	59.06	12.55	7.29	6.89
Stripped 2020 index				
2020		574.04		
Sum		923.91		
Expected index January 2020		2,925.50		
Expected return on stripped index		7.34%		
1997 dividend		16.39		
January 1998 index value		923.91		
Prospective dividend yield		2.14%		

percent and that dividends thereafter will grow at 7 percent. Under this relatively optimistic scenario, the expected returns on the near-term strips are very high and returns on the longer-term strips and the 2020 stripped index are about 9.8 percent, or about 300 basis points above the corresponding Treasury yields.

The purpose of this article is not to argue that the current level of the stock market is too high or too low. Rather, the preceding calculations are intended to illustrate the kind of analysis that would be encouraged by the existence of a market for dividend strips—analysis that focuses on the expected growth rate in the underlying fundamental, the dividend stream relative to Treasury strip yields. With the development of markets for price-level-indexed Treasury strips, the focus would also be on the expected real growth rates of dividends.

A Problem and a Possible Solution

Thus far, the assumptions have been that the dividends on the S&P 500 are exogenously determined by nature and that their risk is the ultimate social risk that is to be borne by investors. In reality, the dividends in any year are determined by the decisions of boards of directors, and the dividends are only one component of the net cash flow received by equityholders.[10] This raises two concerns. First, changes in government tax policies may affect corporate dividends.[11] Secondly, to the extent that corporate managements take positions in the dividend strips, they might have an incentive to change corporate dividend policies to the advantage or the detriment of stripholders. These concerns, if taken seriously, would introduce risks for the holders of dividend strips that are not related to the underlying risks in the economy and, therefore, should not exist in an efficient risk-sharing arrangement. The concerns would also make determining the appro-

Table 6. Calculation of Expected Returns on Dividend Strips for Dividend Growth Rate of 7 Percent

Year	Expected Dividend	Imputed Price of Dividend Strip	Expected Return	Treasury Yield
1998	17.54	19.77	−11.30%	5.84%
1999	18.76	19.35	−1.52	5.98
2000	20.08	18.93	1.97	6.13
2001	21.48	18.53	3.77	6.22
2002	22.99	18.13	4.86	6.26
2003	24.60	17.74	5.59	6.33
2004	26.32	17.36	6.12	6.41
2005	28.16	16.99	6.52	6.49
2006	30.13	16.63	6.83	6.54
2007	32.24	16.27	7.08	6.59
2008	34.50	15.93	7.28	6.64
2009	36.91	15.58	7.45	6.69
2010	39.50	15.25	7.59	6.73
2011	42.26	14.92	7.72	6.77
2012	45.22	14.61	7.83	6.80
2013	48.39	14.29	7.92	6.82
2014	51.77	13.99	2.00	6.84
2015	55.40	13.69	8.08	6.86
2016	59.27	13.39	8.14	6.87
2017	63.42	13.11	8.20	6.88
2018	67.86	12.83	8.26	6.89
2019	72.61	12.55	8.31	6.89
Stripped 2020 index				
2020		574.04		
Sum		923.91		
Expected index January 2020		3,630.71		
Expected return on stripped index		8.35%		
1997 dividend		16.39		
January 1998 index value		923.91		
Prospective dividend yield		2.14%		

priate prices of the dividend strips more difficult. Although neither concern seems to be of major importance, both can be allayed by modifying the dividend strip to a "cash flow strip," which is a claim to the net cash flow distributed by the S&P 500, where net cash flow is defined by

Net cash flow = Dividends + Share repurchases − New share issues (+ Other cash distributions).

"Other cash distributions" might include such things as the proceeds from takeovers of firms in the index.

The advantage of the cash flow strip is that it would be immune to changes in corporate dividend policies. The disadvantage is that the S&P 500 Index, which is a price index, would have to be replaced by a redefined index to take account of the net cash flow.[12]

Conclusion

A market in dividend strips on a stock market index could enhance the efficiency of the economy in two major directions. First, such a market would enhance the *allocative* efficiency of the economy by allowing investors to purchase claims that are more closely tied to the current fundamentals in the economy than is the current stock market index.[13] Secondly, the prices of the dividend claims would aggregate and transmit the information in the economy about year-to-year dividend growth rates. This would increase the *informational efficiency* of the economy and facilitate the rational pricing of equities.

How dividend or cash flow strips might be introduced is beyond the scope of this article. The history of the introduction of Treasury strips hints at a role for the investment banks who might buy

Table 7. Calculation of Expected Returns on Dividend Strips for Dividend Growth Rate of 45 Percent in 1998 and 7 Percent Thereafter

Year	Expected Dividend	Imputed Price of Dividend Strip	Expected Return	Treasury Yield
1998	23.77	19.77	20.22%	5.84%
1999	25.43	19.35	14.65	5.98
2000	27.21	18.93	12.85	6.13
2001	29.12	18.53	11.96	6.22
2002	31.16	18.13	11.43	6.26
2003	33.34	17.74	11.08	6.33
2004	35.67	17.36	10.83	6.41
2005	38.17	16.99	10.64	6.49
2006	40.84	16.63	10.50	6.54
2007	43.70	16.27	10.38	6.59
2008	46.76	15.93	10.29	6.64
2009	50.03	15.58	10.21	6.69
2010	53.53	15.25	10.14	6.73
2011	57.28	14.92	10.08	6.77
2012	61.29	14.61	10.03	6.80
2013	65.58	14.29	9.99	6.82
2014	70.17	13.99	9.95	6.84
2015	75.09	13.69	9.92	6.86
2016	80.34	13.39	9.89	6.87
2017	85.96	13.11	9.86	6.88
2018	91.98	12.83	9.84	6.89
2019	98.42	12.55	9.81	6.89

Stripped 2020 index		
2020	574.04	
Sum	923.91	
Expected index January 2020	4,921.06	
Expected return on stripped index	9.79%	
1997 dividend	16.39	
January 1998 index value	923.91	
Prospective dividend yield	2.14%	

the index portfolio and sell off the dividend strips as we have described. Note, however, that the initial pricing of dividend strips would be considerably more difficult than the initial pricing of Treasury strips, which was facilitated by the ability to construct pseudo spot yield curves from the prices of existing coupon bonds. No corresponding securities exist in the equity market to assist in the pricing of long-term dividend strips.[14] So, the risk for the investment bank initiating dividend strips would be correspondingly greater. I have also not attempted to discuss such practical details as taxation, the aggregation of dividends during the year, or the kind of trust vehicle that would be appropriate for issuing such securities. Finally, the analysis has been informal and intuitive. I hope to develop these ideas more formally in a subsequent article.

I am grateful to O. Ledoit, S.A. Ross, and A. Subrahmanyam for constructive comments.

Notes

1. I use the S&P 500 portfolio as convenient shorthand. It should be clear that any comprehensive market index would do as well.

2. Keynes wrote of professional investors that "most of these persons are, in fact, largely concerned, not with making superior long-term forecasts of the probable yield of an investment over its whole life, but with foreseeing changes in the conventional basis of valuation a short time ahead of the general public" (Keynes, 1936, p. 154).

3. I am grateful to Robert Shiller for making these data available.

4. Note that this does not correspond to conventional practice, which defines the dividend yield as the lagged dividend divided by the current price.

5. The logic of the argument is straightforward. Consider a portfolio that is currently worth $100. A promise to receive the first payout on the portfolio, which will be equal to x percent of the value of the portfolio on the payout date, will be worth $x today regardless of the timing of the distribution. Similarly, the second payout, which will be equal to y percent of the value of the portfolio on the payout date, has a current value of $y(100 − x), and so on.

6. The prices that I impute to the dividend strips are not intended as forecasts of the prices at which such strips might trade.

7. Shiller (1993) also discusses the introduction of new markets to improve risk sharing in the economy.

8. The growth rate of year t, g_t, is given by $g_t = (P_t/D_0)1/t(1 + r_{ft})$, where P_t is the price of the year t dividend, D_0 is the Year 0 dividend, and r_{ft} is the zero coupon yield for t years.

9. These rates are the expected growth rates computed with respect to the "equivalent martingale measure" of Harrison and Kreps (1979).

10. The other components are share repurchases, cash purchases of shares in other firms, and new share issues. See Ackert and Smith (1993).

11. The 1936 tax on undistributed corporate profits led to an increase in the median payout ratio from 66 percent in 1935 to 76 percent in 1936, and the median growth in dividends was 25 percent in the first year of the tax. See Christie and Nanda (1994).

12. The price change on the modified index would be equal to the change in the value of the portfolio of S&P 500 firms less the net cash flow as defined in the text. The current index price change is calculated by subtracting only the dividends from the change in the value of the portfolio.

13. Although I explicitly consider only simple claims to the aggregate dividend, a simple extension could consider the nonlinear claims that would probably be required for optimal risk sharing.

14. The maturities of index futures and option contracts are currently too short to provide much assistance.

References

Ackert, L.F., and B.F. Smith. 1993. "Stock Price Volatility, Ordinary Dividends and Other Cash Flows to Shareholders." *Journal of Finance*, vol. 48, no. 4 (September):1147–60.

Bakshi, G.S., and Z. Chen. 1994. "Baby Boom, Population Aging, and Capital Markets." *Journal of Business*, vol. 67, no. 2 (April):165–202.

Brennan, M.J. 1990. "Presidential Address: Latent Assets." *Journal of Finance*, vol. 45, no. 3 (July):709–30.

Christie, W.G., and V. Nanda. 1994. "Free Cash Flow, Shareholder Value and the Undistributed Profits Tax of 1936 and 1937." *Journal of Finance*, vol. 49, no. 5 (December):1727–54.

Froot, K., D.S. Scharfstein, and J.C. Stein. 1992. "Herd on the Street: Informational Inefficiencies in a Market with Short-Term Speculation." *Journal of Finance*, vol. 47, no. 4 (September):1461–84.

Gordon, M.J., and E. Shapiro. 1956. "Capital Equipment Analysis: The Required Rate of Profit." *Management Science*, vol. 3, no. 1 (October):102–10.

Grossman, S.J. 1989. *The Informational Role of Prices*. Cambridge, MA: MIT Press.

Hakansson, N.H. 1978. "Welfare Aspects of Options and Supershares." *Journal of Finance*, vol. 33, no. 3 (September):759–76.

Harrison, M., and D. Kreps. 1979. "Martingales and Arbitrage in Multi-Period Securities Markets." *Journal of Economic Theory*, vol. 20, no. 2 (April):381–408.

Hayek, F.H. 1945. "The Use of Knowledge in Society." *American Economic Review*, vol. 70, no. 2 (June):393–408.

Huang, C-f., and R.H. Litzenberger. 1988. *Foundations for Financial Economics*. Amsterdam: North-Holland.

Keynes, J.M. 1936. *The General Theory of Employment, Interest and Money*. London: MacMillan.

Ross, S.A. 1978. "A Simple Approach to the Valuation of Risky Streams." *Journal of Business*, vol. 51, no. 3 (July):453–76.

Shiller, R.J. 1981. "Do Stock Prices Move Too Much to Be Justified by Subsequent Changes in Dividends?" *American Economic Review*, vol. 71, no. 1 (March):421–76.

———. 1989. *Market Volatility*. Cambridge, MA: MIT Press

———. 1993. *Macro Markets*. Oxford, England: Clarendon Press.

Tuckman, B., and J.L. Vila. 1992. "Arbitrage with Holding Costs: An Arbitrage-Based Approach." *Journal of Finance*, vol. 47, no. 4 (September):1283–302.

PART III

INFORMATION AND PRICE FORMATION IN FINANCIAL MARKETS

[19]

THE JOURNAL OF FINANCE • VOL. LII, NO. 5 • DECEMBER 1997

International Portfolio Investment Flows

MICHAEL J. BRENNAN and H. HENRY CAO*

ABSTRACT

This article develops a model of international equity portfolio investment flows based on differences in informational endowments between foreign and domestic investors. It is shown that when domestic investors possess a cumulative information advantage over foreign investors about their domestic market, investors tend to purchase foreign assets in periods when the return on foreign assets is high and to sell when the return is low. The implications of the model are tested using data on United States (U.S.) equity portfolio flows.

DESPITE THE APPARENT advantages of the international diversification of equity portfolios, demonstrated by Grubel (1968), Levy and Sarnat (1970) and Solnik (1974), and despite the general relaxation of controls on foreign portfolio investments by developed countries that took place in the early 1980s, French and Poterba (1991), Cooper and Kaplanis (1994) and Tesar and Werner (1995) show that there continues to exist a strong domestic bias in national equity portfolios. Explanations that have been offered for this bias include both barriers to capital flows created by higher costs of transacting in foreign securities, withholding taxes, and political risk, as well as other factors such as the failure of purchasing power parity (PPP), information asymmetries, and regulation.

Equilibrium models of international asset pricing that explain the domestic bias in terms of tax and transaction cost barriers to international capital flows have been developed by Black (1974) and Stulz (1981). However, higher transaction costs on foreign transactions could be expected to lead to lower turnover rates on the overseas components of portfolios than on the domestic components, yet Tesar and Werner (1995) find just the opposite: portfolio turnover rates are higher on foreign than on domestic portfolios. Similarly, while withholding taxes on foreign investment income can be expected to cause a home bias in the composition of investment portfolios to the extent that these taxes cannot be offset against domestic taxes, Cooper and Kaplanis (1994) and French and Poterba (1991) find that the expected return differentials that are required to explain the observed degree of home bias exceed what can reason-

* Brennan is from the University of California, Los Angeles, and London Business School. Cao is from the University of California, Berkeley. We are grateful to the Center for International Business Education and Research of the University of California, Los Angeles for financial support. Previous versions of this article were presented at the meetings of AFFI, Geneva 1996, the Northern Finance Association, Quebec City 1996, and the CEPR Summer Workshop, Gerzensee, 1996. The article has been improved as a result of comments from the referee and the editor, René Stulz.

ably be attributed to the effects of differential taxation of foreign investments. Finally, Frankel (1991) shows that for most developed countries political risks, as reflected in the differentials between Euro and domestic interest rates, are too small to account for significant biases in the composition of portfolios.

Adler and Dumas (1983) and Uppal (1993) show that deviations from PPP that lead investors in different countries to choose portfolios to hedge different inflation could also create a home bias in investment portfolios. However, Cooper and Kaplanis (1994) demonstrate that the magnitude of PPP deviations, combined with plausible estimates of the deadweight costs of foreign investing, are sufficient to explain observed portfolio allocations only if investors have very low levels of risk aversion. While residual regulations on foreign portfolio investments remain even in developed countries,[1] they also seem insufficient to account for the magnitude of the domestic bias found in these countries.

In the more recent models of Low (1992), Gehrig (1993), and Kang and Stulz (1994), asymmetric information between domestic and foreign investors leads to a home bias. Kang and Stulz present empirical evidence that foreign investment in Japanese equities is concentrated in the largest firms, which is consistent with foreign investors having relatively less information about small firms than local investors, whereas Carlos and Lewis (1995) demonstrate that informational considerations were of first order importance in explaining British investment in Canadian railroads in the 19th Century; Chuhan (1992) reports that market participants list limited information on emerging markets as one of the major impediments to investing in those markets.

In this article we develop and test the implications of the information asymmetry hypothesis for *flows* of portfolio investment between countries. Thus our analysis complements the previous articles that have explored the static implications of information asymmetry for the composition of equity portfolios. International portfolio flows have received little theoretical analysis,[2] even though they have grown enormously following the liberalization of capital markets in the early 1980s, not to mention the recent fashion for emerging capital markets.

---

[1] Developed countries continue to impose regulations on foreign investments by pension funds and insurance companies: for example Germany limits foreign investments to 5 percent of the value of the portfolio of insurance companies and pension funds; New York State raised the ceiling on foreign investments of insurance companies from 3 percent to 6 percent of asset in 1990; Japan has a 30 percent limitation for insurance companies and pension funds; Canada had a foreign investment limit of 10 percent until 1991. Source: Goldstein and Folkerts-Landau (1994).

[2] Miller and von Neumann Whitman (1970, 1972) combine a portfolio balance model with stock adjustment to explain aggregate U.S. foreign portfolio investment. Other empirical studies include Tesar and Werner (1994, 1995) and Chuhan et al. (1993), who report that the first principal component of several U.S. interest rates and industrial production has some explanatory power for monthly flows of equity capital from the U.S. to Latin America and Asia; Bohn and Tesar (1996) report, consistent with the theory and empirical findings in this article, that monthly U.S. portfolio flows are positively related to the contemporaneous returns in the host market for most large equity markets.

The model we develop abstracts from barriers to investment, currency and political risk, deviations from purchasing power parity, and interest rate differentials in order to focus on the implications of informational differences between foreigners and domestic residents. The model is a dynamic generalization of the noisy rational expectations model of Hellwig (1980), extended by Admati (1985) to a multiasset setting. The basic assumption underlying the model is similar to that of Low (1992), Gehrig (1993), and Kang and Stulz (1994) in that domestic investors are assumed to be better informed about the payoffs on the domestic market than are foreign investors.

Some would argue with this assumption of geographic information asymmetry since communication between countries is now close to instantaneous. Nevertheless, we believe that such an assumption may have considerable descriptive appeal. First, Coval and Moskowitz (1996) find that even portfolios of U.S. domestic mutual funds are geographically biased toward the home of the fund; and problems of distance are dwarfed by problems of language and communication, so that while information about the domestic economy may be acquired virtually costlessly by regular reading of the local press and normal business activities, information about foreign economies requires considerably more effort to acquire—subscriptions to foreign newspapers, translations, and so forth.[3] Our formal model requires only an information asymmetry for the *average* (individual) investor in different countries—there is little doubt that such asymmetry exists between most pairs of countries. Nevertheless, it is probably true that a major part of international portfolio investment is carried out by financial institutions, pension funds, and so forth, and for these investors it might seem that the case for information asymmetry is much weaker. However, while it is true that institutions will often have individuals assigned to monitoring various foreign countries, we believe that it is rare for these informed individuals to have sole responsibility for country allocation.[4] Consistent with the asymmetric information hypothesis, Shukla and Inwegen (1995) report that foreign managed mutual funds in the U.S. are outperformed by domestic funds and that at least part of this performance shortfall is attributable to inferior market timing by the foreign funds. Shiller *et al.* (1996) provide striking evidence that expectations about market returns differ very significantly between countries. Using survey data from a large number of Japanese financial institutions and U.S. institutional investors, they report that: "The Japanese were uniformly more optimistic in their short run expectations for the Japanese market than were the Americans. At a horizon of one

---

[3] The difficulty that foreigners have in obtaining information in some markets is recognized by Price (1994) who remarks of Argentina that "foreigners have been cautioned to use influential intermediaries if they hope to succeed . . . in a market that releases all too little essential investment information . . ."

[4] The dangers of assigning too much local responsibility to an individual simply because he is better informed are well illustrated by the Barings debacle and the more recent Morgan-Grenfell incident in which the manager of an overseas fund greatly exceeded prudent (as well as legal) norms in his allocations to individual companies.

year, there was usually a spread on the order of *20 percentage points*[5] between
the Japanese and U.S. forecasts for the Japanese market." While this is not
direct evidence of differences in information precisions, it does suggest that
geographic location or country of origin may have some bearing on information
acquisition about different country returns.[6]

The assumption of information asymmetry is shown to imply a home-bias in
portfolio holdings relative to a model with homogeneous information, and a
higher turnover rate on foreign than on domestic portfolios, and to place
testable restrictions on the relation between international flows of portfolio
investment and returns on foreign and domestic assets. In order to focus
attention on the role of information asymmetry, exchange risk and interest
rate differentials are ignored, and the analysis is conducted in a model with
many trading periods but only a single terminal consumption period.[7]

The major empirical implications of the model are that purchases of foreign
equities will be a linear function of returns on the domestic and foreign equity
markets; and that the coefficient of the return on the foreign market index will
be positive, provided that foreign investors are less well informed about the
payoffs on stock than are local investors,[8] and provided that the information
advantage of locals is the result of a gradual process of superior information
acquisition rather than of periodic large information leakages to locals. The
sign of the coefficient of the return on the domestic market index is indeterminate.

The intuition for the result is as follows. Foreign and domestic investors
have positions in a national stock market based on their past private information signals, past public signals, and the information about the private signals
received by others that they are able to glean from the price in a noisy rational
expectations equilibrium. Given these portfolio positions, a public signal leads
investors to revise their priors. The assumption of normal distributions implies
that the effect of the public signal on the precision of investors' priors is
independent of the signal realization. However, investors do revise the means
of their predictive distributions in a way that depends on the signal realization. Most importantly, the less well informed (i.e., foreign) investors revise the
means of their distributions by more than do better-informed (i.e., local)
investors. This implies, for example, that if the public signal conveys good
news about the payoff on the domestic market portfolio, foreign investors
increase their assessment of the expected payoff faster than do better informed

---

[5] Emphasis added.

[6] The *Wall Street Journal* frequently carries stories highlighting foreigners' views of U.S.
stocks: Typical headlines include "Cautious foreigners shun U.S. stocks," WSJ December 4, 1995,
"A rare view from abroad: bullish on U.S.," WSJ August 19, 1996.

[7] The single period nature of our model allows us to derive closed form expressions for prices and
trades. Noisy rational expectations models with more than one consumption period such as Wang
(1993) require numerical solution.

[8] The idea that foreigners will be net sellers of equities in bad times is commonly held. For
example, "As stock prices in 'emerging markets' stagger on the bad news from Mexico . . . Mutual
fund managers are rushing for the exits." *Wall Street Journal*, January 13, 1995.

domestic investors; as a result, the price rises to clear the market, and the less well informed foreign investors purchase more of the domestic market portfolio from the better informed domestic investors; the reverse occurs if the news is bad and the price falls. The net effect is that foreign purchases of the market portfolio tend to be positively correlated with the return on the portfolio. The situation is only slightly complicated by news about the payoff on the other market, and indeed if the signal errors in the two markets are independent, then purchases of foreign securities depend only on the return on the foreign market index, and not on the return on the domestic index.

It is important for our theory that the information advantage of domestic investors accrue gradually over time, because the trend following behavior of foreign investors is dependent on their relative information disadvantage *at the start* of the trading period. In fact, if foreign investors enter the period with no information disadvantage, but receive a less precise signal than domestic investors during the trading period, then foreign investors could act as contrarians. The intuition here is that if domestic investors receive a more precise signal than do foreigners then they will revise their priors by more than do foreigners, and this will cause them to be net buyers (and foreigners net sellers) when the average private signal is good so that the price rises. We derive our empirical model by assuming that the information advantage of domestic investors accrues gradually over time from their closer observation of the domestic economy since we believe that it is unlikely that domestic investors would, as a group, be privy to significant information events in any one period that were unknown to foreigners.

We test the association between foreign purchases of equities and the domestic index return by examining U.S. purchases of equities in four developed countries and sixteen emerging markets. We also examine the association between purchases of U.S. equities from the four developed countries and the return on the U.S. market index. We find that U.S. purchases of equities in foreign developed markets tend to be positively associated with the concurrent return in that market; this is consistent with U.S. investors being less well informed about those markets than local investors. However, it is also consistent with exogenous shifts in U.S. investors' demand for foreign securities, that are unrelated to new information, having a price impact on the foreign market, so we are not able to distinguish these hypotheses. There is no association between purchases of U.S. equities by residents of the four developed countries and the concurrent return on the U.S. market index, so there is no indication that investors in these countries are less well informed than U.S. residents about the returns on U.S. equities. It is perhaps to be expected that information asymmetries will be most pronounced in the emerging markets, and for these markets we do tend to find that U.S. purchases are positively associated with the concurrent return on the local market index. While this could be attributable to exogenous shifts in U.S. demands affecting foreign stock prices, we also find some evidence that U.S. purchases are positively related to the *previous* quarter's return; this is not explicable in terms of market impact, but is consistent with the asymmetric information story if this is extended to allow for lagged decision-making by U.S. investors. Finally there is no evidence of wealth effects that would cause purchases of foreign securities to be positively associated with the return on the domestic market index.

The article is organized as follows. Section I presents a general model of a noisy dynamic rational expectations equilibrium with many assets. In Section II this is interpreted within an international context to yield testable predictions about the relation between equity portfolio flows and national stock market returns. Section III describes the data that are used in the empirical tests. The empirical results for developed and emerging markets are described in Sections IV, V, and VI.

I. A General Model

We first consider a dynamic generalization of the multiasset noisy rational expectations model of Admati (1985). The payoffs on the M risky assets are realized at time 1, and are represented by a $M \times 1$ normally distributed random vector $\tilde{U}$ with mean $\bar{U}$ and precision matrix H. Without loss of generality, the riskless interest rate is taken as zero. Each investor i, $i \in [0, 1]$, is endowed at time 0 with quantities of the risky assets represented by the vector X^i; investors are characterized by exponential utility functions defined over time 1 consumption with common coefficient of absolute risk aversion $1/r$. The vector of aggregate per capita supply of the risky assets, $\tilde{X}_0$, is normally and independently distributed with mean $\bar{X}_0$ and precision matrix Φ_0. Unlike Admati who considers only a single trading session, we allow trading to take place in T trading sessions which are held at times $\tau_t = t/T$, $t = 0, \ldots, T - 1$. The asset payoffs are realized and consumption takes place at time 1 after the last trading session: there is no intermediate consumption in the model.

Immediately prior to trading session t, each investor i obtains an $M \times 1$ vector of *private* signals about the asset payoffs, $\tilde{Z}_t^i$, where

$$\tilde{Z}_t^i = \tilde{U} + \tilde{\epsilon}_t^i,$$

$\tilde{\epsilon}_t^i$ is distributed normally and independently of $\tilde{U}$, has mean zero, and is independent of $\tilde{\epsilon}_j^k$, if $k \neq i$ or $j \neq t$. The precision matrix of the private signals received by investor i immediately before session t is denoted by S_t^i. In addition to the private signals, a vector of *public* signals is released immediately before each trading session $t = 0, \ldots, T - 1$. The public signals are represented by the $M \times 1$ vector $\tilde{Y}_t$, where

$$\tilde{Y}_t = \tilde{U} + \tilde{\eta}_t.$$

$\tilde{\eta}_t$ is normally distributed with mean zero and precision matrix N_t. We assume that $N_0 = N_T^{-1} = O$ where O is a zero matrix, to reflect the assumption that there is no public information at time 0 and that all risky asset returns are realized at session T. For notational simplicity, we define $\tilde{Y}_0 = 0$. New liquidity traders are assumed to enter the market in each trading session $t = 1, \ldots,$

$T - 1$ after the initial session; the incremental net supply of these traders is represented by the normally distributed random vectors, $\tilde{X}_t$, which have means, $\bar{X}_t$, and precision matrices, Φ_t. For simplicity we shall impose $\bar{X}_t = 0$, for $t > 0$. In order to retain the less than fully revealing nature of the rational expectations equilibrium described in the theorem below we assume that the total volume of trading is not observable by traders.[9]

The elements of the precision matrices, S_t^i, are assumed to be uniformly bounded, and S_t, the population average of the precision matrix at trading session t, is given by

$$S_t \equiv \int_0^1 S_t^i \, di.$$

We follow the convention used by Admati (1985) in defining the integral of random variables in the continuum economy with multiple risky assets. If $(\tilde{V}^i)_{i \in [0,1]}$ is a process of independent random variables with zero mean and bounded variance, and $(\tilde{W}^i)_{i \in [0,1]}$ is almost surely integrable, then $\int_0^1 (\tilde{V}^i + \tilde{W}^i) \, di = \int_0^1 \tilde{W}^i \, di$. For example, this convention implies that $\int_0^1 \tilde{Z}^i = \tilde{U}$, a.s., and $\int_0^1 S_t^i \tilde{Z}^i = S_t \tilde{U}$, a.s.

Let $\tilde{P}_t$ denote the vector of equilibrium risky asset prices, $\tilde{D}_t^i$ the vector of risky asset demands for investor i in market session t, $\tilde{F}_t$ the public information set including the prices at trading session t, and $\tilde{F}_t^i$ the information set of investor i at trading session t. Then the following theorem describes the risky asset prices and investor asset demands at each market session in a noisy rational expectations equilibrium:[10]

THEOREM: *There exists a partially revealing rational expectations equilibrium in the T trading session economy in which*

(i) the vectors of risky asset prices, $\tilde{P}_t$, and individual asset demands, $\tilde{D}_t^i$, are given by:

$$\tilde{P}_t = K_t^{-1}\left[\left(K_t - \sum_{j=0}^{t} S_j\right)\tilde{\mu}_t + \sum_{j=0}^{t} \{S_j\tilde{U} - \tilde{X}_j/r\}\right], \qquad (1)$$

$$\tilde{D}_t^i = rK_t^i[\tilde{\mu}_t^i - \tilde{P}_t] = r\left[\sum_{j=0}^{t} \{S_j^i\tilde{Z}_j^i - S_j\tilde{U} + \tilde{X}_j/r - (S_j^i - S_j)\tilde{P}_t\}\right], \qquad (2)$$

where

$$\tilde{\mu}_t^i \equiv E(\tilde{U}|\tilde{F}_t^i) = (K_t^i)^{-1}\left(H\bar{U} + \sum_{j=0}^{t}[N_j\tilde{Y}_j + S_j^i\tilde{Z}_j^i + r^2S_j\Phi_jS_j\tilde{Q}_j]\right),$$

---

[9] See Blume *et al.* (1994) for a model in which trading volume is informative.
[10] The proof is given in the Appendix.

$$\bar{\mu}_t \equiv E(\tilde{U}|\tilde{F}_t) = \left(K_t - \sum_{j=0}^{t} S_j \right)^{-1} \left(HU + \sum_{j=0}^{t} [N_j\tilde{Y}_j + r^2 S_j\Phi_j S_j\tilde{Q}_j] \right),$$

$$\tilde{Q}_j = \tilde{U} - r^{-1}S_j^{-1}(\tilde{X}_j - \bar{X}_j),$$

$$K_t^i \equiv \mathrm{Var}^{-1}(\tilde{U}|\tilde{F}_t^i) = H + \sum_{j=0}^{t} [S_j^i + N_j + r^2 S_j\Phi_j S_j],$$

$$K_t \equiv \int_0^1 K_t^i \, di = H + \sum_{j=0}^{t} [N_j + S_j + r^2 S_j\Phi_j S_j].$$

(ii) The optimal trading strategy of the individual investor i is given by

$$\nabla \tilde{D}_t^i \equiv \tilde{D}_t^i - \tilde{D}_{t-1}^i = r \left[S_t^i(\tilde{Z}_t^i - \tilde{P}_t) - S_t(\tilde{U} - \tilde{P}_t) + \frac{\tilde{X}_t}{r} - \sum_{j=0}^{t-1} (S_j^i - S_j)\nabla \tilde{P}_t \right],$$

(3)

where $\nabla \tilde{P}_t \equiv \tilde{P}_t - \tilde{P}_{t-1}$.

Equation (3) shows that the trading strategy of investor i in period t depends on i) the difference between his vector of private signals in period t and the vector of prices, $\tilde{P}_t$, weighted by his private signal precision matrix, S_t^i, ii) the difference between the vector of the average private signal, $\tilde{U}$, and the vector of prices, $\tilde{P}_t$, weighted by the average private signal precision matrix, S_t, iii) the vector of supply shocks due to new liquidity traders in session $\tilde{X}_t$, and iv) the vector of price changes, $\nabla \tilde{P}_t$, weighted by the difference between the investor's private signal precision matrix and the market average precision matrix, $S_j^i - S_j$, accumulated for all sessions up to session $t - 1$.

Since the econometrician observes neither the supply shock nor the private signals, it is convenient to consider the expected trade of investor i conditional on the vector of price changes at time t, $\nabla \tilde{P}_t$; the conditional expected trade vector may be written as:

$$E[\nabla \tilde{D}_t^i|\nabla \tilde{P}_t] = r[\omega_t^i \Gamma_t \nabla \tilde{P}_t + E[\tilde{X}_t/r|\nabla \tilde{P}_t] - \Omega_t^i \nabla \tilde{P}_t],$$

(4)

where

$$\omega_t^i = S_t^i - S_t,$$

$$\Omega_t^i = \sum_{j=0}^{t} \omega_j^i = K_t^i - K_t,$$

$$\Gamma_t = \mathrm{Cov}[\tilde{U} - \tilde{P}_{t-1}, \nabla \tilde{P}_t] \mathrm{Var}^{-1}[\nabla \tilde{P}_t]$$

$$= \left\{ \left[I + K_{t-1}^{-1} \left(\sum_{j=0}^{t-1} S_j + r^{-2}\Phi_j^{-1} \right) \right] [K_{t-1}^{-1} - K_t^{-1}] \right\}$$

$$\times \left\{ [K_{t-1}^{-1} - K_t^{-1}] \left[I + \left(\sum_{j=0}^{t-1} S_j + r^{-2}\Phi_j^{-1} \right) (K_{t-1}^{-1} - K_t^{-1}) \right] \right.$$

$$\left. + K_t^{-1}[S_t + r^{-2}\Phi_t^{-1}]K_t^{-1} \right\}^{-1}.$$

ω_t^i represents the marginal informational (dis)advantage of investor i arising from private signals received at time t, while Ω_t^i represents the cumulative informational (dis)advantage of the investor arising from all the private signals received up to time t. Note first that if the marginal information advantage is zero ($\omega_t^i = 0$) and there is no liquidity shock in trading session t, then each investor's conditionally expected trade will depend only on the final term in expression (4), which is the negative of a matrix representing the investor's cumulative information advantage times $\nabla \tilde{P}_t$, the vector of price changes in session t. On the other hand, if there is no cumulative private information advantage (i.e., $\Omega_t^i = 0$), then, apart from the supply shock, $\tilde{X}_t$, the investor's conditionally expected trade is equal to a matrix representing the investor's information advantage in the current period times the vector, $\Gamma_t \nabla \tilde{P}_t$. Thus the cumulative information advantage from all the private signals, and the marginal information advantage from the current private signal affect the investor's expected trades in quite different ways. Indeed, the following simple results can be obtained in a single security setting: $\Gamma_t > 0$ so that the trades of an investor with no cumulative information advantage ($\Omega_t^i = 0$), but with a positive marginal information advantage ($\omega_t^i > 0$), will be *positively* correlated with the current price change; the trades of an investor with a positive cumulative information advantage ($\Omega_t^i > 0$), but with no marginal information advantage ($\omega_t^i = 0$), will be *negatively* correlated with the price change in the current period.

Thus the relation between the trades of well and poorly informed investors and price changes is critically related to the extent to which the information (dis)advantage arises from a marginal private information advantage in the current period, or from an accumulation of superior private information signals in the past. To derive testable implications from the model it will be necessary to make an assumption about the relative magnitudes of the cumulative and marginal information advantages of domestic investors.

II. International Portfolio Investment

To develop the implications of the model for international portfolio investment, we consider a setting in which there are M countries indexed m. The market portfolio of each country is treated as a single risky asset, currency risk is ignored, and we assume that investors in all countries have access to the same riskless asset whose return is zero.

Let μ^m denote the measure of domestic investors in country m. Then, from equation (4), the vector of conditional expected trades by investors in country m is given by:

$$\mathrm{E}[\nabla \tilde{D}_t^m | \nabla \tilde{P}_t] = r \int_{i \in m} [\omega_t^i \Gamma_t \nabla \tilde{P}_t + E[\tilde{X}_t / r | \nabla \tilde{P}_t] - \Omega_t^i \nabla \tilde{P}_t] \, di. \qquad (5)$$

We further assume that the contribution of noise traders in country m to the aggregate supply shock, $\tilde{X}_t$, is $\mu^m \tilde{X}_t$. Then, adding the trades of noise traders to those of the (rational) investors, and dropping the time subscript, the expectation of the vector of aggregate security purchases by all individuals in country m (including noise traders), $\tilde{\Pi}^m$, conditional on the vector of price changes, $\nabla \tilde{P}$, is

$$E[\tilde{\Pi}^m | \nabla \tilde{P}] = \Theta^m \nabla \tilde{P}, \qquad (6)$$

where

$$\Theta^m \equiv r[\omega^m \Gamma - \Omega^m], \qquad \omega^m \equiv \int_{i \in m} \omega^i \, di, \qquad \Omega^m \equiv \int_{i \in m} \Omega^i \, di.$$

Equation (6) implies that portfolio flows can be written as a linear function of price changes in the M market portfolios plus an orthogonal error term. If there are no differences in information precisions across countries, then $\omega^m = \Omega^m = 0$ and portfolio flows will be independent of market returns. If there are differences in information endowments, the conditional expectations of portfolio flows will be linearly dependent on the vector of price changes.[11]

The aggregate trade of investors in country m in their domestic asset is given by the mth element of the vector $\tilde{\Pi}^m$:

$$\tilde{\Pi}_m^m = \sum_{j=1}^{M} \Theta_{mj}^m \nabla \tilde{P}_j + \tilde{\nu}_m^m. \qquad (7)$$

where $\tilde{\nu}_m^m$ is an orthogonal, mean zero, error term. Similarly, the aggregate trade of investors in country m in the *foreign asset*, k, is

$$\tilde{\Pi}_k^m = \sum_{j=1}^{M} \Theta_{kj}^m \nabla \tilde{P}_j + \tilde{\nu}_k^m, \qquad (8)$$

---

[11] While this result is derived by treating the market portfolio in each country as a single asset, similar results can be obtained when each country has multiple assets if appropriate restrictions are placed on the information endowments.

where $\tilde{v}_k^m$ is an orthogonal, mean zero, error term. Ω^m represents the cumulative information (dis)advantage of the average investor in country m over an average global investor, while ω^m represents the marginal information (dis)advantage of the average investor in country m over an average global investor arising from the precisions of the private information received in the current period. We shall assume that, on average, domestic investors have better information about domestic assets than do foreign investors, and have less information about foreign assets than average foreign investors. In addition, we shall assume that the marginal information (dis)advantage is small relative to the cumulative information (dis)advantage. This is expressed formally in the following assumption:

ASSUMPTION A: Domestic Cumulative Information Advantage.

$$\Omega_{mm}^m > 0, \qquad \Omega_{jj}^m < 0, \qquad |\omega_{mm}^m| \ll |\Omega_{mm}^m|, \qquad |\omega_{jj}^m| \ll |\Omega_{jj}^m|, \qquad j \neq m,$$

which implies that:

$$\Theta_{mm}^m < 0, \qquad \Theta_{jj}^m > 0, \quad j \neq m.$$

Combining Assumption A with equations (7) and (8) yields the following restrictions on the regression of portfolio flows on price changes:

PROPOSITION: *Under Assumption A (domestic cumulative information advantage) i) when the domestic investors' trade in a given foreign market, k, is regressed on the returns of domestic and all foreign markets, the regression coefficient on the market return of country k is positive; ii) when the domestic investor's trade in the domestic market is regressed on the returns on domestic and foreign markets, the regression coefficient on the domestic market return is negative.*

Part (i) of the Proposition implies that under the conditions of Assumption A, foreign investors will tend to behave as trend-followers in a given market, buying in periods when the index rises and selling when the index falls; this will be the focus of the empirical tests that are reported below. Part (ii) of the Proposition is a consequence of market clearing; if foreign investors buy when the domestic index appreciates, then domestic investors must sell.

If we impose additional symmetry on the informational endowments, then expressions (7) and (8) can be greatly simplified. Thus, assume that there is no asymmetry in the off-diagonal elements of the precision matrices S_t^m across m:

ASSUMPTION B: Symmetric Information Endowments.

$$S_{tkl}^m = S_{tkl}, \qquad \forall m; \quad k \neq l.$$

This assumption will be satisfied, for example, if domestic investors have private information only about the domestic asset and not about foreign assets.

Assumption B implies

$$\Theta_{tkl}^m = 0, \qquad k \neq l.$$

Under Assumptions A and B, expressions (7) and (8) for the domestic and foreign investments of individuals in country m can be rewritten as:

$$\tilde{\Pi}_m^m = \Theta_{mm}^m \nabla \tilde{P}_m + \tilde{\nu}_m^m, \tag{9}$$

$$\tilde{\Pi}_k^m = \Theta_{kk}^m \nabla \tilde{P}_k + \nu_k^m, \qquad \forall k \neq m; \tag{10}$$

where $\Theta_{mm}^m < 0$, $\Theta_{jj}^m > 0$, $j \neq m$. This may be stated more formally as:

COROLLARY: *Under Assumption B (symmetric information endowments) the trade of an investor in the domestic market depends only on the domestic market return, and the trade in a foreign market depends only on the foreign market return. Under Assumption A (domestic cumulative information advantage) the domestic market trade is negatively associated with the domestic market return, while the foreign market trade is positively associated with the foreign market return.*

The Corollary implies that under the posited conditions there will be more diversification in a global bull market and more home country bias in a global bear market.

To investigate the tendency towards a *home bias* in investor portfolios under Assumptions A and B, consider the vector of average holdings of investors of country m in the various market portfolios at time t: this is given from equation (2) by

$$E[\tilde{D}_t^m] = X_t + \Omega_t^m K_t^{-1} X_t,$$

where $\bar{X}_t = E[\Sigma_{j=0}^t \tilde{X}_j]$. Let $V_t \equiv K_t^{-1}$ denote the average investor's conditional covariance matrix of asset payoffs at trading session t. Then since Ω_t^m is a diagonal matrix under symmetric information endowments, the expected holding of an average investor in country m of the domestic market portfolio m is:

$$E[D_{tm}^m] = \bar{X}_{tm} + \Omega_{tmm}^m \sum_{j=1}^M V_{tmj} \bar{X}_j,$$

and the expected holding of an average investor in country m of the foreign market portfolio k is:

$$E[D_{tk}^m] = \bar{X}_{tk} + \Omega_{tkk}^m \sum_{j=1}^M V_{tkj} \bar{X}_j, \qquad \text{for} \quad k \neq m.$$

REMARK 1: The necessary and sufficient condition for the expected holdings of the domestic market portfolio of country m by domestic (foreign) investors to exceed (fall short of) the expected average endowment, under Assumptions A and B is that

$$\sum_{j=1}^{M} V_{tmj} \bar{X}_{tj} > 0. \tag{11}$$

Condition (11) is just the requirement that the conditional covariance of the payoff on country m's portfolio with the expected world market portfolio be positive, and the result follows because under Assumption A (domestic cumulative information advantage):

$$\Omega_{tmm}^{m} > 0, \qquad \Omega_{tkk}^{m} < 0, \qquad \forall k \neq m.$$

Remark 1 implies that, on average, domestic investors hold more than their share of the domestic market portfolio and less than their share of each foreign market portfolio. It also predicts that, for a given level of information asymmetry as represented by the cumulative information advantage Ω_{tmm}, the home bias will be greater for countries whose payoffs have a high covariance with the payoff on the expected world market portfolio. Intuitively, when the covariance is large, the benefits of international diversification are small and the home bias created by the informational asymmetry becomes large.[12] The empirical implications of Remark 1 could be tested by running a regression of the degree of home bias for each national market on the covariance of the market return with the return on the world market portfolio.

To understand the effects of information asymmetry on *turnover rates* in foreign and domestic portfolios, define the portfolio turnover rate as the expected trade divided by the expected holding in period t,

$$TO_{tj}^{i} \equiv \left| \frac{E\nabla \tilde{D}_{tj}^{i}}{E\tilde{D}_{(t-1)j}^{i}} \right|, \tag{12}$$

where TO_{tj}^{i} is the turnover rate of investor i in asset j at period t, $\tilde{D}_{tj}^{i}$ is the holding of asset j by investor i in session t, and $\nabla \tilde{D}_{tj}^{i} \equiv \tilde{D}_{tj}^{i} - \tilde{D}_{(t-1)j}^{i}$ is his trade in session t.

REMARK 2: Under the same conditions as those in Remark 1, when $M = 2$ the domestic investors' turnover rate in the domestic market is smaller than that of the foreign investor in the same market.

Proof: See Appendix.

Remark 2 is consistent with the finding of Tesar and Werner (1995) that turnover rates are higher on foreign than on domestic portfolios. The intuition

---

[12] While previous authors have noted that domestic bias can be rationalized by informational considerations, the importance of the covariance with the world market portfolio has not previously been noted.

underlying the result is that the less informed foreign investor will tend to take a smaller position in the foreign market than the domestic investor; then, since the domestic investor's trades are of equal and opposite sign to those of the foreign investor, they constitute a smaller fraction of the domestic investor's portfolio.

We turn now to some empirical tests of the major new empirical prediction of the asymmetric information model, that under Assumptions A and B purchases of a country's equity by foreigners will be positively related to the current return on the national market index.

III. Data

The data on portfolio flows are taken from the U.S. Treasury Bulletin, which reports quarterly data on transactions in equities (and bonds) between U.S. residents and residents of a large number of other countries. We examine equity flows between the U.S. and four developed countries, Canada, Germany, Japan, and the United Kingdom (U.K.), for the period 1982.2 to 1994.4.[13] For these countries we examine both purchases of foreign equities by U.S. residents and purchases of U.S. equities by foreign residents. We also examine net purchases by U.S. residents of equities in 16 emerging markets over the period 1989.1 to 1994.4. The shorter sample period for the emerging markets was selected because it is only in recent years that foreign investment restrictions have been lifted in these markets. We do not examine purchases of U.S. equities by residents of these countries. To take account of the dramatic growth in cross-border equity flows, we normalize each quarter's net flow by the average of the absolute values of the flows over each of the previous four quarters; it is these normalized flows that we attempt to explain in our regressions. For the U.S. and four developed countries, market returns are taken as capital gains computed from the Goldman Sachs-Financial Times-Actuaries (FTA) dollar denominated price indices. For the emerging markets the quarterly returns are calculated from the International Finance Corporation (IFC) total return series in U.S. dollars (USD).[14]

IV. Portfolio Flows between Developed Countries

A. U.S. Portfolio Investment in Developed Markets

We estimate three models of the relation between portfolio flows and equity returns. *Model I*, which corresponds to equation (8), treats portfolio flows as a linear function of returns on all the markets considered plus an orthogonal error term. Under Assumption A (domestic cumulative information advan-

[13] We are grateful to Linda Tesar and Ingrid Werner for making these data available to us. Tesar and Werner (1995) point out that these countries accounted for 84 percent of the total value of world equities in 1990.

[14] We are grateful to Philippe Jorion and Richard Roll for making the return series available to us. For the tests reported in Section VI we also use returns measured in terms of the local currency.

International Portfolio Investment Flows   1865

tage), we expect the coefficient of the return on the market to which the capital flows are directed, the *host market return*, to be positive, as stated in the Proposition. *Model II*, which corresponds to equation (10), treats portfolio flows as a linear function of the return on the host market alone, plus an orthogonal error term; this corresponds to the restriction of symmetric information endowments described by Assumption B. If, in addition, there is a domestic cumulative information advantage as described by Assumption A, then, as stated in the Corollary, we expect the coefficient of the host market return to be positive. *Model III* is an intermediate model that allows portfolio flows to depend not only on the host market return, but also on the *source market return*, which is defined as the return on the equity market in the country which is the origin of the portfolio flows. *Model III* is intended to allow for wealth effects that are not formally included in our model because of the assumption of constant absolute risk aversion. We conjecture that if wealth effects are important, then a positive return on the source market, which will tend to increase the wealth of residents of the source country relative to residents of the host country, will be associated with an increased flow from the source to the host country.

Table I reports the results of seemingly unrelated regressions in which the dependent variables are the (normalized) quarterly purchases of foreign equities in each of the four developed markets by U.S. residents, and the independent variables are the returns on the U.S. and foreign market indices measured in USD. The top panel shows the results for *Model I*. The model explains only 2 percent of the flows to Canada, but 15 to 21 percent for the other three countries. Consistent with Assumption A, the coefficients on the host market returns are positive for Canada, Germany and Japan, and significant for the latter two countries. However, the coefficient for the host market return is negative and significant in the case of the U.K.; this suggests either that Americans are better informed than are U.K. residents about the U.K. market, or that the U.K. residents' informational advantage is relatively short-lived, so that the marginal effect exceeds the cumulative effect.

The second panel shows the results for *Model II* in which the only independent variable is the host market return. Now the coefficient of the host market return is positive in every case, and statistically significant except in the case of the U.K. A likelihood ratio test of the restrictions of *Model II* implied by symmetric information endowments, that the coefficients of the nonhost market returns are zero, yields a χ^2 statistic of 24.43 with 16 degrees of freedom, and an associated p-value of 0.08. Thus, we are unable to reject the restrictions implied by symmetric information endowments. Under this assumption, the parameter estimates are consistent with American residents being at an informational disadvantage in Canada, Germany, and Japan, but not in the U.K. It is possible that the major U.S. banking presence in London is what distinguishes the results for the U.K. from those for the other countries.

The third panel of Table I shows the results for *Model III* in which the source market return is included along with the host market return to allow for possible wealth effects. The results are somewhat mixed. On the one hand, the

Table I

U.S. Purchases of Equities in Developed Foreign Markets

Seemingly unrelated regressions of normalized quarterly U.S. purchases of foreign equities in four developed markets on U.S. and foreign equity returns measured in United States (U.S.) dollars for the period 1982.2 to 1994.4. Normalized purchases are net purchases in quarter t expressed as a proportion of the average absolute level of net purchases over the previous four quarters. Returns are quarterly capital gains computed from Goldman-Sachs Financial Times Actuaries (FTA) dollar-denominated price indices. D-W: Durbin-Watson statistic. Nobs: Number of observations. LL: value of the log likelihood for the system. (absolute value of t-ratios in parentheses). Coefficients in bold are positive under the domestic cumulative information advantage hypothesis of Assumption A.

	Constant	R_{US}	R_{CAN}	R_{GER}	R_{JAP}	R_{UK}	R^2 D-W	LL Nobs
Model I								−418.11
Canada	0.58	−3.02	**5.09**	2.91	1.11	2.54	0.02	51
	(1.99)	(0.52)	**(1.11)**	(1.10)	(0.53)	(0.68)	1.61	
Germany	0.60	6.61	−6.91	**8.37**	−0.48	−3.21	0.15	51
	(2.16)	(1.18)	(1.57)	**(3.28)**	(0.24)	(0.90)	1.57	
Japan	0.29	15.87	5.14	0.66	**7.68**	−13.47	0.21	51
	(0.68)	(1.85)	(0.76)	(0.17)	**(2.50)**	(2.47)	1.86	
United Kingdom	0.99	10.77	4.59	0.19	4.16	**−8.55**	0.17	51
	(3.25)	(1.75)	(0.95)	(0.07)	(1.89)	**(2.19)**	2.33	
Model II								−430.39
Canada	0.69		7.19				0.05	51
	(2.57)		(2.51)				1.56	
Germany	0.60			6.83			0.15	51
	(2.20)			(3.00)			1.48	
Japan	0.61				4.79		0.09	51
	(1.41)				(2.08)		1.61	
United Kingdom	1.30					1.53	0.01	51
	(4.02)					(0.59)	1.99	
Model III								−425.86
Canada	0.71	−0.76	**7.29**				0.03	51
	(2.49)	(0.14)	**(1.65)**				1.56	
Germany	0.64	−1.78		**7.26**			0.13	51
	(2.25)	(0.49)		**(3.00)**			1.47	
Japan	0.27	13.84			**3.23**		0.16	51
	(0.61)	(2.48)			**(1.36)**		1.76	
United Kingdom	1.02	13.06				−2.08	0.13	51
	(3.30)	(2.99)				(0.71)	2.32	

coefficient of the host market returns remains positive for Canada, Germany, and Japan, and remains insignificant for the U.K. On the other hand the coefficient of the source market return (i.e., U.S. market return) is positive and significant for Japan and the U.K., which is consistent with wealth effects' being important. However, they are also consistent with informational effects. A positive sign on the source market return implies under Assumption A (cumulative domestic information advantage) that $\Omega_{mk}^m < 0$; this would be the case for example if the off diagonal elements of the correlation matrix of signal errors were the same and positive across countries while residents of each country received a more precise signal of the domestic market return than foreigners. A likelihood ratio test of the restrictions that the coefficients of the host country returns are jointly zero yields a χ^2 statistic of 9.04 with 4 degrees of freedom, and an associated p-value of 0.06, so that we marginally fail to reject the null of no wealth effects.

While the results for Canada, Germany, and Japan are consistent with the hypothesis that foreign investors are less well informed, as we have suggested, a possible concern is that exogenous shifts in the U.S. demand for foreign equities, that are not caused by new information, will give rise to an increase in U.S. purchases of foreign equities, and that the price impact of these purchases will create a spurious association between the return on the foreign index and U.S. portfolio flows. This is a problem that we cannot entirely rule out, although the lack of a positive coefficient for the U.K. suggests that the price impact of U.S. transactions is unlikely to be the whole story. The data reported by Tesar and Werner (1995) imply, for example, that U.S. holdings of Canadian equities amounted to 10.4 percent of the total Canadian equity market in 1990, while Kang and Stulz (1994) estimate that *total* foreign ownership of Japanese equities has fluctuated in the range of 4 to 11 percent in our sample period. It is not clear whether the changes that have taken place in these portfolio positions would have created a large enough price impact to affect our results. It is worth noting also in this context that Tesar and Werner (1995) report that the turnover of foreign equities held by U.S. residents is some two and one half times the rate of turnover of domestic equities; this alone suggests that the transactions costs, which include price impact in the foreign markets, cannot be very significant.

When we replace the foreign return in the regression by the lagged foreign return the coefficients become insignificant, though all except Japan are positive. When a single coefficient on the lagged foreign return is estimated across all four countries it is positive, but only significant at the 54 percent level. It is difficult to interpret these results, since the lack of a significant lagged effect of returns on portfolio flows is consistent with the contemporaneous effect being the spurious result of price impact caused by shifts in U.S. demands for foreign securities that are not related to new information; but it is also consistent with the predictions of the model which imply that the association between returns and flows will be contemporaneous. A test for Granger causality between foreign returns and U.S. portfolio flows using two lags yielded ambiguous results. On the one hand we could reject the null that German returns are not (Granger) caused by U.S. purchases; on the other hand we could reject the null that U.S. flows to Japan are not (Granger) caused by Japanese returns. The other results are not significant. While the finding for Japan is consistent with a lagged version of the asymmetric information hypothesis, the finding for Germany does not imply that price impact is important, since we are aware of no theory that predicts a *lagged* price impact, and it is difficult to conceive of the mechanism for such an effect.

Table II
Purchases of U.S. Equities by Residents of Developed Foreign Countries

Seemingly unrelated regressions of normalized foreign purchases of U.S. equities by residents of four developed countries on United States (U.S.) and foreign equity returns measured in U.S. dollars for the period 1982.2 to 1994.4. Normalized purchases are net purchases in quarter t expressed as a proportion of the average absolute level of net purchases over the previous four quarters. Returns are quarterly capital gains computed from Goldman-Sachs Financial Times Actuaries (FTA) dollar-denominated price indices. D-W: Durbin-Watson statistic. Nobs: Number of observations. LL: value of the log likelihood for the system. (absolute value of t-ratios in parentheses). Coefficients in bold are positive under the domestic cumulative information advantage hypothesis of Assumption A.

	Constant	R_{US}	R_{CAN}	R_{GER}	R_{JAP}	R_{UK}	R^2 D-W	LL Nobs
Model I								−391.03
Canada	0.62	**−5.32**	7.55	−4.49	2.98	−2.62	0.06	51
	(2.22)	**(0.94)**	(1.70)	(1.75)	(1.48)	(0.73)	1.06	
Germany	0.22	**−7.45**	5.22	3.37	4.00	−1.48	0.02	51
	(0.74)	**(1.24)**	(1.10)	(1.23)	(1.86)	(0.39)	1.48	
Japan	0.23	**−3.08**	3.27	2.89	3.75	−1.74	0.00	51
	(0.77)	**(0.50)**	(0.68)	(1.04)	(1.71)	(0.45)	1.92	
United Kingdom	−0.09	**−0.59**	4.93	4.59	0.53	1.99	0.21	51
	(0.43)	**(0.14)**	(1.49)	(2.39)	(0.35)	(0.74)	1.40	
Model II								−402.00
Canada	0.52	**−0.76**					0.00	51
	(1.80)	**(0.21)**					1.17	
Germany	0.36	**0.74**					−0.02	51
	(1.18)	**(0.20)**					1.31	
Japan	0.37	**2.73**					−0.01	51
	(1.20)	**(0.73)**					1.71	
United Kingdom	0.01	**8.13**					0.13	51
	(0.04)	**(3.02)**					1.29	
Model III								−399.44
Canada	0.59	**−8.80**	8.95				0.02	
	(2.08)	**(1.73)**	(2.16)				0.98	
Germany	0.31	**−0.23**		1.85			−0.02	
	(1.03)	**(0.06)**		(0.69)			1.32	
Japan	0.23	**−0.67**			4.79		0.03	
	(0.77)	**(0.17)**			(2.56)		1.96	
United Kingdom	−0.03	**4.94**				4.24	0.16	
	(0.14)	**(1.53)**				(1.70)	1.30	

B. Portfolio Investment in the U.S. from Developed Countries

Table II reports the results of estimating the three models using foreign purchases of U.S. equities as the dependent variable. The *Model I* estimates reported in the top panel provide no support for the Proposition: the coefficients of the U.S. market return are uniformly negative and insignificant, which implies that residents of these countries are not at an informational disadvantage relative to U.S. residents about the U.S. market.

The *Model II* estimates in the second panel tell a similar story, except that now it appears that U.K. residents are at an informational disadvantage in the U.S. market, which is consistent with the evidence of Shukla and Inwegen (1995) that U.K. fund managers exhibit inferior market timing ability in the U.S. market. Moreover, a likelihood ratio test of the restrictions implied by Assumption B (symmetric information endowments) and reflected in *Model II* yield a χ^2 statistic of 29.07 with 16 degrees of freedom, and an associated *p*-value of 0.02, so that the restrictions are rejected. The *Model III* estimates are shown in the third panel of the table. Introducing the source country returns has little effect on the coefficients of the host country (U.S.) returns, although the coefficients of all four source market returns are positive, and two are statistically significant. A joint test of the significance of the source market returns yields a χ^2 statistic that is significant only at the 27 percent level.

In summary, our analysis of equity portfolio flows between the U.S. and these four developed markets reveals no evidence that foreign investors are less well informed about the U.S. market than U.S. investors, although there is evidence that is consistent with differences in informational endowments. On the other hand, the results are consistent with U.S. investors being less well informed about the foreign markets (except the U.K.) than the locals in those markets. However, our conclusions are tempered by recognition of the possible confounding effect of exogenous shifts in the U.S. demand for foreign equities that are not associated with new information.

V. U.S. Portfolio Investment in Emerging Markets

Models II and *III* are estimated for U.S. portfolio flows to 16 emerging markets for the period 1989.1 to 1994.4. The shorter sample period and larger number of countries make it necessary to split the country sample into two subsamples of eight countries in order to perform the seemingly unrelated regression procedure. The split was made on an alphabetical basis, and the results are reported in Tables III and IV. There were insufficient data to permit estimation of *Model I*. Table III reports the results of the *Model II* regressions. Of the 16 countries, the coefficient of the host market return is positive, in 14 cases, as the Proposition predicts, and *t*-ratios in excess of two are estimated for five countries. The only significant negative host market return coefficient is that for Chile.

Model III regression estimates are reported in Table IV. The coefficients on the host (i.e., foreign) market return are not affected significantly by the introduction of the source (i.e., U.S.) market return. There is no evidence that the capital flows are driven by wealth effects not encompassed by our model, since the coefficient of the source market return is nowhere significant and is negative in 12 out of 16 cases. Moreover, χ^2 statistics yielded by the likelihood ratio test of the restrictions imposed by *Model II* relative to *Model III* are 5.88

Table III

U.S. Purchases of Equities in Emerging Markets

Seemingly unrelated regressions of normalized quarterly United States (U.S.) purchases of foreign equities in sixteen emerging markets on host market returns measured in U.S. dollars for the period 1982.2 to 1994.4. Normalized purchases are net purchases in quarter t expressed as a proportion of the average absolute level of net purchases over the previous four quarters. Returns for the non-U.S. markets are the International Finance Corporation (IFC) dollar-denominated total return series. D-W: Durbin-Watson statistic. Nobs: Number of observations. LL: value of the log likelihood for the system. (absolute value of t-ratios in parentheses). Coefficients in bold are positive under the domestic cumulative information advantage hypothesis of Assumption A.

Group A	Constant	R_{ARG}	R_{BRA}	R_{CHI}	R_{COL}	R_{GRE}	R_{INDI}	R_{INDO}	R_{KOR}	R^2 D-W	LL Nobs
Model II											−306.05
Argentina	−2.18	**5.44**								0.00	24
	(0.93)	**(3.07)**								2.05	
Brazil	1.76		**1.58**							−0.04	24
	(2.51)		**(1.66)**							1.88	
Chile	2.41			−6.66						−0.00	24
	(5.04)			(3.44)						2.27	
Columbia	1.14				**1.14**					−0.04	24
	(1.43)				**(0.80)**					1.80	
Greece	1.21					**1.53**				−0.10	24
	(2.95)					**(2.21)**				1.81	
India	1.61						**4.18**			0.08	24
	(2.24)						**(1.79)**			1.85	
Indonesia	3.80							**35.11**		0.26	24
	(2.17)							**(4.18)**		1.10	
Korea	1.06								**3.54**	−0.02	24
	(2.60)								**(1.44)**	1.41	

Group B	Constant	R_{MAL}	R_{MEX}	R_{PAK}	R_{PHIL}	R_{PORT}	R_{TAIW}	R_{THAI}	R_{TURK}	R^2 D-W	LL Nobs
Model II											−268.38
Malaysia	1.11	**2.82**								−0.00	24
	(2.59)	**(0.95)**								1.89	
Mexico	1.11		**6.05**							0.18	24
	(2.14)		**(2.49)**							1.61	
Pakistan	1.23			**0.79**						−0.04	24
	(1.78)			**(0.29)**						1.21	
Philippines	1.81				**1.81**					0.00	24
	(4.75)				**(4.75)**					2.34	
Portugal	1.95					**7.17**				0.09	24
	(3.29)					**(1.84)**				(2.18)	
Taiwan	0.49						−0.62			−0.03	24
	(1.27)						(0.49)			1.80	
Thailand	0.58							**2.58**		0.07	24
	(1.59)							**(1.63)**		1.85	
Turkey	4.89								**22.8**	0.01	24
	(0.62)								**(1.10)**	(2.25)	

Table IV

The Influence of U.S. Market Returns on U.S. Purchases of Equities in Emerging Markets

Seemingly unrelated regressions of normalized quarterly U.S. purchases of foreign equities in sixteen emerging markets on U.S. and host market returns measured in U.S. dollars for the period 1982.2 to 1994.4. Normalized purchases are net purchases in quarter t expressed as a proportion of the average absolute level of net purchases over the previous four quarters. Returns for the non-U.S. markets are the International Finance Corporation (IFC) dollar-denominated total return series. D-W: Durbin-Watson statistic. Nobs: Number of observations. LL: value of the log likelihood for the system. (absolute value of t-ratios in parentheses). Coefficients in bold are positive under the domestic cumulative information advantage hypothesis of Assumption A.

Group A	Constant	R_{US}	R_{ARG}	R_{BRA}	R_{CHI}	R_{COL}	R_{GRE}	R_{INDI}	R_{INDO}	R_{KOR}	R^2 D-W	LL	Nobs
Model III												−303.11	
Argentina	−2.24	−4.75	**6.34**								−0.07		24
	(0.89)	(−0.13)	(3.41)								2.08		
Brazil	1.87	−5.64		**1.74**							−0.09		24
	(2.50)	(0.46)		(1.83)							1.84		
Chile	2.46	−3.19			−6.46						0.05		24
	(4.97)	(0.42)			(3.45)						2.21		
Columbia	1.14	1.21				**2.35**					−0.06		24
	(1.43)	(2.95)				(1.14)					1.96		
Greece	1.31	−4.94					**1.58**				−0.13		24
	(3.02)	(0.70)					(2.28)				1.67		
India	1.38	8.11						**5.10**			0.06		24
	(1.70)	(0.60)						(1.94)			1.81		
Indonesia	4.24	−37.26							**35.84**		0.27		24
	(2.41)	(1.26)							(4.47)		1.07		
Korea	1.16	−4.60								**4.38**	−0.06		24
	(2.64)	(0.62)								(1.75)	1.40		

Group B	Constant	R_{US}	R_{MAL}	R_{MEX}	R_{PAK}	R_{PHIL}	R_{PORT}	R_{TAIW}	R_{THAI}	R_{TURK}	R^2 D-W	LL	Nobs
Model III												−271.88	
Malaysia	1.21	−7.65	**4.18**								−0.00		24
	(2.74)	(0.99)	(1.28)								2.11		
Mexico	1.27	−13.25		**7.70**							0.22		24
	(2.46)	(1.46)		(2.94)							(1.95)		
Pakistan	1.46	−10.88			**1.07**						−0.05		24
	(1.99)	(0.94)			(0.39)						1.22		
Philippines	1.66	11.21				−1.41					0.02		24
	(4.36)	(1.55)				(0.82)					2.12		
Portugal	2.01	−3.33					**7.60**				0.05		24
	(3.12)	(0.30)					(1.79)				2.20		
Taiwan	0.35	7.51						−1.14			−0.03		24
	(0.86)	(1.07)						(0.84)			1.82		
Thailand	0.69	−9.99							**3.89**		0.12		24
	(1.91)	(1.50)							(2.19)		1.73		
Turkey	5.85	−47.99								**24.11**	−0.03		
	(0.70)	(0.35)								(1.13)	2.26		

and 6.78 for Groups A and B respectively, with associated p-values of 0.66 and 0.56.[15]

There is no reason to expect that our model of capital flows will be appropriate for markets where portfolio investment is regulated. Therefore Table V arranges the markets according to the estimated t-statistic on the local market return in the regressions reported in Table III, and presents summary information about the openness of the various markets to foreign portfolio investment. Since regulations differ across markets and have been changed at different times, it is not possible to present a single measure of market openness. For each country, where available, the table gives the fraction of trading accounted for by U.S. transactions in 1990, the degree of market integration as estimated by Bekaert and Harvey (1995), and the average premium on the country closed-end fund listed in the U.S. The countries in the first column are those that conform best to the asymmetric information model, and it is notable that these tend to be the most open and least restricted markets with the highest levels of foreign participation. On the other hand, the two countries with negative coefficients, Chile and Taiwan, restrict foreign investment to closed end funds that are not likely to vary their equity participation much, and to authorized financial institutions.

The possibility that the results are distorted by exogenous shifts in U.S. investor demands for foreign securities is probably more serious in the case of emerging markets, since the size of the markets is much less than that of the developed markets. Tesar and Werner (1993) report that U.S. transactions as a proportion of all transactions in 1990 ranged from a low of 0.1 percent in India to a high of 29 percent in Colombia: for the complete figures see Table V. When the host market return is replaced by its lagged value and the coefficient is constrained to be the same across all countries within each group, the coefficient is positive for both groups and the t-statistic was 2.90 for Group A but only 0.17 for Group B. Granger causality tests with two lags between portfolio flows and local market returns reject the null hypothesis that portfolio flows are not Granger caused by local market returns for Argentina, Indonesia, and Turkey at better than the 5 percent level; in no case are we able to reject the null that local market returns are not caused by portfolio flows. Thus, on the whole there is fairly strong evidence of *lagged* trend following by American investors in emerging markets. This might occur if Americans were both less informed and were slow in making investment decisions. Combined with the evidence for the coefficient of the contemporaneous market return, there is fairly strong evidence that equity capital flows from the U.S. to emerging markets are consistent with a model in which U.S. investors behave as rational individuals who are less well informed about local market conditions in emerging markets than are the local investors.

---

[15] Caution should be exercised in interpreting the likelihood ratio statistic in view of the small number of observations.

International Portfolio Investment Flows 1873

Table V
A Comparison of Model Results with Evidence of Capital Flow Restrictions for Emerging Markets

Emerging markets classified by *t*-ratio of coefficient of host market return in regression of normalized United States (U.S.) equity purchases on host market returns. Numbers in brackets are the proportion of total trading volume accounted for by U.S. transactions in 1990 (Tesar and Werner (1993)). Numbers in square braces are the degree of market integration estimated by Bekaert and Harvey (1995). Numbers in curly braces are the average U.S. closed-end country fund premium over the period January 1986 to August 1993 as reported by Bekaert and Urias (1995). Notes on the countries are based on Park and van Agtmael (1993), Price (1994), and de Caires (1988).

t-Stat. > 2.0	2.0 > *t*-Stat. > 0	0 > *t*-Stat
Argentina	Brazil	Chile
(3.6%)[0.26]{12.8%}	(3.5%)[n.a.]{−11.1%}	(n.a.)[0.26]{−5.5%}
No restrictions for foreign	Until 1991 only Brazil Fund and	Only authorized Foreign
capital since November 1989.	similar closed end funds; since then	Capital Investment Funds;
Foreign investors began	foreign institutional investors allowed.	limitations on repatriation of
entering the market in 1991.	Columbia	capital; 2.63% foreign
Greece	(29.0%)[0.14]{n.a.}	ownership in 1990.
(1.3%)[0.86]{n.a.}	10% limit on foreign ownership of	Taiwan
No restrictions for foreign	individual companies lifted 1991, and	(0.05%)[0.90]{26.9%}
capital. It is estimated that	requirement that investment funds	Only closed end funds allowed
foreign investors account for	remain in the country for one year	to invest prior to 1990; since
25% of the activity.	abolished. Institutional investors only.	then authorized institutions
Indonesia	India	allowed to invest up to $100 m
(1.3%)[n.a.]{1.71%}	(0.02%)[0.10]{−3.6%}	each. Total foreign investment
Open to foreigners since	In 1992 market opened to foreign	quota of $5 billion.
1989; 49% limit on foreign	institutional investors who must be	
holdings of most companies.	approved by Securities Board.	
Mexico	Korea	
(12.5%)[0.04]{−17.1%}	(0.26%)[0.99]{54.8%}	
May 1989 rule allowed	Foreign investment limited to closed-	
foreigners to hold	end funds prior to January 1992;	
unrestricted positions in 73%	foreign holdings 2.1% of total	
of companies. Foreign	capitalization in 1989, "less than 4%"	
holdings 18.3% of total	in 1992.	
capitalization at end-1991.	Malaysia	
Philippines	(5.1%)[0.79]{−2.2%}	
(7.07%)[n.a.]{1.7%}	30% limit on foreign holdings of	
Foreigners may purchase	individual companies. At the end of	
special "B" shares	1990 foreigners held 27.4% of equity.	
	Pakistan	
	(n.a.)[n.a.]{n.a.}	
	Most barriers removed 1991; prior to	
	that foreigners required special	
	permission to invest.	
	Portugal	
	(5.1%)[n.a.]{−5.3%}	
	Foreigners hold 60% of free float of	
	shares.	
	Thailand	
	(2.0%)[1.00]{−8.0%}	
	Foreign ownership limited to 49% for	
	individual companies; Foreign	
	transactions accounted for 10.0% of	
	volume in 1987.	
	Turkey	
	(1.6%)[n.a.]{−14.6%}	
	Nonresident investment funds	
	permitted since 1988.	

VI. Currency Effects

To this point we have followed our formal model and ignored the role of currency risk by measuring all of the returns in U.S. dollars. Nevertheless, it is of interest to consider the effect of changes in exchange rates on portfolio flows since the dollar return contains an exchange rate component. We investigate this issue within the context of *Model III* in which the independent variables are the host and source market returns. To test whether U.S. portfolio flows are influenced by exchange rate changes in addition to the host and source market returns measured in USD we add to the *Model III* regressions the change in the host country exchange rate against the USD.[16] Likelihood ratio tests of the null hypothesis that the coefficient of the host country exchange rates are zero yield p-values of 0.33 for U.S. investment in the four developed markets, and 0.63 and 0.006 for investment in the two subsamples of emerging markets; significance in the second subsample is mainly attributable to Malaysia and Pakistan where the investment flows are positively associated with a decline in the value of the local currency. Thus there is little evidence that U.S. flows are associated with exchange rate changes except insofar as these are impounded in the USD returns.

The results are considerably different for investment by residents of the developed countries in the U.S. A likelihood ratio test of the null hypothesis that these flows do not depend on exchange rate changes in addition to the U.S. market return measured in USD is rejected at a p-level of 0.00. Therefore Panel A of Table VI reports the results of regressions in which the exchange rate change is subtracted from the U.S. and source market returns in USD to yield a return in the source country currency. Using source country currency returns does not change the signs of any of the coefficients from those reported in Table II. A likelihood ratio test rejects the null that flows do not depend on exchange rate changes in addition to source country currency returns at the 0.03 level. Therefore Panel B reports regressions that include the return on the source country currency as an additional independent variable—the currency variable is significant only for Japan, and the sign of the coefficient implies that the Japanese increase their foreign investment in quarters in which the yen appreciates. There continues to be no evidence that residents of these countries are at an informational disadvantage in the U.S. market. Finally, we test whether our results are affected by including lagged values of the investment flows as an independent variable. We find no association between current and lagged U.S. flows to either developed or emerging markets, and while we do find lag effects for investment in the U.S. from the developed countries, inclusion of the lag variable does not affect our qualitative conclusion that there is no evidence that residents of these countries are at an informational disadvantage in the U.S. equity market.

---

[16] The exchange rates for developed countries were taken from *International Financial Statistics;* for the emerging markets they were inferred from the difference between market returns measured in USD and in the local currency as reported by IFC.

Table VI

The Influence of Exchange Rates on Purchases of U.S. Equities by Residents of Developed Foreign Countries

Seemingly unrelated regressions of normalized foreign purchases of United States (U.S.) equities by residents of four developed countries on U.S. equity returns measured in source country currency (R^*_{US}), the return on the source country market in local currency (R^*_{Source}), and the change in the USD value of the source country currency (R_X) for the period 1982.2 to 1994.4. Normalized purchases are net purchases in quarter t expressed as a proportion of the average absolute level of the net purchases over the past four quarters. U.S. and foreign equity returns are quarterly capital gains computed from the Goldman-Sachs dollar-denominated price indices less the proportional change in the value of the source country currency measured in USD. D-W: Durbin-Watson statistic. Nobs: Number of observations. LL: value of the log likelihood for the system. (absolute value of t-ratios in parentheses). Coefficients in bold are positive under the domestic cumulative information advantage hypothesis of Assumption A.

	Constant	R^*_{US}	R^*_{Source}	R_X	R^2 D-W	LL Nobs
Panel A						
Canada	0.58	−8.13	8.59		0.02	−294.32
	(2.01)	(1.73)	(1.96)		0.99	51
Germany	0.34	−0.41	1.67		−0.02	
	(1.21)	(0.14)	(0.59)		1.32	51
Japan	0.36	−4.25	4.31		0.01	
	(1.28)	(1.66)	(1.96)		1.94	51
United Kingdom	−0.04	0.14	8.82		0.24	
	(0.19)	(0.06)	(3.31)		(1.18)	51
Panel B						
Canada	0.66	−3.62	0.53	25.11	0.04	−289.02
	(2.37)	(0.68)	(0.1)	(1.94)	(1.13)	51
Germany	0.35	−0.84	2.20	−0.70	−0.04	
	(1.12)	(0.20)	(0.78)	(0.12)	(1.33)	51
Japan	0.04	3.69	1.06	17.11	0.05	
	(0.13)	(0.88)	(0.45)	(2.70)	1.78	51
United Kingdom	−0.04	0.13	8.97	0.07	0.22	
	(0.21)	(0.04)	(3.01)	(0.01)	1.19	51

VII. Conclusion

In this article we develop a model of international equity portfolio flows that relies on informational differences between foreign and domestic investors. The model predicts that if foreign and domestic investors are differentially informed, then portfolio flows between two countries will be a linear function of the contemporaneous returns on all national market indices; and if domestic investors have a cumulative information advantage over foreign investors about domestic securities, the coefficient of the host market return will be positive. If we impose additional symmetry on the informational endowments, we obtain the stronger result that the portfolio flow will depend only on the host market return.

We find empirically that portfolio flows are associated with returns on national market indices as the asymmetric information hypothesis implies. We also find that while U.S. purchases of equities in developed foreign markets tend to be positively associated with the foreign market return, foreign purchases of U.S. equities show no such relation to the U.S. market return. This is consistent with U.S. investors being less well informed about foreign markets than locals, but with foreigners being as well informed about U.S. markets as U.S. residents. An alternative interpretation that we cannot rule out is that the association between U.S. portfolio flows and foreign market returns is due to price impact associated with exogenous shifts in the U.S. demand for foreign securities that is not information related. However, we note that the high turnover rates of U.S. portfolios of foreign equities suggest that price impact effects are not large.

When we examine U.S. portfolio investment in emerging markets we find strong evidence that U.S. purchases are positively associated with local market returns in many countries. There is even evidence that this effect persists when we substitute the lagged local market return for the contemporaneous return. This is consistent with U.S. residents being at an informational disadvantage relative to locals in these markets, and trading on new information with a lag. For neither developed nor emerging markets do we find significant evidence that portfolio flows are affected by host country returns as might be expected if flows were caused by relative wealth shifts between residents of different countries. Our model is able to explain only a small proportion of the variance of international equity portfolio flows. Since these flows are now large and variable, further effort to understand their determinants is called for.

Appendix

Proof of Theorem: We provide the proof for a two trading session economy. The equilibrium in the last trading session is equivalent to the Admati (1985) single trading session model and the proof is neglected. We focus on the proof of the equilibrium in the first trading session. It is straightforward to prove that the price function stated in the theorem clears the market; then we need only to show that the demand of the investors in the first period is optimal, given the public information and each investor's private signal.

Let $\tilde{a}$ denote the price change at trading session 1; $\tilde{b}_t^i$ denote the expected long run excess return for investor i at trading session t; and $\tilde{w}_t^i$ denote the wealth of investor i at trading session t; i.e.,

$$\tilde{a} \equiv \tilde{P}_1 - P_0, \qquad \tilde{b}_t^i \equiv \tilde{\mu}_t^i - \tilde{P}_t, \qquad \tilde{w}_1^i = \tilde{w}_0^i + (\tilde{D}_0^i)'\tilde{a}.$$

In the last trading session, since there is only one trading session left, investor i's trading strategy is characterized by Admati (1985):

$$\tilde{D}_1^i = rK_1^i[\tilde{\mu}_1^i - \tilde{P}_1] = rK_1^i\tilde{b}_1^i. \tag{A1}$$

Given the equilibrium trading strategy in the second trading session, investor i's expected utility conditional on his information at the second trading session is:

$$E[U^i|F_1^i] = E[U^i|F_0^i, \tilde{a}, \tilde{b}_1^i] = -\exp\left\{ -\frac{\tilde{w}_1^i}{r} - \frac{(\tilde{b}_1^i)' K_1^i \tilde{b}_1^i}{2} \right\}, \qquad (A2)$$

The first term in the exponential comes from the investor's wealth, and the second term represents the gains in expected utility from returns in the second period. Note that the effect of public and private signals on investor i's expected utility is manifested through the variable $\tilde{b}_1^i$. Since all the random variables are multi-normally distributed, the conditional mean $\tilde{\mu}_1^i \equiv \tilde{b}_1^i + \tilde{P}_0$ is the sufficient statistic for all information in calculating expectations at session 1.

To determine the optimal strategy of investor i, we need to calculate his expected utility given any strategy D_0^i at time 0, i.e., $E[U^i|F_0^i]$. This can be determined in two steps:

$$E[U^i|F_0^i] = E[E[U^i|F_0^i, \tilde{a}]|F_0^i] = E[E[E[U^i|F_0^i, \tilde{a}, \tilde{b}_1^i]|F_0^i, \tilde{a}]|F_0^i].$$

We can rewrite $\tilde{a}$ as:

$$\tilde{a} = A(\tilde{u} - P_0 + \delta)$$

where $A = K_1^{-1}(K_1 - K_0)$, $\tilde{\delta} = (K_1 - K_0)^{-1} [N_1 \eta_1 - (rS_1\Phi_1 + r^{-1})\tilde{X}_1]$.
Define:

$$\Lambda^i \equiv \text{Var}^{-1}[\tilde{u}|\tilde{a}, F_0^i]$$

$$\tilde{\mu}_{\tilde{b}_1^i} \equiv E[\tilde{b}_1^i|F_0^i, \tilde{a}] = B^i \tilde{a} + C^i \tilde{b}_0^i,$$

$$\mu_{\tilde{a}}^i \equiv E[\tilde{a}|F_0^i] = A\tilde{b}_0^i,$$

$$B^i \equiv [I - C^i]A^{-1} - I,$$

$$C^i \equiv (\Lambda^i)^{-1}K_0^i,$$

$$\Gamma^i \equiv \text{Var}^{-1}[\tilde{b}_1^i|F_0^i, \tilde{a}] = [\text{Var}[\tilde{u}|\tilde{a}, F_0^i] - \text{Var}[\tilde{u}|\tilde{a}, \tilde{b}_1^i, F_0^i]]^{-1}$$

$$= [(\Lambda^i)^{-1} - (K_1^i)^{-1}]^{-1},$$

$$\Psi \equiv \text{Var}^{-1}[\tilde{a}|F_0^i] = (A')^{-1}[(K_0^i)^{-1} + (\Lambda^i - K_0^i)^{-1}]^{-1}A^{-1} = (B^i + I)'K_0^iA^{-1}.$$

We can now calculate the expected utility conditional on $\tilde{a}$; dropping irrelevant terms, this is given by:

$$E[U^i|F_0^i,\tilde{a}] \propto \int_{R^M} \exp\left[-\frac{(D_0^i)'\tilde{a}}{r} - \frac{(\tilde{b}_1^i)'K_1^i\tilde{b}_1^i}{2} - \frac{(\tilde{b}_1^i - \tilde{\mu}_{\tilde{b}_1^i})'\Gamma^i(\tilde{b}_1^i - \tilde{\mu}_{\tilde{b}_1^i})}{2} \right] d\tilde{b}_1^i$$

$$\propto -\exp\left[-\frac{(D_0^i)'\tilde{a}}{r} - \frac{\tilde{\mu}_{\tilde{b}_1^i}^t \Gamma^i \tilde{\mu}_{\tilde{b}_1^i}}{2} + \frac{\tilde{\mu}_{\tilde{b}_1^i}^t \Gamma^i (K_1^i + \Gamma^i)^{-1}\Gamma^i \tilde{\mu}_{\tilde{b}_1^i}}{2} \right]$$

$$= -\exp\left[-\frac{(D_0^i)'\tilde{a}}{r} - \frac{\tilde{\mu}_{\tilde{b}_1^i}^t((K_1^i)^{-1} + (\Gamma^i)^{-1})^{-1}\tilde{\mu}_{\tilde{b}_1^i}}{2} \right] \qquad (A3)$$

$$= -\exp\left[-\frac{(D_0^i)'\tilde{a}}{r} - \frac{\tilde{\mu}_{\tilde{b}_1^i}^t \Lambda^i \tilde{\mu}_{\tilde{b}_1^i}}{2} \right]$$

$$= -\exp\left[-\frac{(D_0^i)'\tilde{a}}{r} - \frac{(B^i\tilde{a} + C^i\tilde{b}_0^i)'\Lambda^i(B^i\tilde{a} + C^i\tilde{b}_0^i)}{2} \right].$$

Taking the expectation with respect to $\tilde{a}$ we get,

$$E[U^i|F_0^i]$$

$$\propto - \int_{R^M} \exp\left[-\frac{(D_0^i)'\tilde{a}}{r} - \frac{(B^i\tilde{a} + C^i\tilde{b}_0^i)'\Lambda^i(B^i\tilde{a} + C^i\tilde{b}_0^i) - (\tilde{a} - \mu_{\tilde{a}}^i)'\Psi^i(\tilde{a} - \mu_{\tilde{a}}^i)}{2} \right] d\tilde{a}$$

$$\propto -\exp[(F^i)'G^iF^i/2 - (\tilde{b}_0^i)'H^i\tilde{b}_0^i/2], \qquad (A4)$$

where

$$F^i = D_0^i/r + (B^i)'\Lambda^iC^i\tilde{b}_0^i - \Psi^i\mu_{\tilde{a}}^i, \qquad (A5)$$

$$G^i = [(B^i)'\Lambda^iB^i + \Psi^i]^{-1}, \qquad (A6)$$

$$H^i = (C^i)'\Lambda^iC^i + A'\Psi A = (C^i)'K_0^i + [(B^i + I)A]'K_0^i = [C^i + I - C^i]'K_0^i = K_0^i. \qquad (A7)$$

Since Λ^i, Ψ^i are positive definite, G^i is positive definite. The first order condition simplifies to:

$$F^i = 0. \qquad (A8)$$

This implies that the optimal demand for the first trading session is

$$\tilde{D}_0^i = r[\Psi^i\mu_{\tilde{a}}^i - (B^i)'\Lambda C^i\tilde{b}_0^i] = r[(B^i + I)' - (B^i)']K_0^i\tilde{b}_0^i = rK_0^i[\tilde{\mu}_0^i - \tilde{P}_0]. \qquad (A9)$$

International Portfolio Investment Flows 1879

The optimal demand in expression (21) has the same form as (13) except for the time subscript. Thus the optimal demand at session t is unaffected by the existence of future trading sessions. Substituting equations (19) and (20) back into equation (16), we have

$$E[U^i|F_0^i] \propto - \exp\left[-\frac{w_0^i}{r} - (\tilde{b}_0^i)' K_0^i \tilde{b}_0^i/2 \right]. \tag{A10}$$

Expression (22) has the same form as expression (14) except for the time subscript which shows that we can easily extend the proof to the general case of T trading sessions.

Proof of Remark 2: In equation (12) the numerator is the same for a domestic and foreign investor but the denominator is higher for the domestic investor. This implies that the domestic investor has the lower turnover rate under the same conditions as Remark 1.

REFERENCES

Adler, Michael, and Bernard Dumas, 1983, International portfolio choice and corporation finance: A synthesis, *Journal of Finance* 38, 925–984.

Admati, Anat, 1985, A noisy rational expectations equilibrium for multi-asset securities markets, *Econometrica* 53, 629–657.

Bekaert, Geert, 1995, Market integration and investment barriers in emerging equity markets, *The World Bank Economic Review* 9, 75–107.

Bekaert, Geert, and Campbell R. Harvey, 1995, Time-varying world market integration, *Journal of Finance* 50, 403–444.

Bekaert, Geert, and Michael S. Urias, 1995, Diversification, integration and emerging market closed end funds, NBER Working paper No. 4990.

Black, Fischer, 1974, International capital market equilibrium with investment barriers. *Journal of Financial Economics*, 337–352.

Blume, Lawrence, David Easley, and Maureen O'Hara, 1994, Market statistics and technical analysis: The role of volume, *Journal of Finance* 49, 153–182.

Bohn, Henning, and Linda L. Tesar, 1996, U.S. equity investment in foreign markets: Portfolio rebalancing or trend chasing, *American Economic Review* 86, 77–81.

Brennan, Michael J., and Avanidhar Subrahmanyam, 1995, The determinants of average trade size, Working paper No. 7-95, University of California, Los Angeles.

Carlos, Ann M., and Frank D. Lewis, 1995, Foreign financing of Canadian railroads, in Michael D. Bordo and Richard Sylla, Eds.: *Anglo-American Financial Systems* (Irwin, New York).

Chuhan, Paul, 1992, Sources of portfolio investment in emerging markets, Working paper, World Bank, International Economics Department, Washington, D.C.

Chuhan, Paul, Claessens, Stijn, and N. Mamingi, 1993, Equity and bond flows to Latin America, Working paper No. 1160, World Bank, Washington, D.C.

Cooper, Ian A., and Evi Kaplanis, 1994, Home bias in equity portfolios, inflation hedging, and international capital market equilibrium, *Review of Financial Studies* 7, 45–60.

Coval, Joshua, and Toby Moskowitz, 1996, Home bias at home: Local equity preference in domestic portfolios, Unpublished manuscript, University of California, Los Angeles.

de Caires, Bryan (Editor), 1988, *The GT Guide to World Equity Markets* (Euromoney, London).

Frankel, Jacob A., 1991, Quantifying international capital mobility in the 1980's, in Douglas Bernheim and John B. Shoven, Eds.: *National Savings and Economic Performance*, (University of Chicago Press, Chicago).

French, Kenneth R., and James M. Poterba, 1991, Investor diversification and international equity markets, *American Economic Review*, Papers and Proceedings 81, 222–226.

Gehrig, Thomas P., 1993, An information based explanation of the domestic bias in international equity investment, *The Scandinavian Journal of Economics* 21, 7–109.

Goldstein, Morris, and David Folkerts Landau, 1994, *International Capital Markets: Developments, Prospects, and Policy Issues* (International Monetary Fund, Washington, D.C.).

Grubel, Herbert, 1968, Internationally diversified portfolios, *American Economic Review* 58, 1299–1314.

Hellwig, Martin F., 1980, On the aggregation of information in competitive markets, *Journal of Economic Theory* 22, 477–498.

Kang, Jun-Koo, and René M. Stulz, 1994, Why is there a home bias? An analysis of foreign portfolio equity ownership in Japan, *Journal of Financial Economics*, forthcoming.

Levy, Haim, and Marshall Sarnat, 1970, International diversification of investment portfolios, *American Economic Review* 50, 668–675.

Low, Aaron, 1992, Essays on asymmetric information in international finance, Ph.D. dissertation, University of California, Los Angeles.

Miller, Norman C., and Marina von Neuman Whitman, 1970, A mean-variance analysis of United States long-term portfolio foreign investment, *Quarterly Journal of Economics* 84, 175–196.

Miller, Norman C., and Marina von Neumann Whitman, 1972, Alternative theories and tests of U.S. short-term foreign investment, *Journal of Finance* 28, 1131–1150.

Park, Keith K.H., and Antoine W. van Agtmael, 1993, *The World's Emerging Stock Markets* (Probus, Chicago, Illinois).

Price, Margaret M., 1994, *Emerging Stock Markets: A Complete Investment Guide to New Markets around the World* (McGraw-Hill, New York).

Shiller, Robert J., F. Kon-Ya, and Yoshiro Tsutsui, 1996, Why did the Nikkei crash? Expanding the scope of expectations data collection. *Review of Economics and Statistics* 78, 156–164.

Shukla, Ravi, and Gregory van Inwegen, 1995, Do locals perform better than foreigners?, *Journal of Economics and Business* 47, 241–254.

Solnik, Bruno, 1974, Why not diversify internationally rather than domestically? *Financial Analysts' Journal* 30, 48–54.

Stulz, René, 1981, On the effects of barriers to international investment, *Journal of Finance* 36, 923–934.

Tesar, Linda L., and Ingrid Werner, 1993, U.S. equity investment in emerging markets, Research paper 1278, Stanford University.

Tesar, Linda L., and Ingrid Werner, 1994, International equity transactions and U.S. portfolio choice, in Jacob A. Frankel, Ed., *The Internationalization of Equity Markets* (University of Chicago Press, Chicago).

Tesar, Linda L., and Ingrid Werner, 1995, Home bias and high turnover, *Journal of International Money & Finance* 14, 467–492.

Uppal, Raman, 1993, A general equilibrium model of international portfolio choice, *Journal of Finance* 48, 529–554.

Wang, Jiang, 1993, A model of intertemporal asset prices under asymmetric information, *Review of Economic Studies* 60, 249–282.

THE JOURNAL OF FINANCE • VOL. XLVI, NO. 5 • DECEMBER 1991

Stock Prices and the Supply of Information

MICHAEL J. BRENNAN and PATRICIA J. HUGHES[*]

ABSTRACT

We develop a model in which the dependence of the brokerage commission rate on share price provides an incentive for brokers to produce research reports on firms with low share prices. Stock splits therefore affect the attention paid to a firm by investment analysts. Managers with favorable private information about their firms have an incentive to split their firm's shares in order to reveal the information to investors. We find empirical evidence that is consistent with the major new prediction of the model, that the number of analysts following a firm is inversely related to its share price.

THE CLASSICAL THEORY OF finance assigns great importance to the aggregate market value of the equity of a firm, but has no role for the number of shares in a firm's capital stock, or for the price of a single share. Consequently, the attention paid to this seemingly irrelevant variable by firms, investors, and brokers, as well as by legal and regulatory authorities, has so far defied plausible explanation. It is clear that firms attempt to manage the unit price of their shares by stock splits and occasional reverse splits, and there is a strong relation between the price per share and the size of the firm.[1] Moreover, investors pay attention to stock splits, the abnormal return consequent on a split announcement being strongly related to the projected post-split share price. This reaction has been explained by Brennan and Copeland (1988a) as the rational response to a costly signal by the firm. The basis of their argument is that it is costly for a firm to reduce its share price by splitting because the structure of brokerage commissions makes it more costly to trade in low priced shares. The relation between splits and trading

[*] Irwin and Goldyne Hearsh Professor of Banking and Finance at University of California, Los Angeles, and University of Southern California, respectively. We are grateful to Craig Holden and Jim Brandon for research assistance. We also thank Yuk-Shee Chan, Linda DeAngelo, John Hand, Prem Jain, Pat O'Brien, Brett Trueman, Ivo Welch, Fred Weston, workshop participants at Cornell, London Business School, London School of Economics, Stanford, UC Berkeley, UCLA, UC Riverside, USC, and University of Texas (Austin), and the referees and Rene Stulz for helpful comments. A previous version of this paper was presented at the 1990 meetings of the American Accounting Association, the French Finance Association, the IMI in Rome, and the Western Finance Association.

[1] Stoll and Whaley (1983) show that, based upon portfolios formed on firm size, average price per share is monotonically increasing in size, and both the mean portfolio return and beta are monotonically decreasing in size.

costs has been acknowledged in the business press,[2] and the signaling argument finds support in the work of McNichols and Dravid (1990) and others who show that stock splits are followed by unexpected increases in earnings. Less easy to explain is the change in stock price behavior following the date the split becomes effective. Ohlson and Penman (1985) observe an increase in the variance of returns following the split ex-date, and Brennan and Copeland (1988b) find that the systematic risk of firms also increases following the split.

The Brennan and Copeland signaling model is at best a partial explanation of the stock price reaction to split announcements, for it relies on the observed structure of brokerage commissions which is taken as exogenous. Yet why should brokerage commissions depend on such a seemingly irrelevant variable as the share price? And why should legal and regulatory authorities also be concerned about the level of the price per share?[3] In this paper we present a model with an equilibrium in which different firms choose different share prices, smaller firms have lower share prices, brokerage commissions depend on share prices, share prices react to split announcements, the share price behavior and bid-ask spread may change following the split, the number of shareholders increases after a split, and there is cross-sectional variation in the number of analysts following different firms.

We argue that managers with favorable private information will find it advantageous to have independent third parties produce information about their firms for investors.[4] In order to avoid obvious moral hazard considerations, it is necessary that the information producers be independent of the firm.[5] This poses the problem of compensating the information producers for their efforts. We argue that the role of information producer is assumed by brokers who make earnings forecasts about individual firms and receive compensation for their efforts in the form of brokerage commissions from the investors who trade in the particular stocks. Following Merton (1987), we assume in our model that investors will only purchase stocks that they "know about", and that this knowledge is provided in the form of brokers' earnings forecasts. Thus earnings forecasts generate brokerage commissions

---

[2] ' "Stock splits are the biggest ripoff on Wall Street," contends Hans R. Reinisch, a New York investor. "The only thing that changes with a split is the brokerage commissions, and they often go up sharply. If you're an active investor, you have to take into account the transaction costs." ' (*Wall Street Journal*, October 13, 1989).

[3] For example, margin loans are not permitted on stock transactions in which the share price is less than $5.

[4] Diamond (1985) argues that firms have an incentive to make information available to shareholders in order to reduce the costs of private information acquisition.

[5] The lack of credibility of information produced by investment bankers in the employ of the corporation was discussed in a recent *Wall Street Journal* article. An associate research director at Drexel reported "The research department did our darndest to resist pressure from corporate finance. We made it clear when we had a bias, when we had an underwriting relationship. As a result, the thinking was that institutional investors using the Drexel research reports had a red flag, and unless they were completely stupid, they'd do a double check with someone with less involvement." ("Wall Street Grows Treacherous for Analysts Who Speak Out," April 5, 1990)

because investors trade only in those stocks for which the brokers forecast earnings.

In deciding whether to forecast earnings, a broker compares the cost of the forecast with the commission revenue it will generate, which depends on the size of the firm and the total number of brokers making forecasts. Given the commission rate, competition among brokers will determine the equilibrium number of brokers who make forecasts about a particular firm. We consider an equilibrium in which brokers offer a commission schedule which depends on the share price. This permits managers to influence the number of brokers who make earnings forecasts about their firms by changing the share price through a split.[6]

The major new prediction of the model, that the flow of information about firms is an increasing function of firm size and a decreasing function of the share price, is tested by examining the relation between the number of brokerage firm analysts who report earnings forecasts for a firm and its share price and size.[7] We find that the number of analysts is related to both share price and size in the predicted manner.

In the following section we summarize the previous empirical studies of splits. In Section II we present a formal model of the effect of share prices on the flow of information about a firm provided by stockbrokers. Section III discusses the data and reports the result of the empirical tests of the supply of information hypothesis. Section IV concludes.

I. Empirical Evidence on Stock Splits

There have been extensive empirical studies documenting an association between stock splits and various economic variables. We summarize here the empirical regularities that a theory of share prices must address.

Not surprisingly, stock splits follow periods of rising stock prices.[8] However, there also is extensive evidence that share prices rise further on the announcement of a split and fall on the announcement of a reverse split,[9] suggesting that the split announcement serves as a signal of management's

---

[6] A referee has suggested to us an alternative explanation for stock splits and for our empirical results. He argues that small investors who prefer low priced stocks are necessary to provide liquidity in low capitalization stocks, leading to a correlation between size and stock price. Furthermore, "a lower share price corresponds to a wider ownership and implies more potential trading commissions and therefore, more analyst following." However, this argument does not explain the observed relation between splits and subsequent earnings increases (see footnote 11).

[7] Note that our theory relates only to brokerage house analysts whose compensation depends upon stock trading commissions, and not to analysts employed by other financial institutions such as insurance companies.

[8] Fama, Fisher, Jensen, and Roll (1969) find that shares of splitting firms earned abnormal returns for 29 months prior to the split, and Lakonishok and Lev (1987) report that the shares rise by about 70% more than those of their control sample over the four years preceding the split announcement.

[9] See Grinblatt, Masulis, and Titman (1984); Eades, Hess, and Kim (1984); Lamoureux and Poon (1987); and Asquith, Healy, and Palepu (1989).

private information.[10] This notion is confirmed by the finding that stock splits are associated with unexpected increases in earnings.[11] Grinblatt et al. (1984) find that the abnormal announcement return is negatively related to the size of the firm and to a measure of information leakage over the previous week; and they interpret this evidence as consistent with an "attention hypothesis" according to which undervalued firms split their stock in order to attract attention. Arbel and Swanson (1989) find that firms that split had been followed by fewer analysts prior to the split than all firms on average, and conclude that these neglected firms split in order to attract attention from analysts. They also find that the magnitude of the price response to the firm's split announcement is negatively related to the number of analysts following the firm. Brennan and Copeland find that, as predicted by their signaling theory, the announcement return is negatively related to the target post-split share price, which they define as the pre-split price divided by the split factor.

It is commonly claimed that the purpose of stock splits is to improve liquidity and increase the number of shareholders. Despite this, several authors (e.g., Copeland (1979)) have found a decrease in trading volume following a split. However, Lakonishok and Lev (1987) show that it is the trading volume prior to the split which is abnormally high, and that it returns to normal within two months of the split. Conroy and Flood (1989) find that, despite the decline in the dollar volume of trade, there is an increase in the number of transactions, which implies that the average transaction size falls. They also find an increase in the number of individual shareholders subsequent to the split.

Stock splits also appear to be associated with increases in risk.[12] While Amihud and Mendelson (1988) attribute this finding to the discreteness of stock prices and increases in the bid-ask spread following splits, Sheikh (1989) finds an increase in the volatility implied by option prices following the split ex-date, which suggests that the phenomenon is real rather than due to measurement error. Brennan and Copeland (1988b) report a major increase in the beta coefficient on the ex-date (but not on the announcement date). Wiggins (1990) finds that the magnitude of this increase is sensitive to the return measurement interval, and explains the Brennan and Copeland finding as the result of a more rapid response of security returns to market information following the split date.

The Brennan and Copeland signaling model relies on the fact that brokerage commissions depend upon share prices. Table I summarizes the results of a study by Coler and Schaefer (1988) which compares typical commissions charged by full service brokers with those charged by discount brokers. Not

---

[10] More puzzling is the finding of additional abnormal returns on the ex-date of the split. See Grinblatt, Masulis, and Titman (1984).

[11] See Lakonishok and Lev (1987), Doran and Nachtmann (1988), and McNichols and Dravid (1990). Asquith, Healy, and Palepu (1989) find that large increases in earnings prior to the split are not reversed in the four years following the split.

[12] See Ohlson and Penman (1985), French and Dubofsky (1986), and Dravid (1987).

Stock Prices and the Supply of Information 1669

Table I

Typical Full Service Brokerage Commissions as Per Cent of Trade Value for Selected Transactions* (Average Discount Broker Commissions in Parentheses)

Size of Trade	Share Price				
	10	20	30	40	50
$3,000			2.600 (1.180)		
$4,000		2.625 (1.101)		2.225 (0.922)	
$5,000	2.980 (1.086)				1.940 (0.755)
$6,000			2.233 (0.846)		
$8,000				2.100 (0.700)	
$9,000			2.089 (0.716)		
$10,000		2.040 (0.734)			1.870 (0.589)
$12,000				1.850 (0.587)	
$15,000					1.720 (0.499)

*Constructed from Table 2 in Coler and Schaefer (1988).

only is the discount broker commission (in parentheses) about one-third that of the full service broker, but, for both types, the commission charged as a proportion of the trade declines as a function both of the size of the trade and of the price of the shares traded.[13] Branch (1985) argues that, although some processing fees and costs paid by brokers do depend upon the number of shares traded, these are of relatively minor importance, and the bulk of the costs to be recovered are fixed costs. He concludes that there is no justification for the current system which discourages trading in low priced stocks, and remarks that "While a company's per share price is essentially arbitrary, as a matter of practice companies with low priced stocks tend to be smaller, younger and more prone to be owned by individual investors" (op. cit., p11). He concludes that the current system discourages trading in low priced stocks. This leaves open the question why these companies choose to have low priced shares.

Since full service brokers survive the competition from discounters, they must provide additional services. According to Coler and Schaefer, the most significant consideration is that, unlike the full service broker, the discounter

---

[13] See Smidt (1990) for an historical perspective on New York Stock Exchange commission rates. Commission rates depended on share prices from 1919 until the end of the fixed commissions era. In 1964, the commission rate on $20 shares was 4.58 times that on $200 shares.

will not provide security recommendations or research analyses, or offer access to new stock issues. Thus it seems that the additional charge of the full service broker is to cover research costs, and that these brokers are able to prevent investors from free riding by meting out the quantity and timeliness of research they provide to customers according to their volume of trading. If the commission schedule were as arbitrary as Branch suggests, it is difficult to see how it could withstand competition. Thus, according to the evidence in Table I, a full service broker charges $97 for a $5000 transaction in a $50 stock, and an extra $52 ($= (0.298 - .0194) \times 5000$) for the same size transaction in a $10 stock. The discounter however charges only $16.55 extra ($= (0.01086 - 0.00755) \times \$5000$) for the transaction in the low priced stock. Therefore, assuming that this represents the incremental execution costs of both types of brokers,[14] it is apparent that the full service broker is making an additional profit of $35.45 ($= 52 - 16.55$) on the low priced stock. It seems unlikely that this could persist in equilibrium unless there is some additional cost incurred by the full service broker for the low priced stock. In our model, this is an additional cost of research per dollar of transaction.

In summary, there is substantial evidence that stock splits serve as signals of management's private information about future earnings. They also lead to an increase in the number of shareholders, wider bid-ask spreads, and higher brokerage commissions. After the split becomes effective, the variance is higher and the response to market-wide information is more rapid.[15] However, the only attempt to explain how a split announcement can serve as a credible signal is the transaction cost model of Brennan and Copeland which is incomplete because it offers no rational justification for the dependence of brokerage commission rates on stock prices. In the following section we develop a more complete model.

II. An Equilibrium Model of the Supply of Information

In order to capture the notion that full service stockbrokers are compensated for their research costs by commissions on share transactions,[16] we consider an economy in which investors only invest in the securities of firms that they "know about",[17] and that the only way in which investors get to know about firms is through their personal brokers. Investors are loyal and

---

[14] Execution costs may be higher for small illiquid companies which typically have low share prices.

[15] Kryzanowski and Zhang (1990) find similar security price behavior for a sample of Canadian firms.

[16] "For years, big institutional investors such as pension funds and insurers have paid for Wall Street research reports by directing stock trades to the brokerage firms that produce them. The four to six cents in trading commissions that Allstate and other institutions dole out serve as payment for a variety of services, from trading expertise to research reports on the food industry." (from "Challenge to Wall Street: What's Research Worth?" *Wall Street Journal*, December 14, 1989)

[17] For a similar assumption see Merton (1987) and Arbel and Swanson (1989).

remain with brokers, receiving information from them and trading through them, as long as the charges of the broker are competitive.[18] In particular, we shall assume that brokers who charge more than the average commission charged by full service brokers lose all of their clients; moreover, clients conjecture that brokers who offer commissions less than the average of full service brokers are not providing *bona fide* forecasts. Consequently, in equilibrium all full service brokers charge identical commissions.[19] For simplicity we assume that the volume of trading done by an individual investor is determined by life-cycle considerations and is therefore insensitive to the level of brokerage commissions. The expected rate of return on a security, however, will reflect the cost of transacting in the security, so that securities in which it is expensive to trade will have low prices *ceteris paribus*.[20]

Let f denote the cost to an individual broker of making an earnings forecast for a particular firm and let t denote the present value of the total brokerage revenues to be earned from trading in the shares of the firm as a proportion of its end of period value, x. We assume that the marginal cost of transacting is zero to brokers, and consider an equilibrium in which all investors are identical, and all brokers charge the same commission and have the same number of clients. Then, since investors are loyal to their brokers and trade only in shares they know about, the total brokerage commissions will be divided equally among the brokers who make forecasts. Competition among brokers ensures that total brokerage revenue is equal to the total cost of making forecasts, so that N, the equilibrium number of brokers making forecasts for a firm with end of period value $\tilde{x}$, is given by

$$N = E[t\tilde{x}]/f \qquad (1)$$

where $E[\ ]$ denotes the expectations operator.[21] Thus the equilibrium number of brokers making a forecast about a particular company depends on both the size of the company as measured by its expected end of period value, $E[\tilde{x}]$, and the brokerage commission rate, t.[22]

---

[18] In practice brokers restrict the flow of information to investors who do not trade through them.

[19] "Also, the lack of variation in trading commissions assumes that one firm's research is as good as another." (*Wall Street Journal*, December 4, 1989)

[20] For a similar assumption see Brennan and Copeland (1988a); for empirical evidence that equilibrium rates of return do depend on the cost of transacting see Amihud and Mendelson (1987).

[21] Implicit in expression (1) is the assumption that trading volume is invariant to the commission rate. A weaker sufficient condition for what follows is that aggregate commissions be increasing in the commission rate. This condition is consistent with Copeland's (1979) finding that aggregate brokerage revenue increased following a split, despite the decrease in trading volume.

[22] A further reason that increased commissions may attract more analysts is that at many brokerage houses, trading commissions generated by analysts are used to determine the annual bonuses, which can account for more than 50% of the analysts' compensation. ("Are Analysts Putting Their Mouths Where the Money Is?" *Business Week*, December 18, 1989, p118)

Consistent with observed commission schedules discussed in the preceding section, we assume that the brokerage commission depends on the price, P, at which an individual share of the security trades, $t(P)$, where $t'(P) < 0$. Then companies with low share prices will have relatively high commission costs, and for their size, will have a relatively large number of brokers making forecasts about them. Conversely, firms that have high share prices will, for their size, have a relatively small number of brokers making forecasts about them. Moreover, by choosing the price at which their shares trade by splitting, managers are able to control the attention paid to their firms by the brokerage industry.[23]

Consider now the problem faced by the manager of a company who has private information about its future earnings and wishes to communicate it to the market. Let us suppose that there exists no credible mechanism by which the private information can be communicated costlessly to the market. One possibility is for the manager to incur communication costs, for example by employing a third party (such as an auditor) to verify the signal. However, if the third party is paid directly by the manager there is a moral hazard problem which reputational considerations will only partially alleviate.[24] The only alternative that we consider here is the manager's decision to change the stock price by means of a split. Splits affect the incentive of brokerage houses to provide earnings forecasts which serve to reveal the manager's private information, with a precision which is proportional to the number of earnings forecasts.[25]

We assume that initially all investors and the manager of the firm have homogeneous beliefs about the end of period value of the firm. The manager receives a private signal about the end of period value and decides whether to split. If a decision is made to split, the manager announces the new number of shares to be outstanding after the stock split. The stock split will change the stock price, P, which determines the rate of brokerage commission $t(P)$; and this in turn determines the number of analysts who make earnings forecasts according to relation (1). The timing of events is as follows:

τ_0: investors and the manager have homogeneous prior beliefs about the firm's final payoff, x.

τ_1: the manager receives a private signal about x and announces the new number of shares, n, through a stock split.

τ_2: N analysts gather information and announce forecasts of the end of period value.

---

[23] Note that it is the commission schedule that makes the attention hypothesis of Grinblatt, Masulis and Titman (1984) economically rational.

[24] Thakor (1982) models third-party information production by debt insurers in a similar setting of information asymmetry where moral hazard considerations preclude direct disclosure of default probabilities.

[25] The role of multiple analysts' forecasts is similar to that of multiple ratings for bond issuers. Hsueh and Kidwell (1988) find that 46% of their sample of municipal bonds had two bond ratings. They find that a second rating reduces borrowing costs.

τ_3: the end of period value is realized and analysts are compensated by the brokerage commission.

We assume that all individuals are risk neutral, that prior beliefs about x are represented by a normal distribution with mean x_0 and precision s_0,[26] and that the interest rate is zero. The market value of the firm at τ_0 then is

$$V_0 = x_0(1 - t). \qquad (2)$$

At τ_1 the manager receives a noisy signal about the end of period value:

$$y_m = x + \tilde{\epsilon}_m, \qquad (3)$$

where $\tilde{\epsilon}_m$ is normally distributed with mean zero and precision s_m. After observing the signal y_m the manager announces n, the number of shares that will be outstanding after the split. Knowing n, investors infer that the manager's signal was $\hat{y}_m(n)$. They then revise their beliefs about x in accordance with Bayes' Rule:

$$E(x \mid n) \equiv \hat{x}(n) = \frac{x_0 s_0 + \hat{y}_m(n) s_m}{s_0 + s_m}, \qquad (4)$$

where $s_0 + s_m$ is the new precision. When n is announced, the market value of the firm changes to $V_1(n)$, which reflects the new information, the new commission, and the fixed administration costs of executing the split, C[27]:

$$V_1(n) = E[x(1 - t(x/n)) \mid n] - C. \qquad (5)$$

In (5), x/n is the τ_3 share price. The expected aggregate brokerage commission, $T(n)$, is given by

$$T(n) = E[xt(x/n) \mid n]. \qquad (6)$$

Assuming that $T(n)$ is monotonic,[28] the same information is conveyed by an announcement of T or of n, and it will be analytically convenient to assume that the manager announces T. Equation (5) then becomes

$$V_1(T) = \hat{x}(T) - T - C, \qquad (7)$$

where $\hat{x}(T) = E[x \mid T]$ at τ_1.

Then, defining $F = f^{-1}$, the number of analysts who make forecasts is, from (1)

$$N(T) = FT. \qquad (8)$$

The forecast of each analyst is y_i $(i = 1, \ldots, N(T))$, where

$$y_i = x + \tilde{\epsilon}_i, \qquad (9)$$

---

[26] Precision is defined as the inverse of the variance.

[27] The administrative costs of splitting include the costs of printing and distributing new stock certificates, and the buying and selling of fractional shares.

[28] It is shown below that a sufficient condition for this is that aggregate brokerage commissions are increasing in firm size for a given number of shares.

and $\tilde{\epsilon}_i$ is drawn from an independent normal distribution with mean zero and precision s. Define $\bar{y}$ as the average value of y_i.

Then the value of the firm at τ_2, *after* all the analysts forecasts have been publicly revealed is $V_2(T, \bar{y})$ where

$$V_2(T, \bar{y}) = \frac{x_0 s_0 + \hat{y}_m(T) s_m + \bar{y} FTs}{s_0 + s_m + FTs} - E\big[xt(x/n) \,|\, T, \hat{y}_m, \bar{y} \big] - C. \quad (10)$$

Since the number of analysts making forecasts is increasing in T (from (8)), the effect of a higher commission T is to increase FTs, the precision of the average brokerage forecast, $\bar{y}$. Clearly then, the greater the number of analysts making earnings forecasts, the greater will be the weight that investors place on the average brokerage forecast in valuing the firm. This provides the motivation for a manager with good news to seek attention from analysts.

We assume that the objective of the manager at τ_1 is to choose the new number of shares n (or equivalently, the expected aggregate brokerage commission T), in order to maximize the expectation, conditional on his private information, of the value of the firm at τ_2 when all of the analysts' information will have been revealed. Note that

$$E[\bar{y} \,|\, y_m] = \frac{x_0 s_0 + y_m s_m}{s_0 + s_m} \quad (11)$$

and

$$E\big[\{ xt(x/n) \,|\, T, \hat{y}_m, \bar{y} \} \,|\, y_m \big] = T. \quad (12)$$

After substituting (11) and (12) into (10), the manager's expectation at τ_1 of the τ_2 value of the firm is

$$E[V_2(T) \,|\, y_m] = \frac{x_0 s_0 + \hat{y}_m(T) s_m + \left\{ \dfrac{x_0 s_0 + y_m s_m}{s_0 + s_m} \right\} FTs}{s_0 + s_m + FTs} - T - C. \quad (13)$$

Note that the numerator of (13) is a weighted average of the investors' prior beliefs, what they infer about the manager's current information, and what the manager believes about the future information to be provided by analysts. The objective of the manager then is to maximize expression (13) through the choice of the new aggregate brokerage commission T.

Combining the first order condition for a maximum of (13) with respect to T with the equilibrium condition that $\hat{y}_m(T) = y_m$ yields the following differential equation for the investors' inference schedule $\hat{y}_m(T)$.

$$\hat{y}'_m(T) = \frac{s_0 + s_m + FTs}{s_m}. \quad (14)$$

The solution to (14) is

$$\hat{y}_m(T) = \frac{s_0 + s_m}{s_m} T + \frac{Fs}{2 s_m} T^2 + K, \tag{15}$$

where K is a constant of integration.

Due to the fixed costs of administering a split, not all managers will find it advantageous to announce a split after receiving private information. In order to determine the value of K, it is necessary to determine the minimum y_m which is disclosed through a split announcement. Let n_0 be the number of shares initially outstanding and let y_m^s denote the signal level at which a manager is indifferent between announcing a split and not.[29] If the manager does not announce a split, the expected aggregate brokerage commission is $\bar{T} \equiv E[\,xt(x/n_0)\,|\, y_m \le y_m^s]$. Similarly, $T(n_0)$, the expected brokerage commission if the manager announces the minimum split factor of one, is defined by $T(n_0) \equiv E[\,xt(x/n_0)\,|\, y_m^s]$. Then the condition for the manager who receives a signal y_m^s to be indifferent to splitting is that the expected value of V_2 conditional on y_m and no split be equal to the expected value to be obtained by announcing the minimum split factor of one, less the costs of the split, or:

$$E\big[\, E(\,x\,|\, y_m \le y_m^s,\, \bar{y})\,|\, y_m^s,\, s(\bar{y}) = F\bar{T}s\big] - \bar{T}$$

$$= \frac{x_0 s_0 + y_m^s s_m + y_m^s F T(n_0) s}{s_0 + s_m + F T(n_0) s} - T(n_0) - C. \tag{16}$$

The left-hand side of condition (16) is the expectation of the τ_2 value of the firm of a manager who has received the signal y_m^s, when the market infers from the absence of a split that $y_m < y_m^s$, and receives the average analyst forecast $\bar{y}$ which has precision $F\bar{T}s$. Condition (16) and the definition of $\bar{T}$ suffice to determine y_m^s, the signal of the marginal splitting firm: note that y_m^s depends upon the prior distribution of management signals. The constant of integration in (15) is then identified by considering the inference of investors for the minimum split factor of one. Since the manager who receives the signal y_m^s will announce $T = T(n_0)$, consistent inference requires that

$$\hat{y}_m(T = T(n_0)) = \left(\frac{s_0 + s_m}{s_m}\right) T(n_0) + \frac{Fs}{2 s_m} T(n_0)^2 - K \equiv y_m^s. \tag{17}$$

The solution for K from (17) is

$$K = \frac{Fs}{2 s_m} T(n_0)^2 + \frac{Fs}{2 s_m} T(n_0) - y_m^s. \tag{18}$$

---

[29] For simplicity we ignore the possibility of reverse splits, which we consider in the Appendix. We assume that even an incipient stock split in which the split factor is one cannot be accomplished without incurring the fixed administrative costs.

The second order condition for a maximum of (13) is always satisfied because $\partial^2 E[V_2(T) \mid y_m]/\partial T^2 = -Fs(s_0 + s_m + FsT) < 0$.

The investors' inference of y_m is an increasing and convex function of the expected aggregate brokerage commission T (for $T > \overline{T}$). Since the inference function (15) depends upon the prior precision s_0, it differs from the more common inference schedule in signaling models where investors ignore their prior beliefs when inferring the manager's information from the observed signal. A further departure from the standard signaling model is that the manager does not care about the current τ_1 value of the firm, but is maximizing the expectation of the future value when the analysts' information is revealed.

Since investors are able to infer the manager's signal y_m at τ_1, it follows that the value of the firm at τ_1 may be written as its expected value at τ_2, conditional on $\hat{y}_m$:

$$V_1(T) = E\left[V_2(T) \mid \hat{y}_m(T)\right] - C$$

$$= \frac{x_0 s_0 + \hat{y}_m(T) s_m + \left\{\dfrac{x_0 s_0 + \hat{y}_m(T) s_m}{s_0 + s_m}\right\} FTs}{s_0 + s_m + FTs} - T - C \quad (19)$$

$$= \frac{x_0 s_0 + \hat{y}_m(T) s_m}{s_0 + s_m} - T - C, \quad (20)$$

which is identical to expression (7).

It remains to be shown that $T(n) \equiv E[xt(x/n) \mid n]$ is increasing in n as assumed. Under this assumption we have established that the distribution of x conditional on the announcement of n (or $T(n)$) is normal with mean $x_0 s_0 + \hat{y}_m(T) s_m$ and precision $s_0 + s_m$ as shown in expression (20). Therefore the effect of an increase in n (or $T(n)$) is to shift the distribution to the right. A sufficient condition for this to increase $T(n)$ is that $xt(x/n)$ is increasing in x, or that brokerage commissions be increasing in firm size for a given number of shares.

It is easy to show that $dV_1(T)/dT > 0$, so that the post-announcement value of the firm is monotonically increasing in the signal T. Since $T'(n) > 0$, and the projected share price x_0/n is negatively related to n, it follows that the market reaction to the split announcement will be negatively related to the target share price x_0/n, as found by Brennan and Copeland (1988a).

Consistent with the evidence discussed in Section I, the model also predicts that a split will be followed by an increase in the number of shareholders as more investors learn about the firm. After the split becomes effective and brokers communicate their information to investors to stimulate trade at the higher commission rates, there will be more private information in the market. This would explain the observed increases in the bid-ask spread and the variance of returns according to the theories of Copeland and Galai (1983) and Glosten and Milgrom (1985), and Holthausen and Verrecchia

(1990) respectively. On a more speculative note, the increased attention from analysts to splitting firms could lead to the more rapid response of security returns to market-wide information as found by Wiggins (1990). Since, for a given share price the number of analysts is increasing in firm size,[30] a smaller firm must choose a lower share price in order to gain the same analyst following as a larger firm. It is likely that this accounts for the observed positive correlation between share prices and firm size. The model also predicts that stock splits will be followed by an increase in the number of earnings forecasts provided by analysts. As there is no prior evidence on this hypothesis, in the next section we turn to consider the empirical relation between share prices, stock splits, and analyst following.

An extension of the model to include reverse stock splits appears in the Appendix. We find that reverse splits convey bad news about the firm, and should occur infrequently because of the associated administrative costs. The empirical evidence on reverse splits is consistent with these predictions.

III. Data and Empirical Tests

Data on the number of analysts following individual stocks were drawn from the I/B/E/S tape for the years 1976–1987.[31] Data on stock prices, returns, and numbers of shares were drawn from the CRSP NYSE-AMEX and NASDAQ tapes. The criteria for a stock to be included in the analysis in a given year were that it was included on both the CRSP and the I/B/E/S databases on December 31 of that year, and that it was reported in the same CRSP database at the end of each of the prior five years.

Descriptive statistics for the sample appear in Table II. There is significant cross-sectional variation in the number of analysts following individual firms. The modal number of analysts for the sample firms on all exchanges for all years is one, except for the NYSE in 1987 when it is two.[32] The maximum number of analysts following a single firm is 44, and the distribution shows considerable skewness. The increase in the number of firms followed by I/B/E/S analysts over the twelve years is 60% for NYSE, 198% for AMEX, and 555% for NASDAQ. The median number of analysts is greatest for NYSE firms, which is not surprising given that these firms are larger. It also appears that NASDAQ firms have a slightly larger following

---

[30] Bhushan (1989) suggests that large firms generate more transactions, and finds that the number of analysts is positively related to the size of the firm.

[31] The authors gratefully acknowledge Lynch, Jones, and Ryan for making this tape available. I/B/E/S was developed by Lynch, Jones, and Ryan in order to systematically collect and distribute earnings forecasts from Wall Street and Regional brokerage firms. Brown, Foster, and Noreen (1985) found that, as of 1984, over 80 brokerage firms provided earnings forecasts for more than 2700 firms.

[32] Since firms are included in the sample only if they are on the I/B/E/S database, each firm must be followed by at least one analyst.

Table II

Descriptive Statistics For the Sample for the Time Period 1976 to 1987

Number of analysts is defined as the number making one-year ahead forecasts of earnings in December as reported on the I/B/E/S database. Firm size is the total market value of equity in $ millions on December 31. Price per share is the share price on December 31.

	Number of Firms	Number of Analysts		Firm Size		Price per Share	
		Mean	Median	Mean	Median	Mean	Median
NYSE							
1976	702	7.0	4	785	314	$30.02	$26.69
1977	806	6.3	4	650	264	26.10	23.50
1978	1140	6.8	5	503	175	22.65	19.69
1979	1171	7.1	6	598	215	25.90	23.13
1980	1163	7.6	6	786	253	29.33	24.75
1981	1187	8.9	7	717	250	24.83	22.50
1982	1186	9.5	8	840	317	28.30	24.50
1983	1202	10.3	8	1011	408	29.98	26.69
1984	1202	10.5	8	1102	381	26.84	24.38
1985	1196	12.2	10	1390	436	31.48	27.25
1986	1207	12.1	10	1613	486	30.13	25.75
1987	1123	12.4	10	1731	522	25.40	21.63
AMEX							
1976	66	2.3	1	99	40	18.18	14.25
1977	82	2.1	1	86	42	17.93	17.07
1978	139	2.6	1	75	37	15.91	14.00
1979	152	2.9	1	104	50	19.35	17.76
1980	153	2.9	2	164	66	22.98	21.00
1981	173	3.0	2	112	52	17.23	15.75
1982	211	3.1	2	119	57	18.37	15.50
1983	222	3.5	2	156	79	19.06	17.07
1984	235	3.4	2	127	59	15.49	12.75
1985	218	3.9	2	165	75	17.97	13.88
1986	219	4.1	2	182	72	16.16	13.50
1987	197	4.0	2	191	63	13.51	10.25
NASDAQ							
1976	200	3.0	1	117	57	21.22	19.13
1977	265	2.8	1	90	53	20.26	17.88
1978	430	3.1	2	78	46	18.75	16.13
1979	439	3.5	2	107	58	22.27	19.31
1980	384	3.8	2	139	78	23.60	20.57
1981	476	4.2	3	130	75	20.52	18.38
1982	620	4.1	3	144	84	21.94	19.57
1983	865	4.1	3	154	80	20.14	17.63
1984	1142	4.0	2	121	60	15.90	13.00
1985	1150	4.6	3	164	77	18.70	15.50
1986	1276	4.6	3	177	75	16.53	13.50
1987	1309	4.8	3	170	60	12.91	10.25

than do AMEX firms although their size and stock price distributions do not differ significantly.

The NYSE firms are large compared to the other groups. The distributions of AMEX and NASDAQ firm sizes appear similar. The increase in average firm size over the twelve years is 121% for NYSE, 93% for AMEX, and 45% for NASDAQ, which may be due to NASDAQ firms moving onto the NYSE or AMEX as they grow.

The time-series growth in firm size is not matched by a comparable increase in share price. To show the effect of stock splits on stock prices, Figure 1 plots the time series of the logarithms of the annual CRSP equal weighted price relatives with and without adjustment for stock splits and stock dividends. It is apparent that stock prices decrease when the market goes down, but do not increase correspondingly when the market goes up. This is consistent with the prior evidence that stock splits tend to occur after a rise in stock prices.

Table III provides statistics about the firms for which there was a change in the cumulative split factor reported on the CRSP tape during the year.[33] Reverse stock splits are very rare, and stock splits occur more frequently than do stock dividends. It is clear from Table III that only a minority of firms split in any given year. These numbers appear to be consistent with the findings of Lakonishok and Lev (1987) who analyze all CRSP NYSE and AMEX firms for the years 1963-1982 and find that in most of the years, 5-10% of the firms split their stock.

In addition, as Lakonishok and Lev (1987) have found, splitting firms have higher than average share prices, with the median price for splitting firms in our sample being $42.13 for NYSE, $26.50 for AMEX, and $24.75 for NASDAQ. As our theory predicts, prices for reverse splitting firms tends to

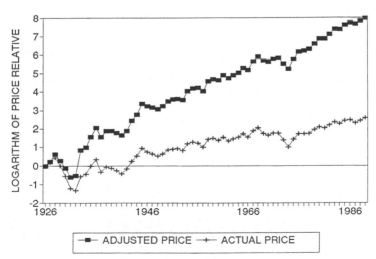

Figure 1. The effect of splits on average, 1926-1989. Logarithm of the CRSP equally weighted price relative with and without adjustment for stock splits.

---

[33] The data upon which Table III is based consists of *all* firms on the CRSP tape, not only those which are also carried by I/B/E/S.

Table III

Descriptive Statistics For Firms Listed on the CRSP Database Which Had a Change in The Split Factor in The Year

	Firms with Stock Splits					Firms with Reverse Splits					Firms with Stock Dividends				
	No. of Splits	% of Total	Max	Min	Med	No. of Splits	% of Total	Max	Min	Med	No. of Divs	% of Total	Max	Min	Med
NYSE															
1976	114	7	3[a]	1.25	2	1	0	5[b]	5	5	97	6	1.20[c]	1.01	1.04
1977	107	7	3	1.25	1.55	1	0	4	4	4	87	6	1.20	1.01	1.05
1978	129	8	4	1.25	1.5	1	0	4	4	4	86	6	1.20	1.01	1.05
1979	141	9	5	1.25	1.5	0					74	5	1.20	1.02	1.05
1980	183	12	4	1.25	2	0					65	4	1.25	1.02	1.05
1981	197	13	5	1.25	2	1	0	2	2	2	60	4	1.20	1.02	1.05
1982	84	5	2	1.25	1.5	1	0	3	3	3	58	4	1.20	1.01	1.05
1983	246	16	10	1.25	2	2	0	5	4	5	53	4	1.20	1.02	1.05
1984	121	8	5	1.25	1.5	0					56	4	1.20	1.02	1.05
1985	129	9	3	1.25	2	1	0	2	2	2	42	3	1.20	1.02	1.05
1986	237	16	5	1.25	2	4	0	50	10	14	45	3	1.15	1.02	1.05
1987	213	14	5	1.25	2	6	0	50	2	10	38	2	1.20	1.02	1.05
AMEX															
1976	52	5	2	1.25	1.5	2	0	3	2	3	96	9	1.20	1.02	1.05
1977	52	5	3	1.25	1.5	1	0	5	5	5	94	9	1.20	1.02	1.05
1978	70	7	3	1.25	1.5	1	0	5	5	5	97	10	1.20	1.01	1.05
1979	69	8	5	1.25	1.5	1	0	3	3	3	101	11	1.20	1.01	1.07
1980	108	12	7	1.25	1.5	0					110	13	1.25	1.01	1.06
1981	96	11	10	1.25	1.5	2	0	10	7.14	10	88	10	1.20	1.02	1.05
1982	58	7	2	1.25	1.5	3	0	3	2	2	66	8	1.20	1.02	1.05
1983	133	16	5	1.25	1.5	1	0	3.33	3.33	3.33	75	9	1.20	1.01	1.05
1984	43	5	3	1.25	2	0					61	8	1.20	1.02	1.05
1985	68	9	4	1.25	1.5	3	0	15	3	5	47	6	1.20	1.02	1.05
1986	67	9	10	1.25	1.5	1	0	3	3	3	42	5	1.20	1.01	1.06
1987	63	8	4	1.25	1.5	4	1	6	2.5	5	33	4	1.20	1.04	1.07

Table III—Continued

	Firms with Stock Splits		Change in Split Factor			Firms with Reverse Splits		Change in Split Factor			Firms with Stock Dividends		Change in Split Factor		
	No. of Splits	% of Total	Max	Min	Med	No. of Splits	% of Total	Max	Min	Med	No. of Divs	% of Total	Max	Min	Med
NASDAQ															
1976	152	6	5	1.25	1.5	7	≈0	50	1.5	5	208	8	1.20	1.01	1.05
1977	170	7	3	1.25	1.5	4	0	10	4	10	222	9	1.22	1.01	1.06
1978	260	10	7	1.25	1.5	7	0	10	2	5	227	9	1.22	1.02	1.08
1979	167	7	10	1.25	1.5	5	0	25	2.5	10	243	10	1.21	1.01	1.10
1980	273	11	10	1.25	1.5	5	0	8	2	3	210	8	1.20	1.02	1.10
1981	344	13	10	1.25	1.5	12	0	10	2	5	208	8	1.20	1.01	1.10
1982	183	6	5	1.25	1.5	20	1	50	1.5	5	193	6	1.20	1.02	1.07
1983	521	17	5	1.25	2	32	1	50	1.33	5	178	6	1.20	1.01	1.06
1984	243	7	10	1.25	1.5	31	1	40	2	10	196	5	1.20	1.01	1.07
1985	390	10	20	1.25	1.5	36	1	100	2	8	183	5	1.20	1.02	1.07
1986	527	14	40	1.25	1.5	22	1	200	2	10	164	4	1.20	1.01	1.06
1987	383	9	10	1.25	1.5	61	1	200	2	10	177	4	1.20	1.02	1.10

[a] A change of 3 means that 3 new shares are issued in exchange for 1 old share.
[b] A change of 5 means that 1 new share is issued in exchange for 5 old shares.
[c] A change of 1.2 means that a 20% stock dividend was issued.

be very low: the median is \$1.25 for NYSE, \$1.50 for AMEX, and \$0.69 for NASDAQ.

In order to test the implication of the model that the number of analysts making earnings forecasts about a firm is negatively related to the share price, and positively related to the size of the firm, the following equation was estimated by ordinary least squares for each year from 1976 to 1987 for all firms in the sample.

$$N_{it} = a_{0t} + a_{1t} \text{Log Size}_{it} + a_{2t}(1/P_{it}) + a_{3t}\text{Var}_{it}$$
$$+ a_{4t}\text{Log } R_{it} + a_{5t}\text{Log } R_{it-1} + \cdots + a_{8t}\text{Log } R_{it-4} + e_{it}, \quad (21)$$

where

N_{it} = the number of analysts reporting a one-year ahead earnings forecast for firm i in December of year t

Size_{it} = the market value of the equity of firm i on December 31 of year t

P_{it} = the share price of firm i on December 31 of year t

Var_{it} = the variance of returns for firm i estimated over the last 200 days prior to December 31 of year t

R_{it} = the rate of return on the shares of firm i in year t, excluding dividends.

The first two terms in regression equation (21) are derived from the theory in the preceding section. We include the variance of returns because there is prior evidence[34] that the variance is positively related to the number of analysts and we wish to determine if the share price exerts an independent effect on the number of analysts.[35]

The lagged log returns are included in the regression to allow for a possible spurious relation between share price and analyst following due to a lagged relation between number of analysts and firm size. If the number of analysts reported on the I/B/E/S tape adjusts slowly to changes in firm size, then a firm that earns negative returns will tend to have a larger analyst following than that predicted on the basis of its current size (as measured by market value of equity). It will also have a relatively low stock price, thereby inducing a spurious relation between share price and number of analysts. Inclusion of the logarithm of the lagged (dividend adjusted) returns is equivalent to including lagged size variables to the extent that size changes are due to capital gains and losses rather than stock issues and retirements. In addition, while the model predicts a simultaneous change between share

[34] Bhushan (1989) includes the variance of returns in his empirical study of the determinants of analyst following. He hypothesizes that the value of private information should be positively related to return variability because it increases the conditional expected return.

[35] Our model assigns no role to the variance as influencing the number of analysts. However, Kim and Verrecchia (1990) show that the absolute value of price changes may be positively related to the volume of trading. Under our assumption about competition in the brokerage industry, an increase in the volume of trading will lead to an increase in the number of analysts.

price and analyst following, there is evidence that some of the I/B/E/S data may not be current.[36]

The regression results for equation (21) are presented by year for all firms in the sample in Table IV.[37] As Bhushan (1989) finds, the influence of the size variable is positive and highly significant, and in 10 of the 12 years, there is a significantly positive relation between analyst following and the variance

Table IV

Determinants of the Number of Analysts Forecasting Earnings for a Firm

Estimation of expression (21) for the entire sample of firms. N_{it} is the number of analysts reporting a one-year ahead earnings forecast for firm i in December of year t. $Size_{it}$ is the market value of the equity of firm i on December 31 of year t. P_{it} is the share price of firm i on December 31 of year t. Var_{it} is the variance of returns for firm i estimated over the last 200 days prior to December 31 of year t. R_{it} is the rate of return on the shares of firm i in year t, excluding dividends. n is the sample size and t-statistics appear in parentheses.

$$N_{it} = a_{0t} + a_{1t}\text{Log Size}_{it} + a_{2t}(1/P_{it}) + a_{3t}\text{Var}_{it} + a_{4t}\text{Log } R_{it}$$
$$+ a_{5t}\text{Log } R_{it-1} + \cdots + a_{8t}\text{Log } R_{it-4} + e_{it}$$

t	n	a_0	a_1	a_2	a_3	a_4	a_5	a_6	a_7	a_8	R^2
1976	967	−34.02	3.24	10.58	98.15	−3.75	0.55	−1.27	0.35	0.59	0.59
		(21.45)	(28.60)	(2.43)	(3.10)	(7.53)	(1.67)	(4.00)	(1.16)	(2.23)	
1977	1152	−29.85	2.89	6.70	152.53	−1.98	−1.60	−0.03	−0.87	0.51	0.59
		(23.75)	(30.39)	(2.27)	(4.37)	(5.11)	(4.89)	(0.14)	(3.50)	(2.14)	
1978	1707	−33.06	3.29	7.50	59.00	−0.99	−0.68	−1.34	−0.05	−0.41	0.62
		(34.39)	(44.00)	(4.56)	(4.17)	(3.82)	(2.69)	(6.04)	(0.26)	(2.33)	
1979	1699	−31.29	3.16	4.22	66.89	−2.33	−0.16	−0.22	−0.92	0.38	0.65
		(38.86)	(50.26)	(3.52)	(4.05)	(11.32)	(0.77)	(1.11)	(4.79)	(2.35)	
1980	1699	−33.85	3.35	8.17	33.11	−1.62	−1.82	0.07	−0.19	0.49	0.65
		(38.10)	(49.30)	(5.05)	(2.09)	(7.29)	(7.93)	(0.33)	(0.91)	(2.48)	
1981	1835	−37.84	3.71	9.80	3.44	−1.55	−0.69	−0.75	0.14	0.00	0.66
		(41.02)	(52.26)	(6.67)	(0.21)	(7.30)	(3.61)	(3.68)	(0.69)	(0.01)	
1982	2016	−41.95	4.04	8.29	8.76	−0.78	−0.66	−0.06	−0.18	0.07	0.67
		(48.11)	(59.09)	(6.61)	(0.94)	(5.10)	(3.51)	(0.37)	(0.98)	(0.48)	
1983	2288	−43.82	4.19	5.26	50.99	−0.85	−0.35	−0.43	0.08	0.07	0.67
		(50.33)	(61.77)	(4.70)	(4.29)	(5.73)	(2.47)	(2.66)	(0.52)	(0.44)	
1984	2577	−40.24	3.93	4.29	33.88	−1.43	−0.34	−0.23	−0.32	0.21	0.66
		(53.91)	(65.65)	(7.20)	(4.25)	(8.63)	(2.78)	(1.83)	(2.17)	(1.73)	
1985	2560	−46.39	4.55	0.91	29.75	−3.11	−0.94	−0.47	−0.33	−0.33	0.67
		(56.88)	(69.02)	(3.50)	(5.01)	(13.45)	(5.58)	(3.51)	(2.36)	(2.19)	
1986	2700	−44.51	4.33	3.35	23.45	−2.06	−1.07	−0.74	−0.30	−0.12	0.67
		(55.07)	(67.26)	(5.71)	(4.11)	(11.48)	(5.70)	(5.29)	(2.40)	(0.97)	
1987	2628	−43.81	4.26	3.00	24.69	−1.56	−0.62	−0.43	−0.53	−0.20	0.66
		(53.27)	(65.42)	(6.14)	(5.89)	(7.57)	(4.67)	(3.17)	(4.22)	(1.73)	

[36] O'Brien (1988) and Brown, Foster, and Noreen (1985) describe characteristics of the I/B/E/S data.

[37] Results for the individual exchanges, which were included in an earlier version of this paper, are available from the authors.

of stock price. The major new prediction of our model, that the number of analysts will be negatively related to share price, is strongly supported by the finding that the coefficient of the reciprocal of share price is positive and strongly significant in each year.[38] The coefficients of the lagged return variables are negative and strongly significant for short lags, which is consistent with the discussion above of slow analyst adjustment. Since the coefficient for a lag of five years is generally insignificant and of variable sign, it appears that the adjustment is complete after five years so that share price is not a proxy for a lagged size term.

Results for the individual exchanges are similar in nature, but less significant, due to reduced sample sizes. The coefficient on the reciprocal of share price is positive for NYSE firms in 10/12 years, for AMEX firms in 11/12 years, and in 12/12 years for NASDAQ firms.

While these results are consistent with the predictions of our model, it is possible that they are due to a common factor which is associated with low shares prices and a large analyst following—for example, an industry association. In such a case, the number of analysts following a firm would not be affected by a stock split, as we hypothesize. Therefore, a more direct test of the effect of a split on analyst following is a regression of the change in the number of analysts following a firm on current and lagged values of the split factor and the capital gains as follows.

$$\Delta \text{Log } N_{it} = a_{0t} + a_{1t} \Delta \text{Log } F_{it} + a_{2t} \Delta \text{Log } F_{it-1} + \cdots$$
$$+ a_{5t} \Delta \text{Log } F_{it-4} + a_{6t} \text{Log } R_{it} + \cdots + a_{10t} \text{Log } R_{it-4} + e_{it}, \quad (22)$$

where $\Delta \text{Log } F_{it}$ is the change in the CRSP split factor in year t and, as before, R_{it} is the capital gain on the stock in year t.[39]

Under the null hypothesis, $a_{1t} = a_{2t} = \cdots = a_{5t} = 0$, whereas our model and, more generally, the Attention Hypothesis of Grinblatt, Masulis, and Titman (1984), predicts that at least some of these coefficients will be positive.

Table V reports the results of estimating equation (22) by year together with an F-test of the null hypothesis that the coefficients on the lagged changes in the split factor are all equal to zero. The null hypothesis is rejected in 7 of the 12 years at the 1% level, and in 3 additional years at the 5% level. Weighting the parameter estimates for each year by their precisions, the point estimates suggest that a doubling of the split factor (i.e., a two-for-one split) is associated with a 24% increase in the number of analysts reported by I/B/E/S in the current year, and a 54% increase by the end of

---

[38] We obtained similar but slightly less consistent results when we replaced the reciprocal of the stock price with the logarithm of the stock price.

[39] We adopted the log specification because it allows for the effect on the number of analysts of price changes associated both with returns (and therefore with changes in size) and with stock splits in a simple additive fashion.

five years. The effect is relatively weak for NYSE firms where a doubling of the split factor is associated with only a 19% increase in the number of analysts after five years. The corresponding numbers for AMEX and NAS-DAQ firms are 130% and 36%. The effect seems most consistent for NASDAQ firms for which it is concentrated in the year of the split.

The timing of the increase in the number of analysts reflects not only the predicted influence of the split, but also the efforts of Lynch, Jones, and Ryan to increase the coverage of their database. An interesting feature of the results is the large and highly significant negative coefficient on R_{it}, the log of the current year's dividend-adjusted return. While this is consistent with our hypothesis that a lower share price will be associated with a larger number of analysts, the effect seems too great for this explanation. We conjecture that analysts tend to turn their attention from firms whose stocks have appreciated either because, a major source of value having been discovered, the future prospects for further value discoveries are relatively slight, or because such firms are more likely to be overvalued and analysts tend to avoid making sell recommendations.[40] Clearly this phenomenon bears further investigation.

IV. Summary and Conclusions

We assume that investors trade only in stocks that they "know about", and trade through brokers who analyze those firms which will generate the greatest trading volume and brokerage fees. A manager with private "good news" has an incentive to attract the attention of security analysts so that they will discover the good news and inform their clients through earnings forecasts. In our model the manager does this by announcing a stock split, thereby reducing the share price and increasing the trading commission revenue which will result from research activity by brokerage houses. Investors accordingly interpret a stock split as a signal that the manager has favorable information, which explains the positive abnormal returns observed around split announcements. The model also predicts that there will be an increase in the amount of information generated by analysts after the ex-date; this may account for the increase in price volatility observed after the ex-date, the wider bid-ask spread, and the increase in the number of shareholders.

The predictions of the model are tested and confirmed on a sample of firms listed on the I/B/E/S database during 1976–1987. The number of analysts making forecasts is negatively related to share price, and the change in analyst following is positively related to the magnitude of stock splits.

---

[40] There is some indirect evidence that analysts are less willing to make sell recommendations than buy recommendations. Lloyd-Davies and Canes (1978) identify 597 buy recommendations, but only 188 sell recommendations in their study. Some explanations for this reluctance are offered by Galant (1990).

Table V
Determinants of the Change in the Number of Analysts Forecasting Earnings for a Firm

Estimation of expression (22) for the entire sample of firms. N_{it} is the number of analysts reporting a one-year ahead earnings forecast for firm i in December of year t. $\Delta \log F_{it}$ is the change in the logarithm of the CRSP split factor in year t. R_{it} is the rate of return on the shares of firm i in year t, excluding dividends. n is the sample size and t-statistics appear in parentheses.

$$\Delta \log N_{it} = a_{0t} + a_{1t} \Delta \log F_{it} + a_{2t} \Delta \log F_{it-1} + \cdots + a_{5t} \Delta \log F_{it-4}$$
$$+ a_{6t} \log R_{it} + \cdots + a_{10t} \log R_{it-4} + e_{it}$$

t	a_0	a_1	a_2	a_3	a_4	a_5	a_6	a_7	a_8	a_9	a_{10}	R^2	n
1976	−3.02	0.06	10.47	0.27	−0.23	0.16	−1.00	−3.27	−0.14	−0.02	−0.12	.08	967
	(46.06)	(0.36)	(2.34)	(1.82)	(0.48)	(1.09)	(7.62)	(3.23)	(1.46)	(0.05)	(1.40)	2.40*[a]	
1977	−1.22	0.57	0.78	−0.13	−0.00	−0.22	−1.76	−0.11	−1.03	0.08	0.61	.05	1152
	(9.77)	(1.60)	(2.19)	(0.11)	(0.00)	(0.43)	(6.38)	(0.42)	(2.26)	(0.38)	(1.47)	1.43[a]	
1978	−1.83	1.19	1.03	1.32	−1.98	0.11	−1.18	−0.51	−0.44	0.33	0.49	.04	1708
	(15.27)	(3.23)	(2.96)	(3.81)	(1.48)	(0.36)	(5.16)	(2.05)	(1.96)	(0.91)	(2.77)	7.35**[a]	
1979	−0.13	0.31	0.51	0.39	0.41	−1.07	−0.87	−0.74	−0.48	−0.20	0.39	.06	1761
	(1.91)	(1.40)	(2.25)	(1.94)	(1.83)	(1.64)	(7.28)	(5.70)	(3.44)	(1.49)	(2.05)	3.36**[a]	
1980	−0.18	0.44	0.18	0.54	0.18	−0.06	−0.40	0.04	−0.45	0.03	0.04	.03	1699
	(3.64)	(2.85)	(1.14)	(3.57)	(1.19)	(0.35)	(4.40)	(0.37)	(4.77)	(0.33)	(0.42)	4.75**[a]	
1981	−0.36	−0.07	0.76	0.68	0.83	0.41	−0.45	−0.43	−0.21	−0.54	0.03	.05	1835
	(6.31)	(0.53)	(4.13)	(3.30)	(4.49)	(2.23)	(4.32)	(4.10)	(1.88)	(4.81)	(0.27)	10.23**[a]	
1982	−0.15	0.08	0.07	−0.06	0.09	0.05	−0.73	0.06	−0.11	0.08	0.15	.12	2016
	(4.18)	(1.08)	(0.80)	(0.62)	(0.74)	(0.43)	(14.87)	(0.95)	(1.82)	(1.22)	(2.50)	0.55[a]	
1983	−0.17	0.30	−0.12	0.12	0.12	−0.03	−1.07	0.35	−0.14	0.01	0.18	.22	2288
	(4.53)	(5.23)	(1.62)	(1.41)	(1.09)	(0.27)	(21.59)	(7.70)	(2.61)	(0.27)	(3.11)	7.02**[a]	

Table V — *Continued*

t	a_0	a_1	a_2	a_3	a_4	a_5	a_6	a_7	a_8	a_9	a_{10}	R^2	F	n
1984	−0.42	0.29	0.12	−0.10	0.14	0.12	−0.79	−0.06	0.09	−0.08	0.05	.08	6.23**[a]	2577
	(12.80)	(4.64)	(1.96)	(1.25)	(1.61)	(1.21)	(14.41)	(1.25)	(1.98)	(1.51)	(1.12)			
1985	−0.01	0.19	0.10	0.09	0.06	0.11	−0.36	0.06	0.04	−0.01	0.09	.02	2.89*[a]	2562
	(0.49)	(2.71)	(1.94)	(1.81)	(0.96)	(1.63)	(6.82)	(1.48)	(1.16)	(0.20)	(2.43)			
1986	−0.27	0.38	0.15	0.05	−0.00	0.06	−0.71	0.14	−0.08	0.05	0.10	.11	9.95***[a]	2700
	(10.59)	(6.82)	(2.24)	(0.83)	(0.01)	(0.98)	(16.56)	(3.09)	(2.39)	(1.57)	(3.09)			
1987	−0.26	0.17	0.05	0.04	−0.01	0.05	−0.37	0.09	−0.02	0.03	−0.02	.03	2.51*[a]	2627
	(11.58)	(3.24)	(1.03)	(0.78)	(0.23)	(0.94)	(9.12)	(2.93)	(0.76)	(0.97)	(0.72)			

[a] F-statistic for the null hypothesis $a_1 = a_2 = \cdots = a_5 = 0$.
* Significant at the .05 level.
** Significant at the .01 level.

Appendix

Reverse Stock Splits

The model presented in Section II can be extended with minor modification to include reverse stock splits. We assume that there is a minimum brokerage commission T_{min} available to the firm, and that the next lowest commission is $T_1 = T_{min} + \delta$, where δ is strictly positive.[41] Depending upon parameter values, there may exist several different types of equilibria. Figure 2 illustrates the inference schedule for the equilibrium in which the most information is revealed, given that there is a cost of splitting or reverse-splitting. The values of $\hat{y}_m(T)$ corresponding to $T \in [(T_1, T_2), (T_3, \infty)]$ satisfy equation (15) for $K = K_1$ and K_2, respectively. The constants of integration and $y_m^0, y_m^r, y_m^s, T_2, T_3,$ and $\bar{T}$ are defined as follows.

The values of y_m^0 and K_1 follow from conditions analogous to those in equations (16) and (17): that is, that the firm with the signal y_m^0 is indifferent between remaining in the pool of firms selecting T_{min}, and identifying itself by choosing T_1, and that investors make the correct inference. These conditions are:

$$E\left[E\left(x \mid y_m \leq y_m^0, \bar{y} \right) \mid y_m^0, s(\bar{y}) = FT_{min}s \right] - T_{min}$$

$$= \frac{x_0 s_0 + y_m^0 s_m + y_m^0 FT_1 s}{s_0 + s_m + FT_1 s} - T_1, \quad \text{(A-1)}$$

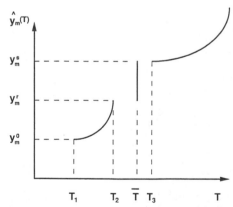

Figure 2. The inference schedule for a model of stock splits and reverse splits. T is the expected aggregate brokerage commission. $\hat{y}_m(T)$ is investors' inference of y_m based upon T. y_m^s is the signal of the marginal splitting firm. y_m^r is the signal of the marginal reverse splitting firm. $\bar{T}$ is the aggregate brokerage commission for a firm that does not split.

---

[41] It is necessary that δ be positive so that the pool of firms selecting T_{min} does not unravel. Since the inference schedule is convex and y_m is unbounded, a pool of firms must exist at the lower bound on T. Note that if y_m had a fixed support, the lower boundary condition for the inference schedule would be provided by the condition that the firm with the lowest possible signal would choose the minimum commission rate in equilibrium.

and

$$\hat{y}_m(T_1) = \left(\frac{s_0 + s_m}{s_m}\right)T_1 + \frac{Fs}{2 s_m}T_1^2 - K_1 \equiv y_m^0. \qquad \text{(A-2)}$$

The value of y_m^r, the signal level of the marginal firm to choose a reverse split, and T_2 are determined by the condition that (T_2, y_2) lies on the inference schedule, and that the firm with the signal y_m^r is indifferent to announcing a reverse split and remaining in the pool of firms choosing $\overline{T}$. The conditions are:

$$E\big[\,E(x \,|\, y_m^r \leq y_m \leq y_m^s, \bar{y})\,|\, y_m^r, s(\bar{y}) = F\overline{T}s\big] - \overline{T}$$

$$= \frac{x_0 s_0 + y_m^r s_m + y_m^r F T_2 s}{s_0 + s_m + F T_2 s} - T_2 - C, \quad \text{(A-3)}$$

where $\overline{T} \equiv E[\,xt(x/n_0)\,|\, y_m^r \leq y_m \leq y_m^s]$, and

$$\hat{y}_m(T_2) = \left(\frac{s_0 + s_m}{s_m}\right)T_2 + \frac{Fs}{2 s_m}T_2^2 - K_1 \equiv y_m^r. \qquad \text{(A-4)}$$

Condition (A-3) depends upon y_m^s, the signal level of the marginal splitting firm. This, along with K_2, is identified by conditions analogous to (A-3) and (A-4). Finally, T_3 is defined by

$$T_3 \equiv E\big[\,xt(x/n_0)\,|\, y_m^s\big]. \qquad \text{(A-5)}$$

For appropriate parameter values, the nonlinear set of equations can be solved to yield the inference schedule shown. An interesting feature of the equilibrium is that no firms choose brokerage commissions $T_2 < T < \overline{T}$.[42] It is therefore necessary to show that the equilibrium is supported by reasonable beliefs about out-of-equilibrium choices of T. It is readily shown that an equilibrium in which $\hat{y}_m(T) = y_m^r$ for $T \in (T_2, \overline{T})$ satisfies the Cho-Kreps (1987) Intuitive Criterion.

Reverse splits convey negative information in this equilibrium.[43] Firms do not announce small reverse stock splits because they also are costly. Large savings in commissions are required to offset the administrative and information costs of a reverse split. Small stock splits, however, do occur in equilibrium. This implication of the model is consistent with the empirical evidence presented in Table III.

Note that as $\overline{T}$ is reduced (by reducing $E(x/n_0)$, T_2 will approach T_1 until the first continuous portion of the inference schedule is eliminated. Finally, as $\overline{T}$ declines or C increases, reverse splits will disappear completely,[44] although regular splits will continue to occur. Thus the model is consistent with the empirical finding (see Table III) that reverse splits are much less frequent than regular splits.

---

[42] Note that values of T such that $T_{\min} < T < T_1$ or $\overline{T} < T < T_3$ are technically infeasible.
[43] Lamoureux and Poon (1987) report a negative abnormal return of 3% associated with reverse stock splits. Dravid (1987) finds a decrease in the variance of returns.
[44] A sufficient condition for the absence of reverse splits is that $\overline{T} > C$.

REFERENCES

Amihud, Y. and H. Mendelson, 1987, Trading mechanisms and stock returns: An empirical investigation, *Journal of Finance* 42, 533-553.

———, and H. Mendelson, 1988, Liquidity and asset prices: Financial management implications, *Financial Management* 17, 5-15.

Arbel, A. and G. Swanson, 1989, Why do firms undertake stock splits? The role of incomplete information, Working paper, Cornell University.

Asquith, P., P. Healy, and K. Palepu, 1989, Earnings and stock splits, *The Accounting Review* 64, 387-403.

Bhushan, R., 1989, Firm characteristics and analyst following, *Journal of Accounting and Economics* 11, 255-274.

Branch, B., 1985, Low-priced stocks: Discrimination in the brokerage industry, *AAII Journal*, 7, 9-11.

Brennan, M. J. and T. E. Copeland, 1988(a), Stock splits, stock prices, and transactions costs, *Journal of Financial Economics* 22, 83-101.

———, and T. E. Copeland, (1988b), Beta changes around stock splits: A note, *Journal of Finance* 43, 1009-1013.

Brown, P., G. Foster, and E. Noreen, 1985, *Security Analyst Multi-Year Earnings Forecasts and the Capital Market*, Studies in Accounting Research #21, (American Accounting Association).

Cho, I-K. and D. Kreps, 1987, Signaling games and stable equilibria, *Quarterly Journal of Economics* 102, 179-221.

Coler, M. D. and A. Schaefer, 1988, 70% off! Discount brokers still offer big savings, *AAII Journal*, 10, 12-14.

Conroy, R. M. and M. Flood, 1989, The effect of stock splits on marketability: Transaction rates and share ownership, Working paper, University of Virginia.

Copeland, T. E., 1979, Liquidity changes following stock splits, *Journal of Finance* 34, 115-141.

———, and D. Galai, 1983, Information effects on the bid-ask spread, *Journal of Finance* 38, 1457-1469.

Diamond, D. W., 1985, Optimal release of information by firms, *Journal of Finance* 40, 1071-1094.

Doran, D. T. and R. Nachtmann, 1988, The association of stock distribution announcements and earnings performance, *Journal of Accounting, Auditing, and Finance*, 113-132.

Dravid, A. R., 1987, A note on the behavior of stock returns around ex-dates of stock distributions, *Journal of Finance* 42, 163-168.

Eades, K., P. Hess, and H. Kim, 1984, On interpreting security returns during the ex-dividend period, *Journal of Financial Economics* 13, 3-34.

Fama, E. F., L. Fisher, M. C. Jensen, and R. Roll, 1969, The adjustment of stock prices to new information, *International Economic Review* 10, 1-21.

French, D. W. and D. A. Dubofsky, 1986, Stock splits and implied price volatility, *Journal of Portfolio Management*, 12, 55-59.

Galant, D., 1990, The hazards of negative research reports, *Institutional Investor*, 24, 73-80.

Glosten, L. R. and P. R. Milgrom, 1985, Bid, ask and transaction prices in a specialist market with heterogeneously informed traders, *Journal of Financial Economics* 14, 71-100.

Grinblatt, M. S., R. W. Masulis, and S. Titman, 1984, The valuation effects of stock splits and stock dividends, *Journal of Financial Economics* 13, 461-490.

Holthausen, R. W. and R. E. Verrecchia, 1990, The effect of informedness and consensus on price and volume behaviour, *The Accounting Review* 65, 191-208.

Hsueh, L. P. and D. S. Kidwell, 1988, Bond ratings: Are two better than one? *Financial Management* 17, 46-53.

Kim, O. and R. E. Verrecchia, 1990, Trading volume and price reactions to public announcements, Working paper, UCLA.

Kryzanowski, L. and H. Zhang, 1990, Anomalous behaviour around Canadian stock splits, Working paper, Concordia University.

Lakonishok, J. and B. Lev, 1987, Stock splits and stock dividends: Why, who, and when, *Journal of Finance* 42, 913–932.

Lamoureux, C. G. and P. Poon, 1987, The market reaction to stock splits, *Journal of Finance* 42, 1347–1370.

Lloyd-Davies, P. and M. Canes, 1978, Stock prices and the publication of second-hand information, *Journal of Business* 51, 43–56.

McNichols, M. and A. Dravid, 1990, Stock dividends, stock splits, and signaling, *Journal of Finance* 45, 857–879.

Merton, R. C., 1987, A simple model of capital market equilibrium with incomplete information, *Journal of Finance* 42, 483–510.

O'Brien, P. C., 1988, Analysts' forecasts as earnings expectations, *Journal of Accounting and Economics* 10, 53–83.

Ohlson, J. A. and S. H. Penman, 1985, Volatility increases subsequent to stock splits: An empirical aberration, *Journal of Financial Economics* 14, 251–266.

Scott, D., 1983, *The Investor's Guide to Discount Brokers*, (Prager, New York).

Sheikh, A. M., 1989, Stock splits, volatility increases and implied volatilities, *Journal of Finance* 44, 1361–1372.

Smidt, S., 1990, Long run trends in equity turnover, *Journal of Portfolio Management* 17, 66–73.

Stoll, H. R. and R. E. Whaley, 1983, Transaction costs and the small firm effect, *Journal of Financial Economics* 12, 57–80.

Thakor, A. V., 1982, An exploration of competitive signalling equilibria with 'third party' information production: The case of debt insurance. *Journal of Finance* 37, 717–739.

Wiggins, J. B., 1990, Beta changes around stock splits revisited. Working paper, Cornell University.

[21]

Investment Analysis and the Adjustment of Stock Prices to Common Information

Michael J. Brennan
University of California at Los Angeles

Narasimhan Jegadeesh
University of California at Los Angeles and University of Illinois at Urbana-Champaign

Bhaskaran Swaminathan
University of California at Los Angeles

In this article we are concerned with the effect of the number of investment analysts following a firm on the speed of adjustment of the firm's stock price to new information that has common effects across firms. It is found that returns on portfolios of firms that are followed by many analysts tend to lead those of firms that are followed by fewer analysts, even when the firms are of approximately the same size. Many analyst firms also tend to respond more rapidly to market returns than do few analyst firms, adjusting for firm size. This relation, however, is nonlinear, and the marginal effect of the number of analysts on the speed of price adjustment increases with the number of analysts.

In a recent paper Lo and MacKinlay (1990) report that current returns on a portfolio of small stocks are correlated with lagged returns on a portfolio of large stocks, but not vice versa. While such a finding could be the result of infrequent trading in small stocks, the authors demonstrate that unrealistically high nontrading frequencies would be required to account for their empirical results. This evidence, therefore, seems attributable to the fact that some stocks react faster

---

We thank Andrew Lo, Patricia O'Brien (the referee), and Chester Spatt for valuable comments. We are also grateful for the comments and suggestions of seminar participants at INSEAD, the London Business School, the University of Michigan and the University of Turin. Address correspondence to Narasimhan Jegadeesh, 340 Commerce West, College of Commerce and Business Administration, University of Illinois at Urbana-Champaign, Champaign, IL 61820.

The Review of Financial Studies Winter 1993 Vol. 6, No. 4, pp. 799–824
© 1993 The Review of Financial Studies 0893-9454/93/$1.50

The Review of Financial Studies / v 6 n 4 1993

than others to new information that has value implications across stocks, and which we therefore term *common information*.

This paper examines the relation between the speed of price adjustment to common information and the number of investment analysts following a firm. Recent theory suggests that the number of analysts may have an effect on the speed of adjustment to new information. For instance, Holden and Subrahmanyam (1992) and Foster and Viswanathan (1993), in important extensions to the classic model of Kyle (1985), have shown that as the number of informed investors increases, the share price will reflect new information more rapidly; this would suggest an association between the number of analysts and the speed of adjustment, if the number of analysts can be regarded as a proxy for the number of informed investors.

In looking for the effects of the number of investment analysts on the speed of adjustment we hold firm size constant. We do this because we already know from the results of Lo and MacKinlay (1990) that size is related to the speed of adjustment; since there is a positive association between size and the number of analysts following a firm [Bhushan (1989)], finding that the number of analysts is positively associated with the speed of adjustment would not allow us to distinguish the number of analysts hypothesis from a pure size effect. Lo and MacKinlay offer no explanation for why size may be an important determinant of the speed of adjustment; one possibility is that size is positively associated with the number of individuals who are interested in a firm and therefore *know* about it [Merton (1987)], either because they already own the stock or because they gain information about the firm in the normal course of their business. A second possibility is that firm size proxies for trading volume and the latter may be related to the speed of price adjustment because of its effect on the informativeness of the stock price [see Admati and Pfleiderer (1988)]. By including the logarithm of firm size as well as the logarithm of share turnover in some of our tests we are able to determine whether there is an effect associated with size that is independent of trading volume and the number of analysts following the stock.

Broadly, our tests are of three kinds. First, we employ Granger causality regressions to determine whether, holding firm size constant, the returns on portfolios of *many analyst* firms (Granger) cause the returns on portfolios of *few analyst* firms and whether there is reverse causality.[1] We develop restrictions on the parameters of the Granger causality regressions that allow us to test the speed of adjustment hypothesis—that the many analyst firms react faster to common

---

[1] One variable is said to Granger-cause another if its lagged values are useful in predicting future values of the other. See Granger (1969) and Sims (1972).

information than do the few analyst firms. We find reliable support for this hypothesis.

The second test examines the pattern of price response of zero net investment, or "arbitrage," portfolios that are long in many analyst firms and short in few analyst firms of similar sizes to returns on the value-weighted index (VWI) and the equal-weighted index (EWI).[2] The returns on these market indices may be viewed as proxies for common information. We find that the returns on these arbitrage portfolios are negatively related to lagged returns on the EWI, which is consistent with slower price adjustment for the few analyst firms. Similar results are obtained for the two larger firm size quartiles when a VWI is used, but the results are more mixed for the smaller firm quartiles.

Finally, we examine whether the individual security betas with respect to the lagged returns on the VWI and the EWI are systematically related to firm size, share turnover, and number of analysts following the firm. Our results indicate that firm size, share turnover, and number of analysts are all highly significant in explaining lagged beta. The relation between the number of analysts and the speed of adjustment, however, appears to be nonlinear; a small number of analysts has little effect on the speed of adjustment.

The rest of the paper is organized as follows: Section 1 presents a simple model of lagged price adjustment and develops restrictions that form the basis for our tests. Section 2 presents the data, and Section 3 presents the Granger causality tests. Section 4 examines the timeliness of stock price reaction to the market, and Section 5 concludes.

1. A Simple Model of Lagged Price Adjustment

In order to lay the groundwork for our empirical analysis we consider in this section a simple model in which the returns on two portfolios respond to common information variables at different rates. Let $R_{M,t}$ and $R_{F,t}$ denote the returns on portfolios M and F on day t, where M and F refer to the portfolios of firms followed by *Many* and *Few* analysts respectively, and suppose that these returns can be written as lagged functions of the current and lagged values of K common factors, $z_{k,t}$, whose values are independently and identically distributed:

$$R_{M,t} = \alpha_M + \sum_{k=1}^{K} \beta_{M,k}(z_{k,t} + a_M z_{k,t-1}) + \epsilon_{M,t}, \qquad (1)$$

---

[2] Both VWI and EWI are constructed with all firms in the New York and American Stock Exchanges and the NASDAQ.

The Review of Financial Studies / v 6 n 4 1993

$$R_{F,t} = \alpha_F + \sum_{k=1}^{K} \beta_{F,k}(z_{k,t} + a_F z_{k,t-1}) + \epsilon_{F,t}, \tag{2}$$

where $\epsilon_{M,t}$ and $\epsilon_{F,t}$ are the idiosyncratic shocks to the return processes $R_{M,t}$ and $R_{F,t}$. In the analysis in this section we assume that $\text{Var}(\epsilon_{F,t}) = \text{Var}(\epsilon_{M,T}) \equiv \sigma^2$.

In this model $\beta_{M,k}$ and $\beta_{F,k}$ determine the response of the portfolio returns to the contemporaneous common factors; a_M and a_F are lag response ratios, which provide a measure of the timeliness of stock price reactions. The lag response ratios are assumed to be the same for all factors. Without loss of generality, we assume that $\sigma^2_{z_k} = 1$ and, in keeping with our hypothesis that portfolio M responds more rapidly to new information, that $a_F > a_M$. Then the difference between the cross-serial covariances of $R_{F,t}$ and $R_{M,t-1}$ and of $R_{M,t}$ and $R_{F,t-1}$ is $(a_F - a_M)(\sum_{k=1}^{K} \beta_{F,k}\beta_{M,k})$, which is positive whenever the factor sensitivities of the two portfolios are of the same sign for each factor. In other words, the covariance between the current return on the more rapidly responding portfolio M and the lagged return on the less rapidly responding portfolio F is always less than the covariance between the current return on F and lagged return on M provided that the factor sensitivities are of the same sign. Under this assumption, the relative speeds of response can be assessed by examining the cross-serial covariances. In contrast, the autocovariances of the returns of portfolios M and F, $a_M \sum_{k=1}^{K} \beta^2_{M,k}$ and $a_F \sum_{k=1}^{K} \beta^2_{F,k}$, are not restricted by the assumption that portfolio M responds more quickly than portfolio F to new information. For example, if the return of portfolio F responds only to the lagged common factors,[3] then its serial covariance will be zero while the serial covariance of M will be positive for $a_M > 0$. On the other hand, if $a_M = 0$ and $a_F > 0$, then portfolio F will have a larger serial covariance than M. Therefore, we follow Lo and MacKinlay (1990) and focus on cross-serial covariances or correlations in our speed of adjustment tests rather than on autocovariances.

In order to derive a simple test for differences in the speed of adjustment, we perform Granger causality regressions that allow us to determine whether the returns on portfolio M are more useful in predicting the returns on portfolio F than vice versa. To understand the relation of the speed of adjustment to the Granger causality regressions, consider the following simplified version of the Granger causality regressions, in which each portfolio's return is regressed on its lagged value and the lagged value of the other portfolio return:

---

[3] In other words, $z_{k,t}$ does not appear in Equation (2).

$$R_{M,t} = b_0 + b_F R_{F,t-1} + b_M R_{M,t-1} + u_{M,t}, \tag{3}$$

$$R_{F,t} = g_0 + g_F R_{F,t-1} + g_M R_{M,t-1} + u_{F,t}. \tag{4}$$

The relation between the coefficients of the Granger causality regressions (3) and (4) and the speed of adjustment coefficients and factor sensitivities of Equations (1) and (2) are described in the following proposition, which is proved in the Appendix.

Proposition 1. *If the lag response ratio of portfolio F exceeds that of portfolio M (i.e., if $a_F > a_M$), then*

(a) $g_M > b_F$.

(b) If, in addition, the total factor sensitivities of M and F are equal—that is, $\beta_{M,k}(1 + a_M) = \beta_{F,k}(1 + a_F) \ \forall k$, then $b_M > b_F$ and $g_M > g_F$.

It should be noted that the cross-equation restriction in part (a) of the proposition obtains whenever the speed of adjustments differ in the hypothesized manner. The own equation restrictions in part (b) of the proposition, however, require somewhat stronger assumptions. Intuitively, the assumption in part (b) requires that the portfolios M and F be alike in all respects except the lag response ratio.

As discussed earlier, we control for the effect of size-related differences in the speed of adjustment by implementing the Granger causality tests with portfolios comprising firms of similar sizes. In order to control for the effect of other exogenous variables in our further tests of the speed of adjustment hypothesis, we employ a single measure of the speed of adjustment. To understand the nature of this measure, consider the Dimson-type regressions

$$R_{j,t} = a + b_{j,0} I_t + b_{j,1} I_{t-1} + u_t, \tag{5}$$

where $I_t \equiv \sum_{k=1}^{K} w_k z_{k,t}$ is a linear combination of the common factors.

The coefficients of regression (5) are related to the factor sensitivities and lag response coefficients in expressions (1) and (2) by

$$b_{j,0} = \frac{1}{\sigma_I^2} \sum_{k=1}^{K} w_k \beta_{j,k},$$

$$b_{j,1} = a_j b_{j,0}, \qquad j = M, F.$$

Although $b_{j,1}$ seems to be an obvious measure of lagged response to common information since it measures the lagged response to index I, it depends on $b_{j,0}$ as well as the lag response ratio a_j. Therefore, $b_{M,1} > b_{F,1}$ need not imply $a_M > a_F$. However, if $b_{M,0} > b_{F,0}$, then $b_{M,1} < b_{F,1}$ does imply that $a_M < a_F$. For later reference we state this as

The Review of Financial Studies / v 6 n 4 1993

Result 1. *A necessary condition for $b_{M,1} < b_{F,1}$ when $b_{M,0} > b_{F,0}$ is that $a_M < a_F$.*

It follows from this result that when $R_{M,t} - R_{F,t}$ is regressed on current and lagged values of I, a positive coefficient on I_t and a negative coefficient on I_{t-1} will imply that the speed of response of portfolio F is less than that of portfolio M.

In the empirical analysis we report below, we run the Granger causality tests and Dimson regressions with multiple lags to allow for a more general setting in which information lags may exceed one period. We present tests of the restrictions corresponding to those developed in this section on the sum of the lagged response coefficients in these regressions.

2. Data

Daily stock returns and trading volume data for all firms were obtained from the CRSP NYAM-NASDAQ tapes from January 1977 to December 1988. The number of investment analysts following each firm was taken from the I/B/E/S tapes.[4] Our sample contains stocks in the I/B/E/S universe that were also in the CRSP database for five years.[5] The number of analysts following a particular firm in a given year was defined as the number of analysts making an annual earnings forecast in December of the previous year.[6]

At the beginning of each year, firms were initially assigned to quartiles based on their market values of equity on the preceding December 31. Within each size quartile the firms were further divided into four size-ranked subgroups. Within each of these groups, four subgroups were formed based on the number of analysts following the firms, yielding 16 subgroups based on size and number of analysts ranks within each size quartile. Four portfolios were then formed from the 16 subgroups within each size quartile as follows: The subgroups with the fewest number of analysts in each of the four size classifications were combined to form the *Few* analysts portfolio. The *Many* analysts portfolio was formed by combining the subgroups having the most analysts within each size classification. Two intermediate analysts portfolios were formed in a similar fashion, yielding a total of four analyst-ranked portfolios within each size quartile. This procedure, designed to minimize the association between size and

---

[4] We are grateful to Lynch, Jones, and Ryan for giving us access to the I/B/E/S tapes.

[5] We use the same sample as Brennan and Hughes (1991).

[6] If a firm was included in the I/B/E/S database but was not followed by any analyst in a given year, then the number of analysts was taken as zero. We also repeated our tests excluding the zero-analysts groups and found results similar to those reported here.

Investment Analysis and Price Response Timeliness

Table 1
Statistics of size-analyst portfolio returns

Port-folio size, analyst	n	Mean, %	Std. dev., %	VR_3	VR_5	VR_{10}	VR_{20}
1, 1	112.7	0.1262	0.8587	1.571	1.567	2.044	2.654
1, 2	115.9	0.0996	0.8459	1.539	1.599	2.109	2.670
1, 3	114.9	0.0925	0.8617	1.565	1.599	2.047	2.569
1, 4	116.1	0.0933	0.9041	1.617	1.678	2.060	2.480
2, 1	119.4	0.0840	0.8572	1.513	1.524	1.824	2.117
2, 2	116.8	0.0817	0.8487	1.589	1.624	1.915	2.411
2, 3	117.1	0.0814	0.9219	1.617	1.633	1.994	2.413
2, 4	122.4	0.0792	0.9796	1.593	1.644	1.950	2.256
3, 1	120.0	0.0685	0.8451	1.549	1.560	1.850	2.109
3, 2	118.3	0.0776	0.8204	1.570	1.633	1.883	2.054
3, 3	119.9	0.0751	0.8885	1.603	1.666	1.952	2.142
3, 4	122.8	0.0670	0.9683	1.519	1.562	1.847	2.107
4, 1	121.5	0.0665	0.9469	1.342	1.402	1.575	1.579
4, 2	118.5	0.0675	0.9325	1.336	1.425	1.558	1.527
4, 3	121.2	0.0594	0.9391	1.307	1.376	1.472	1.418
4, 4	125.7	0.0606	0.9729	1.235	1.294	1.392	1.325

Statistics of daily returns of size-analyst portfolios over 1977–1988. *Size 1* refers to the smallest size portfolio, and *Size 4* refers to the largest size portfolio. Similarly *Analyst 1* refers to the fewest number of analysts, and *Analyst 4* refers to the greatest number of analysts. The number of daily returns for all portfolios from 1977 to 1988 is 3033. n refers to the average number of firms in each portfolio over 1977–1988. VR_k refers to the k-day variance ratio, where $VR_k = [\mathrm{var}(R_{t,t-k})/k\,\mathrm{var}(R_{t,t-1})]$; and $R_{t,t-k}$ and $R_{t,t-1}$ are continuously compounded k-day and 1-day returns.

number of analysts within each size quartile, yielded 16 portfolios ranked first on size and then on number of analysts.[7] There were on average about 118 firms in each portfolio.

Table 1 reports the portfolio characteristics. There is some tendency within each size group for the mean return to decrease as the number of analysts increases, and the portfolio of small firms with the fewest analysts has by far the highest mean return.[8] Table 2 reports the median and average size of the firms in each portfolio and the median and average number of analysts following each firm in the portfolio. The median sizes of the firms in the different number of analyst portfolios within each size quartile are virtually the same. This indicates that we have been quite successful in reducing the association between size and number of analysts.

[7] We also considered forming a four-analysts group within each size quartile without the intraquartile size sorting. This simpler procedure, however, did not adequately control for size across the different analysts portfolios within a given size quartile.

[8] This is consistent with the findings of Arbel, Carrell, and Strebel (1983). However, Fama–MacBeth (1973) style regressions in which the mean returns on the 16 portfolios were regressed on estimated betas and number of analysts yielded no significance for the number of analysts.

The Review of Financial Studies / v 6 n 4 1993

Table 2
Statistics of size-analyst portfolio size and number of analysts

Portfolio	Size		Analysts	
Size, analyst	Median	Mean	Median	Mean
1, 1	0.0204	0.0197	0.4167	0.3546
1, 2	0.0214	0.0219	0.5833	0.6916
1, 3	0.0216	0.0228	1.2500	1.1769
1, 4	0.0215	0.0229	2.3750	2.6483
2, 1	0.0680	0.0702	0.5833	0.6795
2, 2	0.0695	0.0726	1.4167	1.6329
2, 3	0.0688	0.0731	2.7500	2.8810
2, 4	0.0690	0.0733	5.4167	5.8784
3, 1	0.2045	0.2178	1.5000	1.7615
3, 2	0.2050	0.2217	4.0833	4.0856
3, 3	0.2056	0.2250	6.2083	6.4435
3, 4	0.2056	0.2268	10.5833	10.9666
4, 1	0.9880	1.4325	6.6667	7.3437
4, 2	1.0021	1.6723	11.3750	12.3066
4, 3	0.9960	1.8012	15.4167	16.0158
4, 4	1.0073	2.5415	21.0833	21.6350

Statistics of size (in billions of dollars) and number of analysts making yearly forecasts in December for size-analyst portfolios obtained over 1977–1988. *Size 1* refers to the smallest size portfolio, and *Size 4* refers to the largest size portfolio. Similarly *Analyst 1* refers to the fewest number of analysts, and *Analyst 4* refers to the greatest number of analysts. Statistics of portfolio size and number of analysts are obtained as follows: first the cross-sectional statistics (median and mean) of size and number of analysts are computed for each portfolio, each year; then the yearly cross-sectional statistics of each portfolio are averaged over time and reported above.

3. Granger Causality Tests

Table 1 reports the variance ratios for our 16 portfolios. If slow adjustment to new information manifests itself in positive autocorrelation, then we should expect to find that the few analyst, more slowly adjusting, portfolios have higher variance ratios. All of the variance ratios exceed unity which is consistent with the findings of Lo and MacKinlay (1988) and others of positive autocorrelation in portfolio returns at short horizons. There is a strong tendency for the small firm portfolios to have higher variance ratios than the large firm portfolios; however, only within the large size group is there much evidence that the portfolios with fewer analysts have higher variance ratios than those with more analysts. However, as we argued in Section 1, autocovariances, and therefore serial correlations, are unlikely to yield reliable inferences about the relative speeds of adjustment. Therefore, we turn to tests based on cross-serial correlations.[9]

---

[9] For comparison with Lo and MacKinlay (1990) we also computed cross-correlation matrices for lags up to five days (these results are not reported here in order to conserve space but are available from the authors on request). We found that, within size quartiles, returns on portfolios with fewer analysts had greater correlation with lagged returns of portfolio with many analysts than for the reverse case. As explained in Section 1, this is consistent with the many analyst firms adjusting to new common information more rapidly.

Investment Analysis and Price Response Timeliness

Table 3
Granger causality regressions for the size-analyst portfolio returns

Size (1)	LHS (2)	Few (3)	Many (4)	R^2 (5)	F_1 (6)	F_2 (7)
			A: 5 Lag regressions			
1	Few	0.1042	0.3517*	0.12	3.80†	1.99
	Many	0.2170*	0.2377*	0.10	0.02	
2	Few	0.0650	0.2635*	0.08	1.61	4.55†
	Many	0.0027	0.3872*	0.09	4.68†	
3	Few	0.0482	0.3139*	0.09	3.53‡	20.43*
	Many	−0.1914†	0.5123*	0.08	18.51*	
4	Few	0.1483	0.1034	0.05	0.05	1.34
	Many	−0.0704	0.2420†	0.03	2.15	
			B: 10 Lag regressions			
1	Few	0.0978	0.4215*	0.12	2.98‡	2.34
	Many	0.2080	0.2645*	0.10	0.08	
2	Few	0.0394	0.3153*	0.08	1.54	4.82†
	Many	−0.0638	0.4389*	0.09	3.98†	
3	Few	0.0487	0.3204*	0.10	2.03	14.70*
	Many	−0.2568†	0.5503*	0.08	13.36*	
4	Few	0.1790	0.0554	0.04	0.19	0.26
	Many	−0.0499	0.1894	0.02	0.66	

In column (2), Few (Many) indicates that the LHS variable is the return on the fewest (greatest) analysts portfolio within each size quartile. In columns (3) and (4), Few and Many refer to the sum of the slope coefficients of the lagged fewest analysts portfolio returns and most analysts portfolio returns respectively. F_1 is the F-statistic corresponding to the null that the sum of regression coefficients of "Few" is equal to that of "Many." F_2 is the F-statistic corresponding to the cross-equation restriction $\Sigma_{k=1}^{K} b_{F,k} = \Sigma_{k=1}^{K} g_{M,k}$. This restriction implies that the impact of "Few" on "Many" (as measured by the sum of lagged regression coefficients) is equal to that of "Many" on "Few." R^2 refers to the adjusted coefficient of determination. * means significant at 1 percent level; † means significant at 5 percent level; ‡ means significant at 10 percent level.

In order to proceed more formally, and to reduce the number of statistical tests, we restricted our attention to the two portfolios within each size quartile that had the smallest and the largest number of analysts. These portfolios are referred to as *Few* (*F*) and *Many* (*M*) respectively. For each of the four pairs of portfolios, the following Granger causality regressions, which are generalizations of regressions (3) and (4), were run using daily returns:[10]

$$R_{M,t} = a_M + \sum_{k=1}^{K} b_{F,k} R_{F,t-k} + \sum_{k=1}^{K} b_{M,k} R_{M,t-k} + u_{M,t}, \qquad (6)$$

$$R_{F,t} = a_F + \sum_{k=1}^{K} g_{F,k} R_{F,t-k} + \sum_{k=1}^{K} g_{M,k} R_{M,t-k} + u_{F,t}. \qquad (7)$$

These regressions were fitted with 5 and 10 lags—with $K = 5$ and K

---

[10] If some stocks did not trade on a given day, then those stocks were dropped on that day and the portfolio return was computed as the average return of the other stocks in the portfolio.

The Review of Financial Studies / v 6 n 4 1993

= 10. If portfolio M adjusts to new information faster than portfolio F, then we expect from Proposition 1a that the sums of the coefficients on lagged values of R_M in (7) will exceed the sum of the coefficients on lagged values of R_F in (6).

Table 3 presents the sums of the coefficients on the lagged values of R_M and R_F. Consider the estimates of the five-lag regression first. For the first three size quartiles the values of R_M reliably predict the returns on both portfolios M and F, while the sums of the coefficients on lagged values of R_F are typically not different from zero. For the largest size quartile there is no evidence that either set of lagged returns helps in predicting returns on portfolio F; however, the returns on the portfolio M are predicted by their own lagged returns but not by the lagged returns on portfolio F.

The sums of the coefficients are consistent with the restriction corresponding to Proposition 1a; that is, $\Sigma_{k=1}^{5} b_{F,k} < \Sigma_{k=1}^{5} g_{M,k}$ for each of the four pairs of regressions. The F-statistic (F_2 in Table 3) indicates rejection of the hypothesis that $\Sigma_{k=1}^{5} b_{F,k} = \Sigma_{k=1}^{5} g_{M,k}$ at the 5 percent and 1 percent levels for size quartiles 2 and 3 respectively. The F-statistic under the hypothesis that this restriction holds jointly for all the four size quartiles is 7.08, which indicates rejection at the 1 percent level. Turning to the restriction implied by Proposition 1b, we find that the sum of the coefficients on the lagged values of R_M exceeds the sum of the coefficients on the lagged values of R_F in seven out of eight regressions and the differences in the sums are statistically significant in four regressions. The F-statistic under the hypothesis that sums of these coefficients in the eight regressions are jointly equal—$\Sigma_{k=1}^{5} b_{F,k} = \Sigma_{k=1}^{5} b_{M,k}$ and $\Sigma_{k=1}^{5} g_{F,k} = \Sigma_{k=1}^{5} g_{M,k}$—is 4.29, which is significant at the 1 percent level.

Finally, we note that in three out of four cases the returns on portfolio F are more predictable than the returns on portfolio M, as measured by the R^2; this is as we should expect if the prices of firms with few analysts react more slowly to new common information than those of firms with many analysts.

The results of the 10-lag regressions are similar to that for the 5-lag regressions. Moreover, the sums of the coefficients for the 10-lag regressions are close to the corresponding sums for the 5-lag regressions, indicating that there is little stock price reaction to information at lags longer than five days.

So far we have found that the lagged returns on portfolio M are more important than those of portfolio F in predicting returns on both portfolios, which is consistent with portfolio F adjusting more slowly to new information. In the following section we consider the role of the number of analysts in determining the speed of adjustment to new information contained in an index of market returns.

4. Timeliness of Reaction to Stock Market Returns

We first examine the speed of adjustment of portfolio values to market returns for the various size-analysts portfolios using the following regression:

$$R_{j,t} = a + \sum_{k=-K}^{K} b_{j,k} R_{m,t-k} + u_{j,t}, \tag{8}$$

where $R_{m,t}$ is the market portfolio return on day t. An estimate of the total sensitivity of portfolio j's return to the market is given by the sum of the slope coefficients, $\Sigma_{k=-K}^{K} b_{j,k}$.

The market return may be viewed as a linear combination of the contemporaneous common factors $z_{k,t}$. Define $LAG_j \equiv \Sigma_{k=1}^{K} b_{j,k}$, the sum of the coefficients on lagged market returns, and $LEAD_j \equiv \Sigma_{k=-K}^{-1} b_{j,k}$. LAG_j is a measure of the lagged price adjustment to common information. Similarly, $LEAD_j$ is a measure of the degree to which the returns on portfolio j anticipate or lead the returns on the market portfolio.

In order to determine the effect of the number of analysts on the rate at which security prices adjust to marketwide information, we estimated Equation (8) for each of the 16 size-analyst portfolios, using the VWI and the EWI. Figures 1a and 1b plot the cumulative fraction of the stock price reaction to market information realized by day d ($\Sigma_{k=-10}^{d} b_k / \Sigma_{k=-10}^{10} b_k$) for each portfolio using VWI as the market proxy. For instance, the value at $d = 0$ denotes the fraction of the information in the index returns incorporated in the prices on the date that the index returns are observed. For VWI returns, the graph is flat for $d < 0$ in all size quartiles, reflecting the fact that portfolio returns do not predict VWI returns. The large increase in the plots for $d = 0$ corresponds to the contemporaneous response coefficient. Most significant for our purposes is the increase in the level of the plots for $d = 1$, which corresponds to LAG_j. As one would expect, LAG_j is heavily influenced by firm size. Figures 2a and 2b plot the normalized cumulative slope coefficients using EWI as the market proxy. The results are qualitatively similar, although the large firms seem to forecast the EWI returns. Indeed, for the largest size quartile the sum of the slope coefficients on lagged EWI returns is negative for all analyst groups. To see that this result is to be expected when large firms adjust to new information more rapidly than the equal-weighted index, suppose that the returns on the EWI, $R_{E,t}$, and the returns on a large firm portfolio L, $R_{L,t}$, are functions of the current and lagged values of market index, I_t:

$$R_{L,t} = a_1 I_t + a_2 I_{t-1} + \epsilon_{L,t}, \tag{9}$$

$$R_{E,t} = b_1 I_t + b_2 I_{t-1}. \tag{10}$$

The Review of Financial Studies / v 6 n 4 1993

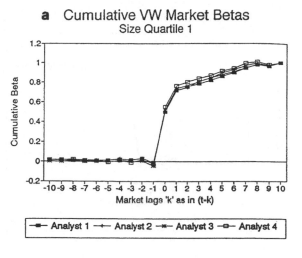

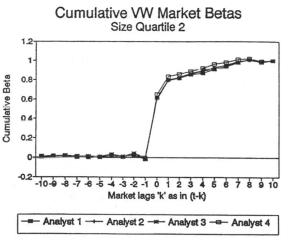

Figure 1
Normalized Cumulative Sums of the elements of the Dimson Beta Estimator using Value-Weighted (VW) Market Index
The figures plot $\Sigma^d_{k=-10}\, b_{j,k}/\Sigma^{10}_{k=-10}\, b_{j,k}$ for $d=,-10, 10$ where $b_{j,k}$ are the coefficients from the regression $R_{j,t} = a + \Sigma^{10}_{k=-10}\, b_{j,k}\, R_{m,t-k} + u_{j,t}.$

Then it is easy to show that in a regression of $R_{L,t}$ on current and lagged values of $R_{E,t}$, the coefficient on $R_{E,t-1}$ is $[(b_1 a_2(b_1^2 + b_2^2) - b_1 b_2(a_1 b_1 + a_2 b_2))]/[(b_1^2 + b_2^2)^2 - b_1^2 b_2^2]$, which will be negative when $b_1/b_2 < a_1/a_2$—that is, when portfolio L responds more rapidly than portfolio E. Moreover, the coefficient decreases as the ratio a_1/a_2 increases—that is, the more timely are the returns on portfolio L.

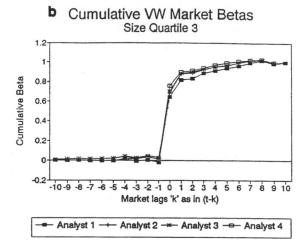

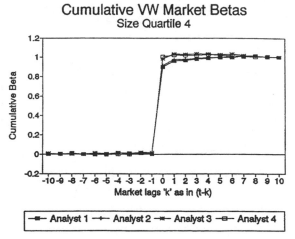

Figure 1 *Continued*

A formal test for the difference between the speed of response to common information of portfolios M and F was constructed as follows. For each size quartile the return on a zero net investment *arbitrage* portfolio denoted by O, which is long in portfolio M and short in portfolio F, was regressed against leads and lags of the return on the market portfolio:

$$R_{O,t} = a_O + \sum_{k=-K}^{K} b_{O,k} R_{m,t-k} + u_{O,t}. \tag{11}$$

The Review of Financial Studies / v 6 n 4 1993

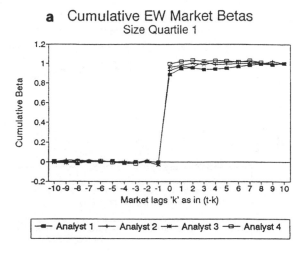

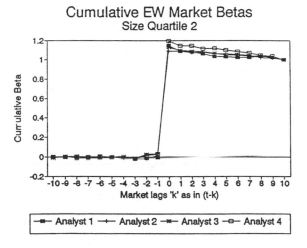

Figure 2
Normalized Cumulative Sums of the elements of the Dimson Beta Estimator using Equal-Weighted (EW) Market Index
The figures plot $\Sigma_{k=-10}^{d} b_{j,k} / \Sigma_{k=-10}^{10} b_{j,k}$ for $d=,-10, 10$ where $b_{j,k}$ are the coefficients from the regression
$R_{j,t} = a + \Sigma_{k=-10}^{10} b_{j,k} R_{m,t-k} + u_{j,t}.$

Since $b_{O,k} = b_{M,k} - b_{F,k}$, the lag coefficients in regression (11) provide evidence on the relative speed of adjustment. Table 4 reports the results of these regressions for the four size quartiles using the VWI as the market proxy.

There is little evidence that current returns on the arbitrage port-

Investment Analysis and Price Response Timeliness

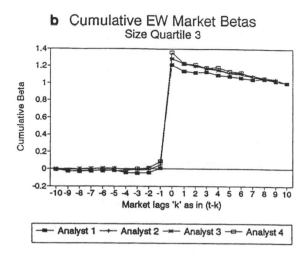

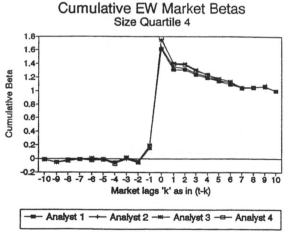

Figure 2 *Continued*

folios are associated with future returns on the value-weighted market portfolio. The value of $b_{0,0}$ is significantly positive for all size quartiles, indicating that M is more sensitive than F to contemporaneous market returns. Then Result 1 implies that if the sum of the coefficients on lagged returns is less than zero ($\sum_{k=1}^{K} b_{0,k} < 0$), then the speed of adjustment of portfolio F is less than that of portfolio M. However, a positive sum of lagged return coefficients does not necessarily imply that the reverse is true, since $b_{0,0} > 0$ (see Result 1).

The Review of Financial Studies / v 6 n 4 1993

Table 4
Regressions of arbitrage portfolio on value-weighted index

Size	LHS	$\Sigma_{k=1}^{K} b_{0,k}$	$b_{0,0}$	$\Sigma_{k=-1}^{-K} b_{0,k}$	R^2
		A: 5 Leads/lags			
1	$R_{1,4,t} - R_{1,1,t}$	0.0094	0.0921*	−0.0089	0.02
2	$R_{2,4,t} - R_{2,1,t}$	0.0681*	0.1413*	−0.0112	0.11
3	$R_{3,4,t} - R_{3,1,t}$	−0.0524*	0.1649*	0.0323‡	0.12
4	$R_{4,4,t} - R_{4,1,t}$	−0.1014*	0.0460*	0.0054	0.04
		B: 10 Leads/lags			
1	$R_{1,4,t} - R_{1,1,t}$	−0.0482	0.0921*	−0.0117	0.03
2	$R_{2,4,t} - R_{2,1,t}$	0.0181	0.1413*	0.0071	0.11
3	$R_{3,4,t} - R_{3,1,t}$	−0.1080*	0.1642*	0.0340	0.12
4	$R_{4,4,t} - R_{4,1,t}$	−0.1251*	0.0464*	−0.0036	0.04

This table provides the results from regressing the difference between the returns on most analysts and fewest analysts portfolios within each size quartile, on CRSP (NYAM-NASDAQ) value-weighted market returns. Here $\Sigma_{k=1}^{K} b_{0,k}$ refers to the sum of lagged betas, $\Sigma_{k=-1}^{-K} b_{0,k}$ refers to the sum of leading betas, and $b_{0,0}$ refers to the contemporaneous beta. * means significant at 1 percent level; † means significant at 5 percent level; ‡ means significant at 10 percent level.

The sum of the lag coefficients is reliably negative for the two largest size quartiles for both 5 and 10 lags. For the smallest quartile, the lag sum in the 10-lag regression is negative but not significant. For the second size quartile the lag sum is positive in both cases and significant in the five lag regressions (as noted, this is not inconsistent with a slower speed of adjustment for portfolio F since $b_{0,0} > 0$). The analysis was repeated using the EWI and the results are reported in Table 5. Now the lag sum is negative in all cases and significant except in one, despite the fact that $b_{0,0}$ is positive (except for the largest size quartile, where the lag sum is significantly negative in any case). These results are generally consistent with portfolio M, showing a faster speed of adjustment to common information.

4.1 Lagged betas of individual securities
The results documented so far, based on our size-number of analysts-ranked portfolios, are consistent with the hypothesis that the prices of firms followed by fewer analysts adjust more slowly to common information for a given firm size. It is possible, however, that we have not controlled for the effect of other firm specific variables such as the volume of transactions. Controlling for firm-specific variables that may be related to the speed of price adjustment is particularly important in interpreting our evidence, given the analysis in Brennan (1990). Brennan (1990) suggests that the number of analysts following a particular stock may be determined by its speed of price adjustment to new information.[11] In this case the speed of adjustment is exoge-

---

[11] When the number of analysts is endogenously determined by the speed of adjustment as in Brennan (1990), the nature of the relation between these two variables is ambiguous. On the one hand,

Investment Analysis and Price Response Timeliness

Table 5
Regressions of arbitrage portfolio on equal-weighted index

Size	LHS	$\sum_{k=1}^{K} b_{0,k}$	$b_{0,0}$	$\sum_{k=-1}^{-K} b_{0,k}$	R^2
		A: 5 Leads/lags			
1	$R_{1,4,t} - R_{1,1,t}$	−0.0686*	0.1347*	−0.0044	0.02
2	$R_{2,4,t} - R_{2,1,t}$	−0.0138	0.1595*	0.0322‡	0.08
3	$R_{3,4,t} - R_{3,1,t}$	−0.1220*	0.1563*	0.0744*	0.07
4	$R_{4,4,t} - R_{4,1,t}$	−0.0821*	−0.0112	0.0248	0.01
		B: 10 Leads/lags			
1	$R_{1,4,t} - R_{1,1,t}$	−0.1245*	0.1359*	0.0022	0.03
2	$R_{2,4,t} - R_{2,1,t}$	−0.0753*	0.1615*	0.0430‡	0.08
3	$R_{3,4,t} - R_{3,1,t}$	−0.1689*	0.1564*	0.0817*	0.08
4	$R_{4,4,t} - R_{4,1,t}$	−0.0860*	−0.0097	0.0215	0.01

This table provides the results from regressing the difference between the returns on most analysts and fewest analysts portfolios within each size quartile on CRSP (NYAM-NASDAQ) equal-weighted market returns. Here $\sum_{k=1}^{K} b_{0,k}$ refers to the sum of lagged betas, $\sum_{k=-1}^{-K} b_{0,k}$ refers to the sum of leading betas, and $b_{0,0}$ refers to the contemporaneous beta. * means significant at 1 percent level; † means significant at 5 percent level; ‡ means significant at 10 percent level.

nously determined, and it is not affected by the number of analysts. By controlling for firm-specific factors such as size and turnover, we attempt to control for exogenous factors that affect the speed of price adjustment. If we find any relation between the speed of price adjustment and the number of analysts keeping these exogenous factors constant, then the results will provide stronger support for the speed of adjustment hypothesis than otherwise.

For each year from 1977 to 1988, regression (8) was estimated for individual securities in our sample that traded on the NYSE, AMEX, or NASDAQ, in order to estimate $LAG_{j,t}$. The following cross-sectional regressions were then run every year from 1977 to 1988:

$$LAG_{j,t} = a_{1,t} + a_{2,t}D_{j,t}^{nasd} + a_{3,t}\text{Ln } SZ_{j,t} + a_{4,t}(D_{j,t}^{nyam} \times \text{Ln } TO_{j,t})$$
$$+ a_{5,t}(D_{j,t}^{nasd}\text{Ln } TO_{j,t}) + a_{6,t}ANALSYT_{j,t} + u_{j,t} \qquad (12)$$

and

$$LEAD_{j,t} = \alpha_{1,t} + \alpha_{2,t}D_{j,t}^{nasd} + \alpha_{3,t}\text{Ln } SZ_{j,t} + \alpha_{4,t}(D_{j,t}^{nyam} \times \text{Ln } TO_{j,t})$$
$$+ \alpha_{5,t}(D_{j,t}^{nasd}\text{Ln } TO_{j,t}) + \alpha_{6,t}ANALYST_{j,t} + u_{j,t}, \qquad (13)$$

where the subscripts j and t refer to firm j and year t respectively. Ln SZ is the natural logarithm of the market value of equity (in billions of dollars) at the end of the previous year and Ln TO is the logarithm of the average daily share turnover, where daily share turnover is

---

when stocks respond slowly to new information, there is more scope for discovering mispricing; on the other hand, the reward for discovering mispricing is received sooner for more rapid price adjustments. These countervailing effects give rise to two possible equilibria: one in which many analysts collect information for stocks that respond rapidly to information, and the other in which many analysts collect information for stocks that respond slowly to information.

The Review of Financial Studies / v 6 n 4 1993

defined as the ratio of the number of shares traded per day to the number of shares outstanding at the end of the day. Since the product of firm size and share turnover is (approximately) equal to the value of shares traded, this formulation is roughly equivalent to one in which the logarithms of size and trading volume (instead of turnover) are included. The dummy variable $D_{j,t}^{nyam}$ ($D_{j,t}^{nasd}$) is assigned a value of 1 if firm j trades on NYSE or AMEX (NASDAQ) in year t, and 0 otherwise. Since NASDAQ is a dealership market, unlike NYSE and AMEX where orders are frequently crossed between investors, the trading volume on this market is not directly comparable to that on the other two markets. For this reason different turnover variables are used for stocks traded on NASDAQ and NYSE/AMEX.[12] *ANALYST* is the number of analysts following the firm at the end of the previous year. Thus, if the number of analysts following a firm increases its speed of adjustment to economywide information, we should expect the coefficient of *ANALYST* in Equation (12) to be negative.

The results of the annual regressions for five lags and leads are reported in Table 6.[13] The means and t-statistics of the coefficients from the annual regressions are reported at the foot of the table. The estimated coefficient of *ANALYST* in regression (12) is negative in every year but one,[14] consistent with the speed of adjustment hypothesis. The t-statistic on the mean coefficient of *ANALYST* is highly significant.

The slope coefficients on Ln SZ and Ln TO are both negative and reliably different from zero. Interestingly, for NYSE/AMEX stocks the coefficients of Ln SZ and Ln TO are insignificantly different from each other. This implies that if we had used the log of dollar volume as the independent variable in the place of Ln SZ and Ln TO,[15] there would be little change in the explanatory power of the regression. This result suggests that firm size affects the informativeness of the stock prices only through its effect on trading volume, as discussed by Admati and Pfleiderer (1988), and does not exert an independent influence. On the other hand, for NASDAQ firms the slope coefficient on Ln TO is significantly positive. A possible explanation for this result is that low-turnover firms on NASDAQ have systematically lower sensitivities to the VWI returns.

When the dependent variable is $LEAD_j$, the coefficients of both turnover variables are positive and statistically significant, suggesting

---

[12] The NASDAQ stocks enter the sample only from 1983 for the tests here since their trading volume is not available on the CRSP prior to 1983.

[13] The results for 10 leads and lags were similar and hence not reported.

[14] For the 10-lag regressions, it is negative in 10 out of 12 years.

[15] Note that Ln SZ + Ln TO equals the log of dollar volume.

Table 6
Cross-sectional regressions of lead and lag betas (value-weighted market index) on firm size, turnover, and number of analysts for individual securities

Dep. var.	Sum of lag betas					Sum of lead betas					
YEAR	Ln SZ	Ln TO (NYAM)	Ln TO (NASD)	DUMMY (NASD)	ANALYST	Ln SZ	Ln TO (NYAM)	Ln TO (NASD)	DUMMY (NASD)	ANALYST	n
1977	−0.0549	−0.1423	—	—	−0.0096	0.0005	0.0592	—	—	0.0023	1359
1978	−0.1209	−0.1653	—	—	−0.0032	−0.0045	−0.0240	—	—	0.0039	1391
1979	−0.0939	−0.2177	—	—	0.0026	0.0252	0.0617	—	—	−0.0047	1371
1980	−0.0165	−0.1000	—	—	−0.0165	0.0114	−0.0435	—	—	0.0039	1343
1981	−0.0740	−0.0920	—	—	−0.0039	0.0106	0.0408	—	—	0.0004	1302
1982	−0.0185	−0.0825	—	—	−0.0128	−0.0022	0.0257	—	—	0.0013	1264
1983	−0.0965	−0.0887	0.0063	−0.0277	−0.0067	0.0461	0.1011	0.1313	0.0155	−0.0080	1684
1984	−0.0364	−0.0428	0.0798	0.0384	−0.0146	0.0291	0.0761	0.0761	0.0398	−0.0068	2045
1985	−0.0308	−0.0296	0.0362	0.1691	−0.0111	0.0054	0.0272	0.0736	0.0493	−0.0012	2222
1986	0.0298	−0.0071	0.0403	0.1091	−0.0124	0.0340	0.0503	0.0434	0.0493	−0.0060	2174
1987	−0.0701	0.0660	0.0177	0.1388	−0.0079	0.0275	0.0046	−0.0113	0.0657	0.0014	2288
1988	−0.0219	0.0018	0.0756	−0.0366	−0.0073	−0.0208	0.0204	0.0299	−0.0821	0.0021	2164
MEAN	−0.0504	−0.0750	0.0426	0.0744	−0.0086	0.0135	0.0333	0.0571	0.0229	−0.0010	
	(−4.10)	(−3.31)	(3.50)	(2.35)	(−5.53)	(2.44)	(2.81)	(2.89)	(1.04)	(−0.78)	

Cross-sectional regressions of the sums of five lead and five lag betas on log size (Ln SZ), log turnover for NYAM firms (Ln TO (NYAM)), log turnover for NASDAQ firms (Ln TO (NASD)), dummy variable for NASDAQ firms (DUMMY (NASD)) and number of analysts (ANALYST). The betas are obtained by regressing daily returns of each firm on lead and lag daily returns of CRSP (NYAM-NASDAQ) value-weighted index, each year. The summed betas are then regressed on Ln SZ, Ln TO (NYAM), Ln TO (NASD), and ANALYST. The sample period is 1977–1988 for NYAM firms and 1983–1988 for NASDAQ firms. n refers to the number of firms in cross-sectional regressions. The numbers in parentheses are t-statistics.

The Review of Financial Studies / v 6 n 4 1993

Table 7
Cross-sectional regressions of lead and lag betas (equal-weighted market index) on firm size, turnover, and number of analysts for individual securities

Dep. Var.	Sum of lag betas					Sum of lead betas					
YEAR	Ln SZ	Ln TO (NYAM)	Ln TO (NASD)	DUMMY (NASD)	ANALYST	Ln SZ	Ln TO (NYAM)	Ln TO (NASD)	DUMMY (NASD)	ANALYST	n
1977	-0.1141	-0.4516	—	—	-0.0191	0.0119	0.1770	—	—	0.0033	1359
1978	-0.1088	-0.3686	—	—	0.0003	-0.0121	0.0004	—	—	0.0039	1391
1979	-0.0744	-0.3298	—	—	0.0052	0.0481	0.0933	—	—	-0.0036	1371
1980	-0.0441	-0.2569	—	—	-0.0059	0.0459	0.0471	—	—	0.0025	1343
1981	-0.1480	-0.2918	—	—	0.0110	0.0406	0.1327	—	—	-0.0032	1302
1982	-0.0672	-0.2719	—	—	-0.0145	0.0371	0.1210	—	—	0.0023	1264
1983	-0.1404	-0.2935	-0.2917	0.1419	-0.0023	0.0383	0.1612	0.1895	0.0250	-0.0050	1684
1984	-0.0753	-0.2255	-0.2690	0.1083	-0.0167	0.0642	0.1608	0.0949	0.0341	-0.0069	2045
1985	-0.0529	-0.1616	-0.3112	0.5149	-0.0169	0.0064	0.0505	0.1037	-0.0174	0.0037	2222
1986	-0.0055	-0.0866	-0.1126	0.3240	-0.0136	0.0465	0.1039	0.0622	0.1343	-0.0047	2174
1987	-0.0982	-0.1067	-0.2255	0.3425	-0.0018	0.0354	0.0991	0.0490	0.0412	0.0040	2288
1988	-0.0411	-0.0655	0.0168	-0.0698	-0.0171	-0.0215	0.0420	0.0884	-0.1918	0.0032	2164
MEAN	-0.0808	-0.2425	-0.1989	0.2269	-0.0076	0.0284	0.0991	0.0980	0.0042	-0.0000	
	(-6.59)	(-7.09)	(-3.83)	(2.68)	(-2.62)	(3.75)	(6.22)	(4.86)	(0.10)	(-0.03)	

Cross-sectional regressions of the sums of five lead and five lag betas on log size (Ln SZ), log turnover for NYAM firms (Ln TO (NYAM)), log turnover for NASDAQ firms (Ln TO (NASD)), dummy variable for NASDAQ firms (DUMMY (NASD)) and number of analysts (*ANALYST*). The betas are obtained by regressing daily returns of each firm on lead and lag daily returns of CRSP (NYAM-NASDAQ) equal-weighted index, each year. The summed betas are then regressed on Ln SZ, Ln TO (NYAM), Ln TO (NASD), and *ANALYST*. The sample period is 1977–1988 for NYAM firms and 1983–1988 for NASDAQ firms. *n* refers to the number of firms in cross-sectional regressions. The numbers in parentheses are *t* statistics.

Investment Analysis and Price Response Timeliness

Table 8
Cross-sectional regressions of lag betas on firm size, turnover, and number of analysts for individual securities by exchange groups

EXCH	Dependent variable: lag beta with respect to the value-weighted index			Dependent variable: lag beta with respect to the equal-weighted index		
	Ln *SZ*	Ln *TO*	*ANALYST*	Ln *SZ*	Ln *TO*	*ANALYST*
NYSE	−0.0645	−0.0812	−0.0072	−0.0843	−0.2462	−0.0078
	(−4.50)	(−3.25)	(−4.74)	(−5.62)	(−6.40)	(−3.48)
AMEX	−0.0526	−0.0474	−0.0012	−0.0965	−0.2622	0.0025
	(−1.93)	(−1.69)	(−0.18)	(−2.45)	(−8.33)	(0.21)
NASDAQ	−0.0058	0.0365	−0.0119	−0.0655	−0.1782	−0.0240
	(−0.45)	(2.86)	(−2.70)	(−4.38)	(−3.75)	(−3.02)

Summary results from the cross-sectional regressions of the sums of five lag betas on log size (Ln *SZ*), log turnover Ln *TO*, and number of analysts (*ANALYST*) by exchange. The betas are obtained from time-series regressions of daily returns of each firm on lead and lag daily returns of CRSP (NYAM-NASDAQ) value-weighted and equal-weighted indices respectively, each year. The sample period is 1977–1988 for NYAM firms and 1983–1988 for NASDAQ firms. The number of firms in the cross-sectional regressions varies from 1062 to 1143 in NYSE, 191 to 296 in AMEX, and 468 to 1054 in NASDAQ. The numbers in parentheses are *t*-statistics.

that heavily traded firms tend to lead the value-weighted market index. On the other hand, the number of analysts variable is insignificant.

Table 7 reports the estimates of regressions (12) and (13) using security betas estimated with respect to the EWI. The results are qualitatively similar to that using the VWI, except that the slope coefficient of the NASDAQ turnover variable is now significantly negative.

4.2 Exchange groups

The effect of the number of analysts on the speed of adjustment may differ across markets because of the differences in the market structures, and disclosure and listing requirements. This subsection examines the relation between number of analysts and speed of adjustment separately in each of the three markets using regression (12).

Table 8 presents the means of the annual regression estimates for the three markets using lagged betas estimated with respect to the VWI and the EWI. The slope coefficients on *ANALYST* are significant for the NYSE and NASDAQ. Interestingly, the slope coefficient on *ANALYST* is larger in magnitude for NASDAQ than for NYSE or AMEX using both EWI and VWI lagged betas, which raises the possibility that investors may rely more on information provided by analysts for NASDAQ stocks than for exchange-listed stocks.

The *ANALYST* coefficient, however, is not significant for AMEX stocks. One possible explanation for this is that the variation in the number of analysts is small for AMEX stocks, which in turn will reduce the precision with which the slope coefficient on *ANALYST* is esti-

The Review of Financial Studies / v 6 n 4 1993

mated.[16] In fact, the standard error of this slope coefficient is much larger for AMEX than for NYSE or NASDAQ.

The average number of analysts following AMEX firms is 2.16, which is smaller than the average number of analysts following NYSE and NASDAQ stocks (8.77 and 4.11 respectively). The evidence that the *ANALYST* coefficient is not significant for AMEX suggests the possibility that the effect of number of analysts on speed of response is nonlinear. We consider this possibility in the following section.

4.3 Nonlinear effect of number of analysts

Holden and Subrahmanyam argue that even a few analysts have a dramatic effect on the speed of adjustment, which suggests that there will be a convex relation between the number of analysts and the speed of adjustment. On the other hand, the AMEX evidence discussed suggests that a small number of analysts following a firm may not affect the speed of stock price response to information significantly.

To explore the possibility of a nonlinear effect of the number of analysts on the speed of adjustment, we fitted the regression

$$LAG_{j,t} = a_{1,t} + a_{2,t}D_{j,t}^{nasd} + a_{3,t}\text{Ln } SZ_{j,t} + a_{4,t}(D_{j,t}^{nyam} \times \text{Ln } TO_{j,t})$$

$$+ a_{5,t}(D_{j,t}^{nasd}\text{Ln } TO_{j,t}) + \sum_{k=1}^{8} a_{k+5,t}D_{j,k,t} + u_{j,t}, \qquad (14)$$

where $D_{j,k,t}$ is a dummy variable that equals 1 if the number of analysts following the firm falls into group k, and 0 otherwise.[17] The mean of the annual coefficients from these regressions are reported in Table 9.

The results reveal a distinct nonlinear relation between the number of analysts and the speed of adjustment. The coefficient of the analyst dummy declines after the first analyst group (zero analysts) when lagged VWI betas are used to compute LAG_j, but is then virtually flat or marginally increasing for the next five groups (up to 11 analysts) and then declines sharply. A similar nonlinear pattern emerges when LAG_j is computed using lagged EWI betas as well.[18]

This result suggests that the speed of adjustment is a nonlinear function of the number of analysts; few analysts have little effect, but once a threshold is reached an increase in the number of analysts

---

[16] The cross-sectional standard deviation of the number of analysts for the AMEX is 3.47, compared with that of 8.01 for the NYSE and 4.20 for NASDAQ.

[17] The groups, which were chosen to ensure a roughly equal number of firms in each, correspond to 0, 1, 2, 3–4, 5–7, 8–11, 12–15, and greater than 15 analysts.

[18] The coefficients on the analyst dummies are displaced downward in the regression with LAG_j computed with the lagged EWI betas relative to that with lagged VWI betas. The reason is that the lagged EWI betas are on average smaller than the lagged VWI betas, since the EWI responds more slowly to common information than the VWI.

Investment Analysis and Price Response Timeliness

Table 9
Cross-sectional regressions of lag betas on firm size, turnover, and dummy variables for number of analysts

	MEAN	t-Statistics	Analysts
A: Lagged betas with respect to value-weighted index			
Ln *SZ*	−0.0722	−5.29	
Ln *TO* (NYAM)	−0.0837	−3.72	
Ln *TO* (NASD)	0.0231	1.91	
DUMMY (NASD)	0.0785	2.24	
ANALYST 1	0.2103	1.53	0
ANALYST 2	0.1155	4.21	1
ANALYST 3	0.1465	4.92	2
ANALYST 4	0.1805	7.81	3.43
ANALYST 5	0.1865	6.80	5.92
ANALYST 6	0.1795	9.96	9.37
ANALYST 7	0.1237	6.96	13.42
ANALYST 8	0.0128	0.64	21.89
B: Lagged betas with respect to equal-weighted index			
Ln *SZ*	−0.1002	−7.23	
Ln *TO* (NYAM)	−0.2492	−7.11	
Ln *TO* (NASD)	−0.2123	−4.01	
DUMMY (NASD)	0.2290	2.60	
ANALYST 1	−0.3275	−3.62	0
ANALYST 2	−0.3327	−7.70	1
ANALYST 3	−0.2997	−6.56	2
ANALYST 4	−0.2899	−7.37	3.43
ANALYST 5	−0.2717	−6.89	5.92
ANALYST 6	−0.2960	−7.74	9.37
ANALYST 7	−0.3499	−7.91	13.42
ANALYST 8	−0.4464	−7.45	21.89

Summary results from the cross-sectional regressions of the sums of five lag betas on log size (Ln *SZ*), log turnover for NYAM firms (Ln *TO* (NYAM)), log turnover for NASDAQ firms (Ln *TO* (NASD)), dummy variable for NASDAQ firms (DUMMY (NASDAQ)) and dummy variables for various analyst groups for all firms in CRSP. The dummy variables assume a value of 1 if the number of analysts for a firm belong to the corresponding group and 0 otherwise. There are eight groups based on the following grouping: 0, 1, 2, 3–4, 5–7, 8–11, 12–15, >15. The variables *ANALYST 1* to *ANALYST 8* refer to the eight dummy variables corresponding to the eight groups. The betas are obtained from time-series regressions of daily returns of each firm on lead and lag daily returns of CRSP (NYAM-NASDAQ) value-weighted and equal-weighted indices respectively, each year. *ANALYSTS* refers to the mean number of analysts in the eight groups over 1977–1988. The sample period is 1977–1988 for NYAM firms and 1983–1988 for NASDAQ firms. The number of firms in these regressions vary between 1200 and 2300.

does increase the speed of adjustment. This is in contrast to the Holden and Subrahmanyam (1992) theory, in which even a few analysts have a dramatic effect on the speed of adjustment.

5. Conclusion

We have examined the empirical relation between the number of analysts following a firm and its speed of adjustment to new information that has common effects across firms. We found little effect of the number of analysts on the serial correlation of portfolio returns. However, Granger causality regressions revealed that the returns on many analyst firm portfolios tend to anticipate those on few analyst

The Review of Financial Studies / v 6 n 4 1993

firm portfolios. Moreover, many analyst firm portfolios respond more rapidly to new information contained in returns on the value-weighted and the equal-weighted market indices. Examination of individual security returns shows a distinct nonlinear relation between the speed of adjustment and the number of analysts.

Appendix

As a preliminary to the proof of Proposition 1, note that the probability limits of the slope coefficients of the Granger causality regression (3) and (4) are given by

$$b_F = \frac{\text{var}(R_M)\text{cov}(R_{M,t}, R_{F,t-1}) - \text{cov}(R_{M,t}, R_{F,t})\text{cov}(R_{M,t}, R_{M,t-1})}{\text{var}(R_M)\text{var}(R_F) - [\text{cov}(R_{M,t}, R_{F,t})]^2}, \quad \text{(A1)}$$

$$b_M = \frac{\text{var}(R_F)\text{cov}(R_{M,t}, R_{M,t-1}) - \text{cov}(R_{M,t}, R_{F,t})\text{cov}(R_{M,t}, R_{F,t-1})}{\text{var}(R_M)\text{var}(R_F) - [\text{cov}(R_{M,t}, R_{F,t})]^2}, \quad \text{(A2)}$$

$$g_F = \frac{\text{var}(R_M)\text{cov}(R_{F,t}, R_{F,t-1}) - \text{cov}(R_{M,t}, R_{F,t})\text{cov}(R_{F,t}, R_{M,t-1})}{\text{var}(R_M)\text{var}(R_F) - [\text{cov}(R_{M,t}, R_{F,t})]^2}, \quad \text{(A3)}$$

$$g_M = \frac{\text{var}(R_F)\text{cov}(R_{F,t}, R_{M,t-1}) - \text{cov}(R_{M,t}, R_{F,t})\text{cov}(R_{F,t}, R_{F,t-1})}{\text{var}(R_M)\text{var}(R_F) - [\text{cov}(R_{M,t}, R_{F,t})]^2}. \quad \text{(A4)}$$

Proof of Proposition 1a. Since the denominators in (A1) and (A4) are the same and positive, we need to compare only the numerators. Denote the numerator of each expression with the superscript n; hence, b_F^n denotes the numerator of b_F from (A1). From (1) and (A1),

$$
\begin{aligned}
b_F^n &= \left\{ \sum_{k=1}^{K} \beta_{M,k}^2 (1 + a_M^2) + \sigma^2 \right\} a_M \sum_{k=1}^{K} \beta_{M,k}\beta_{F,k} \\
&\quad - \left\{ \sum_{k=1}^{K} \beta_{M,k}\beta_{F,k}(1 + a_M a_F) \right\} a_M \sum_{k=1}^{K} \beta_{M,k}^2 \\
&= \sigma^2 a_M \sum_{k=1}^{K} \beta_{M,k}\beta_{F,k} + a_M^2(a_M - a_F) \sum_{j=1}^{K} \sum_{k=1}^{k} \beta_{M,j}^2 \beta_{M,k}\beta_{F,k}. \quad \text{(A5)}
\end{aligned}
$$

Using similar steps we get

$$g_M^n = \sigma^2 a_F \sum_{k=1}^{K} \beta_{M,k}\beta_{F,k} + a_F^2(a_F - a_M) \sum_{j=1}^{K} \sum_{k=1}^{K} \beta_{F,j}^2 \beta_{M,k}\beta_{F,k}. \quad \text{(A6)}$$

Since $a_F > a_M$, the first term in (A6) is greater than the first term in (A5), and the second term in (A6) is positive while that in (A5) is negative. It follows that $g_M > b_F$. In fact, from (A5), it can be seen that if the variance of the idiosyncratic component of return (σ^2) is sufficiently small, then h_F would be negative.

Proof of Proposition 1b. If $\beta_{M,k}(1 + a_M) = \beta_{F,k}(1 + a_F)$ for all k and $a_F > a_M$, then $\beta_{M,k} > \beta_{F,k}$ and $\beta_{M,k}a_M < \beta_{F,k}a_F$. Some algebraic manipulations of the numerators of (A2) and (A1) yields

$$h_M^n - h_F^n = \sigma^2 a_M \sum_{k=1}^{K} (\beta_{M,k}^2 - \beta_{M,k}\beta_{F,k})$$

$$+ a_M(1 + a_M a_F) \sum_{k=1}^{K} \beta_{M,k}\beta_{F,k} \left\{ \sum_{j=1}^{K} \beta_{M,j}^2 - \sum_{j=1}^{K} \beta_{M,j}\beta_{F,j} \right\}$$

$$+ \sum_{i=1}^{K} \beta_{M,i}^2 \sum_{j=1}^{K} \beta_{F,j} \sum_{k=1}^{K} (a_F \beta_{F,k} - a_M \beta_{M,k}).$$

Now, $h_M^n > h_F^n$ since each of the three terms in this expression is positive. The proof that $g_M > g_F$ is similar.

References

Admati, A., and P. Pfleiderer, 1988, "A Theory of Intraday Patterns: Volume and Price Variability," *Review of Financial Studies,* 1, 3–40.

Arbel, S. C., and P. Strebel, 1983, "Giraffes, Institutions and Neglected Firms," *Financial Analysts Journal,* 39, 57–63.

Bhushan, R., 1989, "Firm Characteristics and Analyst Following," *Journal of Accounting and Economics,* 11, 255–274.

Brennan, M. J., 1990, "Presidential Address: Latent Assets," *Journal of Finance,* 45, 709–730.

Brennan, M. J., and P. J. Hughes, 1991, "Stock Prices and the Supply of Information," *Journal of Finance,* 46, 1665–1691.

Fama, E. F., and J. D. MacBeth, 1973, "Risk, Return and Equilibrium: Empirical Tests," *Journal of Political Economy,* 81, 607–636.

Foster, F. D., and S. Viswanathan, 1993, "The Effect of Public Information and Competition on Trading Volume and Price Volatility," *Review of Financial Studies,* 6, 23–56.

Granger, C. W. J., 1969, "Investigating Causal Relations by Econometric Models and Cross-Spectral Models," *Econometrica,* 37, 424–438.

Holden, C., and A. Subrahmanyam, 1992, "Long-Lived Private Information and Imperfect Competition," *Journal of Finance,* 47, 247–270.

Kyle, A. S., 1985, "Continuous Auctions and Insider Trading," *Econometrica,* 53, 1315–1335.

Lo, A., and C. MacKinlay, 1988, "Stock Market Prices Do Not Follow Random Walks: Evidence from a Simple Specification Test," *Review of Financial Studies,* 1, 175–206.

The Review of Financial Studies / v 6 n 4 1993

Lo, A., and C. MacKinlay, 1990, "'When Are Contrarian Profits due to Stock Market Overreaction," *Review of Financial Studies*, 3, 175–206.

Merton, R. C., 1987, "A Simple Model of Capital Market Equilibrium with Incomplete Information," *Journal of Finance*, 42, 483–510.

Sims, C. A., 1972, "Money, Income and Causality," *American Economic Review*, 62, 540–552.

22

ELSEVIER   Journal of Financial Economics 38 (1995) 361–381

Investment analysis and price formation in securities markets

Michael J. Brennan[a,b], Avanidhar Subrahmanyam[*,a,c]

[a]*Anderson Graduate School of Management, University of California, Los Angeles, CA 90024, USA*
[b]*London Business School, London NW1 4SA, UK*
[c]*Graduate School of Business, Columbia University, New York, NY 10027, USA*

(Received October 1993; final version received September 1994)

Abstract

This paper investigates the relation between the number of analysts following a security and the estimated adverse selection cost of transacting in the security, controlling for the effects of previously identified determinants of liquidity. Using intraday data for the year 1988, we find that greater analyst following tends to reduce adverse selection costs based on the Kyle (1985) notion of market depth. This result is consistent with the analysis of Admati and Pfleiderer (1988). Estimates of structural parameters of a version of the Admati and Pfleiderer model of endogenous information acquisition provide qualified support for the model.

Key words: Security analysis; Market depth; Asymmetric information
JEL classification: G14; D82

1. Introduction

The important paradigms of price formation in securities markets developed by Kyle (1984, 1985) and Admati and Pfleiderer (1988) suggest that trading by investors who possess superior information imposes significant liquidity costs on other market participants due to adverse selection, which we call *the adverse selection costs of transacting*. These theoretical models have stimulated the

---

*Corresponding author.

We are indebted to John Long (the editor) and an anonymous referee for their detailed and insightful suggestions. We also thank Larry Harris, Richard Roll, and participants at the UCLA finance seminar for helpful comments.

development of empirical techniques for measuring the effect of informed trading on market liquidity in Glosten and Harris (1988), Madhavan and Smidt (1991), and Hasbrouck (1991), among others. Although these papers report significant evidence of adverse selection costs due to information-based trading in financial markets, for the most part they provide little empirical evidence on the cross-sectional determinants of the size of these costs. A notable exception is the paper by Glosten and Harris (1988), which reports a very weak association between an estimate of adverse selection costs and a measure of insider holdings, which is taken as a proxy for the intensity of informed trading.

We provide further evidence on the effect of information-based trading on liquidity costs by analyzing the empirical relation between the number of investment analysts following a stock and the estimated adverse selection cost of transacting in the stock, controlling for the effects of trading volume, price level, and return volatility. The number of investment analysts researching a firm is a simple proxy for the number of individuals producing information about the value of the firm, based on Brennan, Jegadeesh, and Swaminathan (1993), who find that stocks that are followed by many analysts react faster to common information than stocks that are followed by few analysts. The adverse selection cost is defined as the price impact of a marginal dollar of trade, and, apart from a price scale factor, is proportional to the inverse of the Kyle (1985) measure of market depth (in the Kyle, 1985, and Admati and Pfleiderer, 1988, models, depth is given by the reciprocal of the regression coefficient of the price change on the order flow). Recent theoretical work leads us to expect a relation between the adverse selection cost of transacting in a security and the number of individuals producing information about the security.

Thus the Admati–Pfleiderer model, which assumes that the information asymmetry is short-lived, predicts either a positive or a nonmonotone (Subrahmanyam, 1991) relation between the number of informed traders and market depth. However, when information is long-lived, an increase in the number of informed traders will tend to increase the rate at which private information comes to be reflected in price; consequently, market depth will be lower in the early rounds of trading, when the information disadvantage of the market maker is greatest, but the effect will be reversed in later rounds as the market maker gains more information from the order flow. Holden and Subrahmanyam (1992) present an explicit model of market depth with multiple informed traders and long-lived information.

While the number of analysts following a stock is an imperfect proxy for the number of informed traders, the influence of security analysis on market depth is an issue of interest in its own right, since security analysis is a costly activity whose social benefits remain largely unexplored (see, however, Brennan, Jegadeesh, and Swaminathan, 1993; Arbel, Carvell, and Strebel, 1983). The empirical relation between the number of analysts and market depth is particularly relevant in light of the positive relation between market illiquidity and required rates of return derived, for example, in Amihud and Mendelson (1986).

Our empirical results may be summarized as follows. Other things equal, an increase in the number of investment analysts tends to be associated with a reduction in the adverse selection costs of transacting, as would be predicted by the model of Admati and Pfleiderer (1988). Structural estimates of a non-linear simultaneous equation specification of the model of endogenous information acquisition developed by Admati and Pfleiderer are broadly supportive of the model. However, a more general specification which allows the number of analysts to depend on the degree of institutional participation, as in Bhushan (1989), performs better in characterizing the market for information.

In Section 2 we briefly summarize some of the recent theoretical literature on the effect of informed traders on market depth. In Section 3 we describe the data used in the empirical tests. Section 4 describes the estimation of the measures of market depth, while Section 5 presents the empirical results relating market depth to the number of investment analysts following a stock. Section 6 concludes.

2. Competition and market depth

To see the effect of the number of informed traders on market depth in a single-period setting, consider a special case of the model of Admati and Pfleiderer (1988), in which n risk-neutral traders receive a perfectly informative signal about the final payoff, u, on an asset. The informed traders, as well as uninformed noise traders, place market orders with a competitive, risk-neutral market maker who fills the orders at a single price, P, which depends on the total order flow q:

$$P = E[u] + \lambda q, \tag{1}$$

where $E[u]$ is the unconditional expectation of the asset payoff. Admati and Pfleiderer show that λ, *the inverse of* market depth, is given by

$$\lambda = \frac{\sqrt{n}}{n+1} \sqrt{\frac{\text{var}(u)}{\text{var}(z)}}, \tag{2}$$

where var(z) is the variance of the orders placed by noise traders.

Eq. (2) implies that λ is decreasing in n, the number of informed traders, for $n > 1$, so that market depth is increasing in the number of informed traders. Admati and Pfleiderer also show that if there is a fixed cost of acquiring information, c, and the number of informed traders is determined endogenously, then n, the equilibrium number of informed traders, satisfies (except for the integer constraint):

$$\frac{\text{var}(u)}{(1 + n)^2 \lambda} = c. \tag{3}$$

In general, λ depends on the sensitivity of the total order flow, q, to the information signal. Subrahmanyam (1991) shows that a risk-neutral market maker will set λ according to

$$\lambda = \frac{t \, \text{var}(u)}{t^2 \, \text{var}(u) + \text{var}(z)}, \tag{4}$$

where t, the intensity of informed trading, is equal to the coefficient of the perfectly informative signal of u in the informed traders' aggregate order function. While t is monotone increasing in n in the model of Subrahmanyam (1991), it can be seen from Eq. (4) that λ is a nonmonotonic function of t. In the model of Admati and Pfleiderer, in which the informed traders are risk-neutral, t is always sufficiently large that $\partial \lambda / \partial t < 0$, and therefore $\partial \lambda / \partial n < 0$. In Subrahmanyam (1991), however, risk aversion reduces the intensity of trading by the informed traders so that, for small n, $\partial \lambda / \partial t > 0$, and therefore $\partial \lambda / \partial n > 0$ for small n. In summary, the model of Admati and Pfleiderer predicts a negative relation between λ and the number of informed traders, while Subrahmanyam's model with risk-averse traders predicts that the relation will be negative only when the number of informed traders is sufficiently large. Eq. (3) shows that the number of informed traders cannot be taken as exogenous, but will be determined in equilibrium by the costs and benefits of becoming informed.

When information is long-lived, predictions regarding market depth are more ambiguous. Holden and Subrahmanyam (1992) show that in a model with a Kyle (1985) market maker and competing informed traders, the informed investors trade much more aggressively than in the monopoly case considered by Kyle. As a result, the price reflects their private information much more rapidly than in the monopoly case, which causes the market depth to increase with the number of informed traders, except possibly in the first few auctions if the number of informed traders is small. Overall, this analysis strongly suggests that market depth, though time-varying, will be higher on average the greater is the number of informed traders. It also suggests that the effect of an increase in the number of informed traders will be nonlinear, being greatest when the number of informed traders is small.

Thus, while models in which private information is short-lived suggest that an increase in the number of informed traders will increase market depth, models in which private information is long-lived have more ambiguous predictions, so that empirical evidence on the issue is of particular interest.

M.J. Brennan, A. Subrahmanyam / Journal of Financial Economics 38 (1995) 361–381   365

Our empirical work focuses on the relation between the number of analysts following a firm and estimates of the (inverse of) market depth, λ, holding constant factors which previous authors have found to be associated with market liquidity (see Benston and Hagerman, 1974; Branch and Freed, 1977). Glosten and Harris (1988) estimate λ for a small sample of NYSE securities and find that the estimated adverse selection trading costs for average size transactions are negatively related to the number of shareholders in the firm and (insignificantly) positively related to the concentration of insider holdings in the firm. They interpret their results as consistent with a Kyle-type model in which the adverse selection problem faced by the market maker is an increasing function of insider concentration, and the volume of noise trading is proxied by the number of shareholders. They suggest (p. 140) that the coefficient of the insider concentration variable may be insignificant because 'the information from which market makers must protect themselves is related to superior analytical ability among some investors rather than information obtained by legally defined insiders'. We examine whether the information from which market makers must protect themselves is related in particular to the superior analytical ability and investment in information of security analysts.

In our empirical work, we rely primarily on the procedures developed by Glosten and Harris (1988) and Madhavan and Smidt (1991) to measure the adverse selection costs of transacting. However, to assess the robustness of the results to the estimation procedure for the Kyle λ, we also follow a procedure used by Foster and Viswanathan (1993) which is based on Hasbrouck (1991).

3. Data

The data employed in the empirical tests reported below were provided by the Institute for the Study of Security Markets and consist of intraday quotes as well as transaction prices and quantities for 1,550 common stocks that were listed continuously on the NYSE for the calendar year 1988. To minimize data errors, the data were screened as follows. First, quotations and transactions reported out of sequence were excluded. Second, the overnight price change and the closing quotes were omitted to eliminate price effects associated with opening and closing procedures, dividend payments, and overnight news arrival. Third, an error filter was used to screen out intraday reporting errors. The error filter discards a trade if the trade price is too far outside the price range defined as the minimum range that includes the *preceding* bid and ask quotations and the *immediately following* trade price or bid and ask quotations. If the price falls outside this range by more than four times the width of the range, the trade is discarded. This filter is conservative and discards fewer than one in 40,000 observations in the sample considered.

For each security, the number of investment analysts following the firm is defined as the number of analysts making an annual earnings forecast for that firm in December 1987, according to the Institutional Brokerage Earnings Estimates tape.[1] The daily return variance, the average daily trading volume in shares, and the average daily closing price are computed using data for 1988 from the Center for Research in Security Prices' New York Stock Exchange/ American Stock Exchange daily tape. Finally, the *S&P Security Owners' Stock Guide* provides the number of institutions reported as owning shares in each company and the number of shares held by institutions as of December 1987. Forty-two companies in the sample did not have these data available, leaving 1,508 companies for which data on all variables were available.

4. Estimation of adverse selection costs

Before examining the relation between adverse selection costs and the number of analysts following a stock, we estimate λ, the inverse of market depth in a Kyle-type model. To facilitate comparison with earlier studies, we initially estimate λ using two different procedures developed by Glosten and Harris (1988) and Madhavan and Smidt (1991), respectively. The analysis of Glosten and Harris follows Kyle (1985) in assuming that investors can place only unconditional market orders. This assumption is implicit in the manner in which they model the adverse selection component of the spread [see Eq. (1a) of their paper]. Madhavan and Smidt, on the other hand, explicitly assume that informed investors condition their order flow on the price. Since the NYSE allows both market and limit orders, neither measure of (the inverse of) market depth is entirely appropriate, and by using both measures in our regressions we are able to assess the sensitivity of our results to the assumptions made about the order submission protocol.

To understand how Glosten and Harris relate λ to the time-series behavior of prices, let m_t denote the expected value of the security conditional on the market maker's information set at time t. Then, consistent with the Kyle (1985) model in which informed traders place market orders, the expectation will evolve according to

$$m_t = m_{t-1} + \lambda q_t + y_t, \qquad (5)$$

where q_t is the (signed) order flow at time t and y_t is the public information innovation. It is standard in the empirical microstructure literature to allow for a fixed cost component of the price impact of a trade. This component compensates the market maker for the costs associated with operating a market. To

---

[1] We are grateful to Lynch, Jones, and Ryan for making these data available.

model the fixed cost component of the price response to a transaction, Glosten and Harris proceed as follows.[2] Let D_t denote the sign of the incoming order at time t ($+1$ for a buyer-initiated trade and -1 for a seller-initiated trade). Denoting the fixed-cost component by ψ, we can write

$$p_t = m_t + \psi D_t . \tag{6}$$

Substituting out m_t using (5), we have

$$p_t = m_{t-1} + \lambda q_t + \psi D_t + y_t . \tag{7}$$

However, since $p_{t-1} = m_{t-1} + \psi D_{t-1}$, we obtain

$$\Delta p_t = \lambda q_t + \psi [D_t - D_{t-1}] + y_t . \tag{8}$$

Eq. (8), which ignores the discrete nature of price quotes, is used to estimate the Glosten–Harris λ for each NYSE-listed stock for the year 1988. (Glosten and Harris find that their estimates of λ are not sensitive to the precise specification of the distribution of the equation error.)

To relate λ to the time-series behavior of prices in the Madhavan and Smidt (1991) model, let the μ_t denote mean of the private information. The order flow, q_t, which (contrary to the assumption of the Kyle model) depends on the price, p_t, can then be written as

$$q_t = \alpha(\mu_t - p_t) + z_t , \tag{9}$$

where z_t is the liquidity trading component. The risk-neutral market maker who sees $\tau_t \equiv p_t + \alpha^{-1} q_t$ as a noisy measure of μ_t will set the price according to

$$p_t = m_t + \psi D_t = \pi \gamma_t + (1 - \pi)\tau_t + \psi D_t , \tag{10}$$

where γ_t is the market maker's prior mean of the asset's value and π is the Bayesian weight placed on the prior observation. Now,

$$p_{t-1} = m_{t-1} + \psi D_{t-1} ,$$

which can be written as

$$\gamma_t = p_{t-1} - \psi D_{t-1} + \eta_t ,$$

where $\eta_t \equiv \gamma_t - m_{t-1}$. Substituting for γ_t in (10), we have

$$p_t = \pi(p_{t-1} - \psi D_{t-1} + \eta_t) + (1 - \pi)[p_t + \alpha^{-1} q_t] + \psi D_t . \tag{11}$$

Rewriting,

$$\Delta p_t = \lambda q_t + \frac{\psi}{\pi} D_t - \psi D_{t-1} + \eta_t , \tag{12}$$

---

[2]Glosten and Harris (1988) ignore inventory holding costs, which appear to be small in an intraday setting (see, for example, Stoll, 1989; George, Kaul, and Nimalendran, 1991; Madhavan and Smidt, 1991).

where $\lambda \equiv \alpha^{-1}(1 - \pi)/\pi$. Madhavan and Smidt (1991) show that the error term η_t follows an MA(1) process in their framework. Further, Eq. (12) differs from Eq. (8) in the coefficients of D_t and D_{t-1}: the difference arises from the different assumptions about the dependence of the order flow on the price. Eq. (12) is used to obtain our estimate of the Madhavan–Smidt λ.

To estimate λ from either Eq. (8) or Eq. (12), it is necessary first to estimate D_t, the sign of the order quantity. We use the procedure suggested by Lee and Ready (1991): if a transaction occurs above the prevailing quote mid-point, it is regarded as a purchase, and if it occurs below the prevailing quote mid-point, it is regarded as a sale. If a transaction occurs exactly at the mid-point, it is signed using the 'tick' test, which assigns a positive sign to the trade if the price move from the previous transaction price is upward, and vice versa. If the price is the same as the previous transaction price, the test is applied using the last price following which there was a move.

Given the series of prices and signed order quantities, λ is estimated from both Eqs. (8) and (12). In conformance with the theoretical specifications of the Glosten and Harris (1988) and Madhavan and Smidt (1988) models, we assume an i.i.d. error process in the Glosten–Harris specification and an MA(1) error process in the Madhavan–Smidt specification. Further, to take account of possible misspecifications, we allow for intercepts in each of the two regression specifications. A significant assumption underlying empirical measures of market depth that rely on an analysis of the relation between price change and order flow is that the public information innovation [y_t in Eq. (8) and η_t in Eq. (12)] is uncorrelated with the order flow, q_t.[3] For example, if, contrary to the assumption of the Kyle (1985) model, market makers systematically 'lean against the wind' by contrarian trading, the estimated value of λ will be biased, which will affect our point estimates of trading costs. However, there is no reason to believe that the bias is related to the number of analysts following the stock, which would be necessary if it were to affect our inferences about the effect of investment analysis on market depth.

Of the 1,508 companies in the original sample, 87 yielded negative estimates for at least one of the λ's and were eliminated from the sample to facilitate estimation of the log-linear specifications we posit below. For each measure of λ, the adverse selection cost of transacting is estimated by dividing λ by the average daily closing price, *PRI*.

In the Kyle model, the total adverse selection cost of trading q shares is λq^2. Given the price, P, the marginal cost per dollar of transaction when q shares are traded is thus $2\lambda q/P$. Table 1 provides summary statistics on the marginal cost per dollar of transaction for the two measures of λ (in the table q is set equal to

---

[3]See Glosten and Harris (1988), Hasbrouck (1991), Madhavan and Smidt (1991), and Foster and Viswanathan (1993).

Table 1
Summary statistics of estimated market depth for the year 1988 and analyst following as of December 1987 for a sample of 1,421 stocks continuously listed on the NYSE for the year 1988 for which complete data were available on institutional holdings as of December 1987 and for which nonnegative estimates of market depth were obtained

λ_{GH} is the estimate of the inverse of market depth from the Glosten–Harris specification:

$$\Delta p_t = \lambda q_t + \psi [D_t - D_{t-1}] + y_t;$$

λ_{MS} is the estimate of the inverse of market depth from the Madhavan–Smidt specification:

$$\Delta p_t = \lambda q_t + \frac{\psi}{\pi} D_t - \psi D_{t-1} + \eta_t.$$

Δp_t is the price change at transaction t, q_t is the signed trade size, D_t is a dummy variable that is equal to $+1$ for a trade classified as a buy and -1 for a sell, and y_t and η_t are error terms. The Glosten–Harris model is estimated assuming that y_t is i.i.d., while the Madhavan–Smidt model is estimated assuming that η_t is MA(1). *PRI* is the average daily closing price for 1988.

Number of firms = 1,421	Mean	Median	Standard deviation
$(1,000)\lambda_{GH}/PRI$	0.0314	0.0082	0.0701
$(1,000)\lambda_{MS}/PRI$	0.0156	0.0046	0.0371
Number of analysts	8.90	5	9.99

500 shares). The mean of the marginal cost of purchasing 500 shares is 3.14% for the Glosten–Harris specification and 1.56% for the Madhavan–Smidt specification. The Glosten–Harris measure is approximately twice as variable in the cross-section as the Madhavan–Smidt measure. The correlation between the two measures of adverse selection cost is 0.93. To assess the sensitivity of our results to model specification, we use both estimates in our analysis.

Table 1 also provides summary statistics for the number of analysts following each firm. The distribution is highly skewed: the mean number is 8.9 while the median is 5, and 438 out of the total sample of 1,421 were not covered by the I/B/E/S service.

5. Empirical results

5.1. Cross-sectional determinants of the adverse selection cost of transacting

Ordinary least-squares (OLS) regressions in which the dependent variable is an estimate of the adverse selection cost are likely to be biased and inconsistent, because trading volume, a primary determinant of this cost, and the number of analysts, which is the key variable in our analysis, may both be affected by the cost of transacting. We therefore adopt a simultaneous equations approach. Following the earlier empirical work on the determinants of the bid–ask spread (Benston and Hagerman, 1974; Branch and Freed, 1977), the first equation explains the logarithm of the adverse selection cost, LTC, as a linear function of the logarithm of the volume of trading ($LVOL$), as measured by the average number of shares traded per day during the year, the logarithm of the stock price ($LPRI$) measured by the average daily closing price during the year, and the logarithm of the daily return variance measured over the year ($LVAR$). To introduce the number of analysts in a consistent manner, $LANAL$ is defined as the logarithm of one plus the number of analysts allowing us to include in the regression firms for which no analyst is reported by I/B/E/S. This definition is also consistent with the notion that there is some informed trading even in the absence of security analysis reported on the I/B/E/S tape.

The second equation explains $LANAL$, the (log) number of analysts, in terms of the adverse selection cost variable, LTC, and the logarithms of variance, size, and price. Following Bhushan (1989), it also includes five industry dummies and $LNINST$ and $LPINST$, the (log) number of institutions holding shares in the company and the (log) percentage of shares held by institutions, respectively. The third equation explains $LVOL$, the logarithm of trading volume, in terms of the trading cost variable, LTC, as well as $LANAL$ and $LSIZE$. Thus the following equation system was estimated by two-stage least squares:

$$LTC = a_{S0} + a_{S1}LANAL + a_{S2}LVOL + a_{S3}LPRI + a_{S4}LVAR + e_{TC},$$

$$(13)$$

$$LANAL = a_{A0} + a_{A1}LTC + a_{A2}LVAR + a_{A3}LSIZE + a_{A4}LPRI$$

$$+ \sum_{i=1}^{5} a_{Ai+4}IND_i + a_{A10}LNINST + a_{A11}LPINST + e_{ANAL},$$

$$(14)$$

$$LVOL = a_{V0} + a_{V1}LTC + a_{V2}LANAL + a_{V3}LSIZE + e_{VOL}, \qquad (15)$$

where IND_i is a dummy variable corresponding to one of five industry classifications; the industry classifications are obtained from the COMPUSTAT tapes and follow Bhushan (1989). The first and third equations in the above system are identified, while the second is underidentified. Table 2 reports the two-stage least-squares parameter estimates for the two identified equations of the system. The analysis is reported for the transaction cost variable, LTC, computed for each of the two measures of λ. The results for both the measures of λ are qualitatively similar.

Considering first the LTC regressions for the determinants of the adverse selection cost, the coefficient of the number of analysts is negative and significant for both measures of λ. This finding is consistent with the prediction of the

Table 2
Two-stage least-squares estimates of determinants of adverse selection cost of transacting, using two empirical measures of λ:

$$LTC = a_{S0} + a_{S1}LANAL + a_{S2}LVOL + a_{S3}LPRI + a_{S4}LVAR + e_{TC},$$

$$LANAL = a_{A0} + a_{A1}LTC + a_{A2}LVAR + a_{A3}LSIZE + a_{A4}LPRI$$

$$+ \sum_{i=1}^{5} a_{Ai+4}IND_i + a_{A10}LNINST + a_{A11}LPINST + e_{ANAL},$$

$$LVOL = a_{V0} + a_{V1}LTC + a_{V2}LANAL + a_{V3}LSIZE + e_{VOL}.$$

The equation for $LANAL$ is not identified.
$LTC_{GH} \equiv \log(\lambda_{GH}/PRI)$ and $LTC_{MS} \equiv \log(\lambda_{MS}/PRI)$ are the logs of the adverse selection costs of transacting. PRI is the average daily closing price.

λ_{GH} is the estimate of the inverse of market depth from the Glosten–Harris specification:

$$\Delta p_t = \lambda q_t + \psi[D_t - D_{t-1}] + y_t;$$

λ_{MS} is the estimate of the inverse of market depth from the Madhavan–Smidt model specification:

$$\Delta p_t = \lambda q_t + \frac{\psi}{\pi} D_t - \psi D_{t-1} + \eta_t.$$

Δp_t is the price change at transaction t, q_t is the signed trade size, D_t is a dummy variable that is equal to $+1$ for a trade classified as a buy and -1 for a sell, and y_t and η_t are error terms. The Glosten–Harris model is estimated assuming that y_t is i.i.d., while the Madhavan–Smidt model is estimated assuming that η_t is MA(1). The sample consists of 1,421 stocks continuously listed on the NYSE for the year 1988 for which complete data were available on institutional holdings as of December 1987 and for which nonnegative estimates of market depth were obtained.

The other variables are defined as follows: $LANAL$ is the logarithm of one plus the number of analysts as of December 1987, $LVOL$ is the logarithm of the average daily trading volume in 1988, $LPRI$ is the logarithm of the average daily closing price during 1988, $LVAR$ is the logarithm of the daily return variance during 1988, and $LSIZE$ is the logarithm of the average daily market value of equity in 1988. $LINST$ and $LPINST$ are logarithms of the number of institutions holding the stock and the percentage of shares held by institutions as of December 1987. IND_i is a dummy variable corresponding to one of five industry classifications, which are obtained using COMPUSTAT tapes and which follow Bhushan (1989).

The t-statistics are in parentheses.

Equation	(13)	(15)	(13)	(15)
Dependent variable	LTC_{GH}	$LVOL$	LTC_{MS}	$LVOL$
Constant	2.300	4.113	− 1.444	5.214
	(5.51)	(9.64)	(2.78)	(7.78)
LANAL	− 0.169	0.897	− 0.258	0.990
	(3.13)	(13.31)	(3.82)	(13.99)
LVOL	− 0.888		− 0.598	
	(26.05)		(14.08)	

Table 2 (continued)

Equation	(13)	(15)	(13)	(15)
Dependent variable	LTC_{GH}	$LVOL$	LTC_{MS}	$LVOL$
LPRI	0.275 (6.42)	−0.907 (15.80)	0.049 (0.92)	−0.919 (18.84)
LVAR	0.638 (18.40)		0.528 (12.23)	
LSIZE		0.615 (12.49)		0.673 (14.53)
LTC_{MS}				0.183 (0.98)
LTC_{GH}		0.023 (0.32)		
R^2	0.75	0.68	0.58	0.63

Admati–Pfleiderer (1988) model and of the Subrahmanyam (1991) model (which incorporates risk aversion) when the number of informed traders is large, that market depth increases with the number of informed traders. The effect of trading volume on LTC is negative, which confirms the intuition that active markets will be deep, and is consistent with prior empirical findings on analyses of the determinants of the bid–ask spread (Branch and Freed, 1977; Stoll, 1978). The coefficient of the log of the stock price ($LPRI$) is positive for both regressions and significant for the LTC_{GH} regression. In interpreting these coefficients it is helpful to bear in mind that, while the marginal cost of transacting for a given number of shares, n, is proportional to λ/PRI, the marginal cost of transacting for a given *dollar* volume, $v \equiv n \ PRI$, is proportional to λ/PRI^2.[4] Thus, while the coefficient of $LTC \equiv \log(\lambda/PRI)$ is positive, it is less than one in all of the regressions, implying that while the marginal cost of transacting for a given *number of shares* is increasing in the share price, the marginal cost for a given *dollar* transaction is decreasing in the share price. Since the value of a transaction is a more natural measure of size than the number of shares involved, the coefficient estimates in the LTC regressions are consistent with the intuition that markets in high-priced stocks are more liquid. Finally, the coefficient of the log of the daily return variance ($LVAR$) is positive and highly

---

[4]The total cost for trading $v = qP$ dollars can be written as $\lambda(v/P)^2$. The marginal cost per dollar for trading v dollars in therefore $2\lambda v/P^2$.

significant in both regressions, consistent with the intuition that adverse selection costs will tend to be higher for stocks for which the flow of new information is higher, and also consistent with Glosten and Harris (1988).

In the *LVOL* regressions, the log trading volume is strongly positively related both to *LANAL*, the log number of analysts, and to *LSIZE*. The former relation suggests that security analysts are able to generate trading volume by their activities, consistent with the notion that security analysts tend to be employed by brokerage houses who benefit from the commissions from the additional trading generated by their analysts. The latter relation is consistent with intuition that the greater the size of the firm, the larger will tend to be the number of shareholders and the volume of noise trading. The coefficients of *LPRI* are close to (but significantly different from) − 1; a value of − 1 would imply that it is the *dollar* volume of trading that is determined by the other variables in the equation. The coefficient of *LTC* in these regressions is positive but it not strongly significant.

It is unclear *a priori* whether the institutional ownership variables that appear in the equation for *LANAL* should also be included in the equations for *LTC* and *LVOL*. (Note that inclusion of these variables in the *LVOL* equation alone will not influence the estimates of the *LTC* equation, as the ownership variables already appear as regressors in the system.) To check for robustness we reestimate the above equation system including *LNINST* and *LPINST* as explanatory variables in both the *LTC* and the *LVOL* equations. The coefficient of *LANAL* remains negative and significant in both the *LTC* and the *LVOL* equations. These results are not reported here for reasons of brevity.

To assess the robustness of the results to the empirical specification of λ we repeat the analysis with λ estimated by yet a third approach suggested by Foster and Viswanathan (1993) (based in turn on Hasbrouck, 1991). The Foster–Viswanathan approach estimates λ by measuring the price response to the *unexpected* component of the order flow. The idea is that if trades are autocorrelated or predictable from past price changes, then part of the current order flow is predictable and should not be included in measuring the information content of a trade. The approach involves first regressing the current order flow on lagged previous order flows and prices. The current price change is then modeled as a linear function of the residual from the order flow regression and the current trade sign minus the lagged trade sign. Finally, the parameter is measured as the coefficient (in the price change regression) of the residual from the order flow regression (see Foster and Viswanathan, 1993, for a detailed exposition and application of this approach). Table 3 provides the two-stage least-squares estimates of the parameters of the identified equations when *LTC* is computed using the Foster–Viswanathan estimator of λ (five lags of trades and prices are used, as in Foster and Viswanathan, 1993). The results are very similar to those for the Glosten–Harris and Madhavan–Smidt specifications; in particular, the magnitude of the *LANAL* coefficient is very close to the corresponding values in Table 2, and remains negative and significant. It thus appears that our results are robust across these three different empirical approaches to estimating λ. As the theoretical models predict, the number of analysts following a stock has a significantly negative effect on the adverse selection cost of transacting in the stock.

Table 3
Two-stage least-squares estimates of determinants of adverse selection cost of transacting, using the Foster–Viswanathan empirical measure of λ:

$$LTC = a_{S0} + a_{S1}LANAL + a_{S2}LVOL + a_{S3}LPRI + a_{S4}LVAR + e_{TC},$$

$$LANAL = a_{A0} + a_{A1}LTC + a_{A2}LVAR + a_{A3}LSIZE + a_{A4}LPRI$$

$$+ \sum_{i=1}^{5} a_{Ai+4}IND_i + a_{A10}LNINST + a_{A11}LPINST + e_{ANAL},$$

$$LVOL = a_{V0} + a_{V1}LTC + a_{V2}LANAL + a_{V3}LSIZE + e_{VOL}.$$

The equation for $LANAL$ is not identified.
$LTC_{FV} \equiv \log(\lambda_{FV}/PRI)$ is the log of the adverse selection costs of transacting. PRI is the average daily closing price.

λ_{FV} is the estimate of the inverse of market depth from the Foster–Viswanathan specification:

$$q_t = \alpha + \sum_{j=1}^{5} \beta_j \Delta p_{t-j} + \sum_{k=1}^{5} \gamma_k q_{t-k} + \tau_t, \qquad \Delta p_t = \zeta + \lambda \tau_t + \psi[D_t - D_{t-1}] + \varepsilon_t.$$

Δp_t is the price change at transaction t, q_t is the signed trade size, and D_t is a dummy variable that is equal to $+1$ for a trade classified as a buy and -1 for a sell. The sample consists of 1,421 stocks continuously listed on the NYSE for the year 1988 for which complete data were available on institutional holdings as of December 1987 and for which nonnegative estimates of market depth were obtained.

The other variables are defined as follows: $LANAL$ is the logarithm of one plus the number of analysts as of December 1987, $LVOL$ is the logarithm of the average daily trading volume in 1988, $LPRI$ is the logarithm of the average daily closing price during 1988, $LVAR$ is the logarithm of the daily return variance during 1988, $LSIZE$ is the logarithm of the average daily market value of equity in 1988. $LINST$ and $LPINST$ are logarithms of the number of institutions holding the stock and the percentage of shares held by institutions as of December 1987. IND_i is a dummy variable corresponding to one of five industry classifications, which are obtained using COMPUSTAT tapes and which follow Bhushan (1989).

The t-statistics are in parentheses.

Equation	(13)	(15)
Dependent variable	LTC_{FV}	$LVOL$
Constant	− 2.000	4.257
	(4.69)	(9.58)
$LANAL$	− 0.185	0.917
	(3.35)	(13.58)

Table 3 (continued)

Equation	(13)	(15)
Dependent variable	LTC_{FV}	$LVOL$
$LVOL$	-0.857	
	(24.59)	
$LPRI$	0.279	-0.920
	(6.36)	(16.16)
$LVAR$	0.643	
	(18.16)	
$LSIZE$		0.630
		(12.91)
LTC_{FV}		0.052
		(0.70)
R^2	0.73	0.67

5.2. Structural estimation of the Admati–Pfleiderer model of endogenous information acquisition

While the two-stage least-squares parameter estimates reported above are consistent with the coefficient sign predictions of current theoretical models, they do not take into account the functional form of the equation for λ implied by the Admati–Pfleiderer Eq. (2) or the determinants of the number of analysts implied by the equilibrium condition (3). Therefore, we turn now to estimates of the structural parameters of the Admati–Pfleiderer model represented by Eqs. (2) and (3).

Dividing both sides of Eq. (2) by the stock price P, we obtain

$$\lambda/P = \frac{\sqrt{n}}{n+1} \sqrt{\frac{\mathrm{var}(R)}{\mathrm{var}(z)}}, \tag{16}$$

where R is the rate of return on the security. Transforming Eq. (3), we obtain

$$\frac{P^2 \, \mathrm{var}(R)}{(1+n)^2 \lambda} = c. \tag{17}$$

We use PRI, the average daily closing price, as a measure of P. Taking logarithms of (16) and (17), defining a new variable, $LINF$, as

$$LINF = \log[\sqrt{n}/(n+1)],$$

recognizing that $LTC = \log(\lambda/PRI)$, and adding error terms to the two equations, the empirical version of the Admati–Pfleiderer model may be written as the following equation system:

$$LTC = a_0 + a_1 LINF + a_2 LSIGR + a_3 \log[\sigma(z)] + e_1, \tag{18}$$

$$\log(1 + n) = b_0 + b_1 LTC + b_2 LSIGR + b_3 LPRI - \log c + e_n, \tag{19}$$

where $LSIGR$ denotes the logarithm of the standard deviation of the rate of return. For empirical purposes, $\log c$, the logarithm of the cost of becoming informed, is assumed to be a function of firm size and industry classification:

$$\log c = k_0 + k_1 LSIZE + \sum_{i=1}^{5} IND_i .$$

The theoretical Admati–Pfleiderer specification implies that $a_0 = b_0 = 0$, $a_1 = a_2 = 1$, $a_3 = -1$, $b_1 = = -0.5$, $b_2 = 1$, and $b_3 = 0.5$.[5] Consistent with our previous specification, n is set equal to one plus the number of analysts reported by I/B/E/S. The log standard deviation of noise trading, $\log[\sigma(z)]$, is initially proxied by $LSIGVOL$, the logarithm of the standard deviation of daily trading volume.

The nonlinear two-stage least-squares estimates of Eq. (18) and (19) are presented in Table 4 for the two definitions of LTC. (The coefficients of the industry dummy variables are not reported to conserve space.) Considering first Eq. (18) for LTC, the coefficients of all three explanatory variables have the predicted sign and are significantly different from zero, except for $LINF$ in the LTC_{GH} specification which is only weakly significant. More importantly, the coefficients are of the predicted order of magnitude; thus the coefficients of $LSIGVOL$ and $LSIGR$ are within about 30% of their predicted values for both specifications and, while the coefficients of $LINF$ conform less well to the theoretical specification, they have high standard errors.

The signs of the coefficient estimates for Eq. (19), which explains the number of analysts, are also consistent with the model predictions and are significantly different from zero. Although the determinants of analyst following are not the primary focus of this paper, it is interesting to note that LTC has a significant negative influence on the number of analysts following a stock, as the Admati–Pfleiderer model predicts. While the estimates of b_1, b_2, and b_3 are significantly different from their theoretical values, they are of the right order of magnitude.

Since the standard deviation of daily volume is an imperfect proxy for $\sigma(z)$, the standard deviation of noise trading, Eq. (18) was reestimated by nonlinear

---

[5]Note that a positive value of a_1 implies that an increase in the number of analysis, holding constant the other explanatory variables in Eq. (18), will reduce the adverse selection cost variable $\log(\lambda/PRI)$.

Table 4
Nonlinear two-stage least-squares estimates of two-equation Admati–Pfleiderer model using standard deviation of daily trading volume as proxy for standard deviation of noise trading:

$$LTC = a_0 + a_1 LINF + a_2 LSIGR + a_3 LSIGVOL + e_1,$$

$$\log(1 + n) = b_0 + b_1 LTC + b_2 LSIGR + b_3 LPRI + k_1 LSIZE + \sum_{i=1}^{5} IND_i + e_n.$$

LTC denotes the logarithm of the adverse selection cost of transacting, $\log(\lambda/PRI)$, where λ is estimated for a sample of 1,421 NYSE stocks using the Glosten–Harris and Madhavan–Smidt methods and PRI is the average daily closing price in 1988. $LINF$ is defined as $LINF = \log[\sqrt{n}/(n + 1)]$, where n is one plus the number of analysts as of December 1987. $LSIGR$ is the logarithm of the standard deviation of the rate of return in 1988, $LSIGVOL$ is the logarithm of the standard deviation of daily volume in 1988, $LPRI$ is the logarithm of the average daily closing price in 1988, $LSIZE$ is the logarithm of the average daily market value of equity in 1988. IND_i is a dummy variable corresponding to one of five industry classifications, which are obtained using COMPUSTAT tapes and which follow Bhushan (1989) (the coefficients on these variables are not reported for brevity).

The t-statistics in parentheses are asymptotic ones for testing whether the relevant coefficient is significantly different from zero. Theoretical values of the coefficients are shown in bold brackets.

Equation	(18)	(19)	(18)	(19)
Dependent variable	LTC_{GH}	$\log(1 + n)$	LTC_{MS}	$\log(1 + n)$
Constant	4.044 (5.19) [0.0]	− 1.912 (6.59)	1.765 (1.42) [0.0]	− 2.728 (7.47)
LINF	1.168 (1.87) [1.0]		4.276 (2.47) [1.0]	
LTC_{MS}				− 0.358 (13.36) [−0.5]
LTC_{GH}		− 0.307 (15.27) [−0.5]		
LSIGR	0.869 (12.08) [1.0]	0.431 (6.33) [1.0]	0.720 (9.39) [1.0]	0.467 (5.94) [1.0]
LSIGVOL	− 1.028 (10.99) [−1.0]		− 0.657 (7.46) [−1.0]	
LPRI		0.322 (7.39) [0.5]		0.210 (4.44) [0.5]
LSIZE		0.081 (4.11)		0.120 (5.88)
R^2	0.75	0.46	0.55	0.27

two-stage least squares with $LSIZE$ replacing $LSIGVOL$ as a proxy for $\log[\sigma(z)]$. [Note that Eq. (19) is now underidentified.] The results, which are given in Table 5, show that the coefficient of $LINF$ is now significantly different from zero and of the correct sign for both empirical LTC specifications. This finding is consistent with the results reported in Section 5.1 in that an increase in the number of analysts reduces the adverse selection cost of transacting, other things equal. In accordance with the role of $LSIZE$ as a proxy for noise trading, its coefficient is negative and significantly different from zero. Though the

Table 5
Nonlinear two-stage least-squares estimates of the first equation of the Admati–Pfleiderer model using firm size as a proxy for variance of noise trading:

$$LTC = a_0 + a_1 LINF + a_2 LSIGR + a_3 LSIZE + e_1 ,$$

$$\log(1 + n) = b_0 + b_1 LTC + b_2 LSIGR + b_3 LPRI + k_1 LSIZE + \sum_{i=1}^{5} IND_i + e_n .$$

LTC denotes the logarithm of the adverse selection cost of transacting, $\log(\lambda/PRI)$, where λ is estimated for a sample of 1,421 NYSE stocks using the Glosten–Harris and Madhavan–Smidt methods and PRI is the average daily closing price in 1988. $LINF$ is defined as $LINF = \log[\sqrt{n}/(n + 1)]$, as where n is one plus the number of analysts as of December 1987. $LSIGR$ is the logarithm of the standard deviation of the rate of return in 1988, $LPRI$ is the logarithm of the average daily closing price in 1988, $LSIZE$ is the logarithm of the average daily market value of equity in 1988. IND_i is a dummy variable corresponding to one of five industry classifications, which are obtained using COMPUSTAT tapes and which follow Bhushan (1989) (the coefficients on these variables are not reported for brevity).

Parameter estimates are given for only the first equation since the second is underidentified. The t-statistics in parentheses are asymptotic ones for testing whether the relevant coefficient is significantly different from zero. Theoretical values of the coefficients are shown in bold brackets.

	LTC_{GH}	LTC_{MS}
Constant	− 4.033	− 5.309
	(12.87)	(15.64)
	[0.0]	**[0.0]**
$LINF$	1.139	2.208
	(2.90)	(5.19)
	[1.0]	**[1.0]**
$LSIGR$	0.136	0.321
	(1.69)	(3.68)
	[1.0]	**[1.0]**
$LSIZE$	− 0.539	− 0.251
	(8.69)	(3.74)
	[−0.0]	**[−0.0]**
R^2	0.59	0.45

Table 6
Nonlinear two-stage least-squares robustness test of two-equation Admati–Pfleiderer model using standard deviation of daily trading volume as a proxy for standard deviation of noise trading:

$$LTC = a_0 + a_1 LINF + a_2 LSIGR + a_3 LSIGVOL + e_1,$$

$$\log(1 + n) = b_0 + b_1 LTC + b_2 LSIGR + b_3 LPRI + b_4 LNINST$$

$$+ b_5 LPINST + k_1 LSIZE + \sum_{i=1}^{5} IND_i + e_n.$$

LTC denotes the logarithm of the adverse selection cost of transacting, $\log(\lambda/PRI)$, where λ is estimated for a sample of 1,421 NYSE stocks using the Glosten–Harris and Madhavan–Smidt methods and PRI is the average daily closing price in 1988. $LINF$ is defined as $LINF = \log[\sqrt{n}(n + 1)]$, where n is one plus the number of analysts as of December 1987. $LSIGR$ is the logarithm of the standard deviation of the rate of return in 1988, $LSIGVOL$ is the logarithm of the standard deviation of daily volume in 1988, $LPRI$ is the logarithm of the average daily closing price in 1988, $LNINST$ is the logarithm of number of insitutions holding the stock as of December 1987, $LPINST$ is the logarithm of the percentage of the firm held by institutions as of December 1987, $LSIZE$ is the logarithm of the average daily market value of equity in 1988. IND_i is a dummy variable corresponding to one of five industry classifications, which are obtained using COMPUSTAT tapes and which follow Bhushan (1989) (the coefficients on these variables are not reported for brevity).

The t-statistics in parentheses are asymptotic ones for testing whether the relevant coefficient is significantly different from zero.

Equation	(18)	(19)	(18)	(19)
Dependent variable	LTC_{GH}	$\log(1 + n)$	LTC_{MS}	$\log(1 + n)$
Constant	4.785	− 0.701	3.402	− 0.858
	(6.77)	(2.52)	(3.03)	(2.94)
LINF	1.594		3.820	
	(2.26)		(2.84)	
LTC		− 0.099		− 0.100
		(4.80)		(4.78)
LSIGR	0.880	0.130	0.831	0.140
	(16.57)	(2.14)	(13.63)	(2.26)
LSIGVOL	− 1.072		− 0.834	
	(15.49)		(11.35)	
LPRI		− 0.001		− 0.034
		(0.02)		(0.81)
LSIZE		0.017		0.032
		(0.38)		(0.73)
LNINST		0.464		0.474
		(6.78)		(6.84)
LPINST		0.119		0.122
		(2.43)		(2.43)
R^2	0.76	0.67	0.59	0.66

coefficient of $LSIGR$ is of the right sign in both regressions, it is significantly different from zero only in the LTC_{MS} regression.

As a further check on the robustness of the results, the two institutional ownership variables, $LNINST$ and $LPINST$, are included in Eq. (19) for analyst following, with the results shown in Table 6.[6] While there is no substantive change in the estimated coefficients for Eq. (18) for LTC, both institutional ownership variables enter significantly in Eq. (19) for the number of analysts, and the R^2 for this equation is considerably higher than the corresponding R^2 in Table 4. Thus, the Admati–Pfleiderer model, although it fares surprisingly well when taken as a literal description of the market for information, and in particular as a model of the adverse selection cost of trading, appears to be too simple to capture all the institutional features of the market for information that affect the number of analysts following a stock; some of these are considered in the informal model of Bhushan (1989).

6. Summary and conclusions

Identification of the cross-sectional determinants of the depth of securities markets is of importance from both an academic and a practical standpoint. Recent models of price formation predict that an important determinant of market depth, which is inversely related to the adverse selection costs of trading, is the number of investors with superior information about the security. The analysis of Admati and Pfleiderer (1988), which assumes short-lived information, suggests that market depth will improve with an increase in the number of informed traders. When information is long-lived, the dynamic model of Holden and Subrahmanyam (1992) implies that the effect of the number of informed investors on market depth will be time-varying, and that depth will improve on average with the number of informed investors.

A simple measure of the number of informed investors in a stock is the number of security analysts who are following the company. In this paper we advance the empirical literature on the determinants of market depth by using intraday data to investigate the relation between the number of analysts and the estimated adverse selection costs of transacting, holding constant previously identified determinants of market liquidity. Consistent with the analysis of Admati and Pfleiderer (1988), the estimated adverse selection cost decreases with the number of analysts, other things equal. In addition, structural estimates of

---

[6]We do not report the estimates of the parameters in Eqs. (18) and (19) for the Foster–Viswanathan specification as the manner in which their measure is estimated is not within the spirit of the Kyle–Admati–Pfleiderer framework. However, qualitatively similar results were obtained using the Foster–Viswanathan specification as well.

the Admati–Pfleiderer model of endogenous information acquisition are consistent with the model. The results support the notion that an increase in analyst coverage leads to deeper markets because of enhanced competition between informed agents.

References

Admati, Anat R. and Paul Pfleiderer, 1988, A theory of intraday patterns: Volume and price variability, Review of Financial Studies 1, 3–40.

Amihud, Yakov and Haim Mendelson, 1986, Asset pricing and the bid–ask spread, Journal of Financial Economics 17, 223–249.

Arbel, Avner, Steven Carvell, and Paul Strebel, 1983, Giraffes, institutions, and neglected firms, Financial Analysts Journal 39, 57–63.

Benston, George and Robert Hagerman, 1974, Determinants of bid–ask spreads in the over-the-counter market, Journal of Financial Economics 1, 353–364.

Bhushan, Ravi, 1989, Firm characteristics and analyst following, Journal of Accounting and Economics 11, 255–274.

Branch, Ben and Walter Freed, 1977, Bid–asked spreads on the AMEX and the big board, Journal of Finance 32, 159–163.

Brennan, Michael J., Narasimhan Jegadeesh, and Bhaskaran Swaminathan, 1993, Investment analysis and the adjustment of stock prices to common information, Review of Financial Studies 6, 799–824.

Foster, F. Douglas and S. Viswanathan, 1993, Variations in trading volume, return volatility, and trading costs: Evidence on recent price formation models, Journal of Finance 48, 187–211.

George, Thomas, Gautam Kaul, and M. Nimalendran, 1991, Estimating the components of the bid–ask spread: A new approach, Review of Financial Studies 4, 623–656.

Glosten, Lawrence and Lawrence Harris, 1988, Estimating the components of the bid–ask spread, Journal of Financial Economics 21, 123–142.

Hasbrouck, Joel, 1991, Measuring the information content of stock trades, Journal of Finance 46, 179–207.

Holden, Craig W. and Avanidhar Subrahmanyam, 1992, Long-lived private information and imperfect competition, Journal of Finance 47, 247–270.

Kyle, Albert S., 1984, Market structure, information, futures markets, and price formation, in: Gary G. Storey, Andrew Schmitz, and Alexander S. Sarris, International agricultural trade: Advanced readings in price formation, market structure, and price instability (Westview Press, Boulder, CT) 45–64.

Kyle, Albert S., 1985, Continuous auctions and insider trading, Econometrica 53, 1315–1335.

Lee, Charles M.C. and Mark Ready, 1991, Inferring trade direction from intradaily data, Journal of Finance 46, 733–746.

Madhavan, Ananth and Seymour Smidt, 1991, A Bayesian model of intraday specialist pricing, Journal of Financial Economics 30, 99–134.

Stoll, Hans R., 1978, The pricing of dealer services: An empirical study of NASDAQ stocks, Journal of Finance 33, 1152–1173.

Stoll, Hans R., 1989, Inferring the components of the bid–ask spread, Journal of Finance 44, 115–134.

Subrahmanyam, Avanidhar, 1991, Risk aversion, market liquidity, and price efficiency, Review of Financial Studies 3, 417–441.

23

ELSEVIER   Journal of Financial Economics 49 (1998) 345–373

Alternative factor specifications, security characteristics, and the cross-section of expected stock returns[1]

Michael J. Brennan[a,b], Tarun Chordia[c], Avanidhar Subrahmanyam[d,*]

[a] *Anderson Graduate School of Management, University of California-Los Angeles, Los Angeles, CA 90095, USA*
[b] *London Business School, Sussex Place, Regents Park, London, NWI 4SA, UK*
[c] *Owen Graduate School of Management, Vanderbilt University, Nashville, TN 37203, USA*
[d] *Anderson Graduate School of Management, University of California at Los Angeles, Los Angeles, CA 90095, USA*

Received 2 December 1996; received in revised form 17 December 1997

Abstract

We examine the relation between stock returns, measures of risk, and several non-risk security characteristics, including the book-to-market ratio, firm size, the stock price, the dividend yield, and lagged returns. Our primary objective is to determine whether non-risk characteristics have marginal explanatory power relative to the arbitrage pricing theory benchmark, with factors determined using, in turn, the Connor and Korajczyk (CK; 1988) and the Fama and French (FF; 1993b) approaches. Fama–Mac-Beth-type regressions using risk adjusted returns provide evidence of return momentum, size, and book-to-market effects, together with a significant and negative relation between returns and trading volume, even after accounting for the CK factors. When the analysis is repeated using the FF factors, we find that the size and book-to-market effects are attenuated, while the momentum and trading volume effects persist. In addition, Nasdaq stocks show significant underperformance after adjusting for risk using either method. © 1998 Elsevier Science S.A. All rights reserved.

JEL classification: G12; G14

Keywords: Asset pricing; Anomalies; Risk factors

* Corresponding author. Tel.: 310/825-5355; fax: 310/206-5455; e-mail: subra@anderson.ucla.edu.

[1] We are especially grateful to Eugene Fama (a referee), an anonymous referee and Bill Schwert (the editor) for insightful and constructive suggestions. We also thank Wayne Ferson, Ken French,

1. Introduction

Early empirical research on the determinants of expected stock returns was concerned with detecting an association between average returns on beta-sorted portfolios and their betas, as predicted by the capital asset pricing model (see, e.g., Black, et al., 1972). Subsequently, Gibbons (1982) and Stambaugh (1982) introduced statistical tests of the null hypothesis that expected returns are determined *solely* by betas.[2] Following the development of the arbitrage pricing theory (APT), a similar series of tests was conducted, in which proxies for the APT factors and factor loadings replaced the market portfolio and betas of the CAPM.[3] Starting with the work of Black and Scholes (1974), Basu (1977), and Banz (1981), researchers began to test these asset pricing models against specific alternatives; these alternative hypotheses posited that expected returns on securities, instead of being determined *solely* by the risk characteristics of the securities, as measured by betas or factor loadings, were also affected by non-risk security characteristics such as size, book-to-market ratios, dividend yields, and earnings-price ratios. The role of some of these non-risk characteristics can be accounted for by frictions within the rational pricing paradigm, or could possibly be accounted for by their statistical properties as proxies for expected returns. However, the role of some other characteristics such as firm size has remained more elusive, so that their apparent importance for expected returns leaves the empirical validity of the rational asset pricing paradigm open to question.

In an important series of papers, Fama and French (FF) (1992a, b, 1993b, 1996) have provided evidence for the continuing validity of the rational pricing paradigm by showing that, with the exception of the momentum strategy of Jegadeesh and Titman (1993, 1995), the cross-sectional variation in expected returns associated with these non-risk characteristics can be captured by only

Footnote 1 continued
Will Goetzmann, Craig Holden, Ravi Jagannathan, Bob Jennings, Bruce Lehmann, Josef Lakonishok, Richard Roll, participants at the 1997 Meetings of the Western Finance Association, the 1997 UCLA/USC/UC Irvine conference, the November 1997 Asset Pricing Meeting of the National Bureau of Economic Research, the Atlanta Forum, and seminars at Columbia, Indiana, Florida, New York, Tulane, and Yale Universities; Eugene Fama and Ken French for providing part of the data used in this study; and Christoph Schenzler for excellent programming assistance. The second author acknowledges support from the Dean's Fund for Research and the Financial Markets Research Center at Vanderbilt University. We are responsible for remaining errors. This paper was formerly titled 'A Re-Examination of Security Return Anomalies'.

[2] Gibbons (1982), Stambaugh (1982).

[3] Roll and Ross (1980), Brown and Weinstein (1983), Shanken (1987), and Lehmann and Modest (1988).

M.J. Brennan er al./Journal of Financial Economics 49 (1998) 345–373 347

two characteristics, namely the firm's size and its book-to-market ratio;[4] and that, moreover (FF, 1993b) these firm characteristics proxy for the security's loadings on priced factors. They show that the firm size and book-to-market effects can be accounted for within a three-factor model in which the factors are the returns on the market portfolio, and on two zero net-investment portfolios, one of which is long in high book-to-market and short in low book-to-market securities (HML), and the other of which is long in small firms and short in large firms (SMB).[5]

An important feature of much of this empirical research on asset pricing is that the analyzed returns are those on portfolios constructed by sorting securities on some criterion of interest. Portfolios are formed either to mitigate problems caused by using estimated betas as independent variables in a two-step estimation procedure or, when a one-step estimation procedure is used, to allow estimation of the covariance matrix of residual returns. This causes two quite different types of problem. First, as Roll (1977) has pointed out, the portfolio formation process, by concealing possibly return relevant security characteristics within portfolio averages, may make it difficult to reject the null hypothesis of no effect on security returns. Lo and MacKinlay (1990) make an almost precisely opposite point, that if the researcher forms portfolios on the basis of characteristics which prior empirical research has found to be related to average returns, he will be inclined to reject the null hypothesis too often due to a 'data-snooping' bias.[6] The resulting problem of inference is illustrated in FF (1996) and Brennan et al. (1996), who present results for six and seven sets of portfolios, respectively, and obtain quite different results depending on the criteria used in portfolio formation.

In this paper we investigate the extent to which expected returns can be explained by risk factors rather than by non-risk characteristics. Our approach differs from that of FF in three principal ways. First, rather than specifying the

---

[4] Fama and French (1992a) show that firm size and the ratio of book to market equity capture the cross-sectional relation between average returns and earnings yield and leverage.

[5] Daniel and Titman (1997) assert that portfolios of firms that have similar characteristics (size and book-to-market), but different loadings on the Fama French factors, have similar average returns, and use this finding to conclude that these security characteristics have an independent influence on expected returns.

[6] Table 5 of Lo and MacKinlay (1990) shows that if the R^2 between the sorting characteristic used to form portfolios and the estimated α's is 0.005, then the probability that a standard F-test will reject the null that the α's are jointly zero at the 5% level is 11.8% if 1000 securities are sorted into 10 portfolios of 100 securities, even though the underlying data satisfy the null hypothesis. If the R^2 is 0.01 the size of a 5% test rises to 36.7% for 1000 securities sorted into 10 portfolios of 100 securities, even though the underlying data satisfy the null hypothesis. If no portfolio aggregation had been performed the size of these tests would be 5%!

risk factors a priori, we follow the intuition of the APT, that the risk factors should be those which capture the variation of returns in large well-diversified portfolios, and use the principal components approach of Connor and Korajczyk (1988) (henceforth CK) to estimate risk factors. We then repeat the analysis using the FF (1993b) factors.[7] Thus, our null hypothesis is that expected returns are determined by the APT with risk factors obtained using the Connor and Korajczyk or the Fama and French approach. Secondly, rather than limiting ourselves to the set of firm characteristics that Fama and French have found to be associated with average returns, notably size and book-to-market ratio, we estimate simultaneously the marginal effects of eight firm characteristics, including dividend yield, and measures of market liquidity such as share price and trading volume, as well as lagged returns. We are able to consider these several characteristics simultaneously because, thirdly, instead of examining the returns on portfolios, we examine the *risk-adjusted* returns on individual securities.[8] Under the null hypothesis, these risk-adjusted returns should be independent of other (non-risk) security characteristics. Not only does this approach allow us to consider the effects of a large number of firm characteristics simultaneously, but it also avoids the data-snooping biases that are inherent in the portfolio-based approaches as discussed above.[9] Our approach also avoids the errors-in-variables bias created by errors in estimating factor loadings, since errors in the factor loadings are impounded in the dependent variable. The costs of this approach are that it imposes the assumption that the zero-beta return equals the risk-free rate, and it incorporates the prediction of the APT that the realized reward per unit of loading on a given factor is equal to the realized return on the underlying factor portfolio.

When we use only size, book-to-market, and lagged returns as the explanatory variables, we find that these variables are significantly related to expected returns even after risk-adjustment using the CK factors. When the analysis is repeated using the FF portfolios as factors, the size and book-to-market effects

---

[7] Campbell (1996), using the intuition of Merton's (1973) intertemporal CAPM, argues that 'priced factors should be found not by running a factor analysis on the covariance matrix of returns ... Instead, innovations in variables that have been found to forecast stock returns and labor income should be used'. It seems likely to us that variables that have a significant effect on the future investment opportunity set are also likely to have a significant effect on contemporaneous returns, so that their traces will be evident in the covariance matrix of returns.

[8] Papers that use risk- *unadjusted* returns for cross-sectional analyses on individual securities include FF (1992a), Litzenberger and Ramaswamy (1979), Miller and Scholes (1982), and Lehmann (1990).

[9] Of course, we are guilty of data-snooping in a different sense: The security characteristics we have chosen to consider are motivated by previous results. But we do avoid the aggravation of the problem caused by sorting to form portfolios. Ferson et al. (1998) also point out the pitfalls in using attribute sorted portfolios as risk factors.

M.J. Brennan er al./Journal of Financial Economics 49 (1998) 345–373   349

are attenuated by a factor of about 1/3, and their significance is weakened as well. Expanding the set of explanatory variables, we find that a return-momentum effect persists, and also that there is a negative and significant relation between returns and trading volume, regardless of whether the risk-adjustment is done with the CK factors or the FF factors. In addition, the introduction of trading volume makes the coefficient of the firm size variable positive and significant. The dividend yield variable is significant with the CK factors but not with the FF factors.

The fact that the 'non-risk' firm characteristics are significant explanators of the 'risk-adjusted' returns implies either that the risk adjustment is incomplete, or that returns are affected by other factors than risk. While the dividend yield effect is present only under the CK risk-adjustment procedure, the trading volume effect we find is rather robust, in that it is present for both types of risk-adjustment, as well as in risk-unadjusted returns; this supports the notion that this variable is acting as a proxy for the liquidity of the market in the firm's shares,[10] rather than as a proxy for the loading on some priced risk factor that is not included in the analysis.

In order to account for the fact that trading volume is measured differently on NYSE/AMEX and Nasdaq, we include separate variables for Nasdaq and NYSE volume. Since the Nasdaq volume is not significant and Reinganum (1990) and Loughran (1993) provide evidence of a 'Nasdaq' effect, we include a dummy variable for Nasdaq membership. We then find that dollar volume is strongly negatively associated with returns for both exchanges, but find that holding constant their factor loadings and other characteristics Nasdaq stocks *underperform* by about 10% per year.

We find that the five CK factors offer a risk-return trade-off that is comparable to that offered by the three FF factors in the sense that the overall squared Sharpe ratios are close; for both sets of factors the null hypothesis that the reward-for-risk ratio equals zero can be rejected at better than the 1% level of significance. However, our analysis suggests that the two sets of factors are not equivalent. Indeed, we find using Gibbons et al. (1989) intercept tests that neither set of factors price the other, though there is evidence that CK factors are priced better by the FF factors than are the FF factors by the CK factors.

The remainder of the paper is organized as follows. In Section 2 we describe the empirical hypotheses we test. In Section 3 the data are described and in Section 4 the statistical model is presented. In Section 5, we present the regression results, while in Section 6, we compare the FF and CK factors, and Section 7 concludes.

---

[10] Glosten and Harris (1988) and Brennan and Subrahmanyam (1995) show that trading volume is a major determinant of market liquidity.

2. Hypotheses

Our null hypothesis is an L-factor version of the APT which implies that the expected excess return on security j is determined solely by the loadings of the security's return on the L factors, $\beta_{jk}(k = 1, \ldots, L)$. Consider the following equation:

$$E(\tilde{R}_j) - R_F = c_0 + \sum_{k=1}^{L} \lambda_k \beta_{jk} + \sum_{m=1}^{M} c_m Z_{mj}, \tag{1}$$

where $\tilde{R}_j$ is the return on security j, R_F is the risk free interest rate, β_{jk} is the loading of security j on factor k, λ_k is the risk premium associated with factor k, Z_{mj} $(m = 1, \ldots, M)$ is the value of (non-risk) characteristic m for security j, and c_m is the premium per unit of characteristic m. Our null hypothesis is that $c_m = 0$ $(m = 0, 1, \ldots, M)$. We include eight non-risk security characteristics (including three momentum-based lagged return variables) as possible determinants of expected returns.

The risk factors are initially taken to be the first five (asymptotic) principal components of excess stock returns estimated over the sample period, and, in turn, the three FF factors. In deciding which non-risk firm characteristics to include as possible determinants of expected returns, attention was given to those variables that had been found to be important in prior studies, as well as those for which there exists a theoretical rationale. Thus firm size is included because of the importance of assessing whether the 'small firm effect' (see Banz, 1981; FF, 1992a) persists after accounting for the five risk factors[11] and other firm characteristics. We also include the ratio of book-to-market equity because this has been found to be strongly associated with average returns (see FF, 1992a; Lakonishok et al., 1994). It has been hypothesized that the low price effect documented by Miller and Scholes (1982) reflects the fact that firms with low prices are often in financial distress, and that financial institutions may be reluctant to invest in them on account of the prudent man rule.[12] Therefore we include the reciprocal of share price as a possible determinant of expected returns.

Amihud and Mendelson (1986) and Brennan and Subrahmanyam (1996) suggest that expected returns are affected by liquidity. Amihud and Mendelson use the bid–ask spread as a measure of liquidity. However, the spread is available only annually, and only for NYSE/AMEX stocks. Brennan and

---

[11] Lehmann and Modest (1988) found that their implementation of a five-factor APT was unable to account for the size anomaly.

[12] Falkenstein (1996) shows that mutual funds 'show an aversion to low-price stocks'.

Subrahmanyam, on the other hand, use the fixed and variable components of trading costs as measures of liquidity. Since their measures require intraday data, which is available only after 1983, their sample period is short. In our study, we include the dollar volume of trading because this variable is associated with liquidity,[13] and because Petersen and Fialkowski (1994) find that the quoted spread is only loosely associated with the effective spread; therefore it is possible that trading volume provides a better measure of liquidity than the bid-ask spread. Further, dollar volume is available monthly, and thus may allow a more powerful test of the liquidity hypothesis.

We include dividend yield because Brennan (1970) suggests that differential taxation of dividends and capital gains could make this variable relevant, and the resulting empirical work of Litzenberger and Ramaswamy (1979) and Miller and Scholes (1978, 1982) has been inconclusive. Finally, we include lagged return variables because Jegadeesh and Titman (1993) have shown these to be relevant, and by including them we should improve the efficiency of the estimates of the coefficients of the other variables.

3. Data

The basic data consist of monthly returns and other characteristics for a sample of the common stock of companies for the period January 1966 to December 1995.[14] To be included in the sample for a given month a stock had to satisfy the following criteria: (1) Its return in the current month and in 24 of the previous 60 months be available from CRSP, and sufficient data be available to calculate the size, price, dollar volume, and dividend yield as of the previous month; (2) Sufficient data be available on the COMPUSTAT tapes to calculate the book-to-market ratio as of December of the previous year. As per Fama and French (1992) we excluded financial firms from our sample. This screening process yielded an average of 2457 stocks per month.

For each stock the following variables were calculated each month as follows:

SIZE – the natural logarithm of the market value of the equity of the firm as of the end of the second to last month.

BM – the natural logarithm of the ratio of the book value of equity plus deferred taxes to the market value of equity, using the end of the previous year

---

[13] Several studies (e.g., Stoll (1978)) find trading volume to be the most important determinant of the bid-ask spread, and Brennan and Subrahmanyam (1995) find that it is a major determinant of their measure of liquidity.

[14] The observation period began in January 1966 because the FF factors are available only from July 1963 onwards, and we required enough lag time to allow loadings to be estimated reliably from past factor realizations.

market and book values. As in FF (1992a), the value of BM for July of year t to June of year $t + 1$ was computed using accounting data at the end of year $t - 1$, and book-to-market ratio values greater than the 0.995 fractile or less than the 0.005 fractile were set equal to the 0.995 and 0.005 fractile values, respectively.

DVOL – the natural logarithm of the dollar volume of trading in the security in the second to last month.

PRICE – the natural logarithm of the reciprocal of the share price as reported at the end of the second to last month.

YLD – the dividend yield as measured by the sum of all dividends paid over the previous 12 months, divided by the share price at the end of the second to last month.

RET2–3 – the natural logarithm of the cumulative return over the two months ending at the beginning of the previous month.

RET4–6 – the natural logarithm of the cumulative return over the three months ending three months previously.

RET7–12 – the natural logarithm of the cumulative return over the 6 months ending 6 months previously.

The lagged return variables were constructed to exclude the return during the immediate prior month in order to avoid any spurious association between the prior month return and the current month return caused by thin trading or bid–ask spread effects. In addition, all variables involving the price level were lagged by one additional month in order to preclude the possibility that a linear combination of the lagged return variables, the book-to-market variable (which is related to the price level in the previous year), and the reciprocal of the price level could provide a noisy estimate of the return in the previous month, thus leading to biases because of bid-ask effects and thin trading.[15]

Table 1 reports the time-series averages of the cross-sectional means, medians, and standard deviations of the raw (i.e., unlogged) security characteristics, and displays the summary statistics associated with both trimmed and untrimmed values of the book-to-market ratio.

The variables display considerable skewness. Therefore, in our empirical analysis we employ logarithmic transforms of all these variables except the dividend yield (which may be zero). Finally, for all of the regressions reported below, the transformed firm characteristics variables for a given month were expressed as deviations from their cross-sectional means for that month; this implies that the average security will have values of each non-risk characteristic that are equal to zero, so that under both the null and the alternative hypotheses its expected return will be determined solely by its risk characteristics. Table 2

---

[15] See Jegadeesh (1990). It is easy to show that thin trading will cause risk-adjusted returns to exhibit first-order negative serial correlation.

M.J. Brennan er al./Journal of Financial Economics 49 (1998) 345–373 353

Table 1
Summary statistics

The summary statistics represent the time-series averages of cross-sectional means for an average of 2457 stocks over 360 months from Jan. 1966 through Dec. 1995. Each stock satisfies the following criteria: (1) Its return in the current month and in 24 of the previous 60 months be available from CRSP, and sufficient data be available to calculate the size, price, dollar volume, and dividend yield as of the previous month; and (2) Sufficient data be available on the COMPUSTAT tapes to calculate the book to market ratio as of December of the previous year. The row titled book-to-market ratio (trimmed) provides summary statistics for the book-to-market ratio after values greater than the 0.995 fractile or less than the 0.005 fractile are set to equal the 0.995 and 0.005 fractile values, respectively.

Variable	Mean	Median	Std. Dev.
Firm size ($ billion)	0.436	0.061	0.099
Book-to-market ratio	2.074	0.836	0.715
Book-to-market ratio (trimmed)	1.250	0.836	0.534
Dollar-trading-volume ($ million per month)	17.627	1.925	13.014
Share price ($)	19.804	15.039	6.767
Dividend yield (%)	2.51	1.67	0.950

reports the averages of the month by month cross-sectional correlations of the transformed variables that we use in our analysis. The largest correlations are between SIZE and DVOL and SIZE and PRICE. The other correlations are smaller than 0.40 in absolute value.

The five CK factors were estimated by the asymptotic principal components technique developed by Connor and Korajczyk (1988)[16] applied to returns in excess of the risk-free rate on all securities listed continuously over the estimation period, where the risk-free rate was taken as the 1 month risk free rate from the CRSP bond files. In order to keep the estimation process computationally manageable, the factors were estimated separately over each of two over-lapping subperiods: July 1963 to December 1979 and January 1975 to December 1995. The three FF factors are the market portfolio, SMB which is intended to mimick the performance of a portfolio that is long in small firms and short in large firms, and HML which is intended to mimic the performance of a portfolio which is

---

[16] Connor and Korajczyk (1993) 'find evidence for one to six pervasive factors generating returns on the NYSE and AMEX over the period 1967 to 1991'.

Table 2
Correlation matrix of transformed firm characteristics

This table presents time-series of monthly cross-sectional correlations between the transformed firm characteristics used in pricing regressions. The variable relate to an average of 2457 stock over 360 months from Jan 1966 through Dec. 1995. RETURN denotes the excess monthly return, i.e., the raw return less the risk-free return. SIZE represents to logarithm of the market capitalization on of firms in billions of dollars. BM is the logarithm of the ratio of book value of equity plus deferred taxes to market capitalization, with the expection that book-to-market ratio values greater than the 0.995 fracticle or less than the 0.005 fractile are set to equal the 0.995 and 0.005 fracticle values, respectively. DVOL is the logarithm of the dollar trading volume. PRICE is the logarithm of the reciprocal of the share price. YLD is the logarithm of the dividend yield; RET2–3, RET4–6, RET7–12 equal the logarithms of the cumulative returns over the second through third, fourth through sixth, and seventh through 12th months prior to the current month, respectively.

	RETURN	SIZE	BM	DVOL	PRICE	YLD	RET2–3	RET4–6	RET7–12
RETURN	1.00	− 0.010	0.030	− 0.006	0.004	0.007	0.009	0.018	0.024
SIZE	− 0.010	1.00	− 0.238	0.753	− 0.790	0.084	0.011	0.013	0.017
BM	0.030	− 0.238	1.00	− 0.146	0.158	0.144	− 0.015	0.040	0.047
DVOL	− 0.006	0.753	− 0.146	1.00	− 0.387	0.028	0.048	0.049	0.067
PRICE	0.004	− 0.790	0.156	− 0.387	1.00	− 0.196	− 0.188	− 0.127	− 0.145
YLD	0.007	0.084	0.144	0.028	− 0.196	1.00	− 0.044	− 0.043	− 0.042
RET2–3	0.009	0.011	− 0.015	0.048	− 0.188	− 0.044	1.00	− 0.005	0.030
RET4–6	0.018	0.013	0.040	0.049	− 0.127	− 0.043	− 0.005	1.00	0.038
RET7–12	0.024	0.017	0.047	0.067	− 0.145	− 0.042	0.030	0.038	1.00

long high book-to-market equity firms and short low book-to-market equity firms.[17]

4. Statistical model

As we have argued above, empirical findings based on the returns on *port-folios* are hard to interpret. Therefore, we report the results from analyzing the returns on individual securities. The null hypothesis against which we evaluate the influence of the non-risk security characteristics is an L-factor APT.

---

[17] As noted in Footnote 14, the FF factors are available only from July 1963 onwards. This is why we start the estimation period for the CK factors in July 1963 as well.

Thus, assume that returns are generated by an L-factor approximate factor model:[18]

$$\tilde{R}_{jt} = E(\tilde{R}_{jt}) + \sum_{k=1}^{L} \beta_{jk}\tilde{f}_{kt} + \tilde{e}_{jt}. \tag{2}$$

Then the exact or equilibrium version of the APT, in which the market portfolio is well-diversified with respect to the factors (Connor, 1984; Shanken, 1985, 1987), implies that expected returns may be written as

$$E[\tilde{R}_{jt}] - R_{Ft} = \sum_{k=1}^{L} \lambda_{kt}\beta_{jk}, \tag{3}$$

where R_{Ft} is the return on the riskless asset, and λ_{kt} is the risk premium for factor k. Substituting from Eq. (3) in Eq. (2), the APT implies that realized returns are given by

$$\tilde{R}_{jt} - R_{Ft} = \sum_{k=1}^{L} \beta_{jk}\tilde{F}_{kt} + \tilde{e}_{jt}, \tag{4}$$

where $\tilde{F}_{kt} \equiv \lambda_{kt} + \tilde{f}_{kt}$ is the sum of the factor realization and its associated risk premium. Our goal is to test whether security characteristics have incremental explanatory power for returns relative to the five-factor CK benchmark or the three-factor FF benchmark.

A standard application of the Fama–MacBeth (1973) procedure would involve estimation of the following equation:

$$\tilde{R}_{jt} - R_{Ft} = c_0 + \sum_{k=1}^{L} \beta_{jk}\tilde{f}_{kt} + \sum_{m=1}^{M} c_m Z_{mjt} + \tilde{e}_{jt}, \tag{5}$$

where Z_{mjt} is the value of characteristic m for security j in month t. Under the null hypothesis that expected returns depend only on the risk characteristics of the returns, as represented by β_{jk}, the loadings on the CK or FF factors, the coefficients c_m ($m = 1, \ldots, M$) will be equal to zero. This hypothesis can be tested in principle by estimating the factor loadings for each month using prior data, estimating a cross-section regression for each month in which the independent variables are the factor loadings and non-risk characteristics, and then averaging the monthly coefficient estimates over time and calculating their time-series standard errors. This standard Fama–MacBeth approach, however, presents problems because the factor loadings are measured with error. One method of dealing with this measurement error problem is to use the information from the first-stage regressions (in which the factor loadings are estimated)

---

[18] See Connor and Korajczyk (1988) for the definition of an approximate factor model.

to correct the coefficient estimates in the second stage regressions.[19] Our approach to correct the bias, however, does not rely on information taken from the first stage regressions.

First, each year, from 1966 to 1995, factor loadings, β_{jk}, were estimated for all securities that had at least 24 return observations over the prior 60 months, with the qualification that since our factor estimation begins in July 1963, the factor loadings in the first month of the regression period (January 1966) were estimated from 30 observations per factor, the next month, 31, and so on till the 60 month level was reached from which point the observation interval was kept constant at 60 months.[20] In order to allow for thin trading, we used the Dimson (1979) procedure with one lag to adjust the estimated factor loadings. The estimated risk-adjusted return on each of the securities, $\tilde{R}_{jt}^*$, for each month t of the following year was then calculated as:

$$\tilde{R}_{jt}^* \equiv \tilde{R}_{jt} - R_{Ft} - \sum_{k=1}^{L} \hat{\beta}_{jk}\tilde{F}_{kt}. \tag{6}$$

As pointed out in the introduction, our risk adjustment procedure imposes the assumptions that the zero-beta equals the risk-free rate, and that the APT factor premium is equal to the excess return on the factor. The risk-adjusted returns from Eq. (6) constitute the raw material for the estimates that we present below of the equation:

$$\tilde{R}_{jt}^* = c_0 + \sum_{m=1}^{M} c_m Z_{mjt} + \tilde{e}_{jt}' \tag{7}$$

Note that the error term in Eq. (7) is different from that in Eq. (4), because the error in Eq. (7) also contains terms arising from the measurement error associated with the factor loadings. We show how this measurement error affects our estimation in the discussion that follows.

We first calculate an estimate of the vector of characteristic rewards $\hat{c}_t$ each month from a simple OLS regression:

$$\hat{c}_t = (Z_t'Z_t)^{-1}Z_t'R_t^*, \tag{8}$$

where Z_t is the vector of firm characteristics in month t and R_t^* is the vector of estimated risk-adjusted returns. Note that although the factor loadings, β_{jk}, are estimated with error, this error affects only the dependent variable, R_t^*, and

---

[19] This is the approach followed by Litzenberger and Ramaswamy (1979) and Lehmann (1990).

[20] We have one set of factors for each of the two overlapping subperiods; since there is no correspondence between factor k in the two subperiods, care was taken to ensure that the factors used for risk-adjustment were the same as those for which the factor loadings were estimated.

while the factor loadings will be correlated with the security characteristics, Z_t, there is no a priori reason to believe that errors in the estimated loadings will be correlated with the security characteristics, so the estimated coefficient vector, $\hat{c}_t$, is unbiased under the null hypothesis.

For each characteristic, m ($m = 0, 1, ..., M$) (including the constant term) the coefficient estimates, for each month from January 1966 to December 1995, are aggregated into an overall estimate in one of two ways. The first, which we call the raw estimate, is given by

$$\hat{c}_{mr} = (j'j)^{-1}j'\hat{c}_m, \tag{9}$$

where j is the unit vector and $\hat{c}_m$ is the vector of monthly estimates of c_m. Thus, Eq. (9) represents the time-series average of the coefficients associated with the characteristics: it is simply the standard Fama–MacBeth estimator except that the dependent variable is the risk-adjusted return, calculated using either the CK or the FF approach. While there is no a priori reason to believe that the errors in the estimated factor loadings will be correlated with the security characteristics, Z_t, to the extent that they are correlated, the monthly estimates of the coefficients of the firm characteristics, $\hat{c}_{mt}$, will be correlated with the factor realizations, and therefore the mean of these estimates which is the Fama–Macbeth estimator will be biased by an amount that depends on the mean factor realizations. Therefore, as a check on the robustness of our results, a purged estimator, $\hat{c}_{mp}$, was obtained for each of the characteristics as the constant term from the regression of the monthly coefficient estimates on the time series of CK or FF factor realizations. This estimator, which was first developed by Black and Scholes (1974), purges the monthly estimates of the factor dependent component, is given by

$$\hat{c}_{mp} = e'(F^{*'}F^*)^{-1}F^{*'}\hat{c}_m, \tag{10}$$

where e is a 6-element vector $[1\ 0\ 0\ 0\ 0\ 0]'$ which serves to pick out the constant of the regression, and F^* is the matrix of factor portfolio returns augmented by a vector of ones. To see that the purged estimator is unbiased even when the errors in the factor loading estimates are correlated with the characteristics, Z, denote the risk-adjusted return under the true factor loadings as $\tilde{R}_{jt}^T$. Then, from Eq. (6), we have

$$\tilde{R}_{jt}^* = \tilde{R}_{jt}^T + \sum_{k=1}^{L} \hat{u}_{jk}F_{kt},$$

where $u_{jk} \equiv \beta_{jk} - \hat{\beta}_{jk}$ is the measurement error in the kth factor loading for security j. Letting c and u be the true coefficient vector of the characteristics and the measurement error matrix, respectively, and F_t be the vector of factor observations in month t, the regression of risk-adjusted returns in month t on the security characteristics yields the following coefficient vector:

$$\hat{c}_t = c + F_t'[(Z'Z)^{-1}Z'u]_t.$$

Thus, the intercept from the regression of $\hat{c}_t$ on F_t will be an unbiased estimate of c so long as the factor realizations are serially uncorrelated.

In sum, $\hat{c}_{mr}$, represents the standard Fama–MacBeth estimator, and $\hat{c}_{mp}$ represents the constant from the OLS regression of the month-by-month Fama–MacBeth estimates on the factor portfolio returns for the purged estimator.[21] The standard error of the estimate is taken from the time series of monthly estimates in the case of the raw estimator, $\hat{c}_{mr}$, and from the standard error of the intercept from the OLS regression in the case of the purged estimator, $\hat{c}_{mp}$. As Shanken (1992) points out, the standard errors of the coefficients yielded by the standard Fama–MacBeth approach are understated because they ignore the additional variation induced by the estimation error in the factor loadings. We show in Section 6, however, that the magnitude of this understatement is small for our sample, and does not affect our basic conclusions.

5. Regression analysis

5.1. Results

To begin our analysis we present the results of Fama–MacBeth regressions of excess (risk-unadjusted) returns on characteristics which are best known to be associated with expected returns, namely, SIZE, BM, and the three lagged return variables. The results are reported in the first column of Table 3.

As can be seen, the coefficients of SIZE and BM are respectively negative and positive, and both are statistically significant, which is consistent with earlier studies such as FF (1992a). In addition, the coefficients of all of the three lagged return variables are positive, and two are strongly significant.

We now consider whether the relation between excess returns and SIZE, BM, and the lagged return variables is maintained when the returns are risk-adjusted returns using the two sets of factors. The raw and purged estimates of the characteristic rewards, $\hat{c}_{mr}$ and $\hat{c}_{mp}$, for risk-adjusted returns using the CK factors are reported in the second and third columns of Table 3. The coefficients of SIZE and BM are essentially unchanged by the risk-adjustment and are highly significant, and the coefficients of all of the three lagged return variables are positive and two of them are significant. There is little difference between the raw and purged estimates as we should expect if the factor loading errors are uncorrelated with the non-risk characteristics. For comparison, the results from

---

[21] Separate estimates are calculated corresponding to the two subperiods for which the principal components were estimated; these were then aggregated using precision weights.

Table 3
Fama–MacBeth regression estimates of Eq. (7) using individual security data

Coefficient estimates are time-series averages of cross-sectional OLS regressions. The dependent variable in the first column is simply the excess return, while in the second and third columns it is the excess returns risk-adjusted using the CK factors, and in the fourth and fifth columns it is the excess returns risk-adjusted using the FF factors (Dimson beats with one lag are used in each case). The independent variables are defined as follows; SIZE represents logarithm of the market capitalization of firms in billions of dollars. BM is the logarithm of the ratio of book value of equity plus deferred taxes to market capitalization, with the exception that book-to-market ratio values greater than the 0.995 fractile or less than the 0.005 fractile are set to equal the 0.995 and 0.005 fractile values, respectively, RET2–3, RET4–6, RET7–12 equal the logarithms of the cumulative returns over the second through third, fourth through sixth, and seventh through 12th months prior to the current month, respectively. The variables are measured as the deviation from the cross-sectional mean in each period. The estimates in the column labeled 'Raw' are the coefficients estimated using Eqs. (8) and (9), while those in the column labeled 'Purged' are from Eqs. (8) and (10). All coefficients are multiplied by 100. t-statistics are in parentheses.

	Excess returns	Risk-adjusted returns using the CK factors		Risk-adjusted returns using the FF factors	
		Raw	Purged	Raw	Purged
Intercept	0.735	0.412	0.101	0.099	0.642
	(2.36)	(0.63)	(1.85)	(1.45)	(0.96)
SIZE	− 0.140	− 0.157	− 0.150	− 0.106	− 0.096
	(2.70)	(4.81)	(4.60)	(2.95)	(2.63)
BM	0.295	0.271	0.264	0.173	0.171
	(4.52)	(4.95)	(4.85)	(3.44)	(3.41)
RET2–3	0.285	0.813	0.510	0.605	0.873
	(0.89)	(3.08)	(2.18)	(1.97)	(2.86)
RET4–6	0.624	0.847	0.693	0.881	1.145
	(2.19)	(3.23)	(3.21)	(3.24)	(4.31)
RET7–12	0.842	0.227	0.302	0.642	0.974
	(5.13)	(1.18)	(1.73)	(3.05)	(5.02)

risk-adjustment using the FF factors are reported in the last two columns. Both the size and book-to-market effects are now reduced by about one third, and their significance is attenuated as well. The lagged returns are highly significant, confirming FF (1996). Although for both sets of factors the intercept term is insignificantly different from zero as predicted by the null hypothesis, it is apparent that neither factor model provides a complete description of equilibrium returns.

In Table 4 we present the results of regressions that use the full set of characteristics: SIZE, BM, PRICE, DVOL, YLD, PRICE, as well as the lagged

Table 4
Fama–MacBeth regression estimates of Eq. (7) using individual security data

Coefficient estimates are time-series averages of cross-sectional OLS regressions. The dependent variable in the first column is simply the excess return, while in the second and third columns it is the excess returns risk-adjusted using the CK factors, and in the fourth and fifth columns it is the excess returns risk-adjusted using the FF factors (Dimson beats with one lag are used in each case). The independent variables are defined as follows; SIZE represents logarithm of the market capitalization of firms in billions of dollars. BM is the logarithm of the ratio of book value of equity plus deferred taxes to market capitalization, with the exception that book-to-market ratio values greater than the 0.995 fractile or less than the 0.005 fractile are set to equal the 0.995 and 0.005 fractile values, respectively. DVOL is the logarithm of the dollar trading volume. PRICE is the logarithm of the reciprocal of the share price. YLD is the logarithm, of the dividend yield; RET2–3, RET4–6, RET7–12 equal the logarithms of the cumulative returns over the second through third, fourth through sixth, and seventh through 12th months prior to the current month, respectively. NYDVOL is the value of DVOL if the stock trades on NYSE/AMEX, and zero otherwise; NADVOL is the value of DVOL if the stock trades on NASdaq; and zero otherwise. The estimates in the column labeled 'Raw' are the coefficients estimated using Eqs. (8) and (9), while those in the column labeled 'Purged' are from Eqs. (8) and (10). All coefficients are multiplied by 100. t-statistics are in parentheses. The variables are measured as the deviation from the cross-sectional mean in each period. The estimates in the column labeled 'Raw' are the coefficients estimated using Eqs. (8) and (9), while those in the column labeled 'Purged' are from Eqs. (8) and (9). All coefficients are multiplied by 100. t-statistics are in parentheses.

	Excess returns	Risk-adjusted returns using the Connor–Korajczyk factors		Risk-adjusted returns using the Fama–French factors	
		Raw	Purged	Raw	Purged
Intercept	0.707	0.004	0.092	0.071	0.035
	(2.25)	(0.06)	(1.69)	(1.02)	(0.51)
SIZE	0.092	0.116	0.143	0.122	0.106
	(1.56)	(2.57)	(3.15)	(2.84)	(2.46)
BM	0.246	0.201	0.188	0.128	0.129
	(5.02)	(4.12)	(3.85)	(2.87)	(2.90)
PRICE	0.196	0.166	0.153	0.109	0.013
	(1.87)	(1.97)	(1.78)	(1.16)	(0.14)
NYDVOL	− 0.130	− 0.190	− 0.199	− 0.162	− 0.173
	(2.68)	(5.02)	(5.34)	(4.17)	(4.38)
NADVOL	− 0.088	− 0.175	− 0.186	− 0.086	− 0.173
	(1.23)	(2.59)	(2.86)	(1.87)	(1.39)
YLD	0.215	1.778	2.371	0.643	0.327
	(0.13)	(1.82)	(3.33)	(0.57)	(0.28)
RET2–3	0.654	1.158	0.706	0.888	1.072
	(2.30)	(4.14)	(2.89)	(2.98)	(3.57)
RET4–6	0.789	1.062	0.849	1.006	1.205
	(3.26)	(3.99)	(3.85)	(2.81)	(4.59)
RET7–12	0.869	0.325	0.365	0.666	0.974
	(5.99)	(1.69)	(2.11)	(3.21)	(5.01)

return variables. Since trading volume is measured differently between NYSE/AMEX and Nasdaq,[22] we split DVOL into two variables: NYDVOL, which equals DVOL if the stock trades on NYSE/AMEX and zero otherwise, and NADVOL, which equals DVOL if the stock trades on Nasdaq and zero otherwise. The results using risk-unadjusted returns are presented in the first column of Table 4.

Now the coefficient of SIZE, which was previously negative and significant, is positive and no longer significant, whereas the coefficients of BM, NYDVOL, and all three lagged return variables are strongly significant.[23] These variables remain significant following risk-adjustment by the CK factors; the coefficient on SIZE and NADVOL now become significant. Particularly striking is the behavior of the coefficient on YLD which becomes large and positive after risk-adjustment. When risk-adjustment is carried out using the FF factors, YLD is insignificant though the coefficient on NYDVOL remains negative and significant. The BM effect is reduced by about 50%, although SIZE remains positive and significant. In summary, risk-adjustment by either set of factors leaves significant SIZE (positive), BM, and NYDVOL effects, as well as lagged return effects; the CK factors also leave a YLD effect and a NADVOL effect.

It is worth noting that the magnitudes of the coefficients on some of the Z variables increase substantially after risk adjustment by the CK factors – for example, the slopes on the volume variables, RET2-3, RET4-6, and particularly the one on YLD which increases by a factor of about nine. While the magnitudes of some of the coefficients also increase after risk-adjustment by the FF factors, the increase is less dramatic and the FF factors significantly reduce the magnitudes of the SIZE and BM coefficients.

The lack of significance of NADVOL, in contrast to the high level of significance of NYDVOL, in the FF regressions leaves the role of trading volume unclear. However, Reinganum (1990) finds that the average returns on NYSE securities exceed those of similar size firms listed on Nasdaq by about 6%

---

[22] It is well-known that Nasdaq volume is considered overstated relative to NYSE/AMEX volume, owing to the inclusion of inter-dealer trading on Nasdaq, and the requirement that most trades on Nasdaq must be submitted to a dealer, whereas crossing between brokers is not included in the reported trading volume on the other exchanges.

[23] We also performed a test of the null hypothesis that the coefficients of the characteristics in these regressions are *jointly* equal to zero. To do this, we calculated the Hotelling T^2 statistic, which, given N time-series observations of p coefficients, is defined as

$$T^2 = N[\bar{\gamma}'S^{-1}\bar{\gamma}],$$

where $\bar{\gamma}$ is the (time-series) mean vector of the coefficients, and S is the estimated variance covariance matrix of the coefficients. Under the null hypothesis, the T^2 statistic is distributed $[(N-1)_p/N - p] F_{p,\ N-p}$. We do not report the results of this test here, because in every regression that we performed, the null hypothesis that the coefficients jointly equal zero could be easily rejected, with p-values ranging from 0.02 to 10^{-20}.

Table 5
Fama–MacBeth regression estimates of Eq. (7) using individual security data, including dummy variable for Nasdaq stocks

Coefficient estimates are time-series averages of cross-sectional OLS regressions. The dependent variable in the first column is simply the excess return, while in the second and third columns it is the excess returns risk-adjusted using the CK factors, and in the fourth and fifth columns it is the excess returns risk-adjusted using the FF factors (Dimson beats with one lag are used in each case). The independent variables are defined as follows; SIZE represents logarithm of the market capitalization of firms in billions of dollars. BM is the logarithm of the ratio of book value of equity plus deferred taxes to market capitalization, with the exception that book-to-market ratio values greater than the 0.995 fractile or less than the 0.005 fractile are set to equal the 0.995 and 0.005 fractile values, respectively. DVOL is the logarithm of the dollar trading volume. PRICE is the logarithm of the reciprocal of the share price. YLD is the logarithm, of the dividend yield; RET2–3, RET4–6, RET7–12 equal the logarithms of the cumulative returns over the second through third, fourth through sixth, and seventh through 12th months prior to the current month, respectively. NYDVOL is the value of DVOL if the stock trades on NYSE/AMEX, and zero otherwise; NADVOL is the value of DVOL if the stock trades on NASdaq; and zero otherwise. The estimates in the column labeled 'Raw' are the coefficients estimated using Eqs. (8) and (9), while those in the column labeled 'Purged' are from Eqs. (8) and (10). All coefficients are multiplied by 100. *t*-statistics are in parentheses. The variables are measured as the deviation from the cross-sectional mean in each period. The estimates in the column labeled 'Raw' are the coefficients estimated using Eqs. (8) and (9), while those in the column labeled 'Purged' are from Eqs. (8) and (9). All coefficients are multiplied by 100. *t*-statistics are in parentheses.

	Excess returns	Risk-adjusted returns using the Connor–Korajczyk factors		Risk-adjusted returns using the Fama–French factors	
		Raw	Purged	Raw	Purged
Intercept	0.797	0.112	0.144	0.149	0.109
	(2.52)	(1.67)	(2.58)	(2.07)	(1.52)
NASDUM	− 0.791	− 0.842	− 0.725	− 0.797	− 0.764
	(6.69)	(6.66)	(5.90)	(6.28)	(5.84)
SIZE	0.637	0.085	0.116	0.099	0.084
	(1.08)	(1.88)	(2.58)	(2.30)	(1.95)
BM	0.235	0.189	0.181	0.120	0.122
	(4.83)	(3.91)	(3.74)	(2.71)	(2.76)
PRICE	0.195	0.165	0.151	0.108	0.012
	(1.86)	(1.96)	(1.77)	(1.17)	(0.15)
NYDVOL	− 0.118	− 0.176	− 0.185	− 0.151	− 0.162
	(2.43)	(4.67)	(5.02)	(3.89)	(4.11)
NADVOL	− 0.296	− 0.404	− 0.312	− 0.306	− 0.301
	(3.56)	(5.03)	(4.63)	(4.05)	(3.88)
YLD	0.220	1.794	2.327	0.656	0.343
	(0.13)	(1.85)	(3.39)	(0.58)	(0.30)

Table 5. Continued.

	Excess returns	Risk-adjusted returns using the Connor–Korajczyk factors		Risk-adjusted returns using the Fama–French factors	
		Raw	Purged	Raw	Purged
RET2–3	0.665	1.170	0.716	0.896	1.080
	(2.34)	(4.18)	(2.93)	(3.02)	(3.60)
RET4–6	0.790	1.067	0.852	1.005	1.203
	(3.27)	(4.00)	(3.86)	(3.80)	(4.59)
RET7–12	0.874	0.329	0.371	0.669	0.977
	(6.02)	(1.71)	(2.14)	(3.22)	(5.02)

per year, so it is possible that the NADVOL variable is playing a dual role, as a volume variable and as a dummy for NASDAQ listing. Table 5 reports the results of including a separate NASDAQ dummy.

The dummy variable is highly significant and the coefficient implies that NASDAQ stocks underperform by about 9.6% per year after adjusting for factor loadings and the non-risk firm characteristics. Moreover, with the addition of the NASDAQ dummy NADVOL becomes highly significant so that trading volume has a similar effect for Nasdaq stocks as it does for the others.

Table 6 reports the results of separate regressions for the NYSE/AMEX subsample (Panel A) and the Nasdaq subsample (Panel B).[24]

Examining the results for NYSE/AMEX subsample, we again see that the book-to-market effect is attenuated considerably (the size of the coefficient is reduced by more than 50%) and its significance is also reduced considerably, when risk-adjustment is done with the FF factors. The purged coefficient of YLD is positive and significant under the CK method of risk-adjustment. Further, the coefficient on DVOL is negative and strongly significant in all of the regressions, while the lagged return effects continue to be positive and significant. The results are in fact very similar to those in Table 5.

The results for the Nasdaq subsample are reported in Panel B. The coefficient of DVOL is again significant and negative in all the regressions. While the coefficients of the other characteristics are insignificant, they are generally of the same magnitude as found in the full sample, so that the lack of significance of those that were significant in Table 5 is likely related to the smaller sample size of Nasdaq stocks. The most striking finding is that the intercept in the

---

[24] The average numbers of stocks in the two subsamples are 1660 and 797, respectively.

Table 6
Fama–MacBeth regression estimates of Eq. (7) using individual security data, sample split by exchange listing (NYSE/AMEX versus Nasdaq).

Coefficient estimates are time-series averages of cross-sectional OLS regressions. The dependent variable in the first column is simply the excess return, while in the second and third columns it is the excess returns risk-adjusted using the CK factors, and in the fourth and fifth columns it is the excess returns risk-adjusted using the FF factors (Dimson beats with one lag are used in each case). The independent variables are defined as follows; SIZE represents logarithm of the market capitalization of firms in billions of dollars. BM is the logarithm of the ratio of book value of equity plus deferred taxes to market capitalization, with the exception that book-to-market ratio values greater than the 0.995 fractile or less than the 0.005 fractile are set to equal the 0.995 and 0.005 fractile values, respectively. DVOL is the logarithm of the dollar trading volume. PRICE is the logarithm of the reciprocal of the share price. YLD is the logarithm, of the dividend yield; RET2–3, RET4–6, RET7–12 equal the logarithms of the cumulative returns over the second through third, fourth through sixth, and seventh through 12th months prior to the current month, respectively. NYDVOL is the value of DVOL if the stock trades on NYSE/AMEX, and zero otherwise; NADVOL is the value of DVOL if the stock trades on Nasdaq; and zero otherwise and NASDUM equals one if the stock is listed on Nasdaq and zero otherwise. The estimates in the column labeled 'Raw' are the coefficients estimated using Eqs. (8) and (9), while those in the column labeled 'Purged' are from Eqs. (8) and (10). All coefficients are multiplied by 100. t-statistics are in parentheses. The variables are measured as the deviation from the cross-sectional mean in each period. The estimates in the column labeled 'Raw' are the coefficients estimated using Eqs. (8) and (9), while those in the column labeled 'Purged' are from Eqs. (8) and (10). In Panel A, the sample consists of an average of 1660 NYSE/AMEX stocks, while in Panel B, of an average of 797 Nasdaq stocks. All coefficients are multiplied by 100. t-statistics are in parentheses.

	Excess returns	Risk-adjusted returns using the Connor–Korajczyk factors		Risk-adjusted returns using the Fama–French factors	
		Raw	Purged	Raw	Purged
Panel A: NYSE/AMEX stocks only					
Intercept	0.777	0.053	0.068	0.083	0.067
	(2.51)	(1.18)	(1.51)	(1.72)	(1.39)
SIZE	0.064	0.079	0.107	0.087	0.074
	(1.04)	(1.81)	(2.49)	(2.02)	(1.70)
BM	0.196	0.133	0.117	0.088	0.081
	(3.85)	(2.79)	(2.45)	(2.10)	(1.92)
PRICE	0.131	0.074	0.079	− 0.001	− 0.087
	(1.22)	(0.87)	(0.91)	(0.007)	(0.91)
DVOL	− 0.144	− 0.207	− 0.215	− 0.178	− 0.189
	(2.86)	(5.56)	(6.02)	(4.63)	(4.84)
YLD	− 0.377	1.450	2.044	0.121	− 0.090
	(0.23)	(1.52)	(3.03)	(0.11)	(0.08)
RET2–3	0.949	1.451	1.241	1.173	1.372
	(3.03)	(4.97)	(4.55)	(3.67)	(4.24)

Table 6. Continued.

	Excess returns	Risk-adjusted returns using the Connor–Korajczyk factors		Risk-adjusted returns using the Fama–French factors	
		Raw	Purged	Raw	Purged
RET4–6	0.889	1.210	0.052	1.103	1.317
	(3.33)	(4.43)	(4.47)	(3.95)	(4.72)
RET7–12	0.972	0.408	0.503	0.733	1.068
	(6.35)	(2.10)	(2.85)	(3.42)	(5.38)
Panel B: Nasdaq stocks only					
Intercept	0.355	− 0.425	− 0.451	0.486	− 0.561
	(0.90)	(3.97)	(3.14)	(3.41)	(3.81)
SIZE	0.160	− 0.024	0.061	0.202	0.181
	(0.83)	(0.10)	(0.39)	(0.90)	(0.80)
BM	0.273	0.302	0.251	0.197	0.185
	(1.89)	(1.77)	(1.79)	(1.20)	(1.13)
PRICE	0.424	0.233	0.063	0.298	0.181
	(1.82)	(0.89)	(0.30)	(1.22)	(0.75)
DVOL	− 0.322	− 0.344	− 0.283	− 0.347	− 0.368
	(2.60)	(2.34)	(2.73)	(2.43)	(2.51)
YLD	4.24	6.38	5.79	3.80	2.77
	(0.95)	(1.24)	(1.64)	(0.81)	(0.58)
RET2–3	1.063	1.095	0.117	1.46	1.638
	(1.38)	(1.22)	(0.15)	(1.68)	(1.83)
RET4–6	0.966	0.575	0.637	1.38	1.585
	(1.64)	(0.81)	(1.16)	(2.12)	(2.38)
RET7–12	0.888	0.595	0.536	0.812	1.088
	(1.87)	(1.00)	(1.27)	(1.56)	(2.04)

risk-adjusted regressions is consistently negative and significant, ranging from *minus* 0.4% to *minus* 0.6% per month, depending on the regression. Since that the non-risk characteristics are scaled to have mean zero, this finding suggests that the average Nasdaq stock underformed relative to the risk model by 5–7% per year, which is consistent with Reinganum's (1990) finding.[25]

---

[25] This contrasts with FF (1993a), who find for a shorter sample period (1973–1991) that the difference between NYSE and Nasdaq returns for size sorted portfolios is not significant after risk adjustment by the FF factors. Loughran (1993) attributes most of Nasdaq stocks' underperformance to the underperformance of initial public offerings which are proportionately more important on Nasdaq.

5.2. Summary of regression results

Our results may be summarized as follows. First, we find as in earlier studies that excess returns are strongly related to SIZE and BM as well as lagged returns. The introduction of PRICE, DVOL, and YLD changes the sign of the coefficient of SIZE before and after risk adjustment,[26] and NYDVOL but not NADVOL is significant. However, when a Nasdaq dummy variable is included, NADVOL becomes significant and a very large negative effect is found to be associated with Nasdaq membership. The factor model that is used to risk-adjust the returns makes relatively little difference to the results; with the exception of the YLD coefficient in the CK regressions, which increases substantially. The most consistent finding is of a strong negative effect associated with trading volume, and introduction of this variable changes the sign of the SIZE coefficient.

While the results plainly reject the null hypothesis that returns are determined by either of these specifications of the APT (or by the corresponding specifications of 'multi-factor equilibrium models' such as Merton's ICAPM) care is required in interpreting the significant coefficients on the firm characteristics for the risk-adjusted returns, especially the YLD coefficient, whose magnitude increases quite dramatically after risk adjustment using the CK factors. One interpretation is that these significant coefficients are evidence that the risk model is mis-specified, and that the priced firm characteristics are proxying for loadings on omitted factors that are priced. It is noteworthy, however, that the significance of SIZE, BM, and the volume and lagged return variables is largely robust to the choice of risk-adjustment even though the two risk models are arrived at in quite different ways, the CK factors being taken as the principal components of returns, and the FF factors being arrived at because of their relation to economic fundamentals.[27] It seems unlikely that both risk models could be misspecified in the same way which would be required if they were to yield similar results for the non-risk characteristics' rewards. For the YLD variable, however, there is a major difference in the result depending on which risk model is used (see Table 5), in that the coefficient of YLD is significant only in the CK regressions. Therefore, while the significance of this variable may be

---

[26] We verified that it is the volume variables that cause the sign of the coefficient of SIZE to change. While in all the regressions without DVOL the coefficient of SIZE was negative and significant, when the DVOL variable alone was added to the regression its coefficient was negative and statistically significant, while the SIZE coefficient became positive and either insignificant or only marginally significant. In addition, the significance of the DVOL coefficient is not a result of the interaction between SIZE and DVOL in that DVOL is negative and significant even if SIZE is omitted from the regressions in Table 6.

[27] FF (1993b, p. 7) note that 'although size and book-to-market equity seem like ad hoc variables for explaining average stock returns, we have reason to expect that they proxy for common risk factors in returns. In FF (1992b) we document that size and book-to-market equity are related to economic fundamentals'.

assigned to the inadequacies of the CK factors (rather than to, say, tax effects of the type described by Brennan, 1970), it seems unlikely that a similar explanation can be given for the other significant coefficients.

For example, the consistently negative relation between returns and DVOL, and the attenuation and sign reversal of the SIZE coefficient when DVOL is included, are consistent with SIZE being a proxy for DVOL, and in turn, for a liquidity premium in asset prices. The magnitude of the DVOL effect may be assessed as follows. The standard deviation of DVOL in the NYSE/AMEX and Nasdaq subsamples is 0.938 and 0.971, respectively. The parameter estimates for the excess return regressions reported in Table 5, imply that a one standard deviation increase in DVOL causes a decrease in excess return of 0.11% per month and 0.29% per month in the NYSE/AMEX and Nasdaq stocks, respectively. These appear to be plausible magnitudes for a liquidity premium. Further it is possible that the positive SIZE effect that we observe when DVOL is included results from the correlation of SIZE with DVOL and a mis-specification of the relation between required returns and volume of trading. The BM and lagged return effects apparent even in the risk-adjusted returns defy such simple explanation. Barberis et al. (1998) and Daniel et al. (1998a, b) offer alternative explanations based on investor psychology.

6. Factor risk premia

We have seen that the two sets of factors yield similar estimates for the coefficients of the non-risk firm characteristics except for the YLD and lagged return variables. In this section we compare the two sets of factor portfolios in terms of the squared Sharpe ratios of the tangency portfolios formed from them, and the ability of each set to price the other set.

MacKinlay (1995) argues that risk-based explanations of asset pricing anomalies are bounded by the plausibility of the (squared) Sharpe ratio of the tangency portfolio that they imply. Table 7 reports the mean excess returns and squared Sharpe ratios on the five CK factor portfolios for each estimation subperiod.

Since we have no assurance that the factor rotations are the same for the two subperiods, they should be treated separately. However, we include a χ^2 test of the joint hypothesis that the mean excess returns of each factor are zero for both subperiods. Only for factors 1 and 2 can we reject the null. The table reports the each factor's squared Sharpe ratio (SSR) for each subperiod, as well as an aggregate SSR for the factor portfolios, which is the SSR of the tangency portfolio formed from the factor portfolios.[28] The largest SSR's are 0.0487 and

---

[28] Since the portfolio returns are orthogonal the SSR of the tangency portfolio is simply the sum of the individual portfolio SSR's. See MacKinlay (1995) and references therein.

Table 7
Excess returns and sharpe ratios for the CK and FF factors, Jan. 1963 through Dec. 1995

Mean monthly excess returns and sharpe ratios for the 5 CK for the two sub-period estimations, and the FF factors for the entire period. The five CK factors are calculated a in Connor and Korajczyk (1988), and the FF factors as in FF (1993). The Sharpe Ratio corresponding to a factor is the ratio of the mean excess return of a factor to its standard deviation. The aggregate squared Sharpe Ratio is the sum of the individual factor portfolio squared Sharpe Ratios, and is the estimated squared Sharpe Ratio of the tangency portfolio formed from the 5 (orthogonal) factor portfolios. The χ^2 statistics are for the null hypothesis that the mean excess returns for the portfolios in each of two subperiods are both equal to zero. The p-value for the combined periods in Panel A aggregates the individual sub-period F-statistics using χ^2 approximations to the F-distribution.

Panel A: factors

Factor	1	2	3	4	5	Aggregate
Period 1: January 1963 to December 1979						
Mean excess return ($\times 100$)	0.784	-0.865	0.788	0.767	0.484	
(*t*-ratio)	(1.56)	(1.72)	(1.57)	(1.52)	(0.96)	
Squared sharpe ratio	0.0123	0.0150	0.0124	0.0117	0.0046	0.0559
(*p*-value)						(0.06)
Period 2: January 1980 to December 1995						
Mean excess return ($\times 100$)	1.243	0.811	-0.015	-0.507	0.154	
(*t*-ratio)	(3.06)	(1.79)	(0.03)	(1.43)	(0.35)	
Squared sharpe ratio (*p*-value)	0.0487	0.0167	0.0000	0.0106	0.0006	0.0767
						(0.02)
Combined periods						
Squared sharpe ratio						0.0663
(*p*-value)						(0.01)
Overall period: H_0 Mean Excess						
Return $= 0$						
χ^2 *p*-value	11.78	6.17	2.45	4.36	1.04	
	(0.00)	(0.05)	(0.29)	(0.11)	(0.59)	

Panel B: FF factors

Factor	Market	SMB	HML	Aggregate
Mean excess return ($\times 100$)	0.480	0.248	0.441	
(*t*-ratio)	(2.09)	(1.66)	(3.28)	
Squared sharpe ratio (*p*-value)	0.0123	0.0076	0.0300	0.672
				(0.00)

0.0167 for factors 1 and 2 in the second subperiod. The estimated SSRs for the tangency portfolio are 0.056 and 0.077 for the two subperiods with p-values of 0.06 and 0.02, respectively.[29] Combining the two subperiods, the average SSR over this 33 year period is 0.066 with an approximate p-value of 0.01.[30]

The aggregate SSR for the FF factors[31] of 0.067 is only marginally higher than the average value for the CK factors. The main contributor to the aggregate SSR of the FF portfolios is the HML portfolio which alone has a SSR of 0.03, or almost three times that of the market portfolio. Thus the reward for risk implied by the FF factors is similar to that implied by the CK factors.

However, the similarity of the Sharpe ratios does not imply that the two sets of factors are economically equivalent. Table 8 reports the intercepts and R^2's from regressions of the CK factors on the FF factors and the FF factors on the CK factors.

The results are reported separately for the subperiods for which the CK factors were estimated. When the CK factors are regressed on the FF factors, factors 3 and 5 have significant intercepts in the first subperiod and factor 1 in the second subperiod; a Gibbons et al. (GRS) (1989) test is able to reject the null hypothesis that the intercepts are jointly zero at with a p-value of 0.00 in the first subperiod, but is unable to reject this hypothesis in the second subperiod. When a χ^2 approximation is used to combine the GRS F-statistics for the two sub-periods, the p-value for the whole period is also 0.00. The regression of the FF factors on the CK factors yields significant intercepts in both subperiods for the market and HML portfolios but not for the SMB portfolio. The hypothesis that the intercepts are jointly equal to zero is rejected for both subperiods and the overall period. Thus, the classical version of the APT, which does not account for frictions such as taxes or illiquidity, appears to be rejected by the data.

While there is evidence that the pricing of the CK factors by the FF factors is better than that of the FF factors by the CK factors, neither set of factors is sufficient to price the other. A possible reason for this is that the average characteristics (e.g., firm size, book-to-market ratio, and trading volume) of the securities underlying the different factors differ; without adjusting for the differences in average characteristics we should not expect either set of factors to price the other. Thus, at first sight, it is surprising to find that the CK factors do not

---

[29] Under the null hypothesis that the factor risk premia are jointly equal to *zero* $[(T - N)/N]$SSR is distributed central $F(N, T - N)$ where N is the number of portfolios and T is the number of time-series observations. See MacKinlay (1995).

[30] The p-value is estimated by combining the two periods using the χ^2 approximation to the F-statistic.

[31] This is given by $\mu'\Omega^{-1}\mu$ where μ is the vector of mean excess returns on the three factor portfolios and Ω is the variance-convariance matrix.

Table 8
Intercepts from the regressions of the estimated CK factors on the FF factors, and vice versa, Jan. 1963 through Dec. 1995

The market factor, MKT, is the excess return of the FF market portfolio. SMB is the difference between the returns of a small and a large firm portfolio; HML is the difference between the returns on a high book to market ratio portfolio and a low book to market ratio portfolio. $CK_k = (k = 1, \ldots, 5)$ denotes the CK factor portfolio returns. The GRS F-statistic is the Gibbons et al. (1989) statistic for testing the hypothesis that the intercepts from the regressions jointly equal zero. The overall χ^2 statistic aggregates the GRS-F-statistics using χ^2 approximations to the F-distribution. The intercepts are multiplied by 100. t-statistics are in parentheses.

Panel A: Intercepts from the regressions of the CK factors on the FF factors

	CK_1	CK_2	CK_3	CK_4	CK_5
July 1963 to December 1979	− 0.088	− 0.736	1.92	0.390	1.23
	(1.12)	(1.78)	(5.92)	(0.77)	(2.97)
R^2	0.98	0.38	0.62	0.06	0.38
GRS F-statistic = 15.22 (p-value = 0.00)					
January 1980 to December 1995	0.189	0.473	− 0.450	− 0.292	0.039
	(2.64)	(1.18)	(1.00)	1.26)	(0.08)
R^2	0.97	0.29			
GRS F-statistic = 1.67 (p-value = 0.14)					
Overall χ^2 statistic = 84.46 (p-value)					

Panel B: Intercepts from the regressions of the FF factors on the CK factors

	MKT	SMB	HML
July 1963 to December 1979	− 0.317	− 0.122	0.80
	(5.76)	(1.42)	(7.40)
R^2	0.97	0.87	0.66
GRS F-statistic = 26.23 (p-value) = 0.00)			
January 1980 to December 1995	0.141	− 0.059	0.438
	(2.52)	(0.70)	(2.84)
R^2	0.97	(0.70)	0.38
GRS F-statistic = 3.77 (p-value = 0.01)			
Overall χ^2 statistic = 90.01 (p-value = 0.00)			

price the FF market portfolio. However, as we have seen in Table 5, there is a significant negative return associated with trading volume, and the market portfolio is strongly weighted towards firms with higher than average trading volume. As we mentioned earlier, Shanken (1985, 1987) points out that the equilibrium APT requires that the 'true' market portfolio be well-diversified with respect to the factors. It is therefore interesting to note that while we cannot be sure the FF market portfolio is the true market portfolio, the CK factors explain 97% of the variation in the FF market factor.

In Section 4 we note that the Fama–MacBeth (1973) approach understates the standard errors of the coefficients because it neglects the effect of estimation errors in the factor loadings. Applying the results of Shanken (1992, Theorem 2),[32] consideration of this estimation error requires the variance of the estimate to be multiplied by one plus the squared Sharpe ratio of the tangency portfolio formed by the factors. The estimates of the SSRs provided in Table 7 indicate a standard error understatement of about 3.3%. Such a magnitude does not alter the basic conclusions described in Section 5.2.

7. Conclusion

In this paper, we have tested a risk-based asset pricing model against specific non-risk alternatives using data on individual securities. Using individual securities is important since, as Roll (1977) and Lo and MacKinlay (1990) have shown, the use of portfolios is problematic. We use two different specifications of the factor model that is used to adjust for risk: the principal components approach of Connor and Korajczyk (1988), and the characteristic-factor based approach of (1993b). Regardless of the method used to risk-adjust returns, we find a strong negative relation between average returns and trading volume, which is consistent with a liquidity premium in asset prices. In addition, the size and book-to-market ratio effects are strong in the CK method of risk-adjustment, while the FF factors attenuate both the magnitude and significance of these effects. There is strong evidence of return momentum both before and after risk-adjustment. Finally, Nasdaq stocks have much lower returns than the other stocks in the sample after adjusting for the effects of the firm characteristics and the factor loadings. The two sets of factors offer similar risk-return tradeoffs, but are not equivalent. In particular, neither set of factors appears to price the other, though there is evidence that the FF factors price the CK factors better than the CK factors price the FF factors.

---

[32] Shanken (1992) assumes conditional homoscedasticity of asset returns. Jagannathan and Wang (1998) derive the asymptotic distribution of the estimators in cross-sectional regressions of the type in Black et al. (1972) and Fama–MacBeth (1973).

References

Amihud, Y., Mendelson, H., 1986. Asset pricing and the bid-ask spread. Journal of Financial Economics 17, 223–249.

Banz, R.W., 1981. The relationship between return and market value of common stocks. Journal of Financial Economics 9, 3–18.

Barberis, N., Shleifer, A., Vishny, R., 1998. A model of investor sentiment. Journal of Financial Economics 49, 307–343 (this issue).

Basu, S., 1977. The investment performance of common stocks in relation to their price-earnings ratios: test of the efficient markets hypothesis. Journal of Finance 32, 663–682.

Black, F., Jensen, M., Scholes, M., 1972. The capital asset pricing model: some empirical tests. In: Jensen, M. (Ed.), Studies in the Theory of Capital Markets. Praeger Publishers, New York.

Black, F., Scholes, M., 1974. The effects of dividend yield and dividend policy on common stock prices and returns. Journal of Financial Economics 1, 1–22.

Brennan, M.J., 1970. Taxes, market valuation, and corporate financial policy. National Tax Journal 4, 417–427.

Brennan, M.J., Subrahmanyam, A., 1995. Investment analysis and price formation in securities markets. Journal of Financial Economics 38, 361–382.

Brennan, M.J., Subrahmanyam, A., 1996. Market microstructure and asset pricing: on the compensation for illiquidity in stock returns. Journal of Financial Economics 41, 341–364.

Brennan, M.J., Chordia, T., Subrahmanyam, A., 1996. Cross-sectional determinants of expected returns. In: Modest, D. (Ed), On Finance: In Honor of Fischer Black. Oxford University Press, Cary, NC, forthcoming.

Brown, S., Weinstein, M., 1983. A new approach to testing asset pricing models: the bilinear paradigm. Journal of Finance 38, 711–743.

Campbell, J., 1996. Understanding risk and return. Journal of Political Economy 104, 298–345.

Connor, G., 1984. A unified beta pricing theory. Journal of Economic Theory 34, 13–31.

Connor, G., Korajczyk, R., 1988. Risk and return in an equilibrium APT: application of a new test methodology. Journal of Financial Economics 21, 255–290.

Connor, G., Korajczyk, R., 1993. A test for the number of factors in an approximate factor model. Journal of Finance 48, 1263–1291.

Daniel, K., Hirshleifer, D., Subrahmanyam, A., 1998a. Investor Psychology, and security market under- and over-reactions. Journal of Finance, forthcoming.

Daniel, K., Hirshleifer, D., Subrahmanyam, A., 1998b. Investor overconfidence, covariance risk, and predictors of security returns. Unpublished working paper, Northwestern University, Evanston, IL.

Daniel, K., Titman, S., 1997. Evidence on the characteristics of cross sectional variation in stock returns. Journal of Finance 52, 1–33.

Dimson, E., 1979. Risk measurement when shares are subject to infrequent trading. Journal of Financial Economics 7, 197–226.

Falkenstein, E.G., 1996. Preferences for stock characteristics as revealed by mutual fund holdings. Journal of Finance 51, 111–135.

Fama, E.F., French, K.R., 1992a. The cross section of expected stock returns. Journal of Finance 47, 427–466.

Fama, E.F., French, K.R., 1992b. The economic fundamentals of size and book-to-market equity. Unpublished working paper. University of Chicago.

Fama, E.F., French, K.R., 1993a. Differences in the risks and returns of NYSE and NASD stocks. Financial Analysts Journal 49, 37–41.

Fama, E.F., French, K.R., 1993b. Common risk factors in the returns on stocks and bonds. Journal of Financial Economics 33, 3–56.

Fama, E.F., French, K.R., 1996. Multifactor explanations for asset pricing anomalies. Journal of Finance 51, 55–84.

Fama, E.F., MacBeth, J., 1973. Risk and return: some empirical tests. Journal of Political Economy 81, 607–636.

Ferson, W., Sarkissian, S., Simin, T., 1998. The alpha factor asset pricing model: a parable. Working paper. University of Washington, Seattle, WA.

Gibbons, M.R., 1982. Multivariate tests of financial models: a new approach. Journal of Financial Economics 10, 3–27.

Gibbons, M.R., Ross, S.A., Shanken, J., 1989. A test of the efficiency of a given portfolio. Econometrica 57, 1121–1152.

Glosten, L.R., Harris, L., 1988. Estimating the components of the bid/ask spread. Journal of Financial Economics 21, 123–142.

Jagannathan, R., Wang, Z., 1998. An asymptotic theory for estimating beta-pricing models using cross-sectional regression. Working paper. Northwestern University, Evanston, IL.

Jegadeesh, N., 1990. Evidence of predictable behavior of security returns. Journal of Finance 45, 881–898.

Jegadeesh, N., Titman, S., 1993. Returns to buying winners and selling losers: implications for stock market efficiency. Journal of Finance 48, 65–92.

Jegadeesh, N., Titman, S., 1995. Overreaction, delayed reaction, and contrarian profits. Review of Financial Studies 8, 973–993.

Lakonishok, J., Shleifer, A., Vishny, R., 1994. Contrarian investment, extrapolation, and risk. Journal of Finance 49, 1541–1578.

Lehmann, B., 1990. Residual risk revisited. Journal of Econometrics 45, 71–97.

Lehmann, B., Modest, D.A., 1988. The empirical foundations of the arbitrage pricing theory. Journal of Financial Economics 21, 213–254.

Litzenberger, R., Ramaswamy, K., 1979. Dividends, short-selling restrictions, tax-induced investor clienteles and market equilibrium. Journal of Financial Economics 7, 163–196.

Lo, A.W., MacKinlay, A.C., 1990. Data-snooping biases in tests of financial asset pricing models. Review of Financial Studies 3, 431–468.

Loughran, T., 1993. NYSE vs NASDAQ returns. Journal of Financial Economics 33, 241–260.

MacKinlay, A.C., 1995. Multifactor models do not explain deviations from the CAPM. Journal of Financial Economics 38, 3–28.

Merton, R.C., 1973. An intertemporal capital asset pricing model. Econometrica 41, 867–887.

Miller, M.M., Scholes, M.S., 1978. Dividends and taxes. Journal of Financial Economics 6, 333–364.

Miller, M.M., Scholes, M.S., 1982. Dividends and taxes: some empirical evidence. Journal of Political Economy 90, 1118–1141.

Petersen, M., Fialkowski, D., 1994. Posted versus effective spreads: good prices or bad quotes. Journal of Financial Economics 35, 269–292.

Reinganum, M.R., 1990. Market microstructure and asset pricing. Journal of Financial Economics 28, 127–147.

Roll, R., 1977. A critique of the asset pricing theory's tests: on past and potential testability of theory. Journal of Financial Economics 4, 129–176.

Roll, R., Ross, S., 1980. An empirical investigation of the arbitrage pricing theory. Journal of Finance 35, 1073–1103.

Shanken, J., 1985. Multibeta CAPM or equilibrium-APT?: a reply. Journal of Finance 40, 1189–1196.

Shanken, J., 1987. Multivariate proxies and arbitrage pricing relations: living with the Roll critique. Journal of Financial Economics 18, 91–110.

Shanken, J., 1992. On the estimation of beta-pricing models. Review of Financial Studies 5, 1–33.

Stambaugh, R.F., 1982. On the exclusion of assets from tests of the two-parameter model: a sensitivity analysis. Journal of Financial Economics 10, 237–268.

Stoll, H., 1978. The pricing of dealer services: an empirical study of NASDAQ stocks. Journal of Finance 33, 1152–1173.

Name index

Acharya, S. 122
Adler, M. 334
Admati, A. 132,141, 335, 338, 358, 391, 407, 416–18, 427, 430, 435
Aghion, P. 140
Alderson, M. 122
Allen, F. 138
Ambarish, R.K. 139
Amihud, Y. 366, 369, 418, 442
Amin, K. 296
Antle, R. 143
Arbel, A. 366, 396, 417
Arrow, K.J. 217
Asquith, P. 80, 138, 366

Barberis, N. 459
Back, K. 292
Bagwell, L.S. 144
Baker, G.P. 140
Bakshi, G.S. 321
Banz, R.W. 438, 442
Basu, S. 438
Bawa, V.S. 41
Baxter, N.D. 29
Bekaert, G. 354–5
Beneviste, L.M. 139
Benston, G. 420, 425
Bergman, Y.Z. 141
Bergstrom, A.R. 186
Berle, A.A. 139
Bhattacharya, S. 139, 142
Bhushan, R. 375, 380–81, 391, 418, 425, 429, 432, 434–5
Bierman, H. 56
Black F. 14, 15, 21, 30, 48,143, 151, 156, 158–9, 162, 164–5, 180, 202, 219, 238–40, 244, 249, 273, 275, 287, 289, 292, 297, 304, 333, 438, 463
Blum, M. 261
Bodie, Z. 57
Bogue, M.C. 56
Bohn, H. 334
Bolton, P. 140–41
Boot, A.W.A. 138, 141
Borch, K. 217
Boyd, J.H. 98
Boyle, P.P. 143, 165
Branch, B. 367–8, 420, 425, 427
Breeden, D.T. 219

Brennan, M.J. 33, 56–8, 60, 139, 142–3, 165, 179, 184, 202, 204, 219, 229, 238–9, 244, 261, 275, 289, 363–4, 366, 368, 374, 405, 417, 439, 442–3, 459
Brown, D.P. 261
Brown, P. 375
Bruner, R.F. 122
Burness, H. 46

Callen, J.L. 141
Campbell, J. 440
Canes, M. 383
Cao, H.H. 296
Carlos, A.M. 334
Carvell, S. 396, 417
Chan, K. 296
Chen, K.C. 122
Chen, Z. 321
Chiesa, G. 140
Cho, I.K. 133, 387
Chuhan, P. 334
Chung, Y.P. 296
Clarke, R.G. 42
Cohn, R.A. 13 1
Coler, M.D. 366–7
Coleridge, S. 115
Connor, G. 437, 440, 445, 455, 460, 463
Conrad, J. 296
Conroy, R.M. 366
Constantinides, G.M. 56, 58, 80 ,121, 139, 142
Cooney, J.W. 144
Cooper, I. 333–4
Cootner, P. 60
Copeland, T.E. 363–4, 366, 368–9, 374
Cornell, B. 128, 141
Coval, J. 335
Cox, J.C. 53–4 ,64, 74, 142, 165–6, 268–9, 180, 202, 240

Daniel, K. 439, 459
Dann, L.Y. 94
Das, S.P. 40
Davis, B.E. 42
De Caires, B. 355
Dean, J. 56
DeAngelo, H. 142
DeLong, J.B. 123, 274
DeMarzo, P.M. 138, 144

Demsetz, H. 141
DeTemple, J. 138, 296
Dewing, A.S. 137
Diamond, D.W. 98-9, 125, 141, 274, 364
Dimson, E. 448
Dofusco, R.A. 140
Donaldson, G. 29, 136
Dorn, W. 168
Dothan, U. 58
Dravid, A. 364, 387
Duffie, D. 138, 144, 256, 289, 291
Dumas, B. 334
Dybvig, P.H. 99, 121, 139

Easley, D. 296
Eckbo, B.E. 80, 122
Emanuel, D. 202
Eppen, G.D. 143

Falkenstein, E.G. 442
Fama, E.F. 137-8, 365, 396, 437-9, 447, 449-50, 455, 463
Farrar, D.E. 3-6, 12
Farrow, S. 121
Fedenia, M. 301
Ferson, W. 261, 440
Fialkowski, D. 443
Figlewski, S. 296
Fisher, I. 56
Fisher, L. 137, 365
Flannery, M.J. 139
Fleming, W.H. 64
Flood, M. 366
Folkerts-Landau, D. 334
Foster, F.D. 391, 420, 428
Foster, G. 375
Frankel, J.A. 333
Franks, J.R. 142
Freed, W. 420, 425, 427
French, K.R. 333, 437-9, 455
Friend, I. 261
Froot, K.A. 143

Galai, D. 151, 157, 374
Galant, D. 383
Gale, D. 138
Gehrig, T.P. 334-5
Gbbons, M.R. 261, 438, 441, 461-2
Gibbons, R. 141
Glosten, L.R. 374, 417, 420-24, 428, 441
Goldstein, M. 334
Gordon, M.J. 46, 322
Gould, J.P. 151, 157
Grammatikos, T. 301
Grant, A.T. 226

Green, R. 92, 140, 142
Greenbaum, S.I. 141
Greenwood, P.R. 110
Grinblatt, M.S. 366, 370, 382
Grossman, S.J. 138, 140, 256, 258, 261, 271, 324
Grubel, H. 333
Grundy, B. 80, 82, 121, 139

Hagerman, R. 420, 425
Hakansson, N.H. 239, 242, 324
Hansen, L. 261
Harrington, D.R. 122
Harris, L. 286, 417, 420-24, 428, 441
Harris, M. 140, 143, 285-6
Hart, O.D. 138, 140, 255
Harvey, C.R. 354-5
Hasbrouck, J. 417, 420, 428
Haugen, R.A. 142
Hayek, F.H. 324
Healy, P. 366
Heaney, W.J. 219
Heinkel, R. 80, 82, 121, 128, 139
Hellwig, M.F. 273-4, 276-7, 303, 335
Hendricks, D. 274
Hendricks, W. 46
Hirshleifer, D. 139-41
Hirshleifer, J. 278
Hite, G. 122
Holden, C.W. 292, 391, 412, 417, 419, 435
Holmstrom, B. 143
Holthausen, R.W. 374
Hsueh, L.P. 370
Huang, C. 256, 289, 291, 324

Ibbotson, R. 233, 260
Ingersoll, J.E. 53-4, 57, 64, 142, 165, 180, 202

Jagannathan, Z. 463
Jarrow, R.A. 74, 138
Jegadeesh, N. 417, 438, 443
Jenning, R. 296
Jensen, M.C. 29, 137-41, 365
John, K. 139
Johnson, H. 296
Johnson, R.R. 140
Jones, R. 239, 244, 249
Jorion, P. 138, 296

Kahneman, D. 140
Kaldor, N. 60
Kang, J.K. 334-5, 349
Kaplanis, E. 333-4
Keynes, J.M. 115, 329

Kidwell, D.S. 370
Kim, E.H. 110
Kim, O. 281, 285, 380
Kingsnorth, G.A. 226
Klein, A. 121
Klevorick, A.K. 41
Knetsch, J.L. 140
Koh, F. 138
Korajczyk, R. 437, 440, 445, 455, 460, 463
Korwar, A.N. 80, 87, 89, 91
Kraus, A. 29,128,139, 204, 289
Kreps, D.M. 133, 255, 387
Kryzanowski, L. 368
Kuhn, T.S. 142
Kyle, A.S. 294, 300, 302, 304, 391, 416–17, 419–23

Laffont, J.J. 289
Lakonishok, J. 365–6, 377, 442
Lamoureaux, C. 296, 387
Latane, H.A. 156
Lee, C.C. 296
Lee, C.M.C. 423
Lehmann, B. 442, 448
Lehn, K. 123, 141
Leland, H.E. 40, 42, 98,138, 220, 223, 225, 239–40, 256, 275
Lev, B. 365–6, 377
Levy, H. 333
Lewis, F.D. 334
Lintner, J. 6
Litzenberger, R.H. 14, 29,142, 219, 324, 443, 448
Lloyd-Davies, P. 383
Lo, A.W. 390–91, 393, 397, 439, 463
Loderer, C. 144
Logue, D. 138
Loughran, T. 441, 457
Low, A. 334–5

MacBeth, J.D. 396, 437, 447, 449–50, 463
MacKinlay, A.C. 390–91, 393, 397, 439, 459, 463
Madhavan, A. 417, 420–24, 428
Majluf, N. 79, 80, 86, 138, 143
Maksimovic, V. 122, 141
Malitz, I.B. 110
Manaster, S. 296
Markowitz, H. 14
Marris, R. 139
Marshall, S.B. 122
Marshall, W.J. 41
Masulis, R.W. 80, 87, 89, 91, 139,142, 366, 370, 382
Maug, E. 141

McCardle, K.F. 292
McConnell, J.J. 110, 121
McCracken, D. 168
McNichols, M. 364
Means, G.C. 139
Meckling, W.H. 29, 137–9
Mendelson, H. 366, 369, 418, 442
Merton, R.C. 15,16, 30, 53, 64,142, 144, 151, 153, 155, 165, 179, 201–2, 219, 239–40, 364, 391, 440
Mikkelson, W.H. 80, 94
Milgrom, P. 276, 293, 374
Miller, M.H. 3, 11, 12, 28–30, 33, 35, 38, 42, 80, 138–9, 142, 442–3
Miller, N.C. 334
Modest, D.A. 442
Modigliani, F. 3, 11, 12, 28–30, 33, 35, 38, 42, 131, 138
Moore, J. 140
Moskowitz, T. 335
Mossin, J. 6, 22, 239
Mullins, D.W. 80, 138
Murphy, K.J. 140–41
Muscarella, C.J. 121
Myers, S.C. 4, 23, 29, 41–2, 79, 80, 86, 138, 140, 143

Narayanan, M.P. 121, 140
Nau, R.F. 292
Noreen, E. 375

O'Hara, M. 138, 296
Ohlson, J.A. 364
Oldfield, G.S. 74

Palepu, K. 366
Park, K.K.H. 355
Parkinson, M. 151, 169
Partch, M.M. 80
Patel, J. 274
Paul, J. 140
Peles, Y.C. 40
Penman, S.H. 364
Penrose, E.T. 139
Perold, A.F. 239, 249
Perrakis, S. 40
Persons, J.C. 139
Petersen, M. 443
Pettit, R.R 15
Pfleiderer, P. 132,141, 391, 407, 416–18, 427, 430, 435
Phillips, P.C.B. 187,189
Pindyck, R.S. 58
Poon, P. 387
Pope, A. 135

Poterba, J.M. 333
Poulson, A. 123
Prescott, E.C. 98
Price, M.M. 335, 355
Pyle, D.H. 98, 138

Rajan, R.G. 142
Ramakrishnan, T.S. 98
Ramaswamy, K. 142, 443, 448
Raviv, A. 140,143, 217, 285-6
Ready, M. 423
Reinganum, M.R. 441, 453, 457
Reinisch, H.R. 364
Rendelman, R.J. 156, 296
Ricart i Costa, J. 143
Richard, S.F. 74, 180, 183
Rishel, R.W. 64
Roberts, G.S. 110
Roberts, R.B. 44, 46
Robichek, A.A. 29, 41
Rock, K. 80, 121, 138-9
Roll, R. 56, 137, 142, 365, 439, 463
Rosansky, V.I. 57
Ross, S.A. 53-4, 57, 60, 64, 113, 138, 142,
        165-6, 168-9, 180, 202, 242, 323
Rothschild, M. 138
Rubinstein, M. 201-4, 206-8, 214, 289

Samuelson, P.A. 16, 64
Sarnat, M. 333
Schaefer, A. 366-7
Scharfstein, D.S. 141, 143
Schleifer, A. 123, 141
Scholes, M.S. 14, 15, 21, 30, 48,142-3, 151,
        156, 158-9, 162, 164-5, 180, 184, 202,
        238, 240, 273, 275, 287, 292, 297, 304,
        438, 442-3
Schwartz, E.S. 33, 57-8, 115, 142, 165,
        179, 202, 229, 238, 289
Selwyn, L.L. 3-6, 12
Senbet, L.W. 142
Shanken, J. 463
Shapiro, A.C. 128, 141, 322
Sharpe, W.F. 6
Sheikh, A.M. 366
Shiller, R. 261, 320, 324, 335
Shukla, R. 335, 351
Sibley, D.S. 41
Sick, G.A. 143
Singleton, K. 261
Sinquefield, R. 233, 260
Skelton, J.L. 142
Skinner, D.J. 295-6
Smidt, S. 56, 417, 420-24, 428
Smith, C.W. 141

Solanki, R. 239, 244, 261, 275
Solnik, B. 333
Solow, R.M. 71
Sparrow, F.T. 42
Spatt, C. 139
Srinivas, P.S. 296
Srivastava, S. 139
Stambaugh, R.F. 438
Stapleton, R.C. 14, 214
Starks, L. 296
Stein, J.L. 40, 121, 139
Stiglitz, J.E. 79, 138
Stokey, N. 276, 293
Stoll, H.R. 363, 427, 443
Strebel, P. 396, 417
Stulz, R.M. 140, 333-5, 349
Subrahmanyam, A. 292, 300, 301, 304, 391,
        412, 417, 419, 435, 441-3
Subrahmanyam, M.G. 214
Summers, L.H. 123, 128
Sundaresan, M. 74
Swaminathan, B. 417
Swanson, G. 366

Telser, L.G. 60
Tepper, I. 143
Tesar, L.L. 333-6, 349, 354-5
Thakor, A.V. 98,138, 140-41, 370
Thaler, R. 140
Thompson, R. 128
Titman, S. 139, 141, 366, 370, 382, 438-9,
        443
Torous, W.N. 142
Tourinho, O.A.F. 59
Townsend, R.M. 98
Trczinka, C. 142
Treynor 14
Turnbull, S. 56
Tuttle, D.L. 14

Uppal, R. 334
Urias, M.S. 355

Van Agtmael, A.W. 355
Van Drunen, L.D. 144
Van Inwegen, G. 335, 351
Vanderhei, J. 122
Vasicek, O. 179
Vermaelen, T. 95
Verrecchia, R.E. 125, 281, 285, 374, 380
Vijh, A.M. 138
Viscione, J.A. 110
Vishny, R.W. 123, 141
Viswanathan, S. 391, 420, 428
Von Neumann Whitman, M. 334

Waldmann, R.J. 123
Walters, T. 138
Wang, J. 336
Wang, R. 463
Warner, J.B. 29, 138, 141–2
Warther, V.A. 141, 285
Webb, G.P. 296
Welch, I. 139
Werner, I. 333–6, 349, 354–5
Westerfield, R. 15
Whaley, R.E. 363
Wiggins, J.B. 366, 375

Wilhelm, W.J. 139
Williams, J. 58,122, 139
Williamson, O.E. 139
Working, H. 60
Wruck, K.H. 142

Zechner, J. 141
Zeckhauser, R. 274
Zender, J.F. 121, 139
Zhang, H. 368
Zorn, T.S. 140